Praise for *Numbers*

"Jay Sklar has provided each section of text with crystal clear and detailed explanation illuminated by helpful charts and summaries, followed by a thought-provoking range of insights into New Testament analogies and robust spiritual and ethical applications for contemporary believers and churches. An exemplary commentary on a regrettably neglected book."

—Christopher J. H. Wright, global ambassador, Langham Partnership

"Jay Sklar is a masterful tour guide of the book of Numbers! With exegetical precision, clarity, and pastoral sensitivity, he draws readers in to one of the most pivotal moments in Israel's history, enticing them to hunger and thirst for the timeless words of warning and encouragement found along the journey. Specialists and non-specialists alike will find this an indispensable addition to their bookshelves!"

—Elizabeth Backfish,
associate professor of Old Testament, Jessup University

"This is an excellent commentary. Those who are planning to teach and preach from the book of Numbers, and those who simply want to acquire a better understanding of the book, will find this to be an invaluable resource. While not aimed at an academic audience per se, the book evidences a wealth of scholarship on the author's part, yet in easily understandable language. In addition to highly lucid comments on each passage, the author has provided helpful maps and many easy-to-follow and enlightening charts. Sklar also helps his readers see the book of Numbers against the backdrop of the entire canon of Scripture, drawing lines to the New Testament, to Jesus Christ, and to the lives of contemporary Christians and the ministry of the twenty-first century church. Take up, read, and enjoy."

—Jerry Shepherd, emeritus professor of Old Testament, Taylor Seminary

"Recounting the protracted journey of the Israelites to the Promised Land, the book of Numbers contrasts the faithlessness of the Israelites, whom God has redeemed from slavery in Egypt, and the faithfulness of God, who graciously fulfils his promises to a new generation of Israelites. Helping readers to navigate this Old Testament book, Prof. Sklar's insightful commentary explains the text with clarity and draws out its implications as God's Word to us in the 21st century. I warmly recommend this commentary for its accessibility and clarity."

> —T.D. Alexander, senior lecturer in biblical studies and director of postgraduate studies, Union Theological College

"Jay Sklar makes the story of the Israelites' wilderness journey in the book of Numbers come alive for modern Christians with exceptionally clear explanations of the text—including its literary, religious, cultural, historical, and geographic aspects—and its profound implications for the larger story of deliverance through Christ and for our own journey with God to the ultimate Promised Land."

> —Roy Gane, professor of Hebrew Bible and ancient Near Eastern languages, Seventh-day Adventist Theological Seminary, Andrews University

The Story of God Bible Commentary Series Endorsements

"Getting a story is about more than merely enjoying it. It means hearing it, understanding it, and above all, being impacted by it. This commentary series hopes that its readers not only hear and understand the story but are impacted by it to live in as Christian a way as possible. The editors and contributors set that table very well and open up the biblical story in ways that move us to act with sensitivity and understanding. That makes hearing the story as these authors tell it well worth the time. Well done."

Darrell L. Bock
Dallas Theological Seminary

"The Story of God Bible Commentary series invites readers to probe how the message of the text relates to our situations today. Engagingly readable, it not only explores the biblical text but offers a range of applications and interesting illustrations."

Craig S. Keener
Asbury Theological Seminary

"I love The Story of God Bible Commentary series. It makes the text sing and helps us hear the story afresh."

John Ortberg
Former Pastor of Menlo Park Presbyterian Church

"In this promising new series of commentaries, believing biblical scholars bring not only their expertise but their own commitment to Jesus and insights into today's culture to the Scriptures. The result is a commentary series that is anchored in the text but lives and breathes in the world of today's church with its variegated pattern of socioeconomic, ethnic, and national diversity. Pastors, Bible study leaders, and Christians of all types who are looking for a substantive and practical guide through the Scriptures will find these volumes helpful."

Frank Thielman
Beeson Divinity School

"I'm a storyteller. Through writing and speaking I talk and teach about understanding the Story of God throughout Scripture and about letting God reveal more of his story as I live it out. Thus I am thrilled to have a commentary series based on the story of God—a commentary that helps me to Listen to the Story, that Explains the Story, and then encourages me to probe how to Live the Story. A perfect tool for helping every follower of Jesus to walk in the story that God is writing for them."

Judy Douglass
Director of Women's Resources, Cru

"The Bible is the story of God and his dealings with humanity from creation to new creation. The Bible is made up more of stories than of any other literary genre. Even the psalms, proverbs, prophecies, letters, and the Apocalypse make complete sense only when set in the context of the grand narrative of the entire Bible. This commentary series breaks new ground by taking all these observations seriously. It asks commentators to listen to the text, to explain the text, and to live the text. Some of the material in these sections overlaps with introduction, detailed textual analysis and application, respectively, but only some. The most riveting and valuable part of the commentaries are the stories that can appear in any of these sections, from any part of the globe and any part of church history, illustrating the text in any of these areas. Ideal for preaching and teaching."

Craig L. Blomberg
Denver Seminary

"Pastors and lay people will welcome this new series, which seeks to make the message of the Scriptures clear and to guide readers in appropriating biblical texts for life today."

Daniel I. Block
Wheaton College and Graduate School

"An extremely valuable and long overdue series that includes comment on the cultural context of the text, careful exegesis, and guidance on reading the whole Bible as a unity that testifies to Christ as our Savior and Lord."

Graeme Goldsworthy
author of *According to Plan*

NUMBERS

Editorial Board
of
The Story of God Bible Commentary

Old Testament general editor
Tremper Longman III

Old Testament associate editors
George Athas
Mark J. Boda
Myrto Theocharous

New Testament general editor
Scot McKnight

New Testament associate editors
Lynn H. Cohick
Michael F. Bird
Dennis R. Edwards

The Story of God Bible Commentary

NUMBERS

Jay Sklar

Tremper Longman III & Scot McKnight
General Editors

ZONDERVAN ACADEMIC

Numbers
Copyright © 2023 by Jay Sklar

Requests for information should be addressed to:
Zondervan, *3900 Sparks Dr. SE, Grand Rapids, Michigan 49546*

Zondervan titles may be purchased in bulk for educational, business, fundraising, or sales promotional use. For information, please email SpecialMarkets@Zondervan.com.

Library of Congress Cataloging-in-Publication Data

Names: Sklar, Jay, author. | Longman, Tremper, III, editor. | McKnight, Scot, editor.
Title: Numbers / Jay Sklar ; Tremper Longman III, Scot McKnight, general editors.
Other titles: Story of God Bible commentary
Description: Grand Rapids : Zondervan, 2023. | Series: The story of God Bible commentary. Old Testament series ; 4 | Includes index.
Identifiers: LCCN 2023015852 (print) | LCCN 2023015853 (ebook) | ISBN 9780310490760 (hardcover) | ISBN 9780310143062 (ebook)
Subjects: LCSH: Bible. Numbers—Commentaries. | BISAC: RELIGION / Biblical Commentary / Old Testament / Pentateuch | RELIGION / Biblical Commentary / General
Classification: LCC BS1265.53 .S55 2023 (print) | LCC BS1265.53 (ebook) | DDC 222/.1407—dc23/eng/20230501
LC record available at https://lccn.loc.gov/2023015852
LC ebook record available at https://lccn.loc.gov/2023015853

All Scripture quotations, unless otherwise indicated, are taken from The Holy Bible, New International Version®, NIV®. Copyright © 1973, 1978, 1984, 2011 by Biblica, Inc.® Used by permission of Zondervan. All rights reserved worldwide. www.Zondervan.com. The "NIV" and "New International Version" are trademarks registered in the United States Patent and Trademark Office by Biblica, Inc.®

Any internet addresses (websites, blogs, etc.) and telephone numbers in this book are offered as a resource. They are not intended in any way to be or imply an endorsement by Zondervan, nor does Zondervan vouch for the content of these sites and numbers for the life of this book.

All rights reserved. No part of this publication may be reproduced, stored in a retrieval system, or transmitted in any form or by any means—electronic, mechanical, photocopy, recording, or any other—except for brief quotations in printed reviews, without the prior permission of the publisher.

Cover design: Ron Huizinga
Cover image: Stockphoto.com
Interior typesetting: Sara Colley

Printed in the United States of America

---

23 24 25 26 27 28 29 30 31 32 /TRM/ 14 13 12 11 10 9 8 7 6 5 4 3 2 1

To my colleagues at Covenant Theological Seminary:
fellow pilgrims following Jesus to the promised land.

"The Lord bless you and keep you;
the Lord make his face shine on you and be gracious to you;
the Lord turn his face toward you and give you peace!"
Numbers 6:24–26

Old Testament series

1. Genesis—*Tremper Longman III*
2. Exodus—*Christopher J. H. Wright*
3. Leviticus—*Jerry E. Shepherd*
4. Numbers—*Jay Sklar*
5. Deuteronomy—*Myrto Theocharous*
6. Joshua—*Lissa M. Wray Beal*
7. Judges—*Athena E. Gorospe*
8. Ruth/Esther—*Marion Ann Taylor*
9. 1–2 Samuel—*Paul S. Evans*
10. 1–2 Kings—*David T. Lamb*
11. 1–2 Chronicles—*Carol M. Kaminski*
12. Ezra/Nehemiah—*Douglas J. Green*
13. Job—*Martin A. Shields*
14. Psalms—*Yohanna Katanacho*
15. Proverbs—*Ryan P. O'Dowd*
16. Ecclesiastes/Song of Songs—*George Athas*
17. Isaiah—*Mark J. Boda*
18. Jeremiah/Lamentations—*Andrew G. Shead*
19. Ezekiel—*Havilah Dharamraj*
20. Daniel—*Wendy L. Widder*
21. Minor Prophets I—*Beth M. Stovell*
22. Minor Prophets II—*Beth M. Stovell*

New Testament series

1. Matthew—*Rodney Reeves*
2. Mark—*Timothy G. Gombis*
3. Luke—*Kindalee Pfremmer DeLong*
4. John—*Nicholas Perrin*
5. Acts—*Dean Pinter*
6. Romans—*Michael F. Bird*
7. 1 Corinthians—*Justin K. Hardin*
8. 2 Corinthians—*Judith A. Diehl*
9. Galatians—*Nijay K. Gupta*
10. Ephesians—*Mark D. Roberts*
11. Philippians—*Lynn H. Cohick*
12. Colossians/Philemon—*Esau McCaulley*
13. 1, 2 Thessalonians—*John Byron*
14. 1, 2 Timothy, Titus—*Marius Nel*
15. Hebrews—*Radu Gheorghita*
16. James—*Mariam J. Kamell*
17. 1 Peter—*Dennis R. Edwards*
18. 2 Peter, Jude—*Abson Joseph*
19. 1, 2, & 3 John—*Constantine R. Campbell*
20. Revelation—*Jonathan A. Moo*
21. Sermon on the Mount—*Scot McKnight*

Contents

Acknowledgments xiii
The Story of God Bible Commentary Series xv
Abbreviations xix
Introduction to Numbers 1
Resources for Teaching and Preaching 37
Maps 39
  1. Numbers 1:1–54 45
  2. Numbers 2:1–34 58
  3. Numbers 3:1–4:49 67
  4. Numbers 5:1–4 91
  5. Numbers 5:5–10 96
  6. Numbers 5:11–31 100
  7. Numbers 6:1–21 112
  8. Numbers 6:22–27 121
  9. Numbers 7:1–89 128
10. Numbers 8:1–4 141
11. Numbers 8:5–26 145
12. Numbers 9:1–14 153
13. Numbers 9:15–10:10 158
14. Numbers 10:11–36 165
15. Numbers 11:1–35 172
16. Numbers 12:1–16 183
17. Numbers 13:1–14:45 190
18. Numbers 15:1–41 209
19. Numbers 16:1–50 221
20. Numbers 17:1–18:7 238
21. Numbers 18:8–32 247
22. Numbers 19:1–22 257
23. Numbers 20:1–29 265
24. Numbers 21:1–22:1 274
25. Numbers 22:2–40 285
26. Numbers 22:41–24:25 297
27. Numbers 25:1–18 315

28. Numbers 26:1–65 322
29. Numbers 27:1–23 334
30. Numbers 28:1–29:40 342
31. Numbers 30:1–16 359
32. Numbers 31:1–54 367
33. Numbers 32:1–42 379
34. Numbers 33:1–49 388
35. Numbers 33:50–34:29 396
36. Numbers 35:1–34 406
37. Numbers 36:1–13 417
Scripture Index 425
Subject Index 459
Author Index 471

Acknowledgments

For two decades my studies have taken me on a journey through Leviticus and Numbers. (Those viewing these books as a wilderness might be tempted to point out I have two decades to go!) Ski, throughout those years and to this day, you have been an indescribable source of encouragement and support. Every time I read Proverbs 18:22, I thank the Lord for the favor he has given me in you!

My journey into Leviticus and Numbers began during my studies under Prof. Gordon Wenham, for whose model of both scholarship and piety I am deeply grateful. Gordon, I know scores of others have exactly the same sentiments.

I am grateful to Tremper Longman for the invitation to write this commentary and very thankful to him and to Myrto Theocharous for reading through the manuscript in its entirety, giving much helpful feedback and making numerous valuable suggestions. My sincere thanks as well to my teaching assistant, Emma Ford, who also read through the entire manuscript, catching numerous mistakes and making many helpful suggestions.

A few years before writing this commentary, I wrote the notes on the book of Numbers for the *NIV Biblical Theology Study Bible* (Grand Rapids: Zondervan, 2018). My thanks to Katya Covrett of Zondervan for permission to make use of those notes in this commentary. This happens infrequently in the commentary proper (more so in the introduction), but when it does, I incorporate them without citation.

This commentary was finished during a sabbatical granted by Covenant Theological Seminary, to whose board and administration I express my sincere thanks. As the dedication to this volume shows, my admiration and love for my colleagues at Covenant runs very deep. Brothers and sisters, you continually challenge and encourage me in my walk with the Lord. What a joy to follow Jesus with you as he leads us to his promised land of rest!

The Story of God Bible Commentary Series

Why another commentary series?

In the first place, no single commentary can exhaust the meaning of a biblical book. The Bible is unfathomably rich, and no single commentator can explore every aspect of its message.

In addition, good commentary not only explores what the text meant in the past but also its continuing significance. In other words, the Word of God may not change, but culture does. Think of what we have seen in the last twenty years: we now communicate predominantly through the internet and email; we read our news on iPads and computers. We carry smartphones in our pockets through which we can call our friends, check the weather forecast, make dinner reservations, and get an answer to virtually any question we might have.

Today we have more readable and accurate Bible versions in English than any generation in the past. Bible distribution in the present generation has been very successful; more people own more Bibles than previous generations. However, studies have shown that while people have better access to the Bible than ever before, people aren't reading the Bibles they own, and they struggle to understand what they do read.

The Story of God Bible Commentary hopes to help people, particularly clergy but also laypeople, read the Bible with understanding not only of its ancient meaning but also of its continuing significance for us today in the twenty-first century. After all, readers of the Bible change too. These cultural shifts, our own personal developments, and the progress in intellectual questions, as well as growth in biblical studies and theology and discoveries of new texts and new paradigms for understanding the contexts of the Bible—each of these elements work on an interpreter so that the person who reads the Bible today asks different questions from different angles.

Culture shifts, but the Word of God remains. That is why we as editors of The Story of God Bible Commentary, a commentary based on the New International Version 2011 (NIV 2011), are excited to participate in this new series of commentaries on the Bible. This series is designed to speak to this generation with the same Word of God. We are asking the authors to explain what the Bible says to the sorts of readers who pick up commentaries so they can understand not only what Scripture says but what it means for today. The Bible does not change, but relating it to our culture changes constantly and in differing ways in different contexts.

As editors of the Old Testament series, we recognize that Christians have a hard time knowing exactly how to relate to the Scriptures that were written before the coming of Christ. The world of the Old Testament is a strange one to those of us who live in the West in the twenty-first century. We read about strange customs, warfare in the name of God, sacrifices, laws of ritual purity, and more and wonder whether it is worth our while or even spiritually healthy to spend time reading this portion of Scripture that is chronologically, culturally, and—seemingly—theologically distant from us.

But it is precisely here that The Story of God Commentary Series Old Testament makes its most important contribution. The New Testament does not replace the Old Testament; the New Testament fulfills the Old Testament. We hear God's voice today in the Old Testament. In its pages he reveals himself to us and also his will for how we should live in a way that is pleasing to him.

Jesus himself often reminds us that the Old Testament maintains its importance to the lives of his disciples. Luke 24 describes Jesus's actions and teaching in the period between his resurrection and ascension. Strikingly, the focus of his teaching is on how his followers should read the Old Testament (here called "Moses and all the Prophets," "Scriptures," and "the law of Moses, the Prophets and Psalms"). To the two disciples on the road to Emmaus, he says:

> "How foolish you are, and how slow to believe all that the prophets have spoken! Did not the Messiah have to suffer these things and then enter his glory?" And beginning with Moses and all the Prophets, he explained to them what was said in all the Scriptures concerning himself. (Luke 24:25–27)

Then to a larger group of disciples he announces:

> "This is what I told you while I was still with you: Everything must be fulfilled that is written about me in the law of Moses, the Prophets and the Psalms." Then he opened their minds so they could understand the Scriptures. (Luke 24:44–45)

The Story of God Bible Commentary Series takes Jesus's words on this matter seriously. Indeed, it is the first series that has as one of its deliberate goals

The Story of God Bible Commentary Series

the identification of the trajectories (historical, typological, and theological) that land in Christ in the New Testament. Every commentary in the series will, in the first place, exposit the text in the context of its original reception. We will interpret it as we believe the original author intended his contemporary audience to read it. But then we will also read the text in the light of the death and resurrection of Jesus. No other commentary series does this important work consistently in every volume.

To achieve our purpose of expositing the Old Testament in its original setting and also from a New Testament perspective, each passage is examined from three angles.

Listen to the Story. We begin by listening to the text in order to hear the voice of God. We first read the passage under study. We then go on to consider the background to the passage by looking at any earlier Scripture passage that informs our understanding of the text. At this point too we will cite and discuss possible ancient Near Eastern literary connections. After all, the Bible was not written in a cultural vacuum, and an understanding of its broader ancient Near Eastern context will often enrich our reading.

Explain the Story. The authors are asked to explain each passage in light of the Bible's grand story. It is here that we will exposit the text in its original Old Testament context. This is not an academic series, so the footnotes will be limited to the kinds of books and articles to which typical Bible readers and preachers will have access. Authors are given the freedom to explain the text as they read it, though you will not be surprised to find occasional listings of other options for reading the text. The emphasis will be on providing an accessible explanation of the passage, particularly on those aspects of the text that are difficult for a modern reader to understand, with an emphasis on theological interpretation.

Live the Story. Reading the Bible is not just about discovering what it meant back then; the intent of The Story of God Bible Commentary is to probe how this text might be lived out today as that story continues to march on in the life of the church.

Here, in the spirit of Christ's words in Luke 24, we will suggest ways in which the Old Testament text anticipates the gospel. After all, as Augustine famously put it, "the New Testament is in the Old Testament concealed, the Old Testament is in the New Testament revealed." We believe that this section will be particularly important for our readers who are clergy who want to present Christ even when they are preaching from the Old Testament.

The Old Testament also provides teaching concerning how we should live today. However, the authors of this series are sensitive to the tremendous impact that Christ's coming has on how Christians appropriate the Old Testament into their lives today.

It is the hope and prayer of the editors and all the contributors that our work will encourage clergy to preach from the Old Testament and laypeople to study this wonderful, yet often strange, portion of God's Word to us today.

Tremper Longman III, general editor Old Testament
George Athas, Mark Boda, and Myrto Theocharous, editors

Abbreviations

ABD	*Anchor Yale Bible Dictionary*
ANEP	*The Ancient Near East in Pictures Relating to the Old Testament.* 2nd ed. Edited by James Pritchard. Princeton: Princeton University press, 1969
ANET	*Ancient Near Eastern Texts Relating to the Old Testament.* Edited by James Pritchard. 3rd ed. Princeton: Princeton University Press, 1969
BA	*Biblical Archaeologist*
BASOR	*Bulletin of the American Schools of Oriental Research*
BBR	*Bulletin for Biblical Research*
BDB	Brown, Francis, Samuel Rolles Driver, and Charles Augustus Briggs. *Enhanced Brown-Driver-Briggs Hebrew and English Lexicon.* Oxford: Clarendon Press, 1977
COS	*The Context of Scripture.* Edited by William W. Hallo. 3 vols. Leiden: Brill, 1997–2002
DOOTP	*Dictionary of the Old Testament: Pentateuch.* Edited by Desmond Alexander and David W. Baker. Downers Grove: InterVarsity Academic, 2003
EBC	Gaebelein, Frank E., John H. Sailhamer, Walter C. Kaiser Jr., R. Laird Harris, and Ronald B. Allen, eds. *The Expositor's Bible Commentary.* Grand Rapids: Zondervan, 1990
ESV	English Standard Version
IBC	Interpretation: A Bible Commentary for Teaching and Preaching
ISBE	*The International standard Bible encyclopedia.* Edited by Geoffrey W. Bromiley. 4 vols. Grand Rapids: Eerdmans, 1979
JETS	*Journal of the Evangelical Theological Society*
JJS	*Journal of Jewish Studies*
JPS	Jewish Publication Society
JSOT	*Journal for the Study of the Old Testament*
NAC	New American Commentary
NASB	New American Standard Bible
NET	New English Translation Bible
NIBC	New International Biblical Commentary

NICNT	New International Commentary on the New Testament
NICOT	New International Commentary on the Old Testament
NIDOTTE	*New International Dictionary of Old Testament Theology and Exegesis*. Edited by Willem A. VanGemeren. 5 vols. Grand Rapids: Zondervan, 1997
NIV	New International Version
NIVAC	NIV Application Commentary
NJB	New Jerusalem Bible
NJPS	*Tanakh: The Holy Scriptures: The New JPS Translation according to the Traditional Hebrew Text*
NRSB	New Revised Standard Bible
RSV	Revised Standard Version
TOTC	Tyndale Old Testament Commentaries
TynBul	*Tyndale Bulletin*
VT	*Vetus Testamentum*
VTSup	Supplements to Vetus Testamentum
WTJ	*Westminster Theological Journal*
ZECOT	Zondervan Exegetical Commentary on the Old Testament
ZIBBC	Zondervan Illustrated Bible Backgrounds Commentary

Introduction[1]

Numbers at a Glance

The book of Numbers should have a certain familiarity to the believer today:

> The story of the book of Numbers is written to a people whose lives are lived between the accomplishing of their redemption and its consummation, between the exodus and the Promised Land. . . . This should all sound familiar to us. We live as they did—between salvation accomplished and salvation completed. We live between the work of God in accomplishing our salvation at the cross and the time when that salvation will be brought to its consummation when Christ returns. We too live between the times.[2]

And, like them, we are called to live by faith, which in the in-between times means "affirm[ing] the reality of God's plot for our lives even when we cannot see it with our own eyes."[3]

The story of Numbers alternates between the heights of obedience and hope and the lows of rebellion and despair. The heights open and close the book and mirror one another like twin majestic peaks (1:1–10:10; 26:1–36:13). The lows occur in between like a dry desert valley that seems to stretch on forever (10:11–25:18). But the peaks and the valley work together to tell a story in which there is one constant: the Lord's faithfulness to his covenant promises and his mercy toward his wayward people.

---

1. As noted in the acknowledgments, I wrote the notes on Numbers for the *NIV Biblical Theology Study Bible* (Grand Rapids: Zondervan, 2018). With Zondervan's permission, portions of those notes are used here. As is well known, Numbers often addresses issues that also arise in Leviticus, making that book especially helpful in illuminating Numbers. Throughout this commentary, I will weave in observations from commentaries I have written on Leviticus but will usually footnote those observations only if the quotation is particularly lengthy. Those commentaries are: Jay Sklar, *Leviticus: An Introduction and Commentary*, TOTC (Downers Grove, IL: InterVarsity Press, 2014), hereafter *Leviticus* (TOTC); and Jay Sklar, *Leviticus: A Discourse Analysis of the Hebrew Bible*, ZECOT (Grand Rapids: Zondervan Academic, 2023), hereafter *Leviticus* (ZECOT).

2. Iain M. Duguid, *Numbers: God's Presence in the Wilderness* (Wheaton, IL: Crossway Books, 2006), 19.

3. Ibid., 20.

The first peak tells the story of the first generation of Israelites, whom the Lord has rescued from Egypt and who are now receiving instructions from him to prepare to march into the land he has sworn to give them (1:1–10:10). The Israelites respond with careful obedience throughout this section (1:54; 2:34; 4:49; etc.), and by its end we have every confidence they will soon be entering the promised land. But the story takes a dramatic turn, plunging into a valley of disobedience and despair as these first-generation Israelites return to their grumbling and complaining ways. Ultimately, they disbelieve the Lord's promises, reject him and his leaders, and turn to other gods for help (10:11–25:18). The Lord brings his justice to bear against them but also responds repeatedly with his mercy, which runs like a stream of grace through this otherwise bleak and depressing wasteland. Finally, after the first generation has died out, the story rises once more to obedience and hope as the second generation carefully follows the Lord's commands and prepares to follow him into the promised land of rest (Numbers 26–36). Thus even the faithlessness of the first generation cannot thwart the Lord's commitment to fulfilling his covenant promises—and the book's ending strongly hints that the fulfillment of those promises is right on the doorstep.

Title, Author, Date, Setting

Title

Numbers is an unfortunate title for this book. As one commentator asks dryly, "Who but a mathematician could rise with joy to a book called 'Numbers'?"[4] The name comes from the Septuagint (the pre-Christian Greek translation of the OT) and was likely inspired by the census counts the book contains (see chs. 1–4; 26). Its Hebrew name, "In the wilderness," refers to its opening words (1:1). But neither title captures its focus. Were length not an issue, a more appropriate title might be "A Tale of the Lord's Ongoing Faithfulness and Mercy to Two Generations of Israelites, One Faithless and One Faithful."

Author and Date

Approaches to the authorship and date of the Pentateuch (the first five books of the Old Testament) divide into two main camps.

---

4. Ronald B. Allen, "Numbers," in *EBC*, ed. Frank E. Gaebelein et al. (Grand Rapids: Zondervan, 1990), 2:700. He proceeds to argue, however, "that these numbers, in their highly stylized environments, are a matter of *celebration of the faithfulness of Yahweh to his covenant people*" (ibid., 700–701, emphasis original; see also at n28 below).

The traditional camp understands Moses to be the substantial author of the Pentateuch, implying a date of sometime between 1440 and 1250 BC (depending on the date assigned to the exodus). This approach views as reliable the Pentateuch's own account of Moses's involvement with its writing and reads it as a cohesive work.

The historical-critical camp, which began in earnest in the nineteenth century, understands the Pentateuch to be composed of sources coming long after Moses (ninth through fifth centuries BC), sources that often conflict with one another in outlook. Understandably, this approach does not view the Pentateuch's account of Moses's involvement with its writing as reliable, nor the final result to have the same cohesiveness.

Significant variations exist within each camp.[5] Those interested in understanding the second camp more fully—along with its potential problems—may refer to one of the many helpful overviews that have been written.[6] My own approach affirms the text's reliability with regard to Moses's involvement in the writing of the Pentateuch, placing me within the first camp. A brief explanation now follows of what I understand the text to indicate about Moses's involvement with Numbers in particular.

While Numbers only identifies Moses as writing down the travel itinerary of 33:3–49 (see 33:2), other reasons support the traditional understanding that he served as the book's primary *source*—that is, the source who passed on the book's contents from the Lord. For instance, much of the book's information is preceded by the phrase "the LORD said (spoke) to Moses," which occurs no less than sixty times (e.g., 1:1; 2:1; 3:5), or is followed by the observation something was done "as the LORD commanded Moses," which occurs no less than twenty times (e.g., 1:54; 2:33, 34).

Moses has also been understood as the book's primary *author*. "Deuteronomy clearly knows the main story of the book of Numbers (cf. Deut. 1–3).[7] . . . And Deuteronomy clearly states that it was written down by Moses (e.g., 31:9, 24). . . . [Therefore,] does it not follow that Numbers . . . must also have been

---

5. And, one might add, other camps besides. See Bill T. Arnold, "Pentateuchal Criticism, History of," *DOOTP*, 622–31, esp. 628–29.

6. T. Desmond Alexander, *From Paradise to the Promised Land: An Introduction to the Pentateuch*, 3rd ed. (Grand Rapids: Baker Academic, 2012), 3–63; Roger N. Whybray, *The Making of the Pentateuch: A Methodological Study*, JSOTSup 53 (Sheffield: JSOT Press, 1987), 17–131 (it may be noted that Whybray is not writing from a conservative position on this issue). My own thoughts on some of these matters may be found in Sklar, *Leviticus* (ZECOT), 5–9.

7. One could add Deut 18:2 (cf. Num 18); 23:4–5 (cf. Num 22–24); and 24:9 (cf. Num 12) (Gordon J. Wenham, *Numbers: An Introduction and Commentary*, TOTC 4 [Downers Grove, IL: IVP Academic, 1981], 23).

his work?"[8] In keeping with this, we see a pattern elsewhere of Moses recording various parts of the Pentateuch at the Lord's command (Exod 17:14; 24:4, 7; 34:27–28; Num 33:2; Deut 31:9, 22–26), with some texts making clear that the words he recorded are the same words he spoke to the Israelites (cf. Exod 24:4 with 24:7; 34:27–28 with 34:32). It is natural, then, to understand he did the same here, namely, writing down the words that he was constantly commanded to speak to the Israelites.

These observations suggest Moses is the book's primary source and author. "Primary" because Numbers itself identifies two brief passages coming from other sources ("the Book of the Wars of the LORD" in 21:13–14 and unnamed poets in 21:27–30). Moreover, Moses likely did not write certain other verses, such as the statement he was "more humble than anyone else on the face of the earth" (12:3) or the description of manna in 11:7–9, which seems to presume a later audience no longer familiar with it. These examples indicate at least some editorial work,[9] though the extent of that work is debated,[10] as is the book's final date.[11] What the above discussion does suggest, however, is

---

8. Gordon J. Wenham, *Numbers*, Old Testament Guides (Sheffield: Sheffield Academic Press, 1997), 69 (hereafter *Numbers* [OT Guides]).

9. While affirming the presence of editorial work sometimes makes conservative scholars nervous, it need not. The Lord can inspire those who edit material as he does those who first write it, as the Gospel of Luke so well attests (Luke 1:1–4). Luke 1:1–4 also affirms inspired editors can make use of sources, which would be true of Moses as well. With regard to non-Mosaic edits in the Pentateuch, we might ask whether these come from a much later time or was the editor someone like Joshua, writing down Moses's words, as did Baruch for Jeremiah (Jer. 36) (this possibility is raised by R. E. Averbeck, "Pentateuchal Criticism and the Priestly Torah," in *Do Historical Matters Matter to Faith? A Critical Appraisal of Modern and Postmodern Approaches to Scripture*, ed. J. K. Hoffmeier and D. R. Magary, [Wheaton, IL: Crossway, 2012], 151–79, esp. 158). See further M. A. Grisanti, "Inspiration, Inerrancy, and the OT Canon: The Place of Textual Updating in an Inerrant View of Scripture," *JETS* 44(4) (2001): 577–98.

10. While those taking a historical-critical approach often classify every Numbers passage according to one source or another, those taking a more traditional approach (or at least affirming some level of Mosaic origins for the book's material) may identify some passages they believe reflect later editing but do not usually claim the list is exhaustive since they are usually less confident in our ability to identify with certainty (or even likelihood) every instance of later editorial activity (e.g., Wenham, *Numbers*, 24; Timothy R. Ashley, *The Book of Numbers*, NICOT [Grand Rapids: Eerdmans, 1993], 6–7). I find myself in this latter group.

11. Among those affirming at least some level of Mosaic involvement in the book's writing, Ashley goes with a preexilic date for the book, tentatively suggesting a more-or-less final form in the united monarchy (*Numbers*, 7); so also Wenham (*Numbers*, 24; cf. A. Noordtzij, *Numbers*, Bible Student's Commentary, trans. Ed van der Maas [Grand Rapids: Zondervan, 1983], 16). A majority of others in this camp either do not comment on a specific date of final editing or imply it was basically in final form at or very shortly after Moses's death (for the latter, see C. F. Keil, *The Pentateuch*, vol. 1 of C. F. Keil and Franz Delitzsch, *Biblical Commentary on the Old Testament*, trans. James Martin, 10 vols. [Grand Rapids: Eerdmans, 1988], 9–10 [*Genesis*, 27–28; for those accessing editions of Keil and Delitzsch in more than ten bindings, these references are also supplied]; R. K. Harrison, *Numbers: An Exegetical Commentary* [Grand Rapids: Baker, 1992], 21–24).

that a substantial amount of the material traces back to the Mosaic era, whose original audience was the first- and second-generation Israelites coming out of Egypt.

Setting

Numbers covers events that happened between 1440 and 1250 BC, depending on the date of the exodus. Geographically, the book opens at Mount Sinai, where the Israelites arrived in Exodus 19 and remained through Leviticus to the opening ten chapters of Numbers. They finally break camp in Numbers 10:11–12, arriving at the southern border of the promised land in 12:16 but rebelling against the Lord's command to enter it (chs. 13–14). Because of this, they spend the next thirty-eight years in the wilderness before finally arriving at the plains of Moab (22:1), just east of the promised land, where they stay for the rest of Numbers (see table, p. 51). Here they receive the book of Deuteronomy and await final orders to enter the land under Joshua (Josh 3).

Historically, events in Canaan at the time of Numbers have been well summarized by Cole (cited at length):

> Archaeologists and historians date the Israelite wilderness sojourn to the middle or latter part of the Late Bronze Age (1550–1200 B.C.) in the ancient Near East. . . . During the fifteenth century B.C. Egypt exacted extensive political and economic control over the region.
>
> Yet in the fourteenth century as the Amarna letters reflect, the Egyptians experienced a significant loss of power among loyal Canaanite puppet-kings because of invasions from the Hapiru, Shasu, and other marauding bands. Then the Nineteenth Dynasty kings Seti I [1294–1279 B.C.] and Ramesses II [1279–1213 B.C.] restored the Egyptian hegemony over much of Canaan, having established a boundary with the Hittites at Qadesh on the Orontes River. Early Hebrew chronologists place the Exodus about 1442 B.C., under either Thutmose III [1479–1425 B.C.] or Amenhotep II [1427–1400 B.C.], placing the forty-year wilderness sojourn during the reigns of Amenhotep II and Thutmose IV [1400–1390 B.C.].[12] Late Hebrew chronologists place both the Exodus and the wilderness period under Ramesses II.

---

12. The dates above follow the so-called low chronology (see K. A. Kitchen, "Egypt, History of [Chronology]," *ABD* 2:329); for other approaches to dating the Pharaohs, see table in John Walton, "Exodus, Date of," *DOOTP* 261.

Whichever chronological scheme is taken, the *terminus ad quem* for Israel's existence in Canaan is the mention of "Israel" in the Merneptah Stele (ca. 1209 B.C.). By that time Israel had established itself as a significant enough entity in the central hill country to be mentioned as one of the peoples defeated in the land of Canaan by the pharaoh Merneptah. By the end of the Late Bronze Age . . . empires such as the Egyptians and Hittites and city-states such as Ugarit experienced dramatic collapse and even destruction.

Most important is that under either chronological scheme, God delivered the Israelites from Egypt during the reign of a powerful pharaoh who oversaw a vast empire that stretched through much of Canaan.[13]

Overarching Structure and Themes

Numbers may be divided into three major sections. The first two focus on the first generation of Israelites coming out of Egypt (1:1–10:10; 10:11–25:18), while the third focuses on their children, the second generation (26:1–36:13).[14]

I. The First Generation: Death in the Wilderness (1:1–25:18)
   A. Organizing and Preparing the Camp in Light of the Lord's Presence among the Israelites as well as the Battles They Will Face in the Promised Land (1:1–10:10)
   B. Departing for the Promised Land but Quickly Rebelling against the Lord and Experiencing His Judgment for Complaining Bitterly, Challenging the Authority Structures He Has Established among Priests and People, and Turning to Other Gods (10:11–25:18)
II. The Second Generation: A New Start for Israel on the Cusp of Entering the Promised Land (26:1–36:13)

The following comments will address one section at a time, highlighting literary and theological themes so the reader can see their emphases and how they contribute to Numbers's story as a whole.

---

13. R. Dennis Cole, "Numbers," in *ZIBBC* (Grand Rapids: Zondervan, 2009), 1:340–41.
14. Technically, the first generation dies before the end of Num 25 (cf. Deut 2:14 with Num 21:12–13), but the book does not begin its focus on the second generation until the second census in Num 26. See further at p. 327n2. Note also that many of my outline titles are longer than those of a standard outline in order to make the narrative themes clearer to the reader.

Organizing and Preparing the Camp in Light of the Lord's Presence among the Israelites as well as the Battles They Will Face in the Promised Land (1:1–10:10)

Numbers' opening section is positive and hopeful. The Israelites are faithful, obedient, and careful to do "just as the LORD commanded" (1:54; cf. 2:34; 4:49; 8:3, 22; 9:5). The chapters focus on preparing to march into the promised land with the Lord's help, and little suggests this will not happen soon.[15]

Organization and Preparation

This section's main theme is organization and preparation in light of two realities: the Lord's presence in Israel's midst and the coming battles Israel will undertake. The focus on organization and preparation thus meets two practical needs.

First, from a logistics standpoint, the Israelites are a massive group traveling through the wilderness toward Canaan where they will engage in warfare. They need to know the size of their fighting forces (Num 1), how to organize their camp (Num 2; 3:13–49), and how to break camp and march (2:3–31; 10:1–10; see diagrams at 2:3–31: The Camp of the Tribes of Israel, Marching Order of the Tribes).

Second, from a theological standpoint, the Lord, the holy King of the universe, has now come to dwell in their midst, setting up his holy palace-tent in the midst of their tents and coming to dwell within it (Exod 40; Lev 9).[16] This has several significant implications.

First, it means the camp must be kept ritually and morally pure (Num 5). Impurity is incompatible with the Lord's holy presence; it attracts his judgment, which destroys it on contact the way light destroys darkness or bleach destroys mold. Impurity also prevents Israel from carrying out their mission to reflect the Lord's blazing holiness to the world. They are to be his holy nation (Exod 19:6).

Second, the Lord's presence in their midst means the Israelites must not trespass on or against his holy presence or property. The tabernacle was the Lord's palace and the most holy place within was his throne room (cf. 2 Sam 6:2; 1 Chr 28:2). One did not simply barge into it. To do so was a severe breach of royal protocol and disrespect (see 1 Kgs 1:15–23; Esth 4:11; cf. John 14:6).

At the same time, the Lord's palace-tent was ritually holy, thus someone

---

15. Num 9:22 alludes to the fact it would ultimately take a long time to get to the promised land, but even here the focus is on Israel's faithfulness to the Lord's direction (see also 9:23).
16. See further at Listening to the Text in the Story, p. 59.

touching its items—such as the altar—had to be in a state of ritual holiness (Num 4:15; 18:3, 7). Otherwise, such people not only profaned the holy item, treating it as a common thing, but also exposed themselves to the lethal power of the Lord's holiness shared by all tabernacle items. As noted at 4:1–20, p. 79, the Lord's holiness can be likened to nuclear radiation. Just as those who approach radioactive material without the proper protection will die from exposure to it, those who approach these holy items without the proper level of protective ritual holiness will die from exposure to them (see esp. 1 Sam 6:19; 2 Sam 6:6–7). In at least some instances, even angels cover their faces in the presence of this holy King (Isa 6:1–3).[17] To protect this from happening, the Lord sets up organizational and physical safeguards.

Organizationally, he sets aside Levi's tribe to work in his sacred precincts on the Israelites' behalf (Num 1:47–53). Within that tribe, he sets aside Aaron's family as priests in charge of the rest of the Levites (3:5–10; 4:16, 28, 33). Through a ritual, Aaron and his sons are made ritually holy (Lev 8) so they may interact with the Lord's holy objects and serve at the altar, presenting the Israelites' sacrifices (Num 18:5, 7). A different rite confers on the rest of the Levites an elevated state of purity (8:5–22) so they can work in the tabernacle environs, including disassembling and reassembling the tabernacle as the camp moves (3:21–37; 4:1–33). (The text is clear, however, that only priests may have direct contact with the holy items [4:15]).

Physically, the Lord sets the tribe of Levi around the tabernacle in the camp (3:21–39) like a protective ring ensuring the Israelites do not carelessly approach it or risk inadvertent contact through camping right next to it (see diagram at 2:3–31, The Camp of the Tribes of Israel).

Importantly, these protective measures were only meant to keep the Israelites from coming before the Lord *improperly*. He still very much wanted them to come into his presence, standing before him in his tabernacle courts (Lev 1:3; 3:2; 12:6; etc.), bringing to him their burdens and their prayers, their worship and their praise. He therefore set aside Levi's tribe to ensure this could happen properly. They would serve as the Lord's servants at his palace, both in place of the Israelites (Num 3:5–10, 44–45; 8:10–11) and on their behalf, with the priests in particular presenting the Israelites' sacrifices (18:7), interceding for them (16:22, 46–48), and praying the Lord's blessing over them (6:22–27; 10:10).

By these organizational means, the Lord can live among his people, who are led by his priestly and Levitical servants so they may worship him, enjoy

---

17. Allen, "Numbers," 734.

fellowship with him, and yet not face judgment for crossing boundaries they should not. It is not yet Eden but is a strong step toward it.

The Israelites' Organizational Structure in Relation to the Lord's Tabernacle

Tribe	Person	Regular Ritual State	Permitted to Do What at Tabernacle?	Summary
Levi, priestly family	High priest	Holiest of priests (cf. Lev 8:12 with 8:30)	Priestly duties in most holy place, holy place, and courtyard	Allowed to have contact with holy items and do priestly duties
Levi, priestly family	Regular priest	Holy (Lev 8:30)	Priestly duties in holy place and courtyard	
Levi, non-priestly family	Levites	Elevated state of purity (Num 8:5–22)	Help with tabernacle tear down and set up, guarding tabernacle, other duties as assigned	Allowed to do tabernacle duties (but not contact holy items or do priestly duties)
Tribe other than Levi	Lay Israelite	Pure	Go into tabernacle courtyard to present offerings and sacrifices	Not permitted to contact holy items or do priestly or tabernacle duties, but welcome in the Lord's courts for fellowship with him and worship of him

The Unity and Parity of the Tribes

A second theme of this first section may be mentioned more briefly: the unity and relative parity existing among the lay tribes.[18] In Numbers 1–2, the

---

18. That is, the tribes other than Levi. While Levi is certainly unified with the other tribes, it differs in terms of tabernacle responsibilities (as just noted above).

descriptions of the census and the arrangement of the outer camp strike many moderns as excessively repetitive, with the same formula repeated for each of the twelve tribes. Similarly, chapter 7 repeats twelve times a lengthy, nearly verbatim description of tribal gifts to the tabernacle (7:12–83)! And yet the repetition may be part of the point, underscoring that each tribe is part of the Lord's people and contributing to his work and worship. Different tribes but one people, all servants of the King. Indeed, while the tribes vary in size (Num 1), each brings the same tabernacle gifts in Numbers 7. In worship, they are not simply unified, but equal.[19]

Departing for the Promised Land but Quickly Rebelling against the Lord and Experiencing His Judgment for Complaining Bitterly, Challenging the Authority Structures He Has Established among Priests and People, and Turning to Other Gods (10:11–25:18)

Whereas Numbers's first section was positive and hopeful, its second section is negative and discouraging. The Israelites turn from belief to disbelief, obedience to disobedience, and ultimately rebel against the Lord, experiencing his repeated judgment (see chart below).

This repetitive pattern is especially evident in this section's major themes. Though at least five may be identified (see below), the two most prominent are rebellion and judgment, making this section a sobering and depressing account to read. Its opening four chapters explode with six different rebellions and corresponding judgments, and further instances of each continue to detonate throughout its remaining chapters. Were it not for the presence of mediators to intercede on Israel's behalf, their future as a nation may well have ended in the wilderness.

Rebellion

The rebellions may be put into six groups. The first is characterized by lack of belief in the Lord's goodness to provide resources and discontent with those he has provided (11:1–3, 4–35; 20:2–13; 21:4–9). This is especially tragic in light of the many ways the Lord had already shown his faithfulness to provide for his people's physical needs, whether of water (Exod 15:22–25; 17:1–7) or food (Exod 16). It is a human tendency to forget the Lord's past faithfulness, doubt his goodness to provide in the present, and treat with contempt whatever he has provided. Israel strongly manifested these tendencies.

---

19. See further p. 139, Which Tribe Matters Most?

Rebellion, Judgment, and Mediators in Numbers 10–25

The Rebellious Act	The Lord's Judgment	The Role of the Mediator(s)
The Israelites complain at Taberah (11:1–3)	The Lord sends fire that consumes the camp's outskirts	Moses prays and the fire dies down
The people wail about food (11:4–35)	The Lord sends a severe plague among the people	Moses initially prays for food, which is provided; no mention of mediation regarding the plague
Aaron and (especially) Miriam reject Moses as the Lord's chief spokesman (12:1–15)	The Lord strikes Miriam with a ritually defiling skin disease	Moses prays on her behalf for healing
Ten of the scouts doubt the Lord's ability to give Israel the promised land (13:28–33); they lead Israel into rebellious unbelief (14:1–4, 36–37)	The Lord strikes them dead with a plague	None
The Israelites rebel against the Lord's command to enter the promised land (14:1–35)	The Lord initially threatens their immediate destruction, but in response to Moses's prayer, forgives them and mitigates their punishment to wandering in the wilderness for forty years and dying before entering the promised land	Moses pleads for the Lord's forgiveness
The Israelites rebel against the Lord's command not to enter the promised land (14:39–45)	The Lord withholds his help so they are defeated soundly before their enemies	None

continued

The Rebellious Act	The Lord's Judgment	The Role of the Mediator(s)
A man breaks the Sabbath (15:32–36)	The Lord decrees the community must execute him	None
Korah, Dathan, and Abiram rebel against the Levites' special role and Moses's leadership (16:1–40)	The Lord has the earth swallow them alive and sends fire to destroy 250 of their followers who offered incense	In response to the Lord's initial decree against the whole community, Moses and Aaron pray he focus his judgment on the rebellion's leaders
The Israelites blame Moses and Aaron for the death of those whom the Lord had executed (16:41–50)	The Lord sends a plague among the people	Aaron makes an incense offering to atone, finally stopping the plague
The people complain about lack of water and oppose Moses and Aaron, ultimately quarreling with the Lord (20:2–13)	None for the Israelites; he provides water	Moses and Aaron pray for the provision of water
Moses and Aaron show unbelief in the Lord by not treating him as holy (20:2–13)	The Lord decrees they will die before entering the promised land	None
The people grow tired of the journey and speak against God and Moses (21:4–9)	The Lord sends venomous snakes among the people	Moses prays for the people and the Lord directs him to make a bronze serpent so the people may be healed
Israelite men commit sexual immorality with foreign women and worship false gods (25:1–15)	The Lord commands the execution of the leaders and sends a plague among the people	Phinehas kills an Israelite and Midianite in the midst of their sexual immorality, in this way atoning for Israel, and the plague is stopped

In the second group of rebellions, the people disbelieve the Lord's ability to fight on their behalf (Num 13:28–33; 14:1–35). His incredulous question in 14:11 stands over this episode: "How long will [the Israelites] refuse to believe in me, in spite of all the signs I have performed among them?" Spiritual amnesia is deadly. Forgetting the Lord's mighty acts of salvation in the past leads to unbelief in the present, and unbelief is the springboard to disobedience.

In the third group of rebellions, the people reject the authority structures the Lord had established among them (Num 12:1–15; 16:1–40). Such rebellions are caused by the twin poisons of envy and desire: envy for what others have and desire for power and glory. The antidote is to be so focused on God's glory you care little for your own. Moses is a perfect example of this (11:26–29). His goal is not to be the main Spirit-led leader; it is for the Lord's people to be led by the Spirit, and he is perfectly content for that to happen through other gifted leaders.

The fourth group of rebellions is characterized by simple disobedience to the Lord's commands (Num 14:39–45; 15:32–36; 25:1–15). The temptations leading to such sins likely varied, but in each case the command was clear, yet the Israelites chose to break it. At its root, sin is always rebellion against the Lord.

A fifth rebellion concerns family and friends of those whom the Lord executed and who hold Moses and Aaron responsible for the deaths (Num 16:41–50). As comments on those verses will indicate (see Chapter 19, p. 230), the Israelites refused to acknowledge the sin of those who died, leaving them no choice but to shift the blame. This response stretches back to Eden (Gen 3:12–13) and forward to our own day. Whether it is the sin of a loved one or our own, our hearts have an amazing ability to rationalize, justify, and shift the blame. Thus the sin is never repented of or dealt with, and it rots us from the inside out.

Finally, Moses and Aaron rebel when they show unbelief in the Lord by not treating him as holy (Num 20:2–13). Later texts make clear the Israelites played a part in this, driving Moses and Aaron to their wits' end with incessant grumbling and complaining (Deut 1:37; 3:26; 4:21; Ps 106:32–33). But the two are still culpable not only because as leaders they are held to a higher standard but also because the nature of their actions was so wrong: they put themselves in the place of God as savior.[20] Leaders are especially vulnerable to

---

20. See at Num 20:9–11, 12 (p. 269), and also pp. 271–73, Why Is the Punishment So Severe?

this sin, making this story a strong warning for them. We do well to repeat regularly with John the Baptist, "I am not the Messiah" (John 1:20).

Judgment

As shown in the chart above, these rebellions lead to judgment. Three observations may be made. First, in several cases, the judgment corresponds ironically to the crime: those who wrongly long for meat receive it but die before they can eat it (Num 11:31–34); the scouts who report that entering the land will result in death are killed (14:36–37); the Israelites have forty days to scout the land but, when they reject it, they must wander in the wilderness forty years as a result (14:34); and those who illicitly present an incense offering are consumed by fire like an offering (16:6–7, 17–18, 35). Though not every judgment is ironic, the overall point is clear: in the Lord's economy, the punishment always fits the crime.

Second, such judgments serve as warnings against repeating the sin. Any parent understands that one reason they punish their children is to warn them. Loving parents long that neither the child nor any watching siblings repeat the wrong. Later biblical passages in fact look back to this section as a warning of how *not* to live before the Lord (Ps 106:13–18, 24–33; 1 Cor 10:1–12; Heb 3:7–4:2). The Lord has created us for life under his blessing, not death under his judgment, and for this reason sends strong warnings to guide us to his life-giving paths.

This leads directly to the third observation: when judgment does not end in death, its goal is to discipline, leading those who have sinned back to the Lord and his ways. One of the most explicit Old Testament passages on discipline is found in Leviticus 26, where the Lord describes the curses he will send to discipline his people if they disobey and break the covenant (26:18). Consider the following comments on that verse:

> The verb "discipline" [Heb. *yissar*] elsewhere describes the discipline a parent exercises with a child (Deut 21:18; Prov 19:18; 29:17), and, in the same vein, the discipline the LORD exercises with his people (Deut 4:36; 8:5). Such discipline could indeed be severe, as [Lev 26] indicates (cf. Pss 38:2[1]; 39:11[12]; 118:18). The Hebrew term is sometimes translated "punish," but the word "discipline" is more appropriate, since it indicates the goal is instruction (cf. Ps 94:12), which is the case here: The Israelites are to learn obedience through these punishments (cf. Hos 5:14–15). Other passages explain God does not discipline his people "merely because

they deserve it, but because he loves them and wants to correct their foolish ways."[21] Currid states it well: "The purpose of these judgments is restoration, not annihilation."[22]

Miriam must therefore learn the respect she owes the Lord's chosen servant (Num 12:1–15), the Israelites must learn to trust the Lord's promises (14:1–35), and Moses and Aaron must learn to show their belief in the Lord through honoring him (20:2–13). In each case, like a good parent, the Lord disciplines those he loves for their greater good, even if the discipline is painful. As the writer of Hebrews notes, "No discipline seems pleasant at the time, but painful. Later on, however, it produces a harvest of righteousness and peace for those who have been trained by it" (Heb 12:11).

The Need for a Mediator, Atonement, and Mercy

The above chart also highlights the central role mediators play, especially in making atonement and appealing to God's mercy. In two instances, the Lord's judgment ends when a priest makes atonement, once by a more regular offering (incense; Num 16:41–50) and once by an irregular "offering" (the slaying of Zimri and Kozbi in the midst of the sin causing the Lord's judgment; 25:6–15). In each case, however, a priest does what only priests are called to do: make atonement on behalf of the people's sin so they might be reconciled to God.

In several other instances, Moses, sometimes joined by Aaron, appeals to the Lord to show mercy in the midst of judgment. The clearest example is in Numbers 14, where the Lord threatens to destroy and disown his people for refusing to enter the promised land. In response, Moses both acknowledges the Lord's right to exercise judgment and prays his mercy will be stronger still. As noted further below,

> Moses . . . appeals to the Lord's character, citing the Lord's earlier self-description as being "slow to anger, abounding in love and forgiving sin and rebellion. Yet he does not leave the guilty unpunished" (14:18a; cf. Exod 34:6–7a). In other words, the Lord is characterized by both mercy and

---

21. Gordon J. Wenham, *Leviticus*, NICOT (Grand Rapids: Eerdmans, 1979), 330–31, citing (among other passages) Prov 3:11–12; Amos 4:6–11; Heb 12:5–11.

22. Sklar, *Leviticus* (ZECOT), 729–30 (verse citations in the ZECOT series follow Hebrew numbering; where different, English versification is noted in brackets); the Currid quote is from John D. Currid, *Leviticus*, Ep Study Commentary (Darlington, UK: Evangelical Press, 2005), 351.

judgment, which is exactly what we will see play out here: mercy in that the Lord will not disown the nation by wiping them out immediately and starting over with Moses, yet judgment in that he will sentence the nation to wandering and dying in the wilderness, never to enter the Promised Land. By citing Exod 34:6–7, Moses acknowledges the Lord's right to administer such justice here, all the while praying that his mercy would also be on full display. He in fact returns to the Lord's love in verse 19, knowing that "God has always bent over backward on the side of love and forgiveness,"[23] and therefore asking the Lord to forgive in keeping with that great love, a love that he has already shown by granting his people forgiveness for their many wrongs since their delivery from Egypt (14:19).[24]

Though other passages are not as detailed, Moses may be seen repeatedly praying on the Israelites' behalf for the Lord's mercy and forgiveness (Num 11:2; 12:13; 16:22; 21:7). The result is not only that the Lord's mercy is shown but also that the people become keenly aware of their need for a mediator. As discussed below (pp. 23, 25), both these realities are put on full display in Jesus.

The Unique Roles of Priests and Levites

Two final themes of this second section may be more briefly addressed. The first concerns the priests' and Levites' unique roles. Described in the discussion of Numbers 1:1–10:10 above (pp. 7–9), these roles resurface in this section because the people rebel against them in Numbers 16. The result is not only judgment (16:28–35) but also an underscoring of the priests' and Levites' unique roles among the people (with the priests taking the lead over the Levites; 17:1–18:7) and an explanation of how the Lord will support priests and Levites through the Israelites' gifts (18:8–32). This emphasis relates to previous themes: in order to avoid judgment for trespassing on the Lord's holy property, and in order to have mediators interceding for them, the Israelites must respect and support their spiritual leaders.

The Lord's Steadfast Faithfulness to His Promises

In the midst of this fairly dark and depressing section, the Lord's steadfast faithfulness breaks through with glorious light. In Numbers 14, the first

---

23. Dennis T. Olson, *Numbers*, IBC (Lousville: John Knox Press, 1996), 83.

24. See comments below at Num 14:13–19. For further discussion on the role of the mediator, see Jay Sklar, "Sin and Atonement: Lessons from the Pentateuch," *BBR* 22.4 (2012): 467–91, esp. 485–91.

generation of Israelites are sentenced to die in the wilderness, but the very next chapter begins with the assurance their children will enter the land: "Speak to the Israelites and say to them: 'After you enter the land I am giving you as a home . . .'" (15:2). The Lord has not forgotten his promise. Similarly, in Numbers 21, Israel is attacked by Canaanites, who take some of the people captive. They cry to the Lord and he delivers the Canaanites into their hand, a foretaste of his faithfulness to defeat the peoples of Canaan on their behalf (21:1–3). The same is seen later in the chapter, with the defeat of Sihon and Og (21:21–35), early assurances of what the Lord will do on a larger scale in Canaan. Finally, the story of Balaam in Numbers 22–24 is littered with allusions to the Lord's patriarchal promises. As noted in the commentary (see below, pp. 301–2), these allusions are ironically expressed in the words of Balaam, a pagan diviner hired to curse Israel, underscoring that the Lord is so sovereign he can use even Israel's enemies to bless them.

Numbers	Genesis
"Who can count the dust of Jacob?" (23:10)	13:16; 28:14
"Like a lion they crouch and lie down, like a lioness—who dares to rouse them?" (24:9)	49:9
"May those who bless you be blessed and those who curse you be cursed!" (24:9)	12:3; 27:29
"A scepter will rise out of Israel" (24:17)	49:10 (cf. Ps 2:9)

In strong contrast to his people, the Lord is always faithful to his promises. This does not mean our faithfulness does not matter; in fact, the main themes of this second section focus on the dire consequences of unfaithfulness. As Hebrews warns, "It is a terrifying thing to fall into the hands of the living God" (Heb 10:31, NET). But God will not let sin ultimately thwart his promises or purposes. And this gives us hope to return to him and follow him with bold confidence as we seek to establish his kingdom of goodness, justice, mercy, and love in this world. The Lord is faithful, and he will do it!

The Second Generation: A New Start for Israel on the Cusp of Entering the Promised Land (26:1–36:13)

In contrast to the preceding section, hope returns in this final section with its focus on the second generation of Israelites. Definite similarities exist between the two generations. Just as the story of the first generation began with censuses (Num 1–4) and preparations for marching into the promised land (5:1–10:10), so the story of the second generation begins with a census (26) and preparations for marching into the promised land (27–36). But whereas the first generation was characterized by disobedience and denied entry to the land, the second generation is characterized by obedience (26:4–63; 31:7, 31; 36:10) and is now at the promised land's border awaiting the Lord's command to enter (36:13). In telling the second generation's story, this section focuses on four major themes.[25]

Transition

The first is transition, which is the focus of the opening two chapters. The story transitions to the second generation (26:1–51), who are headed to a new land (26:52–56) into which they will march under new leadership (27:12–23). This section therefore begins by resetting the narrative, allowing some measure of hope that the story will now proceed as it should have the first time and that Israel will make it into Canaan. This leads to the next theme.

The Land

While the first section opened with discussion of military numbers and the camp's arrangement (Num 1–2), this section opens with discussion of military numbers (26:5–51) and allotment of the promised land (26:52–56, 62), introducing the land as a central focus. The Lord had first promised the land to Israel when he swore to Abraham that his descendants would one day possess it (Gen 15:18–21), and Israel was on the cusp of realizing that promise some forty years earlier before they tragically rebelled and refused to enter (Num 14:1–35). Now the second generation is camped one river-breadth away, on the verge of marching into the land (26:3). This section thus returns repeatedly to issues dealing with the land (see table below).

---

25. Themes from the previous two sections of Numbers are also found, though in more minor ways. These include the unity and (relative) parity of the tribes (26:52–56; 36:8), the importance of providing for priests and Levites (31:28–30; 35:1–8), and the importance of keeping the camp and land ritually pure because of the Lord's presence (31:19–24; 35:32–34).

Preparing for the Promised Land in Numbers 26–36

Passage	Relationship to Theme of the Land
26:52–56	Instructions for allotting the land
27:1–11	A legal case about inheritance in the land
27:12–23	Identifying the leader to take Israel into the land
28:1–29:40	How to celebrate festivals within the land
32:1–42	Two and a half tribes seeking their land inheritance east of the Jordan
33:50–56	Dispossessing the land's inhabitants and distributing it
34:1–15	The land's boundaries
34:16–29	Those who would apportion the land
35:1–8	Cities for the Levites in the land
35:9–34	Cities of refuge in the land
36:1–12	A follow-up to the legal case about inheritance in the land

Such a focus gives the strong impression Israel is on the cusp of the land both physically and temporally. Indeed, each passage functions like a drumbeat drawing repeated attention to the Lord's promise that the land will indeed be theirs, if only they march with faith into it. That they might fail to do so is a real and present danger, as the next theme makes clear.

Warnings against Unfaithfulness

The hope presented by the focus on the land is tempered by the sobering reality of past judgments. Indeed, past unfaithfulness or its judgments keep flashing like a red warning light, as do exhortations to avoid future judgments because of unfaithfulness.

As noted above, the Lord's judgment functioned in part to warn others against repeating the sin. He knows how quickly we can forget such warnings or assume they do not apply to us. It is thus no surprise that the second generation is repeatedly warned against disobedience, just as it is no surprise that Paul, after discussing how the first generation's unfaithfulness served as a warning of how not to live, concludes by saying, "So, if you think you are standing firm, take heed lest you fall!" (1 Cor 10:12, my translation; cf. Matt 26:41). None of us is immune from this risk.

Warnings against Unfaithfulness in Numbers 26–36

Passage	Relationship to Theme of Warnings against Unfaithfulness
26:8–10	Mention of Korah's rebellion and the Lord's judgment
26:61	Mention of the deaths of Nadab and Abihu
26:64–65	Mention that everyone from the first generation (except faithful Caleb and Joshua) had died in the wilderness
27:13	Mention of Moses's coming death
31:2	Mention of Moses's coming death
31:14–16	Mention of the apostasy at Baal of Peor
32:6–15	Accusation that the two and a half tribes are repeating the apostasy of the first generation
33:50–56	Warnings against failing to drive out the land's inhabitants and succumbing to apostasy

Obedience

Given this section's warnings, the second generation's obedience is encouraging. At various points we see them do "as the LORD commanded Moses" (Num 26:4; 31:7, 31; cf. 32:25). Most notably, the book closes with Zelophehad's daughters modeling such obedience (36:10). As noted in the commentary on that passage, the phrase "doing just as the LORD commanded Moses" is the hallmark of Israel when being faithful (Exod 12:28; Lev 24:23; Num 8:22; etc.), and it is embodied here by these women, who are named for the third time (cf. 26:33; 27:1) and serve as a concluding model of faith, both in their belief in an inheritance in the promised land and their obedience to the Lord's commands. If the rest of Israel were to have the faith of these women, all would be well.

Numbers's Theological Themes Summarized and Related to the Larger Biblical Story

In discussing themes, the previous section stayed within the bounds of Numbers. This section will now relate Numbers's theological themes to the larger biblical story, showing how they are emphasized and developed in the Old Testament and the New, and especially how they relate to the person and work of Jesus.

The discussion is organized under three headings: the Lord, the people, and the land. That Numbers should focus on these themes is no surprise. As part of the Pentateuch, Numbers is focused on the promises made to the patriarchs. These promises focus on *the Lord* calling a specific *people* (Israel) to himself and promising them a *land* (Heb. *'erets*) where they could walk in fellowship with him (Gen 12:1–3; 17:1–8). These promises are also in direct keeping with the Lord's intent for humanity from the very beginning. The Bible begins with the story of *the Lord* creating *people* (Adam and Eve) and commanding them to fill all the *earth* (Heb. *'erets*) as they walk in fellowship with him and reflect his image into the world (Gen 1–2). The Lord's intent has always been to enjoy fellowship with his creation and to have them fill all the earth with his character of love, justice, mercy, goodness, and peace. To return to Numbers, this means Israel's purpose is nothing less than carrying out the Lord's creational purpose for humanity: walking in close fellowship with their King as they live out his character, thereby filling the land with his holy kingdom in anticipation of the day his kingdom will fill all the earth.

The Lord

Three themes focus on the Lord:

1. *The Lord's holy presence.* His presence is manifested in the tent of meeting, which serves as his portable royal residence (see at Num 1:1, p. 49). He appears there in a cloud of divine glory, assuring the Israelites he is with them and will march before them into the promised land (10:33–36) and also welcoming them into his courts with their burdens, prayers, worship, and praise. But he is absolutely holy, meaning the Israelites must not only maintain and respect the ritual purity of his tabernacle (19:11–13, 20), camp (5:1–4), and land (35:33–34),[26] they

---

26. See also pp. 7–9, *Organization and Preparation*, for the special role of priests and Levites in maintaining and respecting the tabernacle's ritual purity.

must also obey his commands so they can be his "kingdom of priests and holy nation" (Exod 19:6), reflecting his holiness to the watching world. To disrespect his holiness is to deny who he is, and such denials have severe consequences—as even Moses and Aaron would painfully learn (Num 20:12). In short, the people are to respond to the Lord's holy presence among them by following him with bold confidence into the promised land (see at Num 21:1–3, 21–35; 36:13, pp. 277–78, 279–80, 420) and living holy lives (see at Num 35:33–34, p. 413).

This theme of the Lord's holy presence among his people runs through the Bible. In the Old Testament, it begins before Numbers (Gen 3:8; Exod 29:42–46) and continues after it (1 Kgs 8:10–11). In the New Testament, Jesus becomes the ultimate expression of the holy God dwelling among us (John 1:14), a presence that continues among his people to this day (Rev 1:12–2:1) and will find its complete expression at the last day (21:3–4). As in Numbers, the Lord's ongoing presence should fill his people today with bold confidence in carrying out his kingdom mission (Matt 28:18–20). It should also inspire us to live holy lives of reverence before him (2 Cor 7:1; Heb 12:18–29), especially since our very bodies are living tabernacles in which he dwells by his Holy Spirit (1 Cor 6:19).

2. *The Lord's faithfulness to his covenant promises.* At several points, the book of Numbers makes clear the Lord has been—and continues to be—faithful to the covenant promises he made to Israel's forefathers, whether to be their God (Gen 17:7; 26:24; cf. at Num 10:33–36), to make them a great nation (Gen 12:2; 15:5; 26:4; cf. at Num 1:20–46; 10:33–36; 22:2–4), to give them the promised land (Gen 12:7; 15:18; 26:3; cf. at Num 21:1–3, 21–35; 36:13), to bless the nations through them (Gen 12:3; 26:4; cf. at Num 15:13–16), or, most generally, to bless them (Gen 12:2–3; cf. at Num 6:27; 23:6–10; 24:3–9). "God is not human, that he should lie; not a human being, that he should change his mind" (Num 23:19a). Because he is faithful to his promises the Israelites can follow him, confident that the covenant blessings will be theirs.

The Lord's faithfulness continues after Numbers as Israel experiences the covenant blessings, specifically, making it safely into the long-awaited promised land (see Joshua). The Lord's faithfulness gave the Israelites freedom to pursue covenant living boldly and wholeheartedly, knowing the Lord's promises were certain and sure for those who trusted in him. Correspondingly, the New Testament affirms those who follow Jesus can do so with full confidence that the Lord will be faithful to his covenant promises to us, ensuring we receive all the new covenant blessings, in particular, eternal fellowship with him in the greater promised land to come (John 14:1–3; 1 Cor 1:4–9; 2 Cor 1:20–22; Phil 1:6; 1 Thess 5:23–24; Heb 6:13–20).

3. *The Lord's patience, mercy, and judgment.* He shows patience and mercy repeatedly as he forgives his people rather than unleashing on them the full fury their sins deserve (see esp. at Num 14:10b–12, 13–19, 20–35). In this regard, it is not surprising there is judgment in the Old Testament; it is surprising there is not more. But the Lord's patience does not prevent his justice from coming, sometimes severely so (11:33–34; 12:9–10; 15:32–36; 16:31–35, 47–49; etc.). It serves as a strong warning to Israel—and to us!—not to rebel against the King and Creator. "It is a dreadful thing to fall into the hands of the living God" (Heb 10:31).

The Lord's patience and mercy continues throughout the Old Testament (Pss 30:5; 103:1–18; Mic 7:18) and into the New (Rev 2:21). It shines forth with greatest clarity in Jesus's death on behalf of sinners (John 3:16; Rom 5:8; Eph 5:2; 1 John 4:9–10) and in the Lord's delay of ushering in final judgment (Rom 2:4; 2 Pet 3:9). But the theme of his justice continues as well. It breaks out among the people of God (Acts 5:1–11; 1 Cor 11:30; Jas 5:16) and the nations (Acts 12:21–23), just as it will at the final judgment against those without faith in Jesus (John 3:18, 36; 5:24; 8:24; Acts 4:12; Rom 6:23). Again, this is a stark reminder that we must embrace the Lord's covenant and follow him wholeheartedly.

The People

Five major themes focus on the Israelites:

1. *Unity.* As the Lord's people, they were to be unified in order to carry out their kingdom mission together. This is emphasized repeatedly: in the census lists (which make clear they are "Israelites" [woodenly, "the sons of Israel"] and, thus, blood relatives; Num 1:20–46; 26:4b–51); in the list of tabernacle dedication gifts (which show every tribe participated equally; Num 7:10–88); in sending one spy from each tribe to scout the land (13:2); in sending one thousand from each tribe to fight Midian (31:4); and in requiring the tribes that settled east of the Jordan River to join the battle for Canaan on the west (ch. 32).

The New Testament also emphasizes the necessity of unity among the Lord's covenant people. In his longest-recorded prayer, Jesus prays that his followers may have "complete unity" so the world might know his message is true (John 17:20–23). Paul pictures this unity by describing Jesus as "the chief cornerstone" of "a holy temple" made up of the people of God (Eph 2:20–21). This is a temple "in which God lives by his Spirit" (v. 22) and where his glory is manifested in the earth (3:20–21), especially as his people show one another his love (4:1–6; cf. 1 Cor 12 and 13; see also 1 Pet 2:4–10).

2. *Respecting others' callings.* The Lord's people were to respect the different callings of the individuals among them, whether of Aaron and the priests and Levites, called to the special privilege of tabernacle service (Num 1:47–53; 3:5–39; 4:1–49; 16:1–17:11), or of Moses, called to serve as the people's chief leader (12:6–8). The first-generation Israelites often failed to do this (see esp. chs. 12 and 16).

Believers today are likewise to respect the different callings of their brothers and sisters (1 Cor 12:4–31) and the authority structures the Lord has put in place (1 Thess 5:12–13; 1 Tim 5:17; Heb 13:17). In terms of the latter, the New Testament admonishes believers to respect their leaders (13:17) and provide for their material needs (1 Cor 9:14; Gal 6:6). Moreover, it also emphasizes that Jesus is a leader incomparably greater than any who have gone before. While Moses was a faithful servant *in* God's house, Jesus is the ruling Son of God *over* God's house (Heb 3:1–6); while Aaron was a high priest who temporarily atoned for Israel's sins by sacrifice (10:1–4), Jesus is the great high priest who offered himself as a sacrifice that atones for sins once and for all (10:5–14). If the Israelites were to follow their leaders, how much more are we to follow Jesus (3:7–11)!

3. *Disobedience.* This is found especially in the book's second section (Num 10:11–25:18), where the first-generation Israelites doubt the Lord's provision (11:1–9; 14:1–10; 20:2–5; 21:4–5), question the authority structure he establishes (see above), and are led astray into the worship of other gods (25:1–3). This rebellion not only results in the Lord's judgment (see further above) but also prevents their generation from receiving the covenant promise of land (14:22–23, 28–35).

The theme of the Israelites' disobedience is revisited in the Psalms (95:7–11) and especially in 1 Corinthians 10:1–13 and Hebrews 3:6–4:13, where their faithlessness serves as a warning of the danger of hardening your heart and turning away from the Lord. The New

Testament passages are particularly clear: Do not reject Jesus and therefore fail to receive the eternal promised land of rest awaiting those who follow him (see also Heb 10:19–31).
4. *The people's need for a mediator.* This was especially so when they had rebelled defiantly against the Lord. In these cases, there was no automatic forgiveness by means of sacrifice (see at Num 15:22–31, pp. 213–15). But it was possible for a mediator—such as Moses, Aaron, or a priest—either to stand in the gap and carry out an act that atoned for the people (16:47–48; 25:7–9, 11–13) or to plead that the Lord would be gracious and forgive them (11:2; 12:13; 16:20–24; 21:7).

The New Testament makes clear that any mediation sinners could ever need has been met fully and finally in Jesus, the "one mediator between God and mankind" (1 Tim 2:5), who perfectly fulfills this role because he "gave himself as a ransom for all people" (v. 6; see also Heb 9:12). Moreover, Jesus continues to apply this mediation, and at this very moment is "at the right hand of God . . . interceding for us" (Rom 8:34; see also Heb 7:23–25; 9:24; 1 John 2:1). For this reason, God's repentant people should never fear losing his love. Nothing and no one can "separate us from the love of God that is in Christ Jesus our Lord" (Rom 8:39, see also vv. 34–38).
5. *Obedience.* The Israelites' obedience is especially seen in the first generation in the book's first section (Num 1:54; 2:33–34; 4:49; 8:20, 22; 9:5) and in the second generation in its final section (26:4–63; 31:7, 31; 36:10). Not surprisingly, the Lord's judgment against them is absent in these sections. Instead, the picture is one of the Lord's covenant people enjoying his presence and preparing to follow him into the promised land.

The New Testament also emphasizes showing faith through obedience (John 14:15, 23–24; Jas 2:14–26). Just as the Israelites' obedience was the way by which they lived as a kingdom of priests and holy nation (Exod 19:6), so it is for the Lord's people today (see 1 Pet 2:9–12). As Jesus tells his followers, "Let your light shine before others, that they may see your good deeds and glorify your Father in heaven" (Matt 5:16). Our obedience is indeed for the sake of the nations.

The Land

Two themes concern the land:

1. *Inheritance.* The Israelites will one day inherit the land, that is, Canaan, which the Lord had promised their forefathers in his covenant with

them (Gen 12:7; 15:18; 26:3; see map 2). The land is often in the story's foreground, as when the Israelites faithlessly refuse to enter it (Num 14) or when they assemble on its border forty years later, ready to march in (Num 36:13). It is also often in the background, as with the numerous laws given to inform them how to live once they enter it (see Num 33:50–36:13). In either case, it is abundantly clear that Israel has been promised this land and will one day be in it.

The theme of inheriting the physical land of Canaan is fulfilled in an initial way in the book of Joshua. But the New Testament also applies this theme to the eternal inheritance that awaits those who become God's children through faith in Jesus (Rom 8:1, 12–17; Gal 4:4–7; Eph 1:13–14; Col 1:12–14; Heb 9:13–15; 1 Pet 1:3–6). The fact of this inheritance radically redefines how believers live, since their focus is not on the things of this world but on the praise from their covenant King in the world to come (Matt 6:19–24; 25:21).

2. *Mission.* The land was to have a special place in the Lord's mission of filling the earth with his kingdom. In many ways, the promised land was to function in the world the way the tabernacle functioned in Israel. For example, just as the tabernacle was to be kept pure and holy because the Lord lived there (cf. Lev 15:31), so too was the land of Israel to be kept holy because the Lord lived there: "Do not defile the land where you live and where I dwell, for I, the LORD, dwell among the Israelites" (Num 35:34; cf. Lev 18:24–30; 20:22–26). And just as Aaron's family functioned as priests in the tabernacle, so were the Israelites to function as priests in the earth (Exod 19:6; cf. at Num 15:37–41). In short, the land was to be a place where the nations could see the life the Lord intended for his creation: a holy people, enjoying covenant fellowship with their Creator and King, extending his kingdom of mercy, love, purity, and justice in all the earth.

While the physical land of Canaan was to be a sacred space in Numbers, the area of sacred space was never limited to the actual land of Canaan either in the Old Testament (cf. Psalm 67) or in the New (Acts 1:8). Moreover, the New Testament redefines sacred space in terms of the body of believers, so that it exists wherever they are: a holy place, God's temple (1 Cor 3:16; 2 Cor 6:16; Eph 2:20–22; 1 Pet 2:5). This body of believers—the church—is given the mission to spread and fill the earth, so that God's temple encompasses everything. This is the very thing Jesus teaches us to pray: "Thy kingdom come; thy will be done on earth as it is in heaven" (Matt 6:10, KJV). And he makes clear that we can have confidence to do this because he is the King over all and the King who goes with us in this mission (Matt 28:18–20).

Teaching and Preaching from Numbers

Each chapter of the commentary ends with a section titled Live the Story that discusses how the chapter relates to Christian living. I have divided each discussion into several sections that concentrate on a main point that can be developed in teaching or preaching. Each section begins with a question (instead of a statement) to aid those wanting to approach their teaching or preaching more inductively.[27]

As a further aid, the goal of the following is to identify general interpretive principles for reading Numbers in a way that is sensitive both to its own historical context and to the Bible's larger redemptive-historical context. The discussion is organized to reflect two of Numbers's major genres: law (Num 5–6; 15; 19; 28–30; 35:9–36:13) and narrative (Num 7–14; 16–18; 20–25; 27; 31:1–33:49).[28]

Law

From the perspective of redemptive history, the laws in Numbers (like those of Leviticus) belong to the Sinai covenant, which is no longer in force because Jesus has inaugurated a new covenant (Luke 22:20; Heb 8:6–13). It would therefore be wrong to assume that all these laws are in equal force today.

At the same time, they remain incredibly relevant to Christian living. Laws express the lawgiver's values. For instance, most societies value life and the right to personal property. Therefore they have laws prohibiting murder and theft. Similarly, the laws the Lord gives in Numbers express his values.

Moreover, since the Lord's values flow from his character, which is perfect and constant (Mal 3:6; Heb 13:8; Jas 1:17), we should expect the values behind his laws to have some application today. They give us a window into the Lord's heart, so there is much to learn from them for those seeking to reflect his image well.

In teaching or preaching from a section of law, we should therefore begin

---

27. For possible teaching or sermon series, see Jay Sklar, *Additional Notes on* Numbers *in Zondervan's The Story of God Bible Commentary Series* (St. Louis, MO: Gleanings Press, 2023), Appendix 2—Preaching/Teaching Series on the Book of Numbers.

28. These are the two most significant genres in Numbers. Others will be discussed in the context of the commentary, e.g., for census lists, see comments at pp. 54–55, Why Does It Matter That This King Keeps His Promises?, and p. 139, Which Tribe Matters Most?

by identifying the value(s) being communicated to the original audience. If obeyed, what would that law have taught the Israelites about God's character? About the values he wanted his people to live out in the world? Once these questions are answered, it is a short step to ask, "How does the Lord demonstrate these same values in the New Testament, especially in his Son, Jesus? How does the New Testament command us as Christians to live out these values in the world today?"[29]

Finally, we must remind ourselves and our hearers that law was never given to save us. Law does not *establish* our relationship with the Lord; it *regulates* and *guides* it. The Lord did not say to Israel, "Keep these laws and then I will redeem you." He redeemed them first (Exod 1–19) and then gave them laws to teach them how to live in relationship with him (Exod 20–23). Indeed, to obey the Lord's laws is to respond to the redeeming King with appropriate worship, reverence, and love (cf. Exod 20:2 with 20:3–17). Paul picks up this point in Romans 12, which he begins with a command to obey God ("offer your bodies as a living sacrifice"), doing so as an act of worship ("this is your true and proper worship"). But he introduces the command by referring to the merciful redemption God accomplished in Jesus Christ, which he has just described in Romans 9–11: "*Therefore*, I urge you, brothers and sisters, *in view of God's mercy*, to offer your bodies as a living sacrifice . . ." (12:1, italics added).

Old Testament or New, God's laws are not a to-do list to earn relationship with him; they are loving directions from a heavenly Father that show us how to live in fellowship with him and reflect his character into the world. And while we must repent of failing to obey them and not reflecting his character well, we should teach and preach on law in such a way that our hearers can join the Israelites in praying Psalm 119, rejoicing that God has loved us so much he has given us good laws to guide us in paths that keep us close to him.

Narrative

A large portion of Numbers is devoted to narratives (Num 7–14; 16–18; 20–25; 27; 31:1–33:49), so it is helpful to identify several interpretive

---

29. For a more detailed discussion of how Old Testament laws apply today, see Christopher J. H. Wright, *Old Testament Ethics for the People of God* (Downers Grove, IL: IVP Academic, 2004), 314–24, esp. 321–24 (his discussion complements the above; see also 403–8 for questions related to Israel as a theocratic nation); see also Sklar, *Leviticus* (ZECOT), 33–39. For a helpful summary of various approaches to this question, see Derek Tidball, *The Message of Leviticus: Free to Be Holy*, The Bible Speaks Today (Downers Grove, IL: InterVarsity Press, 2005), 28–31.

questions that may be asked of any narrative, whatever its type, that help us teach and preach it well.[30]

To begin, what does this narrative *as a whole* teach us about the Lord's character? About his ways with humanity? About faithful covenant living? There may be more than one answer, but asking what the narrative as a whole teaches about these things encourages us to ask how the story's different pieces work together. For example, the Israelites' refusal to enter the promised land in Numbers 14 clearly demonstrates: the proper response to the Lord's miraculous deeds is obedient faith (seen in the negative example in 14:1–10a and the Lord's response in 14:10b–12); sinful people need a mediator (seen in the role of Moses in 14:13–19); the Lord is gracious and merciful (seen in the Lord's response to Moses in 14:20); and sin can lead to judgment and discipline (seen in the Lord's response in 14:21–23, 26–37). These points work together to underscore the importance of obedience, the danger of sin, and the need for a mediator and for the Lord's mercy. Keeping the story as a whole before us helps us focus on the main point(s) the Lord is communicating.[31]

It is also important to ask about the overall feel of the passage. Is it one of warning? Of encouragement? Of simple instruction? Answering this helps guide the overall feel our teaching or preaching should take. For example, warning is the overall feel of Numbers 14. Thus the writer of Hebrews alludes to this passage in warning his hearers to stay faithful to God lest they experience his judgment (Heb 3–4). This does not mean our teaching or preaching must end somberly. Even in Numbers 14, there are glimpses of God's mercy (v. 20) that the writer of Hebrews evokes by following his warning with a celebration of Jesus as our great High Priest, the ultimate mediator (Heb 4:14–16). But if we teach or preach on Numbers 14 with no hint of warning or of sin's seriousness, we have missed its thrust.

Finally, we must ask whether we have set the story in the Bible's larger *redemptive*-historical context, meaning the Old Testament context as well as the New Testament context of God's redemption in Jesus. If when preaching or teaching on Numbers 14 we simply say, "God hates sin; don't sin," we have missed its Old Testament context: the Lord is Israel's *redeemer*, who has lovingly set them apart as his treasured possession to reflect his character into this world. Their sin is not simply breaking the rules of a cosmic deity but betraying a relationship, committing treason against their loving and

---

30. For homiletical (as opposed to hermeneutical) suggestions on how to present narratives in teaching or preaching, see Sklar, *Additional Notes*, Appendix 1—Four Ways of Preaching Stories.

31. See further discussion in Richard Pratt, *He Gave Us Stories: The Bible Student's Guide to Interpreting Old Testament Narratives* (Phillipsburg, NJ: P&R Publishing, 1990), esp. 107–402.

redeeming King. Moreover, this King is not simply a rule-giver: he desires their fellowship and will forgive their sin so that they might again be in relationship with him (Num 14:20; see also 15:1–29).

These truths are seen with even greater clarity in the New Testament. In Jesus we see the Lord's ultimate act of redemption, which demonstrates beyond a doubt the Lord's love and desire to forgive us so that we might be in relationship with him. Such magnificent grace also helps us to see our sin as a similar act of betrayal, a treasonous rebellion against a loving and redeeming King. It also provides us with the right context to invite people to turn from their sin to the arms of a holy, merciful God, who both hates sin and shows tremendous love for sinners in his Son Jesus, the ultimate mediator on our behalf.

Interpretive Challenges

Large Numbers in the Book of Numbers

Numbers 1 and Numbers 26—which occur roughly forty years apart—each contains a census of the Israelites "twenty years old or more" (1:18; not counting Levites, 1:47). The totals are 603,550 (1:46) and 601,730 (26:51), respectively. How these numbers should be understood is widely debated. Four main approaches are:[32]

1. *The numbers should be taken at face value.* While the most traditional approach is taking the numbers at face value, this creates tensions with biblical and archaeological data.[33] For example, Israel is called "the fewest of all peoples" (Deut. 7:7) and their small numbers are the reason the Lord will drive out the land's inhabitants slowly over time (Ex. 23:30; Deut. 7:22). Yet simply adding a wife and three children per family leads to a total population of at least three million Israelites if we take the numbers at face value. Add older men and the Levites not counted in the census and the number goes as high as four million. Such a population dwarfs the 140,000 people that are estimated to have lived in Canaan between 2000–1500 BC, the period just before Israel entered the land. Even if we multiply that estimation of 140,000 by ten—and it should be noted that the estimation is based on significant amounts of archaeological work and regional surveys—Israel's population would

---

32. For fuller discussion, see Aaron J Goldstein, "Large Census Numbers in Numbers: An Evaluation of Current Proposals," *Presbyterion* 38.2 (2012): 99–108.

33. James K. Hoffmeier, *Ancient Israel in Sinai: The Evidence for the Authenticity of the Wilderness Tradition* (Oxford: Oxford University Press, 2005), 153–56.

still be two times larger, conflicting with the biblical texts cited above. This suggests a different approach is warranted.

2. *The numbers are symbolic.* In the first of two approaches, the symbolism is explained using gematria, a code in which numbers correspond to letters of the alphabet, spelling out different words. In the second, the numbers relate to astronomical phenomena. For example, Benjamin's total of 35,400 (Num 1:37) divided by 100 is the same as the days in a short lunar year: 354. Few have adopted these approaches since they either fail to explain all the data or can explain it only by complex (and many would say arbitrary) calculations.

3. *The word 'eleph has been misunderstood.* The Hebrew word *'eleph*, used in Numbers 1 and 26, usually means "1,000" but can also mean "family" or "clan," and a word built on the same root can mean "tribal leader." Some suggest the text originally referred to one of these other meanings. So, for example, Reuben's 46,500 (Num 1:21) represents 46 *families* totaling 500 people. The problem is such approaches often assume a significant number of scribal errors. (For example, the 603,550 in 1:46 would have to be a later scribal mistake, since it would equal 603 families, totaling only 550 people!) Given the lack of textual evidence for such errors, this approach is highly conjectural.

4. *The numbers involve deliberate hyperbole.* The final approach, which has the fewest problems, understands the numbers to be intentionally inflated. Some suggest an inflation factor of ten, though others say the amount is no longer discernible. Though many moderns believe numbers are either reported with scientific accuracy or they are misleading, numbers were often inflated in the ancient Near East, particularly in military contexts (as demonstrated by Ugaritic and Assyrian texts of the same general time period).[34] Doing so was neither unusual nor extraordinary. Given this convention, the book of Numbers's first audience would have immediately recognized the numbers were inflated. Rather than seeing this as deceptive, they may have seen it as a way to emphasize the Lord had been faithful to his covenant promise to make Abraham into a numerous people (Gen 12:2; 15:5).

In sum, the first approach to the census lists in Numbers 1 and 26 is historically the most common, though the last appears most likely.[35] As noted

---

34. See Goldstein, "Large Census Numbers," 106.
35. If the last approach is most likely for Num 1 and 26, it would also make sense that it applies to other large numbers in the book, such as the census of the Levites in Num 3 and the list of spoils

in the discussion at 1:53, however, both approaches indicate the large size of the numbers underscores that the Lord is a promise keeper; what he had sworn to Abraham has come to pass. And since he had been faithful to that covenant promise, he could be trusted to fulfill his covenant promise to give them a land. Israel could march into Canaan with full confidence in their covenant King.

Ritual Purity and Impurity

In ancient Israel, three ritual states existed: impure, pure, and holy.[36] Ritual states can be likened to how the state of a person's health might impact where they can go at a hospital and what they can do there. A healthy person can enter a hospital and hold a newborn baby; someone with a bad cold cannot. Your state of health determines where you can go and what you can do. Similarly, a ritual state determines where someone could go and what they could do ritually. For example, a ritually holy person could enter the tabernacle; someone simply clean (or unclean) could not. A clean person could eat of a fellowship offering; an unclean person could not.

There is another similarity between a state of health and a ritual state: in both instances, these are not moral states. Being ritually unclean did not make a person less moral than a ritually holy person, just as having a bad cold does not make someone less moral than a healthy person. In other words: just as it is not wrong to get a cold, it was not wrong to become ritually impure.[37] In fact, full obedience to God's word meant people sometimes had to become ritually unclean. His command to "be fruitful and multiply" (Gen 1:28) requires couples to have sex, which results in ritual impurity (Lev 15:18).

So if becoming ritually unclean was not wrong, why all these laws about ritual states? Why command the Israelites to distinguish between clean and unclean and insist they deal properly with their ritual impurity? The concept was well-known among Israel's neighbors,[38] and we may assume it was part of Israel's culture.[39] It seems the Lord made use of this cultural reality as a teaching tool.

---

in Num 31 (though it is also possible it applies uniquely to military contexts, a main area where hyperbolic numbers were used in the ancient Near East; see Goldstein, "Large Census Numbers," 106–7).

36. Some translations use "unclean" and "clean" in place of "impure" and "pure."
37. Except in one instance (Lev 18:19).
38. See Jacob Milgrom, *Leviticus 1–16: A New Translation with Introduction and Commentary*, AB 3 (New York: Doubleday, 1991), 932–33.
39. Cf. Gen 7:2 for the idea that these concepts existed in Israel before Leviticus.

[A]s the Israelites made these distinctions between purity and impurity *from a ritual perspective*, they were constantly reminded that they had been set apart to be a people of purity *from a moral perspective* (cf. Matt 23:25–26 for those who missed the purpose of the reminder). And because they were to make these distinctions in many areas of their everyday life (meals, sickness, bodily processes), all of life became an opportunity for them to remember that they had been set apart as distinct to be the Lord's holy people, reflecting his holy character to the world.[40]

Structure

Many commentators divide Numbers into three sections based on Israel's geographical location (with a few arriving at five by breaking out two travel narratives in 10:11–12:16 and 20:1–22:1).[41] Most take 1:1–10:10 as forming a natural section, with Israel encamped at Sinai. After this, commentators divide significantly, with proposals for the second section ending at 20:13, 21:9, 21:35, and 22:1.[42]

A thematic approach is equally valid. Olson was one of the first to do this, breaking the book into two major parts based on parallels between 1:1–25:18 and 26:1–36:13, the most obvious being the parallel censuses in chapters 1 and 26.[43] In this approach, the first part tells the first generation's story and the second part the second generation's story. The outline below does the same, further dividing the first part into two, thus arriving at three major sections of material: the first generation's preparation to march to the promised land (1:1–10:10), their faithlessness and punishment in the wilderness (10:11–25:18), and the second generation's preparation to march to the promised land (26:1–36:13).

The advantage of this approach is that it recognizes the parallels of chapters 1 and 26 and also aligns beautifully with the distinct feel of each of the

---

40. Sklar, *Leviticus* (TOTC), 49; italics in the original. For further discussion, see ibid., 44–49, on which the above is based, and also discussion at Num 19, Live the Story, and at Num 31, pp. 376–77, What Does Ritual Impurity Have to Do with Us?
41. For the latter, see Wenham, *Numbers*, 54, followed by Ashley, *Numbers*, 15–17.
42. See overview in Allen, "Numbers," 671–73; Wenham, *Numbers* (OT Guides), 16.
43. Dennis T. Olson, *The Death of the Old and the Birth of the New: The Framework of the Book of Numbers and the Pentateuch*, Brown Judaic Studies 71 (Chico, CA: Scholars Press, 1985), 118–24, and more recently Olson, *Numbers*, 4–7. He is followed with various modifications by Allen, "Numbers," 673–75; Roy Gane, *Leviticus, Numbers*, NIVAC (Grand Rapids: Zondervan Academic, 2004), 476–77; R. Dennis Cole, *Numbers*, NAC 3B (Nashville: Broadman & Holman, 2000), 37–42; and David L. Stubbs, *Numbers*, Brazos Theological Commentary on the Bible (Grand Rapids: Brazos Press, 2009), 21–23.

three sections. The first and third are overwhelmingly positive, the second overwhelmingly negative. By picking up on these differences, this approach reflects the book's own emphases, which may aid in making the book's message even clearer.[44] As noted above (n14), many of the titles are longer than those of a standard outline in order to make the narrative themes clearer to the reader.

I. The First Generation: Death in the Wilderness (1–25)
   A. Organizing and Preparing the Camp in Light of the Lord's Presence among the Israelites as well as the Battles They Will Face in the Promised Land (1:1–10:10)
      i. The Census of the Israelite Nation, the Arrangement of Their Sanctuary Camp, and the Distinctions among the People in Terms of Tabernacle Duties (1:2–4:49)[45]
      ii. Various Laws Related to the Camp, Ritual and Moral Purity, and the Priests' Roles (5:1–6:27)
      iii. Flashback: The Dedication of the Tabernacle and Other Matters Related to It (7:1–9:14)
      iv. Transition: Getting Ready to Depart for the Promised Land (9:15–10:10)
   B. Departing for the Promised Land but Quickly Rebelling against the Lord and Experiencing His Judgment for Complaining Bitterly, Challenging the Authority Structures He Has Established among Priests and People, and Turning to Other Gods (10:11–25:18)
      i. Travel from Sinai to the Wilderness of Paran, Initial Acts of Disbelief (10:11–12:16)
      ii. Arrival at Kadesh, Full-Scale Rebellion, the Lord's Judgment (13:1–14:45)
      iii. Further Laws, Emphasizing Especially the Need for Covenant Faithfulness (15:1–41)
      iv. Challenging the Authority Structure the Lord Has Established; the Lord's Reaffirmation of This Structure (16:1–18:32)
      v. Ceremonial Uncleanness from Corpses and How to Cleanse It (19:1–22)

---

44. See pp. 1–2, Numbers at a Glance, and also the helpful discussion in Stubbs, *Numbers*, 22–25.
45. Cf. Rolf P. Knierim and George W. Coats, *Numbers*, The Forms of the Old Testament Literature 4 (Grand Rapids: Eerdmans, 2005), 27.

    vi. Further Rebellion as Israel Travels from Kadesh to the Plains of Moab; Initial Victories (20:1–22:1)
    vii. The Story of Balak and Balaam (22:2–24:25)
    viii. Israel's Faithlessness at Moab and a Priest's Faithful Zeal (25:1–18)

II. The Second Generation: A New Start for Israel on the Cusp of Entering the Promised Land (26–36)
  A. A Second Census of Israel (26:1–65)
  B. Zelophehad's Daughters: A Question about Inheritance (27:1–11)
  C. Joshua Appointed as Moses's Successor to Lead Israel into the Land (27:12–23)
  D. Offerings and Festivals (28–29)
  E. Laws on Vows and Pledges (30:1–16)
  F. The Defeat of Midian and the Division of the Spoil (31:1–54)
  G. The Transjordan Tribes (32:1–42)
  H. Stages in Israel's Journey (33:1–49)
  I. Laws for Life in the Promised Land (33:50–36:13)
    i. Dispossessing the Land's Inhabitants and Distributing the Land (33:50–56)
    ii. The Boundaries of Canaan (34:1–15)
    iii. Those Who Would Apportion the Land (34:16–29)
    iv. Cities for the Levites (35:1–8)
    v. Cities for Refuge (35:9–34)
    vi. Zelophehad's Daughters (36:1–12)
    vii. Conclusion (36:13)

Resources for Teaching and Preaching

As with any biblical book today, commentaries on the book of Numbers abound. The following are those I have found most helpful, with Wenham, Allen, and Ashley as top picks for preachers and teachers. Note also that I have tried to focus in this commentary on the issues most necessary for understanding Numbers well, aiming for concision to help the busy pastor or teacher. Additional comments can always be made, some of which have led to the additional volume mentioned under my name below (and available freely online).

*Allen, Ronald B. "Numbers." Pages 23–456 in vol. 2 of *The Expositor's Bible Commentary*. Rev. ed. Edited by Tremper Longman III and David Garland. Grand Rapids: Zondervan Academic, 2012.
*Ashley, Timothy R. *The Book of Numbers*. The New International Commentary on the Old Testament. Grand Rapids: Eerdmans, 1993.
Bailey, Lloyd R. *Leviticus–Numbers*. Smyth & Helwys Bible Commentary. Macon, GA: Smyth & Helwys Publishing, 2005.
Milgrom, Jacob. *Numbers: The Traditional Hebrew Text with the New JPS Translation*. The JPS Torah Commentary. Philadelphia: Jewish Publication Society, 1990.
Olson, Dennis T. *Numbers*. Interpretation: A Bible Commentary for Teaching and Preaching. Louisville: John Knox Press, 1996.
Sklar, Jay. *Additional Notes on* Numbers *in Zondervan's The Story of God Bible Commentary Series*. St. Louis, MO: Gleanings Press, 2023.
Sprinkle, Joe M. *Leviticus and Numbers*. Teach the Text Commentary Series. Grand Rapids: Baker Books, 2015.
Stubbs, David L. *Numbers*. Brazos Theological Commentary on the Bible. Grand Rapids: Brazos Press, 2009.
*Wenham, Gordon J. *Numbers, an Introduction and Commentary*. Tyndale Old Testament Commentaries 4. Downers Grove, IL: InterVarsity Press, 1981.

Map 1: Exodus and Conquest of Canaan

Copyright © 2023 by Zondervan. All rights reserved.

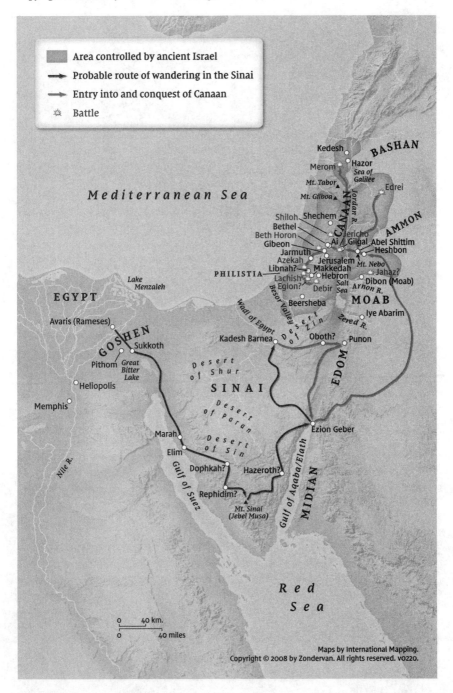

Map 2: The Land of Canaan Explored by the Twelve Spies
Copyright © 2023 by Zondervan. All rights reserved.

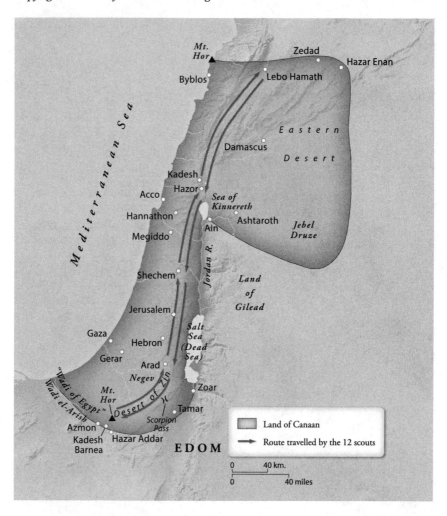

Map 3: Upper Euphrates Region

Copyright © 2023 by Zondervan. All rights reserved.

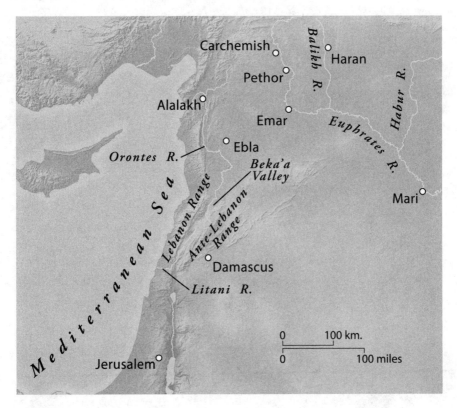

Map 4: The Transjordan Tribes: Reuben, Gad, and the Half-Tribe of Manasseh

Copyright © 2023 by Zondervan. All rights reserved.

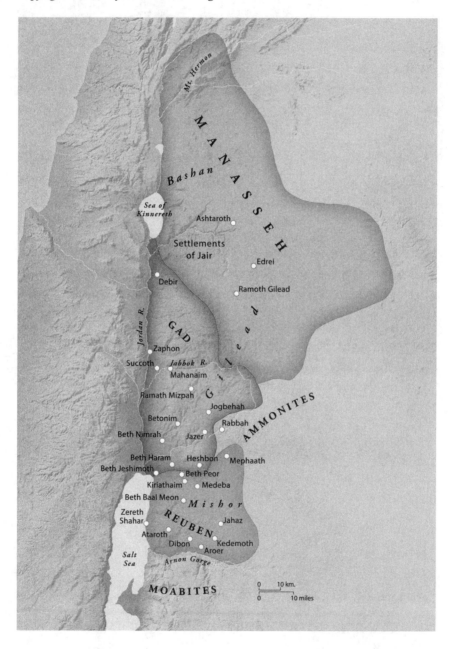

Map 5: Exodus and Wilderness Wanderings

Copyright © 2023 by Zondervan. All rights reserved.

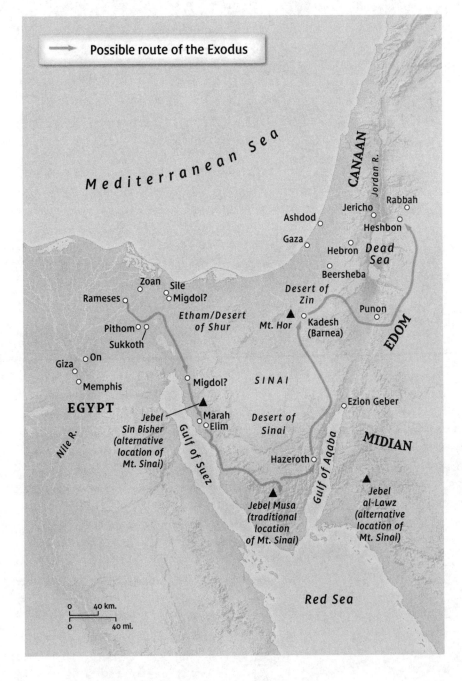

Map 6: Levitical Cities of Refuge

Copyright © 2023 by Zondervan. All rights reserved.

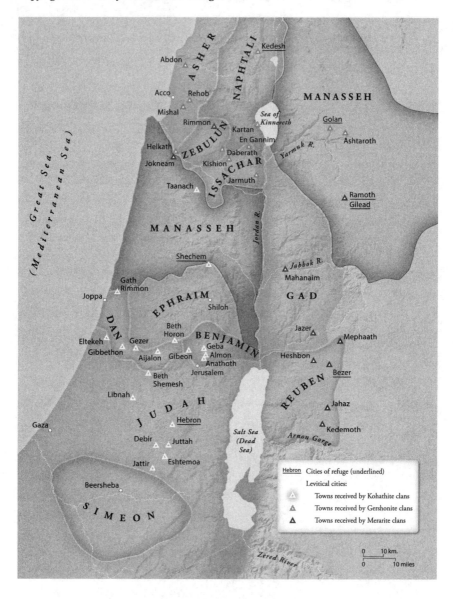

CHAPTER 1

Numbers 1:1–54

 LISTEN to the Story

¹The LORD spoke to Moses in the tent of meeting in the Desert of Sinai on the first day of the second month of the second year after the Israelites came out of Egypt. He said: ²"Take a census of the whole Israelite community by their clans and families, listing every man by name, one by one. ³You and Aaron are to count according to their divisions all the men in Israel who are twenty years old or more and able to serve in the army. ⁴One man from each tribe, each of them the head of his family, is to help you. ⁵These are the names of the men who are to assist you:

from Reuben, Elizur son of Shedeur;

⁶from Simeon, Shelumiel son of Zurishaddai;
⁷from Judah, Nahshon son of Amminadab;
⁸from Issachar, Nethanel son of Zuar;
⁹from Zebulun, Eliab son of Helon;
¹⁰from the sons of Joseph:
from Ephraim, Elishama son of Ammihud;
from Manasseh, Gamaliel son of Pedahzur;
¹¹from Benjamin, Abidan son of Gideoni;
¹²from Dan, Ahiezer son of Ammishaddai;
¹³from Asher, Pagiel son of Okran;
¹⁴from Gad, Eliasaph son of Deuel;
¹⁵from Naphtali, Ahira son of Enan."

¹⁶These were the men appointed from the community, the leaders of their ancestral tribes. They were the heads of the clans of Israel.

¹⁷Moses and Aaron took these men whose names had been specified, ¹⁸and they called the whole community together on the first day of the

second month. The people registered their ancestry by their clans and families, and the men twenty years old or more were listed by name, one by one, [19]as the LORD commanded Moses. And so he counted them in the Desert of Sinai:

[20]From the descendants of Reuben the firstborn son of Israel:
All the men twenty years old or more who were able to serve in the army were listed by name, one by one, according to the records of their clans and families. [21]The number from the tribe of Reuben was 46,500.

[22]From the descendants of Simeon:
All the men twenty years old or more who were able to serve in the army were counted and listed by name, one by one, according to the records of their clans and families. [23]The number from the tribe of Simeon was 59,300.

[24]From the descendants of Gad:
All the men twenty years old or more who were able to serve in the army were listed by name, according to the records of their clans and families. [25]The number from the tribe of Gad was 45,650.

[26]From the descendants of Judah:
All the men twenty years old or more who were able to serve in the army were listed by name, according to the records of their clans and families. [27]The number from the tribe of Judah was 74,600.

[28]From the descendants of Issachar:
All the men twenty years old or more who were able to serve in the army were listed by name, according to the records of their clans and families. [29]The number from the tribe of Issachar was 54,400.

[30]From the descendants of Zebulun:
All the men twenty years old or more who were able to serve in the army were listed by name, according to the records of their clans and families. [31]The number from the tribe of Zebulun was 57,400.

[32]From the sons of Joseph:
From the descendants of Ephraim:

All the men twenty years old or more who were able to serve in the army were listed by name, according to the records of their clans and families. ³³The number from the tribe of Ephraim was 40,500.

³⁴From the descendants of Manasseh:

All the men twenty years old or more who were able to serve in the army were listed by name, according to the records of their clans and families. ³⁵The number from the tribe of Manasseh was 32,200.

³⁶From the descendants of Benjamin:

All the men twenty years old or more who were able to serve in the army were listed by name, according to the records of their clans and families. ³⁷The number from the tribe of Benjamin was 35,400.

³⁸From the descendants of Dan:

All the men twenty years old or more who were able to serve in the army were listed by name, according to the records of their clans and families. ³⁹The number from the tribe of Dan was 62,700.

⁴⁰From the descendants of Asher:

All the men twenty years old or more who were able to serve in the army were listed by name, according to the records of their clans and families. ⁴¹The number from the tribe of Asher was 41,500.

⁴²From the descendants of Naphtali:

All the men twenty years old or more who were able to serve in the army were listed by name, according to the records of their clans and families. ⁴³The number from the tribe of Naphtali was 53,400.

⁴⁴These were the men counted by Moses and Aaron and the twelve leaders of Israel, each one representing his family. ⁴⁵All the Israelites twenty years old or more who were able to serve in Israel's army were counted according to their families. ⁴⁶The total number was 603,550.

⁴⁷The ancestral tribe of the Levites, however, was not counted along with the others. ⁴⁸The LORD had said to Moses: ⁴⁹"You must not count the tribe of Levi or include them in the census of the other Israelites. ⁵⁰Instead,

appoint the Levites to be in charge of the tabernacle of the covenant law—over all its furnishings and everything belonging to it. They are to carry the tabernacle and all its furnishings; they are to take care of it and encamp around it. ⁵¹Whenever the tabernacle is to move, the Levites are to take it down, and whenever the tabernacle is to be set up, the Levites shall do it. Anyone else who approaches it is to be put to death. ⁵²The Israelites are to set up their tents by divisions, each of them in their own camp under their standard. ⁵³The Levites, however, are to set up their tents around the tabernacle of the covenant law so that my wrath will not fall on the Israelite community. The Levites are to be responsible for the care of the tabernacle of the covenant law."

⁵⁴The Israelites did all this just as the LORD commanded Moses.

Listening to the Text in the Story: Genesis 12:1–3; 17:1–8; Exodus 6:6–8; 15:1–21; 19:6

The book of Numbers describes people on a journey. They are the Israelites, Abraham's descendants and inheritors of the promises the Lord made to him (Gen 12:1–3; 17:1–8). Their journey is to Canaan, the land the Lord promised to Abraham (17:8) and the place he is leading them now. Canaan's inhabitants will not be welcoming, but the Israelites need not fear: the Lord has shown himself to be their mighty Warrior-King (Exod 15:1–21) who will be with them as they face war with stronger nations (cf. Num 14:7–9). In this chapter, he begins preparing them for that time.

Numbers' first major section focuses on the first generation of Israelites (chs. 1–25), whom the Lord rescued from slavery in Egypt. Their story starts positively. In Numbers 1:1–10:10, they are faithful, obedient, and careful to do "just as the LORD commanded" (1:54; cf. 2:34; 4:49; 8:3, 22; 9:5, 23). Sadly, this does not last. In Numbers 10:11–25:18, they disbelieve, disobey, and ultimately rebel against the Lord (14:1–10; cf. 11:1–9; 14:39–45; 16:1–14; 20:2–5; 25:1–3). As a result, he disciplines them: they will not enter the promised land; their children will (14:26–35), and the book's second major section will turn its attention to them (chs. 26–36).[1]

But we are not yet at that point. Chapter 1 opens with the Israelites encamped

---

1. For detailed overview of each major section, see discussion starting p. 6, Overarching Structure and Themes.

at Mount Sinai, where they arrived eleven months before in Exodus 19. Since then, the books of Exodus and Leviticus provided instructions and laws guiding the people in holy living (Exod 20–23; 34; Lev 11–27) and holy worship (Exod 25–31; 35–40; Lev 1–10). Now, Numbers turns to preparations for their marching into battle in the promised land with the Lord in their midst (1:1–10:10) and covers such practical matters as troop numbers (1:1–46), tabernacle assignments (1:47–53), and war camp organization (2:1–34).

EXPLAIN the Story

Setting (1:1)

In Exodus, the Lord delivered his people from slavery in Egypt and led them to a mountain in the Sinai wilderness[2] (Exod 1–19; for possible locations, see map 5). There, he made with them a covenant that has come to be known as a "suzerain-vassal" (or "king-servant") covenant. In it, each party had certain obligations. The Lord was Israel's King (suzerain) and would protect them from attacks by foreign nations. Israel was his servant (vassal) and owed him exclusive loyalty: they could not serve any other gods.[3]

But this covenant involved even more. The Lord loved his people and wanted to live among them, so he commanded them to build a tent to serve as his royal palace in their midst (Exod 25–27; 30; 35–40; see image below).[4] At the end of Exodus, his glorious presence descended and filled this tent (40:34–38)—"the tent of meeting"—where he would meet with the Israelites and receive their worship (29:42–46). He would also meet there with Moses, giving him laws for the people (25:22) so they might know how to live in relationship with their heavenly king and carry out their mission as his kingdom of priests and holy nation (19:6), reflecting his goodness, justice, mercy, and love into the world.

In terms of timeframe, the Israelites had arrived eleven months earlier, had just seen the Lord's glory fill the tabernacle the previous month, and had received the laws of Leviticus. They are now receiving these final instructions and will be breaking camp in nineteen days (see table on p. 51). The "second month" means it is April or May. The mention that they "came out of Egypt"

---

2. "Wilderness" or "steppe" is probably better than NIV's "desert" since the Hebrew word can refer to wild pastures where animals could graze (Joel 2:22).
3. See Sandra L. Richter, *The Epic of Eden: A Christian Entry into the Old Testament* (Downers Grove: IVP Academic, 2008), 73–75.
4. See further at pp. 59–61, Listening to the Text in the Story.

reminds them from the very beginning that the Lord is a God who delivers his people (see Exod 12–15), a fact they need to believe fully as they head to battle in the promised land.

The Tabernacle

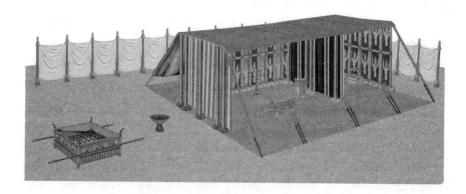

The Census of Israel and Its Military Divisions (1:2–46)

While the battle was ultimately the Lord's (cf. 1 Sam 17:47; Ps 44:1–8), he called his people to show their faith by participating in it. Divine sovereignty and human responsibility work together. The Lord therefore commands Moses and Aaron to take a census of the Israelite men (Num 1:2)[5] and to list them by military divisions (v. 3). These divisions were grouped by tribe (vv. 20–46), and each tribe had more than one division (cf. 2:3). The list was to include all men able to fight (1:3). Many countries to this day have compulsory military service, especially small countries at risk of threat by outside forces (as Israel was). And since in the ancient world kings ordered censuses (cf. 2 Sam 24:2), the Lord's order may have communicated to Israel, "I am your King, who will lead the fight on your behalf in battle."[6]

---

5. A tribe could be divided into "clans and families." In Numbers, "families" (Heb. "house of the fathers") appears to be the broader term, e.g., Levi's tribe has different "families," each of which has different "clans" (3:21–24). ("Leader of the families of the Gershonites" [3:24] in NIV is more accurately "leader of the *family* of the Gershonites," consisting of the "clans" just named; so also for 3:30, 35.)

6. When an Israelite king undertook this action of his own accord, the results could be disastrous (2 Sam 24; see discussion at Num 31:48–54, pp. 374–75, for details). But this case is different: the Lord himself commanded the census to be taken. Whether the text presumes the half-shekel payment of Exod 30:11–16 is unclear.

The Israelites' Location: Where and How Long

Geographical Location	Duration
Deliverance from Egypt (Exod 3:1–15:21)	Several months (?)
Travel to Sinai (Exod 15:22–18:27)	One month, fourteen days (Exod 19:1)[7]
Encamped at Sinai (Exod 19:1– Num 10:10) • From arrival to erecting the tent of meeting • From erecting the tent to the beginning of Numbers • From beginning of Numbers to departing Sinai	Eleven months and nineteen days • Ten months (cf. Exod 19:1 with Exod 40:2) • One month (cf. Exod 40:2 with Num 1:1) • Nineteen days (cf. Num 1:1 with Num 10:11)
Travel to Kadesh (Num 10:11–12:16)	Two to three months (see at Num 13:20; p. 195)
Wandering in area around Kadesh (Num 15:1[?]–19:22 [cf. 33:18–36]), travel to the plains of Moab (20:1–22:1) and stay there (Num 22:2–36:13)	Thirty-eight years (cf. Deut 2:14)
Total	Forty years (Num 32:13)

Tribal leaders help Moses and Aaron with the census (Num 1:4, 16), enabling the numbering to be done accurately and efficiently. One leader

---

7. Exod 19:1 could be woodenly translated, "In the third new moon/month with regard to the children of Israel's going out from the land of Egypt"—that is, not three new moons/months after leaving but the third new moon/month of their departure year—"on that very day, they came into the wilderness of Sinai." Since they came out on the evening of month one day fourteen, they arrive here roughly one and a half months later if "that very day" refers to month three day one, and two months later if "that very day" refers to the day of the third month parallel to their departure day (day fourteen). Arguments in favor of either position are evenly balanced.

is listed from each tribe (vv. 5–15) except for the tribe of Levi, which is not counted (see at 1:47–53 below). (The list still arrives at twelve tribes because Joseph's could count as two: Ephraim and Manasseh; see Gen 48:1, 5.) The list's tribal order is fairly logical:

Tribe	Descended from
Reuben, Simeon, Judah, Issachar, Zebulun	Leah
Ephraim, Manasseh (both from Joseph), Benjamin	Rachel
Dan, Asher, Gad, Naphtali	Leah's and Rachel's handmaids

Next, the congregation assembles, perhaps by the sounding of a ram's horn (Exod 19:13) or trumpet (Num 10:2). All the fighting men are then counted (1:18; cf. vv. 2–3), perhaps in groups of thousands, hundreds, and fifties (cf. Exod 18:25), explaining why the totals are multiples of fifty. (Thus, while everyone was "listed by name," final counts may have been rounded to the nearest fifty.) This was done "as the LORD commanded Moses" (Num 1:19), a repeated theme in the opening ten chapters (1:54; 2:34; 4:49; 8:3, 22; 9:5, 23). At this point, Israel is faithful to the Lord's commands.

The census results follow (Num 1:20–46); three general comments may be made. First, as in 1:5–15, Levi is not mentioned; see below at 1:47–53.

Second, the census shows the Lord has fulfilled his promise to make Abraham a great nation (Gen 12:2; 15:5). This means he can be trusted to fulfill his promise to give Abraham's descendants a land (12:7; 15:18). The Israelites thus have every reason to trust the Lord when they get to the promised land—regardless of the warriors they find there.

Third, great debate surrounds the numbers listed, mainly concerning whether to take them at face value or as hyperbole.[8] Either way, the point is clear: such large numbers underscore that the Lord keeps his promises. His words to Abraham have come to pass.

---

8. See further discussion pp. 30–32, Large Numbers in the Book of Numbers.

The Levites' Special Role[9] (1:47–53)

The Levites will be counted later (Num 3:14–39), not here with the army. Their duty is not fighting but the care and service of the tent of meeting (1:50–53), here called "the tabernacle of the covenant law" (v. 50). *Tabernacle* is an old English term for "dwelling place" and a good translation of the Hebrew term *mishkan*, which can refer to a person's dwelling place,[10] thus strongly reminding Israel that the Lord dwells in their midst. The "covenant law" refers to the stone copies of the covenant placed in the ark of the covenant in the most holy place (Exod 31:18; 40:20), where the Lord sat enthroned as King and divine witness to it (2 Sam 6:2). (Among some of Israel's neighbors, copies of covenants were customarily placed at the feet of the nations' gods so they could serve as divine witnesses.[11]) The phrase "tabernacle of the covenant law" therefore testified that the Lord dwelt in Israel's midst, their King who would be faithful to this covenant and was witness to it, requiring their faithfulness as well.

The Levites' role with the tabernacle included disassembling, transporting, and reassembling it (further details are given in Num 3–4). No one else could do this—on pain of death (1:51). The Hebrew for "anyone else" (v. 51) is "the stranger," that is, a person not appointed to this task, meaning non-Levites (see 18:1–6). The phrase "put to death" suggests death at the hands of the covenant community,[12] which could refer to the Levites in particular (Exod 32:25–28) or to the whole community (Num 15:35–36). This penalty is related to the tent's sacredness; it may only be handled by those who have gone through an extra purifying rite (the Levites go through this in Num 8:5–22).[13] Good hospitals guard the operating room, ensuring the only ones who enter it are surgical staff who are especially clean, thus preventing germs from defiling it and making it unsuitable for use. Similarly, the Levites were to guard the tabernacle, ensuring the only ones who touched it and its holy contents were holy priests or, in some cases, Levites (who were especially pure), thus preventing impurity from defiling it and making it unsuitable for its use as the home of the holy King of heaven.[14]

---

9. The title is from Wenham, *Numbers*, 60.
10. See 16:24, which also uses *mishkan*.
11. See references in Nahum M. Sarna, *Exodus*, The JPS Torah Commentary (Philadelphia: The Jewish Publication Society, 1991), 160.
12. In Exodus to Numbers, the verb's passive form is typically used this way (Lev 24:16; Num 15:35–36; etc.); the active form typically refers to death at the Lord's hands (Lev 10:2; Num 14:37). See further Jay Sklar, *Sin, Impurity, Sacrifice, Atonement: The Priestly Conceptions*, Hebrew Bible Monographs 2 (Sheffield: Sheffield Phoenix Press, 2005), 14–15.
13. For ritual states, see pp. 32–33, Ritual Purity and Impurity.
14. See p. 57, How Should We Respond?

Part of this care involved camping around the tabernacle. While the Israelites provided a protective outer ring, guarding it from outside forces, the Levites provided a protective inner ring, guarding it from unauthorized approach by Israelites (1:52–53; see diagram at 2:3–31, The Camp of the Tribes of Israel).[15] The stakes were high. To defile the Lord's home was to say you thought very little of him and did not care if he remained among you. This was a treasonous act that would call down the Lord's wrath, that is, his just anger against evil and rebellion (1:53). This might be experienced directly from his hand, as when he sends a plague (8:19; 16:46), or more indirectly, as when he withdraws his protective presence and Israel loses in battle (Josh 7:3–9). The Lord wanted neither and surrounded the tabernacle with Levites "so that my wrath will not fall on the Israelite community" (Num 1:53). Because he has created Israel for relationship, not judgment, he puts measures in place so he can dwell among them in fellowship and love.

Summary (1:54)

In this summary, the Israelites' obedience to the Lord's commands is highlighted—and held up as a model to follow.

It is perhaps an understatement to say that many readers of Numbers do not find a census to be an inspiring beginning! But Numbers starts this way for good reason, which we can unpack by asking three questions.

Why Does It Matter That This King Keeps His Promises?

Many Westerners view census lists as repetitive and unimportant and wonder why the Bible would include them. But consider events in our day, such as graduation ceremonies or the Olympics' opening ceremony, where many names are called out and there is much repetition. These ceremonies are important. If your name is not called at graduation, you are not a part of

---

15. Milgrom argues that 1:53b should be translated "the Levites shall do guard duty for the Tabernacle of the Pact" (Jacob Milgrom, *Studies in Levitical Terminology,* Studies in Judaism in Late Antiquity 36 [Leiden: Brill, 1983], 8), but Levine compellingly argues the relevant phrase has several ranges of meaning and that guard duty is not its use here (Baruch Levine, *Numbers 1–20*, AB 4 [New York: Doubleday, 1993], 141–42). A translation such as "perform the duties/obligations of the tabernacle" is probably correct (see further at p. 77n12). As the context here implies, however, part of those duties did involve guarding the tabernacle from illicit contact by lay Israelites.

the graduating class. If your country is not announced at the opening of the Olympics, you are not a participant.

The census list here (Num 1:20–46) is no more repetitive and no less important.[16] Those whose names appeared in this list knew they were members of God's people. What is more, while debate surrounds the size of the numbers,[17] it seems clear that they served, in part, to underscore the Lord's faithfulness to his promise to make Abraham into a great nation (Gen 12:2; 15:5). The Lord is a promise keeper, and it was fundamental that Israel understood this because they were headed to a land filled with warriors far greater and stronger than themselves. Taking it seemed impossible (Num 13:28–29, 32–33), and the only way they could obey the Lord's commands to march in was if they believed he would be faithful to his promise to give it to them (cf. Gen 12:7; 15:18). Their faithfulness had to be rooted in the far greater reality of God's faithfulness.

The same is true for believers today. As God had promised Israel, he rescued them from slavery and led them to a far better land, with he himself dwelling in their midst. But God has done all these things for us at a far deeper level in Jesus, who has rescued us from sin's slavery (Rom 6:5–7), is leading us to a better land (Rev 7:17), and dwells among us by his Spirit (Eph 2:20–22). No wonder Paul can say, "For no matter how many promises God has made, they are 'Yes' in Christ" (2 Cor 1:20a). Because of this, believers today can find the courage and hope they need to obey God in all things. This makes it worthwhile to ask, "Are there areas where I am afraid to obey what God asks of me? How does the faithfulness he shows in Jesus speak into my fears?" This also leads to the next question.

What Does the Almighty King Do and Call His People to Do?

Numbers's opening communicates that the God who redeems us seeks relationship with us and privileges us with his mission. His redemption is manifest in the reminder that the Israelites "came out of Egypt" (Num 1:1) when he rescued them from slavery under one of the mightiest nations on earth (Exod 15:1–21). The relationship he seeks and the mission with which he privileges us are clear from the titles given to his dwelling place. "Tent of meeting" (Num 1:1) reminds the Israelites that there they could come and worship the Lord dwelling in their midst, and there he would give his law to Moses so they would know how to reflect his character into the world (see

---

16. See also discussion in Sklar, *Additional Notes*, introduction, Preaching from Numbers.
17. See further discussion pp. 30–32, Large Numbers in the Book of Numbers.

at 1:1, p. 49). "Tabernacle of the covenant law" (v. 50) reminds them they are in covenant relationship with the Lord dwelling in their midst (see at 1:47–53, p. 53). A covenant was a way to enter into a "relationship that was to be much more personal than a contract, and much more permanent than an ordinary relationship."[18] In this covenant relationship, the Lord was the Israelites' faithful King, rescuing them from slavery and protecting them from foreign nations; the Israelites' were to be his faithful servants, serving him alone and obeying his laws so they could reflect his goodness, justice, mercy, and love into the world (see comments at 1:1 and 1:50). In short, the Lord always redeems for the purpose of both relationship and mission.

The New Testament underscores these same themes of redemption, relationship, and mission. Redemption now comes in and through Jesus, who delivers us from the worst slavery of all. Although it may offend our self-conception as free, self-determining individuals, the Bible describes us as "slaves to sin" because we so often choose to obey evil and its harmful thoughts and desires (John 8:34; Rom 6:16). And sin is a hard master, whose only reward is death (Rom 6:23). But Christ has come "that we should no longer be slaves to sin" (v. 6), freeing us from its power and penalty and giving us life in him.

This leads to a relationship made possible because, in and through Jesus, God has come to live among us. John's Gospel begins by describing Jesus as God in the flesh, who has come to "dwell" among us (John 1:1, 14). The word he uses for "dwell" (*skēnoō*) is directly related to the word used for the "tent" and "tabernacle" (*skēnē*) in the Greek translation of the Old Testament. John's point is clear: in Jesus, God has once again come down to live in our midst. He does this because he loves us and has created us for himself; he cannot and will not stay far away. Biblical religion is not the story of humanity making its way up to God but of a loving God making his way down to redeem us.

But he does not simply redeem us from sin. He redeems us to participate in his mission to return this world to a place that reflects his goodness, justice, mercy, and love. Knowing the Lord and being his representatives in the world always go hand in hand. Having spoken of the freedom from sin Christ wins for us, Paul exhorts, "Offer yourselves to God as those who have been brought from death to life; and offer every part of yourself to him as an instrument of righteousness" (Rom 6:13). God's redemption is always about relationship and mission. This challenges us to consider, "Do I think of redemption as simply

---

18. Sklar, *Leviticus* (ZECOT), 10; adapted from T. Keller, *Preaching: Communicating Faith in an Age of Skepticism* (New York: Viking, 2015), 104.

salvation from sin, or do I also understand it as a call to embody God's own character in the world? Does my life give good evidence that I am on God's mission to fill this world with his goodness, justice, mercy, and love?" These questions lead to a final one.

How Should We Respond When a Holy King Dwells in Our Midst?

As Israel marches toward the promised land, the Lord clearly dwells in their midst as divine King (see at Num 1:1, 47–53, pp. 49, 53). But he is also clearly a holy King, meaning the ritually pure Levites are the only ones to handle and camp around his dwelling place, protecting it from defilement (see hospital analogy at 1:47–53, p. 53). Israel's obedience to this command showed their respect for the Lord and their desire that he remain in their midst. For them to defile his dwelling place would be to show a contempt that said they cared little about whether he remained among them. When you vandalize someone's property, you are telling them to leave the neighborhood.

The New Testament continues to speak of God dwelling in our midst—not in a building but in his people. Sometimes it speaks of all believers as members of God's temple, with Jesus as the cornerstone, and God by his Spirit dwelling in their midst (Eph 2:20–22). Other times it speaks of individual believers as "temples of the Holy Spirit, who is in you, whom you have received from God" (1 Cor 6:19). From either perspective, these modern-day temples of God must be respected. A strong warning is given to any who would create division among the corporate temple of believers—the church: "If anyone destroys God's temple, God will destroy that person; for God's temple is sacred" (3:17a). A strong exhortation is also given to the individual not to defile the temple that is their body with sexual immorality (6:18–19). Both carry the same message: as an act of love and devotion to the holy God who dwells in your midst—who dwells *in you!*—show respect to his sacred dwelling place. In what ways can we do this corporately by seeking the church's peace and purity? And what does it look like to do this individually by honoring God with our bodies (v. 20)? It is sobering to remember that if we vandalize his holy property, we are telling him he is no longer welcome in his home.

CHAPTER 2

Numbers 2:1–34

LISTEN to the Story

¹The Lord said to Moses and Aaron: ²"The Israelites are to camp around the tent of meeting some distance from it, each of them under their standard and holding the banners of their family."

³On the east, toward the sunrise, the divisions of the camp of Judah are to encamp under their standard. The leader of the people of Judah is Nahshon son of Amminadab. ⁴His division numbers 74,600.

⁵The tribe of Issachar will camp next to them. The leader of the people of Issachar is Nethanel son of Zuar. ⁶His division numbers 54,400.

⁷The tribe of Zebulun will be next. The leader of the people of Zebulun is Eliab son of Helon. ⁸His division numbers 57,400.

⁹All the men assigned to the camp of Judah, according to their divisions, number 186,400. They will set out first.

¹⁰On the south will be the divisions of the camp of Reuben under their standard. The leader of the people of Reuben is Elizur son of Shedeur. ¹¹His division numbers 46,500.

¹²The tribe of Simeon will camp next to them. The leader of the people of Simeon is Shelumiel son of Zurishaddai. ¹³His division numbers 59,300.

¹⁴The tribe of Gad will be next. The leader of the people of Gad is Eliasaph son of Deuel. ¹⁵His division numbers 45,650.

¹⁶All the men assigned to the camp of Reuben, according to their divisions, number 151,450. They will set out second.

¹⁷Then the tent of meeting and the camp of the Levites will set out in the middle of the camps. They will set out in the same order as they encamp, each in their own place under their standard.

¹⁸On the west will be the divisions of the camp of Ephraim under their standard. The leader of the people of Ephraim is Elishama son of Ammihud. ¹⁹His division numbers 40,500.

²⁰The tribe of Manasseh will be next to them. The leader of the people of Manasseh is Gamaliel son of Pedahzur. ²¹His division numbers 32,200.

²²The tribe of Benjamin will be next. The leader of the people of Benjamin is Abidan son of Gideoni. ²³His division numbers 35,400.

²⁴All the men assigned to the camp of Ephraim, according to their divisions, number 108,100. They will set out third.

²⁵On the north will be the divisions of the camp of Dan under their standard. The leader of the people of Dan is Ahiezer son of Ammishaddai. ²⁶His division numbers 62,700.

²⁷The tribe of Asher will camp next to them. The leader of the people of Asher is Pagiel son of Okran. ²⁸His division numbers 41,500.

²⁹The tribe of Naphtali will be next. The leader of the people of Naphtali is Ahira son of Enan. ³⁰His division numbers 53,400.

³¹All the men assigned to the camp of Dan number 157,600. They will set out last, under their standards.

³²These are the Israelites, counted according to their families. All the men in the camps, by their divisions, number 603,550. ³³The Levites, however, were not counted along with the other Israelites, as the LORD commanded Moses.

³⁴So the Israelites did everything the LORD commanded Moses; that is the way they encamped under their standards, and that is the way they set out, each of them with their clan and family.

Listening to the Text in the Story: Numbers 1; War Camp of Ramses II at Qadesh

This chapter continues the theme of Israel as a camp preparing for war. In Numbers 1, Israel's military divisions were counted; Numbers 2 describes their place in Israel's camp and their marching order.

At the camp's center is the tent of meeting (see diagram at 2:3–31, The

Camp of the Tribes of Israel). Exodus and Leviticus have already given several signs that the Lord's tent is his royal palace in Israel's midst:

1. The Israelites bring their tribute here (Exod 25:1–9), just as people brought tribute to a king's palace.
2. They come and "stand before" the Lord, just as one "stood before" a ruler or authority figure (1 Kgs 1:28; 3:16; Esth 8:4).
3. The tabernacle's ornate furnishings are unlike those of any other Israelite tent (Exod 25:10–26:37; 30:1–10). This tent is fit for a king.
4. Just as palace servants wore special uniforms to minister before the king (1 Kgs 10:5), so the Lord's priests wear special uniforms to minister before him in his palace-tent (Exod 28, esp. v. 43).
5. The tent has a throne room—the most holy place—where the Lord sits enthroned over the ark in the midst of his heavenly attendants (1 Sam 4:4; Ps 99:1; cf. Isa 6:1–2).[1]

The War Camp of Ramses II at Qadesh
Stephen C. Meyers

The tent's placement in the camp's center confirms it is indeed the Lord's royal palace. An illustration of an Egyptian war camp from about this time (ca. thirteenth c. BC; see the image above) shows the king's tent in the camp's center for maximum protection, with a longer outer room and a shorter inner room. In the inner room is the king's symbol (his cartouche) between two heavenly beings with wings. Similarly, the Lord's tent was set in the center

---

1. Sklar, *Leviticus* (ZECOT), 11.

of Israel's camp, with an outer room (the holy place) twice as long as the inner room (the Most Holy Place). The Most Holy Place was where the Lord manifested his presence above the ark, between the winged cherubim (Exod 25:22). The Lord was Israel's covenant King, dwelling in his royal tent in his people's midst.[2]

Overview: The Tribes Camp around the Tent at Some Distance from It (2:1–2)

The Lord speaks not only to Moses (cf. Num 1:1) but also to Aaron (2:1), perhaps because the tent of meeting is mentioned (v. 2), which was Aaron's special responsibility.

Verse 2 provides an overview; three items are noteworthy. First, the Israelites are grouped according to their "standards" and "banners," which are often understood to refer to a flag or symbol.[3] The "standard" would represent the tribe and the "banner of the family" would represent the next level of division within the tribe ("tribal families"; see at p. 50n5). This is comparable to having a national flag and a state or provincial flag and served to visually organize the Israelites for camping and marching.

Second, the tent of meeting—and the Lord who dwelt within it as King—was at the camp's center. For the significance, see above at Listening to the Text in the Story.

Third, the Israelites must camp "some distance" (Num 1:2) from the tent, providing room for the Levites to camp around it (3:23, 29, 35, 38) and guarding the other tribes from inappropriate contact with it (see at 1:47–53, pp. 53–54). The non-Levite tribes thus provided a protective outer ring around the tabernacle, guarding it from outside forces, while the Levites provided a protective inner ring, guarding it from unauthorized approach by Israelites (1:52–53).

---

2. Such similarities to cultural realities are no surprise: the Lord is a master communicator and conveys his truth to his people in ways they can best understand. Theologians sometimes refer to this as the doctrine of accommodation (or condescension), with Calvin comparing it to the way adults adapt their speaking style when addressing young children (*Institutes*, 1.13.1).

3. See Yigael Yadin, *The Art of Warfare in Biblical Lands* (New York: McGraw-Hill, 1963), 122, 139, for ancient Near Eastern examples. Alternatively, the word for "standard" (*degel*) may refer to a regiment; the text's overall meaning would not be greatly altered.

The Outer Camp's Arrangement and the Tribes' Marching Order (2:3–31)

Three tribes camped on each side of the tabernacle (see diagram below, The Camp of the Tribes of Israel). Since Israelites oriented themselves by the east,[4] the description begins there (Num 2:3–9) and continues clockwise, listing those south (vv. 10–16), west (vv. 18–24), and north (vv. 25–31). The first tribe in each group is the lead tribe, and the camp of that group is named after it (e.g., v. 9). For discussion of the large numbers, see pp. 30–32.

The Camp of the Tribes of Israel
Num 2:1–31; 10:11–33

```
                              N

                        Camp of Dan
                   Asher   Naphtali   Dan*


                          Levites
                         (Merari)

     Camp of Ephraim                          Camp of Judah
        Benjamin                                  Judah*
                     Levites        Levites
  W     Manasseh               Tent of           Issachar    E
                    (Gershon)   Meeting  (Priests)
        Ephraim*                                  Zebulun


                          Levites
                          (Kohath)


                    Gad   Simeon   Reuben*
                       Camp of Reuben


                              S
```

* = leading tribe of the group

In terms of arrangement, some diagrams put the lead tribe in the middle of its group. But assuming each tribe marched out in the order listed (cf. 10:14–16, which does not require this but is plausibly read in this

---

4. The word here for "south" (*teman*, 2:10), is related to the root "right," since the south was on one's right when facing east.

fashion), it would make sense for the lead tribe to be at one end so that when camp is broken, the three tribes could march out in single file.[5] For marching order, see diagram below (and cf. 10:11–28, 33).[6]

Marching Order of the Tribes

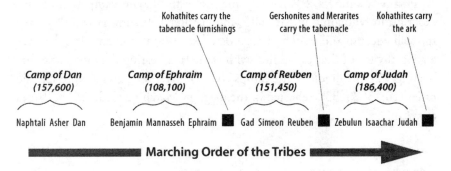

The tribal groupings put like with like (for details, see Gen 29:31–30:24; 35:16–18).

Tribal Grouping	Maternal Descent
Judah, Issachar, Zebulun	Leah
Reuben, Simeon, Gad	Leah, Leah's handmaid (Gad)
Ephraim, Manasseh, Benjamin	Rachel
Dan, Asher, Naphtali	Leah's and Rachel's handmaid

Two general observations on the tribes' groupings are noteworthy. First, the vanguard and rearguard have the largest groups of armies (2:16, 31); this provided maximum security in the outer lines of defense. Second, although Judah is not the firstborn, he is now the first tribe mentioned (cf. 1:20) and

---

5. In the Hebrew, the beginning of 2:5 and 2:7 could be woodenly translated, "And the ones camping to the side of [Judah]: the tribe of Issachar . . . the tribe of Zebulun . . . ." This could mean these tribes are on either side of Judah but could also simply mean that as you look at Judah, the other two tribes are on one side of him.

6. The priests are not specifically named but would presumably depart with the Levites. In particular, Ithamar would be with the Gershonites and Merarites (cf. 4:28, 33) and Eliazar with the Kohathites (cf. 4:15–16).

leads his group (2:3). This is in keeping with his army being the largest (the logical choice to lead the vanguard) and with Jacob's prophetic blessing placing him at the head of his brothers (Gen 49:8, 10; cf. Gen 49:3–4). This blessing would find initial fulfillment in King David, who was of this tribe (1 Sam 17:12), and ultimate fulfillment in King Jesus, the Lord of all (Rev 5:5; 19:16).

Finally, Numbers 2:17 briefly mentions the Levite camp (whose full description will come in the following chapters). It summarizes that they too will encamp and march in an ordered way. As a summary, it only gives a general view of the Kohathites, who came last, bearing the tabernacle furnishings "in the middle of the camps" (v. 17). Later texts give a more specific order (10:13–28, 33), reflected in the diagram Marching Order of the Tribes above, p. 63.

Summary (2:32–34)

These verses correspond to 1:44–54: the total numbers of troops is given (cf. 1:44–46), the Levites are exempted (cf. 1:47–53), and the Israelites do everything as the Lord commanded (cf. 1:54).[7] Their obedience is mentioned twice, thus emphasizing it for the generations to come (2:33, 34). When a King lives in your midst, his laws are to be followed.

LIVE the Story

Are Our Lives Centered around the King?

> It's not about you. The purpose of your life is far greater than your own personal fulfillment, your peace of mind, or even your happiness. It's far greater than your family, your career, or even your wildest dreams and ambitions. If you want to know why you were placed on this planet, you must begin with God. You were born *by* his purpose and *for* his purpose.[8]

So begins the best-selling book by Rick Warren. I wonder if he had been reading Numbers 2.

In this chapter, all the tribal camps are arranged around the Lord's tent. Just as ancient Near Eastern kings had their tent in the camp's center (see above at Listening to the Text in the Story, pp. 59–61), so too does the Lord. Judah is not in the center; neither is Levi. The Lord is. He is Israel's King.

---

7. Cf. Nicholas P. Lunn, "Numbering Israel: A Rhetorico-Structural Analysis of Numbers 1–4," *JSOT* 35.2 (2010): 173–74.

8. Rick Warren, *The Purpose-Driven Life* (Grand Rapids: Zondervan, 2002), 17.

But he is not just any king: he is the King who has rescued them to be in relationship with him and has given them the privilege of filling this world with his kingdom of goodness, justice, mercy, and love. To do so, he must be at their center; he must remain their point of orientation.

It is a general truth that we orient our lives to whatever we put at its center. Whether money, success, love, or family, we spend our time, energy, and resources seeking or guarding whatever we value most. But because we have been made by God and for God, our lives become disoriented if we put anything else at its center. Jesus therefore commands us, "But seek first *his kingdom* and *his righteousness*" (Matt 6:33, italics added). In other words, keep the King at the center. He is a good king, a loving king, and those who keep him at the center will know the joy for which they have been created (25:21).

The picture of the camp, with three tribes per side and the King in its midst, is picked up in Ezekiel to describe a future city with three gates per side, each named after a tribe (Ezek 48:30–36). Revelation identifies that city as heaven (Rev 21:12–14), where the Lord himself will dwell among his people and wipe away every tear from their eyes (vv. 3–4). Death and mourning and crying and pain will be no more, for the old order of things will have passed away, and his people will know the full joy of their King. This picture of the Israelite camp looks forward to that day—and exhorts us even now to keep the King in the center of our lives.

If our priorities were compared to the Israelite camps, would the Lord's tent be at the center? If not, what are the first steps we must take to reorient our priorities? If so, it should help with the next question.

Are We Okay with Not Being First?
In this chapter, the Lord not only organizes the tribes in groups of three, he also establishes a lead tribe in each group after whom it is named (Num 2:9, 16, 24, 31). Order and authority both matter among God's people. When marching, some tribes must take the lead, and that should be okay because all are marching toward the same goal. It does not matter if one tribe has a more prominent role than yours. What matters is carrying out your King's mission.

Paul gets at the same idea when writing to the Corinthians, who seemed to be envying each other's spiritual gifts and roles, especially those considered prominent (1 Cor 12). He compares God's people to a body and acknowledges that some parts have more prominent roles but notes that every part is important to proper functioning (vv. 15–25). Most importantly, he emphasizes we are members of *Christ's* body (v. 27) and thus part of a community meant to embody Jesus in the world. It is all about Jesus and his mission; it is not about us. The more we fix our eyes on these facts—the more we keep Jesus at our life's center—the quicker petty jealousies will disappear.

Thus Paul's pastoral solution to such envy is not to deny differences in gifting or roles but to remind us of our common mission—our common King—and to exhort us to love others who also belong to his body. This leads to the last question.

Are We Committed to His Body?

In Numbers 1 and 2, speaking of the individual is impossible without also speaking of the group to which the individual belongs. Each warrior is counted and yet their number is always part of a tribe. On the one hand, this is a necessary part of being organized along tribal lines. On the other, it is a reminder that God always calls individuals to be a part of a larger community.

This is especially clear in light of the New Testament's metaphors that describe God's people: they are likened to different parts of one body (1 Cor 12:12–18), different stones of one temple (Eph 2:20–22), and different branches of one vine (John 15:5). In each of these metaphors, Jesus is central: *his* is the body to which we belong (1 Cor 12:27); *he* is the chief cornerstone that holds the temple together (Eph 2:20); *he* is the vine from which we draw our life (John 15:5). Again, it is not about us; it is about him. So if we claim to love him, let us work hard to love those connected to him and to serve alongside them as we seek to advance Jesus's mission in this world.

CHAPTER 3

Numbers 3:1–4:49

 LISTEN to the Story

³:¹This is the account of the family of Aaron and Moses at the time the Lord spoke to Moses at Mount Sinai.

²The names of the sons of Aaron were Nadab the firstborn and Abihu, Eleazar and Ithamar. ³Those were the names of Aaron's sons, the anointed priests, who were ordained to serve as priests. ⁴Nadab and Abihu, however, died before the Lord when they made an offering with unauthorized fire before him in the Desert of Sinai. They had no sons, so Eleazar and Ithamar served as priests during the lifetime of their father Aaron.

⁵The Lord said to Moses, ⁶"Bring the tribe of Levi and present them to Aaron the priest to assist him. ⁷They are to perform duties for him and for the whole community at the tent of meeting by doing the work of the tabernacle. ⁸They are to take care of all the furnishings of the tent of meeting, fulfilling the obligations of the Israelites by doing the work of the tabernacle. ⁹Give the Levites to Aaron and his sons; they are the Israelites who are to be given wholly to him. ¹⁰Appoint Aaron and his sons to serve as priests; anyone else who approaches the sanctuary is to be put to death."

¹¹The Lord also said to Moses, ¹²"I have taken the Levites from among the Israelites in place of the first male offspring of every Israelite woman. The Levites are mine, ¹³for all the firstborn are mine. When I struck down all the firstborn in Egypt, I set apart for myself every firstborn in Israel, whether human or animal. They are to be mine. I am the Lord."

¹⁴The Lord said to Moses in the Desert of Sinai, ¹⁵"Count the Levites by their families and clans. Count every male a month old or more." ¹⁶So Moses counted them, as he was commanded by the word of the Lord.

¹⁷These were the names of the sons of Levi:
    Gershon, Kohath and Merari.
¹⁸These were the names of the Gershonite clans:

Libni and Shimei.
¹⁹The Kohathite clans:
Amram, Izhar, Hebron and Uzziel.
²⁰The Merarite clans:

Mahli and Mushi.

These were the Levite clans, according to their families.

²¹To Gershon belonged the clans of the Libnites and Shimeites; these were the Gershonite clans. ²²The number of all the males a month old or more who were counted was 7,500. ²³The Gershonite clans were to camp on the west, behind the tabernacle. ²⁴The leader of the families of the Gershonites was Eliasaph son of Lael. ²⁵At the tent of meeting the Gershonites were responsible for the care of the tabernacle and tent, its coverings, the curtain at the entrance to the tent of meeting, ²⁶the curtains of the courtyard, the curtain at the entrance to the courtyard surrounding the tabernacle and altar, and the ropes—and everything related to their use.

²⁷To Kohath belonged the clans of the Amramites, Izharites, Hebronites and Uzzielites; these were the Kohathite clans. ²⁸The number of all the males a month old or more was 8,600. The Kohathites were responsible for the care of the sanctuary. ²⁹The Kohathite clans were to camp on the south side of the tabernacle. ³⁰The leader of the families of the Kohathite clans was Elizaphan son of Uzziel. ³¹They were responsible for the care of the ark, the table, the lampstand, the altars, the articles of the sanctuary used in ministering, the curtain, and everything related to their use. ³²The chief leader of the Levites was Eleazar son of Aaron, the priest. He was appointed over those who were responsible for the care of the sanctuary.

³³To Merari belonged the clans of the Mahlites and the Mushites; these were the Merarite clans. ³⁴The number of all the males a month old or more who were counted was 6,200. ³⁵The leader of the families of the Merarite clans was Zuriel son of Abihail; they were to camp on the north side of the tabernacle. ³⁶The Merarites were appointed to take care of the frames of the tabernacle, its crossbars, posts, bases, all its equipment, and everything related to their use, ³⁷as well as the posts of the surrounding courtyard with their bases, tent pegs and ropes.

³⁸Moses and Aaron and his sons were to camp to the east of the tabernacle, toward the sunrise, in front of the tent of meeting. They were

responsible for the care of the sanctuary on behalf of the Israelites. Anyone else who approached the sanctuary was to be put to death.

³⁹The total number of Levites counted at the LORD's command by Moses and Aaron according to their clans, including every male a month old or more, was 22,000.

⁴⁰The LORD said to Moses, "Count all the firstborn Israelite males who are a month old or more and make a list of their names. ⁴¹Take the Levites for me in place of all the firstborn of the Israelites, and the livestock of the Levites in place of all the firstborn of the livestock of the Israelites. I am the LORD."

⁴²So Moses counted all the firstborn of the Israelites, as the LORD commanded him. ⁴³The total number of firstborn males a month old or more, listed by name, was 22,273.

⁴⁴The LORD also said to Moses, ⁴⁵"Take the Levites in place of all the firstborn of Israel, and the livestock of the Levites in place of their livestock. The Levites are to be mine. I am the LORD. ⁴⁶To redeem the 273 firstborn Israelites who exceed the number of the Levites, ⁴⁷collect five shekels for each one, according to the sanctuary shekel, which weighs twenty gerahs. ⁴⁸Give the money for the redemption of the additional Israelites to Aaron and his sons."

⁴⁹So Moses collected the redemption money from those who exceeded the number redeemed by the Levites. ⁵⁰From the firstborn of the Israelites he collected silver weighing 1,365 shekels, according to the sanctuary shekel. ⁵¹Moses gave the redemption money to Aaron and his sons, as he was commanded by the word of the LORD.

⁴:¹The LORD said to Moses and Aaron: ²"Take a census of the Kohathite branch of the Levites by their clans and families. ³Count all the men from thirty to fifty years of age who come to serve in the work at the tent of meeting.

⁴"This is the work of the Kohathites at the tent of meeting: the care of the most holy things. ⁵When the camp is to move, Aaron and his sons are to go in and take down the shielding curtain and put it over the ark of the covenant law. ⁶Then they are to cover the curtain with a durable leather, spread a cloth of solid blue over that and put the poles in place.

⁷"Over the table of the Presence they are to spread a blue cloth and put on it the plates, dishes and bowls, and the jars for drink offerings; the bread that is continually there is to remain on it. ⁸They are to spread a

scarlet cloth over them, cover that with the durable leather and put the poles in place.

⁹"They are to take a blue cloth and cover the lampstand that is for light, together with its lamps, its wick trimmers and trays, and all its jars for the olive oil used to supply it. ¹⁰Then they are to wrap it and all its accessories in a covering of the durable leather and put it on a carrying frame.

¹¹"Over the gold altar they are to spread a blue cloth and cover that with the durable leather and put the poles in place.

¹²"They are to take all the articles used for ministering in the sanctuary, wrap them in a blue cloth, cover that with the durable leather and put them on a carrying frame.

¹³"They are to remove the ashes from the bronze altar and spread a purple cloth over it. ¹⁴Then they are to place on it all the utensils used for ministering at the altar, including the firepans, meat forks, shovels and sprinkling bowls. Over it they are to spread a covering of the durable leather and put the poles in place.

¹⁵"After Aaron and his sons have finished covering the holy furnishings and all the holy articles, and when the camp is ready to move, only then are the Kohathites to come and do the carrying. But they must not touch the holy things or they will die. The Kohathites are to carry those things that are in the tent of meeting.

¹⁶"Eleazar son of Aaron, the priest, is to have charge of the oil for the light, the fragrant incense, the regular grain offering and the anointing oil. He is to be in charge of the entire tabernacle and everything in it, including its holy furnishings and articles."

¹⁷The LORD said to Moses and Aaron, ¹⁸"See that the Kohathite tribal clans are not destroyed from among the Levites. ¹⁹So that they may live and not die when they come near the most holy things, do this for them: Aaron and his sons are to go into the sanctuary and assign to each man his work and what he is to carry. ²⁰But the Kohathites must not go in to look at the holy things, even for a moment, or they will die."

²¹The LORD said to Moses, ²²"Take a census also of the Gershonites by their families and clans. ²³Count all the men from thirty to fifty years of age who come to serve in the work at the tent of meeting.

²⁴"This is the service of the Gershonite clans in their carrying and their other work: ²⁵They are to carry the curtains of the tabernacle, that is, the tent of meeting, its covering and its outer covering of durable leather,

the curtains for the entrance to the tent of meeting, ²⁶the curtains of the courtyard surrounding the tabernacle and altar, the curtain for the entrance to the courtyard, the ropes and all the equipment used in the service of the tent. The Gershonites are to do all that needs to be done with these things. ²⁷All their service, whether carrying or doing other work, is to be done under the direction of Aaron and his sons. You shall assign to them as their responsibility all they are to carry. ²⁸This is the service of the Gershonite clans at the tent of meeting. Their duties are to be under the direction of Ithamar son of Aaron, the priest.

²⁹"Count the Merarites by their clans and families. ³⁰Count all the men from thirty to fifty years of age who come to serve in the work at the tent of meeting. ³¹As part of all their service at the tent, they are to carry the frames of the tabernacle, its crossbars, posts and bases, ³²as well as the posts of the surrounding courtyard with their bases, tent pegs, ropes, all their equipment and everything related to their use. Assign to each man the specific things he is to carry. ³³This is the service of the Merarite clans as they work at the tent of meeting under the direction of Ithamar son of Aaron, the priest."

³⁴Moses, Aaron and the leaders of the community counted the Kohathites by their clans and families. ³⁵All the men from thirty to fifty years of age who came to serve in the work at the tent of meeting, ³⁶counted by clans, were 2,750. ³⁷This was the total of all those in the Kohathite clans who served at the tent of meeting. Moses and Aaron counted them according to the LORD's command through Moses.

³⁸The Gershonites were counted by their clans and families. ³⁹All the men from thirty to fifty years of age who came to serve in the work at the tent of meeting, ⁴⁰counted by their clans and families, were 2,630. ⁴¹This was the total of those in the Gershonite clans who served at the tent of meeting. Moses and Aaron counted them according to the LORD's command.

⁴²The Merarites were counted by their clans and families. ⁴³All the men from thirty to fifty years of age who came to serve in the work at the tent of meeting, ⁴⁴counted by their clans, were 3,200. ⁴⁵This was the total of those in the Merarite clans. Moses and Aaron counted them according to the LORD's command through Moses.

⁴⁶So Moses, Aaron and the leaders of Israel counted all the Levites by their clans and families. ⁴⁷All the men from thirty to fifty years of age

who came to do the work of serving and carrying the tent of meeting ⁴⁸numbered 8,580. ⁴⁹At the LORD's command through Moses, each was assigned his work and told what to carry.

Thus they were counted, as the LORD commanded Moses.

Listening to the Text in the Story: Numbers 1:47–53; Hittite "Instructions to Priests and Temple Officials."

After numbering the non-Levitical tribes and describing their placement in the camp (Num 1–2), the text turns to the Levites (chs. 3–4). They were not numbered in the warrior census since they have special tabernacle responsibilities (1:47–53). These are now described in Numbers 3–4 along with the Levites' families and clans, their numbers, and their placement in the camp around the tabernacle. In doing so, these chapters illustrate the importance of guarding holy space, a familiar concept in those days. We have texts from the Late Bronze Age (1550–1200 BC) describing responsibilities of Hittite temple officials in which failure to guard the temple properly was a capital offense.[1] Clearly, respecting holy space was vitally important in the ancient Near Eastern culture and the same was true in ancient Israel: Numbers 1:50–53 implies that Levites bore special responsibility for guarding the Lord's tabernacle; Numbers 18:22–23 implies it was a capital offense if they did not; several verses state that those who approach it improperly must be executed (1:51; 3:10, 38; 18:22). The holy and heavenly King was dwelling in Israel's midst; they must not defile his holy palace or let it be defiled.

EXPLAIN the Story

Introduction: The Account of the Family of Aaron and Moses (3:1)

While Aaron's family is named in what follows (Num 3:2–4), Moses's family is not. Why mention him with Aaron in 3:1? Perhaps because he camps with Aaron's family and is thus named as part of it (3:38; note that Aaron and Moses were brothers [Exod 6:20]).[2] Or perhaps because Numbers 3:1 has all

---

1. See "Instructions to Priests and Temple Officials," trans. Gregory McMahon (*COS* 1.83:10–19) or "Instructions for Temple Officials," trans. Albrecht Goetze (*ANET*, 209–210 [§§10–19]).

2. Jacob Milgrom, *Numbers*, The JPS Torah Commentary (New York: The Jewish Publication Society, 1990), 15.

of Numbers 3–4 in view, and Aaron and Moses, both of Levi's tribe (Exod 6:16–20), were like the tribe's fathers.[3] Either way, Numbers 3 begins a new story focusing on Levi's tribe.

The phrase "at Mt. Sinai" (which may also be translated "on Mt. Sinai") could refer to a time the Lord spoke to Moses on the mountain (cf. Exod 31:18 with 32:1a), in contrast to speaking to him from the tent of meeting "in the wilderness[4] of Sinai" at the mountain's base (Num 1:1; 3:14). If so, then the story of 3:1–13 is recounted here, not earlier in Exodus, to provide background for 3:14 and following.

The Priests: Aaron's Family (3:2–4)

All tabernacle personnel were from Levi's tribe, which included priestly Levites (Aaron and his family) and non-priestly Levites (males not in Aaron's family; in Numbers, the term *Levites* sometimes refers to this second group in particular [3:9; 8:13; 18:6; etc.]). The priests had special responsibilities: "they alone had the right to handle the sacrificial blood, to touch the altar and to enter the tent of meeting. They were the authoritative teachers of the nation (e.g., Lev 10:11; Deut 24:8), the official mediators between God and Israel."[5] They therefore led the tribe (Num 3:9, 32; 4:28, 33) and are naturally described first.

Aaron had four sons. In Leviticus 10, his oldest sons, Nadab and Abihu, "presented unauthorized fire" (Num 3:4; my trans.). Apparently, they brought an offering the Lord did not command, trying to barge into the Most Holy Place—the Lord's very throne room—at a time of their own choosing (cf. Lev 16:1 with 16:2).[6] Since barging into an earthly king's throne room was a sign of treasonous disrespect, barging into the heavenly king's throne room was more so (cf. 1 Kgs 1:15–23; Esth 4:11). The penalty for treason was immediately applied and they "died before the LORD" (cf. Lev 10:1–3). Without sons, their line ended, and their younger brothers served as priests with Aaron (vv. 4–15).

Mentioning this story at the start of Numbers 3–4 was a special warning for priests and Levites. Unlike Nadab and Abihu, they must be completely faithful in carrying out their responsibilities in and with the holy tent. There is no weightier task than handling the Lord's holy things (see above at 1:47–53, pp. 53–54; see also 3:10, 38; 4:15, 18–20; cf. 16:1–35; 2 Sam 6:6–7; Jas 3:1).

---

3. C. F. Keil, *The Pentateuch*, 661 (*Numbers*, 19).
4. For "wilderness" see p. 49n2.
5. Wenham, *Numbers*, 69.
6. For details, see Sklar, *Leviticus* (ZECOT), 293–94. Cf. Est 4:11.

The Levites Serve the Priests in Tabernacle Duties (3:5–10)

Whenever the camp moved, the tabernacle would also be moved, but it was far too large for the priestly family to do so. The Lord therefore assigns the non-priestly Levites to help (Num 3:6).

This meant interacting with the Lord's holy property, so the Levites went through a special cleansing ritual to move into a higher state of ritual purity (Num 8:5–22).[7] This made them ritually purer than regular Israelites but not ritually holy like priests, the spiritual leaders, whose leadership is evident here. The Levites are presented to Aaron (3:6) as before a ruler (Gen 47:7) and "given wholly" to the priests (Num 3:9), placed under their authority to help with tabernacle tasks (cf. 18:6).

Their tasks included tearing the tabernacle down, carrying it, setting it back up, and guarding it from being approached improperly by the Israelites (cf. Num 1:50–53). Failure to care for a king's palace was a serious matter; the Levites exercised such care on Israel's behalf (3:7–8).[8]

Our passage finishes with two important points (Num 3:10). First, in contrast to the Levites, only Aaron and his sons would fulfill priestly duties. The Levites carried and guarded the tent; Aaron and his sons ministered within it (cf. 18:1–7). Second, anyone else approaching the sanctuary would be put to death. In context, this most likely refers to a non-priest approaching the sanctuary to do priestly duties (cf. 18:7), though it would also apply to non-Levites approaching to do Levitical duties. Either was a treasonous act of disrespect and thus a capital crime (see at 1:47–53, pp. 53–54).

The Levites: Taken by the Lord in Place of the Firstborn (3:11–13)

During the final plague on Egypt, the Lord provided for the Israelite firstborn to be saved by means of the blood of a Passover lamb (Exod 12:1–13) and then

---

7. For ritual states, see pp. 32–33, Ritual Purity and Impurity.

8. Other passages show women also helped at the tabernacle (Exod 38:8; 1 Sam 2:22). They are perhaps not mentioned here because they did not participate in the duties of these chapters (transporting and guarding the tabernacle), but other help was needed, e.g., "utensil cleanup, general courtyard cleanup, water resupply, ancillary food preparation, guiding and assisting other women worshipers, [or] washing priests' clothes" (Douglas K. Stuart, *Exodus*, NAC 2 [Nashville: Broadman & Holman, 2006], 767). These tasks may seem mundane—but are no more so than the Levites' work! Indeed, these were important acts of service: without them, the Lord's palace could not function as a place of worship. The same is true today: church only happens after a snowstorm if someone shovels the parking lot. Whatever acts of service these women did, they would have contributed directly to the Lord's people being able to worship.

led them out of the land of slavery.[9] He commanded them to do two things from then on as regular reminders of his rescue: celebrate the Passover meal (Exod 13:3–10) and set aside to him every firstborn human or animal (vv. 1–2, 11–16). In each case, parents performed an action to teach their children the redemption story (vv. 6–8, 12–15).

For setting aside firstborn animals, see at Numbers 18:15–18, p. 251. For firstborn children, being set apart to the Lord could mean serving in his tabernacle (cf. 1 Sam 1:11, 22–28), but instead of disrupting families like this, the Lord normally allowed a five-shekel redemption price to be paid (Num 18:16).

At this one point in history, however, he takes the Levites as substitutes for the firstborn (Num 3:12–13). Though he gave the Levites to help the priests in the Lord's work, ultimately, he has set them apart for himself. The beginning of 3:12 is emphatic in the Hebrew: "*I*—look here!—*I* have taken the Levites . . . " (author's translation and emphasis). They belonged to the Lord in a special way, and as they served him in the Israelites' midst—*in place of the firstborn*—they were a reminder that all the firstborn belonged to the Lord and were therefore a reminder of the exodus story (3:13; 8:16–18). Indeed, because they were set apart to *serve* the Lord, they were a living reminder that the Lord had rescued the Israelites from cruel slavery to an evil ruler in order to enter the glorious service of a good King.

The section closes with the phrase, "I am the Lord" (Num 3:13). When this occurs with the story of the Lord rescuing the Israelites from Egypt with great power, it serves as an exclamation point emphasizing he is the sovereign God and King (Exod 6:6–8; 7:5; 10:2; 12:12). In this context, it becomes a shorthand way to remind the people of his sovereignty: he is the King and has the right to choose who will serve as his palace servants.

The Levites, Part One: Census, Placement in the Inner Camp, and Duties of the Different Tribal Families (3:14–39)

Previous chapters numbered the Israelite warriors and described their place in the camp (Num 1–2); now the Levites and their tabernacle responsibilities are described (Num 3–4). See summary table below.

Because the Levites are taken in place of the firstborn, they are counted (Num 3:14–39), along with the firstborn (vv. 40–43), to see if there are enough

---

9. For further details, see p. 154, Listening to the Text in the Story, and Sklar, *Additional Notes*, at 3:11–13.

Levites to serve as substitutes (vv. 44–48). The command to do so comes "in the Desert of Sinai" (v. 14), meaning the events narrated here happened after the tent had been set up (v. 1).

Levite Clans, Numbers, Placement in the Inner Camp, and Tabernacle Duties (Num 3–4)

Families	Gershon (3:21–26; 4:28, 39–40)	Kohath (3:27–32; 4:16, 35–36)	Merari (3:33–37; 4:33, 43–44)
Clans	Libnites, Shimeites	Amramites, Izharites, Hebronites, Uzzielites	Mahlites, Mushites
Number of Males	7,500	8,300 (see note on 3:39)	6,200
Males 30–50	2,630	2,750	3,200
Placement in the Camp	Tabernacle's west side	Tabernacle's south side	Tabernacle's north side
Levitical Leader	Eliasaph	Elizaphan	Zuriel
Priestly Leader	Ithamar	Eleazar	Ithamar
Tabernacle Items They Transported	Mostly fabrics	Mostly furniture and utensils	Mostly structural elements
How They Did So	With two carts and four oxen (Num 7:7)	By carrying them on their shoulders (Num 7:9)	With four carts and eight oxen (Num 7:8)

Levi had three sons: Gershon, Kohath, and Merari (Num 3:17). These formed "families" within the tribe that could be subdivided into "clans" (vv. 18–20; see table).[10] Today we might use the expression "tribal families" for the former (since we often use "family" to refer to the nuclear family). Every male one month old and older was counted, which was also true of

---

10. See p. 50n5.

the firstborn census (v. 40). The text does not explain the age requirement.[11] Whatever the reason, Israelites would know exactly whom to count.

Having identified the tribe's genealogical structure (Num 3:17–20), the text discusses the three tribal families in turn, identifying their clans, numbers, camp placement, leader, and tabernacle duties[12] (vv. 21–39). The duties are only generally described; chapter 4 will offer more detail (see at 4:1–33, pp. 79–84). Chapter 3 emphasizes, however, the Kohathites are responsible for the sanctuary's holiest items. Not only are these listed (3:31; cf. 4:5–15), but 3:32 names the priest responsible for ensuring the Kohathites carry out their duties faithfully, something not given for the other two tribal families until chapter 4 (cf. 4:28, 33). This suggests the Kohathites' work had to be done with extra care. Indeed, the next chapter states they could not even approach these items until the priests had wrapped them so the Kohathites did not touch them directly (vv. 5–15). Their duties were especially sacred.

For the Levites's placement in the camp, see diagram on p. 62. On the tabernacle's eastern side near its entrance were the tribe's leaders: Moses, Aaron, and Aaron's sons (Num 3:38). Since the priests worked within the tabernacle, this placement made good sense (and gave them a very short commute to work!). The text highlights they were "responsible for the care[13] of the sanctuary on behalf of the Israelites," serving the heavenly King in his earthly palace on Israel's behalf. For anyone else to do so would be an act of treasonous disrespect, so the warning of 3:10 is repeated: any non-priest who draws near is to be put to death (see comments at 1:47–53, pp. 53–54).

The total of the census in the Hebrew is 22,000 (3:39), though the numbers of the three tribal families add up to 22,300 (cf. 3:22, 28, 34). As many have noted, 3:28 likely contains a scribal error and should read 8,300 (see NIV text note), not 8,600. In Hebrew, there is just one letter difference between the words *three* (*sh-l-sh*) and *six* (*sh-sh*).

Firstborn Israelites Redeemed (3:40–51)

This section begins with a command to number the firstborn Israelites (Num 3:40) and a reminder that the Levites will serve as substitutes for them, with their animals serving as substitutes for the firstborn Israelite animals (v. 41;

---

11. For different suggestions, see Sklar, *Additional Notes*, at 3:15.
12. The NIV speaks of the tribal families' being responsible for the "care" of certain aspects of the tabernacle (3:25, 28, 31, 32, 36), but it would be more accurate to translate they were responsible for the "duties/obligations" of the tabernacle. See 3:7–8, where the NIV translates the same Hebrew word in this way; see discussion in Levine, *Numbers 1–20*, 141–42.
13. See n12.

cf. vv. 12–13).[14] The firstborn Israelites are then immediately counted and total 22,273, which is 273 more than the Levites (vv. 42–43; cf. v. 39). Thus a redemption price must be paid for the additional firstborn.[15] In this context, redemption refers to making a payment that transfers the firstborn from the ownership of one party (the Lord) to that of another (the parents). The price is five shekels (v. 47), usually assumed to be about .4 ounces (11–12 g).[16] This was given to Aaron and his sons (vv. 48, 51), who were the Lord's representatives (cf. Exod 30:16). The total came to 1,365 shekels, or about 34 pounds (15–16 kgs), money the priests could use for maintenance of the tabernacle (cf. Exod 30:16) and themselves. (They depended on gifts and donations [cf. Num 18:8–20] because they did not have large land tracts for farming [v. 20].)

The Levites, Part Two: Clans, Tabernacle Duties, Numbers (4:1–49)

Two different Levite censuses were taken. The first counted all the Levites to see if there were enough to substitute for the firstborn Israelites (Num 3:14–48). The second parallels the census of Numbers 1 and thus only counts the Levites of a certain age. In Numbers 1, only military-aged Israelites were counted; here, only the Levites who were the right age to serve at the tabernacle are counted (vv. 34–49).[17] In Numbers 1, those entering the army had to be at least age twenty and thus physically mature enough to fight in war; here, those serving at the tabernacle had to be even older—thirty—perhaps "because the seriousness of their duties called for emotional and mental maturity as well as physical maturity."[18] At age fifty they had to retire from transporting the

---

14. While the Levites are not given large tracts of land for farming (18:23–24), they were allowed flocks and herds to provide for some of their food and clothing needs (cf. 35:2–3).

15. Presumably, the Levites' animals were sufficient to substitute for the Israelites' animals. The Levites serving as substitutes was a one-time event (see at 3:11–13, p. 75). The same would be true with regard to the animals; going forward, the rules of 18:15–18 would be followed.

16. E. M. Cook, "Weights and Measures," *ISBE* 4:1054. The "shekel of the Sanctuary" is perhaps mentioned because it was difficult to standardize weights and measures at this point in history; the text thus makes clear which standard to use.

17. The phrase "all . . . who come to serve in the work at the tent of meeting" (Num 4:3) is more woodenly translated "all . . . coming for the division (*tsaba*) to do work at the tent of meeting." In Num 1, those aged 20 and older were counted in terms of their army "divisions" (*tsaba*; 1:3); here, the Levites aged 30 to 50 are counted in terms of their tabernacle "division" (*tsaba*); so also 4:23, 30, 35, 38, 43.

18. Anastasia Boniface-Malle, "Numbers," in *Africa Bible Commentary*, ed. Tokunboh Adeyemo (Grand Rapids: Zondervan, 2006), 175. Num 8:24 identifies the age as twenty-five; several commentators follow the rabbinical suggestion that this is not a contradiction (rather glaring for an editor to miss) but may be due to an apprenticeship period that began at twenty-five (8:24), with official duties beginning at thirty (4:35, 39, 43) (Allen, "Numbers," 733; Harrison, *Numbers*, 81). If so, the apprenticeship would presumably have involved matters related to disassembling and reassembling the tent as well as instruction on ritual matters more generally.

holy tabernacle (8:25). This is realistic, given the heavy work involved and the shorter lifespans in the ancient world. But they could do other things to help their brothers (v. 26), such as repair wagons, care for animals, or anything else aside from transporting the tabernacle.

The Kohathites' Duties (4:1–20)

Before the census begins, the chapter describes the different responsibilities that are assigned to each of the three Levite tribal branches for moving the tabernacle (Num 4:1–33). It starts with the Kohathites, who will move the most holy furniture. Just as movers today are expected to handle items with care, how much more so here! The tent of meeting is the Lord royal's palace in Israel's midst,[19] meaning the Kohathites had the awesome responsibility of moving the furniture of the King of heaven.

For a description of the holy objects here, see Exodus 25:10–40; 26:31–35; 27:1–8; 30:1–10. All items came from within the tent, aside from the bronze altar and its utensils (Num 4:13–14).

While Levites were at a higher level of ritual purity than regular Israelites (see Num 8:5–22), they were not ritually holy like the priests and so could not directly handle the most holy objects.[20] To do so would be treasonous disrespect for the Lord's holy property and expose them to the lethal power of his holiness that these items shared. To use a modern analogy, the Lord's holiness may be likened to nuclear radiation. Just as those who approach radioactive material without the proper protection will die from exposure to it, so those who approach these holy items without the proper level of protective ritual holiness will die from exposure to them (see esp. 1 Sam 6:19; 2 Sam 6:6–7). In at least some instances, even angels cover their faces in the presence of this holy King (Isa 6:1–3).[21]

Therefore the priests must wrap these objects first. They start in the most holy place (Num 4:5–6), then move outward to the holy place (vv. 7–12) and the court (vv. 13–14). The result will be "six large packages" ready for transport.[22] Only then can the Kohathites approach to carry them away (v. 15).

The chart below summarizes the six packages prepared by the priests. Several observations may be made. First, the cloths used to wrap the tabernacle furniture and accessories are blue, scarlet, or purple, colors associated elsewhere

---

19. See Listening to the Text in the Story, pp. 59–61.
20. For ritual states see pp. 32–33, Ritual Purity and Impurity.
21. Allen, "Numbers," 734.
22. Philip J. Budd, *Numbers*, Word Biblical Commentary 5 (Waco, TX: Word Books, 1984), 50.

with royalty (2 Sam 1:24; Esth 1:6; Ezek 23:6). These items belong to the divine King.

Item	Location in the Tabernacle	Coverings	Method of Carrying
Ark of the covenant law (4:5–6)	Most Holy Place	Shielding curtain, durable leather, blue cloth	Poles
Table of the presence and related items (4:7–8)	Holy Place	Blue cloth, scarlet cloth, durable leather	Poles
Lampstand and related items (4:9–10)	Holy Place	Blue cloth, durable leather	Carrying frame/Pole
Golden incense altar (4:11)	Holy Place	Blue cloth, durable leather	Poles
Other items used in the tabernacle (4:12)	Holy Place	Blue cloth, durable leather	Carrying frame/Pole
Bronze altar and related items (4:13–14)	Courtyard	Purple cloth, durable leather	Poles

Second, they are wrapped in a "color-coded" way: items from the tent are wrapped in blue (and in one case, scarlet); items from the courtyard, in purple. The differing colors may reflect differing levels of holiness.[23] Blue was an especially holy color (note its use in the uniform of the holiest priest [Exod 28:28, 31, 37]). Wrapping the tent items in blue sets them apart as having a higher level of holiness than the courtyard items.

---

23. For differing levels within ritual states, see Sklar, *Leviticus* (TOTC), 45–46; more fully, see Philip Peter Jenson, *Graded Holiness: A Key to the Priestly Conception of the World*, JSOTSup 106 (Sheffield: JSOT Press, 1992), esp. 89–114.

Third, "durable leather"[24] was the final covering for all items except the ark. It was first covered with the "shielding curtain" (traditionally translated "veil"), which separated the most holy place from the holy place (Exod 26:31–33) and was presumably taken down in such a way that the ark remained hidden from view (cf. Lev 16:13). This was followed by a leather covering and finally a covering of blue cloth (note again the association with holiness). This set the ark apart visually from the other items, which is unsurprising: the divine King sat enthroned over it among the cherubim (1 Sam 4:4; Ps 99:1) and it held the "covenant law,"[25] making it supremely important.

Fourth, all these holy items were carried by hand (rather than by cart; cf. Num 7:7–9),[26] which may have been an extra sign of reverence (a later passage will speak of a king being carried by his servants [Song 3:7]). Four of the packages had square or rectangular items made with rings that could hold carrying poles (see table above).[27] Such was not the case for the items of the remaining two packages, so they were wrapped and carried by means of a "carrying frame" (Num 4:10, 12, or perhaps "pole," the way the NIV translates the same word at 13:23).

Fifth, Eleazar, the priest for the Kohathites, bore the responsibility for the holy furnishings and articles (which the Kohathites would carry; Num 4:16; cf. 3:32). Mention is also made in v. 16 of his specific responsibility for four items used in or at the tabernacle: oil for the light (cf. Lev 24:1–4), the fragrant incense (cf. Exod 30:34–38), the regular grain offering (cf. Lev 6:20–23), and the anointing oil (cf. Exod 30:22–33). Perhaps these had their own containers and did not easily fit into the other packages; by mentioning

---

24. The relevant Hebrew word (*tahash*) is widely debated; see Benjamin J. Noonan, "Hide or Hue? Defining Hebrew תַּחַשׁ," *Biblica* 93.4 (2012): 580–89, esp. 586–89, where he concludes the word may well refer to a type of leather.

25. For "covenant law" see at 1:47–53, p. 53.

26. See Sprinkle, *Leviticus and Numbers*, 203, for a picture of Egyptian priests from the time of Ramses II (thirteenth-century BC) carrying sacred boats on poles. Note also the "Anubis Ark" from Tutankhamun's tomb, with rings for the insertion of poles (an internet search for "Anubis Ark" quickly pulls up images).

27. In Num 4:6, many versions translate "put its poles," which seems to conflict with Exod 25:15, where we read that the poles "are not to be removed." One possible explanation is that the poles would be temporarily removed when the ark was wrapped for transport but then immediately reinserted. Alternatively, and perhaps more persuasively, Eichler (Raanan Eichler, *The Ark and the Cherubim* [Tübingen: Mohr Siebeck, 2021], 112–13) has made a good case that there were four poles—two at each end—that were retractable, noting the exact same construction in a fourteenth century BC chest from Tutankhamen's tomb. The poles would be pushed under the ark when at rest (hiding them) and pulled out to be "put [in place]" for carrying when the ark was being moved (Num. 4:6). (For translating the relevant verb [Hb. *sim*] as "put in place," see its use in ESV of Exod 40:28 and see also *DCH*, 135, range of meaning 2.)

them here, the text ensures it accounts for all holy items. Whatever the case, Eleazar presumably could not carry all these things alone, making it likely that "having charge" meant he oversaw the Kohathites carrying these items along with the other holy objects.

Finally, this section warns the Kohathites against overstepping their boundaries. They are forbidden from touching these holy items directly (Num 4:15) or even from looking at them (vv. 19–20), lest they die. As noted above, these items share in the Lord's own holiness, which is lethal when approached improperly. The Kohathites were therefore to show deep reverence to the Lord by not approaching his holy objects improperly (vv. 15, 20), and the priests were to show deep reverence by guarding his holy objects well and prohibiting improper access to them (vv. 18–20).

The Gershonites' Duties (4:21–28)

This section and the next follow the same basic pattern: the text commands the Gershonites and Merarites to be numbered (Num 4:22–23, 29–30), identifies their responsibilities concerning specific tabernacle items (vv. 24–26, 31–32a), underscores that priests will oversee them in this work (vv. 27, 32b),[28] and names the priest specifically responsible for them: Aaron's son Ithamar (vv. 28, 33).

Now that the tabernacle furniture is packed, the next logical step would be the Gershonites' duties: removing the various fabrics that formed the tent walls, coverings, and courtyard and carrying these to the next place. The text focuses on the last step, mentioning "carrying" or "carry" four different times (Num 4:24, 25, 27 [2x]); this is the main work they must do when the camp is on the march.[29]

For a description of the items here, see Exodus 26:1–14, 36–37; 27:9–18. The tent fabrics are mentioned first (Num 4:25),[30] the court fabrics second (v. 26). The amount of material moved totaled about one-quarter the size of an American football field (not including end zones) or one-fifth the size of an average soccer field. Numbers 7:7 implies they used carts to transport these materials. (The chart below assumes an eighteen-inch cubit.)

---

28. The "you" is plural in these verses, referring to Aaron and his sons.

29. The NIV mentions this in addition to "other work" (4:24, 27). Alternatively, the Hebrew may be translated, "This is the service of the Gershonite clans with regard to work, even with regard to carrying/loads" (4:24); "work" is the general category, "carrying/loads" the type of work they must do.

30. The beginning of Num 4:25 is best translated, "They are to carry the curtains of the tabernacle and the tent of meeting." For details, see Sklar, *Additional Notes*, at 4:25.

Item	Measurement (square feet/square meters)
Tabernacle curtains	2,520/234
Tent	2,970/276
Tent covering	2,970/276
Tent outer covering	2,970/276
Tent entrance curtain	Unknown
Courtyard curtains, including entrance curtain	3,375/313
Total	14,805/1,375 (+ tent entrance curtain)

The Merarites' Duties (4:29–33)

The last tabernacle items to be moved were those making up the tent frame and courtyard wall. For a description of the items, see Exodus 26:15–29, 37; 27:9–19; 35:18. Once again, the tent items are mentioned first (Num 4:31), the court's second (v. 32).

Whereas the Gershonites are given two carts to carry the tabernacle fabrics (Num 7:7), the Merarites are given four to carry their items (v. 8), many of which were metal and very heavy. More specifically, their items were either wood (likely the courtyard posts), wood covered in gold (the tabernacle frames, crossbars, posts), or solid metal (bases, tent pegs). The weight would have been considerable. Exodus 38:24–31 lists the amounts of gold, silver, and bronze used in making everything in the tabernacle. Assuming a shekel of .4 oz (11.3 g) and a talent of 75 pounds (34 kg),[31] the metals' weight would be as follows:

Item	Weight (pounds/kgs)
Gold	2,193/995
Silver	7,544/3,422
Bronze	5,310/2,409

---

31. Cook, "Weights and Measures," 4:1054.

Since some of the gold was used to make items carried by the Kohathites (the ark, table, etc.), the Merarites did not have to transport all the above weight, but they were responsible for most of it, which explains their extra carts. (For the marching order of the different Levite branches, see diagram on p. 63 and commentary at 10:14–28.)

Numbering the Levites Old Enough for Tabernacle Service (4:34–49)

Now that the Levites' tabernacle duties have been identified, Moses and Aaron—aided by the community's leaders[32]—can take the census of those able to work there. The number in each of the three Levite branches is given (Num 4:34–45), followed by a summary (vv. 46–49).

Levites Aged Thirty to Fifty	
Kohathites	2,750
Gershonites	2,630
Merarites	3,200
Total	8,580

The text repeatedly notes the numbering is done according to the Lord's command (4:37, 41, 45, 49), perhaps to make clear this was not disobedience to the earlier command of 1:47–49.

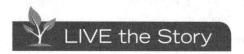

LIVE the Story

At first glance, two chapters focusing on the tabernacle duties of ancient Levite clans seem to have little of practical value for modern people. But they actually have much to teach us, whether by challenging our ideas about authority and independence or encouraging us that our imperfections need not prevent us from relationship with God. We can unpack these themes by asking four questions, the first of which might challenge our understanding of authority.[33]

---

32. On the analogy of 1:4–16, these are probably the leaders of Levi's tribe in particular (3:24, 30, 35).

33. Teachers or preachers may choose to treat each chapter separately. If so, the first two questions relate most naturally to Num 3, allowing a focus on the topic of authority. The third relates most

What Is the Goal of Spiritual Authority?

In business, an "org chart" (organizational chart) outlines a company's authority structure. Were an org chart made for tabernacle roles and responsibilities, the priests would be at the top; they are in charge (Num 3:6, 9, 32; 4:16, 28, 33), and only they can do priestly duties (3:10; 4:15). The Levites would be next; they cannot serve as priests but are responsible for moving the holy tabernacle (3:7–8; 4:1–33). The remaining Israelites would be at the bottom; they would participate in worship at the tabernacle (see Lev 1–5; 23) but can do neither of the things assigned to the priests and Levites. Thus, the priests and Levites are in the primary positions of spiritual authority.

And yet the text is equally clear that those with positions of authority are to carry out their roles *on behalf of the rest of Israel*. Aaron and his sons "were responsible for the care of the sanctuary *on behalf of the Israelites*" (Num 3:38, emphasis added). The Levites "are to perform duties *for [Aaron] and for the whole community* at the tent of meeting by doing the work of the tabernacle" (v. 7, emphasis added). Those with spiritual authority serve others and work on their behalf to ensure the worship of God among his people can carry on well and without interruption.

In short, the Lord establishes a hierarchy among his people not to concentrate power or privilege in the hands of some but to ensure the community can continue in relationship with him. This shows his desire for his people to know him and makes clear that spiritual leadership is for the purpose of serving his people, not being lords over them (cf. 1 Pet 5:3). "Selection is not for privilege, but for service."[34]

Jesus emphasized this by washing his disciples' feet and then exhorting them to follow his example (John 13:5, 12–17). If the King of kings and Lord of lords serves those under his authority so humbly, how could we refuse to do the same? Practically speaking, what might this service look like in our daily lives?

If such questions are for those in authority, a different question may be asked of those under authority.

What Is the Proper Response to Spiritual Authority?

These chapters repeatedly emphasize that the Lord has assigned certain roles involving the tabernacle to the priests and Levites alone (Num 3:7–8, 10, 38;

---

naturally to Num 4, allowing a focus on the proper response to God's authority, while the fourth (though focused on Num 3) follows naturally by showing the good news God provides us in light of our failure to obey him as we should.

34. Thomas B. Dozeman, "Numbers," in *The New Interpreter's Bible*, ed. Leander Keck, 12 vols. (Nashville: Abingdon, 1998), 2:53.

4:15, 18–20). On the one hand, their duties involved handing ritually holy items, and only those set apart into higher ritual states could handle such things (see 1:47–53, pp. 53–54). Since the New Testament does not continue ritual states as a category,[35] this is not immediately applicable to spiritual leadership today.

On the other hand, a deeper principle is at work in terms of the authority structures the Lord establishes among his people. As noted above, the Lord puts priests and Levites in spiritual leadership to serve others and to serve on their behalf. But it must not be missed that he puts them into places of spiritual authority. In the "org chart" of ancient Israel, the priests clearly had the highest level of spiritual authority and the Levites, the next level under. This authority structure was to be recognized and respected (as the tragic story of Numbers 16 so graphically illustrates). In any organized group of people—whether family, business, church, or country—the group's leaders can only serve the group well with the group's support.

The same is true in the church today, which is why the New Testament speaks so emphatically about the importance of respecting those in spiritual leadership in the church:

> Now we ask you, brothers and sisters, to acknowledge those who work hard among you, who care for you in the Lord and who admonish you. Hold them in the highest regard in love because of their work. (1 Thess 5:12–13a)

> The elders who direct the affairs of the church well are worthy of double honor, especially those whose work is preaching and teaching. (1 Tim 5:17)

> Have confidence in your leaders and submit to their authority, because they keep watch over you as those who must give an account. Do this so that their work will be a joy, not a burden, for that would be of no benefit to you. (Heb 13:17)

The words used here go far beyond simple respect, commanding us to "hold them in the highest regard in *love*," "[give them] double *honor*," "submit to their authority . . . so that their work will be a *joy*." It is true that some leaders abuse the spiritual authority given them, and the New Testament provides direction for dealing with this (1 Tim 5:20). But most love the Lord and, despite their weaknesses and imperfections, try their best to love and serve us for Jesus's sake.

---

35. See discussion in Sklar, *Leviticus* (TOTC), 59.

We do well to ask, "What does it mean for us to show them the love and honor we are commanded? How can we help make their work a deep joy?"

While those in a church are under the spiritual authority of others, everyone is under God's authority. This leads to a third major question, one that might challenge our notion of independence.

What Is the Proper Posture to Have before a Holy King?

In the very center of the Israelite camp was the Lord's tent, where he dwelt as holy King in Israel's midst. He dwelt there because he wanted to be among his people, but his holy presence required the Levites to camp around the tent so the Israelites would not experience his wrath, that is, his just anger against evil and rebellion (Num 1:53). Why was there danger of his wrath, and how did the Levites form a buffer of protection from it?

First, they kept the Israelites from barging improperly into the Lord's palace. Barging into the presence of an earthly king was an act of treasonous disrespect; how much more so when it concerned the King of heaven![36] In this case, the disrespect was heightened by the fact that the Lord is a holy King, unique in his purity. Entering his presence with sin or impurity would be like walking across someone's pristine, white carpet wearing muddy boots.

Second, the Levites kept the Israelites from improper exposure to the Lord's holiness, which has a living power to it. As noted above (4:1–20), it may be likened to radioactive material, which requires proper protection to prevent exposure and death. Similarly, those who approached the holy King without the proper level of protective ritual holiness would die from exposure to him (cf. 1 Sam 6:19; 2 Sam 6:7). His holiness destroys sin and impurity the way light destroys darkness. To change the analogy, a holy God living in the midst of a sinful and impure people "is like putting a huge fiery oven in the middle of a fireworks factory. The walls of the oven and careful rules and procedures may keep the fire and the explosive devices separate. But missteps in any of the protective measures will result in explosive danger and death to all who work within the walls of the factory."[37] The Levites thus not only guarded the Israelites from showing treasonous disrespect to the king but also guarded them from improperly drawing near to his holy presence and being consumed in their sin and impurity. There is a reason that Nadab and Abihu are mentioned at the beginning of these chapters: repeat their mistake and you will experience their judgment (Lev 10:1–3).

---

36. See at 3:2–4, p. 73.
37. Olson, *Numbers*, 33.

These chapters therefore focus on respecting the holy King by not entering holy places or performing holy duties without his permission. The Levites are to handle the holy tabernacle, not the Israelites (Num 3:7–8); Aaron's family is to carry out the priestly duties, not the Levites or Israelites (vv. 10, 38). Indeed, the Levites could not even look on the tabernacle's holiest items; only the priests could (4:18–20). To cross these boundaries not only shows you think little of the King's holiness, it can expose you to a deadly demonstration of his power.

Christians today might respond by noting Jesus's sacrifice deals so fully with sin and impurity that these ritual boundaries have been erased. The curtain in front of the Most Holy Place has been torn (Matt 27:51), and we have confidence to enter boldly because of him (Heb 10:19–22). This truth will be revisited below.

But to assume it somehow negates the need to show respect to God as a holy King would be a mistake. The book of Hebrews exhorts us not only to be thankful for what we have in Jesus but also to "worship God acceptably with reverence and awe, for our 'God is a consuming fire'" (Heb 12:28–29, quoting Deut 4:24). His blazing purity burns just as brightly today as it did then—and demands just as much respect. We do this when we reflect the Lord's purity in our lives. Paul speaks of "perfecting holiness out of reverence for God" (2 Cor 7:1) for this reason. The greatest way to show we respect the Lord's holiness is to reflect it in every aspect of life. We might ask, "Do those who watch me get a sense that I follow a God of blazing holiness? In what practical ways does my relationship with a holy God lead me to live differently than my neighbors?"

In asking these questions, we may well become aware of areas where we have not reflected God's holiness well. While this should lead us to repentance, it should not lead us to despair, as the answer to the last major question makes clear.

What Does a Substitute Do?

Several times in Numbers 3, the Lord emphasizes he has taken the Levites in place of the firstborn Israelites (Num 3:12–13, 41, 45); they served as their substitutes. Instead of every firstborn being given over to serve at the tabernacle, the Levites would take on this role (see at 3:11–13, 40–51, pp. 75, 77–78). That is what a substitute does: it stands in for you.

The idea of substitution found here is central to the biblical story. This is especially the case when it comes to the judgment our sins deserve. Repeatedly we read that the Lord, in his mercy and love for his sinful people, provides a substitute to bear that penalty on their behalf.

In the Old Testament sacrificial system, the substitute was a blameless animal whose lifeblood the Lord accepted as a substitute for the sinner's lifeblood (see Lev 17:11). In his comments on Lev 17:11, Levine explains, quoting from Rashi, a famous rabbinic scholar (died 1105):

> Rashi states: "Blood represents life, and it can therefore expiate for life." Basic to the theory of sacrifice in ancient Israel . . . was the notion of substitution. The sacrifice substituted for an individual human life or for the lives of the members of the community in situations where God could have exacted the life of the offender . . .
>
> This explains the specific intent of the Hebrew formula *le-khapper 'al nafshoteikhem*, "for making expiation for your lives." Literally, this formula means "to serve as *kofer* (ransom) for your lives." God accepts the blood of the sacrifices in lieu of human blood.[38]

And he does so as an act of grace: "*I myself* have given it to you on the altar to ransom your lives." He both forgives sin and provides the means of forgiveness.

The idea of substitution is clear also on the great Day of Atonement, when Aaron places his hands on the head of a blameless goat, a scapegoat, confessing the nation's sins and transferring them to this substitute (Lev 16:21). The goat then "will carry on itself all their sins to a remote place" (v. 22), never to return. It bears on its head the Israelites' guilt and the punishment they deserved, so they did not have to.

Isaiah 53 then uses the language of this very passage to describe the suffering servant, the one who bore the responsibility for the penalty of sin on behalf of God's people. Isaiah says the servant, like the goat, will take the people's sins on himself and bear responsibility for them so they do not have to (see chart below).

The idea of substitution finds its greatest fulfillment in Jesus, who is both perfect sacrificial lamb and ultimate Suffering Servant. The apostle Peter can in fact describe him both ways. In 1 Peter 1:18–19, he focuses on Jesus as sacrificial lamb: "You know that it was not with perishable things such as silver or gold that you were redeemed from the empty way of life handed down to you from your ancestors, but with the precious blood of Christ, a lamb without blemish or defect." Then in 2:22–25, he focuses on Jesus as Suffering Servant (with no less than four quotations from Isa 52–53 and four other allusions to it).[39]

---

38. Baruch Levine, *Leviticus*, The JPS Torah Commentary (New York: The Jewish Publication Society, 1989), 115.

39. See D. A. Carson, "1 Peter," in *Commentary on the New Testament Use of the Old Testament*, ed. Greg K. Beale and D. A. Carson (Grand Rapids: Baker Academic, 2007), 1033. Other New

Leviticus 16	**Isaiah 53**
"Aaron must lean both his hands on the head of the live goat, and confess over it all the *iniquities* of the Israelites and all their *transgressions*, with regard to any of their sins" (Lev 16:21a)	"But he was pierced for our *transgressions*, he was crushed for our *iniquities*" (Isa 53:5a)
"So the goat will *bear* on itself all their *iniquities* to a *land cut off*" (Lev 16:22)	". . . he was *cut off* from the *land* of the living . . . He will bear their *iniquities* . . . he *bore* the sin of many" (Isa 53:8b, 11–12)

In this passage, Peter attests that Jesus is the one who suffers sin's penalty on behalf of God's people. "He himself bore our sins in his body on the cross, so that we might die to sins and live for righteousness; by his wounds you have been healed" (1 Pet 2:24). The day of Jesus's crucifixion was thus the ultimate Day of Atonement, when our sins fell on his head, and he was cut off and died, that we might draw near and live. He is the full and final demonstration of the love of the God who provides a third party not only to remove our sin but to bear responsibility for it.[40]

In short, Jesus's death becomes the ultimate demonstration of substitution. Because of it, we can be forgiven and cleansed so deeply that we may boldly approach the throne of God, the holy King (Heb 10:19–22). But it is also the ultimate demonstration of someone with spiritual authority serving others. "For even the Son of Man did not come to be served, but to serve, and to give his life as a ransom for many" (Mark 10:45). His death provides rescue and forgiveness for those who trust their lives to him and calls them to live lives of sacrificial love as they follow him, the King who substituted his life for the lives of his servants.

Testament passages that quote Isa 53 to describe Jesus include Matt 8:17 (cf. Isa 53:4), Luke 22:37 (cf. Isa 53:12), Acts 8:32–33 (applied to Jesus in 8:34–35) (cf. Isa 53:7–8), and Heb 9:28 (cf. Isa 53:12).

40. Sklar, *Leviticus* (ZECOT), 442. For a narrative description of substitutionary atonement, see ibid., The Atonement—A Short Story, 465–67.

CHAPTER 4

Numbers 5:1–4

 LISTEN to the Story

¹The LORD said to Moses, ²"Command the Israelites to send away from the camp anyone who has a defiling skin disease or a discharge of any kind, or who is ceremonially unclean because of a dead body. ³Send away male and female alike; send them outside the camp so they will not defile their camp, where I dwell among them." ⁴The Israelites did so; they sent them outside the camp. They did just as the LORD had instructed Moses.

Listening to the Text in the Story: Leviticus 15:31; Numbers 1–4

The concept of ritual states was well known among Israel and some of her neighbors.¹ Israel recognized three main ritual states: holy, pure, and impure (sometimes translated "holy, clean, and unclean"). These guided Israelites in ritual matters; e.g., a ritually holy person (a priest) could present a sacrifice, while a ritually clean person (a Levite or lay Israelite) could not. Moreover, a ritual state was not a moral category. Ritually impure people were not necessarily morally impure (just as a person with a bad cold is not necessarily morally impure). Ritual impurity simply prohibited the person from participating in certain rituals and entering certain ritual places.²

Ritual states are central to understanding Numbers 5:1–4. The previous chapters described the camp's structure. At its heart was the Lord's holy tent, which had to be treated with the utmost reverence and respect (chs. 1–4).³ This

---

1. For this concept among Israel's neighbors, see Milgrom, *Leviticus 1–16*, 763–65.
2. For fuller explanation, see pp. 30–32, Ritual Purity and Impurity.
3. See esp. p. 72 (Listening to the Text in the Story) and pp. 87–88, What Is the Proper Posture to Have before a Holy King?

section emphasizes the camp must be kept free from severe ritual impurities because of his holy presence (cf. Lev 15:31). Holiness and impurity must never mix.

Maintaining the Camp's Ritual Purity (5:1–4)

Ritual impurities may be divided into minor and major impurities. Their key difference is that minor impurities cannot spread to other people, whereas major impurities are highly "contagious" (like a bad cold).[4] These verses identify people suffering from one of three major impurities:

1. "Anyone who has a defiling skin disease"—traditionally translated "leprosy," though most now agree the Hebrew term refers to various skin conditions that resulted in ritual impurity.[5] The NIV's translation captures the sense well, yet "ritually defiling skin disease" might be even better.
2. "Discharge of any kind"—better translated "everyone with a discharge" (cf. NASB, ESV). The reference is to abnormal genital discharges, described in Leviticus 15:2–15, 25–30, but not including seminal emissions or menstruation, which are covered separately (Lev 15:16–18, 19–24).
3. "Ceremonially unclean because of a dead body"—the impurity coming from a dead person will be fully described in Numbers 19:11–19.[6]

Those with such impurities must be sent outside the camp (undoubtedly keeping company with others having them; cf. 2 Kgs 7:3). This had already been made clear for those with a ritually defiling skin disease (Lev 13:46), but not for those with a discharge (cf. Lev 15:2–15, 25–30). Perhaps leaving the camp was assumed earlier, or perhaps it is added here because the military camp has now formed and may have required an extra level of purity (cf. Deut 23:9–14). In either case, those affected must leave the camp because the holy Lord is dwelling in Israel's midst.

---

4. For further differences see table, p. 259.
5. See fuller discussion in Sklar, *Leviticus* (ZECOT), 361.
6. See fuller discussion at Listening to the Text in the Story, p. 258.

LIVE the Story

While ritual impurity is not a common concept in many cultures today, understanding how it functioned in ancient Israel can nonetheless shed light on who God is and how he wants us to live. Two questions can help make this clearer.[7]

How Do These Laws about the Camp Relate to the Church and to Our Lives?

In ancient Israel, ritual impurity had to be kept separate from anything holy. If holiness could be compared to a white rug, ritual impurity could be compared to muddy boots. The two should never meet. Moreover, if someone with muddy boots intentionally walks across another person's white rug, we immediately see this as serious disrespect. Similarly, to defile the Lord's holy objects or spaces was to show him great disrespect, as though to say, "I couldn't care less whether I disrespect your holy property because I don't respect you."

In this case, the camp was not to be defiled because the Lord dwells in its midst (Num 5:3). The text therefore lists those with the severest ritual impurities—very "muddy boots"—as those who must dwell outside it. These impurities could spread quickly and defile the entire camp, making it impossible for a holy God to continue living in his people's midst. Thus sending those with major impurities outside the camp was not meant to punish them; other texts carefully instruct how their impurities may be cleansed (Lev 14:1–32; 15:13–15, 28–30; Num 19:11–13, 17–19). The goal was to underscore God's holiness and ensure he could continue dwelling among his people. To state it differently: God in his holiness cannot dwell in the midst of impurity and yet longs to live among his impure people; these laws were meant to help make that possible.

The New Testament applies many of these same themes to the church today. It compares Jesus's followers to stones built together into a temple where God dwells by his Spirit (1 Cor 3:16; Eph 2:22) and emphasizes that because God is in their midst, they must be holy. This has two implications. First, those who claim to follow Jesus but engage in serious wrongdoing and are unrepentant may no longer be counted as community members. Like those

---

7. Teachers and preachers wanting to cover more than these four verses in one session may connect 5:1–4 with 5:5–10 under the general theme of "laws related to the tabernacle in Israel's midst" (see Listening to the Text in the Story, p. 96).

with a major ritual impurity, they must be removed (1 Cor 5; 2 Thess 3:14; Titus 3:10–11). Note the ultimate goal of such discipline is not cruelty but repentance and restoration (1 Cor 5:5). But such discipline must take place because of God's holiness. He is utterly distinct in his goodness, purity, and love and calls his people to embody these things in the world, reflecting his true character so the world might know him. When we live in unrepentant sin, we both deny the very heart of who he is and refuse the mission he has given us. We both fling mud in his face and drag his name through the mud in front of others.

This leads directly to the second implication: members of Jesus's community must seek holiness in their personal lives. The Bible connects the Lord's presence in his people's midst today with our need to seek holiness (see 2 Cor 6:16b–7:1). In Jesus, we have become God's holy temple, and we respect his holy presence by seeking to reflect his holiness with our lives, not just individually but corporately. In this light, how might we encourage one another to reflect God's holiness in our midst? What practices might we start or reinforce as we seek to reflect together his holy character in the world?

That we even have to ask such questions means we do not do such things perfectly. This leads to the second major question.

How Does Jesus Deal with Our Impurity?

When the holy King is in your midst, impurity must be kept far away. Other texts make clear what happens when the impure come too close: death itself (Num 1:47–53).

But in Jesus, something radically different happens. Jesus comes into contact with every type of impurity mentioned in these verses. "He touches lepers (e.g., Mark 1:40–45), 'a woman who had been suffering from hemorrhages for twelve years' (5:25–34), and corpses (e.g., 5:21–24, 35–43),"[8] and yet, even though he is God in the flesh, his power does not break out against impure people; it breaks out against impurity itself. "Christ heals lepers, heals the woman, and raises the dead."[9] In this regard, Duguid's comments on Luke 8 are worth citing at length:

> The woman who had had an emission of blood for many years and had tried in vain to find medical relief for her condition came to Jesus and touched him (Luke 8:43–48). From the perspective of the book of

---

8. Stubbs, *Numbers*, 56.
9. Ibid.

Numbers, that was an extremely dangerous act! An unclean woman was deliberately bringing herself into physical contact with the Holy One of Israel. No wonder that when Jesus stopped and demanded to know who had touched him, she came forward trembling. But in Jesus she found physical and spiritual wholeness, rest for her body and peace for her soul. She who was once an outsider, alienated from God and his people, was now brought in through the touch of Jesus.[10]

God's hatred for and incompatibility with impurity had not changed. Rather, in his desire to be among us in our impurity, he had made a way in Jesus to be even closer and, by his touch, to undo the very things that represented our separation from him. This gives us confidence to come to him, no matter what our impurity might be, knowing that "if we confess our sins, he is faithful and just and will forgive us our sins and *purify us* from all unrighteousness" (1 John 1:9, emphasis added). That verse ends with a period, not a comma. No defilement is too difficult for him to cleanse, no sin too foul for him to forgive. It remains for us simply to come to him, like the woman of Luke 8, and seek his healing touch.

---

10. Duguid, *Numbers*, 71.

CHAPTER 5

Numbers 5:5–10

LISTEN to the Story

⁵The Lord said to Moses, ⁶"Say to the Israelites: 'Any man or woman who wrongs another in any way and so is unfaithful to the Lord is guilty ⁷and must confess the sin they have committed. They must make full restitution for the wrong they have done, add a fifth of the value to it and give it all to the person they have wronged. ⁸But if that person has no close relative to whom restitution can be made for the wrong, the restitution belongs to the Lord and must be given to the priest, along with the ram with which atonement is made for the wrongdoer. ⁹All the sacred contributions the Israelites bring to a priest will belong to him. ¹⁰Sacred things belong to their owners, but what they give to the priest will belong to the priest.'"

Listening to the Text in the Story: Leviticus 6:1–7

This passage opens by summarizing an earlier law describing what to do when someone steals or defrauds another and falsely swears in the Lord's name to conceal the crime (Num 5:6–7; cf. Lev 6:1–7). This introduces its real focus, namely, ensuring the Israelites give their sacred contributions to the tabernacle to support the priests (Num 5:8–10). This continues the preceding chapters' theme (the tabernacle's proper functioning in Israel's midst) and reinforces the biblical principle that the Lord's people must provide for their spiritual leaders (1 Cor 9:13–14; Gal 6:6).

 EXPLAIN the Story

Restitution for Wrongs; Priestly Portions (5:5–10)

This section begins with two case laws. A case law describes a situation (the protasis) and then explains what to do (the apodosis). The first law is Numbers

5:6–7, which summarizes the case law of Leviticus 6:1–7. There, a person has committed two wrongs. First, they have defrauded or stolen from someone (Lev 6:2–3 gives several scenarios). Second, they have lied about it by swearing falsely in the Lord's name (vv. 3, 5).[1] Both acts were wrong, the second especially so, since swearing falsely in the Lord's name meant treating it as a very common thing that could be used however one pleased (even for evil), instead of as a very holy thing to be deeply respected.

What makes the person confess? The end of Numbers 5:6 is better translated "and suffers for their guilt," that is, the Lord brings his justice to bear against them in some way,[2] causing them to finally deal with the sin they thought they had gotten away with. The apodosis (what to do in this situation) then begins in v. 7: "then they will confess" (my translation),[3] admitting their wrong and repaying the amount taken plus 20 percent. Note they do not simply admit guilt; they do whatever they can to make things right (cf. Luke 19:8–9). Only then do they bring a guilt offering and correct the wrong committed against the Lord (Num 5:8b; cf. the same order in Matt 5:23–24).

But a question arises: What if the person owed the money is dead or cannot be found,[4] nor their close relatives be found? The amount will then be given to the Lord, presumably as a tabernacle gift (Num 5:8). The result is deeply beautiful, for the Lord entrusts the money to his servants, the priests, meaning the wrong is redeemed by transforming it into a gift that supports the Lord's worship.

The last two verses continue the theme of tabernacle gifts (Num 5:9–10). They focus on the Israelites' "sacred contributions," a term that refers here to various food gifts they give to the Lord by donating them to the tabernacle; the Lord in turn gives them to his tabernacle servants, the priests and Levites (18:13–19, 21–24, 26–29).[5]

In short, this section focuses on taking care not to defraud the Lord's tabernacle of what properly belongs to it. Indeed, 5:8–10 state three times that such gifts belong ultimately to the priests who work there.[6] The overall point

---

1. See further at Sklar, *Additional Notes*, at 5:6–7.
2. ESV's "realizes his guilt" is close but misses the aspect of suffering the word implies. See further at Sklar, *Additional Notes*, at 5:6.
3. Cf. NASB, NET.
4. The text assumes this scenario (there would be no need to seek a close relative of the person wronged if that person was still around).
5. The NIV's translation of 5:10 is unlikely since these contributions now belonged to the Lord, not the person bringing them. Better would be, "So every person's holy gift shall be his [i.e., the priest's]; whatever someone gives to the priest, it becomes his" (my trans.; cf. NASB, ESV).
6. Note also the emphasis in 5:8 of making sure the ram is given to the priest. When the priest made atonement with it, the fat was burned up and the rest of the meat belonged to him (Lev 7:2–7).

is clear: make sure you give that which belongs to the Lord to the tabernacle and in this way support the work of his royal palace in your midst.

What Does True Repentance Look Like?

This section's opening verses summarize an earlier law describing one person defrauding another (Num 5:6–7; cf. Lev 6:1–7). The summary provides a clear picture of God's intent for repentance, highlighting two steps. First, the guilty party must confess. "Taking responsibility for one's actions and agreeing with God that they were wrong is an important part of the process of dealing with sin. As long as we are still excusing our actions, we have not come to recognize their true nature."[7] Second, the wrong must be corrected as far as possible. For theft, this involved repayment plus 20 percent. When we have wronged another, our restitution should go above and beyond in making things right.

The tax collector Zacchaeus beautifully illustrates this (Luke 19:1–10). In Jesus's day, tax collectors were known for extortion, so much so that the titles "tax collector" and "sinner" were interchangeable (v. 7). But when Zacchaeus met Jesus, everything changed for him. He knew repentance meant not only following Jesus in his holy ways of goodness, mercy, and love but also in trying to correct the harm he had caused others. He took this very seriously indeed: "Look, Lord! Here and now I give half of my possessions to the poor, and if I have cheated anybody out of anything, I will pay back four times the amount" (v. 8). So great was his desire to correct his wrongs that he went far beyond the biblical requirement of 120 percent repayment; he would repay 400 percent! And Jesus could see the repentance was real: "Jesus said to him, 'Today salvation has come to this house, because this man, too, is a son of Abraham. For the Son of Man came to seek and to save the lost'" (vv. 9–10). We do well to ask, "When I have wronged others, do I not only ask forgiveness but also, where possible, go above and beyond in repairing the wrong? What might it look like to pay back in full and add 20 percent?"

What Do the Israelites' Holy Gifts Teach Us about Giving Today?

This section finishes by speaking of "sacred contributions" the Israelites were to give to the tabernacle. These included various animal and grain offerings (Num 18:9) and firstfruits of oil, wine, and grain (v. 12). To give such things

---

7. Duguid, *Numbers*, 72.

to the tabernacle was to give them "to the Lord" (5:8); he in turn gave them to the priests or Levites as their "perpetual share" or "inheritance" (18:19, 21). The priests and Levites did not have large land tracts for their inheritance like other Israelites and so were dependent on such gifts to survive and continue serving the tabernacle in Israel's midst. If the Israelites did not faithfully bring such gifts to the Lord, the priests and Levites would be unable to continue their duties, and the Lord's worship would cease (cf. Neh 13:10–11). Refusing to give the Lord the contributions he was due was thus to say you cared very little if his worship continued and he remained in your midst. Supporting the tabernacle was thus crucial.

The New Testament applies these same principles to the support of spiritual leaders in the church today. "Don't you know that those who serve in the temple get their food from the temple, and that those who serve at the altar share in what is offered on the altar? In the same way, the Lord has commanded that those who preach the gospel should receive their living from the gospel" (1 Cor 9:13–14; cf. Gal 6:6). By providing in this way, the church frees its leaders to focus on praying for them, teaching them the things of God, and leading them in his ways and his worship. Hungry shepherds simply cannot care well for their sheep.

CHAPTER 6

Numbers 5:11-31

LISTEN to the Story

¹¹Then the LORD said to Moses, ¹²"Speak to the Israelites and say to them: 'If a man's wife goes astray and is unfaithful to him ¹³so that another man has sexual relations with her, and this is hidden from her husband and her impurity is undetected (since there is no witness against her and she has not been caught in the act), ¹⁴and if feelings of jealousy come over her husband and he suspects his wife and she is impure—or if he is jealous and suspects her even though she is not impure—¹⁵then he is to take his wife to the priest. He must also take an offering of a tenth of an ephah of barley flour on her behalf. He must not pour olive oil on it or put incense on it, because it is a grain offering for jealousy, a reminder-offering to draw attention to wrongdoing.

¹⁶"'The priest shall bring her and have her stand before the LORD. ¹⁷Then he shall take some holy water in a clay jar and put some dust from the tabernacle floor into the water. ¹⁸After the priest has had the woman stand before the LORD, he shall loosen her hair and place in her hands the reminder-offering, the grain offering for jealousy, while he himself holds the bitter water that brings a curse. ¹⁹Then the priest shall put the woman under oath and say to her, "If no other man has had sexual relations with you and you have not gone astray and become impure while married to your husband, may this bitter water that brings a curse not harm you. ²⁰But if you have gone astray while married to your husband and you have made yourself impure by having sexual relations with a man other than your husband"—²¹here the priest is to put the woman under this curse—"may the LORD cause you to become a curse among your people when he makes your womb miscarry and your abdomen swell. ²²May this water that brings a curse enter your body so that your abdomen swells or your womb miscarries."

> "'Then the woman is to say, "Amen. So be it."
>
> ²³"'The priest is to write these curses on a scroll and then wash them off into the bitter water. ²⁴He shall make the woman drink the bitter water that brings a curse, and this water that brings a curse and causes bitter suffering will enter her. ²⁵The priest is to take from her hands the grain offering for jealousy, wave it before the LORD and bring it to the altar. ²⁶The priest is then to take a handful of the grain offering as a memorial offering and burn it on the altar; after that, he is to have the woman drink the water. ²⁷If she has made herself impure and been unfaithful to her husband, this will be the result: When she is made to drink the water that brings a curse and causes bitter suffering, it will enter her, her abdomen will swell and her womb will miscarry, and she will become a curse. ²⁸If, however, the woman has not made herself impure, but is clean, she will be cleared of guilt and will be able to have children.
>
> ²⁹"'This, then, is the law of jealousy when a woman goes astray and makes herself impure while married to her husband, ³⁰or when feelings of jealousy come over a man because he suspects his wife. The priest is to have her stand before the LORD and is to apply this entire law to her. ³¹The husband will be innocent of any wrongdoing, but the woman will bear the consequences of her sin.'"

Listening to the Text in the Story: Exodus 22:11; Code of Hammurabi §132

This passage has clear links to the previous two. Numbers 5:1–4 concerns ritual impurity or defilement in the camp while our passage concerns moral impurity in the camp; in both cases, impurity is described with the same Hebrew root (*t-m-'*); 5:2, 3, 13, 14, 27–29). Moreover, Numbers 5:5–10 concerns a wrong in which someone has been "unfaithful (Heb. *ma'al*) to the LORD" (v. 6), and our passage concerns a wrong in which a wife may have been "unfaithful (Heb. *ma'al*) to" her husband (v. 12).

The passage itself is a long case law addressing suspected adultery. The Lord gives the law to answer a practical question: If no witnesses exist, how may the Israelites know what verdict to pass? He responds that he himself will answer the question by means of a special tabernacle ritual.

This ritual is often called a "trial by ordeal," that is, a "criminal trial in which the guilt or innocence of the accused was determined by subjection to dangerous or painful tests (as submersion in water) believed to be under divine control."[1] The laws of Hammurabi give an example in which one man accuses another's wife of adultery. Law 132 states:

> If the finger was pointed at the wife of a [man] because of another man, but she has not been caught lying with the other man, she shall throw herself into the river for the sake of her husband.[2]

If she makes it out of the river, she is innocent; if not, she is guilty.[3] As with other trials by ordeal, many innocent people would have experienced significant harm—even death.

The ritual of Numbers 5 is entirely different. What the wife drank was no more harmful than the sandy water inadvertently swallowed by swimmers at the beach (v. 17). If harm did come, it was only because the Lord himself brought his justice to bear (v. 21; cf. 1 Kgs 8:31–32). Unlike other trials by ordeal, the danger was only for the guilty; the innocent had nothing to fear.

EXPLAIN the Story

Before turning to an explanation, four introductory comments may be helpful. First, Allen observes that much here strikes us as unjust, especially the wife being put through this rite simply on her husband's suspicions[4]—to which may be added there is no corresponding rite for a suspected husband! But he also notes the law's beneficial function as "a limitation on an angry, suspicious husband—a protection of the wife from his abusive hand."[5] The husband may not use his suspicions to divorce her (exposing her to financial hardship) or abuse her in any way. Justice is taken from his angry hands—and from the hands of any angry mob that might seek her harm—and put into the just hands of the Lord, who would clear an innocent wife's name before her husband and community.

Second, the wife's need for protection might explain the absence of a corresponding law for a husband suspected of adultery. Many laws exist to protect

---

1. "Trial by ordeal," *Merriam Webster*, https://www.merriam-webster.com/legal/trial%20by%20 ordeal; for examples, including modern ones, see "Ordeal trial method," *Britannica*, https://www .britannica.com/topic/ordeal.
2. *ANET*, 171.
3. Cf. Code of Hammurabi §2.
4. Allen, "Numbers," 744.
5. Ibid.

the innocent from potential harm. In an ancient Near Eastern society, the tragic reality was that women needed such protections in ways different than men, who were not at risk of the same financial or physical harm if accused of adultery. The Bible is not affirming that women should be made vulnerable in this way; it simply recognizes this as a reality of a broken world and provides a safeguard. And while this text does not address a man guilty of adultery, we should not assume he went without punishment. If the Lord brought justice to bear on the wife for her secret sin, would he not do so for the man with whom she was involved? The Bible teaches our secret sins are not hidden from the Lord, who will bring us to account for them, whether in this life or the next (cf. Pss 90:8; 101:5; Acts 5:1–11).

Third, a wise husband would view this law as a last resort (and a wise priest would question him closely before proceeding). Wisdom involves trying to solve problems relationally rather than legally. This procedure could cause deep marital pain, and the community would need to support the couple well in piecing their relationship back together.

Fourth, to many moderns this ritual may seem like primitive magic, but this would be unfair to how ancient Israelites understood it. As Wenham notes, "Whether the potion was effective in making a guilty woman sterile no more depends on magic than does intercessory prayer. Prayer and symbolic rituals both depend ultimately on the will of God for their efficacy."[6] Stated differently, this ritual is an enacted prayer; ultimately, "the decision [of guilt or innocence] was not made by any magical powers residing in the water, the dust, and the words [of the curse], but by the Lord's will" (Num 5:21);[7] he would hear the prayer and answer.

The Situation: A Wife Is Suspected of Adultery and the Husband Is Jealous (5:11–14)

From the beginning, this law accounts for two possibilities: a husband's suspicions may be correct (so the law begins by speaking as though adultery occurred [Num 5:12–14a]); but his suspicions can also be horribly wrong (so the law immediately qualifies its opening statement by noting adultery might not have occurred [v. 14b]). It therefore accounts for both scenarios (see also vv. 19–20, 27–28).

As in most societies, adultery in Israel was considered a very great wrong. In Num 5:12, the word translated as "unfaithful" (*maʿal*) is very strong, referring

---

6. Wenham, *Numbers*, 82–83.
7. Noordtzij, *Numbers*, 57.

to severe betrayal, whether in human relationships (as here) or in divine-human relationships (Josh 22:16, 18–19; 1 Chr 5:25; 2 Chr 12:1–2). In either realm, to abandon a covenant partner for other lovers is always a treacherous act.

If the wife is indeed guilty, she would be "impure." In the Pentateuch, the language of purity and impurity is used in two ways. In some contexts, it refers to ritual impurity, as in Numbers 5:2–3 (cf. Lev 12:2; 13:3); in others, it refers to moral impurity, which is clearly the case here (cf. Lev 18:20, 24).[8] Most can identify with the use of such language in a moral context: when we commit great wrong against others, we often feel dirty (cf. Ps 51:2). Evil is not neutral; it is defiling.

But the question remains: is the wife guilty? There were no witnesses, so the husband has only his suspicions, which have led to deep jealousy. While jealousy can be petty or selfish anger (cf. Gen 37:11), it can also be justifiable anger that comes because one person wrongly misplaces their affections. If a wife becomes jealous because her husband has an affair, we recognize such feelings as appropriate—and this would be equally true of a husband in the same situation. But because the husband's feelings might not be based in fact, this law does not affirm them. Rather, it recognizes their reality and protects the wife from their harmful expression. The husband may not divorce her or mistreat her; he must put the situation into the Lord's hands.

The Ritual and Its Results (5:15–28)

To do so, he brings his wife to the priest, along with a standard-sized grain offering (Num 5:15; one-tenth of an ephah).[9] But unlike regular grain offerings, it is made of barley (instead of fine flour) and has no oil or incense placed on it. These differences make clear its different purpose (cf. Lev 5:11) as "a grain offering for jealousy" (Num 5:15; more woodenly, "a grain offering of jealousy"), that is, an offering due to the husband's jealous suspicions his wife has been unfaithful. It functioned as a prayer for the Lord to make the truth clear, which is why it is called "a reminder-offering to draw attention to wrongdoing" (v. 15). When used of God, the language of "remembering/reminding" in the Bible refers to the Lord showing by his actions his awareness of a certain reality (a promise, an injustice, etc.). Here, the "reminder-offering" asks the Lord to act on any wrongdoing that has been done (cf. Jer 14:10: "[the LORD] will now remember their wickedness and punish them for their sins").

The priest then takes the lead in the ritual; his actions may be described

---

8. For fuller discussion, see Sklar, *Leviticus* (ZECOT), 488–89.
9. For details, see table on p. 213.

in seven steps. First, he has the wife "stand before the LORD" (Num 5:16); the same language elsewhere refers to presenting someone at the entrance to the Lord's tent (Lev 14:11). The ritual is carried out before him, the just judge who will rule in this case.

Second, he takes a clay jar and puts into it holy water (Num 5:17), perhaps from the courtyard's bronze basin (or laver) (Exod 30:18–21), and then enters the tabernacle and takes dust from its floor (presumably a small amount so the water remains drinkable). The mixture now contains holy water and holy dust, associating it with the holy Lord, who will render the verdict.

Third, he loosens the wife's hair, puts the grain offering in her hands, and takes the water in his own (Num 5:18).[10] Putting the grain offering in her hand connects it to her (cf. Lev 1:4); when it is offered "to draw attention" to possible adultery (Num 5:15), it is clearly requesting the Lord to take stock of any such wrongdoing she may have committed. Why he loosens her hair is unclear. It seems this was a rare public event, being reserved for mourners (Lev 10:6; 21:10) or lepers (13:45). It can be assumed it was more common in the private home, where people could be themselves (cf. the English phrase, "Let your hair down"). In this context, it perhaps indicates the woman is not trying to hide anything from the Lord, but any suggestion of its meaning is a guess.[11]

Fourth, he puts the wife "under oath" (Num 5:19–22). This type of oath is an "imprecatory oath" (*'alah*, translated as "curse" by NIV in v. 21). Some background may be helpful.

> Generally speaking, an oath is a statement or promise whose truthfulness is affirmed by invoking the deity's name . . . By implication, the oath-taker is inviting the deity to act as witness and bring judgment should the statement be false or the promise not kept (cf. Josh 9:20). An "imprecatory oath" . . . makes this judgment explicit. . . . In short, this oath threatens a curse.[12]

In this case, the oath is very basic: if the wife is innocent, the waters will cause no harm (Num 5:19); if she is guilty, they will (vv. 20–22). While debate surrounds the medical conditions verses 21–22 describe, and while

---

10. Specifically, "the bitter water that brings a curse," that is, has the potential to do so if she is guilty.
11. It is sometimes said the act is meant to shame the woman, but since the law clearly acknowledges she may be innocent (5:14b, 19, 28), this interpretation is unfounded.
12. Sklar, *Leviticus* (ZECOT), 159. Along with Num 5:16–22 (esp. 21–22), see also 1 Kgs 8:31–32.

the translation "womb miscarries" might be too specific,[13] it is clear that since she is able to have children if innocent (v. 28), these verses must at least mean she will be unable to do so if guilty (and at most that she will experience some form of further physical suffering). The inability to have children can be exceedingly painful in our day; in biblical times, it seems it was all the more so (Gen 30:1–24; 1 Sam 1:6–16). This was no small penalty. Moreover, because of her guilt and its consequences, she would become "a curse" among her people since her name would now be used in imprecatory oaths: "May the Lord treat you like so-and-so if you are guilty" (cf. Jer 29:22b).

The priest's actions are interrupted by the wife's response, "Amen! Amen!" (Num 5:22b, author's translation; in the Hebrew, the word is repeated.) Elsewhere, this confirms agreement with a previous statement, whether a curse (Deut 27:15–26; Neh 5:13), blessing (Neh 8:6), or praise (Ps 106:48). The repetition underscores full agreement to the curse's terms: "So be it! I have nothing to fear! I am innocent!"

Fifth, "the priest is to write these curses on a scroll and then wash them off into the bitter water" (Num 5:23). The following verse is not the next step in the process (5:24; cf. 5:26b); it simply explains why the priest washes the written curses into the water: so the wife will symbolically drink the harm that comes on the guilty.

Sixth, he presents the grain offering of jealousy (5:25–26a). "Waving" an item was a ritual action that showed an item was given to the Lord.[14] Wave offering texts typically note it comes from the offerer's hand (as here, establishing its connection to the offerer; Exod 29:24; Lev 7:29–30) and then is waved by the priest "before the Lord" (so also Lev 9:21; 14:12). The "memorial offering" was a fistful of the grain offering that was burned on the altar; its rising smoke functioned as a type of prayer: "O Lord, show by your actions that you hear the request I have in bringing this offering to you." In this case, the request was to show the wife guilty or innocent.[15]

Finally, with the prayer offered, the priest has the woman drink the waters, the means by which the prayer will be answered (Num 5:26b). If she is guilty, she will be unable to have children (v. 27), but if she is innocent, she will be "cleared of guilt," sometimes translated "free of punishment" (v. 28). With

---

13. The sense may be general ("unable to have children") as opposed to specific (to "miscarry"); see Sklar, *Additional Notes*, at 5:21.

14. See at 8:11, pp. 147–48.

15. What happens with the rest of the grain offering is not said; normally, the priests ate it (Lev 2:3).

either translation, the point is clear: her husband and community must acknowledge the Lord's verdict of innocence.

Summary and Clarification (5:29–31)

The chapter finishes by briefly summarizing the preceding law (Num 5:29–30)[16] and adding one clarifying point (v. 31). While the wiser course may be to avoid such action (see above, p. 103), a husband has not sinned if his wife is innocent (v. 31a). But if she is guilty, the ritual will have its intended effect (v. 31b), which ends the passage with a warning underscoring that marital fidelity must be maintained. All our ways are before the Lord's eyes. There is no such thing as secret sin (Prov 5:21).

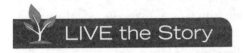

How Does This Law Relate to Our Sexual Practices Today?

In explaining this text to modern audiences, significant time may be needed to answer questions about its fairness and strangeness (see observations beginning the Explain the Story section above). But it will be equally important not to ignore the text's emphasis on marital fidelity. The Bible stresses this in its commands forbidding adultery (Exod 20:14; Lev 18:20; 1 Cor 6:9; Heb 13:4) and exhortations toward marital faithfulness and love (Deut 24:5; Prov 5:18–19; Eph 5:22–33).

The reason makes sense in light of the Lord's larger vision for this world and how sex relates to it.[17] In Genesis 1 and 2, he paints his vision for a society in which humanity can flourish. Central to this are stable families in which a husband and wife are committed to one another in loyalty and love and children are born into that context of relational bedrock and support.[18] In a broken world with broken families (my own family of origin being among them), this vision is often not realized. But this must not make us forget the Lord's vision and desire for his world or how sex relates to it. He has designed sex for marriage and to be used in that context alone. Why?

In *The Meaning of Marriage*, Tim and Kathy Keller address this by

---

16. Num 5:29 may correspond to 5:12–14a and 5:30a to 5:14b (which also begins with "or") (Milgrom, *Numbers*, 347).

17. The following is abridged from Sklar, *Leviticus* (ZECOT), 508–13.

18. Modern studies have repeatedly shown the personal and social benefits of strong families; see Linda J. Waite and Maggie Gallagher, *The Case for Marriage: Why Married People Are Happier, Healthier, and Better off Financially* (New York: Doubleday, 2000).

considering the nature of marriage. In marriage, the husband and wife are said to "hold fast" (ESV; NIV "is united") to one another and to become "one flesh" (Gen 2:24). These phrases elsewhere describe a covenant relationship (Deut 10:20; 30:20), a relationship designed to be more personal than a contract and more permanent than an ordinary social relationship.[19] This means "marriage is a union between two people so profound that they virtually become a new, single person.... In love they donate themselves, wholly, to the other."[20]

It is in this marital context that sex enters the picture, for three reasons. First, God designs sex as a way for a husband and wife to act out the covenant commitment they have already made: "Just as I physically *leave* all others and *cleave* to you in this act of sex, becoming one flesh with you, so I have left every other earthly commitment and alliance to cleave to you in ardent covenant loyalty, not only in this act of sex but in every moment of every day." Sex is marital because it physically embodies the covenant.

Second, God intends sex to be a means to strengthen that commitment.

> [O]nce you have given yourself in marriage, sex is a way of maintaining and deepening that union as the years go by. In the Old Testament, there were often "covenant renewal ceremonies."... This was crucial if the people were to sustain a life of faithfulness.
>
> It is the same with the marriage covenant.... As time goes on, there is a need to rekindle the heart and renew the commitment. There must be an opportunity to recall all that the other person means to you and to give yourself anew. Sex between a husband and a wife is the unique way to do that.[21]

In other words, sex is a symbolic way for spouses to repeat their wedding vows to one another, recommitting to those vows and to the faithful and tender love they have promised each other.

Finally, the above also means that in God's design for sex, when children enter the world, they enter a stable family with a mother and father committed to one another in love and loyalty, working together to provide that child with support and love.

In short, God designs sex as a way to act out and reaffirm a covenant commitment we have made to our spouse in marriage. By its very nature,

---

19. Adapted from Keller, *Preaching*, 104.
20. Timothy Keller with Kathy Keller, *The Meaning of Marriage* (New York: Dutton, 2011), 223.
21. Ibid.

adultery is a betrayal of that covenant commitment. It is an act of personal treachery against our spouse and an act of rebellion against the Lord and the type of society he desires for human flourishing. So why does it happen and how can it be prevented?

How Do We Guard Ourselves from Marital Infidelity?

Psychologists and counselors group affairs into different categories. While there are different ways this is done, it is helpful to identify at least three major types.[22]

> *Category 1:* Often referred to as a "one-night stand," the adulterous person did not wake up that day intending to have a sexual encounter with someone other than their spouse; "it just happened."
>
> *Category 2:* Sexual contact with the non-spouse is the fruit of an emotional closeness that has developed over time. Emotional adultery has already taken place; the physical adultery gives expression to it.
>
> *Category 3:* Some spouses are philanderers, seeking sexual relationships outside marriage regularly and without remorse, while others are addicts, seeking sexual relationships outside marriage regularly and with differing levels of remorse.

Knowing the different types of affairs can help us in guarding ourselves against them.

Category 1: The book of Proverbs gives long and strong exhortation to avoid putting ourselves in compromising situations (Prov 5:8 and esp. 7:6–27). And although the words are addressed from father to son in each instance, the principle applies to men and women: do not put yourself in the way of such danger.

Category 2: This same father in Proverbs exhorts his son to focus his sexual and emotional energy on his wife (Prov 5:18–19). If we are more eager to spend time with another member of the opposite sex than we are with our spouse, we may already be in this category and need to take immediate action.

Category 3: A philanderer needs to clearly understand that those who engage in adultery and are not repentant do not belong to God's people and will not be allowed entry into heaven (1 Cor 6:9–10; Rev 22:15). We cannot continue in such sin and consider ourselves Jesus's follower. A sexual addict

---

22. Cf. the groupings in Frank S. Pittman, *Private Lies: Infidelity and the Betrayal of Intimacy* (New York: Norton, 1990), 132–34, and David Carder and Duncan Jaenicke, *Torn Asunder: Recovering from an Extramarital Affair*, 3rd ed. (Chicago: Moody Press, 2008), 52–60.

needs to heed Jesus's counsel to do whatever it takes to avoid sexual sin (Matt 5:27–29), meaning he or she must not keep the sin hidden but earnestly seek counsel and help in dealing with the addiction.[23]

We should not fool ourselves into thinking that any of the above steps will be easy. Adultery has been a reality throughout history because the temptation of sexual infidelity is very strong. What can help us? What motivates our obedience to the Lord's ways when it comes to honoring him with our bodies in marriage?

What Motivates Us toward Marital Fidelity?

Ultimately, honoring the Lord with our bodies in marriage flows from two motivations. First, it flows out of a fear of God. The Bible speaks frequently of this, but it is often misunderstood today. To many, fearing God sounds extremely negative, as though he is always angry, even petty, and that we are to live our lives groveling before him in fear.

But the reality is far different. Biblically speaking, the idea of fearing God has as its foundation that God, as divine King, directs his just anger toward evil and anything that destroys the world of justice, mercy, and love he intends us to know. This means his anger is not only just, but good. It seeks to preserve a world that reflects his goodness and glory and is for our blessing and joy. When an earthly judge brings justice to bear on anyone who destroys the peace and wellbeing of our society, we do not think evil of the judge; we are thankful justice has been done and society protected. How much more when the heavenly judge does the same?

So we are not to live every moment being afraid of God. But if we are considering evil or are in the midst of doing it, we should be afraid—literally fearful—because the Lord could bring his just and good judgment to bear against us. Parents understand this very well. A good father does not want his child to be afraid of him, but he does want to cultivate a healthy fear in the child that is activated if that child is about to do wrong. So too with our heavenly father.

The Bible therefore speaks of fearing God when we are thinking about sin or are in the midst of it (Lev 19:14; 25:17, 36; Heb 10:26–31). In the context of adultery, we read this warning: "Why, my son, be intoxicated with another man's wife? Why embrace the bosom of a wayward woman? For your ways

---

23. Focus on the Family maintains a list of trained Christian counselors in the U.S. (searchable by the issue being addressed); see https://christiancounselors.network/. See also the list of resources gathered by Mark and Debbie Laaser of Faithful and True Ministries: https://faithfulandtrue.com/resources/.

are in full view of the Lord, and he examines all your paths" (Prov 5:20–21). In other words, even if you hide the sin from others, the Lord, the heavenly judge, sees and knows—and will bring his justice to bear. Fearing God, we should not even draw near to such evil.

But fear is not the only, nor even the primary, motivation. Above all, our motivation to honor the Lord is to be our love for him, which the Bible regularly connects to obeying God and walking in his ways (Exod 20:6; John 14:15; 1 John 5:3). Our love for God springs from a different place. Fear is the response that compels us to stop considering or committing wrong, or to avoid it altogether, knowing the Lord may bring his justice to bear against us. Love is our response to his goodness, mercy, and love and all we have experienced of these things in Jesus. It compels us to honor him through grateful obedience, the proper response to the God who overflows with such goodness and love toward us (Rom 12:1).

In the context of marriage, this means honoring God's plan by faithfully loving our spouse. God has provided the model for us in Jesus's relationship to his followers, which is likened to a marriage, with Jesus as groom and the church as the bride. Jesus has been completely faithful to his bride—to us!—despite all our weaknesses and imperfections. He "loved the church and gave himself up for her to make her holy, cleansing her by the washing with water through the word, and to present her to himself as a radiant church, without stain or wrinkle or any other blemish, but holy and blameless" (Eph 5:25–27). In other words, the model he sets for marriage is one of self-sacrificial love for an imperfect spouse for the sake of the spouse's spiritual well-being and growth. This takes tremendous patience, forgiveness, and love, all three of which we experience richly in Jesus—who now calls us to show the same to our own spouse. And he does not leave us alone to do this but provides us with his Spirit to strengthen us in this task and with his body of believers to encourage and support us in our efforts (Eph 5:18–20). It remains for us to make use of these means, calling out to him the whole time, "O Lord, help me to show to my spouse the same love you have shown to me!"

CHAPTER 7

Numbers 6:1-21

LISTEN to the Story

¹The Lord said to Moses, ²"Speak to the Israelites and say to them: 'If a man or woman wants to make a special vow, a vow of dedication to the Lord as a Nazirite, ³they must abstain from wine and other fermented drink and must not drink vinegar made from wine or other fermented drink. They must not drink grape juice or eat grapes or raisins. ⁴As long as they remain under their Nazirite vow, they must not eat anything that comes from the grapevine, not even the seeds or skins.

⁵"'During the entire period of their Nazirite vow, no razor may be used on their head. They must be holy until the period of their dedication to the Lord is over; they must let their hair grow long.

⁶"'Throughout the period of their dedication to the Lord, the Nazirite must not go near a dead body. ⁷Even if their own father or mother or brother or sister dies, they must not make themselves ceremonially unclean on account of them, because the symbol of their dedication to God is on their head. ⁸Throughout the period of their dedication, they are consecrated to the Lord.

⁹"'If someone dies suddenly in the Nazirite's presence, thus defiling the hair that symbolizes their dedication, they must shave their head on the seventh day—the day of their cleansing. ¹⁰Then on the eighth day they must bring two doves or two young pigeons to the priest at the entrance to the tent of meeting. ¹¹The priest is to offer one as a sin offering and the other as a burnt offering to make atonement for the Nazirite because they sinned by being in the presence of the dead body. That same day they are to consecrate their head again. ¹²They must rededicate themselves to the Lord for the same period of dedication and must bring a year-old male lamb as a guilt offering. The previous days do not count, because they became defiled during their period of dedication.

> ¹³"'Now this is the law of the Nazirite when the period of their dedication is over. They are to be brought to the entrance to the tent of meeting. ¹⁴There they are to present their offerings to the LORD: a year-old male lamb without defect for a burnt offering, a year-old ewe lamb without defect for a sin offering, a ram without defect for a fellowship offering, ¹⁵together with their grain offerings and drink offerings, and a basket of bread made with the finest flour and without yeast—thick loaves with olive oil mixed in, and thin loaves brushed with olive oil.
>
> ¹⁶"'The priest is to present all these before the LORD and make the sin offering and the burnt offering. ¹⁷He is to present the basket of unleavened bread and is to sacrifice the ram as a fellowship offering to the LORD, together with its grain offering and drink offering.
>
> ¹⁸"'Then at the entrance to the tent of meeting, the Nazirite must shave off the hair that symbolizes their dedication. They are to take the hair and put it in the fire that is under the sacrifice of the fellowship offering.
>
> ¹⁹"'After the Nazirite has shaved off the hair that symbolizes their dedication, the priest is to place in their hands a boiled shoulder of the ram, and one thick loaf and one thin loaf from the basket, both made without yeast. ²⁰The priest shall then wave these before the LORD as a wave offering; they are holy and belong to the priest, together with the breast that was waved and the thigh that was presented. After that, the Nazirite may drink wine.
>
> ²¹"'This is the law of the Nazirite who vows offerings to the LORD in accordance with their dedication, in addition to whatever else they can afford. They must fulfill the vows they have made, according to the law of the Nazirite.'"

Listening to the Text in the Story: Leviticus 10:9; 21:1–3, 10–11

Vows were a common practice in the ancient Near East.¹ Israelites vowed to the Lord to perform certain actions, such as sacrifice, if or when their prayer was answered. Properly done, vowing was not a form of haggling with the Lord. Rather, the vow emphasized the seriousness of the worshipper's request—like

---

1. "Vows to the gods . . . were common in the ancient Near East in requests for victory in battle, healing, deliverance, childlessness, or the love of a woman" (Cole, "Numbers," 390).

an exclamation point—and ensured they gave thanksgiving and praise to the Lord when their prayer was answered.[2]

In this case, a person praying about a matter of great importance may have vowed to take on a Nazirite state if their prayer was answered. Others may have made such a vow because they wanted a period of spiritual rededication to the Lord. Either way, this chapter explains the rules governing such vows.

Significantly, comparing some of these rules with those for priests shows that Nazirites were especially holy. Priests were prohibited from alcohol only while on duty (Lev 10:9), but Nazirites could never partake. "The Nazirite was not even 'to smell the cork,' as it were."[3] Moreover, regular priests could draw near to the corpses of their closest family to mourn (Lev 21:1–3), but Nazirites could not (Num 6:7); their rule was closest to that of the high priest (Lev 21:10–11), the holiest priest of all. In short, the rules underscored the vow's main point: for a period of time, Nazirites set themselves apart to the Lord like priests, the Israelites' holiest people, as a sign of their complete devotion to him.

Three Rules for Nazirite Vows (6:1–8)

Like monks and nuns, Nazirites had special rules to follow and were set apart in a special way to the Lord by means of a vow. (Unlike monks and nuns, they were not prohibited from marrying, their vow was typically not lifelong, nor are they required to live separately from society.) The word for "Nazirite" (*nazir*) may in fact be translated as "a person set apart," namely, from the everyday realm into the holy realm and therefore especially dedicated to the Lord (Num 6:2, 8). This happens through a vow described as "special" (v. 2), a word built on a root used to refer to that which is "difficult" (Gen 18:14; Deut 17:8) or "extraordinary, amazing" (Exod 15:11; 34:10; Josh 3:5). This describes Nazirite vows well since they involved a high level of commitment. The vow was typically for a certain period of time (cf. Num 6:13–21), rather than lifelong (Samson and Samuel represent exceptions).[4] Three rules had to be followed, all relating to the Nazirite's ritually holy status.

---

2. Sklar, *Leviticus* (ZECOT), 744. Hannah provides a wonderful example. She prays for a son and vows to dedicate him to the Lord's tabernacle service (1 Sam 1:10–11, 22). When her prayer is answered, she fulfills her vow and then breaks out in a song of praise to the Lord (1 Sam 1:19–2:10).
3. Allen, "Numbers," 750.
4. Judg 13:5; 1 Sam 1:11.

First, "they must abstain" from things related to alcohol, whether the beverages themselves (wine and strong drink), products derived from them (various types of vinegar), or anything related to the grapevine (from which wine is made) (Num 6:3–4). Since priests had to abstain from "wine and strong drink" while on duty so as not to increase their chances of desecrating holy things or their holy state (Lev 10:9), it makes sense that ritually holy Nazirites must as well.

Second, Nazirites could not shave the hair of their head (Num 6:5). Comparable to the distinct clothing of certain monks or nuns, the Nazirites' uncut hair was "the symbol of their dedication to God" (v. 7), the sign that they were ritually "holy" (v. 5) and could therefore not be touched.

Third, they could not go near a dead body (Num 6:6). Corpses were very ritually defiling, and Nazirites had set themselves apart to the Lord as ritually holy (NIV: "consecrated") during the period of their vow (v. 8). To defile their holy status would show great disrespect to the Lord, as though their dedication to him meant nothing. (For how Nazirite rules compare to those of priests, see above, Listening to the Text in the Story.)

Unintentional Defilement (6:9–12)

Ritually holy Nazirites could not intentionally go near ritually defiling corpses (Num 6:6–8), but what if this happens accidentally, as when a person "dies suddenly" beside them (v. 9)? Four results immediately follow. First, the Nazirite has become ritually impure and must address this properly, presumably following the steps outlined in Numbers 19:11–12, 17–19: waiting seven days (as normal for major impurities), being sprinkled with cleansing waters on days three and seven, and washing their clothes and bathing on day seven. Shaving the head is also required on day seven to remove the sign of the broken vow and prepare to make a new vow the following day (vv. 9, 11b–12a).

Second, the Nazirite must address the sin of defiling the hair that symbolized the holy vow, even though such defilement was unintentional (Num 6:9; the death occurred "suddenly"). Just as a driver who speeds unintentionally may be held accountable, so also here. The day after becoming pure, the Nazirite brings two birds to the tent of meeting (v. 10–11), one as a "sin offering," perhaps better translated "purification offering" (NIV footnote)[5]

---

5. The Hebrew name of the sacrifice (*hatta't*) is built on a root (*h-t-*) that can be related to sin (thus "sin offering") but can also be related to "de-sinning," that is, "purifying" (thus "purification offering"). In favor of "purification offering," note this sacrifice's blood is associated with cleansing

and the other as a burnt offering.[6] These are sacrificed to make atonement (*kipper*), a word that refers to the fact that God in his mercy and love—in his desire for fellowship with us—makes a way to deal with our wrongs so we may be made right with him.

Third, the Nazirite must be rededicated to the Lord (6:11b–12a). The former vow had been broken and not fulfilled; now, the vow is retaken.

Finally, the Nazirite must bring a guilt offering[7] (6:12b), which is made elsewhere in cases where the Lord's holy property has been misused (Lev 5:14–6:7). This included broken vows (Lev 6:1–7), since they were typically made in the Lord's name, and failing to keep them was using his name to make a false promise. (Nazirite vows presumably resembled: "As the Lord lives, I will be a Nazirite for X number of days.")

Completion of the Vow (6:13–20)

Anthropologists speak of "rites of passage," ceremonies or events by which a person goes from one state into another; e.g., in a wedding ceremony, a person leaves the state of singlehood and enters the state of marriage. In this ceremony, the Nazirite leaves the ritual state of holiness and enters back into the ritual state of purity.

Offerings were central to the ceremony. As is usually the case, the Israelites could not present animals with physical defects (Num 6:14), which were of far less economic value and would have communicated great disrespect, as though to say, "Lord, you are worthy only of our second best" (cf. Mal 1:8). This ceremony's offerings are most similar to those for the ordination of priests, who also offer purification, burnt, and fellowship offerings,[8] along with various breads (Lev 8:14–29). Each offering may be briefly described. When a purification offering was required, the sin or impurity it addressed "was considered a substance that defiled not only the offerer but also the tabernacle, spreading to it like radiological fallout, unholy 'dust,'[9] or the 'shame' or 'dishonor' one

---

(Lev 8:15; 16:19). Such a translation also explains why it occurs in contexts of sin (Lev 4:20; 5:6) and impurity (Lev 12:7; 15:13–15): both defile, and this sacrifice purifies whatever is stained by them.

6. For fuller descriptions of these offerings, see below at 6:13–20.

7. Perhaps better: "reparation offering," since these made reparation for the guilt of mistreating the Lord's holy property; see discussion in Sklar, *Leviticus* (ZECOT), 173. As for the animal's age, year-old calves and sheep seemed to be ideal sacrificial animals. "Keeping an animal for one year gets it to the point of reaching maximum meat weight with minimum investment" (Oded Borowski, *Every Living Thing* [Walnut Creek: AltaMira Press, 1998], 57).

8. The ordination offering (Lev 8:22) is often understood as a type of fellowship offering, since the offerer ate part of the meat (8:31).

9. Erhard Gerstenberger, *Leviticus: A Commentary* (Louisville: Westminster John Knox Press, 1996), 56.

person can bring on another.[10] By means of [its] blood, the purification offering cleansed the sanctuary and its contents from these defiling effects. And because it was *the offerer's* sin or impurity from which it was cleansed, this benefited the offerer as well."[11]

Burnt offerings had many purposes, including atonement (Lev 1:4) and to serve as an exclamation point to an offerer's prayers, whether prayers of praise and thanksgiving (22:29–30; Num 6:13–20; Ps 66:13–16) or prayers asking the Lord for help in grave situations, such as war (1 Sam 7:9; 13:8–12) or suffering (Ps 20:1–5).

Fellowship offerings were the only offerings of which the offerer ate. Some of the meat was burned to the Lord, some was given to the priest, and the rest was eaten by the offerer, often with family or friends (Deut 12:7, 17–18; cf. 1 Sam 1:3–5, 21). As such, it functioned like a shared meal, which in Israel's day was one way to confirm and celebrate a covenant relationship (Gen 26:28–30; 31:44, 46, 53–54). Not surprisingly, then, when a fellowship offering was presented with atoning sacrifices, it was always made after them (cf. Lev 9:15–21), as though the offerers were saying, "Now that atonement has been made, we offer this fellowship offering to reaffirm and celebrate our covenant relationship with you, O Lord!"[12] Biblically speaking, dealing properly with sin is a necessary first step to enjoy fellowship with the Lord.

In the Nazirite's case, the atoning sacrifices may have been for sins inadvertently committed during the period of the vow. Whatever the reason, the sacrifices together represented full atonement, worship, and fellowship (Num 6:13–17).

The Nazirite then shaves the hair symbolizing their dedication and burns it in the fire under the fellowship offering (Num 6:18). The ritually holy hair is now destroyed, along with any risk of it becoming ritually defiled (the same is done with leftover fellowship offering meat, which is also ritually holy [Lev 19:5–8]).[13]

Returning to the fellowship offering, the priest places several items on the Nazirite's hands (presumably one at a time) and then presents them to the Lord as wave and contribution offerings (Num 6:19–20).[14] Such offerings were

---

10. Roy Gane, *Cult and Character: Purification Offerings, Day of Atonement, and Theodicy* (Winona Lake, IN: Eisenbrauns, 2005), 148–49.

11. Sklar, *Leviticus* (ZECOT), 140.

12. For further details, see Sklar, *Leviticus* (ZECOT), 139–41 (purification offering), 87–89 (burnt offering), and 122–24 (fellowship offering).

13. Milgrom, *Numbers*, 49.

14. NIV's "the thigh that was presented" (6:20) is more woodenly "the thigh of the contribution offering."

often sacrificial portions the offerer gave to the Lord, who in turn gave them to meet tabernacle needs, especially those of the priests and their families[15] since these did not have large land tracts for farming and were dependent on gifts.[16] After the priest received their portions (cf. Lev 7:31–33; 10:14), the remaining breads and meat presumably went to the Nazirite and any of their family and friends who celebrated with them (cf. Lev 8:31; Deut 12:17–18). And since the vow had been fulfilled, the Nazirite would be free to drink wine with the meal (Num 6:20b), as well as engage fully in mourning rites and cut their hair whenever they wanted.

Summary (6:21)

The mention of "in addition to whatever else they can afford" suggests some Nazirites vowed to make offerings beyond the mandatory ones. Because the mandatory offerings were costly, it might have been tempting to avoid making any additional offerings they had vowed, so the text emphasizes Nazirites "must fulfill the vows they have made."

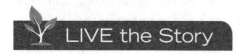

What Were Nazirites Reminders Of?

We often use physical objects as reminders. In my office, I have a photo of my late grandfather to remind me of him. I wear a wedding ring to remind me of the vows of love and faithfulness I have made to my wife, Ski. These physical reminders point beyond themselves to a deeper reality. Nazirites had a similar function in Israel: "The Nazirite was a person who was consecrated to the Lord, just as Israel as a nation was to be consecrated to the Lord [Exod 19:6]. Every time the Israelites saw a Nazirite, therefore, they would have been reminded of their own calling to serve the Lord."[17] Indeed, "Since being a Nazirite is open to all Israelites, men and women of any tribe, it is an especially apt symbol for the calling of all Israel."[18]

Stated differently: when God rescued Israel from Egypt, he called them all to be his "kingdom of priests and . . . holy nation" (Exod 19:6). A priest was set apart to God for specific tasks: praying for people, interceding before God for them, teaching others who God is and what it means to know him, and

---

15. See Exod 29:27–28; Lev 7:32, 34; 10:14–15.
16. See pp. 98–99, What Do the Israelites' Holy Gifts Teach Us about Giving Today?
17. Duguid, *Numbers*, 77–78.
18. Stubbs, *Numbers*, 65.

modeling holy living. In the context of Israel, the Lord set Aaron's family apart for this role toward the Israelites. But in the context of the world, the Lord set Israel apart for this role toward the nations. No Israelite could say, "Holiness is the priests' business, not mine." Anyone belonging to the Lord's people has been called to live as one set apart, and Nazirites, who set themselves apart to the Lord in a special way during their vow, were visible reminders of this reality.

This same call to holy living is true today. In fact, the New Testament uses the language of Exodus 19:6 to describe all who follow Jesus, saying, "But you are a chosen people, a *royal priesthood*, a *holy nation*, God's special possession, that you may declare the praises of him who called you out of darkness into his wonderful light" (1 Pet 2:9, emphasis added). Again, holiness is not only for such "specialists" as pastors or missionaries. All Jesus's followers are set apart by and for him to embody his holy character and to declare the wonder of who God is and what he has done for us through Jesus—so the world may enter into this same wonder and joy. In his love for his world, the Lord sets his people apart and calls each to dedicate their lives to doing this.

What Kind of Dedication Does the Lord Require?

If the Nazirites served to remind Israel to dedicate their lives to the Lord, what was the nature of this dedication? In a word: wholehearted. Dedication to the Lord is to take priority over all else.

Consider mourning rites. Most Israelites could draw near a loved one's body to mourn, but Nazirites could not (Num 6:6–7). Though not prohibited from being sad or crying, they could not engage in mourning rites that would take them near the ritually defiling body since this would profane their holy status and break their vow to the Lord. When a loved one died, Nazirites were therefore faced with an excruciating choice: Do I honor the Lord by keeping my promise or honor my loved one by following my culture's practices?

We might ask, "Why does the Lord not simply make an exception?" Since the vow was made in his name, he certainly could have listed situations in which a person could be released from it. But this would have undermined the very thing the Nazirite embodied: wholehearted dedication to the Lord in which he took priority over all else. When I married Ski, our vows contained no exception clauses. On the contrary: I vowed to love her "in plenty *and in want*, in joy *and in sorrow, in sickness* and in health, as long as we both shall live." The Nazirite was to embody the same wholehearted dedication to the Lord, and this was to remind the Lord's people of the wholehearted dedication each was to have for him. He takes priority over everything else in life.

Jesus put this idea in very stark terms. "If anyone comes to me and does not hate father and mother, wife and children, brothers and sisters—yes, even their own life—such a person cannot be my disciple" (Luke 14:26). He does not mean we must literally hate our loved ones; the Bible is clear that we must honor and care for them (Eph 6:2; 1 Tim 5:4, 8). But Jesus overstates his point to make it clear: if ever we must choose between honoring him and honoring those near to us (or even ourselves), we must honor him—regardless of their expectations, cultural expectations, or our own desires. He is Lord of all our lives or he is not Lord of our lives at all.

Will we do this perfectly? By no means, and he is quick and ready to forgive us when we fail (1 John 1:9). But the Lord does not call us to add him to the various commitments of our lives; he calls us to orient all the commitments of our lives around him. We are to live each day in loving and wholehearted worship of our King. We might pause to consider, "Is that how I think about what it means to follow Jesus? Are there areas of my life where I am not honoring him as Lord? What would surrendering that area to him look like?"

Where Did the Nazirites Live Out This Type of Dedication?

Finally, note the Nazirites did not live out their wholehearted dedication to the Lord by withdrawing from society. Though they did not participate in certain things society expected of most of its members (e.g., mourning rites), there is no indication they stopped living their regular lives: getting up in the morning, carrying on the day's business, interacting with and loving their family and neighbors, doing laundry, etc.

The temptation is to view wholehearted dedication to the Lord as withdrawing from society or taking on a different role (such as pastor or missionary). But no such thing is indicated here, just as there is no indication in the Bible that following Jesus wholeheartedly means withdrawing from society or becoming a pastor or missionary. Certainly, the Lord's followers should be set apart in terms of reflecting his character of goodness, justice, mercy, and love, but they do this in the midst of their everyday, ordinary activities in the world. Thus the New Testament exhorts, "So whether you eat or drink or whatever you do, do it all for the glory of God" (1 Cor 10:31). In short, those who have given themselves wholeheartedly to the Lord are quick to pray: "O Lord, in all I do today, whether big tasks or little ones, exciting or mundane ones, help me to do them as one who does everything for your pleasure and your glory!" If this is our heart's cry, we have learned the lesson of the Nazarite as well.

CHAPTER 8
Numbers 6:22-27

LISTEN to the Story

²²The Lord said to Moses, ²³"Tell Aaron and his sons, 'This is how you are to bless the Israelites. Say to them:

> ²⁴"'"The Lord bless you
> and keep you;
> ²⁵the Lord make his face shine on you
> and be gracious to you;
> ²⁶the Lord turn his face toward you
> and give you peace."'

²⁷"So they will put my name on the Israelites, and I will bless them."

Listening to the Text in the Story: Genesis 1:28; 3:1–19; 9:1; 12:1–3; 22:15–18; Leviticus 26:3–13

Since a benediction can be a concluding action (cf. Lev 9:22–23), these verses naturally conclude Numbers 5–6. They focus on blessing, which is no surprise: the Lord's first words over humanity were words of blessing (Gen 1:28), and though humanity's sin merited his curse (3:1–19), he is relentless in his desire to restore his blessing. He therefore repeats the blessing of creation to Noah (9:1) and makes blessing central to his covenant with Abraham, through whom he will extend such blessing to the entire world (12:1–3; 22:15–18). Because Israelites are heirs of the Abrahamic covenant, blessing is central to their life with God (Lev 26:3–13; Deut 28:1–14), and the priests' prayers for it on their behalf are reminders of that covenant and the Lord's promise of blessing within it.

A Priest's Responsibility: Blessing God's People (6:22–23)

Blessing was an experience of divine favor. Leviticus 26 contains a series of blessings that begins with signs of physical favor, such as safety from enemies and abundant food (vv. 3–10), and culminates with a sign of spiritual favor: experiencing the Lord's presence and fellowship (vv. 11–12). Blessing therefore includes "all of those things that make possible life to the full, life as God intended it at creation. (See also Gen 12:1–3.)"[1]

Here, the Lord commands Israel's priests, Aaron and his sons, to pronounce blessing over the Israelites. Elsewhere when Aaron blesses the people, he lifts his hand (Lev 9:22), which was a posture of prayer (Pss 28:2; 141:2). The words that follow are thus not a magical incantation but a prayer the Lord himself commands the people's spiritual leaders to pray over them, asking him to show his people both physical and spiritual favor. Clearly, one key task of shepherds is to pray for their sheep (cf. Deut 21:5; Phil 1:3–11; Col 1:9–13).

Three Bursts of Blessing (6:24–26)

There are three lines of blessing, which underscores their strength since saying something three times was a way to emphasize it (cf. Isa 6:3). Moreover, in the Hebrew, each line gets progressively longer, with three words in the first, five in the second, and seven in the third. This is a river of blessing whose flow widens and deepens until it finally empties into an ocean of peace—the blessing's final word. Most importantly, these verses emphasize that blessing comes from the Lord. "Grammatically there is no need to repeat God's name, but the repetition emphasizes that the LORD is the source of all Israel's benefits, as does the last clause *I will bless them* (27): 'I' is emphatic in the Hebrew."[2]

As with all blessings, this one focuses on the favor and good that comes to those being blessed. Its different phrases are like voices in a choir, sometimes overlapping, other times harmonizing, but always working together to create a unified piece of beauty. The prayer's sense may be captured in paraphrase:

> *May the* Lord *bless you*, causing you to experience his favor, both physically, such as with safety, health, and material goods, and spiritually, such as with his acceptance, nearness, and fellowship (Lev 26:3–13)!

---

1. Lloyd R. Bailey, *Leviticus–Numbers*, Smyth & Helwys Bible Commentary (Macon, GA.: Smyth & Helwys Publishing, 2005), 422.
2. Wenham, *Numbers*, 90.

May he keep you as the apple of his eye, hiding you in the shadow of his wings and protecting you from all harm (Ps 17:8)!

May he make his face shine upon you, turning it toward you beaming with steadfast love, so that you know his favor and care (Ps 31:16)!

May he be gracious to you, answering your prayers for help and mercy, and making clear that he is your saving God (Pss 30:10; 57:1)!

May he lift up his countenance to you, with favor shining from it, showing he accepts you and delights in you (Ps 4:6)!

May he give you peace, guarding you from all harm, removing every cause for worry, fear, and concern, and leaving you assured of his protective blessing (Lev 26:6; Ps 4:8)!

Conclusion (6:27)

"'And so they will put my name on the Israelites,' wrapping them in it, as with a garment, identifying them as my very own,[3] the ones I myself[4] will bless with divine favor in my love for them and in my desire for the nations to see and know that I am the true God."[5] Again, this is no magic formula, causing blessing to shower down automatically on any Israelite even if they are rebelling against the Lord. As other passages state, the Lord's blessing comes on those who walk in his ways,[6] not because this earns his salvific favor but because they remain close to the Father who delights to reward his faithful children with his blessing and care. Such faithfulness is assumed here, with the emphasis being that the faithful can expect the Lord's blessing. He is our heavenly father and delights to care for his children's needs (Matt 6:25–33; 7:11). Indeed, in the Hebrew, the prayer begins and ends with the word "bless" (Num 6:24, 27). From start to finish, the Lord desires to bless his children.

---

3. Cf. Deut 28:9–10. See discussion in Carmen Joy Imes, *Bearing* Yhwh's *Name at Sinai: A Reexamination of the Name Command of the Decalogue*, BBR Supplements 19 (University Park, PA: Eisenbrauns, 2018), 70–71.
4. As noted above, "I" is emphatic in the Hebrew.
5. For the missional aspects of blessing see Ps 67:1–2 (noted by Imes, *Bearing* Yhwh's *Name*, 71n83).
6. Cf. Lev 26:3 with 26:4–13, and Deut 28:1–2, 9b, 13b-14 with 28:3–9a, 10–13a.

LIVE the Story

What Is Blessing?

How would you answer the question, "What is blessing?" If we view this life as all there is, we might respond in general by saying, "Whatever makes us happy," or by listing particular things that make us happy, such as health, material provision, loving relationships, or doing good. Nothing is wrong with these things. In fact, the Bible commends them! It contains prayers for healing (Pss 6:2; 30:2) and for material provision (Prov 30:8; Matt 6:11), and many of the blessings in our passage would have shown up in very physical ways (see at Num 6:24–26, pp. 122–23). Christianity is not an invitation to ignore our physical or material needs. As for loving relationships and doing good, the Bible teaches us to love our neighbor as ourselves (Lev 19:18; Matt 22:39) and to do good to all people (Luke 6:35; Gal 6:10). Christianity is also not an invitation to be so heavenly minded we are of no earthly good.

But we can have or do these things and still feel empty. At age thirty, Tom Brady was one of the most successful professional quarterbacks in history. During an interview, he reflected on his success and asked, "Why do I have three Super Bowl rings, and . . . still think there's something greater out there for me? . . . There's got to be more than this." The interviewer asked him, "What's the answer?" to which he replied, "I wish I knew! I wish I knew."[7]

Material provision and favor in life are not bad things; they are simply not meant to be foundational or ultimate things. From the Bible's perspective, blessing is founded in relationship with God and finds its ultimate meaning in that relationship. Its story begins by teaching there is a God who loves us and has created us to know him and reflect his goodness and love into the world. Ultimate fulfillment is therefore found in him. St. Augustine's prayer captures it well: "You have made us for yourself, and our heart is restless until it rests in you."[8] The same is seen in our passage: "the LORD make his face shine on you . . . the LORD turn his face toward you" (Num 6:25a, 26a). This intimate language describes the Lord turning his face to us, beaming with love and pleasure. That is true blessing: the King of the universe looking toward you as a loving Father who knows all your needs and then gives you his very self. And this leads to a question.

---

7. "Tom Brady on Winning: There's 'Got to Be More Than This,'" *60 Minutes*, 30 Jan 2019, https://www.youtube.com/watch?v=-TA4_fVkv3c.

8. Augustine, *Confessions*, trans. Henry Chadwick, Oxford World's Classics (New York: Oxford University Press, 2009), 1.1.1.

How Do We Find True Blessing (Part 1)?

This passage goes out of its way to show blessing does not come from priests (or therefore from pastors or other spiritual leaders); it comes from the Lord. True, priests are to pray for blessing, but the Lord is its source. "'*The Lord* bless you and keep you; *the Lord* make his face shine on you and be gracious to you; *the Lord* turn his face toward you and give you peace.' So they will put my name on the Israelites, *and I [myself]*[9] will bless them" (Num 6:24–27, emphasis added). Blessing comes from him.

Significantly, the Lord *desires* to bless his creation. He placed humanity in a garden, not a desert. God's blessing is not something we must work to earn; he comes down to give it. In our passage, the Lord himself commands the priests to pray for his blessing on his people. "Blessing is his idea, his purpose. It is not something his people must beg for, but it is the outreaching of his grace."[10]

The clearest expression of this is found in Jesus. "There's got to be more than this," Tom Brady said. "Yes," the Bible responds, "there *is* more—way more! In Jesus, there is soul-satisfying grace and peace (Eph 1:2)! Because of Jesus, we can have a deep relationship with a heavenly Father who loves us, forgives us, showers his grace on us, grants us his Holy Spirit, and dignifies us with the privilege of reflecting his love and grace into the world (Eph 1:3–14). That is what it's all about! In Jesus, our restless hearts find rest."

How Do We Find True Blessing (Part 2)?

While our text is clear that the Lord is the ultimate source of blessing, it also teaches spiritual leaders are to pray for blessing on those they lead. Aaron does this earlier in Leviticus (Lev 9:22–23). The Levitical priests in Deuteronomy are responsible for doing this (Deut 21:5). Paul often speaks of praying for the churches (Phil 1:3–11; Col 1:9–13). In their love for the sheep, shepherds are to pray regularly for the Lord's blessing, especially because we live in a broken world whose curse touches the Lord's people. Spiritual leaders are therefore to pray for them, earnestly and regularly, that the Lord would protect, watch over, bless, and especially ground his people so deeply in their relationship with him that they would know the deepest peace and joy (Eph 1:15–19; 3:14–19).

If this is to be a priority, churches must examine their expectations for ministers. Do the job descriptions churches write provide time for ministers to pray? Do churches say, "We want you to pray for us," and yet so fill a pastor's day with meetings and events that they leave the pastor little time to pray for

---

9. Emphatic in the Hebrew.
10. Allen, "Numbers," 754.

the people? Shepherds must not only pray for the sheep, they must be given time to do so.

Significantly, such prayers may be offered in great hope, not only because they are offered to the God who loves his people, is at work among them, and will complete the work he has begun in them (Phil 1:6) but also because the Lord himself says he will use the prayers of spiritual leaders to bless his people (Num 6:27). If we are ministers, do our prayers reflect this? Whether privately or publicly, do we pray in a rote, mechanical manner? Do we view benediction as simply a conclusion to a service? Or do we pray hopefully and earnestly, expecting the Lord to strengthen his people, protect them, watch over them, and give them peace? What does it look like for ministers to pray with confident and sincere faith, and what does it look like for those who rest under such prayers to have courage and hope the Lord will hear and respond? This leads to a final question.

How Do We Hope When Blessing Has Not Yet Come?

Most of us can identify areas of our lives that seem to lack blessing, whether material provision, or health, or relationships, or work—the list goes on. Indeed, many of us have been asking for the Lord's favor, protection, and mercy in these places for some time. How can we hope when our prayers seem not to be heard?

The answer comes in remembering where the root of hope is ultimately found. In what has come to be known as his high priestly prayer, Jesus prays for his disciples. His prayer is instructive: He asks that they be spiritually protected (John 17:15), set apart into the service of God's truth (17:17), have perfect fellowship with God, be unified in love (17:21–23), and enter into the joy of eternal life in Jesus's presence (17:24). These requests all focus on our drawing near to God, knowing him and his love, and living out that love before the world. Elsewhere, Jesus will teach us to pray for material provision (Matt 6:11), but that is not his focus here. Such things are not unimportant, but they are not the ultimate source of hope and joy, which are found only in knowing the God who has made us for himself and in fulfilling his mission for us in this world. If we know him, our life is founded on an immovable rock of love, mercy, and hope, enabling us to live his love out into the world no matter what it might throw at us. As the apostle Paul once said, "I have learned the secret of being content in any and every situation, whether well fed or hungry, whether living in plenty or in want. I can do all this through him who gives me strength" (Phil 4:12–13). Paul did not focus on the visible blessings that seemed missing; he focused on the bedrock blessing that put all life in perspective: He belonged to Jesus, who gave him the strength to live with the contentment that belongs to those who know they have the greatest blessing they could ever need because they are held secure in God's loving hand. That is blessing indeed.

CHAPTER 9
Numbers 7:1–89

 LISTEN to the Story

¹When Moses finished setting up the tabernacle, he anointed and consecrated it and all its furnishings. He also anointed and consecrated the altar and all its utensils. ²Then the leaders of Israel, the heads of families who were the tribal leaders in charge of those who were counted, made offerings. ³They brought as their gifts before the LORD six covered carts and twelve oxen—an ox from each leader and a cart from every two. These they presented before the tabernacle.

⁴The LORD said to Moses, ⁵ "Accept these from them, that they may be used in the work at the tent of meeting. Give them to the Levites as each man's work requires."

⁶So Moses took the carts and oxen and gave them to the Levites. ⁷He gave two carts and four oxen to the Gershonites, as their work required, ⁸and he gave four carts and eight oxen to the Merarites, as their work required. They were all under the direction of Ithamar son of Aaron, the priest. ⁹But Moses did not give any to the Kohathites, because they were to carry on their shoulders the holy things, for which they were responsible.

¹⁰When the altar was anointed, the leaders brought their offerings for its dedication and presented them before the altar. ¹¹For the LORD had said to Moses, "Each day one leader is to bring his offering for the dedication of the altar."

¹²The one who brought his offering on the first day was Nahshon son of Amminadab of the tribe of Judah.

¹³His offering was one silver plate weighing a hundred and thirty shekels and one silver sprinkling bowl weighing seventy shekels, both according to the sanctuary shekel, each filled with the finest flour mixed with olive oil as a grain offering; ¹⁴one gold dish weighing ten shekels, filled with incense; ¹⁵one young bull, one ram and one male lamb a

year old for a burnt offering; ¹⁶one male goat for a sin offering; ¹⁷and two oxen, five rams, five male goats and five male lambs a year old to be sacrificed as a fellowship offering. This was the offering of Nahshon son of Amminadab.

¹⁸On the second day Nethanel son of Zuar, the leader of Issachar, brought his offering.

¹⁹The offering he brought was one silver plate weighing a hundred and thirty shekels and one silver sprinkling bowl weighing seventy shekels, both according to the sanctuary shekel, each filled with the finest flour mixed with olive oil as a grain offering; ²⁰one gold dish weighing ten shekels, filled with incense; ²¹one young bull, one ram and one male lamb a year old for a burnt offering; ²²one male goat for a sin offering; ²³and two oxen, five rams, five male goats and five male lambs a year old to be sacrificed as a fellowship offering. This was the offering of Nethanel son of Zuar.

²⁴On the third day, Eliab son of Helon, the leader of the people of Zebulun, brought his offering.

²⁵His offering was one silver plate weighing a hundred and thirty shekels and one silver sprinkling bowl weighing seventy shekels, both according to the sanctuary shekel, each filled with the finest flour mixed with olive oil as a grain offering; ²⁶one gold dish weighing ten shekels, filled with incense; ²⁷one young bull, one ram and one male lamb a year old for a burnt offering; ²⁸one male goat for a sin offering; ²⁹and two oxen, five rams, five male goats and five male lambs a year old to be sacrificed as a fellowship offering. This was the offering of Eliab son of Helon.

³⁰On the fourth day Elizur son of Shedeur, the leader of the people of Reuben, brought his offering.

³¹His offering was one silver plate weighing a hundred and thirty shekels and one silver sprinkling bowl weighing seventy shekels, both according to the sanctuary shekel, each filled with the finest flour mixed with olive oil as a grain offering; ³²one gold dish weighing ten shekels,

filled with incense; ³³one young bull, one ram and one male lamb a year old for a burnt offering; ³⁴one male goat for a sin offering; ³⁵and two oxen, five rams, five male goats and five male lambs a year old to be sacrificed as a fellowship offering. This was the offering of Elizur son of Shedeur.

³⁶On the fifth day Shelumiel son of Zurishaddai, the leader of the people of Simeon, brought his offering.

³⁷His offering was one silver plate weighing a hundred and thirty shekels and one silver sprinkling bowl weighing seventy shekels, both according to the sanctuary shekel, each filled with the finest flour mixed with olive oil as a grain offering; ³⁸one gold dish weighing ten shekels, filled with incense; ³⁹one young bull, one ram and one male lamb a year old for a burnt offering; ⁴⁰one male goat for a sin offering; ⁴¹and two oxen, five rams, five male goats and five male lambs a year old to be sacrificed as a fellowship offering. This was the offering of Shelumiel son of Zurishaddai.

⁴²On the sixth day Eliasaph son of Deuel, the leader of the people of Gad, brought his offering.

⁴³His offering was one silver plate weighing a hundred and thirty shekels and one silver sprinkling bowl weighing seventy shekels, both according to the sanctuary shekel, each filled with the finest flour mixed with olive oil as a grain offering; ⁴⁴one gold dish weighing ten shekels, filled with incense; ⁴⁵one young bull, one ram and one male lamb a year old for a burnt offering; ⁴⁶one male goat for a sin offering; ⁴⁷and two oxen, five rams, five male goats and five male lambs a year old to be sacrificed as a fellowship offering. This was the offering of Eliasaph son of Deuel.

⁴⁸On the seventh day Elishama son of Ammihud, the leader of the people of Ephraim, brought his offering.

⁴⁹His offering was one silver plate weighing a hundred and thirty shekels and one silver sprinkling bowl weighing seventy shekels, both

according to the sanctuary shekel, each filled with the finest flour mixed with olive oil as a grain offering; ⁵⁰one gold dish weighing ten shekels, filled with incense; ⁵¹one young bull, one ram and one male lamb a year old for a burnt offering; ⁵²one male goat for a sin offering; ⁵³and two oxen, five rams, five male goats and five male lambs a year old to be sacrificed as a fellowship offering. This was the offering of Elishama son of Ammihud.

⁵⁴On the eighth day Gamaliel son of Pedahzur, the leader of the people of Manasseh, brought his offering.

⁵⁵His offering was one silver plate weighing a hundred and thirty shekels and one silver sprinkling bowl weighing seventy shekels, both according to the sanctuary shekel, each filled with the finest flour mixed with olive oil as a grain offering; ⁵⁶one gold dish weighing ten shekels, filled with incense; ⁵⁷one young bull, one ram and one male lamb a year old for a burnt offering; ⁵⁸one male goat for a sin offering; ⁵⁹and two oxen, five rams, five male goats and five male lambs a year old to be sacrificed as a fellowship offering. This was the offering of Gamaliel son of Pedahzur.

⁶⁰On the ninth day Abidan son of Gideoni, the leader of the people of Benjamin, brought his offering.

⁶¹His offering was one silver plate weighing a hundred and thirty shekels and one silver sprinkling bowl weighing seventy shekels, both according to the sanctuary shekel, each filled with the finest flour mixed with olive oil as a grain offering; ⁶²one gold dish weighing ten shekels, filled with incense; ⁶³one young bull, one ram and one male lamb a year old for a burnt offering; ⁶⁴one male goat for a sin offering; ⁶⁵and two oxen, five rams, five male goats and five male lambs a year old to be sacrificed as a fellowship offering. This was the offering of Abidan son of Gideoni.

⁶⁶On the tenth day Ahiezer son of Ammishaddai, the leader of the people of Dan, brought his offering.

⁶⁷His offering was one silver plate weighing a hundred and thirty shekels and one silver sprinkling bowl weighing seventy shekels, both

according to the sanctuary shekel, each filled with the finest flour mixed with olive oil as a grain offering; [68]one gold dish weighing ten shekels, filled with incense; [69]one young bull, one ram and one male lamb a year old for a burnt offering; [70]one male goat for a sin offering; [71]and two oxen, five rams, five male goats and five male lambs a year old to be sacrificed as a fellowship offering. This was the offering of Ahiezer son of Ammishaddai.

[72]On the eleventh day Pagiel son of Okran, the leader of the people of Asher, brought his offering.

[73]His offering was one silver plate weighing a hundred and thirty shekels and one silver sprinkling bowl weighing seventy shekels, both according to the sanctuary shekel, each filled with the finest flour mixed with olive oil as a grain offering; [74]one gold dish weighing ten shekels, filled with incense; [75]one young bull, one ram and one male lamb a year old for a burnt offering; [76]one male goat for a sin offering; [77]and two oxen, five rams, five male goats and five male lambs a year old to be sacrificed as a fellowship offering. This was the offering of Pagiel son of Okran.

[78]On the twelfth day Ahira son of Enan, the leader of the people of Naphtali, brought his offering.

[79]His offering was one silver plate weighing a hundred and thirty shekels and one silver sprinkling bowl weighing seventy shekels, both according to the sanctuary shekel, each filled with the finest flour mixed with olive oil as a grain offering; [80]one gold dish weighing ten shekels, filled with incense; [81]one young bull, one ram and one male lamb a year old for a burnt offering; [82]one male goat for a sin offering; [83]and two oxen, five rams, five male goats and five male lambs a year old to be sacrificed as a fellowship offering. This was the offering of Ahira son of Enan.

[84]These were the offerings of the Israelite leaders for the dedication of the altar when it was anointed: twelve silver plates, twelve silver

sprinkling bowls and twelve gold dishes. ⁸⁵Each silver plate weighed a hundred and thirty shekels, and each sprinkling bowl seventy shekels. Altogether, the silver dishes weighed two thousand four hundred shekels, according to the sanctuary shekel. ⁸⁶The twelve gold dishes filled with incense weighed ten shekels each, according to the sanctuary shekel. Altogether, the gold dishes weighed a hundred and twenty shekels. ⁸⁷The total number of animals for the burnt offering came to twelve young bulls, twelve rams and twelve male lambs a year old, together with their grain offering. Twelve male goats were used for the sin offering. ⁸⁸The total number of animals for the sacrifice of the fellowship offering came to twenty-four oxen, sixty rams, sixty male goats and sixty male lambs a year old. These were the offerings for the dedication of the altar after it was anointed.

⁸⁹When Moses entered the tent of meeting to speak with the LORD, he heard the voice speaking to him from between the two cherubim above the atonement cover on the ark of the covenant law. In this way the LORD spoke to him.

Listening to the Text in the Story: Exodus 40:17–33; Leviticus 8:10–11

In Exodus 40:17–33 and Leviticus 8:10–11, the tabernacle is built and anointed. As a portable holy place, it needs a means of transport. Numbers 7:1–9 answers that need by describing carts and oxen brought by Israel's leaders to move it.

It also lists other gifts the leaders brought for the altar's dedication (Num 7:10–88). To many moderns, the list is needlessly repetitive. From a cultural perspective, however, it may simply reflect normal accounting procedures: "The system of numeration employed in Num 7:12–88 . . . directly links biblical records to known methods of ancient Near Eastern accounting. In Num 7:12–88 the sequence of numeration [in the Hebrew] is (a) item, (b) numeral (quantity); for example: . . . 'oxen—2,'" a sequence evident in other ancient Near Eastern texts.[1] Even more importantly, from a theological perspective, this list shows each Israelite tribe contributing equally to the Lord's worship, emphasizing the people's unity and equality before God.

---

1. Levine, *Numbers 1–20*, 261. See further Milgrom, *Numbers*, 362–63.

EXPLAIN the Story

Much of Numbers 7:1–10:10 is chronologically displaced.[2] Numbers 1:1 refers to the first day of the *second month* of the second year after the Israelites left Egypt. Numbers 7:1 refers back to the tabernacle's assembly, which occurred in the *first month* of the second year (Exod 40:17; cf. also Num 9:1). But this flashback makes sense in the larger context. In 10:11, the Lord's cloud will lift from the tabernacle, meaning the Israelites must break camp. As part of this, the Levites will have to dismantle and transport the tabernacle, needing carts and oxen to do so. Chapter 7 describes how the Israelites provide these carts and oxen, along with other precious items, at the tabernacle's dedication, preparing the reader for the climactic moment to come in 10:11.

Setting: The Setting up and Consecrating of the Tabernacle (7:1)

This verse refers back to the tabernacle's assembly and consecration, events detailed in Exod 40:17–33 and Lev 8:10–11. It focuses on the tabernacle and its contents becoming holy through anointing with the holy oil (cf. Exod 30:22–33). This prepared it to be the dwelling place of the Lord, whose holy presence will be the heartbeat of Israel's communal life.

The Tribal Leaders' First Offerings: Carts and Oxen for the Levites (7:2–9)

Since the tabernacle was portable, equipment would be needed to move it. This need is met by Israel's tribal leaders (cf. Num 1:5–15), who present gifts on the tribes' behalf.

Taken together, the gifts are six carts[3] and twelve oxen (Num 7:3), all given to the Levites and used for transporting the tabernacle (v. 5). Two carts and four oxen go to the Gershonites (v. 7), who were responsible for the fabrics (see table, p. 83). Double that amount goes to the Merarites (v. 8), who were responsible for the numerous and heavy structural elements (see

---

2. An exception is 9:16–23, which describes the relationship between the Lord's cloud and the tabernacle during the wilderness wanderings. Less clear is whether 10:1–10 is also chronologically displaced.

3. Or "covered carts" (so NIV), although this translation is uncertain due to the Hebrew term's rarity.

table, p. 83).[4] That leaves the Kohathites, who receive no carts or oxen since they transported the most holy objects by poles and carrying frames (v. 9; see table, p. 80).[5]

The Tribal Leaders' Offerings for the Altar's Dedication (7:10–88)

The text now transitions from gifts for tabernacle transport to offerings "for the dedication of the altar" (Num 7:11), that is, offerings made when the altar began to be used (cf. 1 Kgs 8:62–63; 2 Chr 7:4–9). This happened at some point after it had been made holy through anointing (Num 7:10).[6] In view is the altar of burnt offering, which was the Israelites' lifeline to the Lord. By it, they presented sacrifices to atone for sin and impurity, to express worship and praise, and to underscore prayers of petition. A tabernacle with no functioning altar would be like a body with no heart.

As for the dedication, later in Israel's history, when Solomon dedicates the temple, he presents offerings (as here) (1 Kgs 8:62–64) and also prays that the Lord would be attentive to the worship and prayers offered at the temple (vv. 22–53). It should not surprise us if something similar happened in Numbers 7, with Moses (or the priests) praying on the people's behalf.

The dedication gifts were presented over twelve days, with one tribal leader coming each day (Num 7:11), following the order given in Numbers 2 (see table, p. 63), and each bringing the same offering. This testified to the tribes' unity in worshiping the Lord. It also testified to their equality. Given the disparity in number between tribes (e.g., Judah had 74,600 men, while Manasseh had only 32,200 [2:4, 21]), the equal gifts underscored that every tribe was equally a part of God's covenant people. These twin themes of unity and equality appear throughout the book.[7]

The gifts consisted of dishes and sacrificial animals and are summarized in the tables below. Each tribe brought three types of dishes: one large silver dish[8] (approximately 3.25 pounds [1.5kg]),[9] one silver sprinkling bowl

---

4. For the mention of Ithamar (7:8), see 4:28, 33.
5. Carrying something by hand may have been an extra sign of reverence; the discussion on p. 81.
6. It would be natural to assume this took place soon after the beginning of public worship in Lev 9, when fire from the Lord inaugurated the altar for public use (9:24; cf. 2 Chr 7:1–5).
7. See pp. 23–24, Unity.
8. The Hebrew word (*qeʿarah*) "is related to words that, in the cognate languages, mean 'to be deep,' hence a 'deep dish'" (Ashley, *Numbers*, 162), not a shallow "plate."
9. Each silver dish equaled the price of two adult male servants and one adult female servant (Lev 27:1–8); this suggests they were of great value (Sprinkle, *Leviticus and Numbers*, 224).

(approximately 1.75 pounds [800 g]), and one small gold dish (approximately 4 ounces [115 g]).[10] The first two were filled with fine flour mixed with oil for a grain offering (Num 7:13), which could accompany the burnt or fellowship offerings about to be made on the burnt offering altar (cf. Num 15:3–4, 6, 8–9). The last was filled with incense, which could be presented as an incense offering on the incense altar (cf. Exod 30:1). Going forward, these vessels could be used in various aspects of offerings, including holding cooked or uncooked grain offerings (the silver dishes), drink offerings or sacrificial blood (the silver sprinkling bowls), and incense (the golden dishes). Their presence would be a continual symbolic reminder of each tribe's service and worship to the Lord.

The sacrificial animals were meant for three types of offerings: burnt offerings, which accomplished atonement and served as costly expressions of worship and praise; purification offerings,[11] which removed the offerer's sin and impurity; and fellowship offerings, which functioned as shared covenant meals between the Lord, the priests, and the people.[12] (This explains why the number of fellowship offering animals is greatest: the meat was likely shared by tribal representatives to express this covenant fellowship.) Such offerings allowed each tribe to accomplish a full range of activities before the Lord, from achieving atonement (purification offering, burnt offering), to expressing worship and praise (burnt offering), to celebrating covenant fellowship with him and one another (fellowship offering).

After listing all the gifts and offerings of the twelve days (Num 7:10–83), a summary is given (7:84–88), much the same way we might summarize financial gifts to a church in a budget year.[13]

Dishes Presented

Dish (See Num 7:84–86)	Biblical Weight	Approximate Modern Equivalent
12 silver plates	1,560 shekels	39 pounds (17.9 kilograms)
12 silver sprinkling bowls	840 shekels	21 pounds (9.7 kilograms)
12 gold dishes	120 shekels	3 pounds (1.4 kilograms)

---

10. Assuming .4oz (11–12 g) per shekel. See Cook, "Weights and Measures," 1054.
11. NIV footnote at Num 7:16; see p. 115n5.
12. For details, see at 6:13–20.
13. For "sanctuary shekel" (7:85–86), see p. 78n16.

Animals Offered

Offering	Animals (See Num 7:87–88)
Burnt	12 young bulls, 12 rams, 12 year-old male lambs
Sin	12 male goats
Fellowship	24 oxen, 60 rams, 60 male goats, 60 year-old male lambs

Confirmation of the Lord's Presence in the Tabernacle (7:89)

The concluding verse (Num 7:89) echoes Exodus 25:17–22, where the Lord promises to speak to Moses from above "the ark of the covenant law,"[14] which rested in the most holy place. Given the extreme measures Aaron, the high priest, had to take to enter the most holy place (Lev 16:2–4), Moses presumably does not enter to hear the Lord but stands instead in the holy place on the other side of the veil. Regardless, this verse confirms the Lord's promise (Exod 25:17–22), assuring the Israelites he received their dedicatory gifts with favor and serving as a fitting conclusion: Now that the altar has been dedicated, the tabernacle can fully function, including in its central role as the place where the Lord will speak personally with Moses, giving him commands and instructions for the Israelites.

LIVE the Story

Why Focus So Much on an Altar?

Numbers 7 is the Bible's second longest chapter (after Ps 119) and focuses mostly on gifts brought for the altar's dedication. This would not surprise Israelites. On the altar they presented sacrifices to atone for sin and impurity, express worship and praise, and underscore prayers of petition. Through the sacrificial worship there, the Israelites repaired, maintained, and enjoyed their relationship with the Lord. It was their lifeline to him, and he provided them with the altar and priests to work at it on their behalf so they might know and worship him. The Bible's consistent story is that God has made us for relationship with himself, and in his love, *he* makes ways for this to happen. The tabernacle was his idea, not theirs.

As the Bible's story continues, the focus shifts from human priests offering

---

14. For details, see p. 53 at 1:47–53.

sacrifices on an altar to the God-man Jesus serving as both final priest and sacrifice so that we might know and worship God. Once again, this is God's doing. In love, he sent Jesus to be the ultimate priest who intercedes before him on our behalf (Heb 3:1–2) and to be the ultimate sacrifice to cleanse us of our defiling wrongs (Rom 5:8). Jesus is now our lifeline to God. He is the ladder God has lowered from heaven that we might come to him (John 1:51; 14:6). He is the mirror image of his character that we might know him (John 14:7–11; Heb 1:3). In and through Jesus we can come to know and worship God.

But worshiping God is not simply a spiritual activity. In order to worship the Lord of heaven, earthly needs must be met.

Who's Going to Pay the Electricity Bill?

The Levites had a monumental task: Whenever the Israelites broke camp, it was the Levites' job to disassemble, carry, and reassemble the tabernacle, an enormous tent with heavy curtains and many pieces of solid or plated metal. Exodus lists the weight of the metals (gold, silver, bronze) (Exod 38:24–31), which in modern measurements totals somewhere around 15,000 pounds (ca. 6,800 kgs).[15] Add to this the curtains' weight, and it is clear the Levites had a very practical need in order to carry out their duties: carts and oxen (Num 7:3–9). (Bear in mind they also had their own tents and belongings to transport, thus giving them weight the other tribes did not have.)

Transporting the tabernacle was practical and unexciting work, yet it was crucial for the Lord's worship to continue. Without it, there was no tabernacle and no altar. And to transport the tabernacle, the Levites needed the other tribes to provide for practical, if unexciting, needs. To put it in modern terms, for churches to be open for Sunday morning worship, someone must pay the electricity bill.

In today's context, such provision takes numerous forms. Most basically, it involves supporting those who teach us and lead us in the Lord's worship so they might focus on these things (1 Cor 9:13–14). But it also involves providing for our worship spaces, for instruments used in worship, and even for the training of future ministry leaders and musicians. Providing for these practical needs is not somehow less spiritual; on the contrary, it is saying, "O Lord, what matters to me is that your worship may continue uninterrupted so that you may be glorified and we may experience the joy that comes from knowing you, drawing near to you, and giving you honor and praise."

---

15. Stuart, *Exodus*, 772–74, assuming 75 pounds for the talent and .4 ounces for the shekel (p. 772n300). See also table, p. 83.

The next part of the chapter in fact describes the worship performed by the tribes at the tabernacle. It also answers an important question.

Which Tribe Matters Most?

Where differences exist, comparisons are inevitable: Which is better? Which has more value? Such comparisons are not necessarily bad when considering inanimate objects (such as bicycles or shoes); the problem comes when we compare individuals or groups of people. This could be a strong temptation for Israelites among themselves. Their tribes all descended from Jacob and yet each descended from a different son of his (Exod 1:1–7). The temptation would be to ask, "Which tribe is better? Which has more value? Which matters most?"

This chapter speaks against such comparisons by emphasizing the tribes' unity and equality. Unity because every tribe brings offerings for the Levites' support (Num 7:2–3) and the altar's dedication (7:10–88). Equality because every tribe brings exactly the same gift. Larger tribes, such as Judah (74,600 men), do not bring more, and smaller tribes, such as Manasseh (32,200 men), do not bring less—as the chapter makes clear in painstaking detail!

Indeed, the chapter's detail drives the lesson home. Its seemingly needless repetition actually underscores important points. For example, at our seminary's graduation ceremony each year, it takes more than an hour to recite all the names as each graduate walks across the stage, is hooded, and receives their degree. It would be much quicker to ask all graduates to stand and then to say, "The school declares that everyone standing gets their degree." Quicker, yes, but this would miss the personal involvement of each graduate in the unified body. The ceremony makes clear: *Ben (Lorianne, Craig, Courtney, etc.)* is a member of this graduating class (unity) and has achieved the same degree as everyone else in it (equality). So, too, in this chapter: *Judah (Issachar, Zebulun, Reuben, etc.)* is a member of the Lord's people Israel (unity) and has an equal standing before the Lord (equality). All tribes are personally involved; all stand united in the Lord's worship; all stand equally before him in that worship; all contribute equally to that worship.

The above means that among the Lord's people, asking "Who matters most?" is the wrong question. Luke's Gospel records two different times Jesus's first disciples began arguing among themselves "as to which of them was considered to be greatest" (Luke 22:24; cf. 9:46). Jesus's response could be paraphrased "Wrong question! Focus instead on how you can serve one another in love, just as I, the Lord, have served you in love" (cf. 22:25–27). The Christians in Corinth argued similarly: "We all have different spiritual gifts, and some matter more than others!" (1 Cor 12:15–16). "Wrong focus,"

Paul responds. "You do have different gifts, but you belong to one body! Focus on how you can serve one another in love" (cf. 12:12–14, 20–27; 13:1–8a).

The Bible does not deny differences among the Lord's people. In Numbers 7, the Levites transport the tabernacle, not the other tribes (vv. 5–9); in the New Testament, elders are called to positions of authority in the church, not everyone (1 Tim 3:1–7). But the Bible emphasizes the unity of God's people as they worship and serve him. In Numbers 7, the picture presented is that of the Lord dwelling in his people's midst in the tabernacle, receiving all the honor and glory.[16] The tribes surround him, rejoicing as equal members of his people, assured of his equal love and care, and having the privilege of working together as one to make his praise and glory known.

So, too, for the believer today. In the New Testament, the picture given is that of the Lord dwelling in the midst of his people who are the temple, of which Jesus is the cornerstone (Eph 2:19–22). Once more, God is at the center, receiving all the honor and glory. His people surround him, rejoicing as equal members of his body, assured of his equal love and care, and having the privilege of working together as one to make his praise and glory known. We do well to ask, "Is this what people see in our church? Are we focused on exalting him instead of ourselves and serving our brothers and sisters in love as together we follow Jesus, the one who gave himself for us? If not, what changes might be needed individually and corporately for our community to live out such unified, God-centered love?"

---

16. Cf. Gane, *Leviticus, Numbers*, 552, who notes how the offerings are like tribute brought "to acknowledge the divine King, dwelling . . . in Israel's midst."

CHAPTER 10

Numbers 8:1-4

 LISTEN to the Story

¹The Lord said to Moses, ²"Speak to Aaron and say to him, 'When you set up the lamps, see that all seven light up the area in front of the lampstand.'"
³Aaron did so; he set up the lamps so that they faced forward on the lampstand, just as the Lord commanded Moses. ⁴This is how the lampstand was made: It was made of hammered gold—from its base to its blossoms. The lampstand was made exactly like the pattern the Lord had shown Moses.

Listening to the Text in the Story: Exodus 25:31; 30:7–8; Leviticus 24:1–9

The lighting of the lampstand was one of seven "continual" rites to be carried out at the tabernacle.[1] Along with the continual bread of the presence (Exod 25:30) and the continual incense (30:7–8), this rite occurred in the holy place. The three rites together were rich in symbolism:

> As Averbeck notes, "The combination of the daily lighting of the lampstand and associated burning of incense (Lev 24:3 with Ex 30:7–8) plus the bread constantly on the table impresses one with the fact that the Lord had truly taken up residence in the tabernacle. If there is a lamp burning, incense burning and bread on the table, then someone is 'home.'"[2] Indeed, by doing these things continually, the Israelites acknowledged the Lord was continually in their midst and they were his perpetual servants.[3]

---

1. For a full listing, see Sklar, *Leviticus* (ZECOT), 190.
2. Richard E. Averbeck, "Tabernacle," *DOOTP* 815.
3. Sklar, *Leviticus* (ZECOT), 644.

# EXPLAIN the Story

Lighting the Tabernacle Lampstand (8:1–4)

While chapter 7 described what the tribes did when the tabernacle was set up, this section describes one aspect of what Aaron did: making sure the lampstand worked properly.[4] In terms of its description, I have noted elsewhere:

> The lampstand is described most fully in Exod 25:31–40 and 37:17–24, though its exact shape is unclear. It was made of gold and was tree-like, with a main trunk, six branches, and flowering blossoms on both the trunk and branches. Standing in the Holy Place on the south side (that is, on the left, if facing the tent . . .),[5] it had seven lamps, each containing oil and a wick.[6]

The lampstand was one of three pieces of furniture in the holy place, each of which was to be in continual use: the lamp continually burning (Lev 24:1–4), the golden table continually holding the bread of the presence (Exod 25:30; Lev 24:5–9), and the incense altar continually used morning and evening to burn incense (Exod 30:7–8). As noted above, these highly symbolic rites pointed to the Israelites' continual service before the Lord and to the fact of his presence among them.

The verses here have two emphases. First, the seven lamps lit up the area in front of the lampstand. Since it was on the left side as one entered the holy place, the area in front would have included the holy place and, in particular, the golden table with the bread of the presence (see Exod 40:22–25). See further below for significance (Live the Story: Are We Trying to Make It on Our Own?).

Second, everything is done according to the Lord's command, from the way Aaron lit the lamps (Num 8:2–3; cf. Exod 25:37) to the way the lampstand had been made (Num 8:4; cf. Exod 25:31–36). "It is as if the writer has a list of the commands made in Exodus and is checking them off to assure the reader that the instructions are being fulfilled."[7]

---

4. The focus is on lighting the lamp, but it would be natural to assume Aaron performed the other continual rites of the holy place: placing the showbread on the table and offering incense (Exod 40:22–27).

5. See image at 1:1; see also Exod 40:24–26.

6. Sklar, *Leviticus* (ZECOT), 644.

7. Olson, *Numbers*, 48, who also connects 7:89 with Exod 25:22.

Are We Trying to Make It on Our Own?

This passage is rich with symbolism. Broadly speaking, the light continually burning in the Lord's tabernacle indicates his continual presence (if the lights are on, someone's home), and the high priest's efforts to make it burn continually represent Israel's continual service before him.

But this passage focuses specifically on the high priest's role of ensuring the lampstand casts its light forward (Num 8:2–3), illuminating the holy place and, in particular, the golden table with the bread of the presence. This bread consisted of twelve loaves, representing the twelve tribes. It served as a sign of their covenant relationship with the Lord (Lev 24:8) and as a means of asking him to be faithful and show them his favor (24:7). This adds to the symbolism already noted: not only is the Lord present among his people, who serve him continually, but the light of his presence shines on them, assuring them of his covenant love and favor. Indeed, the Hebrew word for "light up" in Num 8:2 is "exactly the same Hebrew word that the priestly blessing used of God's face shining upon his people (6:25)."[8] As a result, "what we see in Numbers 8:1–4 is a visual metaphor. What the priests declared in the words of their benediction"—The Lord make his face shine on you! (6:25)—"the lampstand of the tabernacle proclaimed as a daily reality: the light of the Lord's blessing rested upon all of the tribes of his people. . . . God's love and acceptance of those who were his was depicted at the very heart of the tabernacle."[9] In short, he delighted to answer their prayer for his love and care. The question for us is whether we are willing to acknowledge our need for these things.

According to the biblical story, we were never intended to try and make it on our own. Acknowledging this is not a sign of weakness but a humble recognition of our finite limitations and our need of the Lord's infinite power and care. A sheep that acknowledges its need of the shepherd's help is not weak, but wise. When the Israelites placed the twelve loaves before the Lord, they acknowledged their need of his favor and help. When the Lord commanded that the light representing his presence shine on those loaves, he acknowledged that caring for the Israelites was the very thing he delighted to do!

He has shown us the same, even more strongly, in Jesus. "In him was life," John announces, "and that life was the light of all mankind" (John 1:4).

---

8. Duguid, *Numbers*, 109.
9. Ibid.

For this reason, Jesus confidently declares "I am the light of the world!" and promises, "Whoever follows me will never walk in darkness, but will have the light of life!" (8:12). Simply stated, "Jesus is the light of God's favor shining in the world,"[10] and he calls us to receive that favor by following him with our whole life into the glorious light of God's love and care.

---

10. Ibid.

CHAPTER 11

Numbers 8:5–26

LISTEN to the Story

⁵The Lord said to Moses: ⁶"Take the Levites from among all the Israelites and make them ceremonially clean. ⁷To purify them, do this: Sprinkle the water of cleansing on them; then have them shave their whole bodies and wash their clothes. And so they will purify themselves. ⁸Have them take a young bull with its grain offering of the finest flour mixed with olive oil; then you are to take a second young bull for a sin offering. ⁹Bring the Levites to the front of the tent of meeting and assemble the whole Israelite community. ¹⁰You are to bring the Levites before the Lord, and the Israelites are to lay their hands on them. ¹¹Aaron is to present the Levites before the Lord as a wave offering from the Israelites, so that they may be ready to do the work of the Lord.

¹²"Then the Levites are to lay their hands on the heads of the bulls, using one for a sin offering to the Lord and the other for a burnt offering, to make atonement for the Levites. ¹³Have the Levites stand in front of Aaron and his sons and then present them as a wave offering to the Lord. ¹⁴In this way you are to set the Levites apart from the other Israelites, and the Levites will be mine.

¹⁵"After you have purified the Levites and presented them as a wave offering, they are to come to do their work at the tent of meeting. ¹⁶They are the Israelites who are to be given wholly to me. I have taken them as my own in place of the firstborn, the first male offspring from every Israelite woman. ¹⁷Every firstborn male in Israel, whether human or animal, is mine. When I struck down all the firstborn in Egypt, I set them apart for myself. ¹⁸And I have taken the Levites in place of all the firstborn sons in Israel. ¹⁹From among all the Israelites, I have given the Levites as gifts to Aaron and his sons to do the work at the tent of meeting on behalf of the Israelites and to make atonement for them so that no plague will strike the Israelites when they go near the sanctuary."

²⁰Moses, Aaron and the whole Israelite community did with the Levites just as the LORD commanded Moses. ²¹The Levites purified themselves and washed their clothes. Then Aaron presented them as a wave offering before the LORD and made atonement for them to purify them. ²²After that, the Levites came to do their work at the tent of meeting under the supervision of Aaron and his sons. They did with the Levites just as the LORD commanded Moses.

²³The LORD said to Moses, ²⁴"This applies to the Levites: Men twenty-five years old or more shall come to take part in the work at the tent of meeting, ²⁵but at the age of fifty, they must retire from their regular service and work no longer. ²⁶They may assist their brothers in performing their duties at the tent of meeting, but they themselves must not do the work. This, then, is how you are to assign the responsibilities of the Levites."

Listening to the Text in the Story: Numbers 3:11–13

Numbers 3 noted that the Levites were taken in place of all the firstborn Israelites to serve at the tabernacle (it may be helpful to review the comments at 3:5–10, 11–13). This passage focuses on the process and the results.[1]

EXPLAIN the Story

Setting Apart the Levites for Tabernacle Service (8:5–22)

In describing how the Levites were taken in place of firstborn Israelites, this text highlights the Levites' purification and their dedication (Num 8:15). First, they are brought into a state of purity higher than that of lay Israelites yet not as high as the priests' ritual holiness (vv. 6, 15, 21).[2] This higher state of purity was necessary for their tabernacle duties and allows them to be dedicated in place of firstborn Israelites to the Lord, who in turn gives the Levites to the priests to perform certain tabernacle duties on the Israelites' behalf (vv. 16–19a). By taking their place, the Levites will "make atonement" for the Israelites (v. 19b), that is, ransom them from any danger that would come

---

1. For the chronological displacement of much of 7:1–10:10, see p. 134, Explain the Story.
2. The Levites are "purified" (8:15, 21) whereas priests are "consecrated" (Lev 8:30), that is, made holy. For details on ritual states, see pp. 32–33, Ritual Purity and Impurity.

(such as a "plague" from the Lord [v. 19]) had the Israelites tried to perform such sacred duties without the proper level of ritual purity.

Five stages of the purification and dedication ceremony may be described.

Stage One: Initial Purification (8:7)

An initial purification rite (Num 8:7) prepares the Levites for being set apart by the Israelites as their representatives (vv. 10–11). First, Moses sprinkles them with "water of cleansing" (v. 7). This water is likely not that described in 19:9, 13, which was prepared long after this event and has a different Hebrew name (a fact obscured by the NIV's use of the same word for both; compare ESV for a better approach). Perhaps this water came from the laver, from which the priests cleansed themselves before tabernacle service (Exod 30:18–21), or perhaps it was spring water, which features in other cleansing rites (cf. Lev 14:51). Either way, water is a natural cleansing symbol. Second, the Levites "shave their whole bodies," as though scraping the skin clean, and "wash their clothes" (Num 8:7), another natural cleansing action. By all of these means, the Levites move into a heightened state of ritual purity (cf. Lev 14:8).

Stage Two: Gathering of Sacrificial Animals and Israelite Congregation (8:8–9)

For a wedding ceremony, one must gather the necessary participants (bride, groom, minister) and objects (rings, wedding license). The same is true for this cleansing and dedication ceremony, which requires the necessary participants (Levites, Israelites) and objects (sacrificial animals).

Stage Three: The People Dedicate the Levites to the Lord on Their Behalf (8:10–11)

In animal sacrifice, the offerer would lean their hand on the animal's head to establish some sort of relationship between the offerer and animal so that the animal would be accepted on the offerer's behalf. Here, the Israelites—perhaps, in particular, their leaders (cf. Lev 4:13–15)—lean their hands on the Levites' heads so they would be accepted on the Israelites' behalf (Num 8:10), in particular, as substitutes "in place of" the firstborn (v. 16).[3]

Aaron then presents the Levites as a wave offering (Num 8:11). "Waving" was a ritual action by which something was dedicated to the Lord, who then usually designates it for the tabernacle in general or the priests in particular

---

3. Derek Kidner, *Leviticus, Numbers, Deuteronomy* (Grand Rapids: Eerdmans, 1971), 38.

(cf. Lev 7:30–31; 10:14–15). Normally, the object was lifted and waved before the Lord, which is impossible here; perhaps Aaron lifted his hands and waved them over the Levites. In any case, they are now set aside on the Israelites' behalf "to do the work of the Lord" (v. 11), which involves disassembling, transporting, and reassembling the tabernacle as well as protecting it from improper approach by the Israelites (see comments at 1:47–53; 3:5–10). Caring for a king's palace was an important duty; the Levites have been dedicated to the Lord to do this on Israel's behalf.

Stage Four: Further Purification: Atoning Sacrifices for the Levites (8:12)
The Levites now present a purification offering[4] and burnt offering for atonement.[5] No specific sin is mentioned, so these offerings may be meant to acknowledge the Levites' general sinfulness and need of atonement when coming into God's presence. The purification offering especially underscored their need to be cleansed and brought into a higher state of purity for their holy tasks (see Num 8:21). Not surprisingly, the priests presented the same type of sacrifices at their ordination (Lev 8:14–20).

Stage Five: Moses Presents the Levites to Aaron and the Priests to Serve Them (8:13)
Moses now takes the atoned and cleansed Levites and "waves" them before the Lord "in front of Aaron and his sons," indicating they are dedicated to the Lord to help the priests in particular (cf. Num 3:5–10; 8:19).

The section ends by summarizing the ceremony (Num 8:21), assuming (but not mentioning) every step outlined in verses 5–13, and underscoring again Israel's obedience in carrying out these commands (v. 20, 22).[6]

Age Restrictions for the Levites' Service (8:23–26)
See at 4:1–49, pp. 78–79.

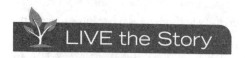

Why Have Age Requirements for the Levites?
Levites had to be aged twenty-five before starting their work and had to retire at fifty (Num 8:23–26). Why?

---

4. NIV footnote; see p. 115n5.
5. For fuller descriptions of these offerings, see at 6:13–20.
6. For 8:14–19, see comments at 3:11–13.

Their primary task involved the heavy work of transporting the tabernacle, so reaching physical maturity first was necessary. But this generally occurs earlier than twenty-five (soldiers started serving at twenty [Num 1:3]), which suggests the requirement also aims at mental, emotional, and spiritual maturity, as appropriate for those handling the Lord's holy possessions.

While the New Testament does not specify age requirements for entering leadership roles, it does emphasize the importance of spiritual maturity. Qualifications for elders and deacons focus on character more than anything else (1 Tim 3:1–13), and Paul's exhortations to those in leadership roles do the same (1 Tim 4:12; 2 Tim 2:22; Titus 2:7). Spiritual maturity matters and comes only from years of walking humbly with the Lord as his Spirit shapes and forms our character. This can happen when we are relatively young (I have seen twenty-five-year-olds who are more spiritually mature than those twice their age), but the New Testament emphasizes that the character traits marking a mature follower of Christ must be present (see again 1 Tim 3:1–13).

As for retiring at fifty, the Levites had to step down from the heavy work of tabernacle transport (Num 8:25), though they could continue helping with other, presumably less taxing, work (v. 26).[7] To this day, mandatory retirement ages are set for certain physically taxing jobs, such as firefighting, and age fifty was realistic for Levites, given the shorter lifespans of the ancient world. But a principle is also present here: our physical abilities diminish as we age, and we are wise to step down at some point from certain leadership roles so other gifted leaders can step into them. Often, we will still be able to help in other ways (v. 26), but our role will become more one of support than of primary leadership.

Noting the Levites' enforced retirement age, an African commentator writes:

> Unfortunately, in many situations in Africa, leaders seem to think that once they have taken office they have to hang on to that office until they die, as if no one else were capable of leading or serving the nation or the church. The pattern that is laid out here in Numbers is a healthier one. The old retire from active service, but are still viewed as wise consultants and counsellors in view of their experience, while younger people take their place. If this approach to leadership were adopted in Africa, it would make a great difference to our continent.[8]

---

7. See at 4:1–49, pp. 78–79.
8. Boniface-Malle, "Numbers," 180–81.

These observations are equally true of church leadership elsewhere. Just as wise parents prepare their children for adulthood and then let them be adults, wise leaders prepare younger counterparts for leadership and then let them lead—which means handing over authority and helping from a support role. What would this look like in our churches? What types of practices or policies might result for leadership positions, whether pastors, elders, deacons, or church staff?

Leadership is about far more than age, however, and this leads to a second question.

What Does God Primarily Require of His Servants?

Many of this chapter's rites focus on ritual purification (see at 8:7 and 8:12 above), a major goal of this ceremony. Note the summary: Aaron "made atonement for them *to purify them*" (v. 21, emphasis added).

Such purification was required because of the Levites' responsibilities with the holy tabernacle. In a hospital, a higher level of physical cleanliness is required for surgeons than for others; entering the operating room dirty would show great disrespect for their role and the space in which they work. Similarly, the Levites require a higher level of ritual purity; for them to handle the Lord's holy property while ritually impure or defiled would show great disrespect for that property and its owner: the Lord! The Lord's servants show their respect for his holiness by cleansing themselves of defilement and seeking to be pure.

The focus here is on ritual purity, but such requirements were to remind Israelites of the far greater need for moral purity, that is, to be unstained by evil and wrongdoing and characterized instead by good and upright behavior.[9] And while all God's people need such purity (Lev 19:2), this passage focuses on the Levites, who have a leadership role at the tabernacle. Though they are not the main leaders (they are under the priest's authority [Num 8:19, 22]), they are leaders nonetheless and must model purity.

The New Testament emphasizes that all leaders must model purity. This is true of the church's main leaders, the elders (1 Tim 3:2–7), who, like priests, have spiritual authority (1 Tim 5:17; cf. Num 17:2–11) and focus on teaching (1 Tim 3:2; cf. Lev 10:11). And it is equally true of deacons, who, like Levites, have a service-oriented role (Acts 6:1–4) but also have a list of character requirements just as high as that for elders (cf. 1 Tim 3:1–7 with 3:8–9, 12–13)! In short, church leaders regardless of role must show respect for God's holiness by keeping themselves unstained by evil and reflecting

---

9. See pp. 32–33, Ritual Purity and Impurity.

God's pure goodness and love into the world. In this way, they will help lead the Lord's people in his paths of goodness, justice, mercy, and love so that every local congregation becomes a beacon of God's character. But this only happens as those in leadership serve as reminders and models of this calling, which leads to a final question.

What Are the Levites Reminders Of?

Clearly, the Levites are substitutes for the Israelites' firstborn sons (Num 8:16–18).[10] But the passage equally emphasizes that they are dedicated to the Lord (vv. 16, 18) and therefore are constant visual reminders that the Israelites' firstborn sons are dedicated to him. Moreover, since the firstborn sons represent all Israel (cf. Exod 4:22), the Levites ultimately remind every Israelite of their own dedication to the Lord. He is the one who redeemed them from slavery to be his firstborn son, faithfully serving their heavenly father in reverent obedience and love. This especially made sense in Israel's historical context. "The firstborn son in the ancient world was . . . the one who would represent the father in many ways as he came into maturity and the father gave him more and more responsibility."[11] Israel's role collectively and individually was to represent the Lord in this world, reflecting into it his goodness, justice, mercy, and love.

Parallels to our modern context are not hard to find. Like elders and deacons today, Levites had a unique calling with unique responsibilities. But just as lay Israelites were not to look at them and say, "They are dedicated to the Lord; I don't need to be," lay Christians must not look at church leaders and say, "They do the Lord's work; I don't have to." The opposite is true. The Levites were to remind the Israelites of the dedication they must also show the Lord. Furthermore, the dedication shown by Christian leaders should remind Christians of their own dedication to the Lord. When Paul exhorts pastor Timothy to "set an example for the believers in speech, in conduct, in love, in faith and in purity" (1 Tim 4:12), he clearly implies every believer is to live these out in their service to God. Our sphere of service may be different, but our level of dedication is to be just as wholehearted.

Only one leader models such dedication blamelessly. Jesus Christ alone has shown us perfectly what it means to live a life of complete dedication to God. The ultimate firstborn Son of God (Rom 8:29; Heb 1:6), Jesus lived a life of perfect purity, unstained by evil and wrongdoing and living out instead

---

10. See further p. 88, What Does a Substitute Do?
11. Stuart, *Exodus*, 146.

complete goodness and love in a perfect representation of the Father in this world. Indeed, he does far more than the Levites ever could. In his role as substitute, he becomes the sacrifice on our behalf to make us pure (2 Cor 5:21). The proper response to such a gift is to follow him in reverent love, offering our lives up to God in wholehearted dedication (Rom 12:1). Does this characterize our life? Where might we be out of step with Jesus in living lives of purity and wholehearted dedication to the Lord? We must come to him honestly about these things, not holding anything back, and can do so confidently, knowing he delights to cleanse us (1 John 1:9), make us whole, and strengthen us to be sons and daughters who represent the Father well in this world!

CHAPTER 12

Numbers 9:1–14

 LISTEN to the Story

¹The LORD spoke to Moses in the Desert of Sinai in the first month of the second year after they came out of Egypt. He said, ²"Have the Israelites celebrate the Passover at the appointed time. ³Celebrate it at the appointed time, at twilight on the fourteenth day of this month, in accordance with all its rules and regulations."

⁴So Moses told the Israelites to celebrate the Passover, ⁵and they did so in the Desert of Sinai at twilight on the fourteenth day of the first month. The Israelites did everything just as the LORD commanded Moses.

⁶But some of them could not celebrate the Passover on that day because they were ceremonially unclean on account of a dead body. So they came to Moses and Aaron that same day ⁷and said to Moses, "We have become unclean because of a dead body, but why should we be kept from presenting the LORD's offering with the other Israelites at the appointed time?"

⁸Moses answered them, "Wait until I find out what the LORD commands concerning you."

⁹Then the LORD said to Moses, ¹⁰"Tell the Israelites: 'When any of you or your descendants are unclean because of a dead body or are away on a journey, they are still to celebrate the LORD's Passover, ¹¹but they are to do it on the fourteenth day of the second month at twilight. They are to eat the lamb, together with unleavened bread and bitter herbs. ¹²They must not leave any of it till morning or break any of its bones. When they celebrate the Passover, they must follow all the regulations. ¹³But if anyone who is ceremonially clean and not on a journey fails to celebrate the Passover, they must be cut off from their people for not presenting the LORD's offering at the appointed time. They will bear the consequences of their sin.

> [14] "'A foreigner residing among you is also to celebrate the LORD's Passover in accordance with its rules and regulations. You must have the same regulations for both the foreigner and the native-born.'"

Listening to the Text in the Story: Exodus 12:1–28

The Passover was one of the most significant celebrations of the Israelite calendar. And no wonder.

> The Passover was first celebrated while the Israelites were enslaved in Egypt (Exod 12:1–28). . . . Every Israelite household was required to slaughter a year-old sheep or goat at twilight on the fourteenth day of the month, apply the animal's blood to their doorposts, and roast and eat the animal the same night with unleavened bread and bitter herbs (Exod 12:1–10). The first celebration was especially significant since the final plague occurred that night (the plague on the firstborn), when the LORD spared the firstborn of the Israelites who had applied the Passover animal's blood to their doorposts (Exod 12:12–13). They were finally released from Egypt the next day (Exod 12:29–36), and thereafter the Passover was to be celebrated to recount how the LORD rescued them in the midst of judgment and led them from the land of slavery (Exod 12:25–27, 42). Indeed, he commands the Israelites to begin their calendar year with this month (Exod 12:2) so that each year began with the reminder: "The LORD is a redeeming God, the one who rescues us from our enemies."[1]

EXPLAIN the Story

Celebrating the Second Passover (9:1–5)

This passage picks up one year after the first Passover (Num 9:1). Since it is the first month,[2] the Lord commands the Passover be celebrated at the proper time ("the fourteenth day of this month") and in the proper way ("in accordance with all its rules and regulations," v. 3). As is common in 1:1–10:10, the Israelites obeyed completely (9:5; see 1:54; 2:34; 8:20).

---

1. Sklar, *Leviticus* (ZECOT), 627.
2. Since 7:1 already mentioned setting up the tabernacle, which happened in the first month (Exod 40:2), this passage naturally follows.

Laws about Celebrating the Passover (9:6–14)

But some Israelites could not obey because they "were ceremonially unclean on account of a dead body" (Num 9:6; cf. 19:11–14). Since the Passover was a "sacred assembly" (Lev 23:4–5), those with ritual impurity could not partake (cf. Lev 7:19–21). The realms of the holy and the impure were not to be mixed (just as in a hospital the realms of the sterile and the unsanitary are not to be mixed).[3] This meant the Passover meal was out of bounds, yet the unclean Israelites wanted to partake, so they come to Moses to see whether this is possible (Num 9:7).

Moses brings their situation to the Lord (Num 9:8), who provides three guiding laws. First, if someone is ritually impure or away on a long journey, they will celebrate the Passover one month later (vv. 10–11a). In his grace, the Lord provides a way his servants may come and worship him. But grace was not license; they still had to follow all other Passover regulations, a few of which are mentioned by way of example (vv. 11b–12; cf. Exod 12:8, 10, 46).

Second, if someone is neither unclean nor away on a journey and yet does not celebrate the Passover, "they must be cut off from their people" (Num 9:13), a phrase referring to exile or even death.[4] This punishment fits the crime. The Passover celebrates the Lord's powerful redemption of Israel from slavery. To partake of it was to proclaim allegiance to the Lord and his redeemed community. To refuse to partake was to deny such allegiance and sever oneself from the Lord and his people; being "cut off" simply sealed that decision.

Third, any resident alien[5] among the people may[6] partake of the Passover but must follow its regulations (Num 9:14), which would include circumcising any males.[7] To partake of the meal celebrating the Lord's redemption of his covenant people, one must have the covenant sign, indicating allegiance to the Lord. Permitting resident aliens to do this is clear testimony to the Lord's desire for his salvation to spread far beyond his people Israel (cf. Gen 12:3).

---

3. For further discussion of ritual realms, see pp. 32–33, Ritual Purity and Impurity.
4. For details, see Sklar, *Leviticus* (ZECOT), 41–42.
5. NIV's "foreigner" is not exact enough. The Hebrew term refers to a non-native who has the same rights as citizens with a few exceptions (e.g., they did not own land, which belonged to native Israelites [Josh 13–19]). This is comparable to resident aliens today: non-natives who have the same rights as citizens with a few exceptions (e.g., they cannot vote in certain elections).
6. NIV's "a foreigner . . . *is also* to celebrate" could imply they must celebrate the Passover. Most versions understand that this law simply indicates what resident aliens must do *if* they choose to celebrate it (ESV, NASB, etc.).
7. Males were the leaders of households and represented all those in it, explaining why females (mercifully) did not require circumcision.

# LIVE the Story

Why Was the Passover to Be Regularly Celebrated?

The Passover celebrated the greatest act of deliverance in Israel's history: the Lord rescuing his people from slavery in Egypt. This was an especially important reminder for Israel at this point in their history. In just over a month,[8] they would leave as the Lord had commanded for the promised land, which was filled with a hostile people they could defeat only with his help. They could find courage to obey by remembering how he had already shown his mighty deliverance.

The Lord's Supper functions similarly for the Christian. Jesus instituted this meal during the Passover (Matt 26:17, 26–28), which was also the time of his crucifixion (Matt 26:17; 27:15–26). The New Testament writers did not miss the connection, calling him "our Passover lamb" (1 Cor 5:7) and even noting that like that lamb, "not one of his bones [was] broken" (John 19:36; cf. Num 9:12). To partake of this meal is to proclaim, "We follow Jesus, God in the flesh, who in his great power and deep love has rescued us and called us into the glorious freedom of his service!" In doing so, we find courage and grace to live our lives fully for him. Celebrating the Lord's acts of deliverance and love in the past is crucial for obeying his commands in the present.

In certain situations, however, the Passover could not be celebrated—at least not at its proper time. This leads to a second question.

What Model Do These Israelites Provide?

Some Israelites were ritually impure at the time of the Passover and thus could not partake (see at 9:6–14). Their response to the situation models two positive behaviors.

First, they treat this meal as holy and not to be eaten in an unworthy manner. This response forms another link between Passover and the Lord's Supper since Christians are strongly warned not to partake "in an unworthy manner" (1 Cor 11:27). In context, partaking in an unworthy manner means refusing to treat other believers as equally valued members of Christ's body, especially when they are of lower economic or social status (1 Cor 11:18–22).[9]

Second, they model a proper desire to celebrate the Passover, so much so their case goes before the Supreme Court: the Lord himself (Num 9:7–8)!

---

8. Cf. Num 9:1 with 10:11.

9. See discussion in Gordon D. Fee, *The First Epistle to the Corinthians,* NICNT (Grand Rapids: Eerdmans, 1987), 531–36 (esp. 535–36), 540–42.

Because this meal is an opportunity to celebrate the Lord's redemption and proclaim allegiance to him and his redeemed community, they view participating as a high priority. Seeing this perspective is a good opportunity for Christians to ask, "When it comes to the Lord's Supper, are we more like these Israelites or those the Lord warns in 9:13, who view the meal as having little importance? Has individualism or a negative view of ritual caused us to see this communal celebration of God's deliverance as less important than it really is? What does prioritizing the Lord's Supper look like in our lives and our church's life?"

The passage finishes by turning from Israelites to non-Israelites, leading to a final question.

Why Have a Law for Non-Israelites?

The final law anticipates non-Israelites will come to believe in the Lord and embrace his covenant (Num 9:14; cf. Exod 12:48). The Israelites should not be surprised. The Lord had told their founding father, Abraham, that through him "all peoples on earth will be blessed" (Gen 12:3). One tangible way this blessing was to occur was when nations living in Israel's midst saw and understood the glories of the God Israel worshiped and chose to put their faith in him. Indeed, by requiring "the same regulations" for resident aliens as for native-born (Num 9:14), this verse encourages Israel to treat the nations in their midst with the same love and mercy they themselves have received from God (cf. Lev 19:34, which commands the same).

Christians do well to ask whether they take a similar loving approach to those who do not yet follow Jesus. Yes, clearly a distinction should be maintained. In Israel, non-Israelites could not partake of the Passover unless they decided to show their allegiance to the Lord by having the covenant sign (circumcision) applied (see at Num 9:14, p. 155). The parallel today is that the Lord's Supper is only for those who have decided to show their allegiance to the Lord by having the covenant sign (baptism) applied. Yet such distinctions must not detract Christians from demonstrating the same love to those outside the church that they themselves have received from God (cf. Titus 3:1–2 with vv. 3–7). Is this our heart's desire? Why or why not? What does it look like to embody God's love in such practical ways that others can see we follow a God worthy of allegiance, who has formed us into a community of goodness and love that would be the deepest blessing to join?

CHAPTER 13

Numbers 9:15–10:10

 LISTEN to the Story

⁹:¹⁵On the day the tabernacle, the tent of the covenant law, was set up, the cloud covered it. From evening till morning the cloud above the tabernacle looked like fire. ¹⁶That is how it continued to be; the cloud covered it, and at night it looked like fire. ¹⁷Whenever the cloud lifted from above the tent, the Israelites set out; wherever the cloud settled, the Israelites encamped. ¹⁸At the Lord's command the Israelites set out, and at his command they encamped. As long as the cloud stayed over the tabernacle, they remained in camp. ¹⁹When the cloud remained over the tabernacle a long time, the Israelites obeyed the Lord's order and did not set out. ²⁰Sometimes the cloud was over the tabernacle only a few days; at the Lord's command they would encamp, and then at his command they would set out. ²¹Sometimes the cloud stayed only from evening till morning, and when it lifted in the morning, they set out. Whether by day or by night, whenever the cloud lifted, they set out. ²²Whether the cloud stayed over the tabernacle for two days or a month or a year, the Israelites would remain in camp and not set out; but when it lifted, they would set out. ²³At the Lord's command they encamped, and at the Lord's command they set out. They obeyed the Lord's order, in accordance with his command through Moses.

¹⁰:¹The Lord said to Moses: ²"Make two trumpets of hammered silver, and use them for calling the community together and for having the camps set out. ³When both are sounded, the whole community is to assemble before you at the entrance to the tent of meeting. ⁴If only one is sounded, the leaders—the heads of the clans of Israel—are to assemble before you. ⁵When a trumpet blast is sounded, the tribes camping on the east are to set out. ⁶At the sounding of a second blast, the camps on the south are to set out. The blast will be the signal for setting out. ⁷To gather the assembly, blow the trumpets, but not with the signal for setting out.

> ⁸"The sons of Aaron, the priests, are to blow the trumpets. This is to be a lasting ordinance for you and the generations to come. ⁹When you go into battle in your own land against an enemy who is oppressing you, sound a blast on the trumpets. Then you will be remembered by the LORD your God and rescued from your enemies. ¹⁰Also at your times of rejoicing—your appointed festivals and New Moon feasts—you are to sound the trumpets over your burnt offerings and fellowship offerings, and they will be a memorial for you before your God. I am the LORD your God."

Listening to the Text in the Story: Exodus 40:34–38

The Israelites are on the verge of breaking camp and departing for the promised land (Num 10:11). The text now covers two items relevant to their imminent departure. First, it refers back to Exodus 40:34–38, where the Lord descended on the tabernacle in a cloud of glory representing his presence as divine King in Israel's midst.[1] That cloud will now visually lead the Israelites through the wilderness (Num 9:15–23).

Second, it discusses the silver trumpets, which are an auditory way of giving the camp more specific instructions (Num 10:1–8) as well as a means for priests to pray on Israel's behalf (vv. 9–10). We gain possible insight into their shape by considering examples from Egypt, where the Israelites had been living. "A particularly well-known example, also made of silver, was discovered in Tutankhamen's tomb (mid-fourteenth cent. BC),"[2] the same general timeframe the Bible places Moses. Its length is 23 inches (58.2 cm), with a tube starting at .66 inches (1.7 cm) near the mouthpiece, growing to 1 inch (2.6 cm) at the bell, which flares to a width of 3.5 inches (8.2 cm).[3] Recordings of these trumpets being blown can be easily found online.[4]

---

1. For the Lord's presence as King in Israel's camp, see pp. 59–61, Listening to the Text in the Story.
2. Ashley, *Numbers*, 187.
3. Sprinkle, *Leviticus and Numbers*, 241.
4. e.g., "King Tutankhamun's Trumpets played after 3000+ years," https://www.youtube.com/watch?v=Qt9AyV3hnlc (a search for "King Tut's trumpets" brings up several examples). I am thankful to George Bryan for bringing these recordings to my attention.

EXPLAIN the Story

The Cloud of Glory: The Lord's Guiding Presence among His People (9:15–23)

The Hebrew of Numbers 9:15–23 marks the passage as a long but important aside describing the cloud's presence and function.[5] In terms of presence (vv. 15–16), the cloud had first descended on the tabernacle when it was set up (Exod 40:2, 34) and protected the Israelites from full exposure to the Lord's lethally overwhelming radiance (33:20). If the cloud's appearance on Mt. Sinai is a guide, it was lit up with fire and lightning (19:18; 20:18–21), making the Lord's power known and his presence among his people clear, especially at night when the cloud "looked like fire," a nuclear night light of the Lord's glory (Num 9:15–16).[6] But day or night, it "continued to be" there (v. 16), a constant reminder the Lord was with Israel at the tabernacle where he dwelt as covenant King in their midst.[7]

In terms of function (Num 9:17–23), the Lord used the cloud to tell the Israelites when to break camp and where to set it up. The highly repetitive verses explain the same point from different angles to emphasize: by day or night, after a short time frame or long, the Israelites obediently followed the Lord's guidance by cloud. Their King was leading them to the land he had promised, and they were faithfully following (cf. Exod 13:21–22; 40:36–38).

One Use of Trumpets: Giving Direction to the Israelites (10:1–7)

Trumpets were of two basic types: those made of a ram's horn (Josh 6:4) and those made of metal. This passage focuses on metal trumpets, in this case, silver and meant especially for priests (Num 10:2, 8). Unlike modern trumpets, which have different parts, these were presumably one piece of hammered silver (cf. Exod 25:36).[8]

While the cloud guided the Israelites generally, trumpet signals provided more specific direction about gathering and dispersing (Num 10:2). Two gathering signals are given. When both trumpets are blown (10:3), the whole congregation gathers before Moses at the tent, perhaps to receive instruction

---

5. Hebrew narrative usually has a series of clauses beginning with verbal forms known as *wayyiqtols*. When *wayyiqtols* are avoided (as happens in 9:15–23), the text is often providing background information.
6. Cf. Gane, *Leviticus, Numbers*, 556.
7. See n1; for "tabernacle" and "tent of the covenant law" (9:15) see at 1:47–53.
8. See also at Listening to the Text in the Story, p. 159.

(Exod 35:1) or partake in special ceremonies (Lev 8:3; 9:5; Num 8:9). When one is blown (10:4), only the leaders gather, perhaps to receive direction about duties (1:4–16). As for dispersing, the trumpets are blown with a special "blast" (10:5), distinct from the other signals and repeated each time a different part of the camp is to set out (10:6–7).[9] "This . . . function raises our anticipation for the long-awaited march that is set to begin immediately in Num. 10:11."[10]

Related Commands (10:8)

The trumpets are to be used throughout coming generations (Num 10:8b) and are to be blown by the priests (v. 8a). The priests' involvement makes good sense. As the Lord's servants, they would be giving direction from him (vv. 1–7); as the people's mediators, they would be praying for them (vv. 9–10).

A Second Use of Trumpets: Musical Prayers for the Lord's Help and Favor (10:9–10)

The trumpet blasts served as musical prayers for the Lord to "remember" his people (Num 10:9),[11] not because he had forgotten them (cf. Isa 49:15–16) but because the language of remembrance describes the Lord showing his people they are in the forefront of his thoughts. He does this by granting them favor (Gen 8:1; 19:29) and, in particular, by demonstrating faithfulness to his covenant promises (Gen 9:15, 16; Exod 2:24). In war, the trumpet blasts were prayers for the Lord's help and deliverance (Num 10:9).[12] In worship, they were prayers the Lord would accept offerings with favor (v. 10).[13] Either way, he would delight to answer these prayers made on the Israelites' behalf. He is "the LORD [their] God" (v. 10), who will continue to deliver and shine his favor on his people as they follow him in obedience and love.

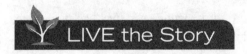

What Is the Proper Response to a King of Glory?

The Lord appears to Israel in a cloud because beholding him with the naked eye is more dangerous than staring at the sun. He is a king of such power and

---

9. For the march's full order, see 10:11–28.
10. Olson, *Numbers*, 54.
11. The word "memorial" (10:10) is built on the same root.
12. For narrative examples, see Num 31:1–7 and 2 Chr 13:1–19, esp. vv. 12–16.
13. For a narrative example, see 2 Chr 29:25–28.

purity that seeing him as he is would be a power surge of goodness and glory that would overwhelm mortal capacities. A filter is needed.

And so he comes near in a cloud, which shades the Israelites from full exposure to his radiance and yet is bursting with glory, a clear sign by day or night that this King, the Lord, is with them (Num 9:15–16). They needed to know this; they were in a wilderness, heading to a land filled with enemies. Their only hope of survival was for their great King to go before them, delivering them in his power and caring for them in his love. The cloud promised them exactly this, and so they followed, day or night, wherever it led (vv. 17–23). We know from later passages their obedience was far from perfect (Num 14!). But our text focuses on those times they did obey and, in so doing, modeled for the coming generations the proper response to a King so powerful and good: follow him.

The New Testament makes clear how the Lord's kingly presence among his people is fulfilled in Jesus. Just as God dwelt over the tabernacle in Israel's midst and revealed his glory in the cloud, so God came to "tabernacle" among us in the person of Jesus. The incarnation was the filter through which God showed us his glory and manifested his presence (John 1:14). And just as God was present in his people's midst as King, so Jesus is present with us as King. "All authority in heaven and on earth has been given to me" (Matt 28:18), Jesus said. He is the one we are to follow—and to exhort others to follow (v. 19). If this seems impossible or overwhelming—if the wilderness seems too hard or the future too frightening—he reminds us of the most important promise of all: "And surely I am with you always, to the very end of the age" (v. 20). The King is with us! His powerful presence means we have nothing to fear, and his goodness means his guidance is trustworthy. What does it look like for us to follow him with confident obedience no matter what our wilderness may be?

As the Israelites followed the Lord in the wilderness, they had more than a cloud for guidance; they also had trumpet sounds, which leads to a second question.

What Does a Trumpet Sound Do (Part 1)?

Fire alarms, school bells, and church bells share a common feature: they communicate information quickly to large groups of people. In the ancient world, trumpet signals did the same (see Judg 3:27–28; 2 Sam 2:28). Our passage describes different signals, each with its own message for the people (see at Num 10:1–7) and always to be sounded by priests (10:8). The priests' involvement leads to two observations.

First, for proper communication to occur, the different sounds had to be made well, requiring skill borne of long practice. Thus the priests who did this "were not casual players who would 'jam' from time to time; they were professional players whose making of music was as serious as the work of a soldier on the battlefield [cf. v. 9!] and as sacred as any task done by a sacrificing priest in the tabernacle courts [cf. v. 10!]."[14] From the beginning, skillful musicians have had a role in leading God's people.

Second, the fact the signals are sounded only by priests (Num 10:8), as the Lord's servants, underscores that *the Lord* is using these signals to lead his people. On Israel's way to the promised land, he will tell them when to disperse and when to gather. In the New Testament, Jesus picks up on this gathering trumpet call in a profound way. In describing the end times (Matt 24:30–31), he combines the imagery of a cloud, glory, and a trumpet call when he speaks of himself as "the Son of Man, who descends from heaven in glory on a cloud," with "accompanying angels [taking] over the priestly role of blowing the trumpets to assemble the elect from around the world."[15] This is a hope-filled message! "In Europe the faithful have traditionally been called to worship by church bells, but in the last day the elect will once again be summoned 'with a loud trumpet call', 'and the dead shall be raised incorruptible' (Mt. 24:31; I Cor. 15:52 AV; cf. Rev. 8–9)."[16] Trumpet sounds can thus serve as reminders of the future glory promised to God's people.

But in our passage they also serve as "reminders" to the Lord, leading to a final question.

What Does a Trumpet Sound Do (Part 2)?

The Psalms contain prayers asking the Lord to remember his people (Pss 74:2; 106:4; 119:49; etc.) or rejoicing because he has (Pss 105:8, 42; 106:45; etc.). As noted above (Num 10:9–10), to ask the Lord to remember his people is to pray, "O Lord, make clear that your people are in the forefront of your thoughts by delivering them and showing them your favor in practical ways." As mere human beings, we are in desperate need of the Lord's help and favor; by asking for it, we acknowledge our finite weakness and his infinite strength.

Our need for God's help is no different today, so it is not surprising that Jesus tells "his disciples a parable to show them that they should always pray and not give up" (Luke 18:1). In it, he speaks of a widow who continues coming to a godless judge, pleading for deliverance. The judge finally grants

---

14. Allen, "Numbers," 779.
15. Dozeman, "Numbers," 91.
16. Wenham, *Numbers*, 102.

her request, not out of care but to be rid of the nuisance (vv. 2–5)! Jesus then turns the story on its head: if that happens with a powerless widow's plea before a godless judge, how much more will it happen for God's powerless children who bring their requests before the one who has chosen them as his very own (vv. 6–8a)! He delights showing his children favor and help. Indeed, our passage ends by reminding that he is "the Lord [our] God" (Num 10:10), meaning we come to him as a child to a loving father, as a servant to a good and gracious king. We do well to ask, "How should this affect the way we pray? How often we pray? What does the life of prayer look like for those convinced of their need of God's help—and of his delight to help them?"

CHAPTER 14

Numbers 10:11-36

 LISTEN to the Story

¹¹On the twentieth day of the second month of the second year, the cloud lifted from above the tabernacle of the covenant law. ¹²Then the Israelites set out from the Desert of Sinai and traveled from place to place until the cloud came to rest in the Desert of Paran. ¹³They set out, this first time, at the Lord's command through Moses.

¹⁴The divisions of the camp of Judah went first, under their standard. Nahshon son of Amminadab was in command. ¹⁵Nethanel son of Zuar was over the division of the tribe of Issachar, ¹⁶and Eliab son of Helon was over the division of the tribe of Zebulun. ¹⁷Then the tabernacle was taken down, and the Gershonites and Merarites, who carried it, set out.

¹⁸The divisions of the camp of Reuben went next, under their standard. Elizur son of Shedeur was in command. ¹⁹Shelumiel son of Zurishaddai was over the division of the tribe of Simeon, ²⁰and Eliasaph son of Deuel was over the division of the tribe of Gad. ²¹Then the Kohathites set out, carrying the holy things. The tabernacle was to be set up before they arrived.

²²The divisions of the camp of Ephraim went next, under their standard. Elishama son of Ammihud was in command. ²³Gamaliel son of Pedahzur was over the division of the tribe of Manasseh, ²⁴and Abidan son of Gideoni was over the division of the tribe of Benjamin.

²⁵Finally, as the rear guard for all the units, the divisions of the camp of Dan set out under their standard. Ahiezer son of Ammishaddai was in command. ²⁶Pagiel son of Okran was over the division of the tribe of Asher, ²⁷and Ahira son of Enan was over the division of the tribe of Naphtali. ²⁸This was the order of march for the Israelite divisions as they set out.

²⁹Now Moses said to Hobab son of Reuel the Midianite, Moses' father-in-law, "We are setting out for the place about which the Lord said, 'I will

give it to you.' Come with us and we will treat you well, for the LORD has promised good things to Israel."

³⁰He answered, "No, I will not go; I am going back to my own land and my own people."

³¹But Moses said, "Please do not leave us. You know where we should camp in the wilderness, and you can be our eyes. ³²If you come with us, we will share with you whatever good things the LORD gives us."

³³So they set out from the mountain of the LORD and traveled for three days. The ark of the covenant of the LORD went before them during those three days to find them a place to rest. ³⁴The cloud of the LORD was over them by day when they set out from the camp.

³⁵Whenever the ark set out, Moses said,

"Rise up, LORD!
    May your enemies be scattered;
    may your foes flee before you."

³⁶Whenever it came to rest, he said,

"Return, LORD,
    to the countless thousands of Israel."

Listening to the Text in the Story: Numbers 1:1–10:10

As noted earlier, the first major section of Numbers (chs. 1–25) focuses on the first generation of Israelites and has two halves.[1] The first starts positively and is characterized by the Israelites' regular obedience (1:1–10:10). The second becomes negative and is characterized by their regular rebellion (10:11–25:18).[2]

But in Numbers 10:11–36 the negativity has not yet started. Israel has been encamped at Mt. Sinai since Exodus 19; now they depart in battle formation "at the LORD's command through Moses" (Num 10:13). This demonstrates how their camp will look when they march toward the promised land (vv. 14–28) and underscores that the Lord continues in their midst as divine King to guide and protect (vv. 33–36). Their departure marks the beginning

---

1. See p. 48, Listening to the Text in the Story.
2. For a detailed overview of this second section, see discussion starting at p. 10.

of a travel narrative that continues until 12:16, when they finally arrive at the destination identified in 10:12: the desert of Paran.

The Cloud Lifts and the Israelites Depart (10:11–13)

At long last, the cloud of the Lord's guiding presence lifts from the tabernacle (Num 10:11),[3] and the Israelites begin their journey toward the promised land (v. 12). The "second month" places this in April or May. They have been at Mt. Sinai for eleven months and nineteen days,[4] which, from the reader's perspective, has taken fifty-nine chapters![5] With the Israelites now ready to depart, verse 10:12 summarizes the coming journey, naming the desert of Paran as the camp's first major destination (intermediary stops will be named along the way, e.g., 11:3, 34–35). This was on Canaan's southern border, a natural entry point into the land (see at 12:16 for details, p. 187). The Israelites will arrive there at the end of chapter 12, with our passage emphasizing they are embarking in accordance with the Lord's command through Moses (10:13).[6] The Lord is guiding Israel, and at this point, Israel is obediently following.

The Marching Order Described (10:14–28)

Mention of Israel's "divisions" and "standards" reminds us Israel is headed for war in the promised land. For a diagram of the tribes' marching order and related comments, see at 2:3–31 (pp. 62–64; reviewing those comments at this point would be helpful). Numbers 10 provides a bit more detail on the Levites (cf. 2:17), specifying that the Gershonites and Merarites dismantle the tabernacle (cf. 4:21–33), set out after Judah's camp (10:17), and are followed first by Reuben's camp (v. 18) and then by the Kohathites, who carry the tabernacle furniture (v. 21; cf. 4:1–20).[7] This order allows the tabernacle to be reassembled on the other end so the furniture can simply be "moved in" when the Kohathites arrive (v. 21).

---

3. For "tabernacle of the covenant law," see at 1:47–53, p. 53.
4. See table, p. 51.
5. That is, Exod 19–Num 10; noted by Peter Enns, *Exodus*, NIVAC (Grand Rapids: Zondervan Academic, 2000), 386.
6. "Through Moses" is perhaps a reference to the trumpet signals just described (Num 10:1–7; cf. 9:23).
7. See diagram, p. 63. The only exception to the above arrangement is the ark, which most clearly represents the Lord's presence and therefore marches ahead of the entire camp; see at 10:33–36, pp. 168–69.

Request for Hobab to Stay (10:29–32)

Moses's father-in-law, a Midianite[8] named Reuel, was first introduced in Exodus 2:18; this verse introduces his son, Hobab, Moses's brother-in-law.[9] Moses asks him to come along, promising the Israelites will share with him whatever good the Lord does for them, in this way treating him as one of their own (Num 10:29, 32). This was in keeping with the Lord's intent for the Israelites: through them, all the families of the earth would be blessed (Gen 12:3).

Hobab initially refuses (Num 10:30), perhaps because of a natural desire to stay connected to his own land and people or perhaps because he was following custom by declining first, thus allowing Moses to repeat his request more forcefully.[10] Either way, Moses insists, stating, "You know where we should camp in the wilderness, and you can be our eyes" (v. 31). Since the Lord is guiding Israel, this statement could refer to Hobab providing specific logistical advice about desert living once they arrive at a camping spot. (Just as the Israelites needed skilled shepherds even though the Lord would bless their flocks and herds, so they needed skilled guides even though the Lord would show them where to camp.) No further refusal is recorded, so Hobab presumably agreed.

The Lord Guides the Israelites by His Ark and Cloud (10:33–36)

The narrative resumes the Israelites' departure, noting they leave Mt. Sinai on a three-day journey (perhaps to Taberah; Num 11:3). Mt. Sinai is here called "the mountain of the Lord" (10:33), a phrase occurring elsewhere only in Genesis 22:14 in the famous saying, "On the mountain of the Lord it will be provided." And while Genesis 22:14 does not refer to Mt. Sinai, the use of the phrase here seems to frame their departure with the reminder that the Lord will faithfully provide for all their needs.

The graphic picture now presented underscores this. As the Israelites depart Mt. Sinai (Num 10:33), the cloud of the Lord's presence rests over them (v. 34), guiding them and providing protective shade whenever they travel

---

8. Also referred to as a Kenite (Judg 1:16; 4:11); the "Midianites" may have been a larger grouping of which "Kenites" were a part (Milgrom, *Numbers*, 78, citing William J. Dumbrell, "Midian: A Land or a League?" *VT* 25 [1975]: 323–37), although there is no scholarly consensus at this point in time.

9. For a survey of approaches to the relationship between Reuel (Exod 2:18; Num 10:29), Jethro (Exod 3:1; 4:18; 18:1; etc.), and Hobab (Num 10:29; Judg 4:11), see Ashley, *Numbers*, 194–97, who suggests (with many commentators) that the simplest understanding is that Reuel and Jethro are two names for the same person, and Hobab is his son. See further discussion in Sklar, *Additional Notes*, at 10:29.

10. NET marginal note; cf. Gen 23:7–16.

by day (cf. Ps 105:39). At their head is the "ark of the covenant of the LORD" (Num 10:33). In the Hebrew, this is the first time the word "covenant" occurs together with the ark.[11] This highlights what the ark represents: the Lord is the God who has entered into covenant relationship with Israel and will keep his covenant promises to them. He will rise up in power to scatter his (and their) enemies (v. 35) and will dwell among them, the ones to whom he has already shown his faithfulness by multiplying them into "countless thousands" (v. 36; cf. Gen 15:5; 24:60).

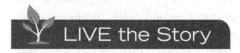

What Keeps Us from Being Afraid?

From a human perspective, the Israelites had every reason to fear. They were heading to a land they had never visited, filled with an enemy they had never seen. Uncertainty is the hardest part. If the only thing you know for certain is that your future will involve great difficulty, there is every reason to fear.

But this story makes clear the Israelites knew one other fact with certainty: the Lord himself would go with them, overshadowing them with his protective cloud (Num 10:34) and marching at their head by means of his ark (v. 33). The ark receives special focus. For the first time it is called "the ark of the covenant of the LORD" (v. 33), a reminder that Israel's covenant-keeping God is in their midst and would be faithful to his promises to bless and protect (see at 10:33–36, pp. 168–69). Moses, in fact, immediately prays for these promises to be fulfilled: that the Lord would defeat his and their enemies (v. 35) and that he would dwell in their midst (v. 36). The Lord's faithful presence changes everything. He is a God who delivers his people. They had nothing to fear.

The writer of Psalm 68 saw this clearly. Looking back to this passage (68:1; cf. Num 10:35), he elaborates on the result of the Lord's delivering presence: enemies melt like wax, while his people are filled with joy (Ps 68:2–3); the Lord is a father to the fatherless and a protector of widows (v. 5); he scatters kings before them, providing for their needs and giving them a home (vv. 7–10, 12, 14); he bears their burdens daily and delivers them from death (vv. 19–20); he gives his people power and strength (v. 35). No matter our uncertainty about the future, we need not fear. If the Lord is our God, he is with us, and he is

---

11. NIV's "ark of the covenant law" (Exod 25:22; Num 4:5; etc.) is usually translated "ark of the testimony" (the Hebrew root for "covenant" does not occur in those verses). After Num 10:33, the phrase "ark of the covenant of the LORD" is commonly used (14:44; Deut 10:8; Josh 3:3: 4:7; etc.).

mighty to save. How can this reality speak to our fears or worries? What does it mean for us to trust in his powerful presence in our lives?

As this passage goes on to show, there is more good news to be had. The Lord is not simply a God who delivers his people, he is also one who leads his people.

Where Does the Lord Lead His People To?

"The ark of the covenant of the Lord went before them during those three days to find them a place to rest" (Num 10:33). In this verse, "place to rest" refers to the first place of encampment the Lord led Israel. But it also recalls the Lord's promise to give Israel their own land (cf. Deut 12:9), a far greater "resting place" where they could settle. Simply put, the Lord leads his people to a place of rest.

Other verses make clear what this "rest" involves. For Israel, it especially meant security and freedom from worry about enemies (see Deut 12:10; Josh 21:44). Such rest implies having peace and tranquility, being unburdened by fear and care, and it assumes these come because the Lord is with his people. As the psalmist says, "He makes me lie down in green pastures, he leads me beside quiet waters" (Ps 23:2), more woodenly translated, "waters *of rest.*" The picture is one of calm and peace, a place the sheep can rest without fear or concern because their good shepherd is with them.

As the story of the Bible moves on, the Lord provides his own son as a shepherd to give us soul-satisfying rest. "Come to me, all who labor and are heavy laden, and I will give you rest," says Jesus. "Take my yoke upon you, and learn from me, for I am gentle and lowly in heart, and you will find rest for your souls. For my yoke is easy, and my burden is light" (Matt 11:28–30, ESV). To take on his yoke is to submit to his direction and guidance. Far from being a burden, however, Jesus's yoke provides rest for our souls because he leads us in the Lord's ways, the very ways we have been created to follow. These are green pastures where we can flourish, waters of rest where we can have calm and peace. In light of this, we might consider: are there areas of our lives where we are refusing his yoke? Are there places where our lack of rest is tied directly to our unwillingness to trust his guidance?

While the passage focuses on the ways in which Israel was to enter this rest, it also makes clear it was not meant only for Israel.

Who Is This Rest For?

We read here of a short conversation between Moses and his brother-in-law Hobab (Num 10:29–32). Hobab is not an Israelite; he is from Midian (v. 29).

But Moses immediately invites him to come with Israel to the promised land (v. 29) and share in "whatever good things the LORD gives us" (v. 32).[12] Simply put, Moses models that the Lord intends his people to share their covenant blessings with the world, in direct keeping with the Lord's original words to Israel's forefather, Abraham: "in you all the families of the earth shall be blessed" (Gen 12:3, ESV).

In the context of our passage, a certain tension arises since Israel is on their way to engage in warfare in the promised land and fight against the nations. This will be discussed in further detail at Numbers 21.[13] But Israel's normal function was to be a "kingdom of priests and a holy nation" (Exod 19:6). Within Israel, priests were to help people in their relationship with God in a number of different ways. Within the world, Israel was to have that same function.

> As a kingdom of priests, Israel is called to represent the nations before God, to mediate God's redemptive purpose in the world. A priest stands between God and the people, representing each to the other. The fundamental purpose of priests in Israel was to represent the people before God through their sacrificial and intercessory ministry. Yahweh here summons Israel as an entire nation to act as a priest, a covenantal mediator between him and the rest of the world. In this priestly service, he expects Israel to pray for, love, minister to, and witness to the nations.[14]

In the New Testament, followers of Jesus are called to step into this priestly role (1 Pet 2:9). In this role, we are expected "to pray for, love, minister to, and witness to the nations," inviting them into the same soul-satisfying rest we have found in Jesus. We do well to ask, "What does it mean for us to carry out that role in our relationships today? What does it mean for this to be a priority in our lives? Who are the Hobabs in our lives and how might we get to a place where we can invite them to know God's rest in Jesus?"

---

12. True, Moses at one point says Hobab should come with them to be a wilderness guide (Num 10:31), but he does not start there (v. 29), giving the impression this is more of an excuse to get him to come along than the primary motivation.

13. See pp. 281–83, Why Such Severe Destruction?

14. Michael D. Williams, *Far as the Curse is Found: The Covenant Story of Redemption* (Phillipsburg, NJ: P&R Publishing, 2005), 138.

CHAPTER 15

Numbers 11:1-35

 LISTEN to the Story

¹Now the people complained about their hardships in the hearing of the LORD, and when he heard them his anger was aroused. Then fire from the LORD burned among them and consumed some of the outskirts of the camp. ²When the people cried out to Moses, he prayed to the LORD and the fire died down. ³So that place was called Taberah, because fire from the LORD had burned among them.

⁴The rabble with them began to crave other food, and again the Israelites started wailing and said, "If only we had meat to eat! ⁵We remember the fish we ate in Egypt at no cost—also the cucumbers, melons, leeks, onions and garlic. ⁶But now we have lost our appetite; we never see anything but this manna!"

⁷The manna was like coriander seed and looked like resin. ⁸The people went around gathering it, and then ground it in a hand mill or crushed it in a mortar. They cooked it in a pot or made it into loaves. And it tasted like something made with olive oil. ⁹When the dew settled on the camp at night, the manna also came down.

¹⁰Moses heard the people of every family wailing at the entrance to their tents. The LORD became exceedingly angry, and Moses was troubled. ¹¹He asked the LORD, "Why have you brought this trouble on your servant? What have I done to displease you that you put the burden of all these people on me? ¹²Did I conceive all these people? Did I give them birth? Why do you tell me to carry them in my arms, as a nurse carries an infant, to the land you promised on oath to their ancestors? ¹³Where can I get meat for all these people? They keep wailing to me, 'Give us meat to eat!' ¹⁴I cannot carry all these people by myself; the burden is too heavy for me. ¹⁵If this is how you are going to treat me, please go ahead and kill me—if I have found favor in your eyes—and do not let me face my own ruin."

¹⁶The LORD said to Moses: "Bring me seventy of Israel's elders who are

known to you as leaders and officials among the people. Have them come to the tent of meeting, that they may stand there with you. ¹⁷I will come down and speak with you there, and I will take some of the power of the Spirit that is on you and put it on them. They will share the burden of the people with you so that you will not have to carry it alone.

¹⁸"Tell the people: 'Consecrate yourselves in preparation for tomorrow, when you will eat meat. The Lord heard you when you wailed, "If only we had meat to eat! We were better off in Egypt!" Now the Lord will give you meat, and you will eat it. ¹⁹You will not eat it for just one day, or two days, or five, ten or twenty days, ²⁰but for a whole month—until it comes out of your nostrils and you loathe it—because you have rejected the Lord, who is among you, and have wailed before him, saying, "Why did we ever leave Egypt?"'"

²¹But Moses said, "Here I am among six hundred thousand men on foot, and you say, 'I will give them meat to eat for a whole month!' ²²Would they have enough if flocks and herds were slaughtered for them? Would they have enough if all the fish in the sea were caught for them?"

²³The Lord answered Moses, "Is the Lord's arm too short? Now you will see whether or not what I say will come true for you."

²⁴So Moses went out and told the people what the Lord had said. He brought together seventy of their elders and had them stand around the tent. ²⁵Then the Lord came down in the cloud and spoke with him, and he took some of the power of the Spirit that was on him and put it on the seventy elders. When the Spirit rested on them, they prophesied—but did not do so again.

²⁶However, two men, whose names were Eldad and Medad, had remained in the camp. They were listed among the elders, but did not go out to the tent. Yet the Spirit also rested on them, and they prophesied in the camp. ²⁷A young man ran and told Moses, "Eldad and Medad are prophesying in the camp."

²⁸Joshua son of Nun, who had been Moses' aide since youth, spoke up and said, "Moses, my lord, stop them!"

²⁹But Moses replied, "Are you jealous for my sake? I wish that all the Lord's people were prophets and that the Lord would put his Spirit on them!" ³⁰Then Moses and the elders of Israel returned to the camp.

³¹Now a wind went out from the Lord and drove quail in from the sea. It scattered them up to two cubits deep all around the camp, as far as a

> day's walk in any direction. ³²All that day and night and all the next day the people went out and gathered quail. No one gathered less than ten homers. Then they spread them out all around the camp. ³³But while the meat was still between their teeth and before it could be consumed, the anger of the LORD burned against the people, and he struck them with a severe plague. ³⁴Therefore the place was named Kibroth Hattaavah, because there they buried the people who had craved other food.
>
> ³⁵From Kibroth Hattaavah the people traveled to Hazeroth and stayed there.

Listening to the Text in the Story: Exodus 15:22–24; 17:1–7; Numbers 1:54; 2:34; 4:49; 8:2, 32; 9:5, 23

With this chapter, the book of Numbers takes a tragic turn. Up to this point, the Israelites have been generally faithful, being careful to do "just as the LORD commanded" (Num 1:54; cf. 2:34; 4:49; 8:3, 22; 9:5, 23). Now, the grumbling and complaining that marked some of their behavior in Exodus (15:22–24; 17:1–7) begins to characterize all they do (cf. 14:39–45; 16:1–14; 20:2–5; 25:1–3). Chapters 11–12 introduce this tragic turn with three stories in which rebellious complaint is met with the Lord's discipline or judgment, a warning for Israel not to repeat such rebellious behavior (and sadly, a warning that goes unheeded).

EXPLAIN the Story

The People Complain at Taberah (11:1–3)

One goal of this short story is to explain why the Israelites' first stop was named Taberah (Num 11:3; see below). But a larger goal is to give us a template of what will happen repeatedly in chapters 11–25: the people sin, the Lord's judgment comes (or is announced), Moses intercedes as mediator, and the Lord's anger is turned away.[1]

In this story, the people's complaints start as soon as they depart for the promised land (Num 11:1). This will be the first of three complaint stories found in Numbers 11–12 and, since repeating something three times

---

1. For fuller discussion, see pp. 10–16, Departing for the Promised Land.

was a way to emphasize it (cf. Isa 6:3), it becomes clear that grumbling and complaining characterized this generation.

The complaint's cause is not mentioned here. Moving through the wilderness as a large group was undoubtedly difficult, but the Lord's provision, both past and present (cf. Num 11:4–6), meant such complaints were a shocking denial of the Lord's goodness (cf. 10:29), a form of saying, "Lord, despite all you've done to provide to this point, you cannot be trusted, and we turn away from you and your past provision with utter contempt" (14:11). The Israelites are like children who know better but choose to turn away scornfully from a parent who has loved and cared for them well. The Lord responds with justified anger and, as happens elsewhere, sends a literal fire of judgment (11:1; cf. 16:35). Whether this was a series of lightning strikes or a more dramatic pillar of fire descending from heaven is not stated; either way, the living and powerful God is clearly among them. Mercifully, the burning takes place at "the outskirts of the camp" (11:1), not in its densely populated midst, presumably serving as a warning. The people get the message and immediately cry out for help to Moses, who once more intercedes on their behalf (cf. Exod 32:11–14). The Lord hears his prayer and relents (Num 11:2), but the place is named Taberah (Heb. for "burning"), a constant reminder of the rebellion that happened here—and a warning not to repeat it. Sadly, the lesson was not learned, as the next story shows.

More Grumbling, Help for Moses in Leading the People, the Lord's Judgment (11:4–35)

This story consists of four scenes. In the first (Num 11:4–9), the "rabble"[2]—or perhaps simply "mixed multitude" (NET)[3]—begins "to crave other food" (v. 4), and their complaints spread like a fast-growing cancer to all Israel. The Israelites primarily desire meat, though they also long for other types of foods they ate in Egypt (v. 5). But their memory is incredibly selective, focusing on the very few pleasures they knew in Egypt while ignoring the host of trials and sufferings they experienced (cf. Exod 2:23–24; 3:7, 9; 6:5, 9). They are like freed prisoners looking back with nostalgia on prison food.

Their complaints about what they lack are coupled with ingratitude for what they have: the sweet manna the Lord freely provided (Num 11:6–9; cf. Exod 16:31). The Israelites would turn it into a type of flour they could use for

---

2. Since this group is contrasted with "the Israelites" later in the verse, it likely consists of non-Israelites that joined Israel during the exodus (cf. Exod 12:38).

3. The Hebrew term occurs only here and is built on a root meaning "to gather"; it is not clear it implies the negative connotation of "rabble."

making breads and had a fresh supply each morning, miraculously provided by the Lord (see Exod 16 for the full story). Despite this, they refuse to believe he really loves them and wants their best. They view trials, or simply a lack of abundance, as proof the Lord is indifferent and uncaring.

In the second scene (Num 11:10–23), a conversation takes place between the Lord and Moses. The complaints have definitely infected all the people (v. 10), and the Lord is again angry, but this time "exceedingly" (v. 10; cf. v. 1). This hints the coming judgment will be more severe than last time. As for Moses, the people's response deeply troubles him, leading to impassioned prayer (vv. 11–15).

His prayer is both respectful (note his use of "your servant," Num 11:11) and achingly honest.[4] His leadership feels like a punishment (v. 11), a burden impossibly too large to bear (vv. 12, 14), and required because of the Lord's promises, not his (v. 12). Indeed, the burden is so great he feels death would be better (v. 15). Significantly, the center of his prayer identifies the burden's main source: the people's complaints, which are impossible for him to meet (v. 13). Even a leader with granite resolve can be worn down by incessant drips of grumbling.

The Lord first responds by addressing Moses's need for help in carrying the leadership burden (Num 11:16–17). Previously, Moses had appointed leaders over the people to help with legal disputes (Exod 18:25–26); now he is to gather a subset of seventy leaders whom the Lord will anoint with a special portion of the Spirit to help Moses. One person cannot carry a ton, but a ton spread among seventy people becomes twenty-nine pounds each, which is very doable, all the more so because of the special anointing these fellow leaders will receive for the task (see further below).

In contrast to his attitude toward Moses, the Lord's anger toward his people is clear as he highlights their rebellious words and thoughts: "We were better off in Egypt! Why did we ever leave Egypt!" (Num 11:18, 20). This is a blasphemous declaration that the Lord's glorious redemption was an oppressive mistake. In a punishment fit to the crime, the Lord declares he will provide so much meat they will become sick of it (vv. 19–20). In the meantime, the Israelites must consecrate themselves (v. 18), implying the Lord is about to miraculously manifest his power (cf. Exod 19:10–11, 14–15), in this case, by providing abundant quail.

Moses's response is incredulous (Num 11:21–22), though perhaps more

---

4. This is a lament. For differences between lament and complaining, see pp. 181–82, What's the Difference?

earnest than doubtful, as his response of faith will momentarily suggest (v. 24).[5] The Lord's question in return—"Is the LORD's arm too short?" (v. 23)—is a way to ask, "Is the power of the Lord limited?"[6] The implied answer is a resounding, "No!," and Moses, *without yet knowing how this will come to pass*, obediently goes and prepares the people (v. 24). This is remarkable faith indeed.

In the third scene (Num 11:24–30), the Lord "came down in the cloud" (v. 25)—the typical manifestation of his special presence (cf. Exod 19:9, 16; 24:15–16; etc.)—and "took some of the power of the Spirit that was on him and put it on the seventy elders" (Num 11:25).[7] This is clearly the Lord's Spirit,[8] who not only works in the context of salvation and sanctification but also to equip people with special gifts and abilities for various tasks, whether building the tabernacle (Exod 31:2–5) or leading the people (Judg 3:10), the latter of which is the case here (cf. Num 11:17).

To make this empowerment clear, the text notes "they prophesied" (Num 11:25). While this word can refer to someone in self-control delivering a message from the Lord (1 Kgs 22:17–18), it can also refer to someone overcome by the Spirit in such a way that they exclaim words from or about God with great emotion and physical gestures (1 Sam 10:5–6, 10–11; 19:20–24). It seems the latter happens here: the Spirit overcomes the elders, who respond, body and soul, with passionate exclamations of words from God. But this was a one-time occurrence (they "did not do so again," Num 11:25), underscoring that Moses's unique role as *the* prophet of Israel continues (cf. 12:6–8).

A brief interlude shows us something of Moses's nature as leader (Num 11:26–29). For reasons not explained, two of the elders did not go to the tent (v. 26). Nonetheless, the Spirit came upon them and they suddenly started prophesying. Joshua, who was introduced in Exodus as Moses's assistant (Exod 24:13; 33:11; cf. 17:9–14; 32:17), urges Moses to stop them, apparently out of loyalty to Moses and fear that these elders—who are doing this right in the people's midst—will become exalted as leaders. Moses responds, "Are you jealous for my sake? I wish that all the LORD's people were prophets and that

---

5. Cf. Mary's earnest question in Luke 1:31–34 with that of Zechariah's doubting question in 1:18–20.
6. Cf. Isa 59:1.
7. There is no hint Moses's power is in some way diminished, making the sharing of the Spirit here more like the sharing of fire: seventy new flames are kindled without diminishing the first (Keil, *The Pentateuch*, 697 [*Numbers*, 70]).
8. Cf. Num 11:29 (emphasis added): "I wish . . . the LORD would put *his* Spirit on [all his people]!"

the LORD would put his Spirit on them!" (Num 11:29). He does not care about his own glory; like all good spiritual leaders, his greatest desire was to see a work of God among God's people. In particular, Moses's goal is not to be the main Spirit-led leader; it is for the Lord's people to be led by the Spirit, and he is perfectly content for that to take place through others' gifts. The scene finishes with Moses and the elders leaving the sanctuary and returning to the camp (v. 30); the problem of a lack of leadership "has come to a satisfactory conclusion."[9]

In the final scene (Num 11:31–34), the Lord judges the people for their treasonous rejection of him and their blasphemy against his deliverance. He causes a wind to drive flocks of quail into the camp, which spread out as far as the eye could see and up to two cubits (3 feet [.91 m]) deep in places (v. 31). The people responded by gathering all that day and night and next day, with the smallest amount gathered being 10 homers (v. 32), estimated at anywhere from 33 to 111 U.S. bushels (1175 to 3900 liters).[10] Even at the low end of this range, the amount is significant, with 33 bushels equaling 4,915 cups (4,651 metric cups). That's a lot of quail soup!

But these large amounts of meat were not to be enjoyed. If we maintain the translation "before [the meat] could be consumed" (Num 11:33), then the phrase is likely hyperbole since the people undoubtedly ate some of the meat during those two days (cf. Ps 78:29). Alternatively (and perhaps preferably), this phrase could be translated "before it [the meat] was cut off," that is, the judgment fell before all the meat could be consumed.[11] Either way, the Lord's judgement matched the crime: the very piles of meat they longed for would never be eaten (cf. Ps 78:30–31)! The Lord struck the people with a severe plague, that is, some form of disaster/calamity (Num 11:33).[12] The type of disaster is not named, but it would be suiting if the sickness came from the quail (cf. Ps 106:15, which suggests a "wasting disease" of some sort). What is clear is a great number died because of it, leading to the place's name, "Kibroth Hattaavah" ("graves of the craving," 11:34). The name picks up on the word for "craving" in v. 4 that began this story, tying it together in a depressing bow of judgment: those who rebelled in their craving experience the Lord's judgment for it. The story will resume on their next stop, Hazeroth (v. 35)—where yet another rebellion is about to unfold.

---

9. Ashley, *Numbers*, 217.
10. Cf. Cook, "Weights and Measures," 1051, with Milgrom, *Leviticus 1–16*, 895.
11. Cf. Ashley, *Numbers*, 219; cf. BDB 504.4.
12. Cf. 1 Sam 4:8, which uses the same Hebrew term to refer to the plagues of Egypt.

LIVE the Story

What Leads to Complaining?[13]

Complaining does not come simply because we experience hardship. It comes when we experience hardship while forgetting God's goodness. And once his goodness is forgotten, it is very soon denied.

This is exactly what happens in these two stories. The Israelites had already seen the Lord do so much good for them: delivering them from slavery in Egypt by mighty signs and wonders (Exodus 1–15), defeating their enemies in the wilderness (17:8–16), and providing for their needs of water and food (15:22–25; 17:1–7)—including one earlier miraculous provision of quail (16:1–13)! The Lord's past provision should have led them to trust him for present and future needs.

But here, all his goodness is both forgotten and denied. As noted above, the Israelites' complaints—"We were better off in Egypt! Why did we ever leave Egypt?" (Num 11:18, 20)—were a blasphemous declaration that the Lord's glorious redemption was an oppressive mistake, like a Christian saying to Jesus, "I wish you had not died for me! Leave me alone!"[14] Even the daily blessings the Lord gives (sweet-tasting manna) are redefined as part of the burden (v. 6).

That is the tragic endpoint to which a spirit of complaining leads. And no wonder. "Grumbling distorts your vision. It reimagines the past as a golden land, it despises the good gifts that God has surrounded you with in the present, and it completely ignores God's promises for the future."[15] In short, forgetting God's goodness not only leads to complaining; complaining causes us to forget God's goodness all the more.

This explains why Paul so clearly exhorts Christians not to imitate Israel in these ways: "Do everything without grumbling or arguing, so that you may become blameless and pure, 'children of God without fault in a warped and crooked generation'" (Phil 2:14–15a). To complain is to indulge our hearts in the belief that God is not at work in our midst and cannot be trusted; it is, in fact, to *strengthen* our hearts in a denial that he is good, and it will inevitably lead us to further acts of unbelief. Complaining does not bring us

---

13. While some may teach and preach this by following the type of outline below, others will simply want to tell the story scene by scene, incorporating the points made below into the telling of the story. See resource listed on p. 29n30.
14. Allen, "Numbers," 793.
15. Duguid, *Numbers*, 150.

closer to God; it takes us further from him because it causes us to deny who he is—which leads to the next question.

How Does God View Complaining?

We tend to view complaining as something we simply do with our mouths. But a husband or wife who falsely accuses their loving spouse of unfaithful behavior is not simply making a verbal mistake; they are betraying a relationship, which is exactly what Israel is doing to the Lord.

The Israelites have willingly entered into a covenant in which the Lord is their King and they are his servants. They committed to absolute loyalty to his laws and absolute trust in his protection and provision. Israel abandons that commitment constantly, all the while accusing the Lord—who has been completely faithful—of being untrustworthy and having only their worst in mind. Just as we do not look down on kings who punish treason or on parents who punish severe disobedience, we should not look down on the Lord for punishing his treasonous, disobedient people.

The surprising thing is not that the Lord responds with anger *but that he has taken so long to do so!* Imagine a husband who is completely loving and faithful to his wife, but she is unfaithful to him. Imagine that she is unfaithful ten different times and each time he forgives her and takes her back. If he responds with anger the eleventh time and files for divorce, do we blame him or do we stand in awe because he was so merciful and forgiving the first ten times?

So too with the Lord. He is the completely faithful and merciful husband, and Israel is the faithless bride, repeatedly betraying him. These stories make clear there are serious consequences for doing so. We cannot turn our backs on God and think it will have no impact on us.

But complaining not only leads to negative consequences for us; it leads to very negative consequences for our leaders.

How Does Complaining Impact Our Leaders (and How Should They Respond)?

With leadership comes an increase in responsibilities, and these can weigh heavily on the leader. Many leaders therefore resonate deeply with Moses's claim that leading the people is a burden too heavy for him (Num 11:14); the weight of leadership can be crushing.

This weight grows exponentially when those being led grumble and complain, asking of the leader things he or she is incapable to give. The Israelites' complaints made the leadership burden so heavy for Moses he despaired of life itself, asking the Lord: "Please go ahead and kill me . . . and do not let me face my own ruin!" (Num 11:15). Moses may be using hyperbole, but doing so underscores how oppressive the situation has become. The Israelites' complaints have made death more appealing than life. Little wonder the New Testament exhorts Christians to submit to our leaders' authority in the church, recognizing the weight of their responsibility and responding to them in such a way "that their work *will be a joy*, not *a burden*" (Heb 13:17, emphasis added). We do well to pause and consider two or three steps we might take to make this a reality for our own spiritual leaders.

As for his part, Moses models for leaders what to do when they feel the burden of their role: take it to the Lord and ask for his help (Num 11:11–15). He recognizes his limits and knows when he cannot go further without breaking. (The importance of leaders following this example cannot be stated strongly enough—for their own good and the good of those they lead.) Moreover, when his prayer is answered, and the Lord provides seventy other Spirit-anointed leaders to help bear the burden (vv. 24–27), Moses is not jealous others will now share in having authority; he is thrilled the Lord's people have Spirit-anointed leaders over them—and wishes for more (v. 29)! He shows the goal of leadership is not to be the main Spirit-led leader who receives all the glory but for the people to be led by the Spirit so the Lord might be glorified. Leaders may well ask themselves, "To what extent is this a description of my own heart? Are there ways in which I am focused on my own glory instead of the Lord's? Jealous of others' gifts? How can I encourage others to use their gifts?"

But there is one final thing Moses models here, not simply for leaders but for all of God's people: the importance of honesty before the Lord with our own struggles and burdens. While we are not to complain about our burdens, we are very welcome to lament them.

What's the Difference between Complaining and Lamenting?

Moses has a very frank conversation with God about how difficult life has become (Num 11:11–15). He does so respectfully—note that he calls himself "your servant" (v. 11), showing he recognizes he is speaking to a King—but he does so honestly. His words mirror laments found elsewhere in the Bible, in which difficulties are named and help is asked for.

The difference between lament and complaint is crucial. In laments, the sufferer is honest about their pain and suffering but also looks to God for help and deliverance.[16] This is what Moses does: the depth of his pain is obvious

---

16. For biblical examples, see Pss 3–7, 13, 22, 31, 44.

(he feels he would be better off dead!), but he is coming to the Lord for help. The Israelites' complaints were entirely different:

> [These complaints] were not part of a prayer directed to God, but were simply a grievance directed against God and their leaders. . . . Their scorn for God's gift [of manna] was accompanied by a desire to reject his greater gift of freedom and a promised land, and to return to Egypt, the land of slavery! In short, there is a sharp contrast between prayers of lament and [prayers of] grumbling and complaining.[17]

In lament, we still look to our loving King for help. In complaint, we deny his loving kingship. Ann Voskamp captures it beautifully: "Lament is a cry of belief in a good God, a God who has His ear to our hearts, a God who transfigures the ugly into beauty. Complaint is the bitter howl of unbelief in any benevolent God in this moment, a distrust in the love-beat of the Father's heart."[18]

Jesus himself lamented in the midst of the most severe trial imaginable: his death on behalf of humanity. At one point on the cross, he cries out, "My God! My God! Why have you forsaken me?" (Matt 27:46). Jesus is quoting Psalm 22:1, which comes from a lament psalm written by an Israelite believer in severe trial. The words are brutally honest but are still a prayer. And that is the point: the psalmist still looks to God in his suffering, and Jesus does the same. Indeed, lament psalms typically include honest expressions of grief together with deep expressions of trust and hope. Significantly, Jesus's final words on the cross—"Into your hands I commit my spirit" (Luke 23:46)—also come from a lament psalm (Ps 31:5) and are rooted in his knowing that no matter what trial we go through, God is there in the midst of it, is good, and will listen to our prayers. What does it look like for us to do this in the midst of our trials? And how does the fact Jesus has already done this encourage us to look to him for strength to do the same?

---

17. Boniface-Malle, "Numbers," 183.
18. Ann Voskamp, *One Thousand Gifts: A Dare to Live Fully Right Where You Are* (Grand Rapids: Zondervan, 2011), 175.

CHAPTER 16

Numbers 12:1-16

 LISTEN to the Story

¹Miriam and Aaron began to talk against Moses because of his Cushite wife, for he had married a Cushite. ² "Has the LORD spoken only through Moses?" they asked. "Hasn't he also spoken through us?" And the LORD heard this.

³(Now Moses was a very humble man, more humble than anyone else on the face of the earth.)

⁴At once the LORD said to Moses, Aaron and Miriam, "Come out to the tent of meeting, all three of you." So the three of them went out. ⁵Then the LORD came down in a pillar of cloud; he stood at the entrance to the tent and summoned Aaron and Miriam. When the two of them stepped forward, ⁶he said, "Listen to my words:

> "When there is a prophet among you,
>   I, the LORD, reveal myself to them in visions,
>   I speak to them in dreams.
> ⁷But this is not true of my servant Moses;
>   he is faithful in all my house.
> ⁸With him I speak face to face,
>   clearly and not in riddles;
>   he sees the form of the LORD.
> Why then were you not afraid
>   to speak against my servant Moses?"

⁹The anger of the LORD burned against them, and he left them.

¹⁰When the cloud lifted from above the tent, Miriam's skin was leprous—it became as white as snow. Aaron turned toward her and saw that she had a defiling skin disease, ¹¹and he said to Moses, "Please, my lord, I ask you not to hold against us the sin we have so foolishly committed.

> ¹²Do not let her be like a stillborn infant coming from its mother's womb with its flesh half eaten away."
>
> ¹³So Moses cried out to the Lord, "Please, God, heal her!"
>
> ¹⁴The Lord replied to Moses, "If her father had spit in her face, would she not have been in disgrace for seven days? Confine her outside the camp for seven days; after that she can be brought back." ¹⁵So Miriam was confined outside the camp for seven days, and the people did not move on till she was brought back.
>
> ¹⁶After that, the people left Hazeroth and encamped in the Desert of Paran.
>
> *Listening to the Text in the Story:* Numbers 11:1–35

This marks the third of three complaint stories that began in chapter 11 (see p. 174, Listening to the Text in the Story). Whereas the first two stories involve complaints against Moses by the people, this one involves complaints against him by fellow leaders—in this case, his siblings! The Lord himself vindicates Moses and highlights his unique role as Israel's prophetic leader.

The Complaint of Miriam and Aaron against Moses (12:1–3)

Fueled by envy and rivalry, Miriam and Aaron, Moses's siblings (Num 26:59), team up against him. In the Hebrew, attention is drawn to Miriam in particular,[1] suggesting she leads in the complaint (and explaining why she becomes the focus of judgment).

The surface reason for the complaint is Moses's wife (12:1). Since his first wife, Zipporah, was a Midianite (Exod 2:21), this text appears to refer to a second wife, coming from Cush, a kingdom to Egypt's south with dark-skinned inhabitants (cf. Jer 13:23) and not as closely related to the Israelites as the Midianites (cf. Gen 10:1, 6 with Gen 11:10–26 and 25:1–4). Whether Zipporah was still living is unclear, but Israelite law did not forbid marrying non-Israelites in general, only certain nations from within Canaan that did

---

1. She is named first and the verb for "speak (against)" is feminine singular (even though it refers to both Miriam and Aaron).

not include Cush (Exod 34:15–16; Deut 7:1–3). This makes it hard to see Miriam and Aaron's antagonism as anything other than an unwillingness to embrace their Israelite role of seeking the blessing of all the families of the earth (cf. Gen 12:3), an unwillingness perhaps fueled by an underlying racism.

But there is a deeper reason for their complaint: Miriam and Aaron believe they should be just as elevated in leadership as Moses himself since the Lord has also spoken to them (Num 12:2). To be sure, the Lord did speak directly to Aaron (Lev 10:8; 11:1; 13:1; etc.), and Miriam was a prophetess (Exod 15:20), but nowhere does the Lord's communication to them come close to the communication he had with Moses—as the Lord will make clear in a moment (Num 12:6–8). Moreover, their charge implies Moses has somehow been self-seeking, which is baseless, as shown by his initial desire to avoid a leadership role (Exod 4:10–17) and especially by his recent joy in leadership being shared among God's people (Num 11:24–29).

The text immediately confirms Miriam and Aaron's complaint should be viewed negatively. First, it states "the LORD heard" (Num 12:2), the exact same language used in 11:1, where wrongful speech came to the Lord's ears and was met with judgment. Second, it notes Moses was not self-seeking but just the opposite: one of the planet's humblest people (12:3). While the relevant Hebrew word (*'anaw*) can refer to those who are "afflicted" through oppression or difficulty (Pss 9:12, 18; 10:12), it can also refer to those who are "humble" and reliant on the Lord in contrast to those who are proud and evil (Prov 3:34). This fits the context very well since it addresses (and denies) the heart of Miriam and Aaron's complaint. This also makes it likely an editor included these words (since it would be hard to make such a comment about oneself),[2] though it is not impossible Moses could have made the statement as a simple protestation of innocence: "My record shows that I am not self-seeking but look to the Lord and follow him as meekly as possible!" (cf. Num 11:26–29). Either way, Miriam and Aaron's complaint is without merit—as the Lord will now make abundantly clear.

The Lord's Vindication of Moses and His Anger toward Aaron and Miriam (12:4–9)

Summoning Moses, Aaron, and Miriam to the tent, the Lord descends in the pillar of cloud (cf. at 11:25) and ominously narrows the "three of them" to "two of them," calling Aaron and Miriam to draw near (Num 12:4–5). Their claim to receive direct communication from the Lord is about to be confirmed—but as a sign of judgment, not favor!

---

2. See fuller discussion pp. 2–5, Author and Date.

The Lord's speech focuses on Moses's prophetic role, explaining how it is unique and why it is granted to Moses. The role's uniqueness is shown by way of contrast: with other prophets, the Lord speaks in visions or dreams (Num 12:6), which often communicate indirectly by means of symbolism that must be interpreted (v. 8). With Moses, the Lord does not use symbolism or riddle; he speaks to him directly, like a live, face-to-face conversation (v. 8). The word "like" is important here since elsewhere the Lord tells Moses, "You cannot see my face, for no one may see me and live" (Exod 33:20). This means the phrase "face to face" in Numbers 12:8 is hyperbole (a common device in poetry), underscoring the directness of the Lord's communication to Moses. This is emphasized by the phrase "he sees the form of the LORD," where the word "form" refers not to a full vision of God as he is (cf. Exod 33:20) but to some type of visual appearance that gives Moses an idea of God's being (cf. vv. 21–23) and is unique to Moses in terms of intensity and regularity (cf. Deut 4:15). Such a unique role is granted to Moses because of his faithful behavior (Num 12:7). In ancient Israel, large households often had one or more servants, and those who were especially faithful could be put in charge of the entire household (Gen 24:2; 39:4). From the Lord's perspective, all Israel was his household, Moses was his faithful servant that he put in charge of it (cf. Heb 3:2, 5), and so he spoke with him very directly, as one does with a trusted worker or friend (Exod 33:11).

Moses's special role as chief servant also explains the Lord's closing question to Aaron and Miriam, "Why then were you not afraid to speak against my servant Moses?" (Num 12:8). When we slander a beloved child to his or her parents, they rightly respond with deep anger; when one slanders a king's beloved servant, he responds similarly, explaining well why the Lord's anger burns against Aaron and Miriam (v. 9).

Miriam's Judgment and Its Aftermath (12:10–15)

As the cloud departs, the Lord's judgment becomes clear: Miriam is severely afflicted with a ritually defiling skin disease. Detailed in Leviticus 13, this malady refers not to leprosy (Hansen's disease) but to a range of skin conditions, often resulting in flaking skin ("white as snow"), that made the person ritually impure and required they leave the camp so as not to defile it (Lev 13:45–46; Num 5:1–4). The punishment appears to focus on Miriam since she took the lead in the rebellion (see at 12:1, p. 184).[3]

On seeing this, Aaron turns immediately to Moses for help (Num 12:11–12).

---

3. This is not sexism; elsewhere, even harsher judgments fall on men who take the lead in rebelling against Moses's leadership (Num 16:1–35).

Clearly, he now recognizes Moses's leadership role is unique and far above his own. Not only does he call Moses "my lord," he confesses their accusation against him was foolish sin (v. 11). Moreover, he asks Moses for mercy, not because Moses brought this calamity about but because the sin was against Moses and only he, as the Lord's faithful servant, can appeal successfully to the Lord for healing (cf. Job 42:7–9). And healing was greatly needed, for the disease had ravaged Miriam's body, making it corpse-like in appearance (Num 12:12).

In a further demonstration of his humility, Moses urgently cries out on behalf of the one who had just been persecuting him (Num 12:13). The Lord hears Moses's prayer but makes clear there will still be discipline (v. 14). In ancient Israel, as in many cultures today, one reason to spit on someone was to say their behavior was utterly shameful (cf. Deut 25:9 for an example of a woman spitting in a man's face). Apparently, when a father spit in his daughter's face for some wrong, she would be in a state of public humiliation for seven days. The Lord begins with this example as a way to say, "Suffering leprosy is a far greater penalty than that, and therefore even after Miriam's healing she should experience a similar state of public humiliation by being confined outside the camp seven days" (Num 12:14). (This means exclusion because of ritual impurity is a secondary issue here, not a primary issue.) Her discipline was indeed evident to all since the Israelites did not move on until she was allowed to reenter their midst (v. 15). The Lord does not hesitate to discipline leaders publicly (cf. 1 Tim 5:20).

Travel Notice (12:16)

In Numbers 10:12, the Israelites set out from the wilderness of Sinai and have now arrived at Kadesh (also known as Kadesh Barnea, 32:8), in the wilderness of Paran (13:26). That wilderness was in between Egypt and Midian (1 Kgs 11:18), placing it northeast of the traditional Mt. Sinai and south of the promised land (see map 1). It seems to have been amorphous enough to overlap with the wilderness of Zin since Kadesh is identified as being in both places (Paran: 13:26; Zin: 20:1; 27:14; 33:36). This understanding also explains why Paran is not mentioned "in the itinerary list of Num. 33, since, on this hypothesis, many or most of the sites would be located within the wilderness of Paran."[4] In any case, it is on the way to Canaan and the reader may expect the Israelites to enter Canaan soon from the south. Sadly, the next two chapters will dash this hope, and the Israelites will take almost forty years before they make good progress from this area toward the promised land (cf. Deut 2:14).

---

4. Ashley, *Numbers*, 193.

LIVE the Story

What Do Bad Leaders Look Like?[5]

If you were to ask ancient Israelites to identify some of their key leaders in addition to Moses, the names Miriam and Aaron would have been at the top of the list (cf. Mic 6:4). But sometimes those with the most power and authority are least satisfied; having begun to taste honor and glory, they will not rest until they have more of these things than anyone else. And that is the heart of the problem: once we focus on honor and glory *for ourselves*, we will be jealous and envious of anyone with whom we have to share these things. The problem is especially real for leaders, who can become accustomed to power and praise and feel especially offended when others have more. Miriam and Aaron illustrate this with their complaints against Moses, but the problem continues throughout the biblical story. In Paul's day, envy and rivalry led to certain leaders preaching the gospel fervently, not in order to win people to Jesus but apparently to increase their leadership role at the expense of Paul's (Phil 1:15–17). That is how twisted we become with envy: we turn something as beautiful as preaching the gospel into an opportunity to advance our reputation over that of others. Bad leaders are characterized by envy and rivalry because they care most about themselves.

What Do Good Leaders Look Like?

Moses provides a totally different leadership model. In the previous chapter, when others were given a special portion of the Lord's Spirit to enable their leadership, Moses responds with deep thankfulness (Num 11:29). He views his role ultimately as one of service to the Lord in order to bring him glory and honor—and the more people who can help the better! Moses's servant-like approach to leadership is identified by the Lord himself, who describes Moses as "my servant" who "is faithful in all my house" (12:7). Because he knew himself to be the Lord's servant, Moses was exceedingly humble instead of self-seeking (v. 3). It is hard to seek your own glory when your eyes are fixed on bringing glory to your heavenly Father.

The Scriptures repeatedly model and exhort such servant-leadership (e.g., 1 Cor 3:5; 2 Cor 4:5). Indeed, note how Paul responds to those preaching the gospel from envy and hoping to hurt him in doing so: "But what does it matter? The important thing is that in every way, whether from false motives

---

5. For an alternative homiletical approach, see p. 179n13.

or true, Christ is preached. And because of this I rejoice!" (Phil 1:18). He recognizes so clearly that he is a servant whose job is to bring glory and honor to the one he serves; that is all that matters to him. Especially if we are leaders, we might stop to ask, "Are we acting out any feelings of jealousy or envy toward others with leadership roles? What should it look like when we think of our role as leaders through the lens of '*servant* of God' instead of through the lens of gaining glory and honor for ourselves?"

What Do Good Servants Look Like?

But this story is not simply about how to lead; it is also about how to respond to the Lord's authority. Note how Deuteronomy returns to this story as a warning. After exhorting the Israelites to "follow carefully what [the Lord has] commanded" (Deut 24:8), the very next verse says, "Remember what the LORD your God did to Miriam along the way after you came out of Egypt" (v. 9). In other words, "Obey God's word! Do not be like Miriam! She rejected Moses, the one who spoke God's very words, and that was equivalent to rejecting God himself!"

In moving to today's context, we may consider two related ideas. First, since the Bible itself represents God's very words, our posture before it is to be one of humility and reverence. We do not sit over the Bible, picking and choosing what we want to listen to and what to ignore; we are to sit under it, humbly, reverently, treating it as God's very voice and looking to it to direct us in his paths and ways. That's what good servants always want to do: obey their king's voice. What does it mean for us today to have such a posture? What types of thoughts and actions would demonstrate we really do value the Bible as that which will help us in serving God?

The second idea is immediately related: Jesus himself is described as God's Word, perfectly reflecting God to us because he came as God in the flesh. "In the beginning was the Word, and the Word was with God, and the Word was God. . . . [And] the Word became flesh and made his dwelling among us" (John 1:1, 14a). If rejecting Moses was a serious wrong, how much more if we reject Jesus (cf. Heb 3:1–11)! In short, to submit to Jesus and serve him is to submit to God himself, while to reject him is to reject God himself. This is why Jesus could boldly say, "I and the Father are one. . . . No one comes to the Father except through me" (John 10:30; 14:6b). Such claims are ludicrous unless Jesus is indeed who the Bible says he is, in which case, such claims are the truest statement in the world—and the most wonderful invitation to enter into relationship with God and serve him.

CHAPTER 17

Numbers 13:1–14:45

LISTEN to the Story

¹The LORD said to Moses, ²"Send some men to explore the land of Canaan, which I am giving to the Israelites. From each ancestral tribe send one of its leaders."

³So at the LORD's command Moses sent them out from the Desert of Paran. All of them were leaders of the Israelites. ⁴These are their names:

from the tribe of Reuben, Shammua son of Zakkur;
⁵from the tribe of Simeon, Shaphat son of Hori;
⁶from the tribe of Judah, Caleb son of Jephunneh;
⁷from the tribe of Issachar, Igal son of Joseph;
⁸from the tribe of Ephraim, Hoshea son of Nun;
⁹from the tribe of Benjamin, Palti son of Raphu;
¹⁰from the tribe of Zebulun, Gaddiel son of Sodi;
¹¹from the tribe of Manasseh (a tribe of Joseph), Gaddi son of Susi;
¹²from the tribe of Dan, Ammiel son of Gemalli;
¹³from the tribe of Asher, Sethur son of Michael;
¹⁴from the tribe of Naphtali, Nahbi son of Vophsi;
¹⁵from the tribe of Gad, Geuel son of Maki.

¹⁶These are the names of the men Moses sent to explore the land. (Moses gave Hoshea son of Nun the name Joshua.)

¹⁷When Moses sent them to explore Canaan, he said, "Go up through the Negev and on into the hill country. ¹⁸See what the land is like and whether the people who live there are strong or weak, few or many. ¹⁹What kind of land do they live in? Is it good or bad? What kind of towns do they live in? Are they unwalled or fortified? ²⁰How is the soil? Is it fertile or poor? Are there trees in it or not? Do your best to bring back some of the fruit of the land." (It was the season for the first ripe grapes.)

²¹So they went up and explored the land from the Desert of Zin as far as Rehob, toward Lebo Hamath. ²²They went up through the Negev and came to Hebron, where Ahiman, Sheshai and Talmai, the descendants of Anak, lived. (Hebron had been built seven years before Zoan in Egypt.) ²³When they reached the Valley of Eshkol, they cut off a branch bearing a single cluster of grapes. Two of them carried it on a pole between them, along with some pomegranates and figs. ²⁴That place was called the Valley of Eshkol because of the cluster of grapes the Israelites cut off there. ²⁵At the end of forty days they returned from exploring the land.

²⁶They came back to Moses and Aaron and the whole Israelite community at Kadesh in the Desert of Paran. There they reported to them and to the whole assembly and showed them the fruit of the land. ²⁷They gave Moses this account: "We went into the land to which you sent us, and it does flow with milk and honey! Here is its fruit. ²⁸But the people who live there are powerful, and the cities are fortified and very large. We even saw descendants of Anak there. ²⁹The Amalekites live in the Negev; the Hittites, Jebusites and Amorites live in the hill country; and the Canaanites live near the sea and along the Jordan."

³⁰Then Caleb silenced the people before Moses and said, "We should go up and take possession of the land, for we can certainly do it."

³¹But the men who had gone up with him said, "We can't attack those people; they are stronger than we are." ³²And they spread among the Israelites a bad report about the land they had explored. They said, "The land we explored devours those living in it. All the people we saw there are of great size. ³³We saw the Nephilim there (the descendants of Anak come from the Nephilim). We seemed like grasshoppers in our own eyes, and we looked the same to them."

¹⁴:¹That night all the members of the community raised their voices and wept aloud. ²All the Israelites grumbled against Moses and Aaron, and the whole assembly said to them, "If only we had died in Egypt! Or in this wilderness! ³Why is the LORD bringing us to this land only to let us fall by the sword? Our wives and children will be taken as plunder. Wouldn't it be better for us to go back to Egypt?" ⁴And they said to each other, "We should choose a leader and go back to Egypt."

⁵Then Moses and Aaron fell facedown in front of the whole Israelite assembly gathered there. ⁶Joshua son of Nun and Caleb son of Jephunneh, who were among those who had explored the land, tore their clothes ⁷and

said to the entire Israelite assembly, "The land we passed through and explored is exceedingly good. [8]If the Lord is pleased with us, he will lead us into that land, a land flowing with milk and honey, and will give it to us. [9]Only do not rebel against the Lord. And do not be afraid of the people of the land, because we will devour them. Their protection is gone, but the Lord is with us. Do not be afraid of them."

[10]But the whole assembly talked about stoning them. Then the glory of the Lord appeared at the tent of meeting to all the Israelites. [11]The Lord said to Moses, "How long will these people treat me with contempt? How long will they refuse to believe in me, in spite of all the signs I have performed among them? [12]I will strike them down with a plague and destroy them, but I will make you into a nation greater and stronger than they."

[13]Moses said to the Lord, "Then the Egyptians will hear about it! By your power you brought these people up from among them. [14]And they will tell the inhabitants of this land about it. They have already heard that you, Lord, are with these people and that you, Lord, have been seen face to face, that your cloud stays over them, and that you go before them in a pillar of cloud by day and a pillar of fire by night. [15]If you put all these people to death, leaving none alive, the nations who have heard this report about you will say, [16]'The Lord was not able to bring these people into the land he promised them on oath, so he slaughtered them in the wilderness.'

[17]"Now may the Lord's strength be displayed, just as you have declared: [18]'The Lord is slow to anger, abounding in love and forgiving sin and rebellion. Yet he does not leave the guilty unpunished; he punishes the children for the sin of the parents to the third and fourth generation.' [19]In accordance with your great love, forgive the sin of these people, just as you have pardoned them from the time they left Egypt until now."

[20]The Lord replied, "I have forgiven them, as you asked. [21]Nevertheless, as surely as I live and as surely as the glory of the Lord fills the whole earth, [22]not one of those who saw my glory and the signs I performed in Egypt and in the wilderness but who disobeyed me and tested me ten times—[23]not one of them will ever see the land I promised on oath to their ancestors. No one who has treated me with contempt will ever see it. [24]But because my servant Caleb has a different spirit and follows me wholeheartedly, I will bring him into the land he went to, and his descendants will inherit it. [25]Since the Amalekites and the Canaanites are

living in the valleys, turn back tomorrow and set out toward the desert along the route to the Red Sea."

²⁶The Lord said to Moses and Aaron: ²⁷"How long will this wicked community grumble against me? I have heard the complaints of these grumbling Israelites. ²⁸So tell them, 'As surely as I live, declares the Lord, I will do to you the very thing I heard you say: ²⁹In this wilderness your bodies will fall—every one of you twenty years old or more who was counted in the census and who has grumbled against me. ³⁰Not one of you will enter the land I swore with uplifted hand to make your home, except Caleb son of Jephunneh and Joshua son of Nun. ³¹As for your children that you said would be taken as plunder, I will bring them in to enjoy the land you have rejected. ³²But as for you, your bodies will fall in this wilderness. ³³Your children will be shepherds here for forty years, suffering for your unfaithfulness, until the last of your bodies lies in the wilderness. ³⁴For forty years—one year for each of the forty days you explored the land—you will suffer for your sins and know what it is like to have me against you.' ³⁵I, the Lord, have spoken, and I will surely do these things to this whole wicked community, which has banded together against me. They will meet their end in this wilderness; here they will die."

³⁶So the men Moses had sent to explore the land, who returned and made the whole community grumble against him by spreading a bad report about it—³⁷these men who were responsible for spreading the bad report about the land were struck down and died of a plague before the Lord. ³⁸Of the men who went to explore the land, only Joshua son of Nun and Caleb son of Jephunneh survived.

³⁹When Moses reported this to all the Israelites, they mourned bitterly. ⁴⁰Early the next morning they set out for the highest point in the hill country, saying, "Now we are ready to go up to the land the Lord promised. Surely we have sinned!"

⁴¹But Moses said, "Why are you disobeying the Lord's command? This will not succeed! ⁴²Do not go up, because the Lord is not with you. You will be defeated by your enemies, ⁴³for the Amalekites and the Canaanites will face you there. Because you have turned away from the Lord, he will not be with you and you will fall by the sword."

⁴⁴Nevertheless, in their presumption they went up toward the highest point in the hill country, though neither Moses nor the ark of the Lord's

covenant moved from the camp. ⁴⁵Then the Amalekites and the Canaanites who lived in that hill country came down and attacked them and beat them down all the way to Hormah.

Listening to the Text in the Story: Genesis 12:7; 13:15; 15:18; 17:8; Exodus 32; Numbers 11–12; tablets from Ebla, Mari, and el-Amarna

For the first time in Numbers, the term "Canaan" occurs (Num 13:2). This term occurs elsewhere in a Mari tablet (ca. 1800 BC) and a cuneiform tablet "found at el-Amarna in Egypt (ca. 1400 BC). . . . Thus at the time of the exodus and conquest, the 'land of Canaan' was a definite geopolitical entity."[1]

Significantly, the Lord's promise to give Abraham and his descendants Canaan was central to his covenant with him (Gen 12:7; 13:15; 15:18; 17:8; etc.). To agree to enter the land will be a clear declaration that the Lord will be faithful to that promise; to refuse to enter will be a clear declaration that he cannot be trusted. Going into the land is not first and foremost a decision about military probabilities; it is a decision about divine faithfulness.

Sadly, the Israelites decide the Lord cannot be trusted, and the grumbling and complaining of Numbers 11 and 12 turn into full-scale apostasy and revolt in chapters 13 and 14. These chapters, in fact, highlight parallels with the Israelites' previous grand failure: the golden calf (Exod 32). Similar to that incident, the Lord threatens to disown Israel and start over with Moses, Moses pleads on Israel's behalf, and the Lord mitigates his originally stated penalty. A key difference, however, is that in Exodus the Lord still has the Israelites depart for the promised land; here, they are barred from it.[2] The Lord is indeed "slow to anger," but even his patience has limits. Severe rebellion may be met with severe discipline.

EXPLAIN the Story

The Twelve Scouts Explore the Land (13:1–25)

The Israelites are at Kadesh (also known as Kadesh Barnea, Num 32:8) in the northern wilderness of Paran (12:16; 13:26), south of the promised land (see

---

1. Carl G. Rasmussen, *Zondervan Atlas of the Bible*, rev. ed. (Grand Rapids: Zondervan Academic, 2010), 106. For its boundaries in the biblical text, see map 2.
2. Bailey, *Leviticus-Numbers*, 465.

map 1). The Lord commands that twelve men to be sent "to explore the land of Canaan, which I am giving to the Israelites" (13:2).[3] In the Hebrew, "I am giving" has an immediacy about it, describing an action already in progress and/or on the verge of happening. The Lord is about to fulfill his covenant promise; at least, that is how the story is supposed to go.

The twelve men are to come from each tribe and be leaders, acting as representatives on their tribe's behalf. Of the twelve men listed (Num 13:4–15), ten are never mentioned again; the reasons for this are tragic and will unfold shortly. Two men, however, will be mentioned later on in the biblical story and praised for their faithfulness (cf. 32:12): Caleb (13:6) and Hoshea (v. 8), the latter of whom Moses renames Joshua (v. 16). We do not know when this name change took place (the name "Joshua" is already used several times in Exodus, e.g., 17:9; 24:13), but it is significant theologically: "Hoshea" means either "he saved" or "salvation," while "Joshua" means either "the Lord saves" or "the Lord is salvation."[4] In making this change, Moses made clear for all Israel that the Lord is their help; Israel's job is to believe this in faith when it comes to taking the promised land.

When Moses sends the scouts (Num 13:17), he gives them various instructions. Some of these relate to the upcoming battles that Israel is to undertake with the land's inhabitants; moving forward in faith does not mean moving blindly. Moses thus commands them to find out about the land's inhabitants: their strength in battle, numbers, and fortifications (vv. 18b, 19b). Other instructions relate more directly to verifying that this is a land "flowing with milk and honey" (14:8), which would confirm that the Lord was indeed being faithful to his promise for such a land. Moses therefore commands them to learn about the land's fertility and tree population[5] and to bring back food samples (13:20a). A quick note tells us the grape season has just begun (v. 20b), placing this event as early as July—just a few months after leaving Mt. Sinai in April or May (see at 10:11–13, p. 167)—and preparing us for the upcoming scene of the fruit the scouts bring back.

The scouts head northward through the wilderness of Zin, then through the Negev in the south of Canaan into the hill country (Num 13:17, 21), which starts in the Negev's highlands and continues northward like a hilly spine. Their final journey took them as far north as Rehob, in the area of Lebo

---

3. Deuteronomy 1:22 informs us that the people requested the sending of spies, implying the Lord's command in Num 13:2 came in response to this request.
4. In the Greek translation, "Joshua" is translated as "Jesus"; cf. Matt 1:21.
5. Trees were necessary for fuel and everyday items. Undoubtedly, the scouts would also be expected to report on what kinds of trees were there and especially whether there were fruit trees.

Hamath (v. 21), thought to be north of Damascus (see map 2); the text, however, focuses on their experience in Hebron (v. 22) and the Valley of Eshkol (vv. 23–24), since both places provide important background information for the scouts' final report.[6]

Hebron was in the south of the land, about nineteen miles south-southwest of Jerusalem (see map 2). It was inhabited by the descendants of Anak (Num 13:22), described elsewhere as "great and tall" (Deut 9:2) and identified later in this chapter as being in the line of the Nephilim (Num 13:33), who were known as "the heroes of old, men of renown" (Gen 6:4), apparently famous for their strength and valor.[7] This highlights the challenge Israel will face and provides background to explain the negative report about to be given by ten of the scouts. But Hebron's mention should have led to a much different reaction. "It was near Hebron that God first promised Abraham that he would inherit the land (Gn. 13:14–18). . . . It was in Hebron that [Abraham] acquired his only piece of real estate for the burial of his wife, and where he and the other patriarchs were buried (Gn. 23; 25:9; 35:27–29; 50:13)."[8] In short, it was the clearest possible reminder of God's promise of Canaan and down payment within it and should have filled the scouts with tremendous hope and faith.[9]

As for the Valley of Eshkol (Num 13:23–24), it was obviously luxuriant, with pomegranates, figs, and grape clusters so large they had to be carried on a pole between two men (the name Eshkol means "grape cluster" in Hebrew). This reality of the land will also feature in the scouts' final report, but again, will fail to provide them with any hope in God's goodness and faithfulness. The scene ends with the scouts returning to the camp after forty days (v. 25), that number becoming central to the Israelites' discipline in the next chapter (14:34).

---

6. The text is not chronological here as much as it is thematic, providing highlights from the scouts' trip that will help the reader understand the events about to unfold in 13:26–33.

7. The word translated "hero" (Heb. *gibbor*) in Gen 6:4 is most often used to describe those with great might, especially in battle (Josh 1:14; 6:2; 10:2; Judg 5:23; etc.).

8. Wenham, *Numbers*, 118–19.

9. The text also notes that Hebron was "built seven years before Zoan in Egypt" (13:22), apparently to testify to Hebron's antiquity and greatness in comparison to another old and important city. Hebron's antiquity is well known, occurring in the biblical story as early as Abraham (Gen 13:18). As for Zoan, if we assume it is the same city mentioned in later biblical texts—which was indeed a key Egyptian city (cf. Isa 19:11, 13; 30:3–4), at one point functioned as a capital, and is now usually identified with the site San el-Hagar—then there is a problem in that it appears not to have been too significant until sometime after the exodus. Perhaps the text originally had a different name here for an earlier capital city in Egypt and this was mistakenly updated to Zoan by a later scribe who confused the two capitals (compare the way a scribe might have correctly updated the name Laish to Dan in Gen 14:14, a name change that took place long after the initial composition of the book of Genesis [see Judg 18:29]).

The Scouts' Report and Undermining of the People's Faith (13:26–33)

The scouts' report starts positively enough, underscoring the land flowed with milk and honey (Num 13:27)—a poetic shorthand to describe a land of incredible fertility, as evidenced by the presence of abundant milk (implying that milk-producing herds and flocks had adequate pastures due to generous rains and water supplies) and honey (one of the sweetest foods available [Judg 14:8] and thus a special treat).[10] But their report quickly turned negative, and they go out of their way to paint the picture as dramatically as possible. One might paraphrase: "The people there aren't simply 'strong' (Num 13:18); they're *fierce* (v. 28)! Their cities are not simply 'fortified' (v. 19); they're *fortified and very large* (v. 28)! The inhabitants are the opposite of 'weak' (v. 18)—among them are the *gigantic descendants of Anak* (v. 28)! The people are not 'few' (v. 18); they're *everywhere*, with Amelekites in the south, Hittites, Jebusites, and Amorites in the central hill country, and Canaanites on either side of the hill country (v. 29)!"

But Caleb (and presumably Joshua with him [Num 14:6]) saw things quite differently. Because the scouts' negative report stirred up the people in complaint against Moses, Caleb first had to quiet them down before he could speak. His words are full of faith and, in the Hebrew, very emphatic: "We should *indeed* go up and so take possession of it, for we can *most certainly* prevail against it!" (13:30, author's translation and emphasis). Sadly, those who had "gone up with him"—and had thus seen things firsthand—contradicted him immediately (v. 31) and then spread an evil report about the land among the people, stating it would devour them[11] and emphasizing that the people there were so big and mighty that the Israelites were like small grasshoppers[12] by comparison (vv. 32–33). As the next chapter will show, this slanderous report spread through the camp like an aggressive spiritual cancer, destroying any faith the Israelites might have had and leading them to give up on the Lord, his leaders, and his promises.

The People's Rebellious Response (14:1–4)

The entire people revolt ("all the members of the community . . . All the Israelites . . . the whole assembly," 14:1–2). With their faith completely

---

10. See further description of the land in Deut 8:7–9.
11. Cf. Lev 26:38 ("the land of your enemies will devour you"), where "land" appears to stand for the inhabitants, who would kill the Israelites (cf. Jer 30:16). Alternatively, this is a reference to there being constant fighting within the land, so that those living in it were frequently killed in battle (Sprinkle, *Leviticus and Numbers*, 266).
12. Cf. the use of the word "shrimp" in English (Milgrom, *Numbers*, 107).

undermined, they weep loudly, and do so "that night" (v. 1), the sense apparently being "into that night and throughout it to the morning." The weeping is mixed with "grumbling" (v. 2), which refers to an expression of strong dissatisfaction with difficult life circumstances that is fueled by a lack of trust in the Lord's goodness and faithfulness (cf. Exod 15:24; 16:2; 17:3). Their grumbling is directed first against Moses and Aaron (Num 14:2), but it quickly becomes apparent the real issue is their lack of trust in the Lord (v. 3). Having heard of the mighty fortresses and warriors of Canaan (13:28–33), they fear certain annihilation of their men in warfare, leaving the women and children as plunder. Their fear is so great they wish they had already died in slavery in Egypt or by starvation in the wilderness (14:2b) and conclude it would be better to abandon Moses, choose another leader, and head back to the land of slavery, where they had been groaning and calling out to the Lord for deliverance (v. 4; cf. Exod 2:23). Somehow, when difficult circumstances are mixed with a lack of belief in God's goodness, bondage to cruel taskmasters becomes an appealing option.

The Faithful Counter-response of Moses, Aaron, Joshua, and Caleb—and the People's Continued Rebellion (14:5–10a)

Moses and Aaron fall on their faces, an action that can show humility before one greater than oneself (Gen 17:3; Lev 9:24), sometimes accompanied by dismay and supplication (Num 16:22; 20:6). This well fits the context here: in dismay and humility, Moses and Aaron plead with the assembly to reconsider their rebellious decision (cf. Num 16:4–6). This understanding finds further support in the actions of Joshua and Caleb, who tear their garments in grief at the assembly's rebellion (14:6; cf. Gen 37:34) and plead with the people to act in faith (Num 14:7–9). They begin by focusing on the land, describing it as "exceedingly good" (v. 7), and then underscoring the Lord's promises to give it to them. Their words could be paraphrased, "If the Lord is pleased with us"—that is, if we do not rebel against him in this matter (see the beginning of v. 9) but respond in faith and go—"then *he* will bring us into this very good land and give it us (v. 8)! So don't be afraid of the people there; their land will not devour you (cf. 13:32), you will devour them! For their divine protection (Hebrew: their 'shade')[13] is gone, since no god can stand before the Lord, the one who is with us, leading us and shading us by the cloud of his presence (cf. Ps 105:39)! So do not fear (Num 14:9)!"

---

13. The word "shade" is "an apt picture of divine protection in the hot lands of the Middle East, Pss. 91; 121:5" (Wenham, *Numbers*, 122).

But the people responded by talking about stoning them (Num 14:10a), that is, not just Joshua and Caleb but likely Moses and Aaron too, who also insisted on going forward into the land. The people's response shows the depth of their anger: it was not enough simply to turn around without these leaders; they thought these leaders deserved to die.

The Lord Appears in Judgment (14:10b)

As all this is going on, the Israelites suddenly see the appearance of the glory of the Lord, which refers to a spectacular display of the Lord's presence and is called "the glory of the Lord" because the proper response to such an awesome display is to give him glory for his strength and majesty.[14] In light of other instances of the Lord's glory appearing, we can imagine that the Israelites would have seen the cloud over the Tent light up with flashes of lightning and divine fire,[15] making it abundantly clear the King of glory was now in their midst and, as his words are about to make clear, coming to hold his rebellious people to account.

The Lord Announces the Initial Judgment (14:11–12)

The Lord begins by stating the reason for the Israelites' judgment: they have "treat[ed] me with contempt" (Num 14:11), which refers to a refusal to follow the Lord in covenant faithfulness and to show by one's actions that he is not worthy of obedience (cf. Deut 31:20). This is made clear by the parallel expression, "they refuse to believe in me" (Num 14:11), that is, not believe that his words are trustworthy and that he is worthy of their confidence (cf. Exod 14:31). This was especially egregious because of "all the signs . . . performed among them" (Num 14:11), from the incredible miracles in Egypt to his miraculous provision for them in the wilderness (v. 11; cf. Num 14:22; Deut 1:30–33).

Having described their guilt, the Lord now pronounces their sentence, mirroring his response after the golden calf incident: he threatens their destruction and offers to make Moses the founder of a new and mighty nation (Num 14:12; cf. Exod 32:10). In the larger context of the Pentateuch, this threat of judgment is well understood as an invitation for Moses to intercede on Israel's behalf. Elsewhere, the Lord tells a trusted servant, such as Abraham or Moses, about a coming judgment, thereby giving the servant a chance to intercede on behalf of those deserving the judgment so they might escape it

---

14. Cf. 1 Kgs 18:37–39; see also the use of "glory" (NIV "honor") in Gen 45:13; Deut 5:24; 1 Chr 16:24.

15. Cf. Exod 40:34–35 and Num 16:42 with Exod 19:16–18; 20:18; 24:16–17.

(Gen 18:17–33; Exod 32:10–14).[16] This is precisely what has happened here, and Moses responds by pleading with the Lord not to destroy the Israelites (Num 14:13–19).

Moses's Intercession on Israel's Behalf (14:13–19)

Moses makes his appeal on two bases: the Lord's honor and the Lord's character. In terms of the former, the Lord had offered to make Moses the head of a new Israelite nation, but Moses's response shows that he was not concerned about his own glory (cf. Exod 32:11–13); he desired the Lord to be honored, which he feared would not happen if the Lord's people died in the wilderness. The Egyptians, who had already seen his power (Num 14:13), might accuse the Lord of delivering his people only to destroy them (cf. Exod 32:12), while the Canaanites, who have already heard of the Lord's very real presence among his people (Num 14:14; cf. Josh 2:9),[17] will conclude the Lord was not great enough to accomplish his promises of giving them the land (Num 14:15–16). In either case, they will defame his name instead of worshiping him as their Lord and creator—and Moses's love for God and his desire for God's goodness to be known could not let him stand this thought. He thus prays that the Lord's strength "be displayed" (v. 17), or perhaps better, "be put on full display," which in this context would happen by his forgiving the people and continuing to care for them (vv. 18–19), in this way showing his strength to watch over and protect them (cf. the use of "power" in v. 13) and thus make clear to the surrounding nations that he is the true God.

But Moses does not stop there; he also appeals to the Lord's character, citing the Lord's earlier self-description as being "slow to anger, abounding in love and forgiving sin and rebellion. Yet he does not leave the guilty unpunished" (Num 14:18a; cf. Exod 34:6–7a). In other words, the Lord is characterized by both mercy and judgment, which is exactly what we will see play out here: mercy in that the Lord will not disown the nation by wiping them out immediately and starting over with Moses, yet judgment in that he will sentence the nation to wandering and dying in the wilderness, never to enter the promised land. By citing Exodus 34:6–7, Moses acknowledges the Lord's right to administer such justice here, all the while praying that his mercy would also be on full display. He, in fact, returns to the Lord's love in Numbers 14:19, knowing that "God has always bent over backward on the side of love and

---

16. Cf. Amos 7:1–9 (Milgrom, *Numbers*, 110).
17. The phrase "face to face" (Num 14:14) is "eye to eye" in Hebrew, an idiom referring not to the Israelites actually seeing the Lord's face (cf. Exod 33:20) but to the fact that his presence in their midst was real and visible (as the rest of the verse makes clear).

forgiveness,"[18] and therefore asking the Lord to forgive in keeping with that great love, a love that he has already shown by granting his people forgiveness for their many wrongs since their delivery from Egypt (v. 19).[19]

As a final observation, it may be noted that Moses's citation of Exodus 34:6–7 includes the phrase, "[the LORD] punishes the children for the sin of the parents to the third and fourth generation" (Num 14:18; Exod 34:7b). What does this mean? It cannot mean the Lord will be angry with a sinner's innocent descendants and make them the focus of his punishment, which goes against other pentateuchal laws that prohibit such actions (Deut 24:16). Closer examination of the historical and literary contexts suggests the idea is that the family in those days often consisted of three to four generations, so that when the parents committed wrong and received the Lord's discipline, the children themselves could be caught up in it, not because the Lord was angry with the children but because the family is a unit, closely connected, so that discipline received by one member often impacts others in that unit until the discipline is complete or the sinner has died. This is, in fact, precisely what will happen here, as made clear by the Lord's later words to those who rebelliously refused to enter the land: "But as for you, your bodies will fall in this wilderness. Your children will be shepherds here for forty years, suffering for your unfaithfulness, until the last of your bodies lies in the wilderness" (Num 14:32–33).[20] In this regard, Exodus 34:7b serves as an incredibly profound warning: do all you can to avoid sin because its discipline often impacts those you love most!

The Lord Declares a Mitigated Judgment on the People (14:20–35)

The Lord begins by addressing Moses directly (Num 14:20–25). He agrees to Moses's request and forgives the people, not carrying out the threatened punishment of immediate destruction (v. 20). But forgiveness does not mean the absence of discipline; just as parents can forgive their children for a great wrong, continue in relationship with them, and yet still exercise discipline, the Lord can do the same with his children, the Israelites.

---

18. Olson, *Numbers*, 83.

19. For further discussion on the role of the mediator, see Sklar, "Sin and Atonement," 467–91, esp. 485–91.

20. Alternatively, the phrase has been understood to mean that the Lord will punish future generations ("to the third and fourth generation") when they commit the same sin as their parents (see Stuart, *Exodus*, 454). Undoubtedly, the Lord would punish future generations in such a situation, but the intended sense of the words is better captured by the above explanation, especially in light of Num 14:32–33. See further Mark J. Boda, *A Severe Mercy: Sin and its Remedy in the Old Testament*, Siphrut 1 (Winona Lake, IN: Eisenbrauns, 2009), 45, and esp. n30.

In this case, the discipline is clear and perfectly fits the wrong: those who have rebelliously refused to enter the land will be barred from ever doing so (Num 14:21–23). The rebellious Israelites had seen multiple instances[21] of the Lord displaying his great power and strength and yet constantly doubted[22] and disobeyed him (v. 22). Most immediately, they had just treated him with contempt by refusing to enter the land and wanting instead to return to Egypt (v. 23). The latter was the final straw of rebellion that broke the back of the Lord's patience, and he thus swears an oath that the discipline he has described will indeed come to pass, an oath that might be paraphrased: "As certainly as I exist, and as certainly as my glory—my great strength and miraculous care—have been evident in the earth, those who have seen clear signs of it and yet still rebelled against me will not make it into the promised land" (vv. 21–23).

But not all rebelled and thus not all will be kept from the land. Caleb will be allowed full entry into the land (Num 14:24), as will Joshua (v. 30);[23] both have shown full confidence in the Lord by believing his covenant promise to give Israel the land and thus both will be able to enter into it. Old Testament or New, covenant faithfulness is necessary to experience covenant blessing (cf. John 15:1–6).

The Lord then provides a related command: in light of the fact this generation of Israelites will not inherit the land, and thus will not have success in battle, make sure not to engage the people of the land in war or attempt to enter into it; turn back south into the wilderness and toward the Red Sea[24] instead of heading north into the land (Num 14:25).[25]

Having announced the judgment to Moses (Num 14:20–25), the Lord

---

21. The phrase "ten times" is often understood as a general expression of emphasis (cf. our expression "I've told you a thousand times"); cf. Gen 31:7; Lev 26:26. Others (including the early rabbis) have attempted to provide a possible list of ten instances, e.g., Allen, "Numbers," 822: Exod 14:10–12; 15:22–24; 16:1–3, 19–20, 27–30; 17:1–4; 32:1–35; Num 11:1–3, 4–34; 14:1–3. In either case, the Israelites' rebellion has been incredibly frequent.

22. When people "test" the Lord, it is always negative, expressing a lack of faith in his goodness and trustworthiness (Exod 17:2–7; Deut 6:16; Pss 78:17–19, 41, 56; 95:9; 106:14).

23. It is not clear why Joshua is not mentioned here in v. 24. Perhaps the text is simply focused on the actions of the common people, of which Caleb was a member, as opposed to those in the circle of Mosaic leadership, of which Joshua was a member. Cf. Deut 1:36–38, where there is a similar focus on Caleb by himself in 1:36, and then the mention of Joshua—and his association with Moses—in 1:38. Others explain the difference by appealing to different sources; for an analysis and critique of such an approach, see Wenham, *Numbers*, 124–26; more broadly, see Wenham, *Numbers* (OT Guides), 68–80.

24. This was a "well-known road . . . [that] stretched from the area of Kadesh to the north shore of the Gulf of Aqabah" (Ashley, *Numbers*, 262).

25. Alternatively, the first part of 14:25 might be connected to the end of 14:24 and translated "and they will inherit it even though the Amalekites and Canaanites are living in the valley" (so Ashley, *Numbers*, 252).

now has it announced to the people (vv. 26–35). The punishment is poetic justice (v. 28): all those twenty and older—who were old enough to fight in faith (1:3) but instead rebelliously declared it would have been better to die in the wilderness (14:2)—would indeed die there (vv. 29, 32)! (The Lord's promise to inherit the land was a covenant promise assuming covenant faithfulness, which is why they would *not* enter the land but why Caleb and Joshua, who expressed true faith, would enter it [v. 30].) Mercifully, the sinful generation's death would not be immediate (which would have destroyed the nation); it would take forty years (corresponding to the number of days the spies went through the land [v. 34]), thus allowing the nation to continue (and preventing other nations from speaking ill of the Lord [vv. 13–16]). But the judgment was sure (v. 35).

Along with this poetic justice, however, there is ironic reversal: while they themselves would "know" the Lord's opposition (Num 14:34), their children, whom they feared would be taken as plunder (v. 3), would "enjoy" (Heb. "know") the land (v. 31)! True, the children would also experience hardship, living as wandering shepherds in the wilderness for forty years while their rebellious parents died out (v. 33);[26] nonetheless, what the parents have sinfully rejected their children will enjoy.

The Lord's Judgment on the Faithless Scouts (14:36–38)

While most of the Israelites would die over the next forty years, the ten faithless spies experienced immediate judgment from the Lord (Num 14:36–37; a brief note makes clear that Joshua and Caleb were not part of this group [v. 38]). The text emphasizes the spies' faithlessness by stating twice that they spread a bad report about the land, making it abundantly clear they were the ultimate source of the people's rebellion. While it is always wrong for a people to sin, those who lead them into sin bear even greater responsibility.

The People Disobey the Lord and Try to Enter the Land (14:39–45)

Upon hearing the Lord's words, the people mourned greatly (Num 14:39; cf. Exod 33:4). They proceed to express repentance in precisely the wrong way. Instead of receiving the Lord's discipline and obeying his voice to turn from the land, they decide to go up into it, hoping they can somehow still gain the promise (Num 14:40).[27] Moses is very clear: this will not work; they have

---

26. Because the family is a unit, discipline coming on the parents impacts the remaining generations under their roof; see above at 14:13–19, p. 201.

27. They decide to try and access it via the hill country, which runs north to south in the land; perhaps this was motivated by the knowledge that the valley area was already occupied (14:25).

already turned from the Lord, and he will not be with them in this endeavor (which means it cannot possibly succeed; vv. 41–43). This would be graphically underscored: neither the ark (representing the Lord's presence) nor Moses (the Lord's leader) would go with the Israelites (v. 44b). The people, however, would go nonetheless, driven by a heedless presumption they could avoid the Lord's discipline (v. 44a). The result was disastrous: without the Lord's presence, they were helpless before their enemies, who beat them into pieces as far as Hormah, a city in the far south[28] of the promised land (but whose exact location is unknown). Interestingly, its name is built on the same root used as the verb "devote to destruction" (*h-r-m*; cf. 21:3); the Israelites, who were to devote the Canaanites to destruction (*haharim*) are instead defeated by the Canaanites as far as Destruction (*hormah*).[29] "The death of the old rebellious generation had begun."[30]

LIVE the Story

We may unpack this story by asking four questions.[31]

What Motivates Our Obedience?
Despite the setbacks of Numbers 11 and 12, chapter 13 starts out incredibly positively. The Lord tells Moses to send twelve scouts into the land he is giving to the Israelites (13:1), and when they come back, they are not only carrying an enormous cluster of grapes between two of them (v. 23), they begin their report by stating, "We went into the land to which you sent us, and it does flow with milk and honey!" (v. 27). Just as the Lord had promised, this was a very good land, and it seems like Israel is moments away from entering into it.

But faith would still be required for this to happen, and for ten of the twelve scouts, faith was in very short supply. They immediately proceed to describe the people of the land as "powerful," giant in stature, and their cities as impregnable (Num 13:28–29). As the day wears on, they convince the rest of the people that trying to enter the land would result in certain death, so that by the next day the Israelites are ready to reverse the exodus,[32] go back

---

28. Cf. Josh 15:21 with 15:30.
29. Cf. J. Gordon McConville, *Deuteronomy*, Apollos Old Testament Commentary 5 (Downers Grove, IL: InterVarsity Press, 2002), 101, 73.
30. Olson, *Numbers*, 86.
31. For an alternative homiletical approach, see p. 179n13.
32. The enormity of this should not be missed; it would be like a Christian wanting to undo Easter.

to Egypt, and kill any leader who thinks entering Canaan is still a good idea (14:1–4, 10a). For the Israelites, there was no question the land was good in terms of its fruitfulness; there was every question whether the Lord was good in terms of his faithfulness. A lack of trust in God can lead us to turn from his ways whenever they appear to go through dangerous land.

Not all the scouts, however, were cut out of the same cloth. Caleb and Joshua modeled true faith for their fellow Israelites, exhorting all to go boldly into the land because "the LORD is with us!" (Num 14:9). And therein lies the difference: the faithless scouts looked at the situation as though they were alone;[33] Joshua and Caleb looked at the situation with full confidence that the God of the universe was with them and could be trusted.[34] Their obedience was not motivated by any confidence in their own abilities and strength but by deep faith in God's abilities and strength, deep faith in his presence, and deep faith in his faithfulness to his promises.

At certain times in our lives, obedience can be very difficult, even scary. Obedience can have relational costs; it can have financial costs; it can cost us in terms of our pride or our reputation. What strengthens us to obey in such times? God's faithful presence with us. In some of Jesus's last words to his disciples, he gave them an incredible mission: spreading his good news among all nations (Matt 28:18–20). For a small group of Jewish fishermen, this might have seemed as impossible as it seemed for the Israelites to go into the promised land! But as Jesus finishes his exhortation, he assures them, "And surely I am with you always, to the very end of the age" (28:20). We can obey simply because the Lord is with us—and he *will* be faithful to his promises! Are there areas in our lives where we are afraid to obey? If so, how might the reality of Jesus's faithful presence with us encourage us to step forward in faith?

Sadly, as the story proceeds, Israel refuses to do this, and their rebellion becomes a story of warning to which many other biblical writers return in order to underscore the importance of faithful obedience. This leads to our second question.

Why Does Obedience Matter?

We can answer this question in three ways. Sometimes we think of sin as simply breaking one of God's rules, but the Bible portrays sin as much more than that: it is to personally despise the Lord. Note the personal language

---

33. "Disbelief is cowardice that correctly assesses the impossibility of a situation but fails to take God into account" (Gane, *Leviticus, Numbers*, 602).
34. "The eye of faith recognizes that in this world, reality is not accurately measured whenever we are 'humanly speaking'" (Duguid, *Numbers*, 171).

he uses to describe the Israelites' sin. In Numbers 14:11 he asks, "How long will these people treat me with contempt?" And in 14:33 he speaks of their "unfaithfulness," a word referring to illicit sexual activity, thus likening Israel to an adulterous spouse.[35] This is highly relational language and for a reason: the Lord is not a distant deity, unmoved and uncaring; he is our creator, a heavenly father wanting relationship with his children, and we betray and turn from that relationship every time we do not obey his commands. Obedience matters because it is impossible to draw close to God without it.

And this leads to the second reason obedience matters. When we turn away from the living God, we turn away from the abundant and eternal life that he offers. The writer of Hebrews makes exactly this point, using the first generation of Israelites in Numbers as a negative example. After describing their faithlessness, the writer states, "See to it, brothers and sisters, that none of you has a sinful, unbelieving heart [like them!] that turns away from the living God" (Heb 3:12). The writer is addressing apostasy—completely rejecting the faith—and the warning comes because those who do so "shall never enter" (4:5, quoting Ps 95:11) the Lord's rest, which in Numbers refers to the promised land but which in Hebrews becomes a way to refer to the far greater gift of eternal life (Heb 4:1–11). The point is not that obedience earns our salvation; the writer makes clear that Jesus, the faithful high priest, is the one who has made a way for our sins to be forgiven (1:3) and that it is those who *believe* the "good news" about Jesus who "enter that rest" (4:2–3). But Jesus calls us to *follow* him (Matt 4:19); if we give up on obedience, choosing to live a life of disobedient rebellion, then we've given up on following Jesus and will stay outside the far greater promised land he came to win us.

There is a final reason that obedience matters. When Moses pleads for the Lord to forgive the Israelites' sin, the Lord agrees to his request—and yet immediately states that the entire first generation of Israelites will die in the wilderness (Num 14:20–22). This should not be surprising. As noted above, forgiveness does not mean the absence of discipline; just as parents can forgive their children for a great wrong, continue in relationship with them, and yet still exercise discipline, the Lord can do the same with his children, the Israelites. And the greater the wrong, the more severe that discipline can be. Obedience definitely matters, and this leads to our third question.

---

35. The metaphor helps to put God's judgment in context: what spouse would not be furious at adultery, especially if it had already happened "ten times" (Num 14:22)? That there is judgment in the Old Testament is not surprising; what is surprising is that there is not more.

What Hope Do We Have in Our Disobedience?

If you had been Moses, how would you have prayed for the Israelites at this time? You could not appeal to their character; they were utterly corrupt. So what could you do?

Moses's prayer is driven by two different realities. On the one hand, he had seen God display his glory—his powerful strength and unspeakably good character—and Moses longed for that glory to be seen and recognized by all the nations. If the Lord's people were destroyed, the very opposite would happen, as the nations would conclude that Israel's God was weak or cruel (see at 14:13–19, p. 200), and Moses could not stand the thought of this. And this is the key. Moses is not praying this way because the Lord is like a human king with an ego that needs to be stroked. Rather, Moses has been captivated by the goodness and greatness of who the Lord is and cannot stand the thought that anyone would defame him instead of falling in praise before him. Moses thus models for the Israelites what motivates faithful prayer: a desire for the world's inhabitants to acknowledge him as God. Jesus models the very same when he teaches us to pray, "Our Father in heaven, *hallowed* be your name" (Matt 6:9, emphasis added), that is, "May your name be *recognized as holy*; may people treat you as the holy one you are; may they set you apart in their lives as the God worthy of glory and honor and praise!" Faithful prayer is driven by a desire for God's powerful strength and unspeakably good character to be seen and glorified throughout the earth.

But Moses does not stop there. He realizes the Israelites are still worthy of judgment and so looks to the only thing left that held out hope: the Lord's merciful love. At Mt. Sinai, when the Lord announced his character to Moses, he began by saying. "The LORD, the LORD, the compassionate and gracious God, slow to anger, abounding in love and faithfulness, maintaining love to thousands, and forgiving wickedness, rebellion and sin" (Exod 34:6b–7a). Clearly, he is a God of deep mercy and love. The Lord then continued: "Yet he does not leave the guilty unpunished; he punishes the children and their children for the sin of the parents to the third and fourth generation" (v. 7b). Clearly, he is also a God who takes sin very seriously.[36] In short, the Lord is a God of incredible mercy and yet of incredible justice. Moses acknowledges both but appeals in particular to the Lord's merciful, steadfast love. He knows

---

36. For the explanation of these verses, see at 14:13–19 above, p. 201.

that God "[bends] over backward on the side of love and forgiveness,"[37] and he appeals to that now, repenting on Israel's behalf. For Moses, deep hope for disobedient sinners can be found in the merciful love of God.

How much more so in Jesus! If ever there was a time that God "bent over backward on the side of love and forgiveness," it was in sending Jesus to bear the justice that our sin deserved so that we might be forgiven and put right with God. In Jesus's sacrifice, God carries out judgment for the sins of the world and yet in such a way that his merciful love is made available to all who believe (Rom 3:25–26); in Christ, judgment and mercy meet. And this means that no matter how deep our disobedience and rebellion has been, there is hope for us, if only we come to him in repentant faith, trusting in the merciful love shown to us in Jesus.

But our story in Numbers 13–14 is not over yet, and this leads to our final question.

How Does the Story End?

We might hope that Israel had learned her lesson by now, that hearing of the Lord's discipline would have led them to new depths of obedience, closely following his word and rejoicing that although the discipline was severe, the Lord in his love and mercy would continue in relationship with them. But this is not what happens.

Upon hearing of the Lord's decision not to give them the land, the Israelites acknowledge their sin but decide to try and take the land in their own strength (Num 14:39–45). Even in repentance, the Israelites find a way to rebel. They have not understood that the Lord's covenant promises are a gift of his grace, to be received through faith, instead of something they can earn on their own.

And that is the difference between human religion and biblical faith. Human religion teaches you to acknowledge your sin but to be the one who makes up for it to save yourself; biblical faith teaches you to acknowledge your sin and cast yourself on Jesus as the only one who can save you. Human religion allows you to maintain some semblance of pride, because at the end of the day you can fix yourself; biblical faith requires absolute humility, because at the end of the day only God can fix you. The good news is that he delights to do so and, in Jesus, bends over backward to show us love and forgiveness, if only we humble ourselves and put our trust in him.

---

37. Olson, *Numbers*, 83. One author defines God's forgiveness as his "gritty patience and willingness to continue on in relationship in spite of the past" (Stubbs, *Numbers*, 133).

CHAPTER 18

Numbers 15:1-41

 LISTEN to the Story

¹The LORD said to Moses, ²"Speak to the Israelites and say to them: 'After you enter the land I am giving you as a home ³and you present to the LORD food offerings from the herd or the flock, as an aroma pleasing to the LORD—whether burnt offerings or sacrifices, for special vows or freewill offerings or festival offerings—⁴then the person who brings an offering shall present to the LORD a grain offering of a tenth of an ephah of the finest flour mixed with a quarter of a hin of olive oil. ⁵With each lamb for the burnt offering or the sacrifice, prepare a quarter of a hin of wine as a drink offering.

⁶"'With a ram prepare a grain offering of two-tenths of an ephah of the finest flour mixed with a third of a hin of olive oil, ⁷and a third of a hin of wine as a drink offering. Offer it as an aroma pleasing to the LORD.

⁸"'When you prepare a young bull as a burnt offering or sacrifice, for a special vow or a fellowship offering to the LORD, ⁹bring with the bull a grain offering of three-tenths of an ephah of the finest flour mixed with half a hin of olive oil, ¹⁰and also bring half a hin of wine as a drink offering. This will be a food offering, an aroma pleasing to the LORD. ¹¹Each bull or ram, each lamb or young goat, is to be prepared in this manner. ¹²Do this for each one, for as many as you prepare.

¹³"'Everyone who is native-born must do these things in this way when they present a food offering as an aroma pleasing to the LORD. ¹⁴For the generations to come, whenever a foreigner or anyone else living among you presents a food offering as an aroma pleasing to the LORD, they must do exactly as you do. ¹⁵The community is to have the same rules for you and for the foreigner residing among you; this is a lasting ordinance for the generations to come. You and the foreigner shall be the same before the LORD: ¹⁶The same laws and regulations will apply both to you and to the foreigner residing among you.

"'17"The LORD said to Moses, 18"Speak to the Israelites and say to them: 'When you enter the land to which I am taking you 19and you eat the food of the land, present a portion as an offering to the LORD. 20Present a loaf from the first of your ground meal and present it as an offering from the threshing floor. 21Throughout the generations to come you are to give this offering to the LORD from the first of your ground meal.

22"'Now if you as a community unintentionally fail to keep any of these commands the LORD gave Moses—23any of the LORD's commands to you through him, from the day the LORD gave them and continuing through the generations to come—24and if this is done unintentionally without the community being aware of it, then the whole community is to offer a young bull for a burnt offering as an aroma pleasing to the LORD, along with its prescribed grain offering and drink offering, and a male goat for a sin offering. 25The priest is to make atonement for the whole Israelite community, and they will be forgiven, for it was not intentional and they have presented to the LORD for their wrong a food offering and a sin offering. 26The whole Israelite community and the foreigners residing among them will be forgiven, because all the people were involved in the unintentional wrong.

27"'But if just one person sins unintentionally, that person must bring a year-old female goat for a sin offering. 28The priest is to make atonement before the LORD for the one who erred by sinning unintentionally, and when atonement has been made, that person will be forgiven. 29One and the same law applies to everyone who sins unintentionally, whether a native-born Israelite or a foreigner residing among you.

30"'But anyone who sins defiantly, whether native-born or foreigner, blasphemes the LORD and must be cut off from the people of Israel. 31Because they have despised the LORD's word and broken his commands, they must surely be cut off; their guilt remains on them.'"

32While the Israelites were in the wilderness, a man was found gathering wood on the Sabbath day. 33Those who found him gathering wood brought him to Moses and Aaron and the whole assembly, 34and they kept him in custody, because it was not clear what should be done to him. 35Then the LORD said to Moses, "The man must die. The whole assembly must stone him outside the camp." 36So the assembly took him outside the camp and stoned him to death, as the LORD commanded Moses.

> ³⁷The Lord said to Moses, ³⁸"Speak to the Israelites and say to them: 'Throughout the generations to come you are to make tassels on the corners of your garments, with a blue cord on each tassel. ³⁹You will have these tassels to look at and so you will remember all the commands of the Lord, that you may obey them and not prostitute yourselves by chasing after the lusts of your own hearts and eyes. ⁴⁰Then you will remember to obey all my commands and will be consecrated to your God. ⁴¹I am the Lord your God, who brought you out of Egypt to be your God. I am the Lord your God.'"

Listening to the Text in the Story: Leviticus 1; 3–5; 23

Previous chapters in the Pentateuch have gone into extensive detail about different types of animal sacrifices (Lev 1; 3–5; 23); they have not, however, given a standardized description of the grain and drink offerings that should accompany these sacrifices. This chapter addresses that need (Num 15:1–16).

Many pictures from the second millennium BC show that tassels were worn by different peoples on their garments.[1] While the exact significance of the tassels for other nations is unknown, their function for Israelites is clearly stated: they are to be visual reminders to keep the laws of their covenant King (15:37–41).[2]

EXPLAIN the Story

Laws for the Promised Land: Grain and Drink Offerings (15:1–16)

In the previous chapter, the Lord states that the rebellious first generation of Israelites would not enter the promised land but promises their children would. This chapter's opening words (Num 15:2–3a) confirm that promise: not only will the second-generation Israelites enter the promised land, the Lord will accept their faithful worship when they get there. These are strong words of hope;[3] the Lord remains Israel's covenant-keeping God.

---

1. See *ANEP*, plates 6, 7, 45, 476. For fuller discussion, see Stephen Bertman, "Tasseled Garments in the Ancient East Mediterranean," *BA* 24 (1961): 119–28.
2. See further detail p. 216.
3. Ashley, *Numbers*, 277.

When Israel entered the land, they would continue presenting offerings, including burnt and fellowship offerings.[4] These could be brought for "special vows," which were personally or financially costly,[5] "freewill offerings," which were brought voluntarily, and "festival offerings" (v. 3), which were required at Israel's annual festivals, such as Passover, the Festival of Booths (Succoth), etc. (see Lev 23; Num 28–29).[6] In each case, the goal was to offer these as a "pleasing aroma," a phrase that conveys the Lord is pleased with the offerer and favorably accepts the smoke as representing a legitimate sacrifice presented with heartfelt worship (cf. Gen 8:21; Ezek 20:41).

The chapter then describes the grain and drink offerings accompanying these sacrifices (Num 15:4–10).[7] One metaphor for sacrifice was that of a meal. In ancient Israel, a special meal would consist of meat and bread and wine (1 Sam 16:20), and the offerings described here make the sacrificial meal complete, complementing the meat (sacrificial animal) with bread (grain offering) and wine (drink offering).

Grain offerings were brought to the burnt offering altar by the priest, who would burn a handful of the offering on the offerer's behalf; the remainder would normally go to the priests (Lev 6:15–17; cf. v. 23). Drink offerings were also brought to the burnt offering altar by the priest and presumably poured out upon it (cf. Exod 30:9). The size of grain and drink offerings differed in accord with the size of the animal presented; these verses describe three types of animals, from smallest to largest, and their corresponding offerings (see table below).[8]

These offering rules are to be followed for each sacrificial animal offered (Num 15:11–12) and apply equally to native Israelites and to non-Israelites living in their midst (vv. 13–16). The application to non-Israelites was important in order to avoid syncretism, since it made clear that any worship of the Lord had to be done exactly as he commanded; no foreign worship could

---

4. For fuller descriptions of these offerings, see at 6:13–20, pp. 116–17. When mentioned with burnt offerings, fellowship offerings are sometimes simply referred to as "sacrifices" (Num 15:3; cf. Lev 23:37; Josh 22:26). The Hebrew term translated "food offerings" (NIV) is perhaps better translated "fire offerings" (so RSV; see Levine, *Leviticus*, 7–8); it is most often used to describe portions of offerings burned up on the altar to the Lord (see Lev 2:2; 3:3–5; 7:5; 8:28).

5. Such as the dedication of a person (Lev 27:2), or a Nazirite vow, which involved strict lifestyle obligations (Num 6:2).

6. This may have also included non-festival occasions, such as the daily, Sabbath, and monthly offerings (Num 28:2–15).

7. There is no evidence grain and drink offerings were made with purification (sin) or guilt offerings.

8. Adapted from Sklar, *Leviticus* (ZECOT), 106. Identifying modern equivalents for many biblical measures is difficult. Those in the chart on Biblical Measurement are based on Cook, "Weights and Measures," 1051. Most authorities lean toward the lower end of these ranges.

intrude. But it also reminds the Israelites that coming before the Lord is not to be restricted to themselves; the goal is for all nations to worship him.⁹

	Biblical Measurement (and Rough Modern Equivalent)		
Animal	Lamb (sheep in the first year) or kid (young goat) (Num 15:4–5, 11)	Ram (adult male sheep) (Num 15:6–7)	Bull (adult male bovine) (Num 15:8–10)
Fine Flour	1/10 ephah = 8.8 to 16.3 cups (8.3 to 15.4 metric cups), weighing between 2.8 to 5.1 lb (1.3 to 2.3 kg)	2/10 ephah = 17.6 to 32.6 cups (16.6 to 30.8 metric cups), weighing between 5.6 to 10.2 lb (2.5 to 4.6 kg)	3/10 ephah = 26.4 to 48.9 cups (24.9 to 46.2 metric cups), weighing between 8.4 to 15.3 lb (3.8 to 6.9 kg)
Olive Oil, Wine	1/4 hin = .24 to .43 gallons (.9 to 1.63 liters)	1/3 hin = .32 to .59 gallons (1.2 to 2.2 liters)	1/2 hin = .48 to .86 gallons (1.8 to 3.25 liters)

Laws for the Promised Land: First Loaf (15:17–21)

Like the previous verses, Numbers 15:17–21 give offering instructions to follow in the promised land. The word used here for "offering" (*terumah*) refers to an item that is given to the Lord that he in turn gave to support the tabernacle and its workers.¹⁰ Several texts require the Israelites to present firstfruits to the Lord (Exod 23:19; 34:26; Lev 23:9–14); this text specifies that a loaf of bread from the firstfruits of the ground meal¹¹ also be brought.

Unintentional Sin versus Defiant Sin (15:22–31)

Like the chapter's beginning, this section discusses animal sacrifices with their grain and drink offerings, and it includes the resident alien.¹² Its goal, however, is to contrast unintentional and defiant sins. The former may be forgiven by means of sacrificial atonement; the latter may not. This contrast is especially

---

9. Olson, *Numbers*, 93, notes also 1 Kgs 8:41; Isa 56:7; see further Ps 67.
10. See Lev 7:14; Ezek 44:30.
11. The word for "ground meal" is rare; others translate as "dough" or "kneading trough." What is clear is that a loaf is the final result of this offering.
12. Cf. Num 15:24 with 15:3–16 and 15:26 with 15:14–16.

important following the defiant sin of Numbers 14, and the overall effect is to warn, "The only type of sin you should ever commit is that done completely by mistake!" Any other type of sin is already one step too close to rebellious apostasy.[13]

First addressed are unintentional sins of the community (Num 15:22–26), which occur when they "unintentionally fail to keep"[14] any of the Lord's commands through Moses, whether those already given or those yet to be given (vv. 22–23). No examples are named, but such sin might take place if the community got the calendar wrong and celebrated a feast on the incorrect day. When such sin happens, the Israelites are to bring the appropriate sacrifices (v. 24b),[15] the priest will offer them on the people's behalf, make atonement, and they will be forgiven (v. 25a), that is, by the Lord. The phrases "make atonement" and "be forgiven" occur naturally together, since making atonement regularly involves giving a lesser penalty (a ransom) in place of the one deserved and forgiving regularly involves allowing a lesser penalty in place of the one deserved.[16] In this case, the animal sacrifices are the ransom payment, which the Lord graciously accepts so the people might be forgiven. A closing verse affirms that such forgiveness extends to resident aliens since they would have sinned with the community (v. 26). The Israelites thus knew they did not need to cast them out of their midst and were again reminded that the Lord's desire is that non-Israelites, too, be in right relationship with him (cf. at 15:13–16, pp. 212–13).

Unintentional sins of an individual are addressed next (Num 15:27–29). Again, the individual Israelite must bring the appropriate offering to be forgiven (vv. 27–28), as must also the non-Israelite (v. 29).

The text now describes what to do when a person sins "defiantly" (Num 15:30–31) or, more woodenly, sins "with an uplifted hand," a phrase used elsewhere to describe raising one's hand in defiant rebellion against a human

---

13. See further discussion in Sklar, "Sin and Atonement," esp. 482–85.

14. This is not limited to sins of "omission" (failing to do something); as Ashley (*Numbers*, 285) notes, 15:24 and 15:29 speak of the sinner doing something (sins of "commission"). "Any of the Lord's commands" are in view.

15. For fuller descriptions of these offerings, see at 6:13–20, pp. 116–17. Lev 4:13–21 calls for a bull for a purification offering (instead of a goat) and does not require a bull burnt offering. Why? Gane (*Cult*, 85n46) surveys responses and gives a contextual suggestion: since Num 15:22–24 comes after the community's rebellion in Num 14 (including their grumbling against Aaron, the high priest), the Lord makes their purification offering lesser than the high priest's to remind them of their place and requires a bull as a burnt offering to make up for the lesser purification offering animal.

16. See further discussion in Sklar, *Leviticus* (ZECOT), 146. An example of such forgiveness just happened in Num 14; see comments at 14:20–35, pp. 201–2.

king (rendered "rebelled against" twice in 1 Kgs 11:26–27a). When done against the Lord, the heavenly King, this refers to apostate rebellion; the person has not simply sinned but completely rejected faith in the Lord through disobedient action, "blaspheming the Lord" and utterly "despising" his word (Num 15:30–31).[17] Such a person must be "cut off" (v. 31), a phrase referring to exile or even death.[18] For unintentional sin, the Lord guarantees an automatic means of forgiveness: sacrifice.[19] But for apostasy, no such automatic means is guaranteed. Kings do not typically encourage treason by providing an automatic way of escape from it.

The Penalty for Defiant Sin Illustrated (15:32–36)

Coming immediately after a description of defiant sin, this story provides an illustration of it. It begins with the Israelites finding a man gathering wood on the Sabbath. Keeping the Sabbath was foundational to Israelite faith since the Sabbath was the sign of the Sinai covenant.[20] To fail to keep it was to deny the covenant relationship and the Lord of that relationship (Exod 31:12–17), like ripping off and trampling a wedding ring—the sign of covenant relationship with a spouse—only much more serious, since this was an act of treason against the very King of heaven. Not surprisingly, other laws state that those breaking the Sabbath face the penalty usually given to the treasonous: death (Exod 31:14–15).

In this instance, however, the Israelites are unsure what to do and approach the Lord for legal direction (Num 15:34).[21] Perhaps their uncertainty is because earlier laws explicitly forbid building a fire on the Sabbath (Exod 35:3) but not collecting sticks, making them unsure if the Sabbath had been broken. Or perhaps they understood the death penalty to function like a maximum sentence but also thought that lesser sentences might be allowed and thus asked how to proceed in this instance.

In either case, the Lord's response is clear: this man must be put to death. The Lord knew the act was not "unintentional" sin (Num 15:27–29) but "defiant" sin, a rebellious "blaspheming of the LORD" and "despising his word" (vv. 30–31). In short, this man was not simply collecting wood; he

---

17. See further Sklar, "Sin and Atonement," 472–76.
18. For details, see Sklar, *Leviticus* (ZECOT), 41–42.
19. But for important qualifications, see the end of this chapter: Live the Story: Why Does Grace not Make Sin Safe?
20. See Exod 31:16–17.
21. The same happens in Lev 24:10–23; Num 9:6–14; 27:1–11; 36:1–9.

"was committing an act of rank apostasy, denying the Lord's covenant as well as profaning that which he had set apart as holy."[22] This was intentional treason and the penalty for the treasonous is applied; this man had chosen his own fate.

Executions were performed outside the camp (cf. Lev 24:23), perhaps to ensure the ritually defiling dead body (Num 19:11) did not pollute the camp. Bringing the man "outside of the camp" would also have been a fitting picture: the one who had rejected the Lord was now forcibly removed from the Lord's people. That the Israelites did just as "the LORD commanded Moses" (15:36) is a welcome note of obedience after the rebellion of Numbers 14.[23]

Tassels on Garments: A Reminder to Obey (15:37–41)

Coming on the heels of the wood-gatherer's rebellion, a visual reminder of obedience is appropriate. Similar reminders are given elsewhere (cf. Deut 6:8–9). In this case, it is tassels on the Israelites' garments, with other texts specifying all four of the garment's corners (or "extremities, wings"; 22:12),[24] with one blue cord for each, the cord perhaps fastening the tassels to the corners (cf. Exod 28:28, 37). The tassels were to help the Israelites remember and obey all the Lord's commands (Num 15:38–39), and no wonder: blue was a royal color (Esth 1:6; 8:15) and was used in the heavenly King's earthly palace, the tabernacle (Exod 26:1), and in the clothing of his royal servants, the priests (28:6, 8, 33). Tassels involving a blue thread were thus a good reminder for the Israelites to be a "kingdom of priests and a holy nation" (19:6) and to obey all the King's commands.

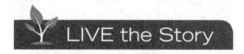

Even though this chapter has strong warnings and judgment, its theme note is that of grace. Four questions will help to make this clear.[25]

How Does the Lord Demonstrate His Grace?

In this chapter, the Lord demonstrates grace in numerous ways: (1) despite the Israelites' treachery in the last chapter, he begins this chapter by stating that

---

22. Sklar, "Sin and Atonement," 478.
23. Cf. Ashley, *Numbers*, 292.
24. Meaning either: (a) garments had four literal corners; (b) tassels were to be spread equally around the garment's bottom (like the four points of a compass); or (c) garments had four "scalloped hems resembling wings" (Milgrom, *Numbers*, 127.
25. For an alternative homiletical approach, see p. 179n13.

their children will inherit the promised land (Num 15:2) and come before him in worship (vv. 3–16), thus affirming they continue to be his people; (2) he would provide for their needs once in the promised land (vv. 17–21); (3) he provides sacrificial atonement so they might be forgiven of their sin (vv. 22–29); and (4) he finishes the chapter by underscoring he is their redeeming God (v. 41). In short, the Lord will show his faithfulness and love not simply by staying in relationship with them but also by taking care of their deepest needs. This includes physical needs, such as the food that comes from harvests, and spiritual needs, such as forgiveness for wrongs and continued relationship with the Lord. Both types of needs are fundamental to us as human beings and the Lord provides generously for both, just as a good father does for his children. He truly is full of love and grace.

What Is the Proper Response to Grace?
Responding properly to such grace takes on different forms. In worshiping the Lord, for example, we will want to do so exactly as he commands (cf. Num 15:1–16). In the ancient world, as in the modern, there was a certain protocol to follow when coming into a king's presence (cf. Esth 5:1–2). Following the protocol showed appropriate honor and respect to one who was so great and yet had invited you to spend time with him. And if that was true for an earthly king, how much more for the King of heaven! He is a gracious king but a king nonetheless, and we must always be sure to approach him on his terms, not our own.

Another example of a proper response to grace is seen in the giving of the firstfruits (Num 15:17–21). Doing so was a physical way for the Israelite to celebrate the Lord's faithfulness in providing food for them. Indeed, because the firstfruits were viewed as the harvest's very best (Num 18:12), the Israelites were demonstrating the Lord was worthy of the most honor they could give. This is worship fueled by deep thankfulness for the Lord's gifts and deep acknowledgement that all we have is from him.[26] Those with such a posture can indeed be "cheerful givers"—the very type of givers the Lord loves (2 Cor 9:7). If this is a struggle, we might want to ask ourselves, "Have I stopped being thankful for the material blessings God has given me? How might I begin to remember again that all I have is from him and given to me in love?" Answering such questions can help us move from asking "Do I have to give?" to "How much am I able to give?"[27]

---

26. Duguid, *Numbers*, 186.
27. Ibid., 187.

While responding properly to grace is incredibly important, it is equally important we do not take grace for granted. This leads to the next question.

Why Does Grace Not Make Sin Safe?
While the Lord is exceedingly gracious, this does not mean that it is safe to sin. This passage makes this clear by stating that sacrificial atonement is available for unintentional sin (Num 15:22–29) but not for "defiant" sin (vv. 30–31), that is, completely rejecting the Lord, turning our back on him, and going our own way. The wood gatherer is a tragic example of this (vv. 32–36); those who turn their back on the Lord experience the most fearful thing possible: the Lord turning his back on them.

Three points may be made by way of clarification. First, although not mentioned here, there is a third category of sin that falls in between unintentional and defiant sins. Leviticus gives examples of sins that are not unintentional and yet sacrificial atonement can be made for them, meaning they are not in the "defiant" category (Lev 5:1, 5–6; 6:1–7). Just what qualifies a sin for this category is debated,[28] but the category exists.[29] So why does Numbers 15 not mention it? Given the context of defiant sin in Numbers 14, the simplest explanation is perhaps that intentional sin, of whatever type, must be avoided at all costs. After all, it is not the person who sins by mistake that is in danger of apostasy but the person who sins intentionally; the step between intentional sin and defiant sin is very short, very slippery, and very easy to make. This chapter therefore leaves the middle category out in order to underscore: "Whatever you do, do not sin intentionally; avoid intentional sin of whatever type as though your life depends on it—because it does!" We do well to ask, "Is this our perspective when it comes to sin? Do we view it as a mortal enemy and do all we can to fight it, or do we view it simply as a spiritual inconvenience that we might need to pay a bit more attention to?"

---

28. "One plausible suggestion is that certain sins were considered automatic signs of apostasy and rebellion (e.g., idolatry), while others might have been viewed as being due more to human weakness than apostate intent. For example, in the case of [Lev] 5:1, the witness may fail to come forward because of 'friendship or shame or fear' (Milgrom, *Leviticus 1–16*, 294), and similar motivations—especially shame and fear—may have prompted the false oath of 5:20–26 (6:1–7)" (Sklar, *Leviticus* [ZECOT], 20).

29. "Duguid (*Numbers*, 191) compares them to our legal category of crimes of passion, that is, crimes we did not set out to commit but commit in the heat of the moment: 'These sins flow out of the war that goes on inside us between our sinful natures and our transformed hearts.' But they differ from defiant sins in that our response to them is one of repentance and turning back to the LORD instead of turning away from him in hardened rebellion" (Sklar, *Leviticus* [ZECOT], 20n47).

Second, forgiveness for defiant sin was still possible, as the previous chapter makes clear (Num 14:11–35). Instead of sacrificial atonement, however, a mediator interceded on the people's behalf,[30] and even when forgiveness was granted, the resulting discipline could still be severe: the first generation of Israelites will die outside the promised land, not inside it.

This leads naturally to the third point: Jesus's sacrifice is so great that it can atone for any category of sin, and yet the New Testament still repeats dire warnings against committing defiant sin. How does this work? Because Jesus's sacrifice is so powerful, it can cleanse any sin, no matter how deep the stain (Heb 10:14–22). To switch the metaphor, he is a priestly mediator who "always lives to intercede for [us]" (7:25). This means we can come to him with bold confidence for forgiveness and cleansing for our sin, no matter how dark or deep! But if we do not—if we reject him, turning our backs and walking away—then we have rejected our only hope of forgiveness.[31] This explains the warnings of places like Hebrews 10:

> If we deliberately keep on sinning after we have received the knowledge of the truth" [that is, if we continue in a life of rebellion even though we have learned about Jesus, then] no sacrifice for sins is left, but only a fearful expectation of judgment and of raging fire that will consume the enemies of God. Anyone who rejected the law of Moses died without mercy on the testimony of two or three witnesses. How much more severely do you think someone deserves to be punished who has trampled the Son of God underfoot? . . . It is a dreadful thing to fall into the hands of the living God. (vv. 26–29a, 31)

This is sobering language; many moderns will not feel comfortable with it, but our discomfort does not lessen its truth. If the consequences for treason against earthly rulers results in grave penalty, how much more for treason against the King of heaven.

But the chapter does not end on this note. Once more, it returns to grace.

What Has the Lord Graciously Called Us to Be?

The Lord's desire for us is life, not judgment; he has created us for his blessing, not his curse. He therefore commands the Israelites to wear tassels as a visual

---

30. For a discussion of this pattern in the Pentateuch, see Sklar, "Sin and Atonement," 485–90.
31. "The problem is not for God to be willing to forgive, but for a sinner to want to be forgiven" (Gane, *Leviticus, Numbers*, 628).

reminder that they are a kingdom of priests, serving the heavenly King, and must be careful to follow his commands.[32] Doing so would have two results.

First, it would protect them from acting to "prostitute [themselves] by chasing after the lusts of [their] own hearts and eyes" (Num 15:39). This is strong language; the words translated "prostitute" and "chasing" are in fact built on the same roots as the words used to describe the "faithlessness" (14:33) and "scouting" (v. 34) of the faithless scouts,[33] thus recalling their rebellion. The language is also deeply personal: the Israelites are not simply breaking rules when they act this way; like an adulterous spouse, they are betraying a faithful covenant partner, the Lord. This was the very thing the wood gatherer did; the Israelites were not to repeat his rebellion.

Second, following his commands would result in the Israelites being "consecrated to [their] God" (Num 15:40), that is, their obedience would show that they indeed belonged to him. The Lord underscores this relationship as the chapter closes, with words that could be woodenly translated: "I am the LORD your God, who brought you out of Egypt to be to you for a God" (v. 41a). The language "to be to person *x* for role *y*" is highly relational and similar to the language describing adoption and marriage, thus referring to a very close relationship.[34] In this context, it underscores that the Lord is a redeeming King, a caring father; in each case, he is in the position of authority but exercises that authority with tender care. As a result, the Israelites are not to view obedience as an impersonal checklist but as a highly relational act of love for their God, the one who had redeemed them and privileged them with the task of showing forth his holy character to the world as his holy priestly servants and children.[35]

What visual reminders might we make use of to remind us of this holy calling? What other reminders might we incorporate into our lives to encourage us to carry out the privilege of reflecting God's character into the world?

---

32. "Sight leads to memory and memory to action" (Milgrom, *Numbers*, 128, citing the rabbis [Babylonian Talmud, Menahot 43b]).

33. Milgrom, *Numbers*, 127.

34. See Jan Joosten, *People and Land in the Holiness Code: An Exegetical Study of the Ideational Framework of the Law in Leviticus 17–26*, VTSup 67 (Leiden: Brill, 1996), 102–3. For adoption, see Exod 2:10a; 2 Sam 7:14a; 1 Chr 17:13; 22:10; 28:6; Jer 31:9b. For marriage, see Gen 20:12; 24:67a; Num 36:11.

35. See further discussion in Sklar, *Leviticus* (ZECOT), 478–79.

CHAPTER 19

Numbers 16:1-50

 LISTEN to the Story

¹Korah son of Izhar, the son of Kohath, the son of Levi, and certain Reubenites—Dathan and Abiram, sons of Eliab, and On son of Peleth—became insolent ²and rose up against Moses. With them were 250 Israelite men, well-known community leaders who had been appointed members of the council. ³They came as a group to oppose Moses and Aaron and said to them, "You have gone too far! The whole community is holy, every one of them, and the Lord is with them. Why then do you set yourselves above the Lord's assembly?"

⁴When Moses heard this, he fell facedown. ⁵Then he said to Korah and all his followers: "In the morning the Lord will show who belongs to him and who is holy, and he will have that person come near him. The man he chooses he will cause to come near him. ⁶You, Korah, and all your followers are to do this: Take censers ⁷and tomorrow put burning coals and incense in them before the Lord. The man the Lord chooses will be the one who is holy. You Levites have gone too far!"

⁸Moses also said to Korah, "Now listen, you Levites! ⁹Isn't it enough for you that the God of Israel has separated you from the rest of the Israelite community and brought you near himself to do the work at the Lord's tabernacle and to stand before the community and minister to them? ¹⁰He has brought you and all your fellow Levites near himself, but now you are trying to get the priesthood too. ¹¹It is against the Lord that you and all your followers have banded together. Who is Aaron that you should grumble against him?"

¹²Then Moses summoned Dathan and Abiram, the sons of Eliab. But they said, "We will not come! ¹³Isn't it enough that you have brought us up out of a land flowing with milk and honey to kill us in the wilderness? And now you also want to lord it over us! ¹⁴Moreover, you haven't brought us into a land flowing with milk and honey or given us an inheritance of

fields and vineyards. Do you want to treat these men like slaves? No, we will not come!"

¹⁵Then Moses became very angry and said to the Lord, "Do not accept their offering. I have not taken so much as a donkey from them, nor have I wronged any of them."

¹⁶Moses said to Korah, "You and all your followers are to appear before the Lord tomorrow—you and they and Aaron. ¹⁷Each man is to take his censer and put incense in it—250 censers in all—and present it before the Lord. You and Aaron are to present your censers also." ¹⁸So each of them took his censer, put burning coals and incense in it, and stood with Moses and Aaron at the entrance to the tent of meeting. ¹⁹When Korah had gathered all his followers in opposition to them at the entrance to the tent of meeting, the glory of the Lord appeared to the entire assembly. ²⁰The Lord said to Moses and Aaron, ²¹"Separate yourselves from this assembly so I can put an end to them at once."

²²But Moses and Aaron fell facedown and cried out, "O God, the God who gives breath to all living things, will you be angry with the entire assembly when only one man sins?"

²³Then the Lord said to Moses, ²⁴"Say to the assembly, 'Move away from the tents of Korah, Dathan and Abiram.'"

²⁵Moses got up and went to Dathan and Abiram, and the elders of Israel followed him. ²⁶He warned the assembly, "Move back from the tents of these wicked men! Do not touch anything belonging to them, or you will be swept away because of all their sins." ²⁷So they moved away from the tents of Korah, Dathan and Abiram. Dathan and Abiram had come out and were standing with their wives, children and little ones at the entrances to their tents.

²⁸Then Moses said, "This is how you will know that the Lord has sent me to do all these things and that it was not my idea: ²⁹If these men die a natural death and suffer the fate of all mankind, then the Lord has not sent me. ³⁰But if the Lord brings about something totally new, and the earth opens its mouth and swallows them, with everything that belongs to them, and they go down alive into the realm of the dead, then you will know that these men have treated the Lord with contempt."

³¹As soon as he finished saying all this, the ground under them split apart ³²and the earth opened its mouth and swallowed them and their households, and all those associated with Korah, together with their

possessions. ³³They went down alive into the realm of the dead, with everything they owned; the earth closed over them, and they perished and were gone from the community. ³⁴At their cries, all the Israelites around them fled, shouting, "The earth is going to swallow us too!"

³⁵And fire came out from the LORD and consumed the 250 men who were offering the incense.

³⁶The LORD said to Moses, ³⁷"Tell Eleazar son of Aaron, the priest, to remove the censers from the charred remains and scatter the coals some distance away, for the censers are holy—³⁸the censers of the men who sinned at the cost of their lives. Hammer the censers into sheets to overlay the altar, for they were presented before the LORD and have become holy. Let them be a sign to the Israelites."

³⁹So Eleazar the priest collected the bronze censers brought by those who had been burned to death, and he had them hammered out to overlay the altar, ⁴⁰as the LORD directed him through Moses. This was to remind the Israelites that no one except a descendant of Aaron should come to burn incense before the LORD, or he would become like Korah and his followers.

⁴¹The next day the whole Israelite community grumbled against Moses and Aaron. "You have killed the LORD's people," they said.

⁴²But when the assembly gathered in opposition to Moses and Aaron and turned toward the tent of meeting, suddenly the cloud covered it and the glory of the LORD appeared. ⁴³Then Moses and Aaron went to the front of the tent of meeting, ⁴⁴and the LORD said to Moses, ⁴⁵"Get away from this assembly so I can put an end to them at once." And they fell facedown.

⁴⁶Then Moses said to Aaron, "Take your censer and put incense in it, along with burning coals from the altar, and hurry to the assembly to make atonement for them. Wrath has come out from the LORD; the plague has started." ⁴⁷So Aaron did as Moses said, and ran into the midst of the assembly. The plague had already started among the people, but Aaron offered the incense and made atonement for them. ⁴⁸He stood between the living and the dead, and the plague stopped. ⁴⁹But 14,700 people died from the plague, in addition to those who had died because of Korah. ⁵⁰Then Aaron returned to Moses at the entrance to the tent of meeting, for the plague had stopped.

Listening to the Text in the Story: Exodus 35–40; Numbers 1:47–53; 3:5–10

In Exodus 35–40, the tabernacle was built and the Lord descended in the cloud of glory to take up residence there. Israel's covenant King was now dwelling in his royal palace-tent in his people's midst. But he was a holy King, living in a holy palace; if anything that was not holy came into contact with it, that would profane it (loosely comparable to a person introducing germs or bacteria into an operating room). This would be a severe sign of disrespect, a declaration that the Lord's holy property or his own holiness were of little value (see at 1:47–53, pp. 53–54).

To prevent this from happening, the Lord provided two practical steps. First, he set the tribe of Levi around the tabernacle to guard it and also elevated them into a special level of ritual purity, giving them responsibility for taking down, transporting, and setting up the holy tabernacle (see again at 1:47–53, pp. 53–54) as well as serving the Israelites in various ways at the tabernacle, such as by helping to slaughter and butcher the sacrificial animal (which required significant technical knowledge) so the priests could then offer the animal on the altar (cf. Ezek 44:11). Second, he elevated one family within the Levites—Aaron's family—into the ritual state of holiness so they could serve as priests (thus every priest is a Levite but not every Levite is a priest). This allowed them to have contact with the holy altar and present the Israelites' holy offerings. More generally, they were also the leaders of the Levites, overseeing them in their tabernacle responsibilities (see at 3:5–10, p. 74).

As a result of these two steps, the Lord could remain in the midst of his people so they could enjoy his presence and have fellowship with him. But this arrangement was not to everyone's liking, as illustrated by a series of events in Numbers 16–17, in which the people rebel against the Lord's appointed leaders and the Lord miraculously responds to make clear these are indeed the leaders he has chosen.

EXPLAIN the Story

Numbers 16 contains two rebellion stories: the rebellion led by Korah, Dathan, and Abiram (vv. 1–40) and the people's rebellion (vv. 41–50). As we begin with the first, it may be noted that it describes two different complaints (vv. 1–15) and two vindicating judgments (vv. 16–40):

> A—First complaint: everyone is holy and can be priests, not just Aaron and his family (vv. 1–3)

B—Second complaint: Moses is an unfaithful and poor leader (vv. 12–15)

B′—First vindicating judgment: Moses is the Lord's appointed leader and has acted at his command (vv. 25–34)

A′—Second vindicating judgment: Aaron and his family are the Lord's appointed priests (vv. 35–40)

The Rebellion and Moses's Initial Response (16:1–7)

The chapter begins with a large group of men who gather in rebellion against Moses and Aaron (Num 16:1–2). The group is spearheaded by Korah, a Levite, who is joined by three Reubenites: Dathan, Abiram, and On (cf. 26:8–9). With them are 250 leaders from the nation, recognized and chosen by their fellow Israelites to be leaders and thus (one presumes) speaking on their behalf; this rebellion cuts across the entire nation.[1]

The heart of their initial complaint is that all the nation should be able to carry out priestly duties since every Israelite is holy (which is required for priestly service) and since the Lord is "with them" (Num 16:3; more woodenly, "in their midst," the idea perhaps being he is in their midst as every Israelite's God, not just Moses's and Aaron's God [cf. Exod 29:45]). These are half-truths presented as the whole truth and thus end up being lies. The Israelites had indeed been set apart to be holy in terms of behavior (Exod 19:6; Num 15:40), but only Aaron's family had been set apart to be holy in terms of ritual status (Lev 8). Similarly, the Lord dwelt in the midst of all Israel (Exod 29:45; Num 15:41) but had also made clear that only ritually holy priests could work within his sacred dwelling on Israel's behalf (Num 3:10).

Moses's initial response is to fall facedown (Num 16:4), expressing his humility ("I am not vaunting myself above you! See here: I'm bowing before you!") but also his dismay at this evil rebellion.[2] He then addresses Korah, the rebellion's ringleader, announcing a test on the next day by which the Lord will make clear who is holy and thus who can do priestly duties (v. 5). The test is to present an incense offering, that is, placing burning coals in a metal pan and then adding incense, creating a sweet cloud of smoke that rose as an offering to the Lord (vv. 6–7). Significantly, only priests could present such an offering (v. 40), and the Lord would use this test to show whom he had chosen for priestly duty. We are not yet told how, but if real priests offering incense

---

1. Even if not everyone joined it; cf. Num 27:3.
2. See at 14:5, p. 198.

improperly suffered a miraculous judgment (Lev 10:1–3), non-priests who dared to offer incense might expect the same, if not worse, since they lacked the necessary ritual state for this role: being "holy" (Num 16:7).[3] Holiness was in fact at the debate's center: were Moses and Aaron right to think only Aaron's family had the necessary ritual holiness to serve as priests? Korah insisted they were not, but the Lord himself would be the judge, and Moses's response to Korah gives us a sense of the impending outcome, turning Korah's own words back on him: "You Levites [are the ones who] have gone too far [with this outrageous accusation]!" (v. 7).[4]

Moses's Detailed Interaction with Korah (16:8–11)

Keeping his focus on Korah, Moses next unmasks the reason for his rebellion (Num 16:8–11). He highlights the special privileges the Lord had granted the Levites (vv. 8–10).[5] Indeed, mentioned in 16:1, Korah belonged to the Kohathite branch of Levi, meaning he was privileged with responsibility for the tent's holiest items when it was taken down, transported, and set up (see at 4:1–20, p. 79). As Moses notes, however, Korah wants even more privilege and power (16:10) and so has responded in a jealous rage against Aaron (and Moses), which was in fact rebellion against the one who had called Aaron into priestly service: the Lord (v. 11).

Moses's Detailed Interaction with Dathan and Abiram (16:12–15)

Moses's attention now turns to Dathan and Abiram, who had apparently returned to their tents, causing Moses to summon them (Num 16:12). These two are not driven by a desire for the priesthood but by the bitterness of not receiving the promised land and by the humiliation (so they thought) of submitting to Moses's leadership. Their response to Moses's summons is testimony to how badly sins blinds us to the truth (vv. 13–14). By calling Egypt the land of milk and honey, their former prison has somehow become a paradise;[6] by accusing Moses of failing to take them into Canaan, they are blaming *him* for the results of *their* sin; and by stating he wants to lord his leadership over them, they ignore that it was only because of his humble and loving intercession on their behalf that they were not immediately wiped out for their earlier rebellion

---

3. See above, Listening to the Text in the Story, p. 224.
4. Cf. 16:3. Not all the rebellion's leaders were Levites (cf. 16:1); the term is perhaps used here to make clear that the rebellion originated among the Levites and had Korah (the Levite) as its chief leader.
5. See above, Listening to the Text in the Story, p. 224.
6. Allen, "Numbers," 838.

(Num 14)! Sin distorts our perception so badly we turn every truth into a lie. In this case, it leads them to utterly refuse his summons; they have no interest in seeing him act as leader over them or others (16:14).

Moses responds with justified anger (Num 16:15); as their leader, he has never wrongly taken of their goods or harmed them in any way (cf. 1 Sam 12:3), so he prays the Lord would reject any offering they try to make and thus show he rejects them and their assessment of the situation. This is not vindictiveness on Moses's part; it is looking to the Lord for vindication, and the story now recounts just that (Num 16:16–40).

Preparation for the Vindicating Test (16:16–19a)

Since Dathan and Abiram refused to come, Moses turns his attention back to Korah, instructing him and the 250 gathered with him to bring an incense offering tomorrow (Num 16:16–17). The next day, the instructions are carried out. Korah and the 250 leaders prepare their offering, as does Aaron, and they all meet in the courtyard before the tent of meeting (v. 18). Along with the 250 leaders, Korah gathers "all the assembly against" Moses and Aaron (v. 19a, my translation), that is, representatives of the entire nation.[7] He is supremely confident of his coming vindication; his confidence is about to be shattered into a million pieces.

The Lord Appears in Judgment (16:19b)

As in Numbers 14, the Lord makes his presence miraculously known and comes to announce judgment on the rebellious. See full comments at 14:10b, p. 199.

The Lord's Initial Response and Moses's and Aaron's Intercession (16:20–22)

The announced judgment is the people's immediate destruction; Moses and Aaron are therefore told, "Separate yourselves from this assembly" (Num 16:21). Separating from the guilty is a theme in this chapter (vv. 24, 26, 45), underscoring God's people are not to associate with others in their rebellion and sin.

As noted at 14:1–12, pp. 199–200, the Lord's threat of judgment is often an invitation for Israel's leaders to intercede on the people's behalf. And as happened in chapter 14, Moses and Aaron do just that (cf. 14:11–19). Falling

---

7. The NIV's "all his followers" (16:19) is curious since it translates the exact same word as "assembly" at the end of the verse and in other verses that follow (vv. 21, 22, 24, 26).

humbly on their faces, they appeal to the Lord's merciful love for his creation: "Since you are Lord of all, giving life to all and thus caring for all as a father does for his children, will you take everyone's life because one person has sinned?"[8] They are not denying that Israel has guilt; they are simply emphasizing that the leader (Korah) bears primary responsibility for this situation.[9]

The Lord's Final Response of Judgment and Vindication (16:23–40)
The Lord hears their prayer and focuses his judgment on the rebellion's main leaders: Korah, Dathan, and Abiram, from whom the Israelites must now separate (Num 16:24). Once more, God's people are never to associate with others in rebellion and sin, and the story turns to the judgment itself.

To make sense of what follows, two factors must be remembered. First, the tents of these three men were in two different locations: Korah camped among the Levites; Dathan and Abiram camped among the Reubenites. The narrator's challenge is to show that all three men (and their followers) are being judged, even if this is happening in more than one location, and this sometimes leads to very quick scene changes.[10] Second, there are two separate complaints (Moses's leadership and the restriction of priestly duties to Aaron's family) and thus two corresponding judgments (one to vindicate Moses and the other to vindicate Aaron), and the story goes back and forth between them (see Explain the Story above, pp. 224–25).

The story of the first judgment begins with a focus on Dathan and Abiram (Num 16:25), whose main complaint was about Moses's leadership (vv. 13–14). Since they had refused to answer his summons (vv. 12, 14), he goes to them, along with Israelite elders, who served as the people's representatives. (Whether they are for Moses or against him is not stated; at the least, they would serve as witnesses.) Moses instructs everyone to move back from Dathan's and Abiram's tents, lest they be "swept away" in the judgment that was about to come (v. 26)—the same language used to warn Lot to flee lest he be "swept away" with the punishment of wicked Sodom and Gomorrah (Gen 19:15, 17). We are being prepared for a similar judgment here.

The Israelites obey, and for a moment all three leaders are again mentioned (Num 16:27a). If this were a movie, one imagines the Israelites' obedience carried out in two quickly following scenes, with people melting away from the tents of Korah in one scene and those of Dathan and Abiram in the next. The

---

8. Cf. Gen 18:23.
9. It is also possible that "one person" is hyperbole for "a few" (Korah and other leaders) in contrast to the entire assembly (Sprinkle, *Leviticus and Numbers*, 284).
10. See at 16:27, 32, pp. 228–29.

camera then stays with the latter, who are pictured standing at the entrance to their tents with their families (v. 27b).

Moses addresses their main complaint. They said he wrongly exalted himself as prince and was a horrible leader; it will now be made clear that the Lord has indeed chosen him and sent him to lead Israel in the way that he has ("to do all these things"; Num 16:28). The proof will be in the manner of their death. If they die normally, there is no need to trust that the Lord has appointed Moses as leader. But if they die miraculously—and Moses goes so far as to name exactly what the miracle will be—then it will be clear the Lord has indeed appointed him, meaning the contempt of these men against Moses is in reality contempt against the Lord (vv. 29–30; cf. 14:11, 23).

No sooner does he finish speaking than the judgment takes place exactly as Moses described: the earth splits, opening its mouth in judgment and swallowing them whole (Num 16:31–32a). The camera angle shifts quickly to Korah to let us know the same has happened to him (v. 32b).[11]

The Israelites who see this take place flee, fearing the same judgment may befall them (Num 16:34), either because they sensed their own guilt in having listened to the rebels or simply because fear was the most natural response to such a scene. In either case, for at least a moment, it seems as though the rebellion against Moses's leadership has been put down.

The story of the second judgment quickly follows: fire comes out from before the Lord and consumes the 250 men offering the incense (Num 16:35), mirroring what happened to Nadab and Abihu when they improperly offered incense at the tabernacle (Lev 10:2). Indeed, the last time we saw the 250 men they were at the tabernacle (Num 16:18), so we might imagine the fire bursting forth from the cloud of glory hovering over it (v. 19). If the first judgment made clear that Moses was the Lord's appointed leader, this judgment made clear Aaron was the Lord's appointed priest.

The point is underscored in what happens next as the Lord gives instructions through Moses to Eleazar, Aaron's oldest living son. The scene Eleazar confronts is horrific: the 250 rebels have become 250 smoldering corpses. The 250 metal censers, however, have survived the burning, but since these had been presented to the Lord, they were now ritually holy, as happened with any

---

11. Presumably, Korah has returned to his tent, since he is not mentioned with the 250 at the tabernacle in 16:35. Further, "all those associated with Korah" would refer to those living in his tent (cf. 16:27b); since some of his descendants lived (26:10–11), he either had grown children no longer living with him (and not joining the rebellion) or, as Kidner suggests (*Leviticus, Numbers, Deuteronomy*, 45), had adult children living with him who heeded the warning to get away from his tent, thus rejecting his rebellion.

gift an Israelite brought to the Lord (cf. Lev 22:2; 27:14–19).[12] Eleazar was therefore to take the censers, scatter any remaining coals in them some distance away (as though to underscore the offering made on these coals was rejected?), and then turn them into bronze plating for the altar of burnt offering (Num 16:37–38).[13] This was not only an appropriate use for ritually holy metal, it was also to serve as a "sign" and "reminder" (vv. 38, 40) for the Israelites that only priests were to come and burn incense and, by implication, perform any offering at the altar (since incense offerings were far less involved than other offerings). Thus every time an Israelite brought an offering, they would be reminded that they were not to officiate at the altar lest they, too, suffer fatal judgment. Making offerings was the task of the priests.

Eleazar carried out these commands just as the Lord commanded him through Moses (Num 16:40); the Levite's rebellion is thus contrasted with the priests' obedience. Aaron's family are indeed the Lord's faithful servants.

The People's Rebellion and Aaron's Effective Priestly Intercession (16:41–50)

On the next day, it becomes clear the Israelites' hearts are still rebellious (Num 16:41; cf. 14:2): "*You* [Moses and Aaron] have killed the LORD's people!"[14] Indeed, by calling the rebels "the LORD's people," the Israelites seem to be saying, "The Lord indeed chose them! Yet you caused their deaths!" This claim is outrageous; with yesterday's miracles, *the Lord* clearly brought his judgment to bear, vindicating Moses and Aaron in the process. But for reasons discussed below,[15] the Israelites did not accept these realities and placed the blame squarely on Moses's and Aaron's shoulders.

Once more the Lord appears in judgment. His cloud of glory, lit up with his powerful presence, descends on the tent of meeting (Num 16:42; see at 14:10b, p. 199), and yesterday's events repeat themselves: he tells Moses and Aaron to separate from the guilty so he may consume the people, and Moses and Aaron fall on their faces in humble supplication (v. 45; cf. vv. 21–22). But this time, instead of Moses praying for mercy for a coming judgment, he sees that the judgment has already begun: "Wrath has come out from the

---

12. This explains why Eleazar must retrieve them: only priests could touch that which was ritually holy (cf. Num 4:15).
13. The altar had already been overlaid with bronze (Exod 27:2; 38:30); presumably, this plating was added on top.
14. The "you" is emphatic.
15. See discussion at end of this chapter: Live the Story: How Do the People Respond?

Lord; the plague has started!" (v. 46b). The Lord's "wrath" is his just anger against rebellion; he is a patient and loving king, but a king nonetheless, and rebellion against him can be fatal. In this case, the result is a "plague," an unidentified but deadly punishment. And because it has started, Moses urgently commands Aaron to "hurry to the assembly" and make intercession by means of an incense offering (v. 46a).

The scene is incredibly dramatic: Aaron grabs his censer and a handful of incense, runs to the altar, scoops up live coals, turns and runs into the assembly's midst and hardly stops before throwing the incense on the coals to make a fragrant cloud rise to the Lord, like a sweet-smelling prayer of intercession on behalf of a foul people who have become a stench in the Lord's nostrils (Num 16:47).[16] As a result, the plague—which had been rolling like a tidal wave of death across the people—is now stopped; the Lord has heard Aaron's prayer (v. 48).

The scene is also tremendously ironic: the previous day, those wrongly presenting incense had died; this day, Aaron presents incense so that those who deserve to die might live! That his intercession was accepted shows he is indeed chosen by God to minister as priest (and that he and Moses are not responsible for the people's death but for saving their very lives).

Nonetheless, the plague had swept through quickly enough that 14,700 people died, in addition to those from Korah's rebellion (Num 16:49). (By mentioning the two together, all are joined in the same rebellion.) Aaron returns to Moses at the tent of meeting, where he belongs as the people's high priest, and the chapter concludes by underscoring that the plague was indeed over; his priestly work was effective.

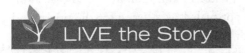

LIVE the Story

Numbers 16 contains two stories that are different in the details but the same in displaying not only our human stubbornness to commit evil but also the Lord's opposition to evil and thus our need for someone to stand in the gap on our behalf to seek the Lord's mercy. We can see these themes play out by asking five different questions.[17]

---

16. This is high-handed sin (or sin "with an uplifted hand"; i.e., defiantly), so no sacrifice is prescribed. Instead, Aaron intercedes as mediator by means of an incense offering. For the role of a mediator in atoning for high-handed sin, see Sklar, "Sin and Atonement," 485–90.

17. For an alternative homiletical approach, see p. 179n13.

What Is the Problem?

The first story begins with a rebellion whose major characters are Korah, Dathan, and Abiram. All three are rebelling against the leadership the Lord has established but they fall into two different camps in terms of why they are rebelling.

In the first camp is Korah, who has incredible special privileges: not only did Levites transport and guard the Lord's own tent, but Korah's branch of the Levites were responsible for the tent's holiest items (see at 16:8–11, p. 226). His focus, however, was not on the great privileges the Lord had already given him but on the greater privileges the Lord had given to the priests (such as ministering at the altar), and this type of comparing led him (as it leads any person) to envy and a deep desire for what others have (cf. Ps 106:16). His response also betrays a significant misunderstanding of leadership. Biblically speaking, when God calls us to positions of authority, it is for the sake of service, not privilege.[18] But Korah was interested in privilege, not service. He refused to accept that God gives each one different gifts and different roles of service. His problem was not with the body having many parts; his problem was that he would not be content until he was the chief part. The result was an envy-fueled rebellion, carried out by means of heretical half-truths (see at 16:1–7, p. 225), meant to gain for himself power and prestige. Sadly, this made him an "archetypal heretic"[19] (cf. Jude 11) and his death a sobering warning, and we do well to ask: do we envy those with greater gifts or authority than ourselves? Do we understand our gifts and positions for the purpose of service or for power and prestige? Do we find ourselves using half-truths to undermine others around us or to exalt ourselves?

In the second camp are Dathan and Abiram. As noted above (at Num 16:12–15, pp. 226–27), they are not fueled by a desire for the priesthood as much as by the bitterness of not receiving the promised land and by the humiliation (so they thought) of submitting to Moses's leadership. If Korah's rebellion is more focused on Aaron (v. 11), their rebellion is more focused on Moses (vv. 12–15). But since it was their fault (not Moses's) that they were not entering the promised land, and since Moses had been an utterly selfless and caring leader (even saving their lives from certain destruction in Num 14),[20] it becomes clear that the roots of their bitterness are found in their unwillingness to acknowledge their own sin. Their approach is to shift the blame as much as possible, and Moses, the leader, becomes the convenient target. Such

---

18. Ashley, *Numbers*, 309.
19. Wenham, *Numbers*, 134.
20. See further at 16:12–15, pp. 226–27.

blame-shifting has gone on since the very beginning (Gen 3:12) and happens to this day every time we refuse to accept responsibility for wrongs we have done and push the blame onto others.

The end result is full-scale rebellion against both the Lord and his leaders. And the Lord does not remain silent, leading to the second question.

How Does the Lord Respond?

For the sake of Moses and Aaron in particular, who stand as two men against a rebellious multitude who are spewing out evil and slanderous accusations, the Lord responds with a test and two vindicating judgments.

The test is straightforward: Korah and his 250 followers, as well as Aaron, are to prepare an incense offering and present it before the Lord (Num 16:4–6, 16–17). Since this was something only ritually holy priests could do (see at 16:1–7, p. 225), the Lord would use this test to make clear whom he had chosen for this role as well as whom he had appointed to lead the people. And he does this by means of the two different judgments.

Once the test begins, the Lord has an initial interaction with Moses and Aaron (see below) and then warns everyone to get away from the tents of Korah, Dathan, and Abiram (Num 16:24). The story zooms in on Dathan and Abiram in particular, whose primary rebellion was against Moses (v. 25). Moses announces a miraculous judgment that only the Lord could bring about and that would be a sign that the Lord had indeed chosen Moses to lead the people: the earth would open its mouth and swallow these rebels whole (vv. 28–30). This is precisely what happens (vv. 31–33), making clear to all that Moses was indeed the Lord's leader. The Lord had vindicated his servant.

The manner of vindication does raise a penetrating question, however, insofar as Dathan and Abiram are swallowed up with their whole families, including their "children and little ones" (Num 16:27).[21] Why should these innocents suffer with the guilty? While answering this question to the satisfaction of all is not possible, the following points may be of help as a framework of response:

- In biblical Israel, the basic family unit was known as "the house of the father," consisting of three to four generations living together.[22] Children

---

21. The Hebrew term for "children" is "sons" and could refer to young children (though older than "little ones") or to adult children (Gen 35:22; 42:1). We might imagine a full range of ages here, with some of the "children" still being quite young and others being young adults.

22. See discussion in Christopher J. H. Wright, *God's People in God's Land: Family, Land, and Property in the Old Testament* (Grand Rapids: Eerdmans, 1990), 53–55.

within this unit benefited from covenant blessings they did not earn when the family head was faithful but could also suffer covenant curses they did not deserve when the family head was unfaithful. We have already seen an example of the latter: "Your children will be shepherds [in the wilderness] for forty years, suffering for your unfaithfulness" (Num 14:33).

- This is not fair, just as it is not fair to this day when a father commits a crime, is imprisoned, and his family suffers social shame and economic difficulty through no fault of their own. But the family is such a tight-knit unit that the impact of one person's sin often ripples through the entire family pond, and from that perspective, these stories strongly warn: Your sin often brings great harm to those you love most.
- Crucially, while Dathan's and Abiram's little ones do suffer as a result of their father's sin, no guilt is ascribed to them. In this regard, it is important to distinguish between temporal life and death and eternal life and death. In terms of eternal life and death, we have little hope of seeing Dathan and Abiram in heaven since they are presented as rank apostates. We need not have such negative expectations, however, about these little ones, who were not only innocent of their parents' wrong but members of Israel's covenant community and to be regarded as such until they proved otherwise (which they had not done). If by means of temporal death God is bringing these children early into his eternal home, it is not injustice on his part. Indeed, from the perspective of these young children in the glories of heaven, would they look at their early homecoming as an unfair curse or as the richest blessing?
- Finally, as for the other adults in these families, it is clear from Numbers 26:10–11 that some of Korah's adult children did heed God's warning, "broke out of their natural covenant loyalty to their father and crossed over to the other side. They joined the rest of the community in leaving the tents of Korah, and so they lived when the rest of their kinfolk died."[23] Those adult family members who did not do so were choosing to rebel with these leaders and, like them, suffered the path of judgment they had chosen for themselves.

The second judgment focuses on vindicating Aaron and follows quickly on the heels of the first. Fire from the Lord breaks out and consumes the 250 men at the tabernacle who are presenting incense, making clear that Aaron

---

23. Duguid, *Numbers*, 206.

is the Lord's chosen priestly representative. By taking their censers in their hands, these men had chosen to take their life in their hands, and the Lord turns their rebellion and death into an object lesson by having their censers hammered into metal sheets and used as plating for the altar, a stark reminder for any Israelite bringing an offering that only Aaron's family could present it at the altar.[24]

While these stories are incredibly sobering, they are also meant to be a strong encouragement to Moses and Aaron (and, through them, to leaders today) that the Lord does indeed watch over, care for, and in due time vindicate his servants (cf. 2 Tim 2:19). This leads to the third question.

How Does Moses Respond?

Two aspects of Moses's response to the people's sin are noteworthy. First, he does not hesitate to rebuke them for their sin. "You Levites have gone too far!" (Num 16:7), he says to Korah, and then proceeds with a lengthy reproof (vv. 8–11). Moses focuses especially on the sin of the leader (Korah) since leaders can do great harm by leading others astray. Similar rebukes of leaders can be found in the New Testament, whether from Jesus himself (Matt 23; Mark 7:6–13) or from Paul (Gal 2:11–14; 2 Tim 2:17–19; see also 1 Tim 5:20). Sometimes godliness means we "overlook an offense" (Prov 19:11), but sometimes godliness means we call sin for the evil and destructive cancer it is, especially when leaders are the ones doing it.

Second, even in giving such rebukes, Moses looks to the Lord for vindication. After the harsh response from Dathan and Abiram (Num 16:12–14), Moses cries out to the Lord for help and vindication (v. 15). And when confronting the false teaching of Korah, he makes clear that "the LORD will show who belongs to him" (v. 5), a verse that Paul quotes to Timothy to assure him of the Lord's vindication in the face of false teachers who, like Korah, are spreading lies (2 Tim 2:19). While a natural reflex in the face of slander and untruth is to take matters immediately into our own hands, the godly reflex is to look first to the Lord, our maker and defender, for deliverance and help.

How Do the People Respond?

Whereas Moses looks to the Lord to bring about justice, the people refuse to accept the Lord's justice. The miraculous nature of the judgments made it abundantly clear they were the Lord's doing, but still the people refused to

---

24. See further details at 16:23–40, pp. 229–30.

accept this and tried to put the blame on Moses and Aaron. How could they be so willingly blind?

While the text gives no explicit answer, various suggestions present themselves from the Israelites' own history and from our own knowledge of human nature. In terms of the Israelites' history, they had been brutally oppressed by Egypt's leadership (Exod 1:11–14; 2:23) and the survival of their very nation had been called into question (1:15–22).[25] It should therefore not surprise us if the severe discipline and death they had just witnessed—of which their leader, Moses, was the messenger—triggered a whole range of past negative emotions and experiences about leadership. That would be a natural response. The problem is that they then chose to view the present through those triggered emotions (thus viewing Moses like an evil Egyptian taskmaster) rather than to bring those triggered emotions to the Lord and to ask for help in seeing clearly.

Perhaps combined with this is our natural human tendency to defend those we love, even when they are clearly wrong. The 250 men that had just been killed by the Lord's fire had come from across the nation (Num 16:2), meaning their deaths touched the nation as a whole. To acknowledge this as an act of the Lord's justice meant to admit these friends and family members were wrong, something many of us resist, especially when it comes to those we love. Whenever human loyalties come before loyalties to God, it will be impossible for us to acknowledge that his ways are right and good if doing so casts someone we love in a negative light. But Jesus was uncompromising in his call to put himself above any other loyalty: "If anyone comes to me and does not hate father and mother, wife and children, brothers and sisters—yes, even their own life—such a person cannot be my disciple" (Luke 14:26). Granted, he is using hyperbole here, since we are not literally to hate those we love (or hate our own life). But hyperbole is used in order to drive a point home, and the point here is clear: our commitment to Jesus is to utterly eclipse any human loyalty we might have. God always comes first.

The Israelites, however, were unwilling to do this. Instead, they sided with those who had rebelled against the Lord and repeated their rebellion by once again rejecting the Lord's leaders.[26] This leads to our last question.

How Does the Story End?

Given that the people are repeating the rebellion of the leaders who had just been judged, it is not surprising that the Lord's judgment comes again. And it

---

25. Cf. Gane, *Leviticus, Numbers*, 648.
26. See at 16:41–50, p. 230.

is severe: a plague breaks out that begins to decimate the people (Num 16:46, 49). The warning is again very strong: when we rebel against the Lord of life, we forfeit our right to live.

But the story does not end here. When the Lord announced his first judgment, Moses and Aaron interceded on behalf of the people as a whole, who had been led astray by false teaching (Num 16:22).[27] After this second announcement of judgment, they intercede again on behalf of the people as a whole, who this time have not been led astray but simply chose to rebel on their own (vv. 45–48). But in either case, despite the fact the people have committed great wrong against Moses and Aaron, they still intercede, choosing to overlook these wrongs for the sake of seeking the Lord's mercy and love for a sinful people. In this second instance in particular, Aaron's priestly intercession atones for the people, appeasing the Lord's just anger against their sin and rebellion, and thus saving their very lives.[28]

The Bible says this is precisely what Jesus does for us, though in a far greater way and on a far deeper level. Like Aaron, he is the priestly mediator who "is able to save completely those who come to God through him, because he always lives to intercede for them" (Heb 7:25). But unlike Aaron, he is both priest and sacrifice. Aaron presented incense on the people's behalf; Jesus presented himself, atoning for our sins "once for all when he offered himself" (v. 27).[29] Aaron's act was costly insofar as he had to *overlook* the wrongs of others in order to intercede for them; Jesus's act was costly in that he had to *suffer* the wrongs of others in order to intercede for them. As Isaiah foretold, "He bore the sin of many, and made intercession for the transgressors" (Isa 53:12).

Are we looking to Jesus as that person who can intercede on our behalf because he has taken the guilt of our wrongs on himself? And if we have, how active are we in interceding on behalf of those who do not yet know him? What does it look like for us to be regularly praying that they would trust in Jesus? And what does it mean for us to do this not simply for those we love, but for those we struggle to love? Whether our struggle to love certain people comes simply from differences of opinion, culture, or tastes, or whether it comes from the fact we are mistreated by them, are we willing to pray on their behalf that the Lord would have mercy on them? Being mistreated did not prevent Moses and Aaron from such prayers on the Israelites' behalf, nor has being mistreated by us prevented Jesus from such prayers on our behalf. Are we willing to follow his lead in praying this way for others?

---

27. See further at 16:20–22, pp. 227–28.
28. See further at 16:41–50, p. 231.
29. Cf. Olson, *Numbers*, 109.

CHAPTER 20

Numbers 17:1–18:7

 LISTEN to the Story

17:1The LORD said to Moses, 2"Speak to the Israelites and get twelve staffs from them, one from the leader of each of their ancestral tribes. Write the name of each man on his staff. 3On the staff of Levi write Aaron's name, for there must be one staff for the head of each ancestral tribe. 4Place them in the tent of meeting in front of the ark of the covenant law, where I meet with you. 5The staff belonging to the man I choose will sprout, and I will rid myself of this constant grumbling against you by the Israelites."

6So Moses spoke to the Israelites, and their leaders gave him twelve staffs, one for the leader of each of their ancestral tribes, and Aaron's staff was among them. 7Moses placed the staffs before the LORD in the tent of the covenant law.

8The next day Moses entered the tent and saw that Aaron's staff, which represented the tribe of Levi, had not only sprouted but had budded, blossomed and produced almonds. 9Then Moses brought out all the staffs from the LORD's presence to all the Israelites. They looked at them, and each of the leaders took his own staff.

10The LORD said to Moses, "Put back Aaron's staff in front of the ark of the covenant law, to be kept as a sign to the rebellious. This will put an end to their grumbling against me, so that they will not die." 11Moses did just as the LORD commanded him.

12The Israelites said to Moses, "We will die! We are lost, we are all lost! 13Anyone who even comes near the tabernacle of the LORD will die. Are we all going to die?"

18:1The LORD said to Aaron, "You, your sons and your family are to bear the responsibility for offenses connected with the sanctuary, and you and your sons alone are to bear the responsibility for offenses connected with the priesthood. ²Bring your fellow Levites from your ancestral tribe to join you and assist you when you and your sons minister before the tent of the covenant law. ³They are to be responsible to you and are to perform all the duties of the tent, but they must not go near the furnishings of the sanctuary or the altar. Otherwise both they and you will die. ⁴They are to join you and be responsible for the care of the tent of meeting—all the work at the tent—and no one else may come near where you are.

⁵"You are to be responsible for the care of the sanctuary and the altar, so that my wrath will not fall on the Israelites again. ⁶I myself have selected your fellow Levites from among the Israelites as a gift to you, dedicated to the LORD to do the work at the tent of meeting. ⁷But only you and your sons may serve as priests in connection with everything at the altar and inside the curtain. I am giving you the service of the priesthood as a gift. Anyone else who comes near the sanctuary is to be put to death."

Listening to the Text in the Story: Numbers 16

As noted earlier, Numbers 16 describes two stories in which the Israelites rebel against the Lord's appointed leaders, particularly with regard to the priesthood, and the Lord responds with miraculous signs to verify these are the leaders he has chosen.[1] These signs came as judgment on the Israelites' rebellion (ch. 16). Now, as though to head off a third rebellion (and judgment!), the Lord intervenes with a final miraculous sign to verify that only Aaron and his family can serve as priests in the tabernacle (17:1–11). The people are convinced and swing to the opposite extreme, now fearing to have God's tabernacle in their midst lest they die like their rebellious countrymen (vv. 12–13)! The Lord reassures them they need not fear—as long as the Israelites, Levites, and priests all stick to their God-ordained roles (18:1–7). (For the importance of the latter, see further at Num 3, Listening to the Text in the Story, p. 72.)

---

1. See pp. 224–25, Listening to the Text in the Story and Explain the Story.

EXPLAIN the Story

The Lord Describes a Second Vindicating Test for the Priesthood (17:1–5)[2]

The test requires each tribal leader to give a staff to Moses (Num 17:2). The Hebrew word for "staff" (*matteh*) can be used to refer to a "tribe" (1:4, 16, 21, etc.) and is also associated with leadership (cf. Gen 49:10; Ps 110:2), making it a perfect symbol for these tribal leaders. This included a staff for Aaron from the tribe of Levi (Num 17:3), making clear (perhaps especially to the other Levites!) that he was that tribe's leader. The staffs were then to be placed in the tent "in front of the ark of the covenant law" (v. 4), which likely refers not to the most holy place but in front of it, in the holy place (just as the incense altar was "in front of the ark of the covenant law" in the holy place; Exod 40:5). This was a very natural place to put them since the Lord reveals his will to the Israelites from within the tabernacle (25:22). In this case, he would do so by making one of these dead pieces of wood sprout with life, indicating he had chosen that staff's owner to serve as priest (Num 17:5a). He finishes by explaining his goal: "I will rid myself of this constant grumbling against you by the Israelites" (v. 5b). The Israelites might be grumbling against Moses and Aaron, but this is felt by the Lord, which is both a warning to Israel (to reject his leadership is to reject the Lord) and an encouragement to Moses and Aaron ("I am aware of the burden you bear and bear it with you").

Moses and the Israelites Follow the Lord's Directions (17:6–7)

The directions having been given, they are immediately carried out. The text keeps our focus on Aaron's rod in the midst of the other twelve (Num 17:6).

The Results of the Test (17:8–11)

Upon entering the tent the next day, Moses sees "that Aaron's staff, which represented the tribe of Levi, had not only sprouted but had budded, blossomed and produced almonds" (Num 17:8).[3] Budding or blossoming might happen in a night, but producing almonds does not. This was clearly a miracle. Significantly, "Moses brought out all the staffs . . . to all the Israelites" and

---

2. For the first test, see 16:16–19a, 35–40, pp. 227, 229–30.
3. Many different guesses have been made as to the possible symbolic significance of the almonds (see Sklar, *Additional Notes on Numbers*, at 17:8). These all remain guesses, however, and preachers and teachers do well to resist presenting any of them as settled facts.

"they looked at them" (v. 9), that is, they were able to examine them and to verify that the blossoming staff was the same one put in the tent yesterday (and that this was not simply some sleight of hand substitute). No further protests occur; these otherwise rebellious and skeptical eyewitnesses were utterly convinced of the miracle's veracity.

In a final step, the Lord commands Moses to put Aaron's staff back "in front of the ark of the covenant law,[4] to be kept as a sign to the rebellious" (Num 17:10a), making it similar to the censers that were hammered into a covering for the altar and also used as a sign to warn against rebellion (16:38).[5] Such signs were for the Israelites' own good since continued rebellion would have the same result of the Lord's lethal justice (17:10b). He desires his people's fellowship and life, not their rebellion and death.

The People's Fear of the Tabernacle (17:12–13)

Now convinced that only Aaron's family can serve in the tabernacle as priests, the people swing to the opposite extreme and are terrified they cannot even come near the tabernacle without dying (Num 17:13). Positively, this means they truly see their need for priestly mediators; this helps prepare the way for the call for them to give the priests and Levites gifts later in chapter 18.[6] Negatively, it could mean they do not draw near at all; the Lord therefore proceeds to explain that the priests and Levites will be responsible for making sure the Israelites do not do anything improper at the tabernacle that would endanger their lives (18:1–7).

The Priests' and Levites' Tabernacle Roles (18:1–7)

Speaking to Aaron directly, the Lord begins with a general overview (Num 18:1). The entire tribe of Levi[7] will bear any punishment[8] connected to sins against the sanctuary since the entire tribe was responsible for it (v. 1a), but only Aaron's immediate family will bear any punishment connected to sins

---

4. That is, place it back in the holy place (see explanation at v. 4 above). Hebrews 9:4 implies that it (and the jar of manna [Exod 16:34]) was at some point put in the ark itself. "Later reference to the tablets bearing the Ten Commandments as the only contents of the Ark may have suggested that something else had once also been located therein" (Gareth Lee Cockerill, *The Epistle to the Hebrews*, NICNT [Grand Rapids: Eerdmans, 2012], 377–78, citing 1 Kgs 8:9 [// 2 Chr 5:10]).

5. Though not in public view, the rod could be brought out at any moment as a reminder of the confirming miracle the Lord had performed.

6. Wenham, *Numbers*, 139.

7. The phrase translated "family" is the same one used in 17:2–3 for "ancestral tribe"; every Levite is responsible to guard the sanctuary.

8. NIV's "responsibility" is a bit weak; the Heb. phrase ("to bear sin") regularly refers to experiencing the punishment due to sin (as in 5:31; 14:34; 30:15; etc.).

against the priesthood since they alone held that office (v. 1b). In either case, the greater privilege of these parties also led to greater responsibility; they had to ensure such sins never happened, whether they committed them (through doing their duties wrongly) or the Israelites did (through illicit contact with the tabernacle's holy property or an illicit attempt to perform priestly duties).

The remaining verses focus first on the non-priestly Levites (Num 18:2–4) and then the priestly Levites (vv. 5–7), drawing together themes from earlier in the book.[9] The non-priestly Levites are to "join"[10] the priests and serve them at the tabernacle (v. 2). They did so by guarding the tabernacle from improper contact by the Israelites (1:47–53) and guarding the priests themselves[11] but perhaps also by helping the Israelites with certain aspects of preparing the animals for sacrifice.[12] Their work did not extend to priestly duties, however, whether inside the tent with "the furnishings of the sanctuary" (such as the lamp [cf. Exod 27:21]) or in the courtyard at "the altar" of burnt offering (Num 18:3). For them to do priestly duties would be a blasphemous breach of the Lord's clear standards and thus to invite certain death, not only for the Levites who did so but also for the faithless priests who let them do so.[13] A concluding verse makes clear no one else may "come near where you [priests] are," that is, come near to join you in working at the tabernacle (v. 4). Israelites could come to the tabernacle to make offerings, but only the non-priestly Levites could help in the tabernacle's work.

As for the priestly Levites (Aaron's family; Num 18:5–7), they were "responsible for the duties[14] of the sanctuary and the altar" (v. 5), that is, anything connected to serving in the tent or at the altar. As long as the priests carried out these duties, the Israelites need not fear the Lord's wrath breaking out, as it did when Korah and his followers tried to act in priestly ways (16:35; cf. v. 46). And while the non-priestly Levites could help in certain ways at the tabernacle (18:6),[15] only Aaron's family could perform priestly functions,

---

9. See at 3:5–10; 4:1–20, pp. 74, 79–80.
10. A play on words; the root for the verb "join" (*l-v-h*) is the basis of the name Levi (*levi*; see Gen 29:34).
11. Num 18:3 could be more woodenly translated, "They are to perform duties regarding you and duties regarding the whole tent." Thus the NIV's "responsible to you" is perhaps better "responsible *for* you" (cf. ESV; NET); just as they had responsibilities for the tent, especially guarding it, so they had responsibilities for watching over the priests in their duties, guarding them (perhaps from being contacted by someone who was ritually impure).
12. See p. 224, Listening to the Text in the Story.
13. The form of the verb "die" suggests death at the hands of the Lord (as happened to Nadab and Abihu, Lev 10:1–2); cf. p. 53n12. For rationale, cf. p. 57, How Should We Respond?
14. NIV "care"; see p. 77n12.
15. For 18:6 see further at 3:11–13 (p. 75) and at 8:13 above.

whether in the courtyard ("the altar" of burnt offering) or in the most holy place ("inside the curtain") or anywhere in between (v. 7). This privilege was the Lord's gift to them and only they could do it. "Anyone else who comes near the sanctuary" to perform priestly duties "is to be put to death" (v. 7) whether by the Levites or priests or by the community.[16]

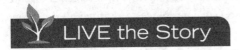

LIVE the Story

Does God Want Us to Know Him?
The Israelites have already seen 250 of their number who were trying to worship God consumed by fire (Num 16:35). Now, in chapter 17, the Lord makes abundantly clear that only Aaron and his family can serve as priests, intermediaries between God and the nation (vv. 1–10). Putting the two together, they conclude (we might paraphrase), "We can't come close to God ourselves! We can't even have his home in our midst without dying!" (vv. 12–13). It seems to them that God did not want them to know him or come near to him.

Nothing could be further from the truth. The reason he provided prophets like Moses was so that they could know his holy will for their lives (Exod 25:22). And the reason he provided priests was to teach them his holy ways, intercede for them, and lead them in joyful worship before him (Lev 8–9; 10:10–11; Deut 33:10). The problem was not that God was unknowable or unapproachable; the problem was trying to know and approach God on their own terms.

This was the very issue in the previous chapter, where Korah and his followers insisted that they could determine how to approach God. But a king is always to be approached on his terms, not our own; otherwise, he is no longer king. As soon as we reject the sovereign God's way of coming into his presence in favor of our own way, we reject him as the sovereign God. And so the Lord makes clear again in Numbers 17 that he has appointed a specific way of entering into his presence and knowing him. He has chosen Aaron and his family as his servants on the people's behalf, able to serve as intermediaries between himself and his sinful people, atoning for their sin and leading them into his presence in worship. And the very reason he does so is so that his people might live (17:10)! In his grace and love, he makes a way for a sinful people to know him, draw near to him, and experience his

---
16. See at p. 53n12.

joy and love. The provision of the priesthood was in fact the greatest proof that the Lord did want his people both to know him and to draw near to him. But the people had to come to him by his appointed means; there was no other.

Those familiar with the biblical story will immediately see the parallels to Jesus. He is the final high priest who atones for our sin, intercedes on our behalf before God, and leads us into God's presence so that we might know and worship him (Heb 4:14–16; 7:25; 10:19–23). He is the God-appointed way—the only God-appointed way (John 14:6)—for us to know and draw close to God. To return to our earlier language, the terms the Lord has given us in order to know him are found only in Jesus. The terms *are* Jesus. To reject him is to reject the King who sent him.

In many societies, this will rub us the wrong way. There is an impulse today to move away from religious claims that feel exclusive, especially because the word "exclusive" has such a negative connotation in spiritual contexts, as though the goal is to keep out—to exclude—as many people as possible. But this is the very opposite of what God intends in sending Jesus!

> Christians . . . believe Jesus came not to exclude people from God's kingdom but to include as many as possible. His invitation to enter it is open to all. Jesus himself says, "For God did not send his Son into the world to condemn the world, but to save the world through him" (John 3:17). In our rebellion and wrong, we have alienated ourselves from God and called forth his judgment of death. In Jesus, God takes that judgment on himself that we might escape it and be restored to him in fellowship and life. That is why Jesus came; he is the ultimate sign of the Lord's love for a rebellious world, a world he desires to be restored to himself and to know the love and joy that comes from relationship with him.
>
> Jesus once expressed this with a metaphor. He compared the kingdom of God to a wedding banquet where God himself is host and, on seeing empty seats, commands: "Go out to the roads and country lanes and compel them to come in, so that my house will be full!" (Luke 14:23). That is the Lord's desire and, in his love, he has sent his only son with the invitation, beckoning us to follow him to the feast so that his table might be full to overflowing, and we might know his love and joy.[17]

---

17. Sklar, *Leviticus* (ZECOT), 613. For further interaction with objections to the exclusive claims of Christianity, see Timothy J. Keller, *The Reason for God: Belief in an Age of Skepticism* (New York: Dutton, 2008), 7–11, and more briefly Sklar, *Leviticus* (ZECOT), 612–13.

Spiritual Leadership: How Hard Can It Be?

Context changes everything. If you're the captain of a soccer team and make bad decisions, you might lead your team to defeat. But if you're the captain of an airplane and make bad decisions, you might kill everyone on board (and scores more on the ground).

The priests and Levites are much more like the captain of an airplane: if they are not faithful in their work, the results could be lethal. This is because of the context within which they work. The tabernacle was nothing less than the palace of the Lord, the heavenly King, blazing in his holiness and purity. To disrespect his home—whether by treating his sacred things as ordinary things, or worse yet, by defiling his sacred things or thinking you could do whatever you wanted in his home—was a treasonous act. When someone vandalizes our property, we take it personally; they have not simply disrespected our home, they have disrespected us. So, too, with the Lord's home: to treat it as ordinary was to say that he was ordinary; to defame it was to defame him.

And that brings us back to the priests and Levites. The Lord appoints them to make sure that such treasonous acts never take place. In this regard, the tabernacle could in some ways be compared to an art museum. In many such museums, you are free to stand before the paintings and soak in their beauty, but there are also guards present and if you get too close to the paintings—or reach out your hand to touch them!—they will quickly come over to stop you. The beauty is there to enjoy, but there are boundaries that must not be crossed. So, too, with the tabernacle. The Israelites were able to come into its courts and stand "before the Lord" (Lev 1:3 ["to"]; 3:1, 7; etc.), worshiping him and basking in his presence. But there were boundaries they must not cross, such as touching the holy objects or performing priestly duties, and the priests and Levites were there to make sure these boundaries were maintained. If they did not guard these boundaries carefully enough, they were the ones held responsible for the wrong (Num 18:1).[18]

This reminds us of the weight that spiritual leaders bear. The book of Hebrews reminds church members that their leaders "are keeping watch over your souls, as those who will have to give an account" (Heb 13:17, ESV). The day of my ordination was both incredibly joyful and incredibly sobering. To be called to shepherd souls—to be responsible to lead people faithfully in the ways of a holy God—these are incredibly weighty duties. No wonder James warns: "Not many of you should become teachers, my fellow believers, because you know that we who teach will be judged more strictly" (Jas 3:1). Captains

---

18. For further analogies and discussion, see pp. 87–88, What is the Proper Posture?

are held to higher standards because their mistakes will impact all those they lead. This leads Paul to exhort pastor Timothy, "Watch your life and doctrine closely. Persevere in them, because if you do, you will save both yourself and your hearers" (1 Tim 4:16).

> The sense is not, "Timothy, you will be their savior!" but, "Timothy, in the absence of faithfulness, great harm may come—harm to you for being unfaithful and harm to them because they will follow you in unfaithfulness! So guard yourself, and lead faithfully, because by faithfulness, you will stay close to the LORD, and you will lead his people to him not away from him!" Leaders cannot be held responsible for every sin their people commit, nor will they be, if they have been faithful in their duties (cf. Ezek 3:18–21). But faithfulness matters.[19]

In this light, leaders do well to ask, "Are there areas where I have been too lax in my duties or too slow to guide and encourage those I lead in the holy ways of God? Do I hold before them both his beautiful love and his blazing holiness?" Leaders also do well, however, to remember both their deep need of the Lord's help as they shepherd and the Lord's deep delight to provide it! So what does it look like for the leaders of his people to look to the Lord for strength, wisdom, courage, and comfort in the midst of their duties? And how can those of us under their leadership show our confidence in them, and submit to their leadership, "so that their work will be a joy, not a burden" (Heb 13:17)?[20] In what practical ways can we "hold them in the highest regard in love because of their work" (1 Thess 5:13a)? They will not be perfect, but they need our encouragement more than our critique and our prayers more than our complaints.

---

19. Sklar, *Leviticus* (ZECOT), 600.
20. For further analogies and discussion, see pp. 87–88, What is the Proper Response?

CHAPTER 21

Numbers 18:8–32

 LISTEN to the Story

⁸Then the LORD said to Aaron, "I myself have put you in charge of the offerings presented to me; all the holy offerings the Israelites give me I give to you and your sons as your portion, your perpetual share. ⁹You are to have the part of the most holy offerings that is kept from the fire. From all the gifts they bring me as most holy offerings, whether grain or sin or guilt offerings, that part belongs to you and your sons. ¹⁰Eat it as something most holy; every male shall eat it. You must regard it as holy.

¹¹"This also is yours: whatever is set aside from the gifts of all the wave offerings of the Israelites. I give this to you and your sons and daughters as your perpetual share. Everyone in your household who is ceremonially clean may eat it.

¹²"I give you all the finest olive oil and all the finest new wine and grain they give the LORD as the firstfruits of their harvest. ¹³All the land's firstfruits that they bring to the LORD will be yours. Everyone in your household who is ceremonially clean may eat it.

¹⁴"Everything in Israel that is devoted to the LORD is yours. ¹⁵The first offspring of every womb, both human and animal, that is offered to the LORD is yours. But you must redeem every firstborn son and every firstborn male of unclean animals. ¹⁶When they are a month old, you must redeem them at the redemption price set at five shekels of silver, according to the sanctuary shekel, which weighs twenty gerahs.

¹⁷"But you must not redeem the firstborn of a cow, a sheep or a goat; they are holy. Splash their blood against the altar and burn their fat as a food offering, an aroma pleasing to the LORD. ¹⁸Their meat is to be yours, just as the breast of the wave offering and the right thigh are yours. ¹⁹Whatever is set aside from the holy offerings the Israelites present to the LORD I give to you and your sons and daughters as your perpetual share. It is an everlasting covenant of salt before the LORD for both you and your offspring."

> [20]The LORD said to Aaron, "You will have no inheritance in their land, nor will you have any share among them; I am your share and your inheritance among the Israelites.
>
> [21]"I give to the Levites all the tithes in Israel as their inheritance in return for the work they do while serving at the tent of meeting. [22]From now on the Israelites must not go near the tent of meeting, or they will bear the consequences of their sin and will die. [23]It is the Levites who are to do the work at the tent of meeting and bear the responsibility for any offenses they commit against it. This is a lasting ordinance for the generations to come. They will receive no inheritance among the Israelites. [24]Instead, I give to the Levites as their inheritance the tithes that the Israelites present as an offering to the LORD. That is why I said concerning them: 'They will have no inheritance among the Israelites.'"
>
> [25]The LORD said to Moses, [26]"Speak to the Levites and say to them: 'When you receive from the Israelites the tithe I give you as your inheritance, you must present a tenth of that tithe as the LORD's offering. [27]Your offering will be reckoned to you as grain from the threshing floor or juice from the winepress. [28]In this way you also will present an offering to the LORD from all the tithes you receive from the Israelites. From these tithes you must give the LORD's portion to Aaron the priest. [29]You must present as the LORD's portion the best and holiest part of everything given to you.'
>
> [30]"Say to the Levites: 'When you present the best part, it will be reckoned to you as the product of the threshing floor or the winepress. [31]You and your households may eat the rest of it anywhere, for it is your wages for your work at the tent of meeting. [32]By presenting the best part of it you will not be guilty in this matter; then you will not defile the holy offerings of the Israelites, and you will not die.'"

Listening to the Text in the Story: Genesis 31:14; Leviticus 25:23; Numbers 16:1–18:7

The previous chapters established the special role that Aaron's family had as tabernacle priests as well as the Levites' special role in helping with tabernacle duties (16:1–18:7). Because priests' and Levites' duties were focused at the tabernacle, and because they were not given large tracts of land like the other tribes (see at 18:20, p. 252), a question arises: How will their material needs be met? The remainder of this chapter explains how the Lord would do so.

One of the principal ways he provided for their needs was through the Israelites' tithes (18:20–32). Duguid puts this practice in its ancient Near Eastern context and explains its significance:

> Throughout the ancient Near East, it was a common practice for kings to tax their people in the amount of a tithe of their produce. The tithe in Numbers 18 seems to function somewhat like these royal taxes of the ancient Near East. The Lord was Israel's Great King, and the tithe was an annual obligation to give 10 percent of their produce for the regular support of Levites, who were the servants of the King.[1]

EXPLAIN the Story

The Priests' Share in the Lord's Offerings (18:8–19)

Verse 8 of chapter 18 provides an overview. As the following verses will show, the term "holy offerings" (v. 8) refers to various food and animal gifts that the Israelites gave to the Lord by giving to the tabernacle, much as one gives tribute to a king at his palace. The Lord makes clear these belong to him ("*I myself*" determine what happens with these; v. 8, emphasis added) but also that he is giving them to his palace servants as a perpetual portion to provide for their needs.

The details now follow, beginning with priestly portions (18:9–19; see the chart below for overview). First mentioned are "most holy" portions (18:9–10), that is, portions of the most holy altar offerings (grain, purification,[2] guilt) that were "kept from the fire" and given to the priests (18:9).[3] Such portions could only be eaten in a ritually "holy place" and only by the ritually holy priests, not their families (Lev 6:16–18; 24:9), and Numbers 18:10 underscores the importance of doing so. To disrespect the king's most holy property is to disrespect the king; the priests had to make sure not to do so.

Next discussed are holy offerings in general (Num 18:11–13). These could be eaten by any ceremonially clean member of a priestly household (cf. Lev 22:10–13). The first mentioned are "the wave offerings of the Israelites" (Num 18:11), that is, items dedicated to the Lord by means of a ritual action in

---

1. Duguid, *Numbers*, 232; see further Richard E. Averbeck, "מַעֲשֵׂר (Tithe)" *NIDOTTE* 2:1035–36.
2. NIV footnote; see p. 115n5.
3. For these portions see Lev 2:1–3 (grain offering), 4:27–31 and 6:24–30 (purification offering), and 7:1–6 (guilt offering).

which the item was waved back and forth (Lev 7:30). Coming immediately after the portions of the "most holy" altar offerings, this verse likely refers to the portion of the "holy" altar offering, namely, the fellowship offering, the breast of which was "waved" before the Lord and given to priestly families (Lev 7:34; cf. Num 18:18).

The Priests' Share in the Offerings

Offering Type (Num 18)	Ceremonial Status of the Offering	Examples	Who Could Eat It
Most Holy Offerings	Most holy	Grain, sin, and guilt offerings	Priests
Wave Offerings	Holy	Breast of fellowship offerings	Priestly households (person had to be ceremonially clean)
Firstfruits	Holy	Olive oil, new wine, grain	Priestly households (person had to be ceremonially clean)
Devoted Items	Most holy	Cows, sheep, goats	Not stated (priests only?)
Firstborn	Holy	Cow, sheep, goats	Priestly households (person had to be ceremonially clean)

Firstfruits are next (18:12–13). Earlier texts had already commanded Israelites to bring these to the Lord (Exod 23:16, 19); he, in turn, shared them with his palace servants. For further comments, see the end of this chapter: Live the Story: What Do We Learn from the Lord's Provision for His Servants?

Next addressed is anything "devoted to the Lord" (Num 18:14). The underlying Hebrew word (*herem*) refers to giving something irrevocably to the Lord, such as a person, an animal, or family land (Lev 27:28). The Lord in turn gave such gifts to the priests. In the case of people, this would mean permanent tabernacle service. In the case of animals or fields, it would mean they passed permanently to the tabernacle to support the Lord's workers there (cf. Lev 27:21).[4]

The final items addressed are firstborn children and animals (Num 18:15–18). At the first Passover, the Lord commanded that all firstborn males be set aside as holy to him in order to commemorate his redemption of Israel, his firstborn son, from Egypt (Exod. 13:2, 12, 14–15). These firstborn males fell into two different groups. Sons or unclean animals were to be "redeemed," that is, the son's parents or animal's owners would make a payment to the tabernacle and the son or animal would continue to belong to the one making the payment (Num 18:15b–16).[5] In the case of sons, the redemption was a visual reminder that the Lord had redeemed Israel, his firstborn son (Exod 4:22; cf. 13:14–15). In the case of unclean animals (such as donkeys), which could not be sacrificed, the redemption provided for tabernacle needs while sparing priests from maintaining the animals.

In the second group were clean animals (cows, sheep, goats), which could not be redeemed because they belonged irrevocably to the Lord (Num 18:17–18).[6] They were to be sacrificed as a visual reminder that the Lord had killed the Egyptians' firstborn (Exod 13:14–15). The meat would then belong to the priestly families (Num 18:18), similar to the breast and thigh of the fellowship offering (cf. Lev 7:34).

Numbers 18:19 summarizes the entire section and identifies these gifts to the priests and their families as a "covenant of salt." This was a way to describe this law's ongoing nature, as demonstrated by the use of the phrase "perpetual share" and the word "everlasting" (cf. 2 Chr 13:5).[7]

---

4. This assumes a non-war context; for war contexts, see pp. 281–83, Why Such Severe Destruction?

5. The payment specified in 18:16 applies to sons (cf. Lev 27:6; Num 3:47); for unclean animals, presumably the law of Lev 27:27 is followed. As for how Lev 27:27 relates to Exod 13:13 and 34:20, it is not entirely clear whether the law of Lev 27:27 is meant to replace the laws of Exod 13:13 and 34:20 or is meant simply to supplement them.

6. For "food offering" see p. 212n4.

7. Wenham (*Leviticus*, 71) notes that "salt was something that could not be destroyed by fire or time or any other means in antiquity, and thus a good symbol of a covenant's enduring nature." This explanation is certainly possible but still speculative; we simply do not have enough information to be conclusive on the reason why salt was associated with an enduring covenant.

The Levites' Share in the Lord's Offerings and the Offerings They Themselves Must Make (18:20–32)

Aaron is again addressed (cf. Num 18:1, 8), this time in his role as leader of the tribe of Levi, including the non-priestly Levites, who are the focus here.[8] The section begins with an important explanation (v. 20), the background to which is that the promised land and all it produced was the Lord's property (Lev 25:23). He in turn gave to the Israelites, his firstborn, large tracts within this land as a portion and inheritance (Num 26:53), much as a father would give a portion and inheritance to his children (cf. Gen 31:14). To the tribe of Levi, however, he gave from his very own table, namely, the holy gifts the Israelites gave to the Lord. We might paraphrase, "You will not have physical land as an inheritance from which to provide for your needs, but you will have my service as an inheritance, and I myself will provide for your needs by means of it" (Num 18:20). In this way, he would not only provide for their material needs but also remind them that the Lord was their ultimate inheritance and hope and use them as a reminder to all the tribes that Israel's ultimate good was found in knowing the Lord.

For the priestly Levites, these gifts consisted of those just described (Num 18:9–19); for the non-priestly Levites, these gifts consisted of the Israelites' tithes (vv. 21–24). Other texts describe tithes and make clear these came from the Israelites' produce (Lev 27:30–31; Deut 14:22–23), which is the focus here (Num 18:27, 30), though tithes were also to come from the Israelites' herds and flocks (Lev 27:32–33).

The biblical and ancient Near Eastern background of the tithe has been described above and underscores that the Lord is the Israelites' divine King and the priests and Levites are his temple servants.[9] This passage makes clear that the tithes are given to the Levites as the Lord's way of providing for their needs (Num 18:20, 24) and in exchange for their work at the tent (v. 21).[10] This work only they could do; lay Israelites could come to the tent to worship but could not draw near to do the Levites' special work, on pain of death (vv. 22–23) (just as the Levites could not draw near it to do the priests' special work, on pain of death; vv. 1–7). Moreover, just as the priests were accountable if they allowed the Levites to do priestly duties (v. 3), the Levites were accountable if they allowed the Israelites to do Levites' duties (v. 23).[11]

---

8. Milgrom, *Numbers*, 154.
9. See Listening to the Text in the Story, pp. 248–49.
10. For their duties see Listening to the Text in the Story, p. 224.
11. Thus the phrase "they commit against it" (18:23) refers to lay Israelites whom the Levites

The Levites in turn gave a tithe of the tithe to the priests (Num 18:26–29). (Since the priests were far fewer in number, this arrangement would adequately supply them.)[12] Even though this did not come from their own harvest, it did count as their income and their giving it to the priests would count as a tithe as much as the other Israelites' tithes did (vv. 27, 30). It was their contribution offering to the Lord ("the LORD's portion") and was to be the very best 10 percent, thus modeling for the Israelites that the Lord deserved the best that they could give (vv. 29, 32).[13] To do otherwise was to say, "You, Lord, are unworthy of our best because you are an unworthy King!" It was also to say, "It matters little to me that you have set aside these Israelite tithes as holy; I will treat them from the very beginning as a very common thing."[14] Such treacherous disrespect would result in the penalty usually given to the treasonous: death (v. 32). But this of course was not the Lord's desire, and the Levites, having properly presented the best 10 percent to honor their King, were then able to enjoy the rest as their portion for their service at the tabernacle and to eat it as ordinary food (that is, it did not have to be eaten in a ritually clean or holy state or a ritually clean or holy place) (v. 31).[15] The Lord loves to provide for his servants' needs.

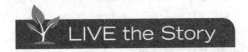

What Do We Learn about Giving to the Lord?

When the Israelites gave their firstfruits to the Lord, they were doing several things at once. To begin, they were expressing thankfulness for God's faithful provision, as though to say, "You, Lord, have been faithful to your covenant promises, delivering us from oppression and slavery, giving us this land, which flows with milk and honey, and blessing us with these good gifts of food"

---

fail to prevent from doing tabernacle duties; by doing these duties, the Israelites commit sin against the tabernacle (for which the Levites will be held responsible).

12. Deuteronomy 14 adds that the tithe was also intended to provide every third year for those who were needy, in this way demonstrating to them the Lord's care (14:28–29). For how these tithing laws relate to those in Leviticus and Deuteronomy, see Jay Sklar, *Additional Notes on* Leviticus *in the Zondervan Exegetical Commentary on the Old Testament Series* (St. Louis, MO: Gleanings Press, 2023), at 27:30–33, where it is argued that all three books refer to one annual tithe, with Deut specifying its distribution at the sanctuary in years 1–2, 4–5 (Deut 14:22–27) and in local towns in years 3 and 6 (Deut 14:28–29; 26:12–15).

13. The phrase "the best and holiest part" (18:29) is perhaps better as "its best part, which is to be dedicated as holy" (cf. ESV). This would be in keeping with the fact it is given to the priests.

14. The NIV's "defile" in 18:32 translates a word (from the root *h-l-l*) that refers to treating a holy object as common (cf. ESV: "profane").

15. Cf. 18:10–11.

(see Deut 26:1–10). What is more, because the firstfruits were viewed as the harvest's very best (Num 18:12), the Israelites were demonstrating the Lord was worthy of the most honor they could give. And finally, by giving of their firstfruits before the full harvest was in, they were demonstrating faith that the Lord would provide so that their own needs would be met.

When Christians give today to support the work of Christ's church, they are doing these very same things. To give back to the Lord is to gratefully acknowledge that he is the one who has provided for us in the first place in his faithful love. To give him our best is to acknowledge he is worthy of the best we have to give. To give generously is to trust in his future provision for us and to remember not only his warning that "whoever sows sparingly will also reap sparingly" but also his promise that "whoever sows generously will also reap generously" (2 Cor 9:6). Keeping all these in mind—his faithful love, his worthiness, his promise of future provision—enables us not only to give but to be cheerful givers (2 Cor 9:7), the very type of givers the Lord loves. Even when a child gives a simple or small gift to a parent, when it is given with a heart full of thankful love, the parent always smiles.

This passage, however, not only speaks of giving to the Lord but also how the Lord used that giving to provide for his tabernacle servants. This leads to the next question.

What Do We Learn about Giving to His Servants?

A key theme of these verses is that the Lord's people must provide for their spiritual leaders' needs. As the Israelites faithfully gave their gifts to the Lord for his servants, it not only reminded the priests and Levites of the Lord's generous provision, it also enabled them to focus on serving at his tabernacle and thus allowed the Lord's worship to continue.

> When the Israelites of Nehemiah's day failed to provide tithes for the Levites . . . [the Levites] had to quit serving in the temple to go in search of work, and the worship of God and ministry of the temple were severely affected (Neh 13:10–11). It was thus vital that the people provide for those who ministered in the LORD's house.
>
> The New Testament applies this principle to the church, teaching that those who devote themselves to serving the church should have their physical needs met by it (1 Cor 9:13–14; Gal 6:6). Paul did not always make use of this right, especially when he believed it might hinder the spread of the gospel in some way (1 Cor 9:12; 1 Thess 2:9; 2 Thess 3:8), but the church should understand it must do all it can to provide for those

who minister within it, both for their sakes and for the sake of the ministry of the gospel. Hungry shepherds cannot care well for their sheep.[16]

In some contexts, congregations are too poor to provide adequately for their leaders, and no guilt should come because of that. But congregations do well to ask, "Are we doing all we can to supply our leaders' material needs?" Indeed, as noted above, the Israelites were to generously bring their very best firstfruits to the tabernacle for the priests (Num 18:12–13). What does it mean for us to give generously and from our best to provide for our leaders? By contrast, a quick search for "sending used tea bags to missionaries" will turn up first-person accounts of people on the mission field who have received such "gifts."[17] Used tea bags are hardly the best of someone's firstfruits! The question is not, "Now that I'm done using this, is there some ministry leader I can give it to?" The question is, "How do I bless those leading in ministry with the best of the bounty the Lord has given me?"

There is a final question we may ask of this passage.

What Do We Learn from the Lord's Provision for His Servants?

Central to this passage is Numbers 18:20. By telling the priests and Levites that instead of having large tracts of land they will have the Lord as their portion and inheritance, he is affirming that he will provide for their needs as his servants. He would do this by sharing from his very own table, taking the Israelites' gifts given to him and giving them to the priests and Levites. As noted above, we might paraphrase, "You will not have physical land as an inheritance from which to provide for your needs, but you will have my service as an inheritance, and I myself will provide for your needs by means of it."

But Numbers 18:20 is far more than a promise of material provision. It is a pointer to life's ultimate goal and good: relationship with the Lord. For the Israelites, the land was certainly central to the covenant promises (Gen 12:1; 13:15; 15:7), and through it they would be able to provide for their physical needs (Exod 3:8; Deut 8:7–10), but above all it was to be the place where

---

16. Sklar, *Leviticus* (ZECOT), 115. With regard to whether tithing laws apply today, since Christians are no longer under the Sinai covenant, the command to tithe does not automatically apply. Like other Old Testament laws, however, the underlying principles continue: Christians are to return material blessings to those who lead them in the Lord's ways (1 Cor 9:6–18), and to the needy (Rom 15:25–28; 2 Cor 8:1–15; Eph 4:28). See further discussion and rationale in Sklar, *Leviticus* (ZECOT), 763–65.

17. To take just one example, see "Used Tea Bags for Missionaries: Notes on a Meme," *Nathan Hobby: A Biographer in Perth*, July 11, 2014, https://nathanhobby.com/2014/07/11/used-tea-bags-for-missionaries-notes-on-a-meme/.

they enjoyed relationship with God (Gen 17:7–8; Lev 26:11–12). The Lord would use the priests and Levites as a reminder of this. For these two groups, the focus is not on the land but on the ultimate good the Israelites are to enjoy in the land: God himself.

The significance of this was not missed by later Israelites, who repeatedly use the language of "portion"[18] to describe the Lord as their ultimate good and ultimate source of hope and strength:

> Lord, you alone are my *portion* and my cup. (Ps 16:5)

> My flesh and my heart may fail,
>   but God is the strength of my heart
>   and my *portion* forever. (Ps 73:26)

> I cry to you, Lord;
>   I say, "You are my refuge,
>   my *portion* in the land of the living." (Ps 142:5)

> I say to myself, "The Lord is my *portion*;
>   therefore I will wait for him." (Lam 3:24)

As a later commentator would write, "Truly, he who possesses God possesses all things."[19]

If Jesus is indeed our portion, what does it look like for us to prioritize our relationship with him as the most important thing in life? How does that show up in how we use our resources and how we make important life decisions? From a different angle, what does it look like for us to find our comfort and hope in him in the midst of distress and hardship? And what does it mean to hope in him when putting him first is costly? We can do so boldly, knowing that he himself has promised, "Everyone who has left houses or brothers or sisters or father or mother or wife or children or fields for my sake will receive a hundred times as much and will inherit eternal life" (Matt 19:29). The Lord indeed loves to provide for his servants!

---

18. NIV translates "share" in Num 18:20 but "portion" in the verses cited above (emphasis added). All these verses use the same Hebrew word (*heleq*).

19. Keil, *The Pentateuch*, 731 (*Numbers*, 118), citing André Masius's commentary on Joshua (*Iosuae imperatoris historia illustrate atque explicita ab Andrea Masio* [Antwerp: Ex officina Christophori Plantini. Architypographi Regii, 1574]).

CHAPTER 22

Numbers 19:1-22

 LISTEN to the Story

¹The Lord said to Moses and Aaron: ²"This is a requirement of the law that the Lord has commanded: Tell the Israelites to bring you a red heifer without defect or blemish and that has never been under a yoke. ³Give it to Eleazar the priest; it is to be taken outside the camp and slaughtered in his presence. ⁴Then Eleazar the priest is to take some of its blood on his finger and sprinkle it seven times toward the front of the tent of meeting. ⁵While he watches, the heifer is to be burned—its hide, flesh, blood and intestines. ⁶The priest is to take some cedar wood, hyssop and scarlet wool and throw them onto the burning heifer. ⁷After that, the priest must wash his clothes and bathe himself with water. He may then come into the camp, but he will be ceremonially unclean till evening. ⁸The man who burns it must also wash his clothes and bathe with water, and he too will be unclean till evening.

⁹"A man who is clean shall gather up the ashes of the heifer and put them in a ceremonially clean place outside the camp. They are to be kept by the Israelite community for use in the water of cleansing; it is for purification from sin. ¹⁰The man who gathers up the ashes of the heifer must also wash his clothes, and he too will be unclean till evening. This will be a lasting ordinance both for the Israelites and for the foreigners residing among them.

¹¹"Whoever touches a human corpse will be unclean for seven days. ¹²They must purify themselves with the water on the third day and on the seventh day; then they will be clean. But if they do not purify themselves on the third and seventh days, they will not be clean. ¹³If they fail to purify themselves after touching a human corpse, they defile the Lord's tabernacle. They must be cut off from Israel. Because the water of cleansing has not been sprinkled on them, they are unclean; their uncleanness remains on them.

¹⁴"This is the law that applies when a person dies in a tent: Anyone

> who enters the tent and anyone who is in it will be unclean for seven days, ¹⁵and every open container without a lid fastened on it will be unclean.
>
> ¹⁶"Anyone out in the open who touches someone who has been killed with a sword or someone who has died a natural death, or anyone who touches a human bone or a grave, will be unclean for seven days.
>
> ¹⁷"For the unclean person, put some ashes from the burned purification offering into a jar and pour fresh water over them. ¹⁸Then a man who is ceremonially clean is to take some hyssop, dip it in the water and sprinkle the tent and all the furnishings and the people who were there. He must also sprinkle anyone who has touched a human bone or a grave or anyone who has been killed or anyone who has died a natural death. ¹⁹The man who is clean is to sprinkle those who are unclean on the third and seventh days, and on the seventh day he is to purify them. Those who are being cleansed must wash their clothes and bathe with water, and that evening they will be clean. ²⁰But if those who are unclean do not purify themselves, they must be cut off from the community, because they have defiled the sanctuary of the Lord. The water of cleansing has not been sprinkled on them, and they are unclean. ²¹This is a lasting ordinance for them.
>
> "The man who sprinkles the water of cleansing must also wash his clothes, and anyone who touches the water of cleansing will be unclean till evening. ²²Anything that an unclean person touches becomes unclean, and anyone who touches it becomes unclean till evening."

Listening to the Text in the Story: Leviticus 11–15

In discussing ritual impurity as it shows up in the Bible, scholars make a distinction between minor and major impurities (see chart below).

But this chart is not quite complete. In between major and minor impurities is the impurity that comes from menstruation (Lev 15:19–24) and corpse contamination (Num 19:11–22). This impurity was similar to major impurities in that it was contagious and lasted at least seven days and similar to minor impurities in that individual sacrifice was not required (perhaps due to the financial burden it would cause). Indeed, as argued below, the provisions of this chapter are a significant act of the Lord's grace, not only in providing cleansing but doing so in a way that spares Israelites financial ruin.[1]

---

1. See pp. 263–64, How Does Cleansing Happen?

	Minor Impurity	Major Impurity
Cleansing Rite(s)	Bathing and/or laundering	Some of the following: bathing, laundering, shaving, sprinkling with cleansing waters or blood, anointing with oil or blood; *always involves sacrifice*
Impurity's Duration	Lasts until sundown	Lasts at least 7 days
Is It Contagious?	No	Yes; for people or objects
Examples	Those who have touched or carried an unclean carcass (Lev 11:24–28); those who have entered, slept or eaten in a house with a ritually defiling infestation (Lev 14:46–47); those who have had intercourse (Lev 15:18)	Those with a skin disease (Lev 13–14); a new mother (Lev 12); a male or female with a discharge (Lev 15:13–15, 28–30)

EXPLAIN the Story

Given the events of Numbers 16, in which nearly fifteen thousand people died (16:31–35, 49), it is no surprise to find instructions here concerning how to cleanse oneself of ritual impurity coming from corpses.

Preparing the Water of Cleansing (19:1–10)

The animal required for the rite is described in several ways (see the table below). It is given to Eleazar (v. 3), Aaron's son, who will lead this rite instead of Aaron, perhaps because the result is ritual impurity (v. 7), which the high priest was to avoid at all costs.

The rite takes place outside the camp, not at the altar, and the animal is to be slaughtered (and later burned) by an unnamed third party, presumably a priest or Levite (Num 19:3). Eleazar then performs a sprinkling rite with its blood (v. 4). Elsewhere, the sprinkling of blood, oil or water is often associated with cleansing or consecrating (Lev 8:30; 14:7, 51–52; etc.), while the number seven connotes completeness and thoroughness, for example, those with a major impurity waited seven days for cleansing, a thorough wait (Lev 12:2; 15:13). Eleazar's act pictures a complete cleansing. That he is to sprinkle this blood "toward the front of the tent of meeting" (Num 19:4) suggests what the overall purpose of the cleansing water will be: to purify not only the defiled person but also the tabernacle itself (see further at Num 19:13, p. 262). Indeed, this sprinkling action is most similar to that of certain types of purification offerings (Lev 4:5–6, 16–17; 16:14, 19), the goal of which was tabernacle cleansing.[2]

Characteristic	Rationale
Red	Every suggested rationale must remain tentative, but since red recalls the color of blood (which has cleansing powers [Lev 8:15]), and since this animal's ashes will be used to create cleansing waters, it is plausible the animal's color was to underscore the waters' cleansing powers (cf. v. 6).
Heifer	Female animals had to be used for the purification offering of individual lay Israelites (Lev 4:28, 32). This fits well here since this is a type of purification offering (Num 19:17) and its ashes used to make purificatory waters for everyday Israelites.
Without defect or blemish	A standard requirement for sacrificial animals (Lev 1:3; 3:1; 4:3; etc.).
Never been under a yoke	For reasons not explained, various peoples in the ancient Near East seemed to view unworked heifers as particularly appropriate for certain important rituals and holy activities (cf. Deut 21:1–9; 1 Sam 6:7–8).

Under the priest's supervision, the entire animal is then burned (Num 19:5), just as certain purification offerings were mostly burned outside the camp (cf. Lev 4:11–12, 21). The priest is to add cedar wood, scarlet material, and hyssop (Num 19:6), items that occur in the cleansing rite of the person with a ritually defiling skin disease (Lev 14:4). Since cedar wood and scarlet material are both red, this again raises the possibility they are associated with blood and its purificatory powers (see at Num 19:3, p. 260). In any case, their

---

2. See Lev 16:14–19.

association with purification is clear (Lev 14:4). As for the hyssop, it also is associated with purification, since it was used as the means by which purifying liquids were applied to others (Lev 14:6–7; cf. Num 19:18). Adding these items to the midst of the burning animal—which is a type of purification offering (v. 17)—would thus underscore the purificatory powers of the waters mixed with its ashes.

For reasons not explained, the priest and the person burning the animal both become ritually impure and must go through the rites often associated with minor impurities (Num 19:7–8).[3] Washing clothes and bathing are natural symbols of cleansing. The text does not explain why one must wait until evening, but the impurity ended with the daylight.

Meanwhile, the ashes are collected by a person who must be ritually pure, presumably so as not to defile the ashes, which are to be kept in a ritually pure place outside the camp and will be used to make "the water of cleansing" (Num 19:9), to be used to ritually cleanse those who are ritually impure due to touching or being near a dead body (v. 12).[4] Again for reasons not explained, the person gathering the ashes also becomes ritually impure and must go through the necessary rites (v. 10a). The final part of verse 10 identifies that the ordinance of preparing these waters is to be ongoing and to serve Israelites and non-Israelites alike (v. 10b).

Cleansing Ceremonial Uncleanness That Comes from Corpses and How to Cleanse It (19:11–22)

The text now explains how to make use of the ashes in order to cleanse people from the ritual defilement coming from corpses (Num 19:11–22). Presumably, the cleansing takes place outside the camp, where those with such defilement were to go so as not to defile the camp in which the holy Lord dwelt (see at 5:1–4, p. 92; cf. 31:19).

Three scenarios for becoming unclean are given (Num 19:11–16). The first is the most general, stating that direct contact with a corpse results in a seven-day impurity (making it like a major impurity; v. 11) and that the

---

3. Regular sacrifices offered at the altar do not defile but, in at least one other instance, the burning of a sacrificial carcass outside the camp results in ritual impurity (Lev 16:27–28). Again, no reasons are given. Milgrom (*Numbers*, 438–39) suggests that purification offerings absorb ritual impurity, thus defiling their handlers, but this fails to explain why these ashes would do so before they are ever used to absorb anyone's impurity (nor is it a scholarly consensus that purification offerings do absorb impurity). The mystery remains.

4. The phrase "it is for purification from sin" (19:9) is perhaps better translated "it is a purification offering" (cf. NJB; ESV; NRSB). The word in question is *hatta't*, the typical word for the purification offering, and translated this way in v. 17 by the NIV (along with many versions). See also Exod 29:14; Lev 4:24; 5:9, 11, 12.

waters of cleansing must be used for the impure person on days three and seven (v. 12). Further details will come on this procedure in a moment (vv. 17–19). In the meantime, the text underscores the importance of cleansing lest the person "defile the Lord's tabernacle" (vv. 12–13). Just as we say that a soldier's dishonorable behavior is a "stain on the uniform," it seems that major impurities resulted in a "stain on the tabernacle."[5] As long as the person dealt properly with their impurity, the tabernacle stain was removed. But failure to deal with their own impurity was to leave the stain on the tabernacle itself, a gross sign of disrespect for the holiness of it and its owner, the Lord. Those who willingly fail to cleanse their defilement from a king's palace are saying they want nothing to do with his kingdom, and the penalty here fits the crime: the person is cut off, a phrase referring to exile or even death.[6]

The second scenario concerns a person who died in a tent (Num 19:14–15). In this case, their impurity acted like a type of defiling mist, settling on anyone entering the tent or already in it and seeping into any container without a lid (vv. 14–15).

In the third case, a person comes in context with a dead body or bone or grave somewhere outside the camp (Num 19:16).[7] Again, the result is a seven-day impurity.

The procedure to follow for cleansing is now described in detail (Num 19:17–22). First, a mixture is made of the ashes and fresh water (v. 17). This has led the ashes to be described as an "instant purification offering."[8] Just as water can be added to instant coffee to prepare coffee, water could be added to these ashes to prepare a mixture that functions like a purification offering.[9]

Next, a ritually clean person takes hyssop, dips it in the cleansing water, and sprinkles it on days three and seven upon anything needing cleansing from the impurity (Num 19:18–19a; cf. v. 12).

Finally, any people who are cleansed must wash their clothes and bathe on day seven and they will be pure (Num 19:19b). The text finishes by underscoring the warning of verse 13 (v. 20) noting that this is a lasting ordinance (v. 21a) and specifies that those who handle the waters become ritually impure,[10] can spread that impurity to others, and must go through the required cleansing rites (vv. 21–22).

---

5. For details, see Sklar, *Leviticus* (ZECOT), 140.
6. For details, see ibid., 41–42.
7. Contact with a dead body was covered in 19:11–13; the repetition here may be to ensure people knew this applied to contact with corpses outside the camp as well as within it.
8. Wenham, *Numbers*, 147.
9. For fuller descriptions of this offering, see at 6:13–20, pp. 116–17.
10. Cf. at vv. 7–8.

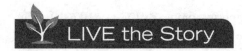

LIVE the Story

What Is Ritual Impurity Anyway?

For the answer to this question, see pp. 32–33, Ritual Purity and Impurity. As noted there, one purpose of laws involving ritual states was to remind the Israelites of moral realities. In this chapter, the reminder comes in the context of properly addressing the ritual defilement that comes from dead bodies, which leads to another question.

Why Are Dead Bodies Ritually Defiling?

The text does not tell us the answer to this question, but that has not stopped people from guessing! The most common approach is to make a connection between purity, holiness, and life on the one hand and impurity and death on the other.[11] The link between impurity and death would make good sense of the laws in this chapter, as well as laws about leprosy, where the person's deteriorating body makes them look like a corpse (cf. Num 12:10–12). But linking impurity with death faces a certain tension when we remember that ritual impurity also comes from having sex and giving birth (Lev 12:1–8; 15:18), two activities intimately related with the production of life.[12]

This tension leads to an important reminder when it comes to trying to explain the rationale behind a ritual state, namely, it is possible we do not have enough information to discern the rationale and equally possible that the Israelites did not know either. Sometimes the origin of a belief is lost in the fog of history. Many Westerners cross their fingers as a sign of good luck, but no one really knows why. Guesses have been made but no one knows for sure and, if you ask most Westerners for a rationale, they will shrug their shoulders and say, "That's just the way it is." We can explain the purpose of the act but not its rationale. The same may be equally true when it comes to the situation of a dead body. An Israelite might not have been able to explain why it was ritually defiling but understood that the purpose of these laws was to help them to address that defilement properly, which leads to a final question.

How Does Cleansing Happen?

At the ritual level, the cleansing happens by means of an "instant purification offering": the ashes of the red heifer are mixed with water to make waters of

---

11. See Milgrom, *Leviticus 1–16*, 1001–3.
12. See further discussion in Sklar, *Leviticus* (TOTC), 47–48.

cleansing that take away the ritual impurity completely (Num 19:17–19). This was a tremendous act of grace on the Lord's part. As noted above (Listening to the Text in the Story), the ritual defilement coming from corpses was a major impurity, which normally requires each person with the impurity to bring a sacrifice. Doing so here could plunge entire families into debt since each member would have become defiled during the mourning rites for their loved one. In his typical grace, the Lord provides a solution: a special purification offering is performed outside the camp and its ashes used to make cleansing waters freely available for the entire community. He not only provides cleansing for the community, he provides it freely.

At this point, someone might well ask, "But how does this all relate to me? After all, the laws about ritual purity and impurity were part of the old covenant, not part of the new covenant." That is certainly true (cf. Mark 7:19). But once it is remembered that these laws about ritual states were reminders about moral realities, we are able to see that Numbers 19 is a profound reminder to us of our need of the Lord to cleanse us. Not ritually, but morally.

Already in the Old Testament, the psalmist recognizes this. In Psalm 51 we find the prayer of someone who has sinned greatly and who feels unclean because of it. Many of us can resonate with this: sin often makes us feel dirty. In Psalm 51, the sinner makes use of imagery from Numbers 19 to express his desire for cleansing to the Lord: "Cleanse me with hyssop, and I will be clean; wash me, and I will be whiter than snow" (v. 7). He knows he needs his sin washed away; he also knows only God can do it.

Not surprisingly, the author of Hebrews therefore alludes to Numbers 19 in describing the cleansing God accomplishes through Jesus and underscores that it is profoundly moral: "The blood of goats and bulls and the ashes of a heifer sprinkled on those who are ceremonially unclean sanctify them so that they are outwardly clean. *How much more*, then, will the blood of Christ, who through the eternal Spirit offered himself unblemished to God, *cleanse our consciences* from acts that lead to death, so that we may serve the living God!" (Heb 9:13–14, emphasis added).

This is profoundly good news. The challenge is to believe it. Our temptation is to want to cleanse ourselves or even to think that some of our sins have stained us so deeply, or are repeated so frequently, that God cannot possibly take them away. But his promises say otherwise. "If we confess our sins, he is faithful and just and will forgive us our sins and purify us from all unrighteousness" (1 John 1:9). Do we believe this? *Will* we believe this? What must not be missed is that verse 9 ends with a period. There are no exceptions. Full and final cleansing is available in Jesus!

CHAPTER 23
Numbers 20:1-29

LISTEN to the Story

¹In the first month the whole Israelite community arrived at the Desert of Zin, and they stayed at Kadesh. There Miriam died and was buried.

²Now there was no water for the community, and the people gathered in opposition to Moses and Aaron. ³They quarreled with Moses and said, "If only we had died when our brothers fell dead before the LORD! ⁴Why did you bring the LORD's community into this wilderness, that we and our livestock should die here? ⁵Why did you bring us up out of Egypt to this terrible place? It has no grain or figs, grapevines or pomegranates. And there is no water to drink!"

⁶Moses and Aaron went from the assembly to the entrance to the tent of meeting and fell facedown, and the glory of the LORD appeared to them. ⁷The LORD said to Moses, ⁸"Take the staff, and you and your brother Aaron gather the assembly together. Speak to that rock before their eyes and it will pour out its water. You will bring water out of the rock for the community so they and their livestock can drink."

⁹So Moses took the staff from the LORD's presence, just as he commanded him. ¹⁰He and Aaron gathered the assembly together in front of the rock and Moses said to them, "Listen, you rebels, must we bring you water out of this rock?" ¹¹Then Moses raised his arm and struck the rock twice with his staff. Water gushed out, and the community and their livestock drank.

¹²But the LORD said to Moses and Aaron, "Because you did not trust in me enough to honor me as holy in the sight of the Israelites, you will not bring this community into the land I give them."

¹³These were the waters of Meribah, where the Israelites quarreled with the LORD and where he was proved holy among them.

¹⁴Moses sent messengers from Kadesh to the king of Edom, saying:

"This is what your brother Israel says: You know about all the hardships that have come on us. ¹⁵Our ancestors went down into Egypt, and we lived there many years. The Egyptians mistreated us and our ancestors, ¹⁶but when we cried out to the LORD, he heard our cry and sent an angel and brought us out of Egypt.

"Now we are here at Kadesh, a town on the edge of your territory. ¹⁷Please let us pass through your country. We will not go through any field or vineyard, or drink water from any well. We will travel along the King's Highway and not turn to the right or to the left until we have passed through your territory."

¹⁸But Edom answered:

"You may not pass through here; if you try, we will march out and attack you with the sword."

¹⁹The Israelites replied:

"We will go along the main road, and if we or our livestock drink any of your water, we will pay for it. We only want to pass through on foot—nothing else."

²⁰Again they answered:

"You may not pass through."

Then Edom came out against them with a large and powerful army. ²¹Since Edom refused to let them go through their territory, Israel turned away from them.

²²The whole Israelite community set out from Kadesh and came to Mount Hor. ²³At Mount Hor, near the border of Edom, the LORD said to Moses and Aaron, ²⁴"Aaron will be gathered to his people. He will not enter the land I give the Israelites, because both of you rebelled against my command at the waters of Meribah. ²⁵Get Aaron and his son Eleazar and take them up Mount Hor. ²⁶Remove Aaron's garments and put them on his son Eleazar, for Aaron will be gathered to his people; he will die there."

²⁷Moses did as the LORD commanded: They went up Mount Hor in the

> sight of the whole community. ²⁸Moses removed Aaron's garments and put them on his son Eleazar. And Aaron died there on top of the mountain. Then Moses and Eleazar came down from the mountain, ²⁹and when the whole community learned that Aaron had died, all the Israelites mourned for him thirty days.

Listening to the Text in the Story: Exodus 12:37–19:1; 17:1–7; Numbers 10:11–12:16

Numbers 20:1–22:1 recounts Israel's third travel narrative. The first took the Israelites from Egypt to Sinai (Exod 12:37–19:1), the second from Sinai to Kadesh (Num 10:11–12:16 [cf. 13:26]), and the third from Kadesh to the plains of Moab (20:1–22:1).[1]

Especially close parallels exist between this section's opening story (Num 20:1–13) and Exodus 17:1–7. In both, the people are in the wilderness, experience a lack of water, quarrel (Heb. *rib*) against their leaders, and accuse them of bringing the Israelites to the wilderness to die. In both, Moses prays to the Lord and is told to take a staff and in front of all the people perform a miracle in which water comes forth from the rock. And in both, the place is named Meribah. While the author clearly understood these to be two separate events,[2] his choice to highlight their similarities emphasizes important themes, most notably, how slow Israel is to trust the Lord. How many times must the Lord provide before they look to him with eyes of faith and not eyes of cynicism and doubt?

An important difference between these two events, however, remains. In the first, Moses carries out the Lord's commands with full obedience. In the second, he does not, nor does Aaron, who is with him. Their disobedience, and its tragic results, become the story's focus.

EXPLAIN the Story

Travel and Death Notice (20:1)
The Israelites now return to the wilderness of Zin at Kadesh, the area where they had rebelliously refused to enter the promised land (Num 13:21;

---

1. Not described here is the wandering they did in the area of Kadesh in between Num 12:16 and 20:1; cf. 33:18–36.
2. Cf. Num 33:14 and 37 (noted by Stubbs, *Numbers*, 158n51).

14:1–4).[3] Exactly how long they've been away from Kadesh is not stated, only that they have now returned in the "first month." The year is not specified, but a combination of verses lead most commentators to assume the fortieth year (cf. 20:1 with vv. 22–28 and 33:38). The fact that it is the fortieth year implies two things: the first generation of Israelites will pass from the scene and the second generation will then enter the land. As a result, the coming chapters narrate different acts of faithlessness that lead to the end of the first generation (21:4–9; 25:1–9) as well as the second generation's departure toward the promised land (20:1–22:1). Miriam's death perhaps introduces the transition from the first generation to the second (20:1). That her death is mentioned at all is a testimony to her significance in the life of the nation (cf. Exod 15:20–21; Num 12).

The Israelites' Complaint (20:2–5)

As soon as they arrive in Kadesh a problem arises: a lack of water. As noted above, the Israelites have been in this situation before and seen the Lord miraculously provide (Exod 17:1–7), but they seem to have no memory of this. Instead of crying out in faith to him, they gather against his appointed leaders (Num 20:2), wish that they had died in the Lord's latest judgment with their fellow Israelites instead of be in this situation (v. 3),[4] and once again blame Moses and Aaron for the situation—even though it is their fault (v. 4)![5] Indeed, verse 5 reads more woodenly, "Why did you[6] bring us up from Egypt in order to bring us to this terrible place?" to which the appropriate answer would be, "We did *not* bring you up from Egypt in order to bring you to *this terrible place*! We brought you up from Egypt to bring you *to the promised land* and *you* refused to go there!"

The Lord's Response (20:6–8)

But instead of speaking to the people, Moses and Aaron seek the Lord, who comes in answer to their prayers (Num 20:6). He commands Moses to take "the staff" (v. 8), an apparent reference to the one placed "before the LORD" in chapter 17 that demonstrated to all that Aaron's family was chosen as the Lord's priests (cf. 20:9 with 17:7, 10) and was a sure sign that a miracle-working God

---

3. See at 12:16, p. 187, for the relationship between the wilderness of Zin and the wilderness of Paran.
4. Cf. this verse with 17:12–13 and 16:31–35, 46–49.
5. See similar complaints in Exod 14:11; 16:3; 17:3; Num 16:13.
6. The "you" is plural.

was in their midst. He then tells Moses and Aaron[7] to "speak" to the rock (20:8), in contrast to Exodus 17 where he told Moses to "strike" the rock (Exod 17:6). The importance of this detail becomes apparent momentarily.

Moses's and Aaron's Obedience and Rebellion (20:9–11)

At first glance, all seems okay: Moses takes the staff as commanded, and he and Aaron gather the people before the rock. But his opening words to them mention nothing of the Lord (cf. Num 16:28–30); he and Aaron remain the focus. The beginning of verse 11 then uses a startling phrase to confirm that all is not right when it says that "Moses *raised his arm*" (emphasis added). Numbers 15:30 uses this same language to describe the person who "sins defiantly" (Heb. "with a *raised arm*"). When followed by a description of Moses "[striking] the rock" (twice!; 20:11) instead of speaking to it as the Lord commanded, it becomes clear that he has taken matters into his own hands (and Aaron with him). They have now put themselves in God's place. And while the Lord graciously provides water for the people (v. 11b), his discipline on Moses and Aaron is swift.

The Lord's Pronouncement of Judgment on Moses and Aaron (20:12)

"You did not trust in me enough to honor me" (Num 20:12) could be more woodenly translated, "You did not believe in me by treating me as holy." We might paraphrase: "By drawing attention to yourself, making yourself out to be the savior, you denied I was my people's redeemer, utterly unique—holy—in my ability to save."[8] This was an act expected of an apostate, which the text makes clear by describing Moses's and Aaron's action with the same words used to describe the apostate Israelites in Numbers 14:11.[9] Not surprisingly, they are likewise given the same sentence: they, too, will not see the promised land (20:12).

The Naming of the Waters (20:13)

The waters are named Meribah in keeping with the events ("Meribah" means "quarreling"). Though the Israelites focused their complaints on Moses and

---

7. The implied "you" of the command "speak" is plural.
8. "They have prevented the full power and might of Yahweh from becoming evident to the people, and have thus robbed him of the fear and reverence due to him" (Budd, *Numbers*, 218, cited in Cole, *Numbers*, 327–28).
9. The Hebrew phrase for "you did not *trust in me*" (20:12, emphasis added) and "they refuse *to believe in me*" (14:11, emphasis added) is the same.

Aaron, their ultimate quarrel was with the Lord. The text also notes that the "LORD . . . was proved holy among them" (Num 20:13) or, perhaps better, "through them he showed himself holy" (so ESV), the idea being that his provision of water showed his redeeming power, which only he had and which set him apart as utterly distinct—holy—in his ability to save.

Edom Denies Israel Passage (20:14–21)

The Israelites are headed to the promised land and will enter it from the plains of Moab, northeast of the Dead Sea (see map 1). One possible route was to go through the territory of Edom, who was descended from Esau (Gen 36:1), the brother of Jacob, the nation of Israel's forefather (Gen 32:3, 28). Moses thus appeals to these "brothers" for passage (Num 20:14), reminding Edom's king of the Israelites' hardships in Egypt and how the Lord miraculously delivered them (vv. 15–16; cf. Exod 14:19). This was perhaps a subtle hint: in light of our God's strength, Edom would be wise to agree to Israel's request (Num 20:16–17). Nonetheless, Edom refuses (v. 18) and continues to do so even after the Israelites make clear they would pay for any of Edom's resources they used (vv. 19–20). Edom backs up this refusal with military force, and the Israelites decide not to head this direction (vv. 20–21), eventually skirting Edom to the east (21:4; Judg 11:18). Including this story thus helps explain why Israel's route to the promised land is not as direct as it might have been.

Aaron's Death and Eleazar's Investiture (20:22–29)

Israel's next stop is Mount Hor, whose exact location is unknown though the text clearly places it in the vicinity of Kadesh and on the edge of Edom's territory (Num 20:22–23).[10] While Moses had called the people rebels at Meribah (v. 10), the Lord here says that Moses and Aaron are the ones who rebelled there and identifies the basic nature of rebellion: disobedience to the Lord's commands (v. 24). In keeping with the Lord's earlier judgment for this sin, Aaron will die here and not enter the promised land.

The Lord commands Moses to go up Mount Hor with both Aaron and Eleazar, Aaron's oldest living son (Num 3:4) and next in line to be high priest (cf. Lev 16:32). Because the high priest wore a distinctive uniform (Lev 8:7–9, 13), this had to be transferred from Aaron to Eleazar so that he could function in that role (Exod 29:29) and the people would know he was doing so (Num 20:26).

Moses immediately obeys, leading Aaron and Eleazar up the mountain in

---

10. See toward the bottom of map 2 for a possible location. (This is not to be confused with the Mt. Hor in the north toward the top of the map.)

view of the people so that the leadership succession would be clear to all (Num 20:27). After the transfer of garments, Aaron dies, and Moses and Eleazar descend alone (v. 28). This triggers a thirty-day mourning period among the Israelites, a sign that Aaron's leadership was of great importance to them (v. 29; cf. Deut 34:8).

LIVE the Story

Isn't the "Rebellion" of Moses and Aaron Understandable?[11]

At first glance, the punishment Moses and Aaron receive in this story far exceeds their crime. For forty years they have put up with the people's whining, complaining, and ungratefulness. For forty years the people have blamed Moses and Aaron for things that were the people's fault. For forty years this has continued despite Moses and Aaron saving the people's lives on more than one occasion, pleading the Lord's mercy and forgiveness for the people's rebellion. Most of us do not blame Moses for responding angrily here; we are amazed he did not do so more regularly! Did he and Aaron really deserve to be kept out of the promised land because of this one outburst of anger? Was this really even something that could be called rebellion?

To complicate the picture even more, several later verses make clear the people share in the blame. In Deuteronomy, Moses tells them three times that "because of you the LORD became angry with me also and said, 'You shall not enter [the promised land]'" (Deut 1:37; see also 3:26; 4:21). This is not bitter blame-shifting on Moses's part. He does not deny his own guilt; he simply makes clear the people share a part in it, an assessment the psalmist agrees with (Ps 106:32–33). Moses is giving honest rebuke, which is especially important for him to do in Deuteronomy because these are his last words to the Israelites before they begin to follow a new leader, Joshua. Moses is underscoring, "Your sin is hard on your leaders! It can lead them to make sinful decisions! Do *not* do to Joshua what you did to me!"

In light of the above, it seems perfectly understandable why a leader would respond with anger in this situation. So why is the punishment so severe?

Why Is the Punishment so Severe?

The answer to the question has two complementary parts. To begin, the punishment is not because of Moses's anger but what he did in that anger. Feeling

---
11. For an alternative homiletical approach, see p. 179n13.

angry and acting out in anger are two very different things. In this case, Moses not only directly disobeyed God in front of all the people, he also put himself and Aaron in God's place, making themselves out to be the people's savior: "Must *we* bring you water out of this rock?" (Num 20:10, emphasis added).[12] If we can imagine the blasphemy of a pastor celebrating communion in his own name, claiming that the bread and wine represent his body instead of Jesus's body, we are beginning to understand the severity of what Moses is doing here (and Aaron along with him). He is denying the very heart of who the Lord is—the powerful redeemer of his people—and such deep unbelief puts him in the same boat as the Israelites only a few chapters earlier when they refused to believe the Lord could deliver them in the promised land.[13] In each case, the sinners have strongly denied the covenant Lord and are thus denied the covenant promise (the land). The punishment fits the crime exactly, and later verses will return to this and similar stories as strong warnings: if such acts of unbelief meant these people did not experience the covenant promises, make sure not to follow their example so that you do not forfeit the covenant promises (2 Cor 4:1–6; Heb 3:7–4:13; cf. Exod 17:1–7; Num 20:1–13). To be clear: the point is not that every time you sin you forfeit these promises. These New Testament passages are using such Old Testament stories as examples of what happens when our disbelief rises to the level of apostasy, a full turning away from the Lord. But these passages are also clear that we arrive at the point of apostasy when we do not turn from sin quickly, allowing it to take root in our lives and turning our hearts into spiritual granite, hardened and dead to faith in God. The Christian does well to ask, "In what ways might I be treating sin too lightly? In what ways am I making decisions that ultimately show a lack of faith in God and his promises?"

The second reason for the punishment's severity is related to the fact Moses and Aaron are leaders. The Scriptures emphasize that leaders of the Lord's people will be held to higher account (cf. Jas 3:1). This is no surprise since a leader's decisions strongly impact the people's well-being, whether for good or for ill. When a captain makes a mistake, everyone on the ship is in danger. By holding leaders to a higher account, the Lord shows how much he cares that his people are well looked after—and underscores to leaders the importance of faithfulness in their duties (Heb 13:17). In this regard, Numbers 20 is one of the Bible's most sobering chapters on leadership. It begins with Miriam dying, ends with Aaron dying, and explains in between

---

12. For this and the following, see comments at vv. 9–12 above, p. 269.
13. See n9 above.

why Moses and Aaron will not enter the promised land. Faithfulness in leadership really matters.

This leads to a final consideration.[14] Though Moses is the main focus in the sin of Numbers 20:9–12, Aaron is right there alongside him, sharing in his guilt (vv. 10, 12) and ultimately dying outside the promised land (vv. 22–29). In short, Aaron is a high priest who is both sinful and mortal, as will be his descendants after him throughout the generations. In terms of priestly sin, the writer of Hebrews says, "The law appoints as high priests men in all their weakness" (Heb 7:28a). But as that writer also notes, a high priest came who was utterly different. With regard to sin, Jesus "is holy, blameless, pure, set apart from sinners, exalted above the heavens. Unlike the other high priests, he does not need to offer sacrifices day after day, first for his own sins, and then for the sins of the people. He sacrificed for their sins once for all when he offered himself" (vv. 26b–27). In terms of priestly mortality, Hebrews notes that "death prevented [those high priests] from continuing in office; but because Jesus lives forever, he has a permanent priesthood. Therefore, he is able to save completely those who come to God through him, because he always lives to intercede for them" (vv. 23b–25)—able to save completely those who come to God through him. That is good news for everyone, and in the context of Numbers 20, especially good news for leaders when they feel the weight of their own inadequacies and failures. Jesus intercedes for us. He will never give up doing so. Let us continually come to God through him!

---

14. The main idea of this paragraph comes from Kidner, *Leviticus, Numbers, Deuteronomy*, 48.

CHAPTER 24

Numbers 21:1–22:1

LISTEN to the Story

²¹:¹When the Canaanite king of Arad, who lived in the Negev, heard that Israel was coming along the road to Atharim, he attacked the Israelites and captured some of them. ²Then Israel made this vow to the Lord: "If you will deliver these people into our hands, we will totally destroy their cities." ³The Lord listened to Israel's plea and gave the Canaanites over to them. They completely destroyed them and their towns; so the place was named Hormah.

⁴They traveled from Mount Hor along the route to the Red Sea, to go around Edom. But the people grew impatient on the way; ⁵they spoke against God and against Moses, and said, "Why have you brought us up out of Egypt to die in the wilderness? There is no bread! There is no water! And we detest this miserable food!"

⁶Then the Lord sent venomous snakes among them; they bit the people and many Israelites died. ⁷The people came to Moses and said, "We sinned when we spoke against the Lord and against you. Pray that the Lord will take the snakes away from us." So Moses prayed for the people.

⁸The Lord said to Moses, "Make a snake and put it up on a pole; anyone who is bitten can look at it ⁹So Moses made a bronze snake and put it up on a pole. Then when anyone was bitten by a snake and looked at the bronze snake, they lived.

¹⁰The Israelites moved on and camped at Oboth. ¹¹Then they set out from Oboth and camped in Iye Abarim, in the wilderness that faces Moab toward the sunrise. ¹²From there they moved on and camped in the Zered Valley. ¹³They set out from there and camped alongside the Arnon, which is in the wilderness extending into Amorite territory. The Arnon is the border of Moab, between Moab and the Amorites. ¹⁴That is why the Book of the Wars of the Lord says:

" . . . Zahab in Suphah and the ravines,
the Arnon ¹⁵and the slopes of the ravines
that lead to the settlement of Ar
and lie along the border of Moab."

¹⁶From there they continued on to Beer, the well where the LORD said to Moses, "Gather the people together and I will give them water."

¹⁷Then Israel sang this song:
"Spring up, O well!
Sing about it,
¹⁸about the well that the princes dug,
that the nobles of the people sank—
the nobles with scepters and staffs."

Then they went from the wilderness to Mattanah, ¹⁹from Mattanah to Nahaliel, from Nahaliel to Bamoth, ²⁰and from Bamoth to the valley in Moab where the top of Pisgah overlooks the wasteland.

²¹Israel sent messengers to say to Sihon king of the Amorites:

²²"Let us pass through your country. We will not turn aside into any field or vineyard, or drink water from any well. We will travel along the King's Highway until we have passed through your territory."

²³But Sihon would not let Israel pass through his territory. He mustered his entire army and marched out into the wilderness against Israel. When he reached Jahaz, he fought with Israel. ²⁴Israel, however, put him to the sword and took over his land from the Arnon to the Jabbok, but only as far as the Ammonites, because their border was fortified. ²⁵Israel captured all the cities of the Amorites and occupied them, including Heshbon and all its surrounding settlements. ²⁶Heshbon was the city of Sihon king of the Amorites, who had fought against the former king of Moab and had taken from him all his land as far as the Arnon.

²⁷That is why the poets say:
"Come to Heshbon and let it be rebuilt;
let Sihon's city be restored.
²⁸"Fire went out from Heshbon,
a blaze from the city of Sihon.
It consumed Ar of Moab,

> the citizens of Arnon's heights.
> ²⁹Woe to you, Moab!
> You are destroyed, people of Chemosh!
> He has given up his sons as fugitives
> and his daughters as captives
> to Sihon king of the Amorites.
> ³⁰"But we have overthrown them;
> Heshbon's dominion has been destroyed all the way to Dibon.
> We have demolished them as far as Nophah,
> which extends to Medeba."
> ³¹So Israel settled in the land of the Amorites.
>
> ³²After Moses had sent spies to Jazer, the Israelites captured its surrounding settlements and drove out the Amorites who were there. ³³Then they turned and went up along the road toward Bashan, and Og king of Bashan and his whole army marched out to meet them in battle at Edrei.
>
> ³⁴The LORD said to Moses, "Do not be afraid of him, for I have delivered him into your hands, along with his whole army and his land. Do to him what you did to Sihon king of the Amorites, who reigned in Heshbon."
>
> ³⁵So they struck him down, together with his sons and his whole army, leaving them no survivors. And they took possession of his land.
>
> ²²:¹Then the Israelites traveled to the plains of Moab and camped along the Jordan across from Jericho.
>
> *Listening to the Text in the Story:* Numbers 14–20; 21–25

After seven chapters of Israel's faithlessness and defeat (Num 14–20), this chapter marks a turn that will stretch until Numbers 25. Rebellion and judgment will continue (21:4–9; 25:1–15), but the section begins with a story of the Israelites defeating the Canaanites in war (21:1–3), goes on to describe further Israelite victories on the Jordan's east side (vv. 21–35), followed by a non-Israelite diviner who ends up speaking the Lord's blessings over Israel (chs. 23–34). While the last wisps of the faithless generation die, their children get a foretaste of the amazing deliverances the Lord will accomplish for them in the promised land.

Chapter 21 is especially known for the bronze serpent story (vv. 4–9), which Jesus uses to explain his own death (John 3:14–15). The story is sometimes described as an example of "sympathetic magic," that is, the ability to control someone or something (such as a snake or its effects) by using its image (in this case, the bronze snake).[1] As we might say, one must "fight fire with fire." The implication would be that the bronze serpent solution is therefore magical, not divine. The story makes clear, however, that the Lord is the source of this solution (and thus of its power).[2] The Israelites might not have been surprised by the Lord's decision to fight fire with fire—indeed, this might have made good sense to them—but this was divine intervention, not magic. "The author of the intertestamental book, the Wisdom of Solomon, put the matter exactly (at Num 16:7), 'For the one who turned toward [the snake] was saved, not by the thing that was beheld, but by you, the Savior of all.'"[3]

An Initial Victory against the Canaanites (21:1–3)

Questions surround the opening verse. The location of "the road to Atharim" is unknown, but "Negev" indicates it is in Canaan's southern area, presumably in the region of Mount Hor near Kadesh (cf. Num 20:22; 21:4). Also unclear is whether "king of Arad" is original or a later insertion.[4] If original, "Arad" likely does not refer to the city traditionally known by that name since it is at least fifty miles from Kadesh (see map 2). It may refer instead to a larger region (note the reference to "cities" in 21:2) or to a different city than the traditional site.

What is clear is that Canaanites fight with Israelites for the first time since defeating them in 14:45. Here, too, the Canaanites win the initial battle, taking Israelite captives (21:1). In a promising sign, the Israelites pray for the Lord's help instead of grumbling, vowing to "totally destroy their cities" (v. 2). The Hebrew for "totally destroy" (from the root *h-r-m*) refers to giving something irrevocably to the Lord (see NIV text note). In this context, instead of taking plunder or captives, the Israelites will devote everything (and everyone)

---

1. Milgrom, *Numbers*, 459.
2. Levine, citing several ancient Near Eastern examples, argues that the only reason sympathetic magic could work in the mind of an ancient Near Eastern person is if the gods empowered it to do so (Baruch Levine, *Numbers 21–36*, AB 4A [New York: Doubleday, 2000], 88–89); the same would be true here.
3. Bailey, *Leviticus-Numbers*, 511.
4. The Hebrew for "the Canaanite" is normally translated "the Canaanites"; using it for an individual is very uncommon (only four other examples exist: Gen 46:10; Exod 6:15; Num 33:40; 1 Chr 2:3). Several thus suggest "king of Arad" is a mistaken scribal insertion based on Josh 12:14 or Judg 1:16–17, which mention Arad and Hormah (but which take place later in Israel's history).

to the Lord like a sacrifice. Their prayer is answered—implying victory as well as recovery of the captives—and they fulfill their vow, completely destroying (Hebrew root *h-r-m*) the people and their cities, leading to the place[5] being called Hormah (*hormah*, i.e. Destruction, from the same root; v. 3). Instead of being defeated by Canaanites at a place called Hormah (14:45), the Israelites defeat Canaanites at a place called Hormah, giving a foretaste of what should happen when they actually march into the land (Deut 7:1–2).

The Bronze Serpent (21:4–9)

Triumph turns quickly to tragedy as the Israelites' abandon their recently expressed faith (Num 21:2) and return to their rebellious complaints (v. 5). Having been refused passage through Edom's land (v. 21), they must take a far less direct route to Canaan (see map 1), undoubtedly increasing their frustration, which now boils over. Previously, they spoke against only their human leaders, even if they were also angry with God.[6] Here they speak out against God as well: they blame him and Moses for difficulties that are their own fault (cf. at 20:4–5), spit out complaints in machine-gun-like fashion, and describe the life-sustaining bread the Lord has provided as "miserable" (21:5; cf. Ps 78:23–25). In condemning it they were condemning God.[7]

The Lord executes judgment by turning the wilderness's dangers against them (cf. Deut 8:15). Venomous serpents bite the people and many die (Num 21:6). In previous judgments, Moses prayed on the people's behalf without their confession or request (14:10–19; 16:41–50; 20:2–8),[8] but here—in another positive sign (cf. 21:2)—the people confess their sin and ask Moses to pray for them (v. 7). In response, the Lord directs Moses to make a bronze serpent and place it on a pole; those bitten needed simply to look at the serpent to be healed (vv. 8–9). For rationale, see further comments at the end of this chapter: Live the Story: How Can we Avoid Such Judgment?

The Journey to Moab (21:10–20)

For the Israelites' possible route since leaving Mount Hor (Num 21:4), see map 1.[9] This itinerary likely summarizes their travels on the Jordan's east side, which brought them to the cusp of Canaan.

---

5. Or perhaps region, since many cities were destroyed.
6. Cf. 20:2 with 20:13.
7. Allen, "Numbers," 876.
8. There is one earlier instance of confession, but it is immediately followed by disobedience (Num 14:39–45).
9. Num 33:41–49 provides a complementary itinerary.

Two of the stopping places are highlighted. The first was at the Arnon River (Num 21:13), which runs east-west between Moab and the Amorites. Its mention leads to what was perhaps a well-known citation (or even song?) from "the Book of the Wars of the LORD" (v. 14), an otherwise unknown work whose title suggests it recounted battles fought in the Lord's name (cf. 1 Sam 18:12–15; 25:28) and with his help.[10] The translation of Numbers 21:14–15 is uncertain at places,[11] but these verses seem to poetically describe the Arnon's topography and its function as a border.

The second place highlighted is Beer (pronounced as two syllables in Hebrew: *be-er*), which means "well (of water)." The poem's exact meaning is somewhat obscure. Since the well was the Lord's provision (Num 21:16), the mention of the princes' and nobles' digging it could suggest he directed them to do so. Whatever the case, the Lord provided and the people understandably rejoiced in song (vv. 16–18).[12]

The passage ends with the people east of the Jordan and north of the Dead Sea encamped near Pisgah, which is either another name for Mount Nebo or is a mountain range of which Mount Nebo was the highest peak (Num 21:20; cf. Deut 34:1). Famously, Balak would bring Balaam to Pisgah to curse the Israelites (Num 23:14), and Moses would go up it to look across the Jordan into the promised land just before dying (Deut 34:1–6). Pisgah was in territory that had recently belonged to Moab (cf. Num 21:26), and the Israelites would remain here until their entry into Canaan.[13]

Victories on the Jordan's East Side (21:21–22:1)

Having summarized Israel's journey to northern Moab (Num 21:10–20), this section flashes back to events that happened along the way (cf. Deut 2:13–3:29). The term "Amorites" (Num 21:21) can refer generally to Canaanites (Gen 15:16; cf. vv. 19–20) or to specific groups in and near Canaan (as here; cf. Josh 5:1; 10:5–6). In this case, their territory extended north from the Arnon River at least to the Jabbok River and was bordered on the east by the Ammonites (Num 21:24). Sihon, the Amorites' king, flatly refuses the Israelites' request for safe passage through his territory and comes to battle them at Jahaz (21:22–23; see map 1). Instead of turning away, as they did with

---

10. Several verses in the Old Testament mention various books or records separate from the Bible that were at times used by biblical authors (Josh 10:13; 2 Sam 1:18; 1 Chr 29:29; Neh 7:5; cf. Luke 1:1–4).
11. See NIV notes.
12. For a similar response to the Lord's help, see Exod 15:1–21.
13. See n19.

Edom (20:21), the Israelites fight,[14] soundly defeating the Amorites and taking over their territory, including the capital, Heshbon (21:24–25).[15]

Heshbon's mention leads both to a description of how Sihon had recently taken over much of this land from Moab (Num 21:26) as well as to another poem (vv. 27–30; cf. vv. 14–15, 17–18). The poem appears to begin with Heshbon in ruins, needing to be rebuilt (v. 27), and then describes its former glory days when its ruler, Sihon, defeated the Moabites (and thus also their god Chemosh, vv. 28–29).[16] Its concluding verse is difficult (v. 30), as witnessed by significant differences in the ancient versions. The NIV's translation understands that the Israelites now describe how they overthrew the victorious Sihon and conquered his territory. This reading is possible and explains why Heshbon is currently in ruins (v. 27). Other translations emend the Hebrew and come closer to the Septuagint, which sees verse 30 as a continuation of the destruction that Sihon wrought (NJB, NRSB), though this does not explain Heshbon's current ruinous state (v. 27). In either case, as verse 31 makes clear, the Israelites have now taken over the Amorites' territory in this region.

After taking even further Amorite territory (Num 21:32),[17] the Israelites engage Og, king of Bashan, a region east and northeast of the Sea of Galilee (see map 1). The Lord's directions are straightforward: "Do not fear, for I am with you; do to him as you did to Sihon" (cf. v. 34). Israel promptly obeys and conquers his territory as well (v. 35).[18]

The text now returns to the same place the story left off in Numbers 21:20.[19] Having conquered much land east of the Jordan, Israel comes to the plains of Moab,[20] opposite Jericho on the Jordan's east side, within striking distance of the promised land. This is the place they will remain until entering the land (22:1; cf. 33:48–51). Their recent series of successful battles, undertaken with the Lord's help, should thus embolden their faith as they prepare to enter into Canaan and accomplish the same there.

---

14. The Lord had forbidden Israel from attacking Edom (Deut 2:4–5) but commanded them to attack the Amorites (Deut 2:24).

15. Heshbon later became part of Reuben's territory (Num 32:2–3, 37). The last phrase of 21:24 is perhaps better translated "for the border of the Ammonites was Jazer" (so Septuagint, followed by NASB, RSV, NJB; cf. 21:32). In other words, Jazer was the last stop before Ammonite territory and mentioned because the Lord prohibited Israel from entering that territory (Deut 2:19).

16. For the belief that defeating an army also meant defeating their gods, cf. 1 Kgs 20:23, 28. For Chemosh, see 1 Kgs 11:7, 33. Little more is known about this god.

17. The location of Jazer is unknown; it later became part of Gad's allotment (32:1, 3, 34–35).

18. It would later be given to Manasseh (32:33; Josh 13:29–30).

19. Cf. 22:1 with 21:20, 23:27–28 and Deut 3:29.

20. Though most recently controlled by the Amorites, it was formerly controlled by Moab (cf. 21:26), leading to the name "the plains of Moab."

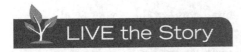

LIVE the Story

Where Does Victory in Battle Come From?[21]

In this chapter, the Israelites' earlier doubts (Num 14:1–4) give way to faith. After an initial defeat by the Canaanites (21:1), the Israelites pray for the Lord's deliverance and he delights to answer their prayer (v. 3). In the later battle against Og and his army, they believe the Lord's promise to deliver them, again winning decisively in battle (vv. 33–35). Not surprisingly, later biblical writers celebrate these chapters' victories as amazing displays of the Lord's saving power (Pss 135:10–12; 136:17–22).[22] In doing so, they remind us that the Lord is the one who fights for his people. Indeed, the Israelites were not wrong to think that the battle for the promised land was impossible to win by themselves; they were wrong to think they had to fight that battle by themselves. The Lord loves his people and fights for them. In this chapter, the Israelites begin to believe this, and in doing so remind us not to fix our eyes on the size of the army in front of us but on the power of the God who goes before us. When God's people believe his promises to be true in the midst of overwhelming odds to the contrary, the Lord has the chance to act on their behalf and show them his redeeming power at work.

Why Such Severe Destruction?

While it is encouraging to think of the Lord's support of his people in their battles, it is disturbing to many to see the type of destruction the Israelites carry out in this chapter. In Deuteronomy, the Lord will command Israel to "totally destroy" (Heb. root *h-r-m*) the Canaanites (Deut 7:1–3), and this is exactly what they to do to the Canaanites in Numbers 21:2–3 as well as to the forces of Sihon and Og (vv. 24, 35; cf. Deut 2:34; 3:3–6). How are we to understand this? At least three questions may be asked to bring further clarity.

First, what does the Hebrew root for "totally destroy" (*h-r-m*) mean? As noted above, this word refers to giving someone or something irrevocably to the Lord (see NIV text note at Num 21:2). In a non-war context, this meant the person or object would serve at the Lord's tabernacle (see at Num 18:14, p. 251). In a war context, it meant the person or object was given over to the

---

21. For an alternative homiletic approach, see p. 179n13.
22. Wenham, *Numbers*, 163.

Lord by death or destruction.[23] In either context, the person or object was given over irrevocably to the Lord.[24]

Second, why was this done? Two main reasons are given. The first is judgment. As early as Genesis 15:16, the Lord had warned of coming judgment for the great evils Canaan's people were committing and would continue to commit, and this reason is returned to again in Deuteronomy (9:3–5). The evils in question are listed in places like Leviticus 18 and 20, which catalogue a vast array of wicked deeds, from various forms of incest and sexual abuse to sacrificing their own children. This evil had reached such a point it had called forth the Lord's judgment (18:24–25; 20:23–24). Clearly, such judgment did not come because of someone's ethnicity but because of their evil behavior, a point underscored by the Lord calling for the same judgment on his own people should they commit great evil (Deut 13:12–16). The second reason this was done was to protect his people's purity, lest those who were committing such evil would lead his own people astray (7:2–6; 20:16–18). Should that happen, Israel's mission of being a blessing to the nations and introducing them to the Lord would be utterly destroyed, leading to further loss for the world.

Third, is it right? Could it not have been done more mercifully? While there is no one answer that is fully satisfying to all people, four comments may be of some help in thinking through this difficult issue. First, this was not the typical way in which Israel carried out war. Normally, the first thing Israelites were to do with a hostile enemy was to offer terms of peace (Deut 20:10–15). "Devote to destruction" warfare was very limited in terms of its geographical and historical scope since it was focused on the Lord's judgment for the evils of specific peoples at a specific point in history.

Second, the Lord does not judge capriciously. In the Atrahasis epic from Mesopotamia, one of the reasons the gods send a flood to destroy humanity is because people are making too much noise for the gods to sleep! In the biblical account of the flood, however, the earth is destroyed because of humanity's evil—evil that grieves the Lord's heart (Gen 6:5–7).

This leads to the third point: these nations were involved in heinous wrongs (see above) and the Lord's judgment comes because of them. The Bible does not hesitate to affirm God's right to judge humanity. He is the creator; we are the created, and the God who has the right to judge us when we die has

---

23. Common to all war contexts is the destruction of life, though the Lord does not always require the destruction of property (see Deut 2:32–35; 3:6–7).

24. ESV translates "devoted to destruction" in war contexts to make clear the idea of giving over to the Lord.

the right to judge us while we yet live. In this regard, the Canaanites' destruction may be thought of as God's end-time judgment breaking into time and space—and serving as a strong warning to repent of our own sin.[25]

There is a final point about the Lord's judgment that may be added, but it is best placed in the context of one last question.

How Can We Avoid Such Judgment?

In the midst of these stories of victory comes another sad tale of the Israelites' lack of faith. Faced with a water shortage, they rail not only against their leaders but against God directly, condemning his care of them and thus condemning God himself (see at Num 21:4–9, p. 278). In response, he sends venomous snakes so that many die. The people repent, Moses prays on their behalf, and the Lord directs that a bronze serpent be made and placed on a pole so that those who looked at it might live.

This solution, while curious to many moderns, had at least two immediate advantages. The first was practical. The "pole" refers to a "signal pole," where a symbol or sign could be placed for large groups of people to see quickly (cf. Jer 4:6). Since speed was of the essence for those bitten, placing the bronze serpent there was the quickest way to make available a public "visual antidote." And because this came at the Lord's direction, it signaled that the healing came from him.[26] The second advantage was pedagogical. The bronze serpent could serve as a physical reminder of warning to future generations, like the bronze censers of Korah's faithless followers (Num 16:36–40) or like Aaron's staff (17:10). In this case, the snake would remind of the very punishment given to those complaining against the Lord and insulting his gracious provision.[27]

To these immediate advantages may be added one of longer term. As the Lord looked down the halls of human history, he knew how this event could serve as an illustration of what his Son would one day do: be lifted up himself on a pole so that those who looked to him with faith would be saved. Jesus did not miss it, saying: "Just as Moses lifted up the snake in the wilderness, so the

---

25. See Meredith Kline, "The Intrusion and the Decalogue," *WTJ* 16 (1953): 1–22 and esp. 15–16; more fully, Tremper Longman III, "Spiritual Continuity," in *Show Them No Mercy: Four Views on God and Canaanite Genocide*, Counterpoints, ed. Stanley N. Gundry (Grand Rapids: Zondervan Academic, 2003), 159–87, and more recently, Tremper Longman III, *Confronting Old Testament Controversies: Pressing Questions about Evolution, Sexuality, History, and Violence* (Grand Rapids: Baker, 2019), 123–206, esp. 195–205. Another instance of such judgment is the flood, which Jesus explicitly points to as a warning to prepare for God's end-time judgment (Matt 24:37–41).
26. See at Listening to the Text in the Story, pp. 276–77.
27. Sadly, later Israelites would turn even this warning into an occasion for idolatry (2 Kgs 18:4).

Son of Man must be lifted up, that everyone who believes may have eternal life in him" (John 3:14–15).

And this leads to the final point to make about the Lord's judgment: he takes it on himself. The Bible consistently states that sin deserves death and calls for God's judgment. It further maintains that we all deserve this judgment: "For the wages of sin is death" (Rom 6:23). But it also underscores that God in his love takes this judgment upon himself in Jesus Christ. "But God demonstrates his own love for us in this: while we were yet sinners"—while we were deserving the judgment of death—"Christ died for us" (5:8), taking our judgment on himself. Jesus allowed himself to be devoted to destruction in our place so that through faith in him we might live. What God's justice demands, his love has provided. Will we accept such love? What does it look like to boldly share such love with those around us?

CHAPTER 25

Numbers 22:2–40

LISTEN to the Story

²Now Balak son of Zippor saw all that Israel had done to the Amorites, ³and Moab was terrified because there were so many people. Indeed, Moab was filled with dread because of the Israelites.

⁴The Moabites said to the elders of Midian, "This horde is going to lick up everything around us, as an ox licks up the grass of the field."

So Balak son of Zippor, who was king of Moab at that time, ⁵sent messengers to summon Balaam son of Beor, who was at Pethor, near the Euphrates River, in his native land. Balak said:

> "A people has come out of Egypt; they cover the face of the land and have settled next to me. ⁶Now come and put a curse on these people, because they are too powerful for me. Perhaps then I will be able to defeat them and drive them out of the land. For I know that whoever you bless is blessed, and whoever you curse is cursed."

⁷The elders of Moab and Midian left, taking with them the fee for divination. When they came to Balaam, they told him what Balak had said.

⁸"Spend the night here," Balaam said to them, "and I will report back to you with the answer the Lord gives me." So the Moabite officials stayed with him.

⁹God came to Balaam and asked, "Who are these men with you?"

¹⁰Balaam said to God, "Balak son of Zippor, king of Moab, sent me this message: ¹¹'A people that has come out of Egypt covers the face of the land. Now come and put a curse on them for me. Perhaps then I will be able to fight them and drive them away.'"

¹²But God said to Balaam, "Do not go with them. You must not put a curse on those people, because they are blessed."

¹³The next morning Balaam got up and said to Balak's officials, "Go back to your own country, for the Lord has refused to let me go with you." ¹⁴So the Moabite officials returned to Balak and said, "Balaam refused to come with us."

¹⁵Then Balak sent other officials, more numerous and more distinguished than the first. ¹⁶They came to Balaam and said:

> "This is what Balak son of Zippor says: Do not let anything keep you from coming to me, ¹⁷because I will reward you handsomely and do whatever you say. Come and put a curse on these people for me."

¹⁸But Balaam answered them, "Even if Balak gave me all the silver and gold in his palace, I could not do anything great or small to go beyond the command of the Lord my God. ¹⁹Now spend the night here so that I can find out what else the Lord will tell me."

²⁰That night God came to Balaam and said, "Since these men have come to summon you, go with them, but do only what I tell you."

²¹Balaam got up in the morning, saddled his donkey and went with the Moabite officials. ²²But God was very angry when he went, and the angel of the Lord stood in the road to oppose him. Balaam was riding on his donkey, and his two servants were with him. ²³When the donkey saw the angel of the Lord standing in the road with a drawn sword in his hand, it turned off the road into a field. Balaam beat it to get it back on the road.

²⁴Then the angel of the Lord stood in a narrow path through the vineyards, with walls on both sides. ²⁵When the donkey saw the angel of the Lord, it pressed close to the wall, crushing Balaam's foot against it. So he beat the donkey again.

²⁶Then the angel of the Lord moved on ahead and stood in a narrow place where there was no room to turn, either to the right or to the left. ²⁷When the donkey saw the angel of the Lord, it lay down under Balaam, and he was angry and beat it with his staff. ²⁸Then the Lord opened the donkey's mouth, and it said to Balaam, "What have I done to you to make you beat me these three times?"

²⁹Balaam answered the donkey, "You have made a fool of me! If only I had a sword in my hand, I would kill you right now."

³⁰The donkey said to Balaam, "Am I not your own donkey, which you have always ridden, to this day? Have I been in the habit of doing this to you?"

"No," he said.

³¹Then the LORD opened Balaam's eyes, and he saw the angel of the LORD standing in the road with his sword drawn. So he bowed low and fell facedown.

³²The angel of the LORD asked him, "Why have you beaten your donkey these three times? I have come here to oppose you because your path is a reckless one before me. ³³The donkey saw me and turned away from me these three times. If it had not turned away, I would certainly have killed you by now, but I would have spared it."

³⁴Balaam said to the angel of the LORD, "I have sinned. I did not realize you were standing in the road to oppose me. Now if you are displeased, I will go back."

³⁵The angel of the LORD said to Balaam, "Go with the men, but speak only what I tell you." So Balaam went with Balak's officials.

³⁶When Balak heard that Balaam was coming, he went out to meet him at the Moabite town on the Arnon border, at the edge of his territory. ³⁷Balak said to Balaam, "Did I not send you an urgent summons? Why didn't you come to me? Am I really not able to reward you?"

³⁸"Well, I have come to you now," Balaam replied. "But I can't say whatever I please. I must speak only what God puts in my mouth."

³⁹Then Balaam went with Balak to Kiriath Huzoth. ⁴⁰Balak sacrificed cattle and sheep, and gave some to Balaam and the officials who were with him.

Listening to the Text in the Story: The Balaam Inscriptions from Tell Deir 'Alla

In 1967, extrabiblical texts were discovered that also speak of "Balaam, son of Beor." They were found at Tell Deir 'Alla (biblical Succoth) and are usually dated to the eighth or seventh century BC.

A general summary of content is as follows: Balaam, son of Beor, receives a message from the gods in a night visitation. The gods express displeasure over the state of affairs on earth (lines 1–2). On the next morning, Balaam is disturbed by his message from the gods (lines 3–4). When asked why he is upset he passes on a message of doom (lines 5–16).[1]

These texts make clear that a man named Balaam was known, at the least, as a "literary character in the Transjordan, in an area within a few miles from where the biblical stories are set, in and before the eighth cent. BC,"[2] and that, like biblical Balaam, he was known for being able to pass on revelations from the gods. Some will conclude from this that the biblical story simply uses a well-known (but imaginary) literary figure to tell its story, but it is just as plausible that "Balaam, son of Beor" was a well-known historical figure that the extrabiblical Balaam texts use in order to tell their story. Both sides agree: Balaam was clearly well-known in the ancient Middle East as one who could communicate with the gods, and these chapters will focus on that ability in a way that completely upends the purposes for which he is hired by Israel's enemies.

As for Balaam's character, a quick read of these chapters might lead one to think of him as basically good, listening to the Lord's words and saying only what the Lord tells him. But on closer inspection, the evidence points to a man motivated by financial gain more than godliness (see at Num 20:2–20 below), requiring the Lord to warn him on pain of death not to disobey his commands (see at 22:21–35 below). It is therefore no surprise that his obedience in chapters 22–24 is short-lived, and he soon returns to warring against God's people (cf. 31:16). Remarkably, one can speak God's very words and yet have a heart so hard that those words take no root there (cf. Matt 7:22–23).

EXPLAIN the Story

Balak Summons Balaam (22:2–20)[3]

As the story opens, Moab is absolutely terrified of Israel's vast army (Num 22:3), now encamped in the plains of Moab, just north of Moabite territory (v. 1; see map 1). The Moabites therefore reach out to the Midianites, who

---

1. Ashley, *Numbers*, 439. The texts are especially fragmented after this, making the flow of thought difficult to follow.
2. Ibid., 439–40.
3. As commentators regularly observe, this story takes place outside of Israelite territory and presumably without the Israelites being aware it was even going on. Just how they became aware of the story is nowhere recounted. Assuming that it accurately reflects events, the information could have come from Balaam himself or the Midianite elders who traveled with him since Israel later engaged Balaam and Midian directly and learned of how they worked together against Israel (31:1–8, 16).

were living nearby,[4] and warn that the Israelites are going to devastate this area like a ravenous beast (v. 4a). If Moab and Midian can work together, perhaps this can be avoided.

Balak, who is Moab's king (Num 22:4b), will take the lead in the joint operation between Moab and Midian against Israel. Their strategy is to hire Balaam, who lives in Pethor, over 370 miles from the plains of Moab (v. 5a).[5] He was apparently well-known in the area, especially for his ability to pronounce effective curses and blessings on the gods' behalf (v. 6). Balak thus sends the elders of Moab and Midian to ask him to put a curse on Israel so that he might defeat them.

The elders go, taking with them the "fee for divination" (Num 22:7).[6] Diviners would perform certain acts by which they would attempt to discern the future, e.g., "For the king of Babylon will stop at the fork in the road, at the junction of the two roads, to use divination:[7] He will cast lots with arrows, he will consult his idols, he will examine the liver" (Ezek 21:21).[8] Importantly, such divination is strongly condemned (Deut 18:10), putting Balaam in a very negative light.

Upon hearing their request, Balaam tells them to spend the night in the hopes he will receive direction from "the LORD" (Num 22:8). As the NIV's small caps indicate, he uses the Lord's proper name here (Yahweh).[9] This is not likely because he is a faithful Yahweh worshipper (despite his suggestions to the contrary, e.g., v. 18). After all, he is not from Israel, makes use of spiritual practices forbidden to Israelites (as just noted), and in fact tries to harm the Israelites later on (cf. 31:16). Rather, his use of the divine name may simply show his recognition that Yahweh is the Israelites' God and must therefore decide these matters. Perhaps it is also a sly way to increase his value

---

4. See Num 25:6, 15–18; 31:2–7; Josh 13:21. At other points in history, Midianites are found in the Sinai region (Exod 2:15–16; 3:1).

5. See map 3. The NIV's "in his native land" in Num 22:5a may also be translated "in the land of the people of Amaw" (so ESV, NET; the underlying Hebrew consonants are the same). "Amaw" is understood to be "a territory between Aleppo and Carchemish, and thus in the same area as posited for Pethor" (Ashley, *Numbers*, 446).

6. Or perhaps "articles for divination"; see Sklar, *Additional Notes*, at 22:7.

7. ESV (the Hebrew root for "to use divination" is the same as our passage); NIV: "to seek an omen."

8. "Royal courts in Assyria and Babylonia had a specialist whose function it was carefully to examine such organs [as livers] in the search for divine guidance as to the future" (Bailey, *Leviticus–Numbers*, 56). "Clay liver models, which testify to this activity, have been found as far afield as Mari, Ugarit, Megiddo, Hazor, and Ebla" (Michael S. Moore, *The Balaam Traditions: Their Character and Development*, Society of Biblical Literature Dissertation Series 113 [Atlanta: Scholars Press, 1990], 42). See further at Listening to the Text in the Story, p. 302.

9. Like most English translations, the NIV puts "LORD" in small caps whenever it translates the divine name Yahweh.

by implying he has an inside track with Israel's God. Whatever the case, the Lord condescends to speak to him throughout these chapters to make clear his sovereignty over Israel's future as well his intention to bless them.[10] He speaks to Balaam that night, presumably in a vision or dream,[11] and commands him not to return with the messengers to curse Israel because he himself has blessed them (22:9–13). Such blessing is an allusion to the patriarchal promises (Gen 12:3; 27:33)[12] and will be returned to in full force in Numbers 23–24.

When the messengers return and report Balaam's refusal to come, Balak sends a second set of messengers more numerous and distinguished than the first (Num 22:15). This was a way to show him esteem and underscored the promise to reward him (Heb. "honor him") handsomely, which Balaam properly interprets to include financial reward (vv. 17–18). Indeed, since this interaction is part of the bargaining process, and since, as noted above, Balaam uses spiritual practices forbidden to the Israelites and later on tries to harm them, his claim that he "could not do anything great or small to go beyond the command of the LORD my God" (v. 18) should be viewed with great suspicion. At this point, these are more likely the words of a "gun for hire" who names great amounts of silver and gold immediately after mention of his supposed faithfulness to Israel's God in order to slyly suggest that buying him off will be very costly.[13]

This time, the Lord tells him to go but also warns him to follow the Lord's commands exactly (Num 22:20). If the Lord's initial refusal was to underscore that Israel was indeed blessed (v. 12), his allowing Balaam to go now was in order to have such blessing publicly proclaimed (chs. 23–24). In either case, the Lord's goal is the same: to emphasize that Israel is indeed blessed by him.

The Rebuke of an Ass (22:21–35)[14]

No sooner does Balaam saddle his donkey to go to Balak than we read of the Lord's great displeasure he was doing so (Num 22:21–22a). But if God had

---

10. "From time to time, Yahweh reveals himself to those outside Israel, usually for the benefit of Israel (see Melchizedek in Gen. 14)" (Ashley, *Numbers*, 448; cf. Gen 20:3; 31:24 cited by Milgrom, *Numbers*, 187).

11. Cf. Gen 20:3 for the latter. The Lord's question in Num 22:9 is not due to his ignorance of the situation; rather, he "uses this rhetorical question . . . to open a conversation (as in Gen 3:9; 4:9)" (Milgrom, *Numbers*, 187), thus allowing Balaam to put the case before the Lord and receive a verdict (cf. 1 Kgs 19:9–14).

12. Sprinkle, *Leviticus and Numbers*, 333.

13. Similarly Wenham, who suggests the mention of silver and gold might have actually been "an oblique demand for a huge fee (cf. Gen 23:11–15)" (*Numbers*, 167). In light of the negative factors noted above, it is not surprising that later biblical authors speak so critically of Balaam, highlighting especially his greed (2 Pet 2:15; Jude 11). See also comments on 22:35 below.

14. The title's ambiguity is intentional: "the rebuke given *by* an ass" and "the rebuke given *to* an ass."

just permitted Balaam to go (v. 20), why was he now angry? Verse 35 provides the clue: by emphasizing that Balaam must "speak only what" the Lord tells him, it implies Balaam was ready to do whatever Balak paid him to do (cf. 2 Pet 2:15; Jude 11). The Lord therefore sends a divine messenger[15] to oppose Balaam on the way (Num 22:22b).

The story now drips with sarcastic irony. Balaam's donkey is more spiritually perceptive than this famed seer from Mesopotamia who stubbornly insists on heading toward certain death. This invites the reader to ask, "Who is the real ass after all?"

There are three encounters between the divine messenger and Balaam and his donkey. In all three, the donkey "sees" the angel while Balaam (the seer!) is blind to this reality (Num 22:23, 25, 27). In all three, Balaam beats her for her behavior, oblivious to the fact she has just saved his life (vv. 23, 25, 27). The irony is especially strong in the last encounter, where Balaam beats her again when his anger boils over—all the while unaware she was rescuing him from the Lord's boiling anger (vv. 26–27)![16]

The donkey now speaks. Israelites of course knew donkeys could not do so, which is why the text explains "the LORD opened the donkey's mouth" (Num 22:28). We are in the realm of miracle and, as Kidner wisely notes, "there seems as little need to fret about the mechanics of this as of any other miracle."[17] Indeed, the miracle only underscores the dullness of Balaam, who not only argues with his donkey—an irrational beast[18]—he loses the argument!

The donkey asks why Balaam has beaten her (Num 22:28). The answer to Balaam seems obvious: she has made a fool of him (one can easily imagine his fellow travelers laughing at his inability to control her; v. 29a). His next words are stunningly blind: "If only I had a sword in my hand, I would kill you right now" (v. 29b), the very fate the donkey had just saved him from three different times![19] The donkey then gives him a lesson in logic (!), forcing him to admit her behavior today was not normal, implying he should have known something was amiss (v. 30). This is perhaps especially the case since "strange actions by animals were often regarded as omens in Mesopotamia. As a specialist in this sort of divination, he ought to have

---

15. The "angel of the LORD" could also be translated "messenger of the LORD"; he occurs frequently as someone who acts and speaks on God's behalf (Gen 16:9–10; 22:11–12; etc.).
16. In Hebrew, the same phrase is used to describe the anger of God (22:22) and Balaam (v. 27).
17. Kidner, *Leviticus, Numbers, Deuteronomy*, 50.
18. Keil, *The Pentateuch*, 767 (*Numbers*, 173).
19. Rembrandt's "Balaam and the Ass" captures the irony beautifully.

realized the deity had a message for him."[20] Once again, his lack of spiritual insight is on full display.

At just this moment, the Lord opens Balaam's eyes to see the spiritual realities his donkey was already aware of, and Balaam falls flat on his face, a sign of deep humility before one greater than himself (Num 22:31; cf. 1 Sam 24:8; 1 Kgs 1:31). The angel rebukes him, explaining his donkey had the eyes to see him and actually saved Balaam's life from certain death (Num 22:32–33).[21] On the one hand, this was deeply humbling, "a deflating reminder to the expert in visions and utterances that under God the very beast he rode could see what he himself was blind to (vv. 23, 31), and prove a better prophet than he."[22] On the other hand, it was the strongest possible warning. Balaam repents for striking the donkey but not for any underlying evil, stating only that he will turn around if his way is "displeasing"—the word could also be translated as "evil" (ESV)—to the angel (v. 34). The angel gives him permission to continue, but warns that he can only speak what the Lord commands (v. 35). The implication is clear: "The reason you faced such opposition is because you were not going to obey the Lord's word! That's why I would have killed you but not the donkey: she was innocent, you were guilty! You have now been warned. Transgress the Lord's command and I will strike you—fatally!"

Balak Greets Balaam (22:36–40)

Some of the messengers presumably go on ahead to let Balak know of Balaam's coming, so Balak goes to meet him at an unnamed city on the edge of his territory (Num 22:36). He greets him with a rebuke, assuming that Balaam ignored such an urgent request because he thought Balak did not have the means to pay him well (v. 37). For Balak, cursing Israel is a financial matter, but the recently chastened Balaam corrects him, noting that he can "speak only what God puts in my mouth" (v. 38).

Balak and Balaam begin heading toward the Israelites, stopping first at the otherwise unknown Kiriath Huzoth, where Balak made sacrifices and gave a feast for Balaam and the recently returned officials (Num 22:39–40). This was just one way to show Balaam honor and reward him, a foretaste that more was to come. Whether such rewards would be enough to get him to do Balak's bidding remains to be seen.

---

20. Wenham, *Numbers*, 170.
21. The translation "is a reckless one" (22:32) is uncertain (see NIV note); fortunately, the context makes clear Balaam's journey angered God (v. 22) and directly implies this was due to the disobedience he would commit (see comments above).
22. Ibid.

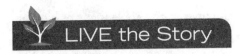
LIVE the Story

While this story takes place, the Israelites are in the plains of Moab (Num 22:1), where they will stay until they cross the Jordan to face fierce nations and fortified towns that they have no earthly hope of defeating. The Lord is aware of this and so has begun encouraging their faith in very palpable ways. In the previous chapter, they defeated Sihon and Og (21:21–35), a foretaste of the victories they would have after crossing the Jordan. In this chapter, he continues encouraging both their faith and their faithfulness. We may consider how he does so by asking three questions.[23]

What Is God's Posture toward His People?

This story begins with two different peoples terrified of the Israelites and wanting to harm them (Num 22:2–4). These peoples' fear should encourage the Israelites, "You don't need to be afraid! God's blessing on you is evident to those who witness your history. Even the nations can see that you are a people blessed by your God!"[24]

At the same time, Israel's enemies do not simply give up. Under Balak's direction, they plan to use spiritual means to change the Lord's blessing into a curse (Num 22:4–7). Some of us will not relate to the fear an Israelite might feel in hearing such a plan. The more we have been affected by modernity, the more we are likely to think, "Simply pronouncing words of blessing or curse do not impact reality." But for the ancients, the pronouncing of blessing and curse was powerful indeed,[25] and many societies to this day believe the same. It should therefore not surprise us if at least some Israelites grew anxious when hearing what Balak hired Balaam to do.

Others, however, should have been able to hear his words with confidence, even amusement, especially his statement to Balaam, "For I know that whoever you bless is blessed, and whoever you curse is cursed" (Num 22:6). Israelites who remembered their own story would know that Balak's words directly contradict the Lord's, who said of Israel's forefather Abraham: "I will bless those who bless you, and whoever curses you I will curse" (Gen 12:3a). They would have known that Balak was actually paying for curses to rain down on his own head! Nor would they have been surprised when the Lord told Balaam, "You must not put a curse on [the Israelites,] because they are blessed" (Num 22:12).

---

23. For an alternative homiletical approach, see p. 179n13.
24. Cf. Rahab's words in Josh 2:9–11.
25. See especially Gen 37:1–41.

And that is the point: God's posture toward his people is one of blessing. His first act toward humanity was to pronounce blessing over them (Gen 1:28). His first words to Abraham included a promise to bless him and his descendants (12:3). The benediction he commands the priests to speak over Israel began with a prayer for his blessing (Num 6:24). Today, God's blessing on Abraham has spread to all peoples who believe in Abraham's ultimate descendant, Jesus (Gal 3:14). In Jesus, God "has blessed us in the heavenly realms with every spiritual blessing" (Eph 1:3). In short, God leans toward his children with blessing in his eyes and love in his arms. Even his discipline is a sign of his love (Heb 12:5–6).

Do we believe that God loves us as his children, or do we picture God as someone who is getting ready to hammer us? What does it look like to believe that God's first posture toward his children is one of blessing? What types of feelings show we believe this to be true? What feelings show we believe the opposite? God regularly assures us in his word of his love for us and his desire to bless us. How do we bring our feelings in line with this reality?

What Is at the Root of Balaam's Wrong?

A second question we may ask is, "What is at the root of Balaam's wrong?" The commentary noted that this chapter casts Balaam in a negative light, especially highlighting his temptation to commit evil for the sake of financial gain.[26] Not surprisingly, the New Testament authors pick up on this. Peter warns of those who "have left the straight way and wandered off to follow the way of Balaam son of Bezer, who loved the wages of wickedness" (2 Pet 2:15), and Jude speaks of those who "have rushed for profit into Balaam's error" (Jude 11b). Balaam is a textbook example of Paul's warning, "For the love of money is a root of all kinds of evil" (1 Tim 6:10a).

The Israelites needed to heed the warning of his negative example. Many of the laws the Lord gives them warn against committing evil because of a love of money, whether by taking bribes to pervert justice (Deut 16:19), using dishonest scales when buying or selling goods (Lev 19:35), or robbing others and not giving them their due wages (v. 13). The love of money is no small sin; it can eventually swallow our souls. As Paul goes on to say, "Some people, eager for money, have wandered from the faith and pierced themselves with many griefs" (1 Tim 6:10). Jesus put the matter even more plainly: "What good is it for someone to gain the whole world, yet forfeit their soul?" (Mark 8:36). And again, "No one can serve two masters. Either you will hate the one

---

26. See above at Listening to the Text in the Story, p. 288.

and love the other, or you will be devoted to the one and despise the other. You cannot serve both God and money" (Matt 6:24).

What about us? Are there areas where we can sense the subtle (or not so subtle) ways that a love for money is taking root in our hearts? What practical steps can we take to tear those roots out and focus instead on loving God, storing up heavenly treasures instead of earthly ones (Matt 6:19–20)?

Who Has the Final Say about Spiritual Realities?

We come finally to the third question we may ask, namely, "Who has the final say about spiritual realities?" Stubbs makes helpful observations on Balak's approach to this question:

> Balak is someone who thinks that spiritual blessing and cursing can be easily manipulated by Balaam and his magical rituals. He certainly recognizes the existence of spiritual powers, but his understanding of them, YHWH included, is that spirits and gods, like other forces in our world, are capable of being controlled by those with the proper know-how and influence. . . . "Blessing and cursing" are marketable spiritual commodities.[27]

This story emphasizes this is not the case. On the one hand, it uses piercing irony to show that when it comes to spiritual realities, one of the most respected pagan spiritual leaders of the day is dumber than an ass. At the same time, it underscores that the Lord is not subject to the whims of any person, no matter what their spiritual standing is in the world's eyes. All are subject to his sovereign power and will (Num 22:20, 35), a point that Balaam himself eventually recognizes (v. 38).

The Israelites greatly needed this lesson. At several points already in Numbers they have heard clearly what the Lord has commanded but decided they could somehow get around it, whether by coming up with new structures of spiritual leadership (Num 16:1–35) or marching into the promised land at the exact moment the Lord had told them not to do so (14:39–45). In either case, their actions showed they believed God's will could be bent to their own.

We repeat this mistake today when we allow the Bible to inform part of our beliefs but not all of them. Whenever this takes place, we are in effect saying, "Lord, I will allow you to speak into certain areas of my life or worldview but not others." In other words, we are saying, "I am the ultimate decision maker

---

27. Stubbs, *Numbers*, 177.

when it comes to spiritual reality. I believe in you, God, but I also believe that my life does not have to bend and shape to fit your spiritual reality."

Such a "god," however, is no longer worthy of our worship, nor can he help us or rescue us in time of need because we have denied the very thing that enables him to do so: his sovereign power. Once we have put ourselves in the position of the Almighty, there is no one who is almighty to help us in our suffering and weakness. The glory of the Bible is that the God it speaks of is both sovereign and good, almighty and caring, the King of kings and yet an adopting Father. He calls us, in love, to enter into relationship with him, but to do so means to acknowledge that he gets all of us.

Jesus said, "Whoever wants to be my disciple must deny themselves and take up their cross daily and follow me" (Luke 9:23). This is a call to die to ourselves as we submit to his loving lordship over all of our lives. Have we heeded this call? Are we willing to stop trying to make God's will fit into our lives and let our lives be bent and shaped to fit his will? Jesus is a loving Savior who loves to save us, but we have to let him be Lord to do so.

CHAPTER 26

Numbers 22:41–24:25

 LISTEN to the Story

^{22:41}The next morning Balak took Balaam up to Bamoth Baal, and from there he could see the outskirts of the Israelite camp.

^{23:1}Balaam said, "Build me seven altars here, and prepare seven bulls and seven rams for me." ²Balak did as Balaam said, and the two of them offered a bull and a ram on each altar.

³Then Balaam said to Balak, "Stay here beside your offering while I go aside. Perhaps the Lord will come to meet with me. Whatever he reveals to me I will tell you." Then he went off to a barren height.

⁴God met with him, and Balaam said, "I have prepared seven altars, and on each altar I have offered a bull and a ram."

⁵The Lord put a word in Balaam's mouth and said, "Go back to Balak and give him this word."

⁶So he went back to him and found him standing beside his offering, with all the Moabite officials. ⁷Then Balaam spoke his message:

> "Balak brought me from Aram,
>   the king of Moab from the eastern mountains.
> 'Come,' he said, 'curse Jacob for me;
>   come, denounce Israel.'
> ⁸How can I curse
>   those whom God has not cursed?
> How can I denounce
>   those whom the Lord has not denounced?
> ⁹From the rocky peaks I see them,
>   from the heights I view them.
> I see a people who live apart
>   and do not consider themselves one of the nations.

> ¹⁰Who can count the dust of Jacob
>   or number even a fourth of Israel?
> Let me die the death of the righteous,
>   and may my final end be like theirs!"

¹¹Balak said to Balaam, "What have you done to me? I brought you to curse my enemies, but you have done nothing but bless them!"

¹²He answered, "Must I not speak what the LORD puts in my mouth?"

¹³Then Balak said to him, "Come with me to another place where you can see them; you will not see them all but only the outskirts of their camp. And from there, curse them for me." ¹⁴So he took him to the field of Zophim on the top of Pisgah, and there he built seven altars and offered a bull and a ram on each altar.

¹⁵Balaam said to Balak, "Stay here beside your offering while I meet with him over there."

¹⁶The LORD met with Balaam and put a word in his mouth and said, "Go back to Balak and give him this word."

¹⁷So he went to him and found him standing beside his offering, with the Moabite officials. Balak asked him, "What did the LORD say?"

¹⁸Then he spoke his message:

> "Arise, Balak, and listen;
>   hear me, son of Zippor.
> ¹⁹God is not human, that he should lie,
>   not a human being, that he should change his mind.
> Does he speak and then not act?
>   Does he promise and not fulfill?
> ²⁰I have received a command to bless;
>   he has blessed, and I cannot change it.
> ²¹"No misfortune is seen in Jacob,
>   No misery observed in Israel.
> The LORD their God is with them;
>   the shout of the King is among them.
> ²²God brought them out of Egypt;
>   they have the strength of a wild ox.
> ²³There is no divination against Jacob,
>   no evil omens against Israel.

> It will now be said of Jacob
> > and of Israel, 'See what God has done!'
> ²⁴The people rise like a lioness;
> > They rouse themselves like a lion
> that does not rest till it devours its prey
> > and drinks the blood of its victims."

²⁵Then Balak said to Balaam, "Neither curse them at all nor bless them at all!"

²⁶Balaam answered, "Did I not tell you I must do whatever the LORD says?"

²⁷Then Balak said to Balaam, "Come, let me take you to another place. Perhaps it will please God to let you curse them for me from there." ²⁸And Balak took Balaam to the top of Peor, overlooking the wasteland.

²⁹Balaam said, "Build me seven altars here, and prepare seven bulls and seven rams for me." ³⁰Balak did as Balaam had said, and offered a bull and a ram on each altar.

²⁴:¹Now when Balaam saw that it pleased the LORD to bless Israel, he did not resort to divination as at other times, but turned his face toward the wilderness. ²When Balaam looked out and saw Israel encamped tribe by tribe, the Spirit of God came on him ³and he spoke his message:

> "The prophecy of Balaam son of Beor,
> > the prophecy of one whose eye sees clearly,
> ⁴the prophecy of one who hears the words of God,
> > who sees a vision from the Almighty,
> > who falls prostrate, and whose eyes are opened:
> ⁵"How beautiful are your tents, Jacob,
> > your dwelling places, Israel!
> ⁶"Like valleys they spread out,
> > like gardens beside a river,
> like aloes planted by the Lord,
> > like cedars beside the waters.
> ⁷Water will flow from their buckets;
> > their seed will have abundant water.
> "Their king will be greater than Agag;
> > their kingdom will be exalted.

⁸"God brought them out of Egypt;
    they have the strength of a wild ox.
They devour hostile nations
    and break their bones in pieces;
    with their arrows they pierce them.
⁹Like a lion they crouch and lie down,
    like a lioness—who dares to rouse them?
"May those who bless you be blessed
    and those who curse you be cursed!"

¹⁰Then Balak's anger burned against Balaam. He struck his hands together and said to him, "I summoned you to curse my enemies, but you have blessed them these three times. ¹¹Now leave at once and go home! I said I would reward you handsomely, but the Lord has kept you from being rewarded."

¹²Balaam answered Balak, "Did I not tell the messengers you sent me, ¹³'Even if Balak gave me all the silver and gold in his palace, I could not do anything of my own accord, good or bad, to go beyond the command of the Lord—and I must say only what the Lord says'? ¹⁴Now I am going back to my people, but come, let me warn you of what this people will do to your people in days to come."

¹⁵Then he spoke his message:

"The prophecy of Balaam son of Beor,
    the prophecy of one whose eye sees clearly,
¹⁶the prophecy of one who hears the words of God,
    who has knowledge from the Most High,
who sees a vision from the Almighty,
    who falls prostrate, and whose eyes are opened:
¹⁷"I see him, but not now;
    I behold him, but not near.
A star will come out of Jacob;
    a scepter will rise out of Israel.
He will crush the foreheads of Moab,
    the skulls of all the people of Sheth.
¹⁸Edom will be conquered;
    Seir, his enemy, will be conquered,

> but Israel will grow strong.
> ¹⁹A ruler will come out of Jacob
>   and destroy the survivors of the city."
>
> ²⁰Then Balaam saw Amalek and spoke his message:
>
> "Amalek was first among the nations,
>   but their end will be utter destruction."
>
> ²¹Then he saw the Kenites and spoke his message:
>
> "Your dwelling place is secure,
>   your nest is set in a rock;
> ²²yet you Kenites will be destroyed
>   when Ashur takes you captive."
>
> ²³Then he spoke his message:
>
> "Alas! Who can live when God does this?
>   ²⁴Ships will come from the shores of Cyprus;
> they will subdue Ashur and Eber,
>   but they too will come to ruin."
>
> ²⁵Then Balaam got up and returned home, and Balak went his own way.

Listening to the Text in the Story: Genesis 1:26–28; patriarchal promises in Genesis (12:3; 13:16; 26:2–4; 27:29; 28:13–15; 49:9, 10)

God's very first words spoken over humanity were words of blessing (Gen 1:26–28), and he never gives up on his intent to bless those he has made. After the flood, he repeated his words of blessing over humanity's new representative, Noah (9:1–3, 7), and after this to Abraham, not only assuring him of blessing but also promising that this blessing would extend through him to all peoples (12:2–3). As Genesis goes on to affirm, Abraham's descendants will indeed be blessed and the source of blessing for all nations (cf. 26:2–4; 28:13–15). God's intent to bring this blessing to bear on Israel is underscored in Numbers 23–24 when the words of Balaam—a pagan diviner hired to curse Israel!—make use of the Genesis promises to describe Israel's present and future reality of blessing (see table below).

Numbers	Genesis
"Who can count the dust of Jacob?" (23:10)	13:16; 28:14
"Like a lion they crouch and lie down, like a lioness—who dares to rouse them?" (24:9)	49:9
"May those who bless you be blessed and those who curse you be cursed!" (24:9)	12:3; 27:29
"A scepter will rise out of Israel" (24:17)	49:10 (cf. Ps 2:9)

In terms of Balaam's role, he presents himself as a "diviner" or "seer," that is, someone who can communicate messages from the gods concerning the future (Num 22:38; 23:12, 26; 24:12–14). Moore identifies different ways that diviners in Mesopotamia and Syro-Palestine would do this (and some of the differences between the practice of divination in these areas). Taken together, some of their methods included: "reading" animal's entrails (similar to how some today "read" tea leaves), especially the liver;[1] looking at various patterns produced by pouring oil or flour into water; examining the patterns and directions of smoke; or using some form of lots (cf. Ezek 21:21).[2] In this situation, Balak either asks Balaam to go beyond the role of diviner (describing the future) to that of a sorcerer (controlling the future by means of the proper curses), or asks him to read the signs of divination in a way that was favorable to Balak and disastrous for Israel. In either case, Balaam has already been soundly warned: he must speak only what the Lord reveals to him (Num 22:21–35).

EXPLAIN the Story

These chapters describe four different times that Balaam delivers an oracle from the Lord. The first three accounts follow a similar pattern (see table below).[3]

---

1. See p. 289n8.
2. For full discussion see Moore, *The Balaam Traditions*, 41–55. See also n7 below.
3. Sprinkle, *Leviticus and Numbers*, 345, following Cole, *Numbers*, 398.

Sequence	First Oracle	Second Oracle	Third Oracle
1. Balak takes Balaam to observation point to view Israel.	22:41	23:13–14a	23:27–28
2. Balaam instructs Balak to offer sacrifices.	23:1	—	23:29
3. Balak sacrifices the animals as instructed.	23:2	23:14b	23:30
4. Balaam tells Balak to stand by his offering altar.	23:3	23:15	—
5. Balaam goes alone, and Yahweh reveals himself.	23:4–5	23:16	24:1–2
6. Balaam returns to Balak standing by his offering.	23:6	23:17	—
7. Balaam obeys Yahweh and speaks the oracle.	23:7–10	23:18–24	24:3–9

After the third oracle, Balak fires Balaam, who responds with a final series of oracles speaking of other nations' ruin and Israel's blessing and victory. In fact, the Lord's blessing of Israel unifies this entire section. And the certainty of that blessing coming is only underscored by the fact it is pronounced, under God's sovereign leading, by the very one who had been hired to curse Israel.

Balaam's First Message (22:41–23:12)

The exact location of Bamoth Baal is unknown but was evidently near the plains of Moab and at good elevation, allowing Balaam a good view of one end of the Israelite camp (Num 22:41). Gane compares it to having a clear line of site "in order to aim his imprecatory 'smart bombs.'"[4]

At Balaam's direction, Balak builds seven altars, gets seven bulls and rams ready, and then he and Balaam offer one of each on each altar (Num 23:1–2).

---

4. Gane, *Leviticus, Numbers*, 693. Note the importance of seeing the people to curse them (22:41; 23:13, 27–28).

Why? Perhaps so Balaam could examine their entrails, which was one method of divination.[5] Alternatively, these sacrifices may be to attract the deity's attention, which would explain why Balaam tells Balak to stay near his sacrifice (he wants to make sure the deity is aware on whose behalf the sacrifice is made; v. 3). Possibly the sacrifices served both goals.

While Balak stays beside the sacrifices, Balaam seeks an audience with the Lord (Num 23:3),[6] who condescends to meet with Balaam and give him direction. Balaam begins by noting he has made lavish sacrifices (v. 4), perhaps to make clear he did not dare approach the Lord empty-handed. The Lord then "put a word in Balaam's mouth" and tells him to give Balak "this word" (v. 5), a reference to his earlier command that Balak speak "only the word that I will tell you" (v. 35, my translation). Just how the Lord gave this word is not said. Possibly it was by direct revelation, whether through the Spirit or a vision or dream. Numbers 24:1, however, suggests that in chapter 23 Balaam practiced divination after the sacrifices were made. The Lord may thus have condescended to Balaam's use of divination here, "speaking" to him by means of lots and Balaam summarizing those decisions in his report back to Balak.[7] In either case, Balaam brings back a message from the Lord to Balak.

He finds Balak where he left him, standing beside his offering, with his officials, undoubtedly hoping his sacrifice has been favorably accepted as he awaited the message from God (Num 23:6). The message Balaam gives him might be paraphrased as follows:

You brought me from my home and asked me to curse Israel (v. 7). But this is impossible because the Lord has not done so (v. 8)! Indeed, from the people's size and strength it is clear they are blessed. They do not consider

---

5. See above, p. 302, Listening to the Text in the Story.

6. The meaning of the word translated "barren height" is greatly debated; see Sklar, *Additional Notes*, at 23:3.

7. It was common for diviners to pose questions to the deity with two options and to receive their answers by means of lots (e.g., Ezek 21:21; for an example from Anatolia, see "Excerpts from an Oracle Report," trans. Gary Beckman (*COS* 1.78); see further Sklar, *Additional Notes*, at 23:5). This might explain Num 23:20a, which in the Hebrew reads, "Behold, I have received 'blessing,'" that is, "I asked the Lord with lots if Israel would be blessed or cursed and received the 'blessing' lot" (cf. Ezek 21:27). If this is the case, the "word" here would be that Israel would not be cursed, which Balaam recounts in poetic form together with his own observations (Num 23:9–10a) and desires (23:10b). For this line of interpretation, I am thankful to Benjamin Wiggershaus, "The Oracles of Balaam in view of Ancient Near Eastern Oracular Reporting" (paper presented at Annual Meeting of the Institute for Biblical Research, Denver, CO, November 16, 2018). His dissertation work expands on this.

themselves a "sub-branch" of any people;[8] they are a mighty nation onto themselves (v. 9), so great, in fact, they are like the dust of the land, and one cannot even count the very end of their camp ("a fourth of Israel"; v. 10a)! To be blessed in such a way must mean they are righteous (and thus worthy of God's blessing),[9] and I long for my life to follow the same path of blessing ("may my final end be like theirs"; v. 10b)!

Balak cannot believe his ears! He has brought Balaam to curse Israel and he has done the exact opposite (Num 23:11)! But Balaam has not forgotten the rebuke and warning of 22:35 and responds that he had no choice; these are not his words but the Lord's, and the only ones he can speak (23:12). The implication is that if Balak is going to be angry at anyone, it must be the Lord.

Balaam's Second Message (23:13–26)

Seeing that things did not go his way from the first vantage point, Balak takes Balaam to the field of Zophim, located "on the top of Pisgah" (Num 23:14), overlooking the valley where the Israelites were encamped (see at 21:20, p. 279). We are not told why Balak thinks that a change in venue might lead to a different outcome (he will try this again in 23:28), nor is it clear why he mentions that Balaam will only see a portion of the people (v. 13).[10] What is clear is that Balak's desire for Israel to be cursed remains as strong as ever.

The previous scene now repeats itself:[11] after sacrifices are made, Balaam departs, receives a word from the Lord, then brings it back to Balak who is waiting by his sacrifice (Num 23:14b–17). Whereas the last message made clear the Lord had not cursed Israel and implied he had blessed them, this one states explicitly the Lord had blessed them and would continue to do so. We might paraphrase as follows.[12]

---

8. Cf. the use of "consider" in Deut 2:11.

9. What Balaam cannot know is that Israel living righteously is more of a goal they have yet to reach than a reality they have already attained. The Lord's blessing has come to them in spite of great unfaithfulness on their part.

10. A plausible suggestion regarding the latter is that this comment makes clear that Balaam has not yet seen all the people, thus explaining why Balak tries a different approach in the next attempt: taking him to see all the people (Ashley, *Numbers*, 475–76, adapting a suggestion made by George Buchanan Gray, *A Critical and Exegetical Commentary on Numbers* [New York: C. Scribner's Sons, 1903], 349–50).

11. See chart above at Explain the Story, p. 303.

12. Debate exists with regard to several of the phrases in this oracle and the ones following in chapter 24. In paraphrasing them, I have tried to summarize what it seems we can know with some degree of certainty while leaving the most uncertain things out of the summary, e.g., the meaning of "Sheth" in 24:17. For further discussion, see comments in Sklar, *Additional Notes*.

Balak, you think of the gods as very powerful humans, standing above humanity in terms of their strength but being like humanity in terms of their nature: untrustworthy and changing their minds in fickle ways. (This is why you try to change the Lord's mind by going to different venues and offering more sacrifices!) But the Lord is not like a very powerful human! He is in a class of his own, standing completely above and apart from humanity in terms of his strength and nature. Unlike humanity, he is always trustworthy and will do what he says (v. 19). In particular, his determination to bless Israel is an irrevocable decree, and no human, including religious experts like myself, can revoke it (v. 20)![13] Because of this blessing, they will not experience misfortune and misery at the hands of others. Indeed, the Lord is with them! Israel shouts with joy because victorious King Yahweh is in their midst (v. 21)![14] This same King has already delivered them powerfully from Egypt and given them the strength of the wild ox, a creature of incredible power and might (v. 22).[15] Even the results of divination and seeking evil omens on my part are unanimous: God is for Israel[16] and this will become exceedingly clear as his deeds on Israel's behalf are observed (v. 23). Because of the Lord, Israel will be like a lion, the fiercest predator of the land, relentless in its pursuit of prey and victory (v. 24)! (So be warned, Balak, lest you become one of his victims!)

With angry frustration, Balak rebukes Balaam, the sense being, "If you absolutely refuse to curse them, then don't say anything at all—especially a blessing!" (Num 23:25). Balaam again reminds Balak of the conditions with which he entered into this partnership: he would speak only what the Lord revealed (v. 26). Once again, the only person for Balak to be angry with is the Lord himself (cf. v. 12).

Balaam's Third Message (23:27–24:14)

Balak would not give up. "The third time's the charm" seems to be his thinking.[17] He either did not hear or refused to believe that Israel's God was absolutely committed to his people's good.

---

13. For "received a command to bless," see n7.
14. See 1 Sam 4:5; cf. Pss 47:5–6 with 47:2–4. Alternatively, Yahweh raises the battle cry in their midst. In either case, King Yahweh fights for them!
15. The verse could also mean the Lord has protected them with his own strength, which is like that of the wild ox (cf. NASB, ESV). For the ox's strength, see Job 39:9–11.
16. That is, the results of Balaam's divination have not come out negatively toward Israel.
17. Wenham, *Numbers*, 176.

The story repeats itself, this time from the top of Peor, whose exact location is unknown but was evidently nearby, overlooking the wasteland[18] and apparently all Israel[19] encamped in it below (Num 23:27–28; cf. 21:20). After the sacrifices are offered (23:29–30), however, a striking contrast is made. Balak had hoped it would "please God to let [Balaam] curse [Israel]" (v. 27), but "Balaam saw that it pleased the LORD to bless Israel" (24:1)! Balaam's approach thus changes. Convinced of the Lord's intent, he does not even bother using divination to ask the Lord his plan. Instead, he turns his face toward the wilderness, where Israel is encamped, fixing his attention there and viewing the people as a whole ("tribe by tribe"; v. 2). For the first time, we are clearly told that God's Spirit comes upon him,[20] and he delivers his third message, which may be paraphrased as follows:[21]

Here is my oracle![22] God has made it clear, opening my eyes to see and speaking in my ears (vv. 3–4a)! The Almighty[23] has given me a vision, causing me to fall in reverent fear before him, and yet opening my eyes—just as he did so I could see the angel (22:31)!—so that I could see this vision clearly (24:4b).[24]

O Israel, your tents are the most pleasing sight (Num 24:5), so fruitful in number they spread out like a lush valley,[25] like a well-watered garden, like prized trees bursting with such growth a divine being, the Lord, must have planted them (v. 6)![26] Israel will have no lack of water going forward, and their seed (and that means descendants!) will flourish as though planted by many waters (v. 7a). What is more, their king will be greater than the

---

18. Also called "the plains of Moab"; see at 22:1, p. 280.
19. Cf. 24:2.
20. Cf. comments at 23:5, p. 304, where it was noted that the Lord may have conveyed his earlier messages by condescending to answer Balaam's divination methods.
21. See at n12.
22. Though Balaam is acting prophetically, the Hebrew word I translate as "oracle" (*ne'um*) is different than the word found in phrases like "the prophecy (*massa*) of Nahum" (Nah 1:1; so also other biblical prophets: Isa 13:1; Hab 1:1; Mal 1:1). This might be to distance Balaam from biblical prophets. Translating "oracle" (so NASB, ESV) instead of "prophecy" (NIV) helps with this possible distinction.
23. Hebrew *shadday*. The translation "Almighty" is based on the Septuagint and Vulgate. "Scholars do not agree on the original meaning of the name and, in a sense, it does not matter, for in Israel it became simply an alternate designation for Yahweh" (Ashley, *Numbers*, 488).
24. Cf. Dan 8:16–17. Alternatively, he fell down in a vision-induced sleep (cf. Gen 15:12; Dan 8:18–19; Levine, *Numbers 21–36*, 194), or he fell down because God's Sprit came powerfully upon him (as with Saul in 1 Sam 19:24; Ashley mentions but does not endorse this option [*Numbers*, 489]).
25. An Arabic roots suggests the word "valley" (*nahal*) could also refer to palm trees (so ESV), which would be in keeping with the tree imagery in the rest of the verse.
26. Cf. Ps 104:16–17.

well-known Agag,[27] and their kingdom highly exalted (v. 7b)! As for Israel's God, he has delivered them powerfully from Egypt and given them the strength of the wild ox, a creature of incredible power and might (v. 8a).[28] Israel will thus devour their enemies, chewing them up and spitting them out (v. 8b)! Israel is like a fierce lion, who no one dares to disturb (on pain of death!) (v. 9a). Whoever blesses this people will in turn be blessed, but whoever curses them will be cursed (v. 9b)—so learn your lesson, Balak, and stop this madness!

Balak explodes with anger, striking his hands together (as someone today might slam their fist on a table; Num 24:10a) and giving his fullest rebuke to date. To paraphrase once again:

To curse my enemies I called you![29] But look here! You have *insisted on blessing them*[30] these three times! So now, flee back home before I harm you![31] I said I would reward you handsomely,[32] but look here: the Lord has kept you from being rewarded (vv. 10b–11)!

He is firing Balaam for breach of contract, giving him no severance pay whatsoever,[33] and excusing such actions by blaming the Lord.

Balaam responds as he did previously, in turn giving his fullest reply to date, reminding Balak he has been completely faithful to do what he said he would do (and perhaps implicitly saying he has not breached his contract and should still be paid; Num 24:12–13). Before returning home, however, he will advise[34] Balak about what Israel will do to Moab in days to come (v. 14),[35] the thought perhaps being, "If you insist on cursing them, this will

---

27. That is, well-known in Balaam's day though still unknown to us today. A king named Agag is also mentioned in 1 Sam 15:8, 9, 20, 32–33, but that is from a much later date. Since the same name could be used by successive kings (e.g., Abimelech in Gen 20:2; 26:1; cf. "King Henry *the Eighth*" more recently), it should not surprise us if the same were true of the name Agag.

28. See n15.

29. "To curse my enemies" comes first in the Hebrew for emphasis.

30. The verb "to bless" is repeated in the Hebrew for emphasis (cf. NASB).

31. NIV's "leave at once" is a bit weak; the Hebrew verb (from the root *b-r-h*) typically describes one person fleeing another to avoid danger (Gen 16:6; 27:43; Exod 2:15; etc.).

32. See 22:17.

33. Olson, *Numbers*, 146.

34. NIV's "warn" is too strong; the Hebrew verb (from the root *y-'-ts*) refers to giving advice (cf. Exod 18:19; 2 Sam 17:11; 1 Kgs 12:6; etc.).

35. The phrase translated "in days to come" or "in later days" can refer to the relatively near future (Deut 31:29) as well as the relatively distant future (Gen 49:1; Deut 4:30; Isa 2:2).

be your outcome!" (vv. 15–19). What is more, he will announce the fate of other nations near Israel: Edom, Amalek, the Kenites, Ashur, and Eber (vv. 20–24).[36]

Balaam's Four Final Oracles (24:15–25)[37]

Balaam turns his attention first to Balak's nation, Moab, and its southern neighbor, Edom (Num 24:15–19). He introduces his oracle as previously (vv. 15–16),[38] underscoring its divine origin, then explains what will happen in the days to come, which may be paraphrased as follows:

> I clearly see a king coming from Israel—not immediately, but coming (v. 17a)! He will have the same majesty and glory as an exalted and shining star and will hold a royal scepter[39] in his hand (v. 17b). He will crush Moab thoroughly, as though driving a spike through his head (v. 17c). Under his leadership, Edom will be defeated in war because Israel will do valiantly[40] in battle (v. 18). Indeed, Israel's enemies will be defeated; no one will survive (v. 19)!

Those reading this during David's reign would see this naturally applying to him, given the thorough ways in which he defeated both Moab and Edom (2 Sam 8:2, 12–14).

Next, Balaam has a prophetic vision ("saw") about Amalek (Num 24:20a). This nation ruthlessly attacked the Israelites on their way out of Egypt (Exod 17:8; Deut 25:17–18), leading the Lord to promise he would blot out Amalek's name from under heaven (Exod 17:14; Deut 25:19). That promise is reiterated here: "Amalek will go from being first to last among the nations and be wiped off the map!" (Num 24:20b, paraphrased). Allowing for the hyperbole of such threats, we can see them fulfilled later in Israel's history, under both Saul (1 Sam 15:3–8) and especially David, who subdued the Amalekites during his reign (2 Sam 8:12).

Next were the Kenites (Num 24:21–22), to whom Moses was related by

---

36. Stubbs, *Numbers*, 194–95.
37. See at n12.
38. Cf. 24:3–4. There is one added phrase: "who has knowledge from the Most High," that is, from the only one who knows the future: the Lord. The title "Most High" stresses the Lord's exalted status as a "great King over all the earth" (Ps 47:2) who is "exalted far above all gods" (Ps 97:9).
39. This very word was used when describing the ruler that would come from Judah (Gen 49:10) and was later used when describing the Lord's anointed king (Ps 2:9, "scepter").
40. So also NASB, ESV.

marriage (Judg 1:16). They lived near the Amalekites and had peaceful relations with Israel at a later point in their history (1 Sam 15:6), though they also had some connection to the Midianites,[41] who were working together here with Balak against Israel (Num 22:7) and who will try to harm Israel in the next chapter (25:6, 16–18). Balaam warns, "Although you currently are as safe as a bird in an unreachable nest,[42] its protective twigs will be burned up when Ashur comes upon you and takes you into exile" (24:21b–22; author's translation). "Ashur" is perhaps best understood not as "the well-known empire of northern Mesopotamia [i.e., Assyria], but [as] a small tribe that lived in northern Sinai, mentioned in several places in the Old Testament (Gen 25:3, 18; 2 Sam 2:9; Ps 83:8). This word then foretells that the Kenites will be subdued by their neighbours, the tribe of Asshur."[43] This reading makes good geographical sense and also fits well with the likely understanding of the following oracle.

Finally, Balaam turns to Ashur and the sea peoples as though to say, "An invading army will come in turn from the north, a sea-faring people (Num 24:23b–24a)![44] They will defeat Ashur and Eber[45] but will themselves be defeated one day (v. 24)." Wenham suggests this refers "to the invasion of the sea-peoples, who swept through the coastal plain of Canaan and attacked Egypt *c.* 1200 BC. The best-known of the sea peoples were the Philistines," whom David subdued along with those mentioned in preceding oracles: Moab, Edom, and Amalek (2 Sam 8:12).[46] Understood this way, these final four oracles—which began with an announcement of a coming victorious Israelite king (Num 24:17)—all anticipate an Israelite king who actually fulfilled them in an initial way.

The chapter ends with Balaam heading out for home (Num 24:25),[47] as Balak had commanded (v. 11), and Balak himself leaving with the very opposite outcome he had wanted. Israel would indeed be blessed!

---

41. Cf. Judg 1:16 with Exod 18:1.
42. The word for "nest" (*qen*) is similar to the word for Kenite (*qeni*).
43. Wenham, *Numbers*, 181, citing Jules de Vaulx, *Les Nombres*, Sources Bibliques (Paris: Gabalda, 1972). So also Ashley, *Numbers*, 508.
44. See NIV footnote on 24:23.
45. Either another name for Ashur or a people somehow related to them (cf. Gen 10:21–24) or living near them.
46. Wenham, *Numbers*, 204.
47. This verse is typical when characters head in different directions at the end of a scene (Gen 18:33; 31:55–32:1a; Milgrom, *Numbers*, 211). Balaam is thus headed home but will stop on the way to advise Midian, which will bring about the disastrous results of the next chapter (cf. 31:16).

LIVE the Story

How Is This Story a Warning?[48]

There are at least two ways in which this story warns. The first warning is actually for those who would say they know and believe God's truth and yet trade the blessing of relationship with the God of the universe for lesser priorities.

Consider Balaam. Four times he insists that he can only speak what the Lord tells him (Num 22:38; 23:12, 26; 24:12–13). Two times he makes clear that God has spoken directly to him and he is faithfully passing on God's word (vv. 3–4; 15–16). He finishes his first oracle by expressing his desire to experience the same God-ordained blessing as Israel: "Let me die the death of the righteous, and may my final end be like theirs!" (23:10). Unquestionably, he knows God's truth and believes it to be true.

But things do not go well for Balaam in the long run. As argued in the comments at chapter 22, greed was a primary driving force in Balaam's life,[49] and while the Lord's warning of death was enough to keep Balaam obedient in these chapters, his obedience was short-lived. In the very next chapter the Midianites will lead Israel into deep sin and rebellion against the Lord, and the architect of their plan was Balaam himself. "[The women of Midian] were the ones *who followed Balaam's advice* and enticed the Israelites to be unfaithful to the LORD" (31:16a). In other words, he found a way to bring harm to Israel and thus do what he was paid to do. As Peter explains, Balaam "loved the wages of wickedness" (2 Pet 2:15) more than the blessing that comes from being in relationship with God, a blessing he longed for at one point in his life (Num 23:10) and yet missed out on at the end because of his greed. Jesus's question at this point is searching: "What good is it for someone to gain the whole world, yet forfeit their soul?" (Mark 8:36). His question is for those who claim to believe God's truth as much as those who deny it. Correct theology is no guarantee of relationship with God. Living faith is what is required, and living faith puts God ahead of all other priorities in our life. Balaam did not have such faith and forfeited his soul for money. Others forfeit it for fame or pleasure or relationships. Whenever we put something else ahead of God in terms of our priorities, we are following in Balaam's footsteps—and will miss out on the greatest blessing possible.

---

48. For an alternative homiletical approach, see p. 179n13.
49. See Listening to the Text in the Story, p. 288.

The second warning of this story is for those who oppose the ones whom God has blessed. When God blesses someone, it is because he has marked them with his love and favor, as a parent does with a child. And just as a parent takes it personally when their child is attacked—and will defend them as strongly as necessary—so too does the Lord. That is why the consequences here are so severe. Consider Balak, king of Moab. He is repeatedly told of God's desire to bless Israel, yet he repeatedly tries to turn that blessing into a curse. As a result, even though the Lord had originally commanded Israel not to harass Moab or engage them in battle (Deut 2:9), he inspires Balaam in his final oracles to speak of Moab's downfall at the hands of an Israelite king (Num 24:17). Several of the other nations mentioned in the final oracles were also openly hostile to Israel (Edom,[50] Amalek,[51] Kenites/Midianites[52]), and presumably the remaining ones are mentioned because their posture to God's people was similar (Ashur, Eber). What they all share in common is a disastrous end. To oppose those whom God has blessed in his fatherly love and care is to invite his protective anger.

To put this in more modern terms, Balak is not a "seeker." He is not entering a dialogue asking honest questions about what the Israelites believe or even someone who is simply skeptical about it. He is hell-bent on destroying them, and in doing so he touches the apple of God's eye. The same happens today when anyone attacks the followers of Jesus. As even a quick reading of Revelation will show, God is bound and determined to protect his church and will do it where necessary with apocalyptic judgment (Rev 6:12–17; 11:1–14; 16:4–7; 18:19–19:2). This story therefore stands as a strong warning: the surest way to quick judgment is to curse those whom God has blessed, for in doing so we incite the wrath of their heavenly Father.

How Is This Story an Encouragement?

In the midst of giving warning, however, this story also gives strong encouragement, especially in emphasizing the Lord's desire to bless. As noted above, God's very first words spoken over humanity were a blessing (Gen 1:26–28), and he never gives up on this intent to bless those he has made.[53] That blessing became focused on Abraham and his descendants, Israel, so that it is no surprise Balaam's first four oracles emphasize that God has not cursed his people but blessed them and would continue to do so. But Israel's blessing was never an end in itself. From the very beginning, God's intent in blessing Israel was

---

50. Num 20:14–21.
51. See at 24:20, p. 309.
52. See at 24:21–22, pp. 309–10.
53. See summary at Listening to the Text in the Story, pp. 301–2.

so that through them "all peoples on earth will be blessed" (Gen 12:3). As the biblical story moves forward, this blessing is made available in the most remarkable way in Abraham's ultimate descendant, Jesus (Gal 3:8, 16). In short, God's first wish is for all peoples to experience his blessing, a blessing that now finds its fulfillment in the joy of knowing our Maker and Redeemer through Christ. Blessing and relationship are thus at the heart of who God is.

We don't always think of God in such ways. Sometimes we think more like Balak: do the right religious things, as formulaic and impersonal as they may be, and God might give you what you want. But the Bible is totally different. It teaches us to enter into relationship with God and experience the joy that comes from knowing the one who loves us and has known our name before the world began. Man-made religion is about rules; biblical religion is about relationship. Jesus himself said, "Now this is eternal life: that they *know* you, the only true God, and Jesus Christ, whom you have sent" (John 17:3, emphasis added). And to those who enter such a relationship of blessing there is a certain and sure promise that God himself will guard them in it. As Jesus also said, "My sheep listen to my voice; I know them, and they follow me. I give them eternal life, and they shall never perish; no one will snatch them out of my hand. My Father, who has given them to me, is greater than all; no one can snatch them out of my Father's hand. I and the Father are one" (10:27–30).

How do these words align with our view of the Lord? What are the implications for how we live before him and talk to him when we see him as a God whose first impulse is to be in relationship with us and bless us? And how does his promise to hold us in an unbreakable grip of eternal love impact how we lean into our fears and worries and anxieties?

Where Is This Story Headed?

A final question to consider is, "Where is this story headed?" In Balaam's fourth oracle he speaks of a coming king: "I see him, but not now; I behold him, but not near. A star will come out of Jacob; a scepter will rise out of Israel" (Num 24:17). The oracle goes on to describe how this king will defeat Israel's enemies and, as noted above, finds initial fulfillment several centuries later in King David.[54]

It has been common in both early Judaism and Christianity, however, to understand that this prophecy finds its ultimate fulfillment in the Messiah, a king far greater than David.[55] Descriptions of the Davidic king often work

---

54. See at 24:15–25, p. 309.
55. See references in Allen, "Numbers," 911. For early Judaism, he cites Targum Onkelos, Targum Jonathan, and sections of the Talmud and the Qumran documents. For early Christianity, he cites

this way. They certainly apply to David and his human descendants, but their grand and exalted language is understood to apply to one far greater than David ever was. From a Christian perspective, that person is Jesus. Thus Psalm 2 speaks of the Davidic king as God's "son" (Num 24:7) and as ruling over the nations (vv. 8–9); the New Testament authors do not hesitate to apply this title and promise to Jesus, the eternal Son of God (Heb 1:5), who does not rule simply over the nations of the Middle East but over those of the entire world (Rev 19:15). Moreover, the Lord says to David, "Sit at my right hand until I make your enemies a footstool for your feet" (Ps 110:1). The New Testament applies this to Jesus in his resurrection from the dead and exaltation as a reigning king at the right hand of God himself in heaven (Heb 1:13). In short, Jesus is great David's far greater Son, and a hint of this is given right from the beginning of Jesus's story.

When the magi came to Israel seeking Jesus, they asked, "Where is the one who has been born king of the Jews? We saw his star when it rose and have come to worship him" (Matt 2:2). They were likely unaware of the prophecy found in this passage, but it would have been very natural for the Jewish readers of Matthew to connect this with Numbers 24:17 and all the other verses associated with it, from the promise of a king from Judah in Genesis 49:10 to the description of the Lord's anointed king and son in Psalm 2:9. This connection would only be strengthened by the magi's mention of "king of the Jews" here, so that the point would be clear: the Lord's long-awaited Messiah had finally arrived!

In Jesus, all the warnings and encouragement of this story come together. In terms of warnings: to put other priorities ahead of him is to forfeit our souls. To fight against him is to fight against God. "Whoever believes in the Son has eternal life, but whoever rejects the Son will not see life, for God's wrath remains on them" (John 3:36). But in terms of encouragement, this is not God's desire. "For God did not send his Son into the world to condemn the world, but to save the world through him" (3:17). And so Jesus is bold to say, "I have come that they may have life, and have it to the full" (10:10). God desires us to have the blessing of abundant life that is found in Jesus. Do we know him? If not, what sorts of questions do we still need answered? What types of sacrifices might we need to be willing to make to put him first in our life? And if we do know him, what does it look like for us to introduce as many people as possible to the joy of the blessing found in him?

Justin Martyr and Athanasius the Great.

CHAPTER 27

Numbers 25:1–18

 LISTEN to the Story

¹While Israel was staying in Shittim, the men began to indulge in sexual immorality with Moabite women, ²who invited them to the sacrifices to their gods. The people ate the sacrificial meal and bowed down before these gods. ³So Israel yoked themselves to the Baal of Peor. And the LORD's anger burned against them.

⁴The LORD said to Moses, "Take all the leaders of these people, kill them and expose them in broad daylight before the LORD, so that the LORD's fierce anger may turn away from Israel."

⁵So Moses said to Israel's judges, "Each of you must put to death those of your people who have yoked themselves to the Baal of Peor."

⁶Then an Israelite man brought into the camp a Midianite woman right before the eyes of Moses and the whole assembly of Israel while they were weeping at the entrance to the tent of meeting. ⁷When Phinehas son of Eleazar, the son of Aaron, the priest, saw this, he left the assembly, took a spear in his hand ⁸and followed the Israelite into the tent. He drove the spear into both of them, right through the Israelite man and into the woman's stomach. Then the plague against the Israelites was stopped; ⁹but those who died in the plague numbered 24,000.

¹⁰The LORD said to Moses, ¹¹"Phinehas son of Eleazar, the son of Aaron, the priest, has turned my anger away from the Israelites. Since he was as zealous for my honor among them as I am, I did not put an end to them in my zeal. ¹²Therefore tell him I am making my covenant of peace with him. ¹³He and his descendants will have a covenant of a lasting priesthood, because he was zealous for the honor of his God and made atonement for the Israelites."

¹⁴The name of the Israelite who was killed with the Midianite woman was Zimri son of Salu, the leader of a Simeonite family. ¹⁵And the name of the Midianite woman who was put to death was Kozbi daughter of Zur, a tribal chief of a Midianite family.

> ¹⁶The LORD said to Moses, ¹⁷"Treat the Midianites as enemies and kill them. ¹⁸They treated you as enemies when they deceived you in the Peor incident involving their sister Kozbi, the daughter of a Midianite leader, the woman who was killed when the plague came as a result of that incident."

Listening to the Text in the Story: Exodus 20:3–6, 23; 32:1–6; 34:15; Leviticus 17:7

In Israel's day, worship of more than one god was the rule, not the exception, and Israel was often guilty of following the culture's lead. Consider:

Even a cursory reading of Israel's history will show that idolatry was one of its greatest temptations.[1] Stuart has summarized various reasons,[2] including:

1. Idols provided an assured, tangible point of access to the divine. . . . Humans have a natural aversion to uncertainty; idols were a way of saying, "You can know you have access to the god."
2. In Israel's day, idolatry was normal (comparable to materialism in many Western cultures today). It would be easy to think, "How could something so normal for most people be wrong?"
3. The worship of more than one god was also normal. In ancient Mesopotamia, people could have a great god and also a personal god, who was often a lesser deity among the many.[3] Israelites might naturally assume they could be faithful to the LORD, the great god of Israel, and to lesser gods as well.
4. Finally, whether the Israelites were eyeing the Canaanites' good crops or the general success of neighboring superpowers (Egypt, Assyria), they would naturally link a nation's success to its idols. It was a large step of faith for Israelites to pursue success by worshiping the LORD alone and not using idols to do so.[4]

---

1. Exod 32:1–6; Num 25:1–3; Judg 2:10–13; 2 Kgs 17:7–16; etc. Cf. the warnings in Exod 20:3–6, 23; Deut 6:14–15; 8:19; etc.
2. Stuart, *Exodus*, 450–54.
3. See Daniel C. Snell, *Religions of the Ancient Near East* (Cambridge: Cambridge University Press, 2011), 27–28.
4. Sklar, *Leviticus* (ZECOT), p. 722.

In this chapter, Israel once more practices idolatry.[5] Their first fateful step toward it begins with sexual immorality, which becomes a sad metaphor for the spiritual adultery they then commit against the Lord.

Israel Betrays the Lord at Moab (25:1–5)

The Israelites are still encamped in the plains of Moab (now at Shittim in particular).[6] Immediately, a crisis is named: Moabite women entice the Israelites with sexual immorality (Num 25:1), which leads quickly to spiritual adultery (cf. Exod 34:15–16), and the Israelites are soon partaking in sacrificial feasts of worship to foreign gods (Num 25:2). Their betrayal is underscored in verse 3 with the metaphor of the double yoke, Israel in one side and Baal of Peor (not the Lord!) in the other.[7] No wonder "the Lord's anger burned against them" (v. 2b). This is the normal and just reaction to severe betrayal.

Though the result of the Lord's anger is unstated here, Israelites would perhaps assume it would be a plague (cf. Num 11:33; 14:37; 16:46–48), which the story will shortly confirm (25:8–9). Atonement will happen by punishing Israel's leaders, who apparently led in this sin (v. 4; cf. v. 14). Their betrayal earns the penalty often inflicted on the treasonous: death. The method of execution is not specified, but their bodies were to be exposed—perhaps by hanging or impaling on a tree (cf. Deut 21:22–23)—"before the Lord" (Num 25:4), that is, like a public sacrifice before him. But the execution was not to be indiscriminate. Only those guilty of the crime were to be executed (Num v. 5).

A Priest's Faithful Zeal (25:6–15)

Before we learn whether this takes place, however, the story quickly changes focus. The plague had begun (Num 25:8), and Moses and the Israelites are weeping at the Lord's tent (v. 6b), undoubtedly earnestly seeking his pardon[8] even as they mourned the loss of life. While this is going on, and in full view of the crowd, an Israelite man brings a Midianite woman into the camp in

---

5. Cf. Exod 32:1–6.
6. Cf. 22:1 and 33:48–49 (it is generally agreed that Shittim and Abel Shittim are the same place).
7. Peor was in the same region as the plains of Moab (23:28) and "Baal of Peor" was the deity worshipped there. "Baal" means "Lord" and was used to describe a significant major deity (1 Kgs 16:31–32) as well as local deities (or perhaps local manifestations of the major deity). Cf. mention of "the Baals" in Judg 2:11.
8. Cf. Joel 2:17.

order to do the very sin that has led to the Lord's judgment and the death of so many (v. 6a; cf. vv. 1–2).[9] Phinehas, son of Eleazar the high priest, sees this and is enraged. Taking a spear, he springs into action, going into the tent after the couple and driving the spear through them. (That it went through both of them suggests they were already embraced in lovemaking.) Immediately we are told the plague stops, though its results were disastrous, with 24,000 dead (24:8b–9).[10] The severity of this punishment, coming just before entry into the land, would underscore the importance of following the Lord's warning not to intermingle with the nations there (cf. Exod 34:15–16).

The Lord then commends Phinehas's actions (Num 25:11–13). The words *zealous* and *zeal* are built on a Hebrew root (q-n-') that can also be translated with "jealous" (so ESV, NASB).[11] While the word *jealous* often has negative connotations, there are contexts where jealousy, and even jealous anger, is not petty but proper. A husband or wife is right to feel jealous anger if their spouse is unfaithful. This explains how the same root can refer to the Lord's jealousy when his people have committed spiritual adultery against him by worshiping other gods (Exod 20:5; Deut 4:24; 5:9) and why it can parallel his anger (Deut 32:16). In this case, Phinehas has the same righteous anger as the Lord, leading him to execute the couple committing the very unfaithfulness that was causing so much harm. Their death was accepted by the Lord like an atoning sacrifice on behalf of the rest of the guilty—two in place of the many—and the plague stopped. The Lord also rewards Phinehas and his descendants with a lasting priesthood,[12] described here as a "covenant of peace" (Num 25:12) because it presumes peaceful relations with the Lord as long as they continue in covenant faithfulness before him.[13]

The story then ties up a loose end by giving background information on the guilty parties, stressing especially that they came from leading families (Num 25:14–15).[14] This underscores the guilt of Israel's leaders

---

9. While Moabite women were also involved (25:1), the fact that a Midianite woman is singled out and also identified as belonging to a leading family shows that the Midianite leaders were involved in trying to harm Israel (cf. 22:4, 7). This also explains why the Midianites are the focus of the Lord's judgment in 25:16–18 and why the Midianite women are focused on in 31:15–16 (cf. Keil, *The Pentateuch*, 790–91 (*Numbers*, 203–4).

10. For how this relates to 1 Cor 10:8, see Sklar, *Additional Notes*, at 25:9.

11. The context favors the latter here (see further comments above); the translation of ESV is thus preferable to NIV in 25:11, 13.

12. Note that the main priestly line is traced through Phinehas in 1 Chr 6:3–15 (see 6:4) and 6:50–53.

13. Cf. Mal 2:5–6 with 2:8–9.

14. Nothing else is known of Zimri or Salu (Num 25:14), but Kozbi's father, Zur, is perhaps the same as one of the Midianites' five main leaders (31:8).

for participating in the sin (cf. vv. 4–5), the righteousness of Phinehas in executing one of them (cf. v. 4), and the guilt of Midian's leaders for leading Israel into sin (cf. vv. 16–18).

The Lord's Judgment on Midian (25:16–18)

The story concludes with the Lord passing judgment on Midian. It is a punishment fit to the crime. The Midianites had treated the Israelites as enemies, leading them into sin that resulted in many of them dying (Num 25:9; cf. 31:16). The Israelites were, in turn, to treat them as enemies and put them to death, a judgment that will find its fulfillment in chapter 31 (and Judg 6–8).

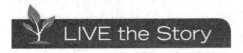

This is a very sobering story that can be very difficult in a day and age where judgment, especially involving death, is viewed very negatively. Three questions might help to put this story in context.[15]

What Is at the Heart of the Problem?

There are two sins here, the first leading to the second. The first is sexual immorality, in this case, by intermingling with those worshiping other gods (Num 25:1). The Lord had warned the Israelites against this in Exodus 34:14–15, since he knows sex's power to knit our heart to someone else so that they have strong influence on how we think and act. This is exactly what happens here, and it leads to the second sin, considered even more grievous: idolatry (Num 25:2).

Reasons for the attraction of idolatry have been noted above.[16] It was not a minor sin. The Israelites had promised the Lord absolute fidelity. To worship other gods was to betray him, leading biblical writers to use the language of "sexual immorality" to describe it (Exod 34:15; Lev 17:7; Deut 31:16; etc.). This was a fitting metaphor, since the Lord himself had entered into covenant relationship with the Israelites, and they betrayed that covenant, like an adulterous spouse, whenever they worshipped other gods.[17] Such language reminds us that the Bible portrays sin as intensely personal. We tend to think of sin as breaking a rule; the Bible thinks of it as betraying a relationship. This is especially the case when we put anything else ahead of the Lord, from actual

---

15. For an alternative homiletical approach, see p. 179n13.
16. See Listening to the Text in the Story, p. 316.
17. Cf. Jer 3:1–2, 6–9; Ezek 16:15–34; 23:1–8.

idols to any other earthly commitment, like family or finances or fame. To do so is to say, "Lord, something else is more worthy of my loyalty and love than you." This sets the background for answering the second question.

Why Is the Punishment So Severe?

A plague kills twenty-four thousand people. A couple are pierced through with a spear in the middle of sex. Why such severity?

The question can be answered in two complementary ways. The first is related to the seriousness of the wrong against God. We get a window into God's perspective on the situation through the response of Phinehas, who embodies God's character, as the Lord himself explains: "He was jealous with my jealousy among [the Israelites]" (Num 25:11, ESV). As noted above, this is not the petty jealousy that we so often see in our own lives and the lives of others.[18] This is the righteous anger of a husband whose wife has been flagrantly and publicly unfaithful to the exclusive love she has promised (cf. v. 6), and that despite the faithful love the Lord has shown in redeeming her from the misery of slavery (Exod 6:5–7; cf. Deut 7:8). But it is more so. Unlike human relationships, where any betrayal is against an equal, Israel has entered into an exclusive relationship with a God who is the King of the universe. Israel's unfaithfulness is thus an act of treason as well as a betrayal of love. They have spit in the face of their great King and faithful husband at the same time.

But the severity of Israel's wrong is even greater still since it is also against God's world. From the Lord's first call of their forefather Abraham, the Lord's intent was to bless Israel and to use them as his channel of blessing to the world (Gen 12:3). One way this would happen was for Israel to be faithful to their call to be "a kingdom of priests" (Exod 19:6) and do what priests do: model holy living to others, minister to their spiritual needs, and help them to know and worship their Lord and Creator. When Israel was unfaithful to this call by abandoning the Lord for idols, they were closing off the channel of God's blessing for his world—and God does not take that lightly. The punishment was severe in order to maintain the purity of his people for the sake of his world. Jesus emphasized the same: "I am the true vine, and my Father is the gardener. He cuts off every branch in me that bears no fruit, while every branch that does bear fruit he prunes so that it will be even more fruitful. . . . This is to my Father's glory, that you bear much fruit, showing yourselves to be my disciples" (John 15:1–2, 8). The Lord's severe discipline of his people

---

18. See comments at 25:6–15, p. 318.

is often the other side of the coin to his extravagant love for his world. And speaking of that love leads to the third question.

How Far Does the Lord's Love Go?

In Numbers 25:4, the Lord's judgment on those who took the lead in this sin was for them to be killed and their bodies exposed, perhaps by being hung up or impaled on a tree.[19] To have your corpse exposed in this way was a shameful thing, so repugnant it served as a sure sign that such a person was cursed by God himself (Deut 21:22–23). In Numbers 25, such an execution was meant to turn away God's wrath by bringing appropriate justice to bear on the guilty. In Jesus's case, however, it turned God's wrath away by means of the innocent bearing justice on behalf of the guilty. Indeed, Phinehas is faithful insofar as the job of the priest was to atone for Israel's sin, which is precisely what he does by slaying the guilty. When Jesus atones for sin, however, he is slain on the guilty's behalf. Indeed, Phinehas impales sinners with a spear; Jesus is impaled for sinners on a cross and by a spear (John 19:34). And the Bible repeatedly explains this as an act of God's love for us. "But God demonstrates his own love for us in this: While we were still sinners, Christ died for us" (Rom 5:8).

And so this story serves, on the one hand, as a severe warning to cling in faithful love to the Lord, putting him ahead of every other loyalty in our lives. What might it look like for us to recommit to this? In which areas of our lives are we most tempted to let other priorities take place over him? What does it mean, practically speaking, for our love for him to be greater than any other love?

On the other hand, this story points forward to the ministry of a great high priest who would become the most unbelievably good display of the Lord's love, making a way for our failures against him to be forgiven. Putting the Lord first is thus not something we do unwillingly or regretfully; rather, it becomes the most natural response in the world to such an extravagant love.

---

19. See at 25:1–5, p. 317.

CHAPTER 28

Numbers 26:1-65

LISTEN to the Story

¹After the plague the LORD said to Moses and Eleazar son of Aaron, the priest, ²"Take a census of the whole Israelite community by families—all those twenty years old or more who are able to serve in the army of Israel." ³So on the plains of Moab by the Jordan across from Jericho, Moses and Eleazar the priest spoke with them and said, ⁴"Take a census of the men twenty years old or more, as the LORD commanded Moses."

These were the Israelites who came out of Egypt:

⁵The descendants of Reuben, the firstborn son of Israel, were:

through Hanok, the Hanokite clan;
through Pallu, the Palluite clan;
⁶through Hezron, the Hezronite clan;
through Karmi, the Karmite clan.

⁷These were the clans of Reuben; those numbered were 43,730.

⁸The son of Pallu was Eliab, ⁹and the sons of Eliab were Nemuel, Dathan and Abiram. The same Dathan and Abiram were the community officials who rebelled against Moses and Aaron and were among Korah's followers when they rebelled against the LORD. ¹⁰The earth opened its mouth and swallowed them along with Korah, whose followers died when the fire devoured the 250 men. And they served as a warning sign. ¹¹The line of Korah, however, did not die out.

¹²The descendants of Simeon by their clans were:

through Nemuel, the Nemuelite clan;
through Jamin, the Jaminite clan;
through Jakin, the Jakinite clan;

¹³through Zerah, the Zerahite clan;
through Shaul, the Shaulite clan.

¹⁴These were the clans of Simeon; those numbered were 22,200.
¹⁵The descendants of Gad by their clans were:

through Zephon, the Zephonite clan;
through Haggi, the Haggite clan;
through Shuni, the Shunite clan;
¹⁶through Ozni, the Oznite clan;
through Eri, the Erite clan;
¹⁷through Arodi, the Arodite clan;
through Areli, the Arelite clan.

¹⁸These were the clans of Gad; those numbered were 40,500.
¹⁹Er and Onan were sons of Judah, but they died in Canaan.
²⁰The descendants of Judah by their clans were:

through Shelah, the Shelanite clan;
through Perez, the Perezite clan;
through Zerah, the Zerahite clan.
²¹The descendants of Perez were:

> through Hezron, the Hezronite clan;
> through Hamul, the Hamulite clan.

²²These were the clans of Judah; those numbered were 76,500.
²³The descendants of Issachar by their clans were:

through Tola, the Tolaite clan;
through Puah, the Puite clan;
²⁴through Jashub, the Jashubite clan;
through Shimron, the Shimronite clan.

²⁵These were the clans of Issachar; those numbered were 64,300.
²⁶The descendants of Zebulun by their clans were:

through Sered, the Seredite clan;
through Elon, the Elonite clan;
through Jahleel, the Jahleelite clan.

²⁷These were the clans of Zebulun; those numbered were 60,500.
²⁸The descendants of Joseph by their clans through Manasseh and Ephraim were:
²⁹The descendants of Manasseh:

through Makir, the Makirite clan (Makir was the father of Gilead);
through Gilead, the Gileadite clan.
³⁰These were the descendants of Gilead:

> through Iezer, the Iezerite clan;
> through Helek, the Helekite clan;
> ³¹through Asriel, the Asrielite clan;
> through Shechem, the Shechemite clan;
> ³²through Shemida, the Shemidaite clan;
> through Hepher, the Hepherite clan.
> ³³(Zelophehad son of Hepher had no sons; he had only daughters, whose names were Mahlah, Noah, Hoglah, Milkah and Tirzah.)

³⁴These were the clans of Manasseh; those numbered were 52,700.
³⁵These were the descendants of Ephraim by their clans:

through Shuthelah, the Shuthelahite clan;
through Beker, the Bekerite clan;
through Tahan, the Tahanite clan.
³⁶These were the descendants of Shuthelah:

> through Eran, the Eranite clan.

³⁷These were the clans of Ephraim; those numbered were 32,500. These were the descendants of Joseph by their clans.
³⁸The descendants of Benjamin by their clans were:

through Bela, the Belaite clan;

through Ashbel, the Ashbelite clan;
through Ahiram, the Ahiramite clan;
^{39}through Shupham, the Shuphamite clan;
through Hupham, the Huphamite clan.
^{40}The descendants of Bela through Ard and Naaman were:

> through Ard, the Ardite clan;
> through Naaman, the Naamite clan.

^{41}These were the clans of Benjamin; those numbered were 45,600.
^{42}These were the descendants of Dan by their clans:

through Shuham, the Shuhamite clan.

These were the clans of Dan: ^{43}All of them were Shuhamite clans; and those numbered were 64,400.
^{44}The descendants of Asher by their clans were:

through Imnah, the Imnite clan;
through Ishvi, the Ishvite clan;
through Beriah, the Beriite clan;
^{45}and through the descendants of Beriah:
> through Heber, the Heberite clan;
> through Malkiel, the Malkielite clan.
^{46}(Asher had a daughter named Serah.)

^{47}These were the clans of Asher; those numbered were 53,400.
^{48}The descendants of Naphtali by their clans were:

through Jahzeel, the Jahzeelite clan;
through Guni, the Gunite clan;
^{49}through Jezer, the Jezerite clan;
through Shillem, the Shillemite clan.

^{50}These were the clans of Naphtali; those numbered were 45,400.
^{51}The total number of the men of Israel was 601,730.
^{52}The LORD said to Moses, ^{53}"The land is to be allotted to them as

an inheritance based on the number of names. ⁵⁴To a larger group give a larger inheritance, and to a smaller group a smaller one; each is to receive its inheritance according to the number of those listed. ⁵⁵Be sure that the land is distributed by lot. What each group inherits will be according to the names for its ancestral tribe. ⁵⁶Each inheritance is to be distributed by lot among the larger and smaller groups."

⁵⁷These were the Levites who were counted by their clans:

Through Gershon, the Gershonite clan;
through Kohath, the Kohathite clan;
through Merari, the Merarite clan.
⁵⁸These also were Levite clans:
the Libnite clan,
the Hebronite clan,
the Mahlite clan,
the Mushite clan,
the Korahite clan.
(Kohath was the forefather of Amram; ⁵⁹the name of Amram's wife was Jochebed, a descendant of Levi, who was born to the Levites in Egypt. To Amram she bore Aaron, Moses and their sister Miriam. ⁶⁰Aaron was the father of Nadab and Abihu, Eleazar and Ithamar. ⁶¹But Nadab and Abihu died when they made an offering before the Lord with unauthorized fire.)

⁶²All the male Levites a month old or more numbered 23,000. They were not counted along with the other Israelites because they received no inheritance among them.

⁶³These are the ones counted by Moses and Eleazar the priest when they counted the Israelites on the plains of Moab by the Jordan across from Jericho. ⁶⁴Not one of them was among those counted by Moses and Aaron the priest when they counted the Israelites in the Desert of Sinai. ⁶⁵For the LORD had told those Israelites they would surely die in the wilderness, and not one of them was left except Caleb son of Jephunneh and Joshua son of Nun.

Listening to the Text in the Story: Numbers 1:1–10:10; 10:11–25:18

As noted earlier, the first major part of Numbers (chs. 1–25) focuses on the first generation of Israelites and has two sections.¹ The first starts very positively and is characterized by the Israelites' regular obedience (1:1–10:10), while the second becomes incredibly negative and is characterized by their regular rebellion (10:11–25:18). As a result, they experience the Lord's discipline: it will not be they who enter the promised land, but their children (14:26–35), and the book's second major part now turns its attention to them (chs. 26–36).

A fitting title for this second part is: The Second Generation: A New Start for Israel on the Cusp of Entering the Promised Land.² Just as the story of the first generation of Israelites began with censuses (Num 1–4) and then further preparations for marching into the promised land (5:1–10:10), so the story of the second generation of Israelites also starts with a census (ch. 26) and then further preparations for marching into the promised land (chs. 27–36). But whereas the first generation was characterized by disobedience to the Lord's commands and denied the land, the second generation is characterized by obedience (26:4–63; 31:7, 31; 36:10) and is now at the border of the promised land awaiting the Lord's command to enter it (36:13).

EXPLAIN the Story

The Lord Commands a Second Military Census (26:1–4a)

Just as the travesty of the Israelites' rebellion in Numbers 14 is followed by the promise in 15:1–2 that they will still inherit the promised land, so also the travesty of their rebellion resulting in the plague in Numbers 25 is followed by the Lord's command for them to take a census of their army—implying that they will soon be marching into the promised land in battle. This is underscored by the mention of Jericho in 26:3, the first city they will attack once they enter the land (Joshua 6), and by Numbers 26:52–56, indicating that a complementary purpose of the census was related to allotting the promised land to the tribes. This chapter thus marks a new beginning that looks ahead with hope to the fulfillment of the Lord's covenant promise to grant Israel

---

1. See Listening to the Text in the Story, p. 48.
2. For detailed overview, see discussion starting p. 18. The first generation died out before Israel reached the plains of Moab in 21:20 (Deut 2:14; cf. Num 21:12–13). From a literary perspective, however, the census of Num 26 most clearly signals that God's judgment on the first generation is complete (cf. 26:64–65) and that Israel's story is restarting with the next generation (Stubbs, *Numbers*, 206).

a land. In doing so, it underscores "one of the great themes of the book of Numbers: God's promises to the patriarchs may be delayed by human sin, but they are not ultimately frustrated by it."[3] (For further comments on the details of these verses, see at 1:2–46, pp. 50–52.)

The Israelites Take a Second Military Census (26:4b–51)

The second census is presumably taken in a way similar to the first (see again at Num 1:2–46 for details). Each tribe's numbers are introduced with a standard formula: the tribe, a listing of its main clans (a grouping somewhere between the tribe and a smaller family unit), and the total number.[4] The overall results to the first census are very similar, though there are significant differences among certain tribes, especially Simeon, Manasseh, Benjamin, and Asher (see table below). The reasons for such dramatic changes are nowhere given and any explanations suggested must remain in the realm of speculation.[5] As Noordtzij bluntly states: "Any attempt to explain these differences is futile; we simply do not have any further data."[6]

Four additional comments may be made. First, 26:9–11 recalls the tragic story of Dathan's and Abiram's participation in Korah's rebellion in Numbers 16:1–35. Dathan and Abiram were Reubenites, so recalling that story while listing his descendants fits logically. Since the text mentions that Korah's line continued (26:11),[7] the implication is that Dathan's and Abiram's line did not, thus emphasizing how they served as a "warning sign": act like them, and you will have no part in Israel! The brief mention of Er and Onan (26:19) serves a similar purpose. Both of them were "wicked in the LORD's sight" and perished (Gen 38:7–10). As a result, their lines do not continue, and the warning is again given not to follow in such wicked ways.

Second, the detail in Numbers 26:33 about Zelophehad's daughters helps prepare for the story in 27:1–11.

Third, while the focus of these lists is on male descendants (through whom the line was traced), Asher's daughter is named in Numbers 27:46, as she is also in Genesis 46:17. The reason for this is not known.

Finally, Israel has basically maintained their numbers, despite the death of

---

3. Wenham, *Numbers*, 190.
4. "Clans" are perhaps the focus because of their role in the land allotments (cf. 26:52–56 with Josh 19:1, 10, 17, etc.). For comparison of the genealogies here to those in Gen 46:8–24, including an explanation of some of the differences, see Keil, *The Pentateuch*, 239–41, 794–96 (*Genesis*, 371–72; *Numbers*, 209–10); and most thoroughly, Ashley, *Numbers*, 525–29, 532–38.
5. For a summary of various suggestions, see Sklar, *Additional Notes*, at 26:4–51.
6. Noordtzij, *Numbers*, 248.
7. See p. 299n11.

the first generation and the difficulties experienced to this point in Numbers. This testifies strongly to the Lord's faithfulness to his promise to make Israel a fruitful people, like the dust of the earth (Gen 13:16; cf. Num 23:10).

The Census Results

Tribe	Numbers 1 Census	Numbers 26 Census	Percent Change
Reuben	46,500	43,730	- 6%
Simeon	59,300	22,200	- 63%
Gad	45,650	40,500	- 11%
Judah	74,600	76,500	+ 3%
Issachar	54,400	64,300	+ 18%
Zebulun	57,400	60,500	+ 5%
Manasseh (Joseph)	32,200	52,700	+ 64%
Ephraim (Joseph)	40,500	32,500	- 20%
Benjamin	35,400	45,600	+ 29%
Dan	62,700	64,400	+ 3%
Asher	41,500	53,400	+ 29%
Naphtali	53,400	45,400	- 15%
Total	603,550	601,730	- 0.3%

How to Distribute the Land (26:52–56)

Having finished the census, the Lord makes clear that it was not simply for the purpose of numbering Israel's army but also to guide them in apportioning Canaan. Two principles are named: the land must be given in proportion to a tribe's numbers (Num 26:53–54) and be awarded by lot (vv. 55–56). The method of lot-casting is not named,[8] but it was done "in the presence of the LORD" (Josh 18:10), meaning not only done at his sanctuary but also that the lot's decision was viewed as his (cf. Prov 16:33). Each tribe's inheritance was thus to be received with thanksgiving instead of comparison or complaint since it was a divine gift (cf. Prov 18:18).

The Census of the Levites (26:57–62)

As in Numbers 1–4, the census of the Israelites is followed separately by the census of the Levites,[9] who were not counted in the main census because they were set apart from the rest of the nation to serve at the tabernacle (instead of in war)[10] and because their inheritance would be gifts deriving from that service (and not large tracts of land).[11]

The census begins by listing the three main Levite clans (Num 26:57) followed by derived subclans (v. 58a),[12] each of the latter being mentioned in the list of 3:18–20. Three subclans are mentioned in that list but not found here, perhaps because they were of less importance at this time.[13] On the other hand, Korahites are not mentioned there but are found here, perhaps to underscore that this clan continued despite Korah's rebellion in chapter 16 (cf. 26:11). Finally, the list concludes by focusing on the priestly line of Levi in particular (vv. 58b–61), which, like the lines of Reuben and Judah, contains its own story of warning in the persons of Nadab and Abihu (v. 61; cf. vv. 9–10, 19).[14] The total number of Levites is given as 23,000 (v. 62), a slight increase (4.5%) from the earlier total of 22,000 (3:39).

Conclusion (26:63–65)

The chapter concludes by noting that none of those counted in the plains of Moab by Moses and Eleazar the high priest was counted at Sinai by Moses and Aaron the high priest (Num 26:63–64). In keeping with the Lord's words (14:29–30), the first faithless generation had indeed died in the wilderness

---

8. Josh 18:6–11 suggests that one set of lots consisted of descriptions of parts of the land and another set of lots consisted of names of the tribes; one of each would be chosen and the match would be made (and presumably adjusted somehow according to the tribe's size; cf. Num 33:54).

9. Cf. Num 1 with Num 3–4.

10. See at 1:47–53, pp. 53–54.

11. Numbers 26:62; see at 18:20–32, p. 252. However, Levites would receive cities to live in (35:1–8).

12. Libnites belonged to Gershon, Hebronites and Korahites to Kohath, and Mahlites and Mushites to Merari (3:17–20; 16:1).

13. Shimeites, Izharites, Uzzielites.

14. For further comments on Nadab and Abihu, see at 3:2–4, p. 73.

except for two among them who had clung to the Lord in faith: Caleb and Joshua (26:65). The conclusion thus serves as both warning ("Do not be like the first generation!") and encouragement ("Those who cling to the Lord in faith will indeed inherit the covenant promises!").

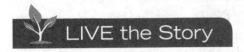

LIVE the Story

When you know your place in the larger story, it can have a tremendous impact on how you live. One of my friends at work is a woman named Alice. She grew up in a small town that her ancestors have inhabited going back one hundred eighty years and she knows that history well. She grew up surrounded by relatives, both close and more distant, who were able to share enough pieces of the story to give her a sense of the whole—and it has left a strong mark. "Growing up, I knew that I was not only a part of a larger story, I knew that the decisions I made would impact the story going forward. I could see how decisions others in my family had made, even long before I was born, impacted the story for good or for ill. This underscored to me the importance of learning from both their mistakes and their wisdom so that I could make the types of decisions that would give my descendants the best chance at experiencing blessing as the story continues."[15]

This chapter makes a similar point. It is a warning and an encouragement, both of which come from the fact that God is faithful to his promises. Two major questions help make this clear.

How Is God's Faithfulness to His Promises a Warning?

As noted above, this chapter concludes by noting that, with the exception of two people, none of those counted in the first census were counted in the second (Num 26:63–64). The Lord had promised to bring his justice to bear on the disobedient (14:29–30) and he was faithful to his word.

What is more, this chapter has three other references to the Lord's judgment coming on the disobedient, whether on lay Israelites, like Dathan and Abiram or Er and Onan (see at Num 26:4b–51, p. 328), or on priests like Nadab and Abihu (see at 26:57–62, p. 330). Each serves as a sober warning: the Lord is indeed compassionate and gracious and forgiving of sin but he "does not leave the guilty unpunished" (Exod 34:7). Because sin is a cancer that destroys his good world, he is diametrically opposed to it and will bring

---

15. Personal communication.

his justice to bear against it. That is his promise. He therefore repeatedly warns against any involvement in sin lest we get caught up in his judgment of it.

In the New Testament, the book of Hebrews looks back on the first generation of Israelites as a special warning to us today (Heb 3–4). The writer notes that because they hardened their hearts against the Lord and disobeyed him in unbelief, he judged them by denying them the promised land. The writer then immediately uses that original promised land as a metaphor for the far greater promised land available in Jesus and warns, "Since the promise of entering his rest still stands, let us be careful that none of you be found to have fallen short of it" (4:1). This happens when our hearts are hardened by sin's deceitfulness (3:13), causing us to turn away from the living God and to disobey him in unbelief (3:12; 4:11). The writer warns strongly against this, knowing that the Lord will bring his judgment to bear against those who have rejected him.

All of this means that we are to look at the first generation as a model of what not to do, especially when it comes to treating sin lightly. How can we tell we are taking this warning seriously in our lives? How should it impact how we view sin, even "small" sins? How should it shape our attitudes toward obedience?

While this chapter does focus on warning, it has an equally strong focus on encouragement. This leads to the second major question.

How Is God's Faithfulness to His Promises an Encouragement?

This chapter's focus on encouragement is evident from its theme: the census. Why even have another one? Because the Israelites will soon be in the land, victoriously defeating its inhabitants, meaning they need to know their numbers for purposes of war (Num 26:2) and for dividing up the land fairly among themselves (vv. 52–54). The census was an encouragement that the Lord's long-awaited promise of the land would shortly come to pass.

This focus on encouragement is also evident in the chapter's final words (26:63–65), which transition from the negative example of the faithless Israelite nation to the positive example of the two faithful spies, Caleb and Joshua, to whom the Lord promised an inheritance in the land (14:24, 30). Their mention here, in contrast to their unfaithful fellow citizens who would not enter the land, was an affirmation that they would enter it (cf. Josh 14:6–15; 19:49). The chapter thus finishes on a note of God's faithfulness to fulfill his covenant promises for his faithful covenant children.

This leads to a related question: Why were Caleb and Joshua faithful? Because they firmly believed that God could be trusted to keep his promises (Num 14:7–8). The believer's obedience is not rooted in their own strength of character but in God's strength of character. The Lord's faithfulness to his promises is what fuels our faithfulness to his commands, leading us to obey boldly, gladly, worshipfully. And if Caleb and Joshua were able to have such faith before seeing the Lord's ultimate faithfulness as expressed in the person of Jesus, how much more do those of us on this side of Jesus's birth, death, and resurrection have reason to believe and obey with full reverence and joy? Because of him, there is a sure and certain hope of a future promised land of such goodness and peace and love that the land of Canaan will seem like only a faint glimmer of light in comparison to that land's blazing brilliance.

How does knowing of his faithfulness to lead us to such a home impact our fears and anxieties? Our views of our current suffering (cf. Rom 8:18–38)? In what ways can it fuel our obedience and love for the Lord? And in answering all these questions, are we remembering the Lord's promise that Jesus is our faithful High Priest, and that because of him we can "approach God's throne of grace with confidence, so that we may receive mercy and find grace to help us in our time of need" (Heb 4:16)? That is a promise we can always count on.

CHAPTER 29

Numbers 27:1-23

 LISTEN to the Story

¹The daughters of Zelophehad son of Hepher, the son of Gilead, the son of Makir, the son of Manasseh, belonged to the clans of Manasseh son of Joseph. The names of the daughters were Mahlah, Noah, Hoglah, Milkah and Tirzah. They came forward ²and stood before Moses, Eleazar the priest, the leaders and the whole assembly at the entrance to the tent of meeting and said, ³"Our father died in the wilderness. He was not among Korah's followers, who banded together against the LORD, but he died for his own sin and left no sons. ⁴Why should our father's name disappear from his clan because he had no son? Give us property among our father's relatives."

⁵So Moses brought their case before the LORD, ⁶and the LORD said to him, ⁷"What Zelophehad's daughters are saying is right. You must certainly give them property as an inheritance among their father's relatives and give their father's inheritance to them.

⁸"Say to the Israelites, 'If a man dies and leaves no son, give his inheritance to his daughter. ⁹If he has no daughter, give his inheritance to his brothers. ¹⁰If he has no brothers, give his inheritance to his father's brothers. ¹¹If his father had no brothers, give his inheritance to the nearest relative in his clan, that he may possess it. This is to have the force of law for the Israelites, as the LORD commanded Moses.'"

¹²Then the LORD said to Moses, "Go up this mountain in the Abarim Range and see the land I have given the Israelites. ¹³After you have seen it, you too will be gathered to your people, as your brother Aaron was, ¹⁴for when the community rebelled at the waters in the Desert of Zin, both of you disobeyed my command to honor me as holy before their eyes." (These were the waters of Meribah Kadesh, in the Desert of Zin.)

¹⁵Moses said to the LORD, ¹⁶"May the LORD, the God who gives breath to all living things, appoint someone over this community ¹⁷to go out and

come in before them, one who will lead them out and bring them in, so the LORD's people will not be like sheep without a shepherd."

¹⁸So the LORD said to Moses, "Take Joshua son of Nun, a man in whom is the spirit of leadership, and lay your hand on him. ¹⁹Have him stand before Eleazar the priest and the entire assembly and commission him in their presence. ²⁰Give him some of your authority so the whole Israelite community will obey him. ²¹He is to stand before Eleazar the priest, who will obtain decisions for him by inquiring of the Urim before the LORD. At his command he and the entire community of the Israelites will go out, and at his command they will come in."

²²Moses did as the LORD commanded him. He took Joshua and had him stand before Eleazar the priest and the whole assembly. ²³Then he laid his hands on him and commissioned him, as the LORD instructed through Moses.

Listening to the Text in the Story: Numbers 20:2–13

Both stories in this chapter look forward to life in the promised land. Zelophehad's daughters want to ensure they inherit property there (Num 27:1–11) and Moses wants to ensure there is someone to lead Israel there (vv. 12–23).

The background to the latter story is found in Numbers 20:9–12, where Moses rebelled against the Lord and was punished by being excluded from the land (see comments there, p. 269). In terms of background to the former story, Stubbs notes that at this point in Israel's history, "land inheritance was patrilineal—a father's land was handed down only to his sons."[1] Why? Stubbs explains:

> It is reasonable to understand that the patrilineal system of inheritance was motivated in part by the desire to preserve the tribal structure.... If the land were equally distributed to both sons and daughters upon their parents' death, marriages between tribes would quickly dissolve the tribal land system.... God's resolution [thus] made clear that the most basic principle of the distribution and inheritance system is not that women cannot possess or inherit land.[2] The ruling showed that the patrilineal

---

1. Stubbs, *Numbers*, 208.
2. Cf. Josh 15:18–19.

system was in service to the more basic concerns that the tribal land structure should remain intact and that there should be an equitable distribution of land to the tribes and the members of the tribes according to their need.[3]

Zelophehad's Daughters Plead Their Case (27:1–4)

Zelophehad's daughters stand before Moses, Eleazar, and the leaders, as one did when pleading a case before a ruler (Num 27:1–2; cf. Gen 43:15). This takes place publicly ("before . . . the whole congregation") and at the tent of meeting, where Moses will ultimately seek the Lord's direction (Num 27:5).

Their case might be paraphrased as follows: "Our father was not among Korah's followers, like Dathan and Abiram, whose lines were wiped out for how they rebelled against the Lord.[4] Our father certainly sinned and died in the wilderness, like the rest of the first generation,[5] but most of their lines continued in their respective clans.[6] Why should our father's line not continue simply because he had no sons? When the land is apportioned, give us a share so we might continue his line" (Num 27:3–4). Their request expresses strong faith since it presumes Israel will inherit the promised land. It also presumes the line's descent is somehow connected to owning property. How? It seems reasonable to suggest that any men who married landowning daughters married into the estate (and thus the family by proxy),[7] just as someone today might marry into the "house" of a wealthy or aristocratic family. By this means, the "house of Zelophehad" would continue through any grandsons that were born.

The Lord Decides Their Case in the Affirmative (27:5–11)

Moses seeks the Lord's legal guidance on the Israelites' behalf (Num 27:5),[8] which underscores that the Lord, not Moses, is Israel's ultimate lawgiver. He agrees with Zelophehad's daughters (v. 7) and gives a new set of laws on land inheritance for cases where a landowner dies without sons (vv. 8–11). In the first instance (v. 8), the land was to go to the daughters, enabling the line of the

---

3. *Numbers*, 208–209.
4. Cf. 26:9–10.
5. Cf. 26:65.
6. Cf. 26:5–51.
7. Cf. 1 Chr 2:34–36; Neh 7:63.
8. See also Lev 24:10–12; Num 9:6–14; 15:32–36.

deceased to continue (see above). If there were no sons or daughters (making continuation of the line impossible), the laws then focus on the larger concern of keeping the land within the clan (vv. 9–11), which was especially important in ancient Israel because land was the most important means for generating income. If land were to be lost when Canaan was apportioned simply because a man did not have a son, the man's entire clan would be disadvantaged and less able to support itself.

Moses Will See the Land but Not Enter It (27:12–14)

The next story keeps its focus on the promised land by answering the question, "Who will lead the people there?" The Lord commands Moses, "Go up into the hill country of the Abarim Range to see the land" (Num 27:12, author's translation).[9] He will eventually do so by climbing Mount Nebo in particular, perhaps the highest in that range,[10] thus providing a good view of the land (Deut 34:1; for possible location, see map 1).[11] Significantly, the Lord speaks of "the land I *have given* the Israelites" (Num 27:12, emphasis added) using a form of the verb that indicates the action is done or as good as done.

He then makes clear that Moses will see this land but, like his brother Aaron, will die without entering it because of his earlier rebellion against the Lord,[12] which put him on the same level as the unfaithful Israelites who were also denied entry into the land (Num 27:13–14; for the nature of Moses's and Aaron's sin, see comments at 20:9–11, 12, 22–29, pp. 269–70).

Moses's Prayer for a Leader for the People (27:15–17)

Moses now shows his love for the Israelites by praying earnestly for them.[13] He combines the language of warfare ("to go out and come in before them," Num 27:17)[14] and shepherding ("like sheep without a shepherd"),[15] the sense of his prayer being, "Since you are Lord of all, giving life to all and thus caring for all as a father does his children, please raise up someone who can lead this people well in the battles they are about to experience—lest they become lost and scattered like sheep and devoured by their enemies!"

---

9. For details see Sklar, *Additional Notes*, at 27:12.
10. See comments at 21:10–20, p. 279.
11. It is traditionally identified with Ras es-Saighah, 10 miles east of the north end of the Dead Sea (Rasmussen, *Zondervan Atlas*, 294).
12. See Deut 32:48–52; 34:1–9.
13. Cf. John 17:6–24 (Stubbs, *Numbers*, 212).
14. Cf. 1 Sam 18:16; 29:6.
15. See the same combination in 2 Sam 5:2.

(vv. 16–17).[16] A lack of good leadership can leave the community vulnerable to division and damage even in the best of cases. In cases involving war, it can be absolutely fatal.

The Lord's Command to Appoint Joshua as Leader (27:18–21)

The Lord answers Moses's prayer by having him get Joshua, a man with just the right makeup for leading the people well (Num 27:18).[17] He had already shown his courage, both in battle (Exod 17:9–14) and by scouting out the land (Num 13:1–16), and had also demonstrated his faith that the Lord would give Israel the land (14:6–9). Having been Moses's assistant since his youth (11:28) would have further prepared him for this role.

Moses is to place him before Eleazar, the leader of the priests, and all the people, so that Joshua's appointment as leader is clear to all (27:19). Moses will then lay his hand on him and commission him, perhaps using words similar to those in Deuteronomy, "Be strong and courageous, for you must go with this people into the land that the LORD swore to their ancestors to give them, and you must divide it among them as their inheritance. The LORD himself goes before you and will be with you; he will never leave you or forsake you. Do not be afraid; do not be discouraged" (Deut 31:7b–8). This act of commissioning would make clear that Joshua now shared in Moses's leadership authority and was deserving of the Israelites' obedience (Num 27:20). As for his responsibilities, one of the most prominent would be leading them in "going out" and "coming in" from battle (v. 21).[18] But he would not do this according to his wisdom. Rather, he would stand before the priest, indicating his submission to the Lord's authority, and seek the Lord's leading by means of the Urim (and Thummim) (v. 21), which were in the high priest's breastplate (Exod 28:30) and appear to have been lots used to enquire of the Lord (see 1 Sam 14:41–42 in NIV). (This seems to indicate that Joshua will not have direct prophetic access to the Lord as Moses did; cf. Num 12:6–8; Deut 34:9–12.)

Moses Obeys and Joshua Is Commissioned as Leader (27:22–23)

Moses follows the Lord's commands exactly and Joshua is commissioned. Since Moses is still present, he will continue in his role as Israel's main leader,

---

16. Cf. Ezek 34:4–6.
17. In 27:18, the Hebrew simply reads, "a man in whom is a spirit," which could refer to the person's gifting (so NIV, NET) or to their courage (the meaning of the word in Josh 2:11 and 5:11, which are also war contexts like our passage). See further Sklar, *Additional Notes*, at 27:18. If "the Spirit" were meant (ESV, NASB, NIV margin) we might expect a definite article ("the Spirit"; cf. Num 11:25–26 with 11:29).
18. See n14.

but the nation now knows his successor. (Later, just before Moses's death, the Lord himself will reaffirm Joshua's commissioning; Deut 31:14, 23.)

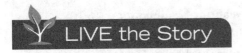

LIVE the Story

As noted above,[19] this chapter's two stories are united by how they look forward to life in the promised land. But each story has unique lessons to teach.

What Do We Learn from Zelophehad's Daughters about Faith?

Generally speaking, Zelophehad's daughters model trust in the Lord's faithfulness. They make their request because they believe that God's promise to grant Israel the land will happen soon (Num 27:3–4). Notably, where their forefathers lacked faith in God's promises, these women boldly step forward to claim them,[20] and the Lord chooses to highlight their actions as the first model of faith we see in the second generation.[21]

More specifically speaking, Zelophehad's daughters model a faith that seeks the Lord and his word to address injustice. In their case, the injustice was particularly related to their lack of opportunity to carry on their father's line (see at 27:1–4, p. 336). But the underlying principle was that this injustice was rooted in cultural practices among God's people, and they looked for a word from the Lord to address it.

This is the opposite of what has often happened in church history, where culture is not challenged in light of God's word, but the teaching of God's word is challenged (or ignored!) in light of cultural concerns. Indeed, the church faces an ongoing danger of enshrining certain cultural values and never letting God's word speak to them—whether values from the wider culture, like materialism or individualism, or values from our respective Christian traditions rooted in extrabiblical rules and laws we have accrued over the years.

Zelophehad's daughters teach us a more excellent way. "There is an injustice among your people, Lord, and we are requesting you to speak to it." What might it look like for us to come to the Lord and his word with a similar attitude? Are we in danger of dismissing injustices too quickly, especially as experienced by those not in power? How can we follow Zelophehad's daughters by seeking a word from the Lord, asking him to bring justice to

---

19. Listening to the Text in the Story, p. 335.
20. Duguid, *Numbers*, 306.
21. Cf. Matt 26:13 (Wenham, *Numbers*, 194).

bear—even asking him to upend cultural assumptions if they are getting in the way of justice?

What Do We Learn from Moses about Leadership?

While the second story begins with a reminder about Moses's failure as a leader (Num 27:12–14), it quickly turns to show us Moses at his best, praying earnestly for his people. His actions and words both model that a good leader is like a good shepherd.

The Bible frequently compares the leaders of God's people to shepherds. This is true for human leaders, such as a king (2 Sam 5:2; Ps 78:70–71) or a leader in general (Jer 3:15; Ezek 34:2–10), and for the Lord himself (Pss 23:1; 78:52; Isa 40:11; John 10:11, 14). The metaphor is very natural to make since those being led are readily comparable to a flock of sheep: just as a flock without a shepherd becomes quickly scattered and easy prey (cf. Ezek 34:5), so also a group of people without a good leader are quickly susceptible to disarray and even danger. Moses, who was himself a shepherd (Exod 3:1), knows these things intimately and thus prays with deep concern for good leadership for God's people (Num 27:16–17).

The shepherd metaphor also points to what should characterize godly leaders, especially protecting and caring for their flock. As Stubbs notes:

> Jesus's commissioning of Simon Peter to lead his "lambs" is carefully structured around this image [of the shepherd] (John 21:15–19). Three times Jesus asks Peter, "Do you love me?" And Peter is told to feed and tend Jesus's people. *Love for Jesus and compassion for God's people are shown to be at the center of Christian leadership.* . . . The images of Jesus as good shepherd, washer of the disciple's feet, and crucified Messiah all combine *to give an image of leadership of God's people in which love, service, and guidance are emphasized*, while prestige and use of coercive power are severely critiqued.[22]

As Jesus himself said, "I am the good shepherd. The good shepherd *lays down his life for the sheep*" (John 10:11, emphasis added). We do well to ask, "What are the first things that come to mind when we think of a great leader? And how do these things compare to the Bible's emphasis on the humble service, protection, sacrifice, and care that should characterize great leaders?" These questions in turn lead to a final one.

---

22. Stubbs, *Numbers*, 213, emphasis added.

What Is the Key to Being a Good Shepherd?

When the Lord identifies Joshua as Israel's next leader, he makes clear that Joshua must follow the Lord's lead (Num 27:21). And that is the key. When we come and stand before the Lord's presence for guidance and direction, we have the opportunity to seek his help and guidance and also to be humbled and remember that his character of protective love and care is what we are to embody in our own leadership. In truth, a leader of God's people is always an under-shepherd, in service of a far greater Shepherd he or she is serving and desiring to imitate. As Peter said to a group of elders, "Be shepherds of God's flock that is under your care, watching over them . . . not lording it over those entrusted to you, but being examples to the flock. And when *the Chief Shepherd* appears, you will receive the crown of glory that will never fade away" (1 Pet 5:2–4, emphasis added).

One of my professors in seminary, himself a pastor, once exhorted us, "Do not let anyone give you the title of 'senior pastor.' Instead, take the title 'senior under-pastor' as a reminder to both you and your congregation that Jesus is your church's ultimate leader." Would such an approach work in our context? (If not, does that actually show how much we need it?) What can we do to help ourselves and our people remember that leadership among God's people is always done in service and imitation of Jesus? Because if we can remember that, we have every hope of shepherding well as we look to him for help and strength.

CHAPTER 30

Numbers 28:1–29:40

 LISTEN to the Story

²⁸:¹The LORD said to Moses, ²"Give this command to the Israelites and say to them: 'Make sure that you present to me at the appointed time my food offerings, as an aroma pleasing to me.' ³Say to them: 'This is the food offering you are to present to the LORD: two lambs a year old without defect, as a regular burnt offering each day. ⁴Offer one lamb in the morning and the other at twilight, ⁵together with a grain offering of a tenth of an ephah of the finest flour mixed with a quarter of a hin of oil from pressed olives. ⁶This is the regular burnt offering instituted at Mount Sinai as a pleasing aroma, a food offering presented to the LORD. ⁷The accompanying drink offering is to be a quarter of a hin of fermented drink with each lamb. Pour out the drink offering to the LORD at the sanctuary. ⁸Offer the second lamb at twilight, along with the same kind of grain offering and drink offering that you offer in the morning. This is a food offering, an aroma pleasing to the LORD.

⁹"'On the Sabbath day, make an offering of two lambs a year old without defect, together with its drink offering and a grain offering of two-tenths of an ephah of the finest flour mixed with olive oil. ¹⁰This is the burnt offering for every Sabbath, in addition to the regular burnt offering and its drink offering.

¹¹"'On the first of every month, present to the LORD a burnt offering of two young bulls, one ram and seven male lambs a year old, all without defect. ¹²With each bull there is to be a grain offering of three-tenths of an ephah of the finest flour mixed with oil; with the ram, a grain offering of two-tenths of an ephah of the finest flour mixed with oil;¹³and with each lamb, a grain offering of a tenth of an ephah of the finest flour mixed with oil. This is for a burnt offering, a pleasing aroma, a food offering presented to the LORD. ¹⁴With each bull there is to be a drink offering of half a hin of wine; with the ram, a third of a hin; and with each lamb, a quarter of

a hin. This is the monthly burnt offering to be made at each new moon during the year. ¹⁵Besides the regular burnt offering with its drink offering, one male goat is to be presented to the LORD as a sin offering.

¹⁶"'On the fourteenth day of the first month the LORD's Passover is to be held. ¹⁷On the fifteenth day of this month there is to be a festival; for seven days eat bread made without yeast. ¹⁸On the first day hold a sacred assembly and do no regular work. ¹⁹Present to the LORD a food offering consisting of a burnt offering of two young bulls, one ram and seven male lambs a year old, all without defect. ²⁰With each bull offer a grain offering of three-tenths of an ephah of the finest flour mixed with oil; with the ram, two-tenths; ²¹and with each of the seven lambs, one-tenth. ²²Include one male goat as a sin offering to make atonement for you. ²³Offer these in addition to the regular morning burnt offering. ²⁴In this way present the food offering every day for seven days as an aroma pleasing to the LORD; it is to be offered in addition to the regular burnt offering and its drink offering. ²⁵On the seventh day hold a sacred assembly and do no regular work.

²⁶"'On the day of firstfruits, when you present to the LORD an offering of new grain during the Festival of Weeks, hold a sacred assembly and do no regular work. ²⁷Present a burnt offering of two young bulls, one ram and seven male lambs a year old as an aroma pleasing to the LORD. ²⁸With each bull there is to be a grain offering of three-tenths of an ephah of the finest flour mixed with oil; with the ram, two-tenths; ²⁹and with each of the seven lambs, one-tenth. ³⁰Include one male goat to make atonement for you. ³¹Offer these together with their drink offerings, in addition to the regular burnt offering and its grain offering. Be sure the animals are without defect.

²⁹:¹"'On the first day of the seventh month hold a sacred assembly and do no regular work. It is a day for you to sound the trumpets. ²As an aroma pleasing to the LORD, offer a burnt offering of one young bull, one ram and seven male lambs a year old, all without defect. ³With the bull offer a grain offering of three-tenths of an ephah of the finest flour mixed with olive oil; with the ram, two-tenths; ⁴and with each of the seven lambs, one-tenth. ⁵Include one male goat as a sin offering to make atonement for you. ⁶These are in addition to the monthly and daily burnt offerings with their grain offerings and drink offerings as specified. They are food offerings presented to the LORD, a pleasing aroma.

⁷"'On the tenth day of this seventh month hold a sacred assembly. You must deny yourselves and do no work. ⁸Present as an aroma pleasing to the LORD a burnt offering of one young bull, one ram and seven male lambs a year old, all without defect. ⁹With the bull offer a grain offering of three-tenths of an ephah of the finest flour mixed with oil; with the ram, two-tenths; ¹⁰and with each of the seven lambs, one-tenth. ¹¹Include one male goat as a sin offering, in addition to the sin offering for atonement and the regular burnt offering with its grain offering, and their drink offerings.

¹²"'On the fifteenth day of the seventh month, hold a sacred assembly and do no regular work. Celebrate a festival to the LORD for seven days. ¹³Present as an aroma pleasing to the LORD a food offering consisting of a burnt offering of thirteen young bulls, two rams and fourteen male lambs a year old, all without defect. ¹⁴With each of the thirteen bulls offer a grain offering of three-tenths of an ephah of the finest flour mixed with oil; with each of the two rams, two-tenths; ¹⁵and with each of the fourteen lambs, one-tenth. ¹⁶Include one male goat as a sin offering, in addition to the regular burnt offering with its grain offering and drink offering.

¹⁷"'On the second day offer twelve young bulls, two rams and fourteen male lambs a year old, all without defect. ¹⁸With the bulls, rams and lambs, offer their grain offerings and drink offerings according to the number specified. ¹⁹Include one male goat as a sin offering, in addition to the regular burnt offering with its grain offering, and their drink offerings.

²⁰"'On the third day offer eleven bulls, two rams and fourteen male lambs a year old, all without defect.²¹With the bulls, rams and lambs, offer their grain offerings and drink offerings according to the number specified. ²²Include one male goat as a sin offering, in addition to the regular burnt offering with its grain offering and drink offering.

²³"'On the fourth day offer ten bulls, two rams and fourteen male lambs a year old, all without defect. ²⁴With the bulls, rams and lambs, offer their grain offerings and drink offerings according to the number specified. ²⁵Include one male goat as a sin offering, in addition to the regular burnt offering with its grain offering and drink offering.

²⁶"'On the fifth day offer nine bulls, two rams and fourteen male lambs a year old, all without defect. ²⁷With the bulls, rams and lambs, offer their grain offerings and drink offerings according to the number specified.

²⁸Include one male goat as a sin offering, in addition to the regular burnt offering with its grain offering and drink offering.

²⁹"'On the sixth day offer eight bulls, two rams and fourteen male lambs a year old, all without defect. ³⁰With the bulls, rams and lambs, offer their grain offerings and drink offerings according to the number specified. ³¹Include one male goat as a sin offering, in addition to the regular burnt offering with its grain offering and drink offering.

³²"'On the seventh day offer seven bulls, two rams and fourteen male lambs a year old, all without defect. ³³With the bulls, rams and lambs, offer their grain offerings and drink offerings according to the number specified. ³⁴Include one male goat as a sin offering, in addition to the regular burnt offering with its grain offering and drink offering.

³⁵"'On the eighth day hold a closing special assembly and do no regular work. ³⁶Present as an aroma pleasing to the LORD a food offering consisting of a burnt offering of one bull, one ram and seven male lambs a year old, all without defect. ³⁷With the bull, the ram and the lambs, offer their grain offerings and drink offerings according to the number specified. ³⁸Include one male goat as a sin offering, in addition to the regular burnt offering with its grain offering and drink offering.

³⁹"'In addition to what you vow and your freewill offerings, offer these to the LORD at your appointed festivals: your burnt offerings, grain offerings, drink offerings and fellowship offerings.'"

⁴⁰Moses told the Israelites all that the LORD commanded him.

Listening to the Text in the Story: Exodus 29:38–42; Leviticus 1–7; 16; 23; Numbers 15:1–29

Previous chapters in the Pentateuch have focused on descriptions of offerings (Lev 1–7; Num 15:1–29) as well as various special days and festivals and their accompanying offerings (Exod 29:38–42; Lev 16; 23). These chapters are most similar to the latter category, though they concentrate especially on the offerings required, thus helping Israel to know how to worship the Lord faithfully. They also maintain the focus on the promised land introduced in the previous chapters insofar as they list festivals that assume a harvest (and thus a land in which to grow crops) and insofar as these festivals point to the ways in which the Lord will bless Israel once they arrive in the promised land:

Every year in future the priests will have to sacrifice 113 bulls, 32 rams and 1086 lambs and offer more than a ton of flour and a thousand bottles of oil and wine. Clearly Israel is destined to be a prosperous agricultural community. These laws about sacrifices then contribute to the note of triumph that grows ever louder as the border of Canaan is reached.[1]

Introduction (28:1–2)

As just noted, the Israelites had already been commanded to bring various offerings to the Lord at appointed times throughout the year (all of which were in addition to individual offerings they chose to make; Num 29:39). While some of these could be observed while in the wilderness (e.g., the daily burnt offering or Sabbath offerings), others were clearly intended for celebration in the promised land when harvests were being gathered (e.g., the Festival of Weeks and of Tabernacles). As in the previous chapter, life in the promised land is on the horizon. Once Israel arrives, the regular worship of the Lord is to a top priority.[2]

As the chapter begins, the Lord first underscores the importance of presenting these offerings (Num 28:2b) and then describes the appointed times and offerings in detail (28:3–29:38). The offerings are listed by frequency: daily (28:3–8), weekly (vv. 9–10), monthly (vv. 11–15), yearly (28:16–29:38; the yearly offerings are listed chronologically). For the size of the offerings, see table on p. 213.

The Hebrew of Numbers 28:2b reads, "my offering, my food, with regard to my offerings by fire,[3] an aroma pleasing to me." The word "food" is used elsewhere for offerings (Lev 3:11; 21:6), not because the Lord was literally hungry (cf. Ps 50:12–13) but because offerings were like a meal, which could express covenant fellowship between two parties,[4] like the fellowship offering, or could honor someone by giving them the very best part of it,[5] like the burnt offering (of which the whole "meal" was given to him).

---

1. Wenham, *Numbers*, 197. For the animals, Duguid (*Numbers*, 311) seems correct in suggesting thirty-seven rams and thirty goats (he agrees with Wenham on the bulls). His number of sheep (1,093) is close enough to Wenham's that the point remains: a large number (over 1,000) are needed!
2. Cf. Ezra 3, where the returnees to Jerusalem put a priority on rebuilding the altar and temple.
3. Translated as "food offering" by NIV; see p. 212n4.
4. See Gen 26:28–30; cf. Exod 24:3–8 (which comes immediately after the Sinai covenant).
5. Gen 43:34; 1 Sam 1:5.

Religious Calendar[6]

Occasion	Date	Burnt Offerings			Sin Offerings
		Bulls	Rams	Male Lambs	Male Goat
Daily (28:1–8)		—	—	2	—
Sabbath (28:9–10)		—	—	2 [4]	—
Monthly (28:11–15)		2	1	7 [9]	1
Passover (28:16)	1/14			1 [3]	
Unleavened Bread (28:17–25)	1/15–1/21	2 (x7)	1 (x7)	7 [9] (x7)	1 (x7)
Weeks (Pentecost) (28:26–31)	50 days after sheaf (cf. Lev 23:15–16)	2	1	7 [9]	1
Trumpets (29:1–6)	7/1	1 [3]	1 [2]	7 [16]	1
Day of Atonement (Yom Kippur) (29:7–11; cf. Lev 16:3–6 for additional offerings)	7/10	1 [2]	1 [3]	7 [9]	1 [3]
Tabernacles (29:12–34)	7/15	13	2	14 [16]	1
	7/16	12	2	14 [16]	1
	7/17	11	2	14 [16]	1
	7/18	10	2	14 [16]	1
	7/19	9	2	14 [16]	1
	7/20	8	2	14 [16]	1
	7/21	7	2	14 [16]	1
Tabernacle's Closing Assembly (29:35)			1	7 [9]	1

6. Modified from Wenham, *Numbers*, 197. The numbers in square brackets are cumulative, e.g., the two Sabbath lambs are in addition to the two daily offering lambs (cf. 28:10, 15). For the dates: the first month was in March/April and the seventh in Sept./Oct.

Daily Offerings (28:3–8)

First commanded in Exodus 29:38–42 (cf. Lev 6:8–13), the Israelites were to present a continual burnt offering of two lambs each day, one in the morning and the other in the evening. The finest ingredients are called for, whether for the animals (year-old lambs without blemish[7]) or for the grain and drink offerings accompanying them (the finest flour, oil from pressed olives,[8] and fermented drink[9]). This was an offering fit for the King.

As noted earlier,[10] burnt offerings had many purposes, including atonement (Lev 1:4) and to serve as an exclamation point to an offerer's prayers, whether prayers of praise and thanksgiving (Lev 22:18–20; Num 6:13–20; Ps 66:13–16), or prayers asking the Lord for help in grave situations, such as war (1 Sam 7:9; 13:8–12) or suffering (Ps 20:1–5). The Israelites' day was thus bordered, morning and evening, with a collective prayer: "You, O Lord our King, dwell in our midst and are worthy of our most costly praise! Look on us with favor! Forgive our sin! Receive our praises and give ear to our cries for help!"

Sabbath Offerings (28:9–10)

Central to Israel's life was the Sabbath. And no wonder. The Sabbath was the sign of the Sinai covenant. To fail to keep it was to deny the covenant relationship and the Lord of that relationship (Exod 31:12–17), like ripping off and trampling a wedding ring—the sign of covenant relationship with a spouse. To keep the Sabbath was to affirm the Lord was Israel's covenant God, like being faithful to one's wedding vows.

The Israelites showed such faithfulness by abstaining from any work on the Sabbath,[11] and the priests marked the day by presenting Sabbath offerings in addition to the regular daily offerings[12] as an extra expression of the Israelites' praise for the Lord and dependence on him.

---

7. For "year old" see p. 115n7; for "without defect" see at 6:13–20, p. 116.

8. The word translated "pressed" (*katit*) "is used exclusively to describe the top-quality olive oil that was produced by gently pounding the olives in a stone mortar . . . and then carefully pouring it off to remove all impurities" (Cornelis Van Dam, "כתת [Beat]" *NIDOTTE* 2:747).

9. The Hebrew term is *shekar*. Its exact identity is unknown, but Num 6 may suggest it derives from the vine (cf. 6:3 with 6:4). This would also explain why Exod 29:40 can use the more general term for "wine" in describing the same offering.

10. See at 6:13–20, p. 117.

11. The same was true for the Day of Atonement (Num 29:7). Other holy days allowed limited work; cf. 28:18, 25, 26; 29:1, 12, 35.

12. Cf. n6.

Monthly Offerings (28:11–15)

In Israel, each month began at the new moon and was to be marked with a special series of sacrifices (the text does not explain why). The sacrifices included a large set of burnt offerings and a purification offering.[13] The purposes of burnt offerings have been described above. As noted earlier, the purpose of purification offerings was to cleanse sin or impurity.[14] In the context of the monthly offerings, this would make it a regular way for Israel to acknowledge sin and seek the Lord's cleansing.[15]

As happened on other worship occasions, the offerings of this day would be accompanied by the sound of trumpets, which were like musical prayers asking the Lord to accept these offerings with favor (see at Num 10:9–10, p. 161). And while it is not clear whether additional feasts accompanied the monthly offerings at this point in Israel's history,[16] at a later point it appears that special feasts were associated with the monthly offerings (1 Sam 20:5–6; Isa 1:13–14). As the text from Isaiah also shows, however, the Lord looked on such religious celebrations with intense hatred if those partaking in them were unrepentant of their evil. Religious duties, no matter how great, mean nothing if they do not proceed from a sincere heart of love for the Lord.

The Passover Festival and the Festival of Unleavened Bread (28:16–25)

The chapter now turns to annual special days and festivals. The first is the Passover (Num 28:16), a time for Israel to remember how the Lord had redeemed them from slavery through the exodus. This was their Easter.[17]

The Passover was accompanied by the seven-day[18] Festival of Unleavened Bread (Num 28:17–25), which began the day after the Passover and shared its purpose: to remember the Lord's deliverance of the Israelites from bondage (Exod 12:17; Deut 16:3). As its name implies, only unleavened bread could be eaten during this time, the same type the Israelites had eaten when leaving Egypt in haste (Exod 12:39). It began and ended with a "sacred assembly"

---

13. Traditionally "sin offering"; see p. 115n5. So also Num 28:22; 29:5, 11, 16, 19, 22, 25, 28, 31, 34, 38.
14. See at 6:13–20, pp. 116–17.
15. Cf. 28:22, 30.
16. The NIV has "New Moon feasts" at 10:10, but the word "feasts" is not in the Hebrew; cf. ESV ("beginnings of your months").
17. For more on the Passover, including links to the events of Easter, see pp. 154–56.
18. For the importance of the number seven throughout these chapters (and elsewhere), see Wenham, *Numbers*, 198–99; Ashley, *Numbers*, 562.

(Num 28:18, 25), in which people assembled together and set the day apart as holy to the Lord, especially by avoiding any "regular work" such as farming. (Other work, such as food preparation, was allowed in keeping with the fact this was a festival; Exod 12:16.) The festival's significance is evident from the elaborate set of offerings required each day (Num 28:19–24), from the fact that it counted as one of three festivals that all Israelite males were to celebrate at the sanctuary (Exod 23:14–17), and from the fact that any Israelite refusing to celebrate it would be "cut off" from the nation (Exod 12:15; see the same for the Passover in Num 9:13).

Taken together, these two festivals, which took place in the first month, began each year with a powerful reminder: The Lord is a redeeming God, the one who rescues us from our enemies![19] Putting these at the head of the festivals is no surprise. Old Testament or New, the Lord's redemption is always the foundation of our relationship with him. Everything else flows from that.

The Festival of Weeks (28:26–31)

This festival is described in a fuller way in Leviticus 23:15–21.[20] In keeping with the rest of Numbers 28–29, the focus in our passage is especially on the animals for the burnt and purification sacrifices and their accompanying offerings. For "sacred assembly" and "do no regular work" see at 28:16–26 above.

The festival was known by three different names: (1) the Festival of Weeks (Exod 34:22; Deut 16:10), since it occurred seven weeks after the offering of the firstfruits of the barley harvest (Lev 23:15); (2) the Festival of the Harvest (Exod 23:16), since it celebrated the firstfruits of the "new grain" of the wheat harvest (Num 28:26; cf. Exod 34:22); and (3) in postexilic times, Pentecost (Tob 2:1; 2 Macc 12:31–32; Acts 2:1) after the Greek word for "fiftieth" (*pentēkostos*), since it occurred on the fiftieth day after the offering of the firstfruits (Lev 23:16).[21] Like the Festival of Unleavened bread, it was very significant and counted as one of three festivals that all Israelite males were to celebrate at the sanctuary (Deut 16:16; in practice, it seems that entire

---

19. It was thus appropriate, centuries later, that the death and resurrection of Jesus took place during this same time (Matt 26:17; 27:15–26, 62–66; 28:1–10), since these were the ultimate acts by which the Lord accomplished redemption in order that we might belong to him.

20. Lev 23:9–14 describes the firstfruits of the barley harvest and vv. 15–21 the firstfruits of the wheat harvest; the latter is the focus here (cf. Num 28:26 with Lev 23:16). See Sklar, *Additional Notes*, at 28:26–31, for a possible reason the former is not discussed and for the small differences between Lev 23:15–21 and our passage.

21. Cf. our use of "the Lord's Supper," "Communion," and "the Eucharist" to describe the same meal.

families often went; v. 11). Its main goal was to celebrate the Lord's provision in the harvest. Indeed, while the Passover and Festival of Unleavened Bread celebrated the Lord's deliverance from the old land (Num 28:16–25), the Festival of Weeks celebrated his provision in the new land. Instead of looking to Canaanite gods, such as Baal, to provide for their agricultural needs (cf. Hos 2:8–9), the Israelites were to remember that the Lord who delivered them from the land of slavery would provide for their needs in the land of promise (Deut 26:10; cf. Ps 145:15–16; Matt 6:19–34).

The Day of Trumpet Blasts (29:1–6)

The number seven was especially significant to the Israelites, so it is not surprising that especially significant rites took place during the seventh month and that the month itself was announced with trumpet blasts. When made in conjunction with offerings, the purpose of trumpet blasts was for the offerer(s) to be remembered before the Lord (Num 10:9–10), that is, for the Lord to shine his favor on them by accepting their offerings and showing his faithfulness to his covenant promises.[22] That purpose would certainly be true of the offerings made this day but perhaps also looked forward to the offerings to come later in the same month, whether those on the tenth day, when the Israelites would seek atonement from all their sins before the Lord (29:7–11), or those of the Festival beginning on the fifteenth day, when they would begin an eight-day festival celebrating the Lord's harvest provision and his redemption (vv. 12–38). Whether in repentance or praise, we are always in need of the Lord's favor, and these trumpet blasts were like musical prayers requesting it.

While there is debate whether early Israelites thought of this day as New Year's Day,[23] it was celebrated as such from at least the fourth century BC. This practice continues today (Rosh Hashanah), and a ram's horn (known after its Hebrew name, *shofar*) is blown to announce it (cf. Lev 25:9, though cf. Num 10:2, 10 for the possibility that silver trumpets were originally used).

The Day of Atonement (29:7–11)

Though not named here, the Day of Atonement is clearly in view (cf. Lev 16:2–34; 23:26–32). Based on its Hebrew name (*yom hakkippurim*), it has come to be known as Yom Kippur and was one of the most solemn days of the Israelite year. While the high priest went through an elaborate series of rituals

---

22. See further at 10:9–10, p. 161.
23. See Milgrom, *Leviticus 23–27*, 2012–13.

and sacrifices (see Lev 16:3–28), the Israelites had two main responsibilities (Num 29:7). First, they had to "deny themselves." At the least, this refers to fasting (cf. Ps 35:13), though it might also refer to other forms of self-denial such as not using ointments (cf. Dan 10:3 with v. 12). Such self-denial often accompanied repentance as an outward sign of a humble, repentant heart (cf. 1 Sam 7:6; Dan 9:3–5). This day's rites mattered little if the Israelites did not acknowledge and turn from their sins (cf. Ps 51:17; Isa 1:11–17). Second, as on the Sabbath, they had to avoid all work, which would help with the requirement to deny themselves since avoiding work would allow for uninterrupted prayer and petition.[24] As the day's name implies, the end result of the repentance and sacrifice would be atonement for the nation's sins and impurities so that the people could continue in close fellowship with their holy Lord (Lev 16:16, 19, 30, 34).[25] Old Testament or New, sin gets in the way of close fellowship with the Lord, and the Lord in his love provides a way to deal with it (cf. Rom 3:24–26; Heb 9:7; 10:3, 19–22).[26]

The Festival of Tabernacles (29:12–38)

This festival was sometimes called the Festival of Ingathering, since it was a harvest festival (Exod 23:16b), and sometimes the "Festival of Tabernacles" (or "Booths"), since the Israelites were to live in temporary structures during the festival (Lev 23:34). (The festival's Jewish name, Sukkoth, is the Hebrew word for these structures.) At least some Israelites lived in such structures when the Lord delivered them out of Egypt (Lev 23:43). By living in them as they feasted on the harvest, the Israelites were to teach their descendants—and to remind themselves—that the blessings of redemption and bountiful provision they enjoyed were gracious gifts from their loving king.

The festival was very significant: it was seven days long (Num 29:12) and included an additional eighth-day closing holy assembly (v. 35); it required extensive offerings (as might be expected during a harvest festival, vv. 13–33);[27] and all males were required to celebrate it at the sanctuary (Deut 16:16; as with the Festival of Weeks, it seems that entire families often went, Deut 16:14).

---

24. Other sacred assemblies allowed certain types of work to be done (see at 28:16–25, pp. 349–50), implying this day was especially holy.

25. It may be noted that the offerings listed in Num 29:8–11 were similar to (or the same as) those of other sacred assemblies and were in addition to the regular daily offerings and those listed in Lev 16 (Num 29:11). The "sin offering for atonement" (29:11) likely refers to what is described in Lev 16:3, 5 (cf. Exod 30:10 with Lev 16:18).

26. Allen, "Numbers," 954.

27. The offerings listed were expected of the whole community, not of every individual or family, most of whom would be bankrupted if they tried to provide all of them.

For a narrative example of this festival, see Nehemiah 8:13–18. Significantly, as the final festival in the religious calendar, it brought the year to a close with tremendous celebration of the Lord's faithful redemption and provision.

Conclusion (29:39–40)

As has been done throughout Numbers 28–29, the first concluding verse underscores that the offerings listed in these chapters are required (29:39).[28] Other offerings can be made throughout the year (such as "vow" or "freewill offerings"),[29] but they may not substitute for the offerings listed here.[30] The second concluding verse ties chapters 28 and 29 together by making clear that Moses was faithful to do as the Lord commanded and passed his words on to the Israelites (29:40; cf. 28:1–2).

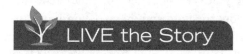

LIVE the Story

Numbers 28–29 look forward to Israel's life in the promised land and describe what their worship was to look like. We may unpack these chapters by asking three different questions.

Why Have So Much Detail on Religious Rituals?

In some circles today, religious rituals are viewed suspiciously. For some, rituals can feel like primitive magic. The better comparison, however, is to prayer. In prayer, we express our heart's deepest longings and needs and hopes. The Israelites were to view rituals as enacted prayers, a way of saying with the body and with ceremony what the heart felt or needed, be that the Lord's help or giving the Lord praise. In a modern context, when a groom puts a ring on his bride's finger, it is not magic but a physical expression of his deepest commitments and desires to show her faithful love. The rituals in these chapters work in similar ways.

To others, rituals can feel impersonal. This was actually a problem in Israel, where rituals could become rote and practiced without living faith in the Lord. When this happened, they were an abomination to him, as he often makes clear (Prov 15:8; Isa 1:10–15; Amos 5:21–24; etc.). Any religious activities we

---

28. Cf. 28:10, 15, 23, etc.
29. Cf. Lev 7:16; 22:18, 21.
30. Verse 39 is perhaps better translated: "All these you shall offer to the Lord at the stated times in addition to your votive and freewill offerings, be they burnt offerings, meal offerings, libations, or peace offerings" (cf. NJPS). For more details, see Sklar, *Additional Notes*, at 29:39.

do are to flow from hearts of love for him. He has created us first and foremost for himself, not for rituals.

Nonetheless, these chapters are unapologetic in their focus on ritual and its importance for faith. As noted above (at Num 28:1–2, p. 346), life in the promised land is on the horizon. Once Israel arrives, the Lord's regular worship is to be a top priority, and these rituals will be essential to that. Indeed, these chapters focus especially on the sacrifices Israelites make to the Lord during these times, underscoring that he is worthy of their worship and that they depend on him for forgiveness and favor.

Importantly, these chapters also emphasize engaging in these activities frequently and regularly. Certain offerings were either daily (Num 28:3–8), weekly (vv. 9–10), or monthly (vv. 11–15). Other offerings were to be made at especially significant times of the year (28:16–29:38). In either case, the Israelites had constant reminders about the Lord and their relationship with him. And they needed it—as we all do—since there is a close connection between forgetfulness and disobedience (Deut 8:11–20; Judg 2:10–12a). When we lose sight of who God is and what he has done for us, it is a short step to start living for others instead of for him. The Lord thus values regular worship habits, not only so we can enjoy fellowship with him but also so they can remind us of who he is, what he has done for us, and how we are to relate to him. Consider:

> Every week, the Sabbath reminded the Israelites they were in covenant relationship with the Lord. Every spring, the Passover and Festival of Unleavened Bread reminded them he had rescued them from Egyptian slavery, while the . . . Festival of Weeks . . . gave them the opportunity to honor him for his provision. As summer gave way to fall bringing the Day of Trumpet Blasts, the Israelites proclaimed the Lord to be their God, and prayed for his favor and continued covenant faithfulness. Just over a week later, they marked the Day of Atonement by coming to him to be cleansed of all impurity and sin . . . Within a week, the Festival of Booths gave them a chance to celebrate that the Lord who cared for their spiritual needs by forgiving their sin was also the God who cared for their physical needs by rescuing them from slavery and giving them a land of bountiful harvests. For the Israelites, this calendar was a classroom, where they regularly acted out, remembered, and celebrated the Lord's character, deeds, and their relationship to him—and taught their children to do the same.[31]

---

31. Sklar, *Leviticus* (ZECOT), 637–38.

Significantly, the Christian church has followed the impulse of these special days and celebrations by creating its own:

> These [days and celebrations in the church] center around Jesus's first coming (Advent, Christmas, Epiphany) and around his death, resurrection, and the coming of the Holy Spirit (Lent, Holy Week, Easter, Pentecost). Sometimes, especially in Protestant circles, these can be viewed negatively. After all, the Bible does not command them, so it can seem that we are adding to God's Word. But the Bible does not forbid them either, and, in light of a chapter such as Lev 23 [or chapters such as Num 28–29], a good case can be made that the church is simply following a biblical pattern, in this case by setting aside special times to remember who the LORD is, why he sent Jesus, and what that means for us as his people. Rightly understood, these times become one more way to help us to remember and to celebrate the LORD's person and work in Jesus—and to teach our children to do the same.[32]

How Were These Special Days and Celebrations to Be Observed?

As we have just seen, they were to be observed regularly, and it goes without saying that they were to be observed just as the Lord commanded. But it may also be noted that they were to be observed communally, and in some cases, lavishly.

Starting with the Passover, the communal nature of these special days and celebrations is evident from their description as "sacred *assemblies*" (Num 28:18, 25, 26; 29:1, 7, 12), implying that Israelites came together to mark these occasions. "The LORD had called Israel to be his covenant community, and they were to remember and celebrate their covenant LORD together. As they did so, they would naturally be reminded that he had called them to be faithful not only in their covenant obligations to him but to one another as well. They were now all part of the same family, and family members are to love and support one another."[33]

In keeping with this, the New Testament exhorts believers to gather regularly in the context of a local church (Heb 10:24–25). The Lord desires his children to be connected to a local church community for encouragement as they seek to serve him faithfully. This can be very challenging for some,

---

32. Ibid., 638–39.
33. Ibid., 639. As Gane (*Leviticus, Numbers*, 758) notes, seeing the communal nature of these celebrations helps us to "gain appreciation for the *corporate* dimension of redemption: The Lord saves people to be a community rather than simply isolated individuals" (emphasis original).

especially if they've experienced significant harm from the local church. Rather than simply withdraw, what does it look like to pray for healing? To seek reconciliation? Or to ask the Lord for a body of believers who really will be an encouragement? The Lord has called us out of the world but into a body and desires we stay strongly connected to it.

Along with the communal nature of these special days and celebrations is the lavish way that some of them were celebrated. This is especially true of the Festival of Tabernacles, which took place at the harvest's conclusion. As noted above (at Num 29:12–38, p. 352), the Israelites were to live in booths during this festival to remind themselves of the temporary structures they lived in when coming out of Egypt. This made it an opportunity to praise the Lord for his past redemption. But as they lived in them, they would have opportunity to feast on the harvest he had so bountifully supplied. This made it an opportunity to rejoice in his current provision. And they did so in lavish ways. During this festival, more animals were sacrificed than the rest of the special days and celebrations combined! And, if other texts involving harvest produce are any guide, they would have engaged in lavish feasting during this time, celebrating the good gifts the Lord had given them (cf. Deut 12:6–7, 11–12; and esp. 14:22–26).

Reading these texts makes me realize that in my early Christian life I would have made a lousy Israelite because I looked at lavishness as worldliness and at excess as poor stewardship. I think especially of the day, during our engagement, that my wife Ski and I were getting some pre-marital counseling from a wise and mature Christian man. I had just said that I wanted to spend as little on the wedding as possible in order to be a good steward. His response startled me: "God is lavish." I didn't like his response at first! For me, stewardship meant saving as much as you could. But I had missed the point. My focus was not on how to celebrate; it was on how to avoid spending. Sitting beside me was the greatest earthly gift the Lord has ever given me, and all I could think about was saving, not celebrating.

This is not to say we can be irresponsible. But it is to say that the Lord sets a pattern of celebrating his lavish goodness and lavish love in lavish ways. The wise and mature Christian man was right: God *is* lavish. He provides good gifts and invites us to partake of them and to celebrate them with gusto because these are the good gifts of our father. Sometimes that will mean money is spent more lavishly than we normally would, though it may also mean we are lavish with our time, spending more of it than we normally would in order to celebrate God's good and precious gifts to us. We do well to ask, "What might this mean for us when Easter and Christmas come around? Or how we might respond with lavish thanks when we see the Lord answer a significant prayer?" When a woman showed Jesus lavish love by breaking a very expensive jar of perfume and anointing him, she was rebuked for "wasting" what could have been spent on the poor. But Jesus saw it as a beautiful demonstration of love—and praised her for it (Mark 14:3–9). How might we do a better job of breaking some jars to show our love for Jesus?

How Do These Special Days and Celebrations Prepare Us for Jesus?

In Colossians 2:16–17, the apostle Paul describes the types of special days and celebrations found in these chapters as "a shadow of the things that were to come," then goes on to say that "the reality . . . is found in Christ." Stated differently, these special days and celebrations foreshadowed deeper realities that came about in Jesus. This becomes especially clear with the Passover (Num 28:16–25) and the Day of Atonement (29:7–11). First, the Passover:

> The New Testament writers use the Passover to explain the death of Jesus, who was crucified at the same general time as the Passover (Matt. 26:17; 27:15–26), and is described as "our Passover lamb" (1 Cor. 5:7). It is a fitting metaphor, since Jesus' sacrifice also delivers us from the Lord's judgment (1 Thess. 1:10) and leads us out of sin's slavery into adoption as the Lord's children (John 1:12; Eph. 1:5; cf. Exod. 4:22). It is during the communion meal, instituted by Jesus at the Passover feast (Luke 22:1–23), that Christians remember and proclaim, "Jesus, you are the mighty Savior, the sacrificial lamb of God who takes away the sin of the world!" (cf. Isa. 53:5–12; John 1:29).[34]

Similarly, the Day of Atonement also foreshadows what Jesus has done on our behalf. In one instance, comparison is made between the cleansing of sin accomplished by the high priest during the Day of Atonement and the cleansing of sin accomplished by Jesus in his death on our behalf (the following paragraph and its accompanying chart are taken from Sklar, *Leviticus* [ZECOT], 441).

> [The book of Hebrews] notes the similarity (a high priest achieving atonement and cleansing by means of sacrifice) but also the significant difference: what the high priest accomplishes in Leviticus is a mere shadow of what Jesus the High Priest accomplishes in the far greater Day of Atonement that was still to come.

---

34. Sklar, *Leviticus* (TOTC), 281.

Reference	Israelite High Priest	Jesus the Great High Priest
Heb 9:12, 24	Enters the Lord's earthly throne room with the blood of sacrificial animals to make atonement	Enters the Lord's heavenly throne room with his own blood to make atonement
Heb 9:25–10:10	Repeats the same sacrifices year after year that cannot deal fully and finally with sin	Has presented himself as the final sacrifice that has dealt with sin once and for all
Heb 9:7; 10:19–22	Only he could enter the Most Holy Place; the cleansing was not sufficient to enable Israelites to enter	The cleansing was so thorough that all God's people may now enter into the Most Holy Place, following behind their Great High Priest, Jesus, and what he has accomplished on their behalf

In another instance, the comparison is made between the scapegoat bearing the penalty for the people's sins and Jesus bearing the penalty for ours. See the table on p. 90, and the surrounding discussion there.

In sum, these two chapters leave us asking, "What does it look like for us to regularly remember and celebrate who the Lord is, what he has done on our behalf, and what he calls us to be? How can we do this in community, and how can we do it lavishly? And how do we do all of these things not from rote, and not to earn God's love, but from a sincere heart of worship and thanksgiving for the amazing gift of love he has given us in Jesus?"

CHAPTER 31

Numbers 30:1–16

 LISTEN to the Story

¹Moses said to the heads of the tribes of Israel: "This is what the LORD commands: ²When a man makes a vow to the LORD or takes an oath to obligate himself by a pledge, he must not break his word but must do everything he said.

³"When a young woman still living in her father's household makes a vow to the LORD or obligates herself by a pledge ⁴and her father hears about her vow or pledge but says nothing to her, then all her vows and every pledge by which she obligated herself will stand. ⁵But if her father forbids her when he hears about it, none of her vows or the pledges by which she obligated herself will stand; the LORD will release her because her father has forbidden her.

⁶"If she marries after she makes a vow or after her lips utter a rash promise by which she obligates herself ⁷and her husband hears about it but says nothing to her, then her vows or the pledges by which she obligated herself will stand. ⁸But if her husband forbids her when he hears about it, he nullifies the vow that obligates her or the rash promise by which she obligates herself, and the LORD will release her.

⁹"Any vow or obligation taken by a widow or divorced woman will be binding on her.

¹⁰"If a woman living with her husband makes a vow or obligates herself by a pledge under oath ¹¹and her husband hears about it but says nothing to her and does not forbid her, then all her vows or the pledges by which she obligated herself will stand. ¹²But if her husband nullifies them when he hears about them, then none of the vows or pledges that came from her lips will stand. Her husband has nullified them, and the LORD will release her. ¹³Her husband may confirm or nullify any vow she makes or any sworn pledge to deny herself. ¹⁴But if her husband says nothing to

> her about it from day to day, then he confirms all her vows or the pledges binding on her. He confirms them by saying nothing to her when he hears about them. ¹⁵If, however, he nullifies them some time after he hears about them, then he must bear the consequences of her wrongdoing."
>
> ¹⁶These are the regulations the LORD gave Moses concerning relationships between a man and his wife, and between a father and his young daughter still living at home.

Listening to the Text in the Story: Leviticus 7:16; Numbers 15:3; 29:39

Since the previous chapter ended by mentioning vows (Num 29:39), this chapter is a logical place to discuss related questions (especially since sacrificial vows might be done during one of the festivals of Num 28–29; cf. 1 Sam 1).[1] It focuses on vows as well as oaths, and many commentators understand this chapter to be using the words to refer to two sides of the same coin.[2] In this context, a vow is a promise to the Lord to give him something, such as a sacrifice (Lev 7:16; Num 15:3),[3] as an expression of thanksgiving and praise for answered prayer (Pss 56:12–13; 66:13–20), while an oath is a promise to the Lord to abstain from something,[4] such as food during a fast, perhaps to pray about a matter of great importance (Ezra 8:21; Ps 35:13).[5] Vows and oaths were voluntary, but it was of fundamental importance to keep them. To break either was to break a promise to God, which became especially tempting when the prayer was answered since thankfulness is one of the first emotions to evaporate. The Bible thus exhorts the prompt payment of vows (Deut 23:21; Eccl 5:4) and wisely advises that "it is better not to make a vow than to make one and not fulfill it" (Eccl 5:5). We are in no place to break our promises to God.

---

1. For vows in the ancient Near East, see p. 113n1.
2. See Wenham, *Numbers*, 207; Milgrom, *Numbers*, 488; Ashley, *Numbers*, 573–74.
3. Other items or actions promised by means of a vow include exclusive worship and monetary gifts (Gen 28:20–22), devoting a conquered enemy's cities to destruction (Num 21:2), or giving a child into the Lord's tabernacle service (1 Sam 1:11).
4. The phrase "deny herself" (30:13) could include fasting (Ps 35:13) or other types of self-denial (Ps 132:2–4; Dan 10:3). Outside of this chapter, an oath may refer broadly to any type of promise made in God's name (Gen 24:3–9) or specifically to a promise inviting God's judgment if not kept (1 Kgs 2:23).
5. See fuller discussion in Milgrom, *Numbers*, 488–90.

EXPLAIN the Story

This chapter opens by addressing the vows and oaths of a man (Num 30:1–2) and then turns to address those of women at different life stages and/or in different marital states (vv. 3–15). The space given to women's vows and oaths makes clear where the chapter's focus lies, as does the conclusion, which directly implies the chapter's goal has been to answer the question, "What happens when a woman under the authority of her father or husband makes a vow or oath?" (v. 16). As such, this chapter assumes the family structure of ancient Israel, in which a young unmarried woman living at home was under her father's authority and a wife was under her husband's authority.

The Vows and Oaths of a Man (30:1–2)

The opening verse may imply the leaders brought a question about vows and oaths to Moses, who then sought the Lord and is now bringing them the answer (Num 30:1).[6] The first law is the most straightforward: a man "must not break his word but must do everything he said" (v. 2). The word for "break" could also be translated "profane." Vows and oaths were considered holy because they involved promises made to the Lord.[7] The law also appears to assume an adult male no longer under the authority of his father. Other scenarios with men, such as a young unmarried man at home under his father's authority, are not considered, perhaps because the chapter's focus is especially on addressing the question of a woman living under the authority of another (see previous paragraph). Possibly, it was assumed that the same principle applied to a young unmarried man living at home as applied to a young unmarried woman living at home.[8]

The Vows and Oaths of a Woman (30:3–15)

A number of different scenarios are now given. In each, the question is, "Does the vow or oath[9] of the woman stand, or are there situations in which it may be annulled?" The basic answer is, "If the woman is under the authority of her

---

6. Cf. 9:6–14; 15:32–36; 27:1–11.

7. For the difference between vows and oaths, see above, Listening to the Text in the Story, p. 360.

8. For evidence that the laws on annulling vows in this chapter are not comprehensive, see discussion at end of this chapter: Live the Story: Are There Any Other Cases When a Vow or Oath May Be Nullified?

9. Verses 10 and 14 mention the pledge made with the oath; the rest of the passage simply mentions the pledges (assuming these are made with oaths). Cf. 30:2.

father or husband, then, when he learns of the vow or oath, he may confirm it through his silence or annul it by saying so. If he does annul it immediately, the Lord will release her from it.[10] If he annuls it later, he will be held responsible. If the woman is under the authority of neither father nor husband, her vow or oath will stand." The following table summarizes the scenarios:

Reference	Woman's Situation	Responsibility of Father or Husband
30:3–5	A young unmarried woman living at home makes a vow or oath (see n9).	Her father may confirm it through his silence or annul it by saying so. If the latter, the Lord releases her from it.
30:6–8	A woman makes a vow or oath and then marries and is now under her husband's authority.	Her husband may confirm it through his silence or annul it by saying so. If the latter, the Lord releases her from it.
30:9	A widow or divorcée makes a vow or oath. It stands since she, like the man in 30:2, is not under another's authority and thus has no one to nullify it (30:9). Like that man, she would have to be very wise when making vows or oaths.	Not applicable.
30:10–12	A woman makes a vow or oath after becoming a wife.	See at 30:6–8 above.
30:13–15	A woman makes a vow or oath after becoming a wife.	The husband's ability to confirm or annul his wife's vow or oath is restated (30:13). The text then underscores that his silence after hearing his wife's vow or oath confirms it (30:14) and warns that if he annuls it at a later date (thus forbidding her from doing it), the Lord will hold him responsible for the broken vow or oath (30:15).

---

10. Heb. "the Lord will forgive her," that is, she need fear no punishment.

Such laws had practical benefits for the woman and her family. On the one hand, they offered her protection if a father or husband prevented her from fulfilling a vow; she was in no way guilty in such cases. At the same time, allowing the husband or father to nullify an oath was also a protection to the family since there were often financial consequences to a vow (such as a promise to sacrifice an animal) that could bring hardship to the family if too extreme (see Num 30:6, which implies rash vows were a reality; cf. Lev 5:4).[11]

Conclusion (30:16)

The conclusion makes clear this chapter has focused on the specific question of a husband's role in confirming or nullifying the vow or oath of his wife and a father's role in the same with his young daughter.

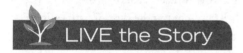

The function of vows has been described at Numbers 6 (Listening to the Text in the Story, pp. 113–14) and of vows and oaths above (Listening to the Text in the Story, p. 360). In order to understand their relevance in this chapter, we may ask three questions.

What's the Point If You're an Israelite?

While this chapter identifies instances when a vow or an oath may be nullified, its underlying principle is that vows and oaths to the Lord must be kept. There are exceptions, but the rule was to stay true to your promises, even if costly.

Psalm 15 emphasizes the same in its list of qualities that describe the person whose life is pleasing to God. The list includes walking blamelessly, having upright speech, and showing the poor compassion, but right in the middle is this quality: "[this person] keeps an oath even when it hurts, and does not change their mind" (v. 4). True love and honor is shown most clearly with costly obedience, and a godly man or woman is characterized by staying true to their commitments to God—even when it hurts—so they may honor him.

In many modern contexts, vows or oaths are not as common among Christians today, but the commitment underlying such vows or oaths must still be true of every believer. To be a Christian is to commit to follow Jesus, no matter the cost, and our obedience to his commands is in this way comparable

---

11. As noted above (see at 30:1–2, p. 361), Israelites possibly assumed the same would apply to a young unmarried man living at home.

to a vow or an oath. To modify the language of Psalm 15:4, a Christian is to be a person who "maintains obedience to Christ even when it hurts, and does not change their mind." Once again, true love and honor is shown most clearly with costly obedience, and Jesus is worthy of all the love and honor we could possibly give.

Can We Still Make Oaths and Vows?

In this passage, vows are promises to God to give him something in response to answered prayer and oaths are promises to God to deny oneself in some way, such as fasting, often for the purpose of focused prayer.[12] Nowhere in the New Testament are these types of vows or oaths forbidden.[13] The book of Acts tells of Paul paying for the costs associated with a vow that four Jewish Christians had made (21:23–24) and of making a vow himself (18:18). And while there is no New Testament example of a Christian making the type of oath Numbers 30 describes, there is no reason to conclude it would be forbidden since it functioned as the other side of the coin to vows.

Christians are thus free to make vows and oaths today, and the most familiar example of the former are wedding vows.[14] At a Christian wedding, these vows are promises made not simply to the person we wed but also to God as a way to say, "O Lord, I promise to you that I will be faithful to these words." In some Christian traditions, other types of vows include vows of celibacy, but vows may be made in many contexts. In my own life, my ordination process was very intense and I spent a lot of time praying for God's help. At that time, my wife and I were on a very tight budget but allowed ourselves a very small amount of "fun money" each month that we could spend however we wanted. I had been saving mine for almost half a year and vowed, "Lord, if you bless this ordination process, I will give thanks to you by giving my fun money to some form of Christian ministry." He did bless the process and I was ordained. When it came time to fulfill my vow, half of my heart did not want to! Thankfulness is one of the first emotions to evaporate, and when it does, what seems like an appropriate expression of thanksgiving in the midst of difficulty can seem like too costly a gift when all is well. The fact that I had promised, however, helped to assure that I did indeed give an expression of thanks that was appropriate.

---

12. See at Listening to the Text in the Story above, p. 360. For other types of oaths, see p. 360n4. The oaths identified there appear to be the type that Jesus (Matt 5:33–37) and James (Jas 5:12) have in mind.

13. See p. n12 above.

14. Even if these are not made in response to answered prayer per se.

Old Testament or New, it is important to remember that vows and oaths are always voluntary.[15] We are not commanded to take them and before doing so we should remember the Bible's own warning: "It is better not to make a vow than to make one and not fulfill it" (Eccl 5:5). We must take this warning very seriously; promises to God must be fulfilled. This leads to a final question.

Are There Any Other Cases When a Vow or Oath May Be Nullified?
It was noted above that this chapter is focused on a very specific question: "What happens when a woman under the authority of her father or husband makes a vow or oath?" (Num 30:16). As such, the chapter is not meant to be comprehensive in its list of possible ways that a vow or oath may be nullified or altered, and other passages fill out the picture helpfully. Two, in particular, may be noted.

The first is Leviticus 27:2–8. There we learn:

Israelites could use a vow to dedicate themselves or others to the LORD (v. 2), that is, to his service at the tabernacle (cf. 1 Sam 1:11). This was obviously a special vow (perhaps better, "difficult vow"), and Israelites making it could redeem those they had vowed [by paying a standard assessment fee]. This was a gracious recognition that people desperate for the LORD's help might make very difficult promises ("I shall give my children to the service of the Lord's tabernacle!"). These laws provide a compassionate way for the person to fulfill the vow and yet not be bound by the full implications of the rash promise.[16]

What is more, if the person could not pay the standard assessment, the priest would name a sum in keeping with the person's means (Lev 27:8). In either case, a person was able to make a substitute payment. The vow was not annulled but modified, and where necessary the modification took into account the person's financial circumstances. Significantly, this was done *under the direction and oversight of spiritual authority*; it was not simply up to the person making the costly vow to decide. As applied today, this would suggest those in spiritual authority in the person's local church would be those in a position to help someone determine if their vow was unrealistic or overly costly, and if so, what they might substitute instead.

The second passage is 1 Samuel 14, where Saul had put the people under

---

15. Cf. the warning of 1 Tim 4:3–4!
16. Sklar, *Leviticus* (TOTC), 327.

an oath not to eat any food, on pain of death, until they had defeated their enemies. His son Jonathan did not know about the oath and ate some honey. When Saul found out, he uttered another oath, "May God deal with me, be it ever so severely, if you do not die, Jonathan" (v. 44). The soldiers first respond with a question, "Should Jonathan die—he who has brought about this great deliverance in Israel?" (v. 45a). This is followed by a counter oath: "'As surely as the LORD lives, not a hair of his head will fall to the ground, for he did this today with God's help.' So the men rescued Jonathan, and he was not put to death" (v. 45b). In this case, the people of God collectively were able to annul the previous oath with one of their own and did so because they recognized that what Saul had sworn was not simply foolish but unpleasing to God and unjust. Once again, the person making the oath was not making the decision; others weighed in and decided the oath should be annulled.

The underlying principle in the above is that vows or oaths should be fulfilled. These are promises to God and the default of the faithful is to fulfill them—even when costly (Ps 15:4). At the same time, the Lord recognizes our weakness and foolishness and how easy it could be to make impossible or unwise promises. (Consider a person who sincerely promises the Lord to become a missionary without realizing they are not really gifted for it.) The Lord thus gives examples above and beyond our passage where vows or oaths can be modified or annulled. Importantly, the final decision is not left to the individual nor to a select group of friends but to those in spiritual authority over the one making the vow or oath or to the body of faithful believers as a whole. On the one hand, we need their help so that we do not try to get out of any of our promises by wrongly labeling them as too costly. On the other hand, we need their help so that we do not carry through with promises that are indeed impossible or unwise. Through it all, what should drive us is a deep desire to honor our commitment to the Lord—even when it is costly (Ps 15:4)—because we long to honor him as the one worthy of our worship and praise.

CHAPTER 32

Numbers 31:1–54

 LISTEN to the Story

¹The Lord said to Moses, ²"Take vengeance on the Midianites for the Israelites. After that, you will be gathered to your people."
³So Moses said to the people, "Arm some of your men to go to war against the Midianites so that they may carry out the Lord's vengeance on them. ⁴Send into battle a thousand men from each of the tribes of Israel." ⁵So twelve thousand men armed for battle, a thousand from each tribe, were supplied from the clans of Israel. ⁶Moses sent them into battle, a thousand from each tribe, along with Phinehas son of Eleazar, the priest, who took with him articles from the sanctuary and the trumpets for signaling.
⁷They fought against Midian, as the Lord commanded Moses, and killed every man. ⁸Among their victims were Evi, Rekem, Zur, Hur and Reba—the five kings of Midian. They also killed Balaam son of Beor with the sword. ⁹The Israelites captured the Midianite women and children and took all the Midianite herds, flocks and goods as plunder. ¹⁰They burned all the towns where the Midianites had settled, as well as all their camps. ¹¹They took all the plunder and spoils, including the people and animals, ¹²and brought the captives, spoils and plunder to Moses and Eleazar the priest and the Israelite assembly at their camp on the plains of Moab, by the Jordan across from Jericho.
¹³Moses, Eleazar the priest and all the leaders of the community went to meet them outside the camp. ¹⁴Moses was angry with the officers of the army—the commanders of thousands and commanders of hundreds—who returned from the battle.
¹⁵"Have you allowed all the women to live?" he asked them. ¹⁶"They were the ones who followed Balaam's advice and enticed the Israelites to be unfaithful to the Lord in the Peor incident, so that a plague struck the Lord's people. ¹⁷Now kill all the boys. And kill every woman who has

slept with a man, ¹⁸but save for yourselves every girl who has never slept with a man.

¹⁹"Anyone who has killed someone or touched someone who was killed must stay outside the camp seven days. On the third and seventh days you must purify yourselves and your captives. ²⁰Purify every garment as well as everything made of leather, goat hair or wood."

²¹Then Eleazar the priest said to the soldiers who had gone into battle, "This is what is required by the law that the LORD gave Moses: ²²Gold, silver, bronze, iron, tin, lead ²³and anything else that can withstand fire must be put through the fire, and then it will be clean. But it must also be purified with the water of cleansing. And whatever cannot withstand fire must be put through that water. ²⁴On the seventh day wash your clothes and you will be clean. Then you may come into the camp."

²⁵The LORD said to Moses, ²⁶"You and Eleazar the priest and the family heads of the community are to count all the people and animals that were captured. ²⁷Divide the spoils equally between the soldiers who took part in the battle and the rest of the community. ²⁸From the soldiers who fought in the battle, set apart as tribute for the LORD one out of every five hundred, whether people, cattle, donkeys or sheep. ²⁹Take this tribute from their half share and give it to Eleazar the priest as the LORD's part. ³⁰From the Israelites' half, select one out of every fifty, whether people, cattle, donkeys, sheep or other animals. Give them to the Levites, who are responsible for the care of the LORD's tabernacle." ³¹So Moses and Eleazar the priest did as the LORD commanded Moses.

³²The plunder remaining from the spoils that the soldiers took was 675,000 sheep, ³³72,000 cattle, ³⁴61,000 donkeys ³⁵and 32,000 women who had never slept with a man.

³⁶The half share of those who fought in the battle was:

337,500 sheep, ³⁷of which the tribute for the LORD was 675;
³⁸36,000 cattle, of which the tribute for the LORD was 72;
³⁹30,500 donkeys, of which the tribute for the LORD was 61;
⁴⁰16,000 people, of whom the tribute for the LORD was 32.

⁴¹Moses gave the tribute to Eleazar the priest as the LORD's part, as the LORD commanded Moses.

⁴²The half belonging to the Israelites, which Moses set apart from that of

the fighting men—⁴³the community's half—was 337,500 sheep, ⁴⁴36,000 cattle, ⁴⁵30,500 donkeys ⁴⁶and 16,000 people. ⁴⁷From the Israelites' half, Moses selected one out of every fifty people and animals, as the LORD commanded him, and gave them to the Levites, who were responsible for the care of the LORD's tabernacle.

⁴⁸Then the officers who were over the units of the army—the commanders of thousands and commanders of hundreds—went to Moses ⁴⁹and said to him, "Your servants have counted the soldiers under our command, and not one is missing. ⁵⁰So we have brought as an offering to the LORD the gold articles each of us acquired—armlets, bracelets, signet rings, earrings and necklaces—to make atonement for ourselves before the LORD."

⁵¹Moses and Eleazar the priest accepted from them the gold—all the crafted articles. ⁵²All the gold from the commanders of thousands and commanders of hundreds that Moses and Eleazar presented as a gift to the LORD weighed 16,750 shekels. ⁵³Each soldier had taken plunder for himself. ⁵⁴Moses and Eleazar the priest accepted the gold from the commanders of thousands and commanders of hundreds and brought it into the tent of meeting as a memorial for the Israelites before the LORD.

Listening to the Text in the Story: Genesis 24:28–31; 34:27–29

In ancient warfare, victory was often followed by taking spoils and captives and by destroying the defeated cities.[1] The spoils would include flocks and herds and any other transportable item of value (Gen 24:30–31; Deut 2:35). The captives could include entire populations (2 Chr 28:5; Isa 14:2) or, in cases where the men had been killed in battle, the women and children who remained (Gen 34:29; Deut 20:14). The children would help strengthen the viability of existing families and the women would help in the creation of new ones. In a world without strong social programs, the family was the social security net, and survival meant having a strong family so that your children could care for you as you aged (just as you cared for your parents as they aged). The importance of belonging to a strong family also meant that when the men in an area had been killed in battle, the taking of women and children captive was of benefit to them, not only their captors, since

---

1. For the latter, see Judg 18:27; 1 Sam 30:3.

the women and children now had opportunity to belong to a family (not to mention the protection it gave them from the potential ravages of famine and from further attack). This is not at all to say the situation was ideal or easy. A law in Deuteronomy even names the sorrow that could accompany a woman leaving her old family to become part of a new one. Remarkably, it makes sure she is given time to grieve (Deut 21:10–13). As Wright notes on that law, "We might like to live in a world without wars and thus without prisoners of war. However, Old Testament law recognizes such realities and seeks to mitigate their worst effects by protecting the victims as far as possible."[2]

This chapter ties up a loose end from the previous section that would have to be addressed before the Israelites went into Canaan (cf. Num 25:16–18). In this way, it keeps the theme of preparing to enter the land as a focus.

Introduction: The Lord's Command to Moses for Battle (31:1–2)

"Take vengeance on the Midianites for the Israelites" (Num 31:2a). In English, the word "vengeance" is often associated with petty or excessive revenge. While the Hebrew word can be used that way to describe the wicked (Ezek 25:12, 15), it frequently describes the Lord's righteous judgment against evil, that is, his avenging, often via human agency, a wrong done, whether the evil his own people commit against him (Ps 99:8; Jer 5:9, 29), the evil other nations commit against him (Mic 5:15; Nah 1:2), or the evil the wicked commit against other people (1 Sam 24:13; Ps 58:10–11). The last of these is in view here. Earlier, the Midianites had treated the Israelites as enemies, purposely leading them into a fatal situation (see at Num 25:16–18, p. 319). As a punishment that fit the crime, the Lord commanded Moses to treat the Midianites as enemies and kill them (vv. 17–18). That command is fulfilled here.

We also learn this is one of the last military acts Moses will do (Num 31:2), reminding us of his imminent death (see at 27:12–14, p. 337) and preparing us for the upcoming transition to Joshua's leadership (see at 27:18–21, 22–23, pp. 338–39).

---

2. Christopher J. H. Wright, *Deuteronomy*, NIBC (Peabody, MA: Hendrickson, 1996), 234. See there for further discussion.

Moses's Commands to the People for Battle (31:3–4)

Moses passes on the Lord's command, making clear that the Israelites are ultimately carrying out the Lord's vengeance on their behalf (Num 31:3). He then specifies that each tribe supply one thousand men for the battle (v. 4).

The Battle and the Taking of Spoil (31:5–12)

The tribes supply the required soldiers and Moses sends them to battle (Num 31:5–6a). With them is Phinehas, son of the high priest, Eleazar (v. 6b). Phinehas has sanctuary articles with him, possibly including the ark of the covenant to show the Lord's presence with Israel (cf. 14:44; Josh 6:2–7; 1 Sam 4:3) and the Urim and Thummim so Phinehas could seek the Lord's direction if needed (cf. Num 27:21; 1 Sam 23:9–12). Alternatively, the phrase "and the trumpets" could be translated "that is, the trumpets," making them the sanctuary articles in view.[3] In either case, the trumpets are presumably those of Numbers 10:1–10, whose primary purpose in a war context was for the priest to sound a musical prayer/shout for the Lord's help so that Israel would be "remembered by the LORD . . . and rescued" in warfare (see comments at Num 10:9–10, p. 161).[4]

Israel's obedience to the Lord's command is highlighted as they go to war, soundly defeating the Midianites and killing the men (Num 31:7). The text highlights five Midianite kings[5] were killed, including Zur, perhaps the father of Kozbi, who was central to the story leading to the current war (v. 8; see 25:6, 14–18). Also killed was Balaam, who apparently stopped at the Midianites on his way home to counsel them how to defeat Israel (cf. 31:16), presumably hoping to receive from them the payment he was denied by Balak.[6] His greed was his undoing.

In keeping with ancient warfare, the soldiers took captives and plunder and burned the cities behind them (Num 31:9–10; see above Listening to the Text in the Story, pp. 369–70). They then brought the captives and plunder to Moses, Eleazar, and the Israelites who had stayed behind and were still encamped on the plains of Moab (vv. 11–12; cf. 26:3).

---

3. So Keil, *The Pentateuch*, 808 (*Numbers*, 225).
4. NIV's "trumpets for signaling" (31:6) is a possible translation but perhaps is too restrictive, given the use of the trumpets in warfare identified in Num 10:9–10. NJPS's "trumpets for sounding the blasts" is an equally possible translation and allows for the rationale of Num 10:9–10.
5. In those days, a "king" was often a leader who ruled a very small area. Cf. Josh 10:1–5.
6. See further p. 311, How Is This Story a Warning?

Moses's Reaction and Further Instructions (31:13–24)

Moses, Eleazar, and other Israelite leaders left the camp to greet the soldiers on their return (Num 31:13). (We will learn momentarily that ritual impurity prevented the soldiers from coming into the camp.) Upon meeting them, Moses became very angry in seeing they had let live the very women who had followed Balaam's advice and led Israel to commit great treachery against the Lord, resulting in twenty-four thousand Israelites dying (31:14–16; cf. 25:9).

Moses's next commands ensure that the Midianite women involved in that sin would die, but they also require the death of all the boys and every woman who had slept with a man—effectively referring to any Midianite wife [7]—but to spare any woman who had not (Num 31:17–18).[8] Why? While the severity of these commands may not be denied, it is also important to place them in their original context. We may begin by noting that this was not the normal approach to warfare with nations outside the promised land. Deuteronomy 20:14 states without qualification that women and children were able to live. In this case, however, there was the added factor that Midian had tried to destroy Israel. As a punishment fit to the crime, the Lord determined that Midian be destroyed. (It should be remembered that the Lord also executed severe punishments on his own people [Num 14:35–37; 16:46–49; 25:9]; his justice shows no favoritism.) In the ancient world, the male line was carried on by sons and the wives who bore them, and, in Israel at least, if a man died without sons, his wife might remarry and the firstborn would carry on the former husband's name (Deut 25:5–6) This meant males and wives had to be killed lest they propagate more Midianites (Num 31:17).[9] Not so for unmarried girls (v. 18), who would marry an Israelite and carry on his line.[10]

Moses next commands for the soldiers to cleanse themselves of any ritual impurity that had resulted from contact with a dead body.[11] Earlier texts prohibited such impurity in the camp (Num 5:1–4) and proscribed a method of

---

7. So also Milgrom, *Numbers*, 259. In Israel, sex and marriage went together (prostitutes being the exception) (Exod 22:16; Deut 22:13–21).

8. See Deut 21:10–14 for the dignity with which the spared women must be treated (and see reference at n2 above).

9. Cf. Judg 21:8–12 for the wiping out of a people group within Israel. When an entire nation is punished, the innocent within it—such as young boys in this instance (Num 31:17)—often suffer as well (see 14:33 and final paragraph of the discussion at 14:13–19, p. 201). A separate question is whether the temporal judgment these non-covenant children experienced means they faced eternal judgment as well. This text does not address the question, but good guidance is found in Abraham's rhetorical question, "Will not the Judge of all the earth do right?" (Gen 18:25).

10. For further discussion of God's judgment, see pp. 375–76, How Is This Story a Warning?

11. For details on impurity from corpses see p. 263, Live the Story: Why Are Dead Bodies Ritually Defiling?

cleansing via special waters being applied to the unclean person on days three and seven (19:11–12, 17–19). Those commands are followed here (31:19). Moses also commands that certain spoils of war are to be cleansed (corpse impurity was a "major" impurity and could thus spread to other people or objects; v. 20).[12] Presumably, this would also involve the special waters for cleansing, but since Numbers 19 does not address this, Eleazar provides specific details: any spoil that is made of metal must be passed through the fire for cleansing and also have the special waters applied (31:21–23a); anything else must be passed through water (perhaps by dipping) and presumably have the special waters applied (v. 23b; cf. Lev 11:32; Num 19:18).[13] As for the people, they must also launder their clothes on day seven (and bathe, v. 19), at which point they are fully cleansed and allowed to come back into the camp (31:24).

Dividing the Spoils (31:25–47)

"The war had been conducted on behalf of the whole congregation of Israel, and hence the spoils of victory were also to be shared by all."[14] Half of the living spoils go to the soldiers and half to the Israelites (Num 31:27; see chart below for totals).[15] Of the soldiers' half, a special contribution was to be made to the Lord by giving one out of every five hundred people or animals (vv. 28–29). These would in turn go to the priests, with whom the Lord shared his portion as a reward for their tabernacle service (cf. 18:8–19). Of the Israelites' half, one out of every fifty people or animals was to go to the Levites as a reward for their tabernacle service (31:30).[16] Taken together, the priests (who were far fewer in number) received one-tenth as much as the Levites (who were far greater in number). The same ratio may be seen in 18:26–28, where the Levites give a tenth of what they receive from the Israelites to the priests.

The total numbers of captured people and animals are now given (Num 31:32–35), followed by the soldier's portion (and what they gave to the priests; vv. 36–41) and the peoples' portion (and what they gave to the Levites; vv. 42–47).

As noted in the introduction, it is debated whether to take all of the numbers in such lists at face value or whether they are inflated in keeping with

---

12. See at 5:1–4, p. 92.
13. I have followed the ESV over NIV in 31:22–23. For further discussion, see Sklar, *Additional Notes*, at 31:23.
14. Boniface-Malle, "Numbers," 205.
15. Cf. Josh 22:8; 1 Sam 30:24. Since the soldiers' numbers were smaller than the remaining Israelites, each soldier received a proportionately bigger share. This appropriately recognized their battle service (see Keil, *The Pentateuch*, 810 [*Numbers*, 228]).
16. See at 1:47–53, pp. 53–54, for details of the Levites' service.

expected ancient Near Eastern practice.[17] In either case, these verses emphasize that all Israel partakes in the victory and that all Israel is faithful in supporting the Lord's tabernacle servants.

	Total	Soldier's Portion	Tribute to the Lord for the Priests	People's Portion	Gift to the Levites
Sheep	675,000	337,500	675	337,500	6,750
Cattle	72,000	36,000	72	36,000	720
Donkeys	61,000	30,500	61	30,500	610
Women	32,000	16,000	32	16,000	320

The Offering on the Soldiers' Behalf (31:48–54)

Moses is now approached by the army's very leaders he had earlier rebuked (Num 31:48; cf. v. 14). They inform him they have taken a census of the soldiers and not one is missing (31:49). As with the numbers in the previous section, interpreters debate whether this statement should be taken at face value or whether it is hyperbole, but even if the latter, the point is clear: the Lord was watching over these soldiers! The commanders then state they are bringing any articles of gold that they found as an atoning offering to the Lord (v. 50).

But why was atonement needed? Because of the census. These verses are full of the very same language used in Exodus 30:11–16, which describes what to do when a census is taken.[18] As that text makes clear, a census put at risk the life of the one being counted. The reason for this is not stated, and while many guesses at the reason have been given,[19] no consensus exists among interpreters

---

17. For discussion of the large numbers see pp. 30–32, Large Numbers in the Book of Numbers.
18. The following words/phrases are the same in both passages in the Hebrew: "counted" (31:49; cf. Exod 30:12); "offering to the Lord" (31:50; cf. Exod 30:13, 14, 15); "to make atonement for ourselves" (31:50; cf. Exod 30:15, 16 ["your lives"]); "a memorial for the Israelites before the Lord" (31:54; cf. Exod 30:16).
19. For an overview, see Song-Mi Suzie Park, "Census and Censure: Sacred Threshing Floors and Counting Taboos in 2 Samuel 24," *Horizons in Biblical Theology* 35 (2013): 21–41, esp. 22–28. These guesses include: numbering people was God's prerogative; a census was proof of sinful ambition on the part of the one taking it; it demonstrated unbelief in God; it recalled the gods' ominous activity of making "lists which determined who among the mortals was to live and who was to die" (ibid., 25, citing [but not endorsing] E. A. Speiser, "Census and Ritual Expiation in Mari and Israel," *BASOR* 149 [1958]: 24).

today. What is not in doubt, however, is the need to make a ransom payment to the tabernacle to rescue one's life and avoid a plague (vv. 12, 15). In the case of Exodus, it was a half-shekel of silver per person (v. 13), which would be six thousand shekels for the twelve thousand troops here. The actual total given (16,750 shekels) not only far exceeds that, it is also gold (not silver). This extravagance perhaps comes from a desire also to thank the Lord for his protection in battle. Moreover, it apparently came from the leaders' own share (Num 31:49–50), meaning they paid on their troops' behalf.[20] It was brought to the tent, where it could be put to use for tabernacle duties (Exod 30:16), and served "as a memorial for the Israelites before the LORD" (Num 31:54b), that is, as a physical expression of their desire that he show them his favor and care,[21] in this case, by delivering them from the otherwise lethal danger of taking a census. That he provided them guidance on how to achieve such atonement was a sign of his desire that his people experience his favor, not his wrath. He has created us for himself and provides what we need to be in right relationship with him.

To understand how this story applies today, we may ask three questions.

How Is This Story a Warning?[22]

God's ultimate vision for this world is one of peace, where "the wolf will live with the lamb" (Isa 11:6). But in a fallen world, war will be necessary, whether "in self-defense or in pursuit of greater justice. We live in a world where evil regularly rears its ugly head and must sometimes be combated directly by force."[23]

One instance of this happens when the Lord calls his people into battle in order to execute his justice, as he does here (Num 31:2–3). This is his war of judgment. As noted earlier,[24] the Bible does not hesitate to affirm God's right to judge humanity. He is the Creator, we are the created. As God, he not only has the right to judge us when we die but also while we yet live. Just as the

---

20. The meaning of 31:53 is debated but seems to contrast the regular soldiers, who were able to keep their share of non-living spoil, with their leaders (31:52, 54), who gave from their spoil on the army's behalf (so also Milgrom, *Numbers*, 265; cf. NJPS).
21. See at 10:9–10, p. 161.
22. For an alternative homiletical approach, see p. 179n13.
23. Duguid, *Numbers*, 329.
24. See pp. 281–83, Why Such Severe Destruction?

Canaanites' destruction in Numbers 21 may be thought of as God's end-time judgment breaking into time and space,[25] so too with the Midianites killed here. Significantly, the judgment for the sin initiated by the Midianites began with the Lord's own people, twenty-four thousand of whom died for their rebellion against him (25:9). His justice breaks out equally against sin and in fact begins with his own people as those who should have known best (cf. Rom 2:9). But his justice now turns to the Midianites, who had led his people into sin. This stands as a warning, even today, that God's judgment against sin will come and we must be ready for it.

Jesus makes just this point in Matthew 24 when he speaks of the need to be ready for the day he returns and final judgment comes. He begins by speaking of the flood, another instance when God's end-time judgment broke into the world because of how great evil had become. He notes that people were carrying on their lives, not thinking about God's will or ways, when the flood came suddenly and took them all away. His point is clear; to paraphrase: "My coming and the end-time judgment it will usher in will be the same. You don't know when it's coming, so be ready now by repenting of evil and following me, lest you, like the people in Noah's day, be swept away in judgment" (see Matt 24:37–51). He warns us because he loves us and wants us to be ready, but his warning is real and his love will not overlook a life of unrepentant rebellion against him. We lessen this warning at our peril.

God's warning of judgment leads naturally to a discussion of ritual impurity, which also had to be cleansed to avoid judgment. But the mention of ritual impurity also leads to our second question.

What Does Ritual Impurity Have to Do with Us?

In Israel, contact with the dead resulted in ritual impurity, which we could liken to polluting radiation that clung to you and could spread to others. No one knows for certain why corpses were ritually defiling,[26] but Israelites accepted it as fact and knew that they had to deal with ritual impurity properly. In particular, they had to make certain that they did not bring this defilement into the camp and defile the Lord's holy tabernacle. To do so would be the highest sign of disrespect, like walking across the white carpet of someone's home with muddy boots, only far worse, because in this instance one stained the very home of the King of kings. To pollute his holy home was to say you

---

25. See p. 283n25 and associated discussion.
26. See p. 263, Why Are Dead Bodies Ritually Defiling?

had no respect for his holiness. The Israelites therefore had to cleanse their impurity before reentering camp. To do so was to say they revered the Lord and respected him for the holy God that he is.

Today, however, most people are unfamiliar with the idea of ritual impurity, and the believer in particular might note that Jesus sets ritual impurity aside when he declared all foods clean (Mark 7:19). What could ritual impurity possibly have to do with us? The answer lies in remembering that ritual states in Israel served as reminders of moral realities.[27] In this case, dealing properly with ritual impurity to show proper reverence to the Lord was a reminder to deal properly with moral impurity to do the same. The Old Testament therefore uses the language of cleansing when speaking of the need to deal properly with sin: "Wash and make yourselves clean. Take your evil deeds out of my sight; stop doing wrong" (Isa 1:16).

Importantly, the same is true in the New Testament. In one instance, after listing various sins, Paul remarks, "Those who cleanse themselves from [such things] will be instruments for special purposes, made holy, useful to the Master and prepared to do any good work" (2 Tim 2:21; cf. vv. 14, 16–18). His point is clear: the Lord cannot use impure instruments for his holy work, so remove moral impurity from your life. Stated differently: how can the Lord pour his holy love into the world with a filthy pitcher? He needs pitchers that are clean.

In another instance, Paul uses cleansing language as he exhorts us to deal properly with sin because the Lord offers us close fellowship with him. "Therefore, since we have these promises [of fellowship with God,] . . . let us purify ourselves from everything that contaminates body and spirit, perfecting holiness out of reverence for God" (2 Cor 7:1). To be unwilling to turn from evil is to say we do not want to know him and do not revere him. We cannot walk with God in his holy ways if we refuse to take our feet out of the mud. Through Jesus, God assures us of cleansing when we confess our sins and turn from them, but turning from them matters, even if done imperfectly, and we do well to ask, "What areas of my life are most in need of cleansing? My speech? Thought life? Interactions with others? Practically speaking, what does repentance in these areas look like?"

One particular area we may ask ourselves about is the way we use our resources. This leads to a final question.

---

27. For further discussion see pp. 32–33, Ritual Purity and Impurity.

How Does the Division of Ancient Spoils Teach Us about Modern Giving?

At least two significant observations may be made about the dividing of the spoils. First, they were divided among all the people, whether or not they went into battle (Num 31:27). The soldiers received a larger share proportionately, as was appropriate given their service in battle,[28] but everyone partook of the fruits of victory. The Israelites viewed themselves as a body and thus shared with the whole body.

This same impulse is evident in the New Testament, whether in the way the early Christians sold excess goods to care for the poor in their midst (Acts 2:44–45), or in Paul's words of exhortation to the Corinthians regarding a financial gift they were to raise for poor believers: "At the present time your plenty will supply what they need, so that in turn their plenty will supply what you need. The goal is equality" (2 Cor 8:14).

The second observation is that the Israelites were to make sure to support the priests and Levites (Num 31:28–30, 36–40). Priests were to teach the people God's word (Lev 10:11), and priests and Levites were central to the tabernacle's functioning and therefore to the Lord's worship (Num 3–4). To support them was to show that learning God's Word and worshiping the Lord properly were top priorities.

Once more, the same impulse is seen in the New Testament, where believers are commanded to support those leading the local church (1 Cor 9:14 [cf. Matt 10:10]; Gal 6:6), for the sake of the leaders and of the gospel. Hungry shepherds cannot care well for their sheep.

In light of the above, Christians should find themselves asking, "How can I share any abundance the Lord has given me with my brothers and sisters in need? And how can I prioritize my giving so that I am supporting the Lord's work through those he has called into vocational ministry?" To do so is to show the world the love that exists within the body of Christ and the desire we have to learn from his Word and to worship him well.

---

28. See p. 373n15.

CHAPTER 33

Numbers 32:1–42

 LISTEN to the Story

¹The Reubenites and Gadites, who had very large herds and flocks, saw that the lands of Jazer and Gilead were suitable for livestock. ²So they came to Moses and Eleazar the priest and to the leaders of the community, and said, ³"Ataroth, Dibon, Jazer, Nimrah, Heshbon, Elealeh, Sebam, Nebo and Beon—⁴the land the Lord subdued before the people of Israel—are suitable for livestock, and your servants have livestock. ⁵If we have found favor in your eyes," they said, "let this land be given to your servants as our possession. Do not make us cross the Jordan."

⁶Moses said to the Gadites and Reubenites, "Should your fellow Israelites go to war while you sit here? ⁷Why do you discourage the Israelites from crossing over into the land the Lord has given them? ⁸This is what your fathers did when I sent them from Kadesh Barnea to look over the land. ⁹After they went up to the Valley of Eshkol and viewed the land, they discouraged the Israelites from entering the land the Lord had given them. ¹⁰The Lord's anger was aroused that day and he swore this oath: ¹¹'Because they have not followed me wholeheartedly, not one of those who were twenty years old or more when they came up out of Egypt will see the land I promised on oath to Abraham, Isaac and Jacob—¹²not one except Caleb son of Jephunneh the Kenizzite and Joshua son of Nun, for they followed the Lord wholeheartedly.' ¹³The Lord's anger burned against Israel and he made them wander in the wilderness forty years, until the whole generation of those who had done evil in his sight was gone.

¹⁴"And here you are, a brood of sinners, standing in the place of your fathers and making the Lord even more angry with Israel. ¹⁵If you turn away from following him, he will again leave all this people in the wilderness, and you will be the cause of their destruction."

[16] Then they came up to him and said, "We would like to build pens here for our livestock and cities for our women and children. [17] But we will arm ourselves for battle and go ahead of the Israelites until we have brought them to their place. Meanwhile our women and children will live in fortified cities, for protection from the inhabitants of the land. [18] We will not return to our homes until each of the Israelites has received their inheritance. [19] We will not receive any inheritance with them on the other side of the Jordan, because our inheritance has come to us on the east side of the Jordan."

[20] Then Moses said to them, "If you will do this—if you will arm yourselves before the LORD for battle [21] and if all of you who are armed cross over the Jordan before the LORD until he has driven his enemies out before him— [22] then when the land is subdued before the LORD, you may return and be free from your obligation to the LORD and to Israel. And this land will be your possession before the LORD.

[23] "But if you fail to do this, you will be sinning against the LORD; and you may be sure that your sin will find you out. [24] Build cities for your women and children, and pens for your flocks, but do what you have promised."

[25] The Gadites and Reubenites said to Moses, "We your servants will do as our lord commands. [26] Our children and wives, our flocks and herds will remain here in the cities of Gilead. [27] But your servants, every man who is armed for battle, will cross over to fight before the LORD, just as our lord says."

[28] Then Moses gave orders about them to Eleazar the priest and Joshua son of Nun and to the family heads of the Israelite tribes. [29] He said to them, "If the Gadites and Reubenites, every man armed for battle, cross over the Jordan with you before the LORD, then when the land is subdued before you, you must give them the land of Gilead as their possession. [30] But if they do not cross over with you armed, they must accept their possession with you in Canaan."

[31] The Gadites and Reubenites answered, "Your servants will do what the LORD has said. [32] We will cross over before the LORD into Canaan armed, but the property we inherit will be on this side of the Jordan."

[33] Then Moses gave to the Gadites, the Reubenites and the half-tribe of Manasseh son of Joseph the kingdom of Sihon king of the Amorites and

the kingdom of Og king of Bashan—the whole land with its cities and the territory around them.

³⁴The Gadites built up Dibon, Ataroth, Aroer, ³⁵Atroth Shophan, Jazer, Jogbehah, ³⁶Beth Nimrah and Beth Haran as fortified cities, and built pens for their flocks. ³⁷And the Reubenites rebuilt Heshbon, Elealeh and Kiriathaim, ³⁸as well as Nebo and Baal Meon (these names were changed) and Sibmah. They gave names to the cities they rebuilt.

³⁹The descendants of Makir son of Manasseh went to Gilead, captured it and drove out the Amorites who were there. ⁴⁰So Moses gave Gilead to the Makirites, the descendants of Manasseh, and they settled there. ⁴¹Jair, a descendant of Manasseh, captured their settlements and called them Havvoth Jair. ⁴²And Nobah captured Kenath and its surrounding settlements and called it Nobah after himself.

Listening to the Text in the Story: Mesha Stele; Numbers 21:21–22:1

In Numbers 21:21–22:1, we learn of various battles Israel wins east of the Jordan, taking over a substantial amount of land. This chapter tells how that land came to be settled by the tribes of Reuben, Gad and half of Manasseh's tribe (see map 4).

The presence of Gad in this area has been confirmed by the Mesha Stele inscription, written by King Mesha of Moab in the ninth-century BC. It also mentions several of the cities named in Numbers 32:34–38. Sprinkle explains:

> Lines 10–12 state, "Now the Gadites had lived in the land of Ataroth forever and the king of Israel had built Ataroth for himself. But I fought against the city and took it, and I killed the entire population of the city, a satiation for Kemosh and Moab." Mesha also practiced "holy war" against Nebo, a city rebuilt by Reuben (Num 32:38), putting its entire population to death and "devoting" it to his god Chemosh (lines 14–18). Sihon had taken this territory from Moab (Num 21:26), and then Israel took it from Sihon (v. 24). In the ninth century Mesha retook this territory from the Israelites.[1]

---

1. Sprinkle, *Leviticus and Numbers*, 400–401.

EXPLAIN the Story

The Gadites' and Reubenites' Request (32:1–5)

The Gadites and Reubenites[2] had large amounts of livestock. When they saw that the land Israel had conquered east of the Jordan provided good pasturage—Jazer and Gilead are singled out in particular (Num 32:1)[3]—they approached Moses, Eleazar, and Israel's leaders with a request. They begin by naming cities the Lord had given into Israel's hand east of the Jordan (vv. 3–4a),[4] then note that these and the surrounding lands are good for livestock (v. 4b) and ask: "Let this land be given to your servants as our possession. Do not make us cross the Jordan" (v. 5).

This does not bode well. To this point in the story, the land the Lord had promised was equated with Canaan, west of the Jordan (Gen 17:8; 48:3–4; Lev 14:34; cf. Num 34:2–12). What is more, while the last request could mean, "Do not make us cross the Jordan *for the sake of inheriting land*, though we will cross for other matters such as warfare," it reads absolutely: "Do not make us cross the Jordan *at all*."

Moses's Angry Response (32:6–15)

Moses is enraged. They are asking to repeat the previous generation's rebellious refusal to enter the promised land, an act that would cause this entire generation to do the same. If ten men had led the first generation astray, how much more would two tribes![5] Moses's response might be paraphrased: "So your brothers will go to fight while you stay here (Num 32:6)? You will totally discourage them from entering the land the Lord has given them, just as your forefathers discouraged the first generation from doing so (vv. 7–9)![6] That was treacherous rebellion against the Lord, and in his just anger, he swore that none

---

2. Reuben is actually listed before Gad in 32:1, perhaps in light of Reuben's firstborn status. The rest of the chapter, however, switches the order (32:6, 25, 29, 31, 33, 34–37), perhaps because Gad led in these events.

3. See map 4 for possible site of Jazer and 21:32 for Israel's defeat of it. Gilead sometimes refers broadly to land east of the Jordan (Judg 20:1), while at other times it refers to certain regions east of the Jordan (see nn. 12 and 17) or even to a city (the latter is perhaps more likely here given its parallel placement to Jazer). See discussion in Sklar, *Additional Notes*, at 32:1.

4. See map 4 for the location (or possible location) of many of these. For further details, see Ashley, *Numbers*, 608. Wherever their exact location, they fell within the territory allotted to Gad and Reuben (cf. Josh 13:15–28).

5. Milgrom, *Numbers*, 268, citing Keter Torah, a fourteenth-century Jewish commentary.

6. See Num 13:17–14:4.

of that adult generation—except faithful Caleb and Joshua[7]—would make it into the promised land (vv. 10–12)![8] The Lord punished them with wandering forty years in the wilderness until they died, and now here you are, you brood of wicked men, acting just like them! Doing this will make the Lord even angrier than before (vv. 13–14)! If you go through with this, turning from him in treacherous rebellion and dragging this people along with you, the Lord will leave them in the wilderness, they will die, and it will be your fault (v. 15)!"

The Reubenites' and Gadites' Proposal and Its Acceptance (32:16–32)

The two tribes then "came up to him" (Num 32:16a), a phrase used elsewhere to describe those coming near to an authority figure in order to plead their case ("went up to him"; Gen 43:19; 44:18). They recognize his anger and approach with a plan to show they will be faithful (Num 32:16b–19). They will build pens for their livestock and fortified cities[9] for their wives and children to protect them from the land's inhabitants, then they will cross over with the rest of the tribes and fight with them until everyone in those tribes has their inheritance.[10] Only then would they return to the Jordan's east side and claim their own inheritance.

Moses agrees to their proposal on condition that they are faithful to their promise (Num 32:20–22). He also warns, however, that breaking their word would be a sin against the Lord, who would surely bring justice to bear against them ("your sin will find you out"; v. 23; cf. Gen 42:21). In between his agreeing and his warning, Moses makes clear this is the Lord's battle. While the Lord is giving the land to the Israelites for an inheritance, the land is his and he will be driving his enemies out of it in judgment (Num 32:21; cf. Lev 18:24; Deut 4:37–38).[11] Israel will be fighting on the Lord's behalf in Canaan.

The Gadites and Reubenites affirm their commitment to the agreement (Num 32:25–27),[12] and Moses makes its details known to those who will lead

---

7. See Num 13:30; 14:6–9, 24, 30.
8. See Num 14:20–35.
9. That is, "rebuild" or "build up" as opposed to build from scratch (see the use of the same verb in 32:34, 37).
10. It might be assumed that some of the men would stay behind to guard the cities and help care for the livestock. Note that forty thousand troops eventually go (Josh 4:13), though Reuben and Gad had 84,230 men old enough for war (Num 26:7, 18), not to mention the troops that would have come from the half-tribe of Manasseh (Josh 4:12). Cf. Milgrom, *Numbers*, 270.
11. For further discussion, see pp. 375–76, How Is This Story a Warning?
12. In 32:26, 29, the term "Gilead" appears to be used in a broader sense than in 32:1 (cf. at n3 above) and is elsewhere called "half the hill country of Gilead" (Deut 3:12), referring to land stretching south from the Jabbok River (Josh 13:25 [cf. 13:30–31]; cf. n17 below).

after him, commanding them to oversee and administer it (vv. 28–30). The Gadites and Reubenites then reaffirm their commitment to faithfulness and underscore that their inheritance will be east of the Jordan (vv. 31–32).

The Property Inherited by Gad, Reuben, and the Half Tribe of Manasseh (32:33–42)

The opening verse describes in a general way their inheritance (Num 32:33), namely, the land and cities once controlled by Sihon and Og but defeated by the Israelites, a territory stretching from the Arnon river in the south to an area north of the Sea of Galilee (see at 21:21–22:1, pp. 279–80, for details; cf. Josh 12:1–6; 13:8–12). These would be for Gad, Reuben, and the half-tribe of Manasseh. The latter is mentioned here because its members would also inherit land east of the Jordan in light of battles they won there (Num 32:39–42). That they are not mentioned previously suggests they were not a part of the earlier negotiations.

More specific descriptions of land allotments now follow, beginning with Gad and Reuben. Along with building pens for their livestock, the Gadites rebuilt eight different fortified cities for their wives and children (Num 32:34–36). The Reubenites rebuilt six different cities, at least some of which were also presumably fortified (such as Heshbon, Sihon's capital city [21:26]; 32:37–38). We also learn that they changed the names of some of these cities,[13] perhaps to avoid their associations with other gods,[14] or perhaps in honor of themselves (cf. vv. 41–42). The new names are not given (perhaps because they were not long lasting?). For possible locations of some of the cities listed in this section, see map 4.[15]

As for the half-tribe of Manasseh, we learn it consists of Makir's descendants,[16] who defeated and drove out the Amorites from Gilead and were thus given that territory (Num 32:39–40).[17] We are also told of two of the tribe's

---

13. The placement of "these names were changed" before Sibmah (32:38a) suggests its name was not changed. Whether all the names before Sibmah were changed is less clear, though the end of 32:38 could imply this.

14. Nebo was the name of a Babylonian god (Isa 46:1), and Baal-Meon could be the name of a Baal worshipped at Meon.

15. These verses simply list the cities these tribes rebuilt for their dependents before their soldiers left for war, not the permanent allotment of these cities to these tribes. Once the allotment did take place (Josh 13:15–28), some of the cities were reassigned (Dibon, Aroer, Heshbon [cf. Josh 21:39 for the latter]). Cf. Wenham, *Numbers*, 215–16.

16. Cf. 26:29, which mentions two major clans within Manasseh: one coming from Makir and one coming from Gilead. For the Makirite clan, see 1 Chr 5:23–24.

17. The term Gilead here again appears to be used broadly, describing the other "half of Gilead" (cf. n12 above), extending northwards from the Jabbok River (Josh 13:29–31).

members who captured particular places: Jair captured various settlements and renamed them "Havvoth Jair" (that is, "settlements of Jair"; v. 41), and Nobah captured Kenath (and its settlements), renaming it Nobah (v. 42).

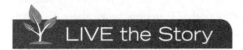

Aren't My Decisions an Individual Matter?[18]

Especially if we live in the West, there is a tendency to think that any decision we make is simply an individual matter. By this we often mean not only that we have the individual right to make whatever decision we want, but also that our decisions primarily affect only ourselves. In reality, however, the individual decisions we make can have a profound impact on others, and this impact can be devastating, not simply because we hurt people but also because we lead them to make unwise and harmful decisions. Even ancient Israelites, who were not at all Western, could underestimate the negative impact of their decisions on others and especially how their decisions could lead others astray. This danger is at the heart of Moses's rebuke of the tribes of Gad and Reuben for their request, "Do not make us cross the Jordan" (Num 32:5). Not only was this request a repetition of the disastrous rebellion that led to forty years of wilderness wandering, but it also risked leading the entire people to follow their example—and to suffer terrifying consequences as a result (see at vv. 6–15, pp. 382–83). Simply put, the "individual" decisions we make can often have a tremendously public impact, and when those decisions are not in keeping with God's ways, their impact can be devastating not only to ourselves but also to those who choose to follow us away from God.

On the one hand, this means we should do all we can to avoid decisions that are not in keeping with God's ways so that we are not modeling such behavior to others or leading others astray. Jesus's warning in this regard is severe: "If anyone causes one of these little ones—those who believe in me—to stumble, it would be better for them to have a large millstone hung around their neck and to be drowned in the depths of the sea. Woe to the world because of the things that cause people to stumble! Such things must come, but woe to the person through whom they come!" (Matt 18:6–7). If the negative behavior of ten men could turn aside an entire nation into ruin (Num 13–14), just imagine what the negative behavior of one man or woman could do in the midst of a small groups of friends, a family, or a congregation (cf. 2 Thess 3:6).

---

18. For an alternative homiletical approach, see p. 179n13.

On the other hand, our decisions can also have a tremendously positive impact when they model the type of behavior that is pleasing to God. "Walk with the wise," Proverbs exhorts, "and become wise" (Prov 13:20a). This leads naturally to important questions: "Am I making the types of decisions that model walking in the Lord's life-giving paths? If people make their decisions according to the values that inform my own, will they be walking more closely with the Lord?" I have been recently struck by Paul's words in Philippians 4:9, "Whatever you have learned or received or heard from me, *or seen in me*—put it into practice" (emphasis added). I'm not sure how comfortable I feel repeating those words—though I deeply long to be. Paul took very seriously Christ's call, "Follow me," and as he followed Christ, he became a living example of what it means to walk like Jesus did. As he says elsewhere, "Follow my example, as I follow the example of Christ" (1 Cor 11:1). And that is Jesus's call to each of us. "Follow me" (Matt 16:24; 19:21). As we do, we model for others what it means to walk with God and to embody his character of goodness, justice, mercy, and love, and our individual decisions become a means of bringing great blessing to his world.

Having said the above, it must also be noted that a life of faithfulness is about far more than individual decisions. This leads to a second question.

Why Is Unity So Important?

In the story of Numbers 32, Reuben and Gad are prepared to let the rest of Israel go into the promised land on their own, not helping them in any way with the many battles they would have to fight in order to achieve what God had promised them (vv. 1–5). After Moses's severe rebuke (vv. 6–15), the solution these tribes come up with centers on their going with the rest of Israel into the land and fighting with them to claim what God had promised (vv. 16–19). The solution is entirely acceptable to Moses (vv. 20–24) and, as later texts will show, was completely carried out (Josh 4:12; 22:1–4). What this models is the importance of God's people maintaining unity as they work together to accomplish God's purposes.

This unity matters because God has chosen to work in this world by means of his people, and his people are always a corporate entity, made up of many individuals. This is true for the nation of Israel in the Old Testament and the church in the New Testament. God always saves us out of this world but into a body, and he has ordained for that body together to be his representative in this world.

Shortly before his arrest, Jesus prayed a lengthy prayer (John 17). In its final section (vv. 20–26), he prays "for those who will believe in me" in days to come (John v. 20), and his very first request is "that all of them may be one, Father, just as you are in me and I am in you" (v. 21a). In other words, this group of people together is to reflect who God is and how he works, and central to that is unity. Just as the Father and the Son are perfectly unified, so too should his followers be. It is no surprise that Jesus therefore goes on to emphasize the importance of unity, saying, "I have given them the glory that you gave me, that they may be one as we are one . . . so that they may be brought to complete unity" (vv. 22–23a). Again, just as the Father and the Son are perfectly unified in glorious love, so too should his people be. And when this happens, Jesus says, "the world will know that you sent me and have loved them even as you have loved me" (v. 23b). To live in the unity that comes from love is to reflect the character of God to the watching world, testifying that we love one another because he has first loved us.

This also means that if the body is divided—if we do not love one another well—we will not be able to carry out God's purposes for us in this world because we cannot show the world who he is. And if they can't see him in us, his people, chances are they will not see him at all. The stakes could not be higher.

Given these realities, it may be especially helpful to ask, "How are we doing at showing love to our fellow believers? Are there any sins we need to confess? Wrongs we need to forgive? And what about believers who are in some way different than us? What about those who come from different denominations? Different countries? Different socioeconomic backgrounds? Do we lean toward them in love? What does it mean to do so?" If one of Jesus's last prayers for us was that we be united in love, shouldn't that be at the top of our list of priorities?

CHAPTER 34
Numbers 33:1–49

 LISTEN to the Story

¹Here are the stages in the journey of the Israelites when they came out of Egypt by divisions under the leadership of Moses and Aaron. ²At the Lord's command Moses recorded the stages in their journey. This is their journey by stages:

³The Israelites set out from Rameses on the fifteenth day of the first month, the day after the Passover. They marched out defiantly in full view of all the Egyptians, ⁴who were burying all their firstborn, whom the Lord had struck down among them; for the Lord had brought judgment on their gods.
⁵The Israelites left Rameses and camped at Sukkoth.
⁶They left Sukkoth and camped at Etham, on the edge of the desert.
⁷They left Etham, turned back to Pi Hahiroth, to the east of Baal Zephon, and camped near Migdol.
⁸They left Pi Hahiroth and passed through the sea into the desert, and when they had traveled for three days in the Desert of Etham, they camped at Marah.
⁹They left Marah and went to Elim, where there were twelve springs and seventy palm trees, and they camped there.
¹⁰They left Elim and camped by the Red Sea.
¹¹They left the Red Sea and camped in the Desert of Sin.
¹²They left the Desert of Sin and camped at Dophkah.
¹³They left Dophkah and camped at Alush.
¹⁴They left Alush and camped at Rephidim, where there was no water for the people to drink.
¹⁵They left Rephidim and camped in the Desert of Sinai.
¹⁶They left the Desert of Sinai and camped at Kibroth Hattaavah.

¹⁷They left Kibroth Hattaavah and camped at Hazeroth.
¹⁸They left Hazeroth and camped at Rithmah.
¹⁹They left Rithmah and camped at Rimmon Perez.
²⁰They left Rimmon Perez and camped at Libnah.
²¹They left Libnah and camped at Rissah.
²²They left Rissah and camped at Kehelathah.
²³They left Kehelathah and camped at Mount Shepher.
²⁴They left Mount Shepher and camped at Haradah.
²⁵They left Haradah and camped at Makheloth.
²⁶They left Makheloth and camped at Tahath.
²⁷They left Tahath and camped at Terah.
²⁸They left Terah and camped at Mithkah.
²⁹They left Mithkah and camped at Hashmonah.
³⁰They left Hashmonah and camped at Moseroth.
³¹They left Moseroth and camped at Bene Jaakan.
³²They left Bene Jaakan and camped at Hor Haggidgad.
³³They left Hor Haggidgad and camped at Jotbathah.
³⁴They left Jotbathah and camped at Abronah.
³⁵They left Abronah and camped at Ezion Geber.
³⁶They left Ezion Geber and camped at Kadesh, in the Desert of Zin.
³⁷They left Kadesh and camped at Mount Hor, on the border of Edom. ³⁸At the LORD's command Aaron the priest went up Mount Hor, where he died on the first day of the fifth month of the fortieth year after the Israelites came out of Egypt. ³⁹Aaron was a hundred and twenty-three years old when he died on Mount Hor.
⁴⁰The Canaanite king of Arad, who lived in the Negev of Canaan, heard that the Israelites were coming.
⁴¹They left Mount Hor and camped at Zalmonah.
⁴²They left Zalmonah and camped at Punon.
⁴³They left Punon and camped at Oboth.
⁴⁴They left Oboth and camped at Iye Abarim, on the border of Moab.
⁴⁵They left Iye Abarim and camped at Dibon Gad.
⁴⁶They left Dibon Gad and camped at Almon Diblathaim.
⁴⁷They left Almon Diblathaim and camped in the mountains of Abarim, near Nebo.

> ⁴⁸They left the mountains of Abarim and camped on the plains of Moab by the Jordan across from Jericho. ⁴⁹There on the plains of Moab they camped along the Jordan from Beth Jeshimoth to Abel Shittim.

Listening to the Text in the Story: Egyptian topographical lists; Assyrian travel itineraries and campaign records

The ancient Israelites were not the only ones to record travel itineraries. Parallels exist in Egyptian topographical lists from the New Kingdom period (between the sixteenth and eleventth centuries BC)[1] and in various Assyrian travel itineraries. On the latter, Milgrom explains:

> [A] letter of Shamshi-Adad I of Assyria (18th cent. [BC]) found in the Mari archive describes the following transport: "from Shubat-Enlil to Tilla, from Tilla to Ashihim, from Ashihim to Iyati, from Iyati to Lakushir, from Lakushir to Sagaratim" (ARM 1.26). Here, just as in Numbers 33, the stations are repeated. The correspondence, however, is not exact since the Mari account is verbless. A more precise parallel is found in the records of the military campaigns of the Assyrian emperors of the ninth century. These utilize the formula "from city A I departed, in city B I spent the night"; and in the next stage, B will occupy the A position.[2]

The existence of such itineraries was thus a well-known phenomenon, and their study can help illuminate the biblical text. Milgrom continues:

> Even more striking is [the example] found in the campaign records of Ashurnasirpal II (883–859):
>
>> I spent the night in the city of Shadikanni
>> The tribute of Shadikanni—silver, gold, lead, vessels of copper and flocks—I received.
>> From the city of Shadikanni I departed.[3]

---

1. See discussion in James K. Hoffmeier, *Israel in Egypt: The Evidence for the Authenticity of the Exodus Tradition* (New York: Oxford University Press, 1997), 176–78.
2. Milgrom, *Numbers*, 497; he cites G. J. Davies, "The Wilderness Itineraries: A Comparative Study," *TynBul* 25 (1974): 46–81.
3. Milgrom, *Numbers*, 497.

He draws attention to the expansions in this example that go beyond simple place names, noting that other expansions in this text deal "with military exploits, river crossings, and the finding of water."[4] From this he observes that similar expansions happen in Numbers 33 (vv. 8, 9, 14, 40) and concludes, "Thus the allegation that these expansions [in Num 33] are editorial glosses is refuted. To the contrary, they are integral to the itinerary since, just as in the Assyrian analogue, they record notable events essential to the journey."[5]

Introduction (33:1–2)

This chapter gives us the Israelites' travel itinerary. The events east of the Jordan are now complete and this itinerary summarizes them, starting in Egypt forty years ago and coming up to the present moment as they are encamped in the plains of Moab,[6] from which they will march into the promised land. Summarizing that journey makes very good sense at this point. Israel is preparing to march into the promised land, the very thing their forefathers refused to do forty years ago. As they prepare to do so, it is vital they remember the mistakes of the past, so they do not repeat them, and the Lord's past faithfulness, so they follow him in obedient trust.

The Israelites' Travel Itinerary (33:3–49)

Broadly speaking, verses 33:3–15 of this itinerary describe the Israelites' journey from Egypt to Sinai and verses 16–49 their journey from Sinai to the plains of Moab.[7] The itinerary lists forty-two travel stations, many of which were not cities that left ruins behind but simply encampments and thus difficult to identify with certainty. There is extensive discussion in the secondary literature on possible locations for several of these sites,[8] and map 5 gives a possible route the itinerary describes (though debate surrounds several important locations; compare also to map 1, whose route differs in places).

---

4. Ibid., 498.
5. Ibid.
6. More specifically, spread out between Beth Jeshimoth to Abel Shittim (33:49), a distance of about five miles (8 km).
7. Olson, *Numbers*, 184.
8. Summaries may be found in the standard Bible atlases. Among the commentators, helpful summaries are found in Ashley, *Numbers*, 626–33, and more succinctly, Cole, "Numbers," 396–99. See also Kitchen, *Reliability of the Old Testament*, 190–99, 254–63, 265–74; Hoffmeier, *Israel in Egypt*, 176–222.

Other itineraries overlap with this one (21:10–20; Deut 1–3),[9] though there are also differences, which is unsurprising since none of these itineraries is complete.[10] For further biblical details on some of the places and events listed in this itinerary, see the cross-references to passages in Exodus and Numbers listed in the following table:

Numbers 33			
vv. 3–4	Exod 12	v. 17	Num 11:35
v. 5	Exod 12:37	v. 36	Num 20:1–13
v. 6	Exod 13:20	vv. 37–39	Num 20:22–29
vv. 7–8	Exod 14:2–15:26	v. 40	Num 21:1–3
v. 9	Exod 15:27	v. 43	Num 21:10
vv. 10–11	Exod 16:1	v. 44	Num 21:11
v. 14	Exod 17	vv. 45, 47	Num 32:3–4
v. 15	Exod 19:2	vv. 48–49	Num 22–32
v. 16	Num 10:11–11:34		

In most instances, the itinerary simply mentions the place the Israelites left and the place they arrived, e.g., "They left Hazeroth and camped at Rithmah" (Num 33:18). In a few instances, further details are mentioned, such as the brief recounting of the exodus (vv. 3–4) or of Aaron's death (vv. 37–39). In either case, many of these names and events trigger powerful memories, whether of Israel's faithlessness, of the Lord's judgment, or of the Lord's

---

9. See the table in Milgrom, *Numbers*, 499.
10. With regard to the itinerary in this chapter, various suggestions have been made as to what led to the selection of the number of places to include. If the starting and stopping places are not counted, the number of stops is forty, exactly the same number as the years of wandering in the wilderness. This similarity suggests to Allen (among others) that there is "some styling of the list, which helps to account for the inclusion or exclusion of some sites" ("Numbers," 984). Others suggest forty-two total names have been chosen so that the list contains six groups of seven (the number seven being especially significant in ancient Israel; Wenham, *Numbers*, 217–19; Bailey, *Leviticus-Numbers*, 595). In either case, the list is selective.

faithfulness and mercy. As noted above and discussed immediately below, learning from these memories would be especially important for Israel as they prepared to enter the promised land.

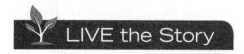

LIVE the Story

Toynbee Crescent. Banff Place. Hewlett Road. For most people, these names mean nothing. But to me they are packed with memories. I grew up on Toynbee Crescent. My grandparents' home was on Banff Place. My wife and I lived on Hewlett Road shortly after getting married. The very mention of these places recalls a flood of memories: some very joyful (Christmas mornings), others filled with sorrow (my grandfather's death), and many quite ordinary (cereal for breakfast). So too with the Israelites and this itinerary. The very mention of these places recalls a flood of memories. Significantly, the memories were to remind them of important lessons. We can consider these lessons by asking two different questions.

What Did Israel Do?

It has often been noted that those who do not learn from history's mistakes are doomed to repeat them. This list is packed with reminders of Israel's past mistakes for that very reason: that Israel might learn *not* to repeat them.

Many of the names in this list would recall mistakes made by the nation as a whole, such as the Israelites' complaining for water at Marah (Num 33:8) and Rephidim (v. 14), their complaining for food in the Desert of Sin and longing to return to Egypt only one month after being redeemed (v. 11), their rebellion with the golden calf in the Desert of Sinai (v. 15), their grumbling for food again at Kibroth Hattaavah (v. 16), their complaining at Kadesh about a lack of water again and causing Moses and Aaron to sin in frustration and be denied the promised land (v. 36), and their rebellion at Abel Shittim with the Moabite women (v. 49).

Other names in the list recall mistakes made by their leaders, such as the rebellion of Miriam and Aaron against Moses at Hazeroth (Num 33:17), and Moses's and Aaron's rebellion, which cost them the promised land and would result in Moses dying on a mountain in the Abarim range (v. 47) and Aaron dying on Mount Hor (vv. 37–39).

There were certainly flashes of faith along the way, but the overall picture is far from positive on Israel's part. We see a people quick to forget the Lord's faithfulness and thus quick to turn from him in the face of difficulty. The current generation was to look back on such behavior as a model of what not to do, especially in light of the consequences. This leads to the second question.

How Did the Lord Respond?

The names in this list give reminders of two main types of responses from the Lord. Some names trigger memories of the Lord's judgment, such as his judgment for the Israelites' idolatry at Sinai (Num 33:15), for their lack of faith and rejection of his redemption at Kibroth Hattaavah (v. 16), for Miriam's and Aaron's speaking against Moses at Hazeroth (v. 17), for Moses's and Aaron's sin at Kadesh (v. 36), and for the Israelites' apostasy at Abel Shittim (v. 49). Israel's experience of the Lord's judgment stands as a strong warning to future generations: do not repeat these sins so that you do not experience the same judgment.

In many contexts today, the idea of God's judgment is very negative, being associated with a God who is simply angry and delights to punish. The biblical picture is far different. It presents a God who is patient, merciful, and longsuffering, who would far rather have our repentance than our judgment (Ezek 18:23) but who will bring his justice to bear against evil. As noted in earlier comments,[11] because sin is a cancer that destroys his good world, the Lord is diametrically opposed to it and will bring his justice to bear against it. That is his promise. He therefore repeatedly warns against any involvement in sin lest we get caught up in its judgment. Many of the places in this list underscore that warning.

The New Testament does the same in 1 Corinthians 10:5–6, where Paul, looking back on the Israelites' behavior during those forty wilderness years, writes, "God was not pleased with most of them; their bodies were scattered in the wilderness. Now these things occurred as examples to keep us from setting our hearts on evil things as they did."[12]

In light of the above, we do well to ask, "What mistakes have we made in the past that we are to learn from?" In answering this, we must not simply focus on our own sins or the sins of individuals who have gone before us but also on those sins committed by corporate groups of believers, be it the church as a whole, a denomination to which we belong, or our own local church. Israel as a whole fell into sinful patterns of behavior and the same rings true for groups of believers throughout the centuries.

---

11. See pp. 331–32, How Is God's Faithfulness to His Promises a Warning?
12. See also Heb 3–4.

Along with the Lord's judgment, however, the names in this list also recall his faithfulness and mercy. We see this in his protecting the Israelites near Migdol with his pillar of fire when Pharaoh's army caught up to them (Num 33:7), his delivering them through the sea (and his wiping out of Pharaoh's army in it; v. 8), his gracious provision of water at Marah (33:8) and Rephidim (v. 14) and his abundant provision of the same at Elim (v. 9), his provision of manna and quail in the desert of Sin (v. 11), his delivering them from the Amalekites at Rephidim (v. 14), his giving them the law and renewing the covenant after their faithlessness at Sinai (v. 15), his provision of quail at Kibroth Hattaavah (v. 16), his giving Dibon Gad and Nebo into their hands (vv. 45, 47), and his causing Balaam to speak a blessing over them instead of a curse while they camped on the plains of Moab (v. 48).

Indeed, one of the few times the list gives extra details, these emphasize the Lord's faithfulness to his people. Numbers 33:3–4 start the itinerary on a note celebrating the Lord's work in saving the Israelites from Egypt by means of the last plague. This was not only a judgment on Egypt but also on their gods (cf. Exod 12:12), who were powerless to help Egypt before the Lord's might. Israel's pilgrimage toward the promised land thus begins with the assurance their God is a redeemer who is totally sovereign, loves them completely, and is therefore worthy of the utmost trust.

The same is true for the believer today. Any pilgrimage toward the far greater promised land begins with Jesus, the ultimate redeemer who displays God's sovereign power and love by rescuing us from the forces of evil and the evil we ourselves have committed. And God's love for us in Christ is secure. "For I am convinced that neither death nor life, neither angels nor demons, neither the present nor the future, nor any powers, neither height nor depth, nor anything else in all creation, will be able to separate us from the love of God that is in Christ Jesus our Lord" (Rom 8:38–39). How should this reality impact our fears? Our unmet desires that discourage us? Our temptations toward sin? And what are the different ways that we can remember not only what the Lord has done for us in Christ but also the many signs of his faithfulness and love that he shows us day by day, week by week? Keeping his faithfulness and mercy before our eyes is like being connected to a spring from which a life of obedient love continually flows.

CHAPTER 35

Numbers 33:50–34:29

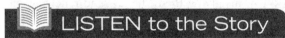
LISTEN to the Story

³³:⁵⁰On the plains of Moab by the Jordan across from Jericho the LORD said to Moses, ⁵¹"Speak to the Israelites and say to them: 'When you cross the Jordan into Canaan, ⁵²drive out all the inhabitants of the land before you. Destroy all their carved images and their cast idols, and demolish all their high places. ⁵³Take possession of the land and settle in it, for I have given you the land to possess. ⁵⁴Distribute the land by lot, according to your clans. To a larger group give a larger inheritance, and to a smaller group a smaller one. Whatever falls to them by lot will be theirs. Distribute it according to your ancestral tribes.

⁵⁵"But if you do not drive out the inhabitants of the land, those you allow to remain will become barbs in your eyes and thorns in your sides. They will give you trouble in the land where you will live. ⁵⁶And then I will do to you what I plan to do to them.'"

³⁴:¹The LORD said to Moses, ²"Command the Israelites and say to them: 'When you enter Canaan, the land that will be allotted to you as an inheritance is to have these boundaries):

³"Your southern side will include some of the Desert of Zin along the border of Edom. Your southern boundary will start in the east from the southern end of the Dead Sea, ⁴cross south of Scorpion Pass, continue on to Zin and go south of Kadesh Barnea. Then it will go to Hazar Addar and over to Azmon, ⁵where it will turn, join the Wadi of Egypt and end at the Mediterranean Sea.

⁶"Your western boundary will be the coast of the Mediterranean Sea. This will be your boundary on the west.

⁷"For your northern boundary, run a line from the Mediterranean Sea to Mount Hor ⁸and from Mount Hor to Lebo Hamath. Then the boundary will go to Zedad, ⁹continue to Ziphron and end at Hazar Enan. This will be your boundary on the north.

¹⁰"'For your eastern boundary, run a line from Hazar Enan to Shepham. ¹¹The boundary will go down from Shepham to Riblah on the east side of Ain and continue along the slopes east of the Sea of Galilee. ¹²Then the boundary will go down along the Jordan and end at the Dead Sea.

"'This will be your land, with its boundaries on every side.'"

¹³Moses commanded the Israelites: "Assign this land by lot as an inheritance. The LORD has ordered that it be given to the nine and a half tribes, ¹⁴because the families of the tribe of Reuben, the tribe of Gad and the half-tribe of Manasseh have received their inheritance. ¹⁵These two and a half tribes have received their inheritance east of the Jordan across from Jericho, toward the sunrise."

¹⁶The LORD said to Moses, ¹⁷"These are the names of the men who are to assign the land for you as an inheritance: Eleazar the priest and Joshua son of Nun. ¹⁸And appoint one leader from each tribe to help assign the land. ¹⁹These are their names:

Caleb son of Jephunneh,
from the tribe of Judah;
²⁰Shemuel son of Ammihud,
from the tribe of Simeon;
²¹Elidad son of Kislon,
from the tribe of Benjamin;
²²Bukki son of Jogli,
the leader from the tribe of Dan;
²³Hanniel son of Ephod,
the leader from the tribe of Manasseh son of Joseph;
²⁴Kemuel son of Shiphtan,
the leader from the tribe of Ephraim son of Joseph;
²⁵Elizaphan son of Parnak,
the leader from the tribe of Zebulun;
²⁶Paltiel son of Azzan,
the leader from the tribe of Issachar;
²⁷Ahihud son of Shelomi,
the leader from the tribe of Asher;
²⁸Pedahel son of Ammihud,

the leader from the tribe of Naphtali."

> [29]These are the men the LORD commanded to assign the inheritance to the Israelites in the land of Canaan.
>
> *Listening to the Text in the Story:*
> See Listening to the Text in the Story at Numbers 13–14, p. 194, for a discussion of "Canaan" in its ancient Near Eastern context and in the biblical story to this point. For its boundaries, see map 2.
> In 33:52 the Lord commands the Israelites to destroy every last trace of false worship in the land. This is no wonder, given the ubiquity of idols in the ancient world and Israel's temptation to worship them. See especially comments at 25:1–18, Listening to the Text in the Story, p. 316.

"When you cross the Jordan into Canaan . . ." (Num 33:51). More than ever before, the book now anticipates life in the promised land. Having just reviewed the Israelites' journey to the plains of Moab on the cusp of Canaan (33:1–49), the book finishes by addressing matters directly related to life in Canaan (33:50–36:13):

1. Dispossessing the Land's Inhabitants and Distributing It (33:50–56)
2. The Land's Boundaries (34:1–15)
3. Those Who Would Apportion the Land (34:16–29)
4. Cities for the Levites in the Land (35:1–8)
5. Cities of Refuge in the Land (35:9–34)
6. Zelophehad's Daughters: A Further Question about Inheritance in the Land (36:1–12)
7. Conclusion (36:13)

Sections 1 through 3 will be addressed here and the remaining sections in the chapters to follow.

Dispossessing the Land's Inhabitants and Distributing It (33:50–56)
The Lord's first commands focus on his people's spiritual purity (Num 33:52), and for good reason: if the Israelites became like these nations the Lord was

judging, they could expect the same judgment (vv. 55–56). To guard their spiritual purity, two related actions were required. First, the Israelites must dispossess the land of its inhabitants (vv. 52a, 53a). In some cases this would happen as the Lord drove out the nations before the Israelites in fear (Exod 23:27–28), and in other cases he would give them over to the Israelites to be destroyed in warfare (Deut 7:1–2; 20:16–18).[1] Either way, the nations living in Canaan had become thoroughly corrupt, and the Lord would use his people to bring his justice to bear upon the evil these nations had done and were doing (Gen 15:16; Lev 18:24–27; 20:23–24).

Second, the Israelites had to destroy every last remnant of the nations' false worship (Num 33:52b). The word for "carved images" (*maskit*) is found in contexts of illicit worship elsewhere (Num 33:52; Ezek 8:12, NIV "idol"), with Ezek 8:10 suggesting it referred in some way to carvings of various creatures. The phrase "their cast idols" (*tsalme massekotam*) refers to gods manufactured, at least in part, by melting metal (cf. Exod 32:4 and 32:24). The language calls to mind the "calf of cast metal" from Exod 32:4, reminding the Israelites not to repeat that tragic event. Finally, the "high places" were cultic sites at which the worship of false gods took place (1 Kgs 11:7; 2 Kgs 17:9). In short, the false gods and their worship places were to be utterly destroyed.

Failure to dispossess the nations would be fatal (Num 33:55–56). The nations would not be a blessing to Israel, or even be neutral neighbors; they would cause excruciating pain, underscored here by comparing them to sharp objects stuck into two of the body's most sensitive areas (the eyes and side; v. 55). Just how the nations would do this is not stated. The images suggest general hostility, even outright oppression, as happened later in Judges (see Judg 2:6–23), but they are broad enough to allow for spiritual harm as well. Indeed, the phrase "they will give you trouble" (Num 33:55) uses the same verb as 25:17–18,[2] which describes the trouble the Midianites gave the Israelites by leading them away from the Lord to the worship of false gods. The same is likely in view here (cf. Exod 23:33; Deut 7:1–5), which explains why the Lord tells Israel, "I will do to you what I plan to do to them" (Num 33:56). In other words, if you repeat their same evils, you must expect their same punishment.

In the midst of the commands and warnings about dispossessing the nations, the Lord reminds the Israelites he has given the land to them as their

---

1. See pp. 281–83, Why Such Severe Destruction?
2. Translated there by NIV as "to treat as an enemy."

inheritance (33:53b; cf. Gen 15:7; 26:3; 28:4). They will gain the promised land because of his faithfulness, not their strength. The Lord also reminds them to divide the land by lot and in proportion to a clan's size (Num 33:54; see comments at 26:52–56, pp. 329–30). On the one hand, this prepares us for some of the next activities described (34:13–29). On the other hand, by framing these verses with commands and warnings about dispossessing the nations and destroying their gods and worship sites (33:52, 54–56), the Lord makes clear how important it is for the Israelites to guard their spiritual purity if they want to experience spiritual blessing. Receiving covenant promises requires covenant faithfulness.

The Boundaries of Canaan (34:1–15)

Having told the Israelites what to do once they get to Canaan (Num 33:50–56), the Lord now describes its borders: south (34:3–5), west (v. 6), north (vv. 7–9), and east (vv. 10–12a). The southern and western of these are generally agreed upon; the northern is somewhat debated, with the eastern more so, though a general enough picture may be given (see map 2). The mention of Zin in the south and Lebo Hamath in the north (vv. 3, 8) recalls the scouts' route in 13:21; what they had scouted out was indeed what the Lord would give Israel.[3] It would not be until David and Solomon that Israel ever gained control of the majority of this area,[4] and their reigns (especially Solomon's) would represent the largest amount of area ever controlled by Israel.[5] Even then, however, not quite all of the area described in Numbers 34 was taken, especially portions along the Mediterranean's eastern shore. The ideal was thus never attained, a stinging rebuke to Israel's lack of faith in God's ability "to do immeasurably more than all we ask or imagine" (Eph 3:20).[6] And yet one must ask: "Would I have fared any better?"

Moses passes on the command, making clear this land will be for the nine and a half remaining tribes because Reuben, Gad and the half-tribe of Manasseh had already taken their inheritance east of the Jordan (Num 34:13–15; cf. 32:33–42).

---

3. Allen ("Numbers," 993) also notes that their scouting would have given the Israelites the data to know about many of the sites listed here.

4. Cf. 1 Kgs 8:65, which mentions Israelites during Solomon's time coming "from Lebo Hamath to the Wadi of Egypt," the same southern and northern boundaries mentioned in Num 34:5, 8 (for David, cf. 1 Chr 13:5). Solomon's borders at one point extended even further north (1 Kgs 4:21–24).

5. During the divided kingdom, a similar-sized area was controlled during the reigns of Azariah (792–740 BC) in the south and Jeroboam II (793–753 BC) in the north. See Rasmussen, *Zondervan Atlas*, 158, 162.

6. Wenham, *Numbers*, 232.

Those Who Would Apportion the Land as an Inheritance (34:16–29)

Having given the land's contours, the Lord now identifies who will help apportion it among the nine and a half tribes once they arrive there. Leading the effort will be Eleazar, who took over as high priest when Aaron died (Num 20:23–28), and Joshua, who will lead Israel into the land once Moses dies (27:12–23; Deut 34:1–9). The manner of dividing the land is described later in Joshua 18:1–10, which finishes by saying, "Joshua then cast lots for them in Shiloh in the presence of the LORD" (v. 10a). In other words, Joshua takes the ultimate lead in casting the lots but does so before the Lord, meaning not only that he does so at his sanctuary (thus Eleazar's presence) but also that the lots' decision was received as the Lord's (cf. Prov 16:33). Each tribe's inheritance was thus to be received with thanksgiving instead of comparison or complaint since it was a divine gift (cf. Prov 18:18).

Helping Eleazar and Joshua would be ten Israelite leaders, one for each of the remaining tribes (Num 34:18–29). (Gad and Reuben, who inherited east of the Jordan, are not included.) Generally speaking, they would serve as the tribe's representative. Specifically speaking, because the land was to be apportioned in keeping with the sizes of different clans within a tribe (26:52–56; 33:54), these leaders would be able to supply the information necessary to apportion fairly.[7] The leaders are listed more or less in their tribes' geographical order from south to north (see map 6). The only leader of these ten that we have heard of elsewhere is Caleb (34:19), one of the original twelve scouts of the land who, along with Joshua, stood against the ten faithless scouts and exhorted the people to march into the land in faith because the Lord was with them (13:30; 14:6–9). As a result of their faithfulness, Joshua and Caleb were promised entry into the land and an inheritance in it (14:24, 30; cf. Josh 14:6–15; 19:49–50). The mention of Joshua and Caleb so closely together here (vv. 17, 19) recalls both their faithfulness as a model for how Israel is to act and also the Lord's delight in blessing his faithful people with his covenant promises.

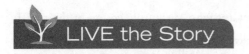

LIVE the Story

At first glance, this section of Scripture seems to hold very little relevance for modern people. Three questions, however, can help us to see ways in which it relates very much to life today.

---

7. See further at 26:52–56, p. 330n8

What Does Dispossessing the Nations Have to Do with Us Today?

One reason Israel had to dispossess the nations was because the Lord had called them to enact his judgment for the gross evil these nations were committing (Gen 15:16; Lev 18:24–27; 20:23–24). As discussed earlier, God's call on his people to do this happened rarely and was very limited in its scope both geographically and historically.[8] This is not a blanket command with ongoing force today.

But dispossessing the nations was not simply to exercise God's judgment; it was also to protect his people spiritually. These nations were utterly corrupt and close association with them would have a disastrous impact on the Israelites' own behavior—which is exactly what happened just a generation later (Judg 2:6–19). And no wonder. "Bad company corrupts good character" (1 Cor 15:33; cf. Prov 13:20; 22:24–25). There is a reason we speak of people "rubbing off" on us; the lives of those closest to us begin to form and shape our own. As one of my friends told his college-bound son, "Your character will become the average of your five closest friends."

There are many different questions we could ask at this point, such as, what are the implications for the types of friends we make? Or the person we marry? Or the groups we join? But we may note a very specific application the New Testament makes in terms of our interactions with those who claim to follow Christ but whose life says the opposite. Writing to believers in Thessalonica, Paul says,

> In the name of the Lord Jesus Christ, we command you, brothers and sisters, to keep away from every believer who is idle and disruptive and does not live according to the teaching you received from us. . . . Take special note of anyone who does not obey our instruction in this letter. Do not associate with them, in order that they may feel ashamed. Yet do not regard them as an enemy, but warn them as you would a fellow believer. (2 Thess 3:6, 14–15)

Paul is not talking about Christians who are simply young in their faith or who are earnestly struggling but sometimes failing in battles with major sins. He is describing those who claim to follow Jesus and yet refuse to live according to Jesus's teaching, which Paul and others passed on. And Paul is very firm: do not continue in close relationship with them as though they belong to Christ. Do not consider them a member of his people. Paul knows

---

8. See pp. 281–83, Why Such Severe Destruction?

this would not only give them false hope, it would also endanger God's people because it would make sin normative. And once sin becomes normative in the church, God's people can no longer do the very mission they have been given: reflecting his holy character into the world. It is impossible for God's people to reflect his light and life while they embrace deeds of darkness and death.

And so, Paul says, if someone is not living like a follower of Christ, we must not treat them as such. Pray for their repentance? By all means! Exhort them in love to surrender their lives to Jesus? Of course! "Do not regard them as an enemy, but warn them as you would a fellow believer" (2 Thess 3:15)! But we harm both them and the church if we treat them as someone who knows Christ when they are not following him at all.

It is not simply others' sin, however, that we must take seriously. The same is true for our own sin. This leads to the second question.

What Does Eradicating Idolatry Have to Do with Us Today?

During Israel's day, the worship of physical idols was not only a living reality, it was normative. This explains in part why the Lord had to warn so strongly against it (note how the Ten Commandments begin, Exod 20:3–6) and why Israel fell into it so often (e.g., Exod 32:1–6; Num 25:1–3). And the reason the Lord treats it so seriously is because idolatry is at its heart an act of betrayal. In fact, the Lord describes idolatry as an act of prostitution (Lev 17:7), an extremely strong but necessary metaphor: The Israelites were not just breaking a law when engaging in such worship, they were betraying their faithful covenant partner. Just as a human spouse takes infidelity seriously, so too does the Lord.

The worship of physical idols was also a living reality in New Testament times (1 Cor 10:14–22) and continues to be such in many cultures today. But even if we live in cultures where we do not make actual gods of wood or stone to bow before, other things can function exactly like idols in our lives. One of the most obvious is money, which Jesus himself warned of as something we could "serve" in place of God (Matt 6:24; cf. Col 3:5). But it need not stop there. If anything in our lives displaces God from being our first love and greatest treasure—be it a career, a lifestyle, a relationship—that thing is functioning like an idol in our lives. We are looking to other lovers for what only God can give.

In the case of physical idols, the clearest solution is the one named here: destroy them! But it gets more complicated if our idol is money (which we actually need to live) or a career (God himself underscores the importance of working, if we're able [1 Thess 4:11; 2 Thess 3:12]). What does "eradicating idolatry" look like in these instances?

As with any sin, the underlying principle is clear: idolatry must be treated as a danger which can drag you into hell—because it can (Matt 5:28–29). And this means we must deal radically with any of the idols in our lives. Is it money? Jesus already gives some guidance: stop storing up more than you need (Matt 6:19) and focus on living life for his kingdom, which is the surest way to take money off the throne in your heart, "For where your treasure is, there your heart will be also" (6:21). Practically speaking, what does it look like to begin to live on less and to shift our financial resources toward kingdom goals? What might it mean, where we are able, to spend less time on making money and more time on serving kingdom needs?

The same types of questions may be asked of other idols in our lives. What are those idols, and what does it mean to deal radically with them? Whatever the answers may be, the goal is not to keep ourselves from certain things as much as it is to gain one unspeakably good thing: deep fellowship with God himself. This leads to the last question.

What Does an Ancient Map Have to Do with Us Today?

The warnings of Numbers 33:50–56 are followed by a reminder of the promise to come: God was leading them to a good land—the contours of which he sketches out here (Num 34)—where he himself would dwell among them. He is not primarily someone who wants to forbid and take away but to give—and to give what is good.

The language used to describe receiving the land is the language of inheritance, which pictures the Lord as the generous father passing on a rich gift to his children. The focus in this chapter is on the land itself, and we must not minimize the simple fact the Lord has made us as physical creatures and therefore provides for our physical needs (cf. Matt 6:11; 1 Tim 4:3). But other texts make clear it is not simply the land that was the good gift, but the land as a place where God himself would walk in Israel's midst. In Leviticus 26, the Lord lists various physical blessings he would provide to his people (vv. 3–10) but crowns the list with his presence among them: "I will put my dwelling place among you, and I will not abhor you. I will walk among you and be your God, and you will be my people" (vv. 11–12). The ultimate inheritance we can have is relationship with him.

The picture of the Lord's covenant people receiving an inheritance from him is used in the New Testament to refer to the eternal heavenly inheritance that awaits those who become his children through faith in Jesus (Col

1:12–14; 1 Pet 1:3–5). In that land, his people will live "before the throne of God and serve him day and night in his temple; and he who sits on the throne will shelter them with his presence. Never again will they hunger; never again will they thirst. The sun will not beat down on them, nor any scorching heat. For the Lamb at the center of the throne will be their shepherd; he will lead them to springs of living water. And God will wipe away every tear from their eyes" (Rev 7:15–17). No earthly idols have any worth compared to such unspeakably profound goodness and joy. So what is keeping us from dealing with them as we should? Why would we hold on to moldy bread when a banquet of God's lavish love for us in Jesus is laid out and ready to enjoy?

CHAPTER 36
Numbers 35:1–34

 LISTEN to the Story

¹On the plains of Moab by the Jordan across from Jericho, the Lord said to Moses, ²"Command the Israelites to give the Levites towns to live in from the inheritance the Israelites will possess. And give them pasturelands around the towns. ³Then they will have towns to live in and pasturelands for the cattle they own and all their other animals.

⁴"The pasturelands around the towns that you give the Levites will extend a thousand cubits from the town wall. ⁵Outside the town, measure two thousand cubits on the east side, two thousand on the south side, two thousand on the west and two thousand on the north, with the town in the center. They will have this area as pastureland for the towns.

⁶"Six of the towns you give the Levites will be cities of refuge, to which a person who has killed someone may flee. In addition, give them forty-two other towns. ⁷In all you must give the Levites forty-eight towns, together with their pasturelands. ⁸The towns you give the Levites from the land the Israelites possess are to be given in proportion to the inheritance of each tribe: Take many towns from a tribe that has many, but few from one that has few."

⁹Then the Lord said to Moses: ¹⁰"Speak to the Israelites and say to them: 'When you cross the Jordan into Canaan, ¹¹select some towns to be your cities of refuge, to which a person who has killed someone accidentally may flee. ¹²They will be places of refuge from the avenger, so that anyone accused of murder may not die before they stand trial before the assembly. ¹³These six towns you give will be your cities of refuge. ¹⁴Give three on this side of the Jordan and three in Canaan as cities of refuge. ¹⁵These six towns will be a place of refuge for Israelites and for foreigners residing among them, so that anyone who has killed another accidentally can flee there.

¹⁶"'If anyone strikes someone a fatal blow with an iron object, that

person is a murderer; the murderer is to be put to death. ¹⁷Or if anyone is holding a stone and strikes someone a fatal blow with it, that person is a murderer; the murderer is to be put to death. ¹⁸Or if anyone is holding a wooden object and strikes someone a fatal blow with it, that person is a murderer; the murderer is to be put to death. ¹⁹The avenger of blood shall put the murderer to death; when the avenger comes upon the murderer, the avenger shall put the murderer to death. ²⁰If anyone with malice aforethought shoves another or throws something at them intentionally so that they die ²¹or if out of enmity one person hits another with their fist so that the other dies, that person is to be put to death; that person is a murderer. The avenger of blood shall put the murderer to death when they meet.

²²'But if without enmity someone suddenly pushes another or throws something at them unintentionally ²³or, without seeing them, drops on them a stone heavy enough to kill them, and they die, then since that other person was not an enemy and no harm was intended, ²⁴the assembly must judge between the accused and the avenger of blood according to these regulations. ²⁵The assembly must protect the one accused of murder from the avenger of blood and send the accused back to the city of refuge to which they fled. The accused must stay there until the death of the high priest, who was anointed with the holy oil.

²⁶'But if the accused ever goes outside the limits of the city of refuge to which they fled ²⁷and the avenger of blood finds them outside the city, the avenger of blood may kill the accused without being guilty of murder. ²⁸The accused must stay in the city of refuge until the death of the high priest; only after the death of the high priest may they return to their own property.

²⁹'This is to have the force of law for you throughout the generations to come, wherever you live.

³⁰'Anyone who kills a person is to be put to death as a murderer only on the testimony of witnesses. But no one is to be put to death on the testimony of only one witness.

³¹'Do not accept a ransom for the life of a murderer, who deserves to die. They are to be put to death.

³²'Do not accept a ransom for anyone who has fled to a city of refuge and so allow them to go back and live on their own land before the death of the high priest.

³³'Do not pollute the land where you are. Bloodshed pollutes the land, and atonement cannot be made for the land on which blood has been shed,

> except by the blood of the one who shed it. ³⁴Do not defile the land where you live and where I dwell, for I, the LORD, dwell among the Israelites.'"

> *Listening to the Text in the Story:* Middle Assyrian Laws; Genesis 1:26–27; 9:6; Exodus 21:12; Levitus 24:17

The Middle Assyrian Laws are found on tablets "datable to about the eleventh century [BC], but are copies of compositions that probably date to fourteenth-century originals."[1] Law 10 on tablet A addresses murder and states that the victim's family was able to choose one of two penalties for the murderer: death or a ransom payment.

> [If either] a man or a woman enters [another man's] house and kills [either a man] or a woman, [they shall hand over] the manslayers [to the head of the household]; if he so chooses, he shall kill them; or if he chooses to come to an accommodation, he shall take [their property]; and if there is [nothing of value to give from the house] of the manslayers, either a son [or a daughter . . .].[2]

Like Numbers 35, this law makes clear that a relative of the victim would be the one to execute justice on the killer (cf. 35:19). Unlike Numbers 35, it allows for a ransom payment—the killer's property—in the case of murder. Numbers 35, however, prohibits ransom payments in cases of murder as well as manslaughter; the shedding of human blood by another human was so serious that no monetary payment was sufficient. This perspective finds its root in the biblical story, which begins by describing that every human, male and female, is created in God's image (Gen 1:26–27). This makes human beings of incalculable worth, so much so that to take the life of an innocent human being was one of the greatest wrongs that could be done. In such cases, the only penalty great enough for spilling human blood was to forfeit one's own (Gen 9:6; Exod 21:12; Lev 24:17). From this perspective, capital punishment was not to say, "The life of the guilty matters very little," but rather to say, "The life of the innocent matters very much!"

---

1. "The Middle Assyrian Laws," trans. Martha Roth (*COS* 2.132, p. 354).
2. Ibid. (*COS* 2.132:10).

EXPLAIN the Story

Cities for the Levites (35:1–8)

In contrast to the other tribes (Num 34), the Levites did not inherit large land tracts (18:21–24) and were therefore to be given forty-eight cities in which to live (35:1–3, 6). This need not mean that only Levites could live there (cf. Josh 21:13 with 2 Sam 2) but would mean they had free permission to settle in them.

When the land was divided, these cities were spread throughout it (see Josh 21:1–48 and map 6), which had at least two benefits. First, since the cities came from the other tribes' inheritance, spreading them throughout the land helped to ensure tribes were giving equally of their inheritance (cf. Num 35:8). Second, since one function of the Levites was to serve as a living reminder that the Israelites' ultimate inheritance was not the land but the Lord (see at 18:20–32, p. 252), the presence of Levites throughout the land would make sure this reminder was everywhere to be seen.[3]

While the Levites were not given large land tracts for farming, they were allowed animals, which were central to providing many daily needs. As a result, the Israelites were to give the Levites pasturelands around the forty-eight cities (35:4–5). There is some debate on how to understand the measurement of the pasturelands described here, but many understand the 1,000 cubits (1,500 feet or about 450 meters) to be the distance from the wall of the city to the edge of the pasturelands (v. 4), and the 2,000 cubits (3,000 feet or about 900 meters) to be the length of the outer edge of the pasturelands when thought of as a square (v. 5). Since the size of the town itself would also have to be accounted for, it is often understood this would have been an assumed addition to the 2,000 cubits (see diagram below),[4] though many of the towns may have been quite small, so that the 2,000 cubits would have been fairly close to the actual measurements.[5]

As for the cities themselves (Num 35:6–8), they were to be distributed proportionately among the tribes (v. 8; cf. 26:53–54; 33:54). Six of them were to be cities of refuge (35:6), which are discussed next (vv. 9–34).

---

3. See further p. 255, What Do We Learn from the Lord's Provision for His Servants?
4. Ashley, *Numbers*, 646; Milgrom, *Numbers*, 503; cf. Keil, *The Pentateuch*, 833–34 (*Numbers*, 259–60). The diagram below is adapted from Milgrom, *Numbers*, 503.
5. Cf. Wenham, *Numbers*, 234–35.

Pasturelands

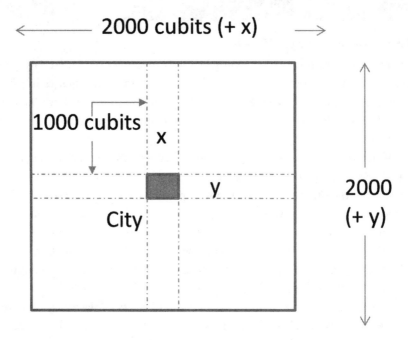

Cities of Refuge (35:9–34)[6]

Cities of refuge were necessary for two reasons. First, when one person killed another, it was common practice for one of the slain person's relatives ("the avenger of blood") to kill the killer (Num 35:19; cf. 2 Sam 3:27). But what if the death was an accident (manslaughter)? The person committing manslaughter was not to be killed and could take refuge in these cities and be protected from the slain person's angry relatives. Second, when innocent blood was spilled, it was considered to have defiled the land. And because the Lord was going to dwell in the Israelites' midst in the land, to defile it was not only to say that his holiness was of no importance, it was also to invite his judgment. Indeed, the Lord was using the Israelites to bring his judgment on those who had defiled his holy land and he would bring the same judgment to bear against them if they did the same (cf. Lev 18:24–30). As discussed below, however, a city of refuge provided a way to address the land's pollution, so that Israel was not punished, while also protecting the person who had killed someone unintentionally (see further discussion at the end of this chapter: Live the Story: What Do the Laws about Cities of Refuge Teach Us about the Lord's View of Human Life?)

---

6. See also Exod 21:12–15; Deut 4:41–43; 19:1–13; Josh 20:1–9.

As for the structure of Numbers 35:9–34, it opens with a general overview (35:9–15). It commands for six cities to be set aside for refuge, three on each side of the Jordan (see Josh 20:7–8 and map 6). Any person, native or non-native, who has killed someone accidentally may take refuge in these cities and be protected from "the avenger"—also known as "the avenger of blood" (Num 25:19, 21, 24, 25, 27)—until a trial is arranged. The avenger was the person who executed justice and is usually understood to be a close relative of the deceased. The word for "avenger" is the same word used elsewhere to describe a "redeemer" (Heb. *go'el*), that is, a relative who looked out for his family's interests, and Deuteronomy 19:6 describes the avenger as being "in a rage," as one would expect of a relative of the person killed.

A series of more specific laws now follows (Num 35:16–34). Since cities of refuge are for someone who has killed unintentionally, the opening laws address the difference between intentional killing (murder; vv. 16–21) and unintentional killing (manslaughter; vv. 22–25).[7] In terms of murder, six different cases are described. The first three are characterized by excessive force: the killer uses a secondary object that anyone would know could cause lethal harm (an iron object, a stone, a wooden object; vv. 16–18). The next three are characterized by intent to harm by a killer who has been storing up their rage and lets it loose fatally, whether through shoving the victim in hatred, lying in wait to throw something,[8] or striking them out of long-standing enmity (vv. 20–21). In any of these situations, they either should have known better (cases 1–3) or they committed lethal action prompted by pre-existing enmity (cases 4–6).[9] Either way, the intent to harm was clear, and the killer is to be held liable for the death. In such cases, and after the appropriate trial (vv. 12, 24–25, 30), the avenger shall execute the murderer (v. 19).[10]

While the last three cases of murder involved pre-existing intent to harm, the three cases of manslaughter are just the opposite: pushing someone "suddenly" but "without enmity," throwing an object but not lying in wait,[11] or dropping a stone on someone without seeing them (Num 35:22–23a). In each

---

7. A third situation—killing in self-defense—is not addressed here, though another law makes clear there was no guilt in such cases (Exod 22:2).

8. See ESV and NASB, which are closer to the Hebrew.

9. Cf. Deut 19:4, which describes the unintentional killer as one who acted "without having hated [the victim] in the past."

10. The phrase "when the avenger comes upon (Heb. root *p-g-'*) the murderer, the avenger shall put the murderer to death" is perhaps better translated, "when the avenger attacks the murderer, the avenger shall put the murderer to death," that is, he will not simply inflict physical punishment in general but capital punishment in particular (so also 35:21). For *p-g-'* with the sense "attack, strike," see Exod 5:3; Judg 18:25; 1 Sam 22:17.

11. See Deut 19:4–5.

case, the killer "was not an enemy and was not seeking the other person's harm" (v. 23b, my translation), which could describe two separate realities (there was no pre-existing enmity and no intent to harm) or be using two phrases to describe the same reality (there was no intent to harm that expresses pre-existing enmity). The former is supported by the fact that this passage and one other provide examples that focus on the fact that no harm at all was intended: the killer drops a stone on someone "without seeing them" (Num 35:23), or "a man may go into the forest with his neighbor to cut wood, and as he swings his ax to fell a tree, the head may fly off and hit his neighbor and kill him" (Deut. 19:5).[12] In such cases, a public trial takes place, and the verdict must be made in keeping with these regulations (v. 24), the assumption being that the court would be able to discern the laws' underlying principles and apply them in a wide variety of situations.[13] When a killing had been ruled unintentional, the assembly was responsible for protecting the unintentional killer from the avenger of blood and returning them safely to the city of refuge (v. 25a).[14]

Significantly, the unintentional killer had to remain there "until the death of the high priest" (Num 35:25b), at which point they were allowed to go free. As many commentators have observed, the high priest's death appears to function as an atoning sacrifice, his blood being taken as a substitute for that of the unintentional killer and cleansing the land of innocent blood. See further comments at the end of this chapter: Live the Story: How Does the Death of the High Priest Prepare Us for the Rest of the Story?

Conversely, if the unintentional killer left the town in advance, they were saying the lifeblood of the slain was of little consequence and had now signed their own death warrant (Num 35:26–28). To view life as so cheap is to forfeit one's own, making yourself fair game for the ultimate judgment of death,

---

12. Some modern bodies of law make a distinction between premeditated murder, in which there is planned intent to harm, and non-premeditated murder (sometimes labeled as a "crime of passion"), in which there is intent to harm but such harm is not preplanned. While the first of these aligns well with how this passage is describing murder in vv. 20–21, it does not align as well with how murder is described in vv. 16–18, which do not focus on premeditation but on whether or not instruments of lethal force are used. As for the modern conception of non-premeditated murder, it does not align neatly with how this passage describes manslaughter since this passage focuses on lack of intent to commit harm (see above discussion). Is it possible an ancient Israelite court might understand the laws of this chapter to allow room for a person to be judged guilty of manslaughter if it was clear they did not intend *lethal* harm (as when two people get into a spontaneous fight and one pushes the other over and they end up striking their head against a stone and dying)? Potentially, but even if such an approach to these laws is possible, it would be important to note the qualifications already present in vv. 16–18 and to consider how these would factor into determination of innocence or guilt.

13. See especially the helpful discussion in Stuart, *Exodus*, 442–45, for how case law functioned in ancient Israel.

14. That they return to the city of refuge suggests the trial took place outside of it, though whether this took place at the crime scene or at the gates of the city of refuge is not clear.

which could be carried out by the avenger of blood without guilt. If this sounds harsh, it might not be because we think too highly of the life of the guilty, but because we think too lowly of the life of the slain.

The chapter finishes with a series of commands related to bloodshed. In the first, the capital penalty may only be applied in cases where there were multiple witnesses (Num 35:30). Because life was so valuable, it could not be taken unless guilt was absolutely clear. And because these laws assume the judge's common sense, the witnesses would have to be deemed reliable.

In the second and third, the Israelites are prohibited from taking ransom from those guilty of killing another. In the case of murder, the murderer had to be executed (Num 35:31); in the case of manslaughter, the guilty had to remain in the city of refuge until the high priest's death (v. 32).

The final commands explain why a ransom payment is prohibited (Num 35:33–34). To begin, innocent lifeblood pollutes the land and could only be atoned for by the lifeblood of the slayer, not by a ransom payment of money (see below: Live the Story: What Do the Laws about Cities of Refuge Teach Us about the Lord's View of Human Life?). To accept a ransom payment is to leave the stain unaddressed (v. 33). What is more, because the Lord dwells in the Israelites' midst in the land, they must keep it free from such pollution, both to honor his holiness and to avoid his judgment (v. 34; cf. opening paragraph at 35:9–34 above). We cannot claim to walk with a holy God if we do not make his holy presence welcome.

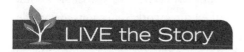

LIVE the Story

What Might It Look Like to Provide Cities for Levites Today?

Unlike the rest of the Israelites, the Levites were not given large land tracts as part of their inheritance. Instead, they had been set aside to serve the priests at the tabernacle so that the Lord's worship could take place regularly, and their inheritance was to consist of the Israelites' tithes to the Lord (Num 18:21–24). When the Lord shared these gifts with the Levites, it was his way of saying, "You will not have physical land as an inheritance from which to provide for your needs, but you will have my service as an inheritance, and I myself will provide for your needs by means of it."[15] Consequently, the Levites became a stark reminder to Israel that the ultimate inheritance one lived for was not real estate but relationship with the living God. As one commentator notes,

---

15. See further p. 255, What Do We Learn from the Lord's Provision for His Servants?

"Truly, he who possesses God possesses all things."¹⁶ By spreading the Levites' cities throughout the land, the Lord ensured this reminder was everywhere to be seen. This was important since we so quickly fix our eyes on material things that we often lose sight of our greatest good.

In today's context, we no longer have Levites, but we do have pastors and ministry leaders who have given up other means of income—often far more lucrative—in order to serve the Lord in a full-time capacity. As we think about such leaders, this chapter's lessons about the Levites apply in two different ways. First, we can let the very fact our leaders have dedicated their lives to such service be a reminder to us that serving the Lord is indeed what we have been called to do. This is not to say that to serve him you must be in Christian vocational ministry full-time (or even part-time). The first person created to bring God glory was a gardener (Gen 2:15), and Paul likewise affirms that all our work—whether vocational Christian ministry or not—is to be done as service unto the Lord (Col 3:23). At the same time, our ministry leaders do remind us that serving and loving God is our greatest and highest good.

Second, the Israelites were to provide for the Levites' needs through their tithes to the Lord (Num 18:21–24) and through the provision of these cities (35:1–8), in this way enabling them to dedicate time to the service of God's tabernacle and his worship. What does it look like for us to do the same? Since we are not going into a new land and dividing it up among a nation, it will not mean setting aside cities per se. But the provision of tithes and cities provided food and shelter, two of our most basic human needs, and Christians should do the same for those who lead them in the Lord's work. Questions to consider include, "Are we paying our ministry leaders a living wage? Are they able to afford housing in our midst, or do they have to live far away from the church in which they serve while the church's members do not?" If we deeply desire for the Lord's worship to continue strongly, we will do everything we can to free up our leaders' time so that they can lead us in that worship without being burdened by the material concerns of this world.

What Do the Laws about Cities of Refuge Teach Us about the Lord's View of Human Life?

In at least three different ways, these laws show how deeply the Lord values human life. First, the city of refuge was there to protect the innocent. In the case of manslaughter, the unintentional killer was not to be put to death (Num 35:22–25), but the avenger of blood might be so enraged by the death

---

16. Keil, *The Pentateuch*, 731 (*Numbers*, 118), citing Masius's commentary on Joshua.

of his family member that he takes matters into his own hands and executes his relative's killer (cf. Deut 19:6). These cities were to prevent that from happening. Second, the highest standards of proof were necessary to convict of a capital crime (Num 35:30). One had to be sure that someone who was about to be executed was indeed guilty. Third, the loss of life was taken with the utmost seriousness. In the case of murder, capital punishment was applied, emphasizing "the sacredness of life. No-one could take a life without surrendering his own."[17] Because of the value life has, taking it is the greatest crime and is met with the greatest penalty.

Each of the above shows how deeply the Lord values life. Even the commandment, "Do not murder," requires much more than simply not killing someone. As Gordon Wenham points out, while biblical laws name a minimum standard of behavior one must follow (what he calls the "floor"), they implicitly point to a higher ethic that one must embody (what he calls the "ceiling").[18] The reason one must not murder (the floor) is because the Lord values life, which means we must do all we can to help life to flourish (the ceiling).[19] In the context of Numbers 35 in particular, we do well to ask, "How can we value life by supporting efforts to reform legal and judicial systems toward increasing standards of justice? In what ways do our legal and judicial systems favor the rich and majority cultures and penalize the poor and minority cultures? At what points do these systems not take certain crimes seriously enough? What might reform look like in all of these areas, and how can we support it so that human life might flourish?" In fighting for these things, we are living out the values of the God we serve.

How Does the Death of the High Priest Prepare Us for the Rest of the Story?

In cases of manslaughter, the unintentional killer had to remain in the city of refuge "until the death of the high priest" (Num 35:25b), at which point they could go free. How may this be explained?

As the passage goes on to make clear, shedding innocent blood pollutes the land (Num 35:33). For one person to shed another's blood is so against God's creation norms that the lifeblood itself is pictured elsewhere as crying out for justice (Gen 4:10) and pictured here as a defiling stain that pollutes the land. Only lifeblood does full justice to such a wrong. When one person has killed another, any other penalty—like paying money—is an insult to

---

17. Tidball, *Leviticus*, 289.
18. Gordon Wenham, "The Gap Between Law and Ethics in the Bible," *JJS* 48.1 (1997): 17–29.
19. Cf. questions 135–136 of the Westminster Larger Catechism.

justice, a cheapening of life. But what if you killed unintentionally? As long as you remained in the city, you acknowledged the greatness of the wrong and the dignity of the life that had been lost; you acknowledged only your lifeblood was great enough to pay for this wrong (cf. Num 35:33), and that acknowledgment was like a temporary atoning sacrifice that allowed the Lord to suspend justice until another means could be found to satisfy it. That means was the death of the high priest, whose lifeblood now served, like a sacrifice, in place of the lifeblood of the guilty, cleansing the land and allowing them to go home. Milgrom, in agreement with the Mishnah and Talmud, summarizes: "As the High Priest atones for Israel's sins through his cultic service in his lifetime (Exod 28:36; Lev 16:16, 21), so he atones for homicide through his death.... The blood of the slain ... is ransomed through the death of the High Priest."[20]

This picture anticipates and prepares us for what Jesus Christ would do. The book of Hebrews emphasizes that Jesus is not only the ultimate High Priest (7:26; 8:1), but that "he sacrificed for ... sins once for all when he offered himself" (7:27; cf. 9:12, 28; 10:10). His lifeblood in place of ours. What is more, this gift is not limited to one particular sin. In Israel's day, the high priest's lifeblood cleansed the land of the pollution caused by manslaughter. Jesus's lifeblood cleanses us of the pollution caused by all our sin. "If we confess our sins, he is faithful and just and will forgive us our sins and purify us from all unrighteousness" (1 John 1:9). Sin often leaves us feeling defiled, impure; Jesus's blood can cleanse, and its power to cleanse knows no limit. When we come to him in repentant faith, *all* unrighteousness is taken away. As noted earlier, 1 John 1:9 ends with a period, not a comma. There is no defilement too difficult for him to cleanse and no sin he is unwilling to forgive. It remains for us simply to come to him and seek his cleansing touch.[21]

---

20. Milgrom, *Numbers*, 294. For the Mishnah, he cites Makkot 2:6; for the Babylonian Talmud, he cites Makkot 11b; he also cites the fifth-century Jewish commentary Leviticus Rabbah 10:6.

21. See further pp. 94–95, How Does Jesus Deal with Our Impurity? and pp. 263–64, How Does Cleansing Happen?

CHAPTER 37

Numbers 36:1–13

 LISTEN to the Story

¹The family heads of the clan of Gilead son of Makir, the son of Manasseh, who were from the clans of the descendants of Joseph, came and spoke before Moses and the leaders, the heads of the Israelite families. ²They said, "When the Lord commanded my lord to give the land as an inheritance to the Israelites by lot, he ordered you to give the inheritance of our brother Zelophehad to his daughters. ³Now suppose they marry men from other Israelite tribes; then their inheritance will be taken from our ancestral inheritance and added to that of the tribe they marry into. And so part of the inheritance allotted to us will be taken away. ⁴When the Year of Jubilee for the Israelites comes, their inheritance will be added to that of the tribe into which they marry, and their property will be taken from the tribal inheritance of our ancestors."

⁵Then at the Lord's command Moses gave this order to the Israelites: "What the tribe of the descendants of Joseph is saying is right. ⁶This is what the Lord commands for Zelophehad's daughters: They may marry anyone they please as long as they marry within their father's tribal clan. ⁷No inheritance in Israel is to pass from one tribe to another, for every Israelite shall keep the tribal inheritance of their ancestors. ⁸Every daughter who inherits land in any Israelite tribe must marry someone in her father's tribal clan, so that every Israelite will possess the inheritance of their ancestors. ⁹No inheritance may pass from one tribe to another, for each Israelite tribe is to keep the land it inherits."

¹⁰So Zelophehad's daughters did as the Lord commanded Moses. ¹¹Zelophehad's daughters—Mahlah, Tirzah, Hoglah, Milkah and Noah—married their cousins on their father's side. ¹²They married within the clans of the descendants of Manasseh son of Joseph, and their inheritance remained in their father's tribe and clan.

> ¹³These are the commands and regulations the LORD gave through Moses to the Israelites on the plains of Moab by the Jordan across from Jericho.

Listening to the Text in the Story: Numbers 27:1–11

Chapter 27 tells the story of Zelophehad's daughters. Normally, land passed on to sons, which kept the land within the clan[1] and enabled the sons to continue the father's line (and therefore name) within Israel. But since Zelophehad died without sons, his land would go to a near relative who would not carry on his name. Zelophehad's daughters therefore requested his inheritance go to them, the idea apparently being that any men who married land-owning daughters married into the estate (and thus the family by proxy),[2] just as someone today might marry into the "house" (and therefore name) of a wealthy or aristocratic family. By this means, the land would stay within the clan and the "house of Zelophehad" would continue through any grandsons born.[3] The daughters' request was granted (27:5–8). The chapter goes on to say if someone died without sons or daughters, the land would go to a clan member; the deceased person's name would not continue but at least the land would stay within the clan (27:9–11).

As the laws are framed, however, a loophole remains.[4] The story of this chapter is driven by a desire to close it.

The Question Posed (36:1–4)

Just as Zelophehad's daughters presented their case before Moses and Israel's leaders (Num 27:1–2), so too do the members of their clan (36:1). They note the Lord commanded Moses to divide Canaan by lot among the tribes, the implication being these allotments should be permanent since they took place at the Lord's command and under his direction (see at 26:52–56, pp. 329–30).

---

1. See pp. 335–36, Listening to the Text in the Story.
2. Cf. 1 Chr 2:34–36; Neh 7:63.
3. Presumably, the groom would have to be a kinsman; cf. Deut 25:5–6.
4. "As is often the case when legislation is promulgated, further legislation becomes necessary" (Ashley, *Numbers*, 658–59).

They also note the Lord commanded Moses to give Zelophehad's inheritance to his daughters since he had died without sons (36:2), which would normally cause no problems since it is generally assumed the custom was to marry within the tribe,[5] meaning the land would stay within it. But custom is different than law, meaning Zelophehad's daughters could marry outside the tribe. If so, they would take that tribe as their own (cf. how women in some societies take their husband's surname). The land they owned would then technically belong to that tribe, diminishing the original tribe's inheritance (v. 3).[6] Moreover, when the Jubilee Year came, there would be a "reset" of property to its proper owner (cf. Lev 25:10), and since the daughters would have taken the new tribe as their own, the land would officially and permanently become the new tribe's territory (Num 36:4).

The Question Answered (36:5–9)

After presumably bringing this case before the Lord (cf. Num 36:5 with 27:5–7a), Moses brings back an answer. The Lord affirms the concern (36:5) and addresses the problem, naming both a freedom and a restriction. The freedom is that "they may marry anyone they please" (v. 6) or, to follow the Hebrew more woodenly, "to the one who is good in their eyes they may marry." Only then is the restriction given: Zelophehad's daughters, and all heiresses in Israel, must marry within the tribal clan so that land never passes out of it (vv. 6–9). See further at the end of this chapter: Live the Story: Is This Fair?

The Obedience of Zelophehad's Daughters (36:10–12)

Zelophehad's daughters obey the Lord, marrying within their tribal clan so the land stayed within it. The problem that was anticipated (Num 36:1–4) is now fully resolved.

Their husbands were their cousins,[7] which will strike some Western readers as strange, though the practice was more common in Western countries in the past, remains a relatively common practice in many societies to this day,[8] and is not prohibited by the incest laws of Leviticus 18 and 20.

---

5. Philip J. King and Lawrence E. Stager, *Life in Biblical Israel*, Library of Ancient Israel (Louisville: Westminster John Knox Press, 2001), 55.

6. Especially when the woman died and the property passed to her sons who would carry on their own father's name, not Zelophehad's (since their father was not Zelophehad's kinsman.

7. Presumably first, though the Hebrew ("the sons of their uncle") could allow for first cousins once removed since the word "sons" can mean "descendants."

8. Worldwide, marriage to a second cousin or closer accounts for 10 percent of marriages. See A. H. Bittles and M. L. Black, "Consanguinity, human evolution, and complex diseases," *Proceedings of the National Academy of Sciences of the United States of America* 107, supplement 1 (2010): 1779–86 (at https://www.pnas.org/content/107/suppl_1/1779). Well-known Westerners marrying a second

The obedience of Zelophehad's daughters is not only mentioned but highlighted, being placed first in the Hebrew of verse 10: "*Just as the* Lord *commanded Moses*, so the daughters of Zelophehad did" (author's translation, emphasis added). This phrase—"Doing just as the Lord commanded Moses"—is the hallmark of Israel when being faithful (Exod 12:28; Lev 24:23; Num 8:22; etc.) and is here embodied by these women, who are personally named for the third time (cf. Num 26:33; 27:1) and serve as a concluding model of faith, both in their belief that there will be an inheritance to be had in the promised land and in their obedience to the Lord's commands. If the rest of Israel could have the faith of these women, all would be well.

Conclusion (36:13)

The language here recalls Numbers 33:50–51. This ties 33:50 to 36:13 together as a unit, its six sections all assuming Israel would soon be in the land and, in this way, ending the book with hopeful anticipation. Indeed, the concluding verse's mention of Jericho anticipates the battle to come there—and the realization of the land promise made so long ago to Abraham: "The whole land of Canaan . . . I will give as an everlasting possession to you and your descendants after you; and I will be their God" (Gen 17:8). As Wenham notes, "On this strong note of hope the book closes, inviting the curious to read on to see how God's purposes were worked out in the subsequent history of Israel."[9]

LIVE the Story

While Numbers's final chapter is relatively short, it still has important lessons for us today. We may get at these by asking three questions.

Is This Fair?

In Numbers 27:1–11, Zelophehad's five daughters gained the right for any daughter to inherit land when a father died without sons. In this chapter, a limitation is introduced: any such daughter needs to marry within the tribal clan. Such a limitation can leave us feeling as though this is a story of two steps forward, one step back.

There are different reasons behind such feelings, but two in particular come to the fore. First, we often think of romance as the primary deciding factor in

---

cousin or closer include Johann Sebastian Bach (second cousin), Charles Darwin (first cousin), Albert Einstein (first cousin), H. G. Wells (first cousin), and Queen Elizabeth II (second cousin).

9. Wenham, *Numbers*, 240.

marriage, making this limitation seem unfair and oppressive. But prioritizing romance is a very modern way of thinking. In biblical times (and throughout much of history), "the various factors in a marriage to be weighed in the negotiations involved social parity, economic advantage and expansion of the kinship network."[10] This does not preclude romance, but it was not the leading factor. This also relates to the second reason we struggle with this passage: because our thinking is so individualistic, we think of marriage as strictly a personal choice, which makes any limitations seem oppressive. In Israel's day, however, they thought corporately: I am a member of a people, and the person who becomes my marriage partner impacts the rest of my clan and tribe. In this case in particular, where land transference was at stake, the "limitation serve[d] the good of the tribe and also the larger good of relative economic equality that the tribal land system itself serves."[11] We therefore have no reason to think Zelophehad's daughters would have agreed with us that this limitation was oppressive; indeed, to choose otherwise may have seemed to them to be incredibly selfish.[12]

In sum, the passage underscores the obedient faith of Zelophehad's daughters, placing them among other female biblical characters that God's people do well to emulate (such as Rahab in Josh 2, Hannah in 1 Sam 1–2, and Mary in Luke 1). This leads to our next question.

What Do These Five Women Model?

In Numbers 27:1–11, emphasis was placed on their faith: they believed that the Lord's promise to give Israel the land would indeed come to pass. In this passage, emphasis is placed on the obedience flowing from their faith. "So Zelophehad's daughters did as the LORD commanded Moses" (36:10). And their obedience meant they were not afraid to accept certain limits on their lives, if that meant being faithful to God's word.

For the believer today, this may indeed impact our choice of marriage partners since this is not the last time the Lord puts limits on whom his people may marry. In describing a Christian widow's right to remarry, Paul uses language similar to our passage when he says, "she is free to marry anyone she wishes, but he must belong to the Lord" (1 Cor 7:39). Freedom, yet limitation (cf. Num 36:6!). And this is generally understood as something that applies to all believers, the implications of which are well explained by Duguid:

---

10. Victor H. Matthews, "Family Relationships," *DOOTP* 294.
11. Stubbs, *Numbers*, 348. See also comments pp. 335–36, Listening to the Text in the Story, and the longer quote from Stubbs in Sklar, *Additional Notes*, at Num 36, Live the Story.
12. Moreover, since their goal was to continue their father's line, they would have wanted to marry within their tribe (perhaps even their clan).

> You are not bound to marry someone from your own clan and tribe: issues of culture, race, social and educational background, interests, and tastes are all secondary to marrying in Christ. . . . Yet as a Christian, you must marry another Christian. This only makes sense, for how could you unite yourself at the deepest level to someone whose fundamental allegiance is to another master? You would be making two commitments that are at war with one another.[13]

Like Zelophehad's daughters, we honor the Lord when we obey his commands and accept this limitation.

But following Christ means obeying him in all aspects of life, and this will require limitations in all sorts of areas that those around us may not accept. With our money, we are not free to spend it simply as we wish; the believer seeks to obey the Lord's command, "Honor the LORD with your wealth, with the firstfruits of all your crops" (Prov 3:9). With our time, we are not free to spend it only on ourselves but will seek to show practical love to others as we seek to honor the Lord's command, "Love your neighbor as yourself" (Lev 19:18; Mark 12:31). Our very lives are no longer ours to do with as we please; they belong to Christ, whose yoke we take on ourselves that we might walk with him in his paths (Matt 11:28–30).

To accept such limits—to deny ourselves for Christ's sake—is to express faith at the deepest level. And, like Zelophehad's daughters, such faith requires knowing that the Lord is faithful to his promises and has made our inheritance in a promised land of blessing and rest an assured reality. This leads to the last question.

What Is the Hope of Our Inheritance?

In Hebrews 3–4, the author uses the wilderness generation as a warning, exhorting Christians not to follow their example of hard-hearted unbelief and disobedience, lest they—like that first generation—fail to enter into the promised land of God's rest (see esp. Heb 3:7–19). In other words, the physical promised land of Canaan with all its blessings is a picture of the far greater promised land of heaven with all its far deeper blessings. And just as belief and covenant faithfulness were required to enter into Canaan, so too belief and covenant faithfulness are required to enter into heaven.

For the believer today, such belief and faithfulness is centered on the Lord Jesus Christ. Hebrews 3, in fact, begins with the exhortation, "Fix your

---

13. Duguid, *Numbers*, 368.

thoughts on Jesus" (v. 1). He is the one who guarantees our future in a land of eternal blessing and rest. He is the one who makes our hope for an inheritance sure. The Israelites were once slaves, but God redeemed them, calling them his own child (Exod 4:23) and giving them as an inheritance the land of Canaan, where he would walk in their midst. Similarly, we were once slaves to sin, but in Christ God redeemed us, calling us his own children (Gal 4:7) and giving us for an inheritance heaven itself, where he will walk in our midst.

Knowing where the path of faith leads, and the One who walks with us on the path, is what enables costly obedience now. It matters not if the path goes through the wilderness; Jesus is with us and is guiding us to the promised land of rest. It matters not if enemies stand in the way; Jesus is with us and will fight for us and take us safely to the promised land of rest. This is a sure and certain hope that enables us to sacrifice joyfully and obey boldly, for our end is sure—and, in Christ, is a promised land beyond all we can ask or imagine.

Scripture Index

Genesis

1	107
1–2	21
1:26–27	408
1:26–28	301, 312
1:28	32, 121, 294
2	107
2:15	414
2:24	108
3:1–19	121
3:8	22
3:9	290
3:12	233
3:12–13	13
4:9	290
4:10	415
6:4	196
6:5–7	282
7:2	32
8:1	161
8:21	212
9:1	121
9:1–3	301
9:6	408
9:7	301
9:15, 16	161
10:1, 6	184
10:21–24	310
11:10–26	184
12:1	255
12:1–3	21, 48, 121, 122
12:2	22, 31, 52, 55
12:2–3	22, 301
12:3	17, 22, 155, 157, 168, 171, 185, 290, 294, 301, 302, 313, 320
12:3a	293
12:7	22, 26, 52, 55, 194
13:14–18	196
13:15	194, 255
13:16	17, 301, 302, 329
13:18	196
14	290
14:14	196
15:5	22, 31, 52, 55, 169
15:7	255, 400
15:12	307
15:16	279, 282, 399, 402
15:18	22, 26, 52, 55, 194
15:18–21	18
15:19–20	279
16:6	308
16:9–10	291
17:1–8	21
17:3	198
17:7	22
17:7–8	256
17:8	48, 194, 382, 420
17:21	48
18:14	114
18:17–33	200
18:23	228
18:25	372
18:33	310
19:15, 17	228
19:29	161
20:2	308
20:3	290
20:12	220
22:11–12	291
22:14	168
22:15–18	121
23	196
23:7–16	168
23:11–15	290
24:2	186
24:3–9	360
24:28–31	369
24:30–31	369
24:60	169
24:67a	220
25:1–4	184
25:3	310
25:9	196
25:18	310

26:1	308
26:2–4	301
26:3	22, 26, 400
26:4	22
26:24	22
26:28–30	117, 346
27–28	4
27:29	17, 301, 302
27:33	290
27:43	308
28:4	400
28:13–15	301
28:14	17, 302
28:20–22	360
29:34	242
30:1–24	106
31:7	202
31:14	248, 252
31:16	310
31:24	290
31:44, 46, 53–54	117
31:55–32:1a	310
32:3, 28	270
34:27–29	369
34:29	369
35:22	233
35:27–29	196
36:1	270
37:1–41	293
37:11	104
37:34	198
38:7–10	328
39:4	186
42:1	233
42:21	383
43:15	336
43:19	383
43:34	346
44:18	383
45:13	199
46:8–24	328
46:10	277
46:17	328
47:7	74
48:1, 5	52
49:1	308
49:3–4	64, 382
49:8	64
49:9	17, 301, 302
49:10	17, 64, 240, 301, 302, 309, 314
50:13	196

Exodus

1–15	179
1–19	28, 49
1:1–7	139
1:11–14	236
1:15–22	236
2:10a	220
2:15	308
2:15–16	289
2:18	168
2:21	184
2:23	198, 236
2:23–24	175
2:24	161
3:1	168, 289, 340
3:1–15:21	51
3:7	175
3:8	255
3:9	175
4:10–17	185
4:18	168
4:22	151, 251, 357
4:23	423
5:3	411
6:5	175
6:5–7	320
6:6–8	48, 75
6:9	175
6:15	277
6:16–20	73
6:20	72
7:5	75
10:2	75
12	392
12–15	50
12:1–10	154
12:1–13	74
12:1–28	154
12:2	154
12:8	155
12:10	155
12:12	75, 395
12:12–13	154
12:15	350
12:16	350
12:17	349

12:25–27	154
12:28	20, 420
12:29–36	154
12:37	392
12:37–19:1	267
12:38	175
12:39	349
12:42	154
12:46	155
12:48	157
13:1–2	75
13:2	251
13:3–10	75
13:6–8	75
13:11–16	75
13:12	251
13:12–15	75
13:13	251
13:14–15	251
13:20	392
13:21–22	160
14:2–15:26	392
14:10–12	202
14:11	268
14:19	270
14:31	199
14:39–45	174, 295
15:1–21	48, 55, 279
15:11	114
15:20	185
15:20–21	268
15:22–24	174, 202
15:22–25	10, 179
15:22–18:27	51
15:24	198
15:27	392
16	10, 176
16:1	392
16:1–3	202
16:1–13	179
16:1–14	174
16:2	198
16:3	268
16:19–20	202
16:27–30	202
16:31	175
16:34	241
17	269, 392
17:1–4	202
17:1–7	174, 179, 267, 268, 272
17:2–7	202
17:3	198, 268
17:6	269
17:8	309
17:8–16	179
17:9	195
17:9–14	177, 338
17:10	174
17:14	4, 309
18:1	168, 310
18:19	308
18:25	52
18:25–26	176
19	5, 49, 166
19–Num 10	167
19:1	51
19:1–2	51
19:1–Num 10:10	51
19:2	392
19:6	7, 22, 25, 26, 48, 49, 118, 119, 171, 216, 225, 320
19:9	177
19:10–11	176
19:13	52
19:14–15	176
19:16	177
19:16–18	199
19:18	160
20–23	28, 49
20:2	28
20:2–5	174
20:3–6	316, 403
20:3–17	28
20:5	318
20:6	111
20:14	107
20:18	199
20:18–21	160
20:23	316
21:12	408
21:12–15	410
22:2	411
22:11	101
22:16	372
23:14–17	350
23:16	250, 350
23:16b	352
23:19	213, 250

23:27–28	399
23:33	399
24:3–8	346
24:4	4
24:7	4
24:13	177, 185
24:15	81
24:15–16	177
24:16–17	199
25–27	49
25–31	49
25:1–3	174
25:1–9	60
25:10–40	79
25:10–26:37	60
25:17–22	137
25:22	49, 61, 142, 169, 240, 243
25:30	141, 142
25:31	141
25:31–36	142
25:31–40	142
25:36	160
25:37	142
26:1	216
26:1–14	82
26:15–29	83
26:31–33	81
26:31–35	60
26:36–37	82
28:37	83
27:1–8	79
27:2	230
27:9–18	82
27:9–19	83
27:21	242
28	60
28:6	216
28:8	216
28:28	80, 216
28:30	338
28:31	80
28:33	216
28:36	416
28:37	80, 216
28:43	60
29:14	361
29:24	106
29:27–28	118
29:29	270
29:38–42	345, 348
29:40	348
29:42–46	22, 49
29:45	225
30	49
30:1	136
30:1–10	60, 79
30:7–8	141, 142
30:9	212
30:10	352
30:11–16	50, 374
30:12	374, 375
30:13	374, 375
30:14	374
30:15	374, 375
30:16	78, 374, 375
30:18–21	105, 147
30:22–33	81, 134
30:34–38	81
31:2–5	177
31:12–17	215, 348
31:14–15	215
31:16–17	215
31:18	53, 73
31:49	374
31:50	374
31:54	374
32	194
32:1	73
32:1–6	316, 317, 403
32:1–35	202
32:4	399
32:10	199
32:10–14	200
32:11–13	200
32:11–14	175
32:12	200
32:17	177
32:24	399
32:25–28	53
33:4	202
33:11	177, 186
33:20	160, 186, 200
33:21–23	186
34	49
34:3	212
34:6–7	200, 201
34:6–7a	15, 16, 200
34:6b–7a	207

34:7	331
34:7b	201, 207
34:10	114
34:14–15	319
34:15	316, 319
34:15–16	185, 317, 318
34:20	251
34:22	350
34:26	213
34:27–28	4
34:32	4
35–40	49, 223, 224
35:1	160
35:3	207
35:18	83
37:17–24	142
38:8	74
38:24–31	83, 138
38:30	230
40	7
40:2	51, 154, 160
40:5	240
40:17	134
40:17–33	133, 134
40:20	53
40:22–25	142
40:22–27	142
40:24–26	142
40:28	81
40:34	160
40:34–35	199
40:34–38	49, 159
40:36–8	160

Leviticus

1	211
1–5	85
1–7	345
1:3	8, 245, 260
1:4	105, 117, 348
2:1–3	249
2:2	212
2:3	106
3–5	211
3:1	245, 260
3:2	8
3:3–5	212
3:7	245
3:11	346
4:3	260
4:5–6	260
4:11–12	260
4:13–15	147
4:13–21	214
4:16–17	260
4:20	116
4:21	260
4:24	261
4:27–31	249
4:28, 32	260
5:1	218
5:4	363
5:5–6	218
5:6	116
5:9	261
5:11	104, 261
5:12	261
5:14–6:7	116
5:20–26	218
6:1–7	96, 97, 98, 116, 218
6:2–3	97
6:3	97, 348
6:4	348
6:5	97
6:8–13	348
6:15–17	212
6:16–18	249
6:20–23	81
6:23	212
6:24–30	249
7:1–6	249
7:2–7	97
7:5	212
7:14	213
7:16	353, 360
7:19–21	155
7:29–30	106
7:30	250
7:30–31	148
7:31–33	118
7:32	118
7:34	118, 250, 251
8	8, 225
8–9	243
8:3	161
8:7–9	270
8:10–11	133, 134
8:12	9

8:13	270
8:14–20	148
8:14–29	116
8:15	116, 260
8:22	116
8:28	212
8:30	9, 146, 259
8:31	116, 118
9	7, 135
9:5	161
9:15–21	117
9:21	106
9:22	122
9:22–23	121, 125
9:24	135, 198
10	73
10:1–2	242
10:1–3	73, 87, 226
10:2	53, 229
10:4–15	73
10:6	105
10:8	185
10:9	113, 114, 115
10:11	73, 150, 378
10:14	118
10:14–15	118, 148
11–15	258
11–27	49
11:1	185
11:24–28	259
11:32	373
12	259
12:1–8	263
12:2	104, 260
12:6	8
12:7	116
13	186
13–14	259
13:1	185
13:3	104
13:45	106
13:45–46	186
13:46	92
14:1–32	93
14:4	260, 261
14:6–7	261
14:7	259
14:8	147
14:11	105
14:12	106
14:34	382
14:46–47	259
14:51	147
14:51–52	259
15:2–15	92
15:13	260
15:13–15	93, 116, 259
15:16–18	92
15:18	32, 259, 263
15:19–24	92, 258
15:25–30	92
15:28–30	93, 259
15:31	26, 91, 92
16	90, 345, 352
16:1	73
16:2	73
16:2–4	137
16:2–34	351
16:3	352
16:3–6	347
16:3–28	352
16:5	352
16:13	81
16:14	260
16:14–19	260
16:16	352, 416
16:18	352
16:19	116, 260, 352
16:21	81, 416
16:21a	90
16:22	89, 90
16:27–28	261
16:30	352
16:32	270
16:34	352
17:7	316, 319, 403
17:11	89
18	282, 419
18:19	32
18:20	104, 107
18:24	104, 383
18:24–25	282
18:24–27	399, 402
18:24–30	26, 410
19:2	150
19:5–8	117
19:13	294
19:14	110

19:18	124, 422
19:34	157
19:35	294
20	282, 419
20:22–26	26
20:23–24	282, 399, 402
21:1–3	113, 114
21:6	346
21:10	105
21:10–11	113, 114
22:2	230
22:10–13	249
22:18	353
22:18–20	348
22:21	353
22:29–30	117
23	85, 211, 212, 345, 355
23:4–5	155
23:9–14	213, 350
23:15	350
23:15–16	347
23:15–21	350
23:16	350
23:26–32	351
23:34	352
23:37	212
23:43	352
24:1–4	81, 142
24:1–9	141
24:3	141
24:5–9	142
24:7	143
24:8	143
24:9	249
24:10–12	336
24:10–13	215
24:16	53
24:17	408
24:23	20, 216, 420
25:9	351
25:10	419
25:17	110
25:23	248, 252
25:36	110
26	14, 122, 404
26:3	123
26:3–10	122, 404
26:3–13	121, 122
26:4–13	123
26:6	123
26:11–12	122, 256, 404
26:18	14
26:18–20	15
26:26	202
26:38	197
27:1–8	135
27:2	212, 365
27:2–8	365
27:6	251
27:8	365
27:14–19	230
27:21	251
27:27	251
27:28	251
27:30–31	252
27:32–33	252

Numbers

1	7, 10, 30, 31, 33, 48, 59, 66, 78, 329
1–2	9, 18, 72, 75
1–4	2, 10, 18, 90, 91, 327, 330
1–10	49
1–25	34, 48, 166, 327
1:1	2, 3, 21, 49, 51, 55, 56, 57, 61, 73, 134, 142
1:1–46	49
1:1–54	45–48
1:1–10:10	1, 2, 6, 7, 16, 33, 34, 48, 49, 154, 166, 326, 327
1:1–25:18	6, 33
1:2	50, 61
1:2–3	52
1:2–46	50, 328
1:2–4:49	34
1:3	50, 149, 203
1:4	51, 240
1:4–16	84, 161
1:5–15	52, 134
1:16	51, 240
1:18	30, 52
1:19	52
1:20	63
1:20–46	22, 23, 50, 52, 55
1:21	31, 240
1:34–39	78
1:37	31
1:44–46	64
1:44–54	64

1:46	30, 31
1:47	30
1:47–53	8, 24, 49, 52, 53, 56, 57, 61, 64, 72, 73, 74, 77, 81, 94, 137, 148, 160, 167, 223, 224, 242, 330, 373
1:50	53, 56
1:50–53	53, 72, 74
1:51	53, 72
1:52–53	54, 61
1:53	32, 54, 87
1:53b	54
1:54	2, 3, 7, 25, 48, 52, 64, 154, 174
2	7, 59, 64, 66, 135
2:1	3, 61
2:1–2	61
2:1–31	62
2:1–34	49, 57–59
2:3	50, 64
2:3–9	62
2:3–31	7, 8, 54, 59, 62, 167
2:5	63
2:7	63
2:9	62, 65
2:10–16	62
2:16	63, 65
2:17	64, 167
2:18–24	62
2:24	65
2:25–31	62
2:31	63, 65
2:32–34	64
2:33	3, 64
2:33–34	25
2:34	2, 3, 7, 48, 52, 64, 154, 174
3	31, 73, 84, 85, 88, 146, 239
3–4	53, 72, 73, 75, 76, 330, 378
3:1	72, 76
3:1–13	73
3:1–4:49	66–42
3:2–4	73, 87, 72, 330
3:4	73, 270
3:5	3
3:5–10	8, 74, 146, 148, 223, 224, 242
3:5–39	24
3:6	74, 85
3:7	85
3:7–8	74, 77, 85, 88
3:9	73, 74, 85
3:10	72, 73, 74, 77, 85, 225
3:11–13	74, 75, 78, 88, 146, 148, 242
3:12	75
3:12–13	75, 78, 88
3:13	75
3:13–49	7
3:14	73, 76
3:14–48	78
3:14–39	53, 75
3:15	77
3:17	76
3:17–20	77, 330
3:18–20	76
3:21–24	50
3:21–26	76
3:21–29	77
3:21–37	8
3:21–39	8
3:22	77
3:23	61
3:24	84
3:25	77
3:27–32	76
3:28	77
3:29	61
3:30	84
3:31	77
3:32	73, 77, 81, 85
3:33–37	76
3:34	77
3:35	61, 84
3:36	77
3:38	61, 72, 73, 77, 85, 88
3:39	77, 78, 330
3:40	77
3:40–43	75
3:40–51	77, 88
3:41	77, 88
3:42–43	78
3:44–45	8
3:44–48	76
3:45	88
3:47	78, 251
3:48	78
3:51	48
4	85
4:1–20	8, 79, 86, 87, 167, 226, 242
4:1–33	8, 77, 79, 85
4:1–49	24, 78, 148, 149
4:3	78

Scripture Index

Reference	Pages
4:5	169
4:5–6	79, 80
4:5–15	77
4:6	81
4:7–8	80
4:7–12	79
4:9–10	80
4:10	81
4:11	80
4:12	81
4:13–14	79, 80
4:15	8, 73, 79, 82, 85, 86, 230
4:15–16	63, 77
4:16	8, 76, 81, 85
4:18–20	73, 82, 86, 88
4:19–20	82
4:20	82
4:21–33	167
4:21–28	82
4:22–23	82
4:23	78
4:24	82
4:24–26	82
4:25	82
4:26	82
4:27	82
4:28	8, 63, 73, 76, 77, 82, 85, 135
4:29–30	82
4:29–33	83
4:30	78
4:31	83
4:31–32a	82
4:32	83
4:32b	82
4:33	8, 63, 73, 77, 82, 85, 135
4:34–35	84
4:34–49	84
4:35	78
4:35–36	76
4:37	84
4:38	78
4:39	78
4:39–40	76
4:41	84
4:43	78
4:45	84
4:46–49	84
4:49	2, 7, 25, 48, 52, 84, 174
5	7, 102
5–6	27, 121
5:1–4	21, 90, 92, 101, 186, 261, 372, 373
5:1–6:27	34
5:1–10:10	18, 327
5:2	101
5:2–3	104
5:3	93, 101
5:5–10	96, 101
5:6	97, 101
5:6–7	96–97, 98
5:7	97
5:8	95, 97, 99
5:8–10	96
5:8b	97
5:9–10	97
5:11–14	103
5:11–31	99–101
5:12	101, 103
5:12–14a	103, 107
5:13	101
5:14	101
5:14b	103, 107
5:15	104, 105
5:15–28	104
5:16	105
5:16–22	105
5:17	102, 105
5:18	105
5:19	105
5:19–20	103
5:19–22	105
5:20–22	105
5:21	102, 103, 105, 106
5:21–22	105
5:22b	106
5:23	106
5:24	106
5:25–26a	106
5:26b	106
5:27	106
5:27–28	103
5:27–29	101
5:28	106
5:29	107
5:29–30	107
5:29–31	107
5:30a	107
5:31	107, 241
5:31a	107

5:31b	107
6	348, 363
6:1–8	114
6:1–21	111–12
6:2	114, 212
6:3–4	115
6:5	115
6:6	115
6:6–7	119
6:6–8	115
6:7	114, 115
6:8	114, 115
6:9	115
6:9–12	115
6:10–11	115
6:11b–12a	115, 116
6:12b	116
6:13–17	117
6:13–20	116, 136, 148, 212, 214, 262, 348, 349
6:13–21	114
6:14	116
6:18	117
6:19–20	117
6:20	117
6:20b	118
6:21	118
6:22–23	122
6:22–27	8, 121
6:24	123, 294
6:24–26	ix, 122, 124
6:24–27	125
6:25	143
6:25a	124
6:26a	124
6:27	22, 122, 123, 126
7	10, 134, 135, 137, 139
7–14	27, 28
7:1	134
7:1–9	133
7:1–89	127–33
7:1–9:14	34
7:1–10:10	134
7:2–3	139
7:2–9	134
7:3	134
7:3–9	138
7:5	134
7:5–9	140
7:7	76, 82, 83, 134
7:7–9	81
7:8	76, 83, 134, 135
7:9	76, 135
7:10	135
7:10–83	136
7:10–88	23, 133, 135, 139
7:11	135
7:12–83	10
7:12–88	133
7:13	136
7:16	136
7:84–86	136
7:84–88	136
7:85–86	136
7:87–88	137
7:89	137
8:1–4	140, 142, 143
8:2	143, 174
8:2–3	142, 143
8:3	7, 48, 52, 174
8:4	142
8:5–13	148
8:5–19	145
8:5–22	8, 9, 53, 74, 79, 146
8:6	146
8:7	147, 150
8:8–9	147
8:9	160
8:10	147
8:10–11	8, 147
8:11	106, 147, 148
8:12	148, 150
8:13	148, 242
8:14–19	148
8:15	146
8:16	147, 151
8:16–18	75, 151
8:16–19a	146
8:18	151
8:19	54, 147, 148, 150
8:19b	146
8:20	25, 148, 154
8:21	146, 148, 150
8:22	7, 20, 25, 48, 52, 148, 150, 174, 420
8:22–26	146
8:23–26	146, 148
8:24	78
8:25	79, 149

8:26	79, 149
8:32	174
8:34–35	90
9:1	134, 154, 156
9:1–5	154
9:1–13	153–54
9:1–14	349
9:3	154
9:5	7, 25, 48, 52, 154, 174
9:6	155
9:6–14	155, 156, 215, 336, 361
9:7	155
9:7–8	156
9:8	155
9:10–11a	155
9:11b–12	155
9:12	156
9:13	155, 157, 350
9:14	154, 155, 157
9:15	157–59, 160
9:15–16	160, 162
9:15–23	159, 160
9:15–10:10	34
9:16	163
9:16–23	134
9:17–23	160, 162
9:22	7
9:23	7, 48, 52, 167, 174
10	167
10–25	11
10:1–7	160, 161, 162
10:1–8	159
10:1–10	7, 134, 371
10:2	52, 160, 351
10:3	160
10:4	161
10:5	161
10:6–7	161
10:8	160, 161, 162, 163
10:8a	161
10:8b	161
10:9	161, 163
10:9–10	159, 161, 163, 351, 371, 375
10:10	8, 161, 163, 164, 349, 351
10:11	51, 134, 156, 159, 161, 167
10:11–13	167, 195
10:11–28	63, 161
10:11–29	165
10:11–33	62
10:11–36	166
10:11–11:34	392
10:11–12:16	33, 34, 51, 266, 267
10:11–25:18	1, 2, 6, 10, 24, 33, 34, 48, 166, 326, 327
10:12	167, 187
10:13	166, 167
10:13–28	64
10:14–16	63
10:14–28	84, 166
10:17	167
10:18	167
10:21	167
10:29	168, 170, 171, 175
10:29–32	168, 170
10:30	168
10:30–36	166
10:31	168, 171
10:32	168, 171
10:33	64, 168, 169, 170
10:33–36	21, 22, 166, 167, 168, 169
10:34	168, 169
10:35	169
10:36	169
11	194, 204
11–12	174, 194
11–25	174
11:1	174, 175, 176, 185
11:1–3	10, 11, 174, 202
11:1–9	24, 48
11:1–35	171–74
11:2	16, 25, 175
11:3	167, 168, 174
11:4	175, 178
11:4–6	175
11:4–9	175
11:4–34	202
11:4–35	10, 11, 175
11:5	175
11:6	179
11:6–9	175
11:7–9	4
11:10	176
11:10–23	176
11:11	175, 181
11:11–15	176, 181
11:12	176
11:13	176
11:14	176, 180

11:15	176, 181
11:16–17	176
11:17	177
11:18	176, 179
11:19–20	176
11:20	176, 179
11:21–22	176
11:23	176
11:24	177
11:24–27	181
11:24–29	185
11:24–30	177
11:25	177, 185
11:25–26	338
11:26	177
11:26–29	13, 177, 185
11:28	338
11:29	177, 178, 181, 188, 338
11:30	178
11:31	178
11:32	178
11:31–34	14, 178
11:33	178, 317
11:33–34	23
11:34	178
11:34–35	167
11:35	178, 392
12	3, 24, 167, 194, 204, 268
12:1	184, 186
12:1–3	184
12:1–15	11, 13, 15
12:1–16	183–84
12:2	185
12:3	4, 185, 188
12:4–5	185
12:4–9	185
12:6	186
12:6–8	24, 177, 185, 338
12:7	186, 188
12:8	186
12:9	186
12:9–10	23
12:10–12	263
12:10–15	186
12:11	187
12:11–12	186
12:12	187
12:13	16, 25, 187
12:14	187
12:15	187
12:16	5, 167, 187, 194, 267, 268
13	194, 204
13–14	5, 207, 385, 398
13:1	204
13:1–16	338
13:1–25	194
13:1–14:45	34, 190–94
13:2	23, 194, 195
13:4–15	195
13:6	195
13:8	195
13:16	195
13:17	195
13:17–14:4	382
13:18	197
13:18b	195
13:19	197
13:19b	195
13:20	51
13:20a	195
13:20b	195
13:21	195–96, 267, 400
13:22	196
13:23	81, 204
13:23–24	196
13:25	196
13:26	187, 194, 267
13:26–33	196, 197
13:27	197, 204
13:28	197
13:28–29	55, 204
13:28–33	11, 13, 198
13:29	197
13:30	197, 383, 401
13:31	197
13:32	198
13:32–33	55, 197
13:33	196
14	16, 26, 33, 29, 162, 194, 214, 216, 218, 227, 232, 327
14–20	276
14:1	198
14:1–2	197
14:1–3	202
14:1–4	11, 197, 205, 267, 281
14:1–10	24, 48
14:1–10a	29
14:1–35	11, 13, 15, 18

14:2 . . . . 198, 203, 230	14:29–30 . . . . 330, 331
14:2b 198	14:30 . . . . 202, 203, 332, 383, 401
14:3 . . . . 198, 203	14:31 203
14:4 198	14:32 203
14:5 225	14:32–33 . . . . 200, 201
14:5–10a 198	14:33 . . . . 203, 206, 220, 234, 372
14:6 . . . . 197, 198	14:34 . . . . 14, 196, 203, 220, 241
14:6–9 . . . . 338, 383, 401	14:35 203
14:7 198	14:35–37 372
14:7–8 332	14:36–37 . . . . 11, 14, 203
14:7–9 . . . . 48, 198	14:36–38 203
14:8 . . . . 195, 198	14:37 . . . . 53, 317
14:9 . . . . 198, 205	14:38 203
14:10–12 227	14:39 203
14:10–19 278	14:39–45 . . . . 11, 13, 48, 203, 208, 278
14:10a 199, 205	14:40 203
14:10b 199, 227, 230	14:41–43 204
14:10b–12 . . . . 23, 29	14:44 . . . . 169, 371
14:11 . . . . 13, 175, 199, 206, 229, 269	14:44a 204
14:11–12 199	14:44b 204
14:11–19 227	14:45 . . . . 277, 278
14:11–23 229	15. . . . . 27, 218
14:11–35 219	15:1–2 327
14:12 199	15:1–16 . . . . 211, 217
14:13 200	15:1–29 . . . . 30, 345
14:13–16 203	15:1–41 . . . . 34, 209–11
14:13–19 . . . . 23, 29, 199, 200, 203, 207, 372	15:1–19:22. 51
14:14 200	15:2 . . . . 17, 217
14:15–16 200	15:2–3a 211
14:17 200	15:3 . . . . 212, 360
14:18 201	15:3–4 135
14:18–19 200	15:3–16 . . . . 213, 217
14:18a 15, 200	15:4–5 213
14:19 . . . . 16, 200, 201	15:4–10 212
14:20 . . . . 29, 30, 201	15:6 135
14:20–22 206	15:6–7 213
14:20–25 . . . . 201, 202	15:8–9 135
14:20–35 . . . . 201, 214, 383	15:8–10 213
14:21–23 . . . . 29, 202	15:11 213
14:22 . . . . 199, 202, 206	15:11–12 212
14:22–23 24	15:13–16 . . . . 22, 212, 214
14:23 . . . . 202, 229	15:14–16 213
14:24 . . . . 202, 332, 383, 401	15:17–21 . . . . 213, 217
14:25 . . . . 202, 203	15:22–23 214
14:26–35 . . . . 48, 203, 327	15:22–24 214
14:26–37 29	15:22–26 214
14:28 203	15:22–29 . . . . 217, 218
14:28–35 24	15:22–31 . . . . 25, 213
14:29 203	15:24 . . . . 213, 214

15:24b	214
15:25a	214
15:26	213, 214
15:27–28	214
15:27–29	214, 215
15:29	214
15:30	269
15:31	215
15:30–31	214, 215, 218
15:32–36	12, 13, 21, 215, 218, 336, 361
15:34	215
15:35–36	53
15:36	216
15:37–41	216
15:37–42	211
15:38–39	216
15:39	220
15:40	220, 225
15:41	217, 225
15:41a	220
16.	16, 24, 86, 224, 231, 239, 259, 330
16–17	224
16–18	27, 28
16:1	226, 330
16:1–2	225
16:1–3	224
16:1–7	225, 232, 233
16:1–14	48
16:1–15	224
16:1–35	73, 186, 295, 328
16:1–40	12, 13, 224
16:1–50	220–23
16:1–8:7	248
16:1–17:11	24
16:1–18:7	248
16:1–18:32	34
16:2	236
16:3	225, 226
16:4	225
16:5	225, 235
16:4–6	198, 233
16:6–7	14, 225
16:7	226, 235, 277
16:8–10	226
16:8–11	226, 232, 235
16:10	226
16:11	226, 232
16:12	226, 228
16:12–14	235
16:12–15	225, 226, 232
16:13	268
16:13–14	226, 228
16:14	227, 228
16:15	227, 235
16:16–17	227
16:16–19	240
16:16–19a	227
16:16–40	224, 227
16:17–18	14
16:18	227, 229
16:19	227, 229
16:19a	227
16:19b	227
16:20–22	227, 237
16:20–24	25
16:21	227
16:21–22	230
16:22	8, 16, 198, 227, 237
16:23–40	228, 235
16:24	227, 228, 233
16:25	228, 233
16:25–34	225
16:26	227, 228
16:27	228, 233
16:27a	228
16:27b	229
16:28	229
16:28–30	233, 269
16:28–35	16
16:29–30	229
16:31–32	268
16:31–32a	229
16:31–33	233
16:31–35	23, 259, 268
16:32	228
16:32b	229
16:34	229
16:35	14, 175, 229, 242, 243
16:35–40	225, 240
16:36	229
16:36–40	283
16:37–38	230
16:38	230, 241
16:40	225, 230
16:41	230
16:41–50	12, 13, 15, 224, 230, 236, 237, 278
16:42	199, 230

16:45	227, 230
16:45–48	237
16:46	54, 237, 242
16:46–48	8, 317
16:46–49	268, 372
16:46a	231
16:46b	231
16:47	231
16:47–48	25
16:47–49	23
16:48	231
16:49	231, 237, 259
17	243, 268
17:1–5	240
17:1–10	243
17:1–11	239
17:1–18:7	16, 238–39
17:2	240
17:2–3	241
17:2–11	150
17:3	240
17:4	240, 241
17:5a	240
17:5b	240
17:6	240
17:6–7	240
17:7	268
17:8	240
17:8–11	240
17:9	241
17:10	243, 268, 283
17:10a	241
17:10b	241
17:12–13	239, 241, 243, 268
17:13	241
18	3, 241, 249, 250
18:1	241, 245, 251
18:1–6	53
18:1–7	74, 239, 241, 252
18:1a	241
18:1b	242
18:2	242
18:2–4	242
18:3	8, 242, 252
18:4	242
18:5	8, 242
18:5–7	242
18:6	74, 242
18:7	8, 74, 243
18:8	249, 251
18:8–19	249, 373
18:8–20	78
18:8–32	16, 247–48
18:9	98, 249
18:9–10	249
18:9–19	249, 252
18:10	249
18:10–11	253
18:11	249
18:11–13	249
18:12	98, 217, 254
18:12–13	250, 255
18:13–19	97
18:14	251, 281
18:15–18	75, 78, 251
18:15b–16	251
18:16	75, 242, 251
18:17–18	251
18:18	250, 251
18:19	99, 251
18:20	78, 248, 252, 255, 256
18:20–32	249, 252, 330, 409
18:21	99, 252
18:21–24	97, 252, 409, 413, 414
18:22	72
18:22–23	72, 252
18:23	252
18:23–24	78
18:24	252
18:26–28	373
18:26–29	97, 252
18:27	252, 253
18:29	253
18:30	252, 253
18:31	253
18:32	253
19	27, 33, 264, 373
19:1–10	259
19:1–22	34, 256–58
19:3	259, 260
19:4	259, 260
19:5	260
19:6	260
19:7	259, 264
19:7–8	261, 262
19:9	147, 261
19:10a	261
19:10b	261

19:11	216, 261
19:11–12	115, 373
19:11–13	21, 93, 262
19:11–14	155
19:11–16	261
19:11–19	92
19:11–22	258, 261
19:12	262
19:12–13	262
19:13	147, 260
19:14–15	262
19:16	262
19:17	260, 261, 262
19:17–19	93, 115, 262, 264, 373
19:17–22	262
19:18	261, 373
19:18–19a	262
19:19	373
19:19b	262
19:20	21, 262
19:21a	262
19:21–22	262
20	272, 273
20–25	27, 28
20:1	267, 268
20:1–13	267, 272, 392
20:1–29	265–67
20:1–22:1	35, 51, 267, 268
20:2	268, 278
20:2–5	24, 48, 268
20:2–8	278
20:2–13	10, 12, 13, 15, 335
20:2–20	288
20:3	268
20:4	268
20:4–5	278
20:6	198, 268
20:6–8	268
20:8	268, 269
20:9	268
20:9–11	13, 269, 337
20:9–12	272, 273
20:10	270, 272, 273
20:11b	269
20:12	13, 22, 269, 273, 337
20:13	33, 269, 270, 278
20:14	270
20:14–21	270, 312
20:15–16	270
20:16–17	270
20:18	270
20:19–20	270
20:21	280
20:20–21	270
20:21–35	288
20:22	277
20:22–23	270
20:22–28	268
20:22–29	270, 273, 337, 392
20:23–28	401
20:23b–25	273
20:24	270
20:26	270
20:26b–27	273
20:27	271
20:28	271
20:29	271
21	17, 171, 276
21–25	276
21:1	277, 281
21:1–3	17, 22, 276, 392
21:1–22:1	274–76
21:2	277, 278, 281, 360
21:2–3	281
21:3	204, 278, 281
21:4	270, 277, 278
21:4–5	24
21:4–9	10, 12, 268, 276, 278, 283
21:5	278
21:6	278
21:7	16, 25, 278
21:8–9	278
21:9	33
21:10	392
21:10–20	278, 279, 337, 392
21:11	392
21:12–13	6, 327
21:13	279
21:13–14	4
21:14	279
21:14–15	279, 280
21:16	279
21:16–18	279
21:17–18	280
21:20	279, 280, 305, 307, 327
21:21	278, 279
21:21–35	17, 22, 276, 293
21:21–22:1	279, 381, 384

21:22–23	279
21:24	279, 281, 381
21:24–25	280
21:26	279, 280, 381
21:27	280
21:27–30	4, 280
21:28–29	280
21:30	280
21:32	280, 382
21:33–35	281
21:34	280
21:35	33, 280, 281
22	311
22–24	3, 17, 288
22–32	392
22:1	5, 33, 280, 288, 293, 307, 317
22:2–4	22, 293
22:2–20	288
22:2–40	285–87
22:2–24:25	35
22:2–36:13	51
22:3	288
22:4	318
22:4–7	293
22:4a	289
22:4b	289
22:5a	289
22:6	289, 293
22:7	289, 310, 318
22:8	289
22:9	290
22:9–13	290
22:12	290, 293
22:15	290
22:17	308
22:17–18	290
22:18	289, 290
22:20	290, 291, 295
22:21–22a	290
22:21–35	290, 302
22:22	291, 292
22:22b	291
22:23	291, 292
22:25	291
22:26–27	291
22:27	291
22:28	291
22:29a	291
22:29b	291
22:30	291, 295
22:31	292, 307
22:32	292
22:32–35	292
22:34	292
22:35	290, 292
22:36	292
22:36–40	292
22:37	292
22:38	292, 295, 302, 311
22:39–40	292
22:41	303
22:41–23:12	303
22:41–24:25	297–301
23	304
23–24	290, 301
23–34	276
23:1	303
23:1–2	303
23:2	303
23:3	303, 304
23:4	304
23:4–5	303
23:5	304, 307
23:6	303, 304
23:6–10	22
23:7	304
23:7–10	303
23:8	304
23:9	305
23:9–10a	304
23:10	17, 302, 311, 329
23:10a	305
23:10b	304, 305
23:11	305
23:12	302, 305, 306, 311
23:13	305
23:13–14a	303
23:13–26	305
23:14	279, 305
23:14b	303
23:14b–17	305
23:15	303
23:16	303
23:17	303
23:18–24	303
23:19	306
23:19a	22
23:20	306

23:20a	304
23:21	306
23:22	306
23:23	306
23:24	306
23:25	306
23:26	302, 306, 311
23:27	307
23:27–28	280, 303, 307
23:27–24:14	306
23:28	305, 317
23:29	303
23:29–30	307
23:30	303
23:35	304
24	305
24:1	304, 307
24:1–2	303
24:2	307
24:3–4	307, 309, 311
24:3–9	22, 303
24:4b	307
24:5	307
24:6	307
24:7	314
24:7a	307
24:7b	308
24:8–9	314
24:8a	308
24:8b	308
24:8b–9	318
24:9	17, 302
24:9a	308
24:9b	308
24:10a	308
24:10b–11	308
24:11	310
24:12–13	308, 311
24:12–14	302
24:14	308
24:15–16	309, 311
24:15–19	309
24:15–24	313
24:15–25	309
24:17	17, 302, 305, 310, 312, 313, 314
24:17a	309
24:17b	309
24:17c	309
24:18	309
24:19	309
24:20	312
24:20–24	309
24:20a	309
24:20b	309
24:21–22	309, 312
24:21b–22	310
24:23b–24a	310
24:24	310
24:25	310
25	6, 276, 321, 327
25:1	317, 318, 319
25:1–2	318
25:1–3	24, 48, 316, 403
25:1–5	317, 321
25:1–8	398
25:1–9	268
25:1–15	12, 13, 276
25:1–18	35, 315–16
25:2	317, 319
25:2b	317
25:4	317, 319, 321
25:4–5	319
25:5	317
25:6	289, 310, 320, 371
25:6–15	15, 317, 320
25:6a	318
25:6b	317
25:7–9	25
25:8	317
25:8–9	317
25:9	318, 319, 372, 376
25:11	318, 320
25:11–13	25, 318
25:12	318
25:13	318
25:14	317, 318
25:14–15	318
25:15–18	289
25:16–18	310, 318, 319, 370
25:17–18	370
25:19, 21, 21, 24, 25, 27	411
26	2, 6, 18, 30, 31, 33, 327, 329
26–36	2, 19, 20, 35, 48, 327
26:1–4a	327
26:1–51	18
26:1–65	35, 322–26
26:1–36:13	1, 6, 18, 33
26:2	332

26:3	18, 327, 371
26:4	20
26:4–51	328
26:4–63	18, 25, 327
26:4b–51	23, 328, 331
26:5–51	18, 336
26:7	383
26:8–9	225
26:8–10	20
26:9–10	330, 336
26:9–11	328
26:10–11	229, 234
26:11	328, 330
26:18	383
26:19	328
26:29	384
26:33	20, 328, 419
26:51	30
26:52–54	332
26:52–56	18, 19, 327, 328, 329, 400, 401, 418
26:53	251
26:53–54	330, 409
26:57	330
26:57–62	330, 331
26:58a	330
26:58b–61	330
26:59	184
26:61	20, 330
26:62	18, 330
26:63–64	330, 331
26:63–65	330, 332
26:64–65	20, 327
26:65	331, 336
26:55–56	330
27	27, 28, 418
27–36	18, 327
27:1	20, 419
27:1–2	336, 418
27:1–4	336, 339
27:1–11	19, 35, 215, 328, 335, 361, 418, 420, 421
27:1–23	334–35
27:3	225
27:3–4	336, 339
27:5	336
27:5–8	418
27:5–11	336
27:7	336
27:8	336
27:8–11	336
27:9–11	337, 418
27:12	337
27:12–13	335
27:12–14	337, 340, 370
27:12–23	18, 19, 35, 401
27:13	20
27:13–14	337
27:15–17	337
27:16–17	338, 340
27:17	337
27:18	338
27:18–21	338, 370
27:19	338
27:20	338
27:21	338, 341, 371
27:22–23	338, 370
27:46	328
28	353
28–29	35, 212, 350, 353, 355, 360
28–30	27
28:1–2	346, 353, 354
28:1–8	347
28:1–29:40	19, 342–45
28:2–15	212
28:2b	346
28:3–8	346, 348, 354
28:3–29:38	346
28:9–10	346, 347, 348, 354
28:10	347, 353
28:11–15	346, 347, 349, 354
28:15	347, 353
28:16	347, 349
28:16–25	349, 350, 351, 352, 357
28:16–29:38	346, 354
28:17–25	347, 349
28:18	348, 350, 355
28:19–24	350
28:22	349
28:23	353
28:24	347
28:25	348, 350, 355
28:26	348, 350, 355
28:26–31	347, 350
28:30	349
29	353
29:1	348, 355
29:1–6	347, 351

29:5	349
29:7	348, 352, 355
29:7–11	347, 351, 357
29:8–11	352
29:11	349, 352
29:12	348, 352, 355
29:12–34	347
29:12–38	351, 352, 356
29:13–33	352
29:16	349
29:19	349
29:22	349
29:25	349
29:28	349
29:31	349
29:34	349
29:35	347, 348, 352
29:38	349
29:39	346, 353, 360
29:39–40	353
29:40	353
30	364
30:1	361
30:1–2	361, 363
30:1–16	35, 359–60
30:2	361, 362
30:3–5	362
30:3–15	361
30:6	363
30:6–8	362
30:9	362
30:10	361
30:10–12	362
30:13	360, 362
30:13–15	362
30:14	361, 362
30:15	241, 362
30:16	361, 362, 365
31	32, 33, 319
31:1–2	370
31:1–7	161, 288
31:1–8	288
31:1–54	35, 367–69
31:1–33:49	27, 28
31:2	20, 370
31:2–3	375
31:2–7	289
31:2a	370
31:3	371
31:3–4	371
31:4	23, 371
31:5–6a	371
31:5–12	371
31:6	371
31:6b	371
31:7	18, 20, 25, 327, 371
31:8	318, 371
31:9–10	371
31:11–12	371
31:13	372
31:13–24	372
31:14	374
31:14–16	20, 372
31:15–16	318
31:16	288, 289, 319
31:16a	311
31:17	372
31:17–18	372
31:18	372
31:19	261, 373
31:19–24	18
31:20	373
31:21–23a	373
31:22–23	373
31:23	373
31:23b	373
31:24	373
31:25–47	373
31:27	373, 378
31:28–29	373
31:28–30	18, 378
31:30	373
31:31	18, 20, 25, 327
31:32–35	373
31:36–40	378
31:36–41	373
31:42–47	373
31:48	374
31:48–54	50, 374
31:49	374
31:49–50	375
31:50	374
31:52	375
31:53	375
31:54	375
31:54b	375
32	23, 386
32:1	280, 382, 383

Scripture Index

32:1–5	382, 386
32:1–42	19, 35, 379–81
32:2–3	280
32:3	280
32:3–4	392
32:3–4a	382
32:4b	382
32:5	382, 385
32:6	382
32:6–15	20, 382, 385, 386
32:7–9	382
32:8	194
32:10–12	383
32:12	195
32:13	51
32:13–14	383
32:15	383
32:16–19	386
32:16–32	383
32:16a	383
32:16b–19	383
32:20–22	383
32:20–24	386
32:21	383
32:23	383
32:25	20, 382
32:25–27	383
32:26	383
32:28–30	384
32:29	382, 383
32:31	382
32:31–32	384
32:33	280, 384
32:33–42	384, 400
32:34	383
32:34–35	280
32:34–36	384
32:32–37	382
32:34–38	381
32:37	280, 383
32:38	381
32:38a	384
32:39–40	384
32:39–42	384
32:41	385
32:41–42	384
32:42	385
33	187, 390, 391, 392
33:1–2	391
33:1–49	35, 388–90, 398
33:2	3, 4
33:3	392
33:3–4	392, 395
33:3–49	3, 391
33:5	392
33:6	392
33:7	395
33:7–8	392
33:8	391, 393, 395
33:9	391, 392, 395
33:10–11	392
33:11	393, 395
33:14	267, 391, 392, 393, 395
33:15	392, 393
33:16	392, 393, 394, 395
33:17	393, 394
33:18	392
33:18–36	51
33:36	392, 393, 394
33:37	267
33:37–39	392, 393
33:38	268
33:40	277, 391, 392
33:43	392
33:44	392
33:45	392, 395
33:47	392, 393, 395
33:48	395
33:48–49	317, 392
33:48–51	280
33:49	391, 393, 394
33:50	419
33:50–51	419
33:50–56	19, 20, 35, 398, 400, 404
33:50–34:29	396–98
33:50–36:13	26, 35, 398
33:51	398
33:52	398, 399, 400
33:52a	399
33:52b	399
33:53a	399
33:53b	400
33:54	330, 400, 401, 409
33:54–56	400
33:55	399
33:55–56	399
33:56	399
34	400, 404, 409

34:1–15	19, 35, 398, 400
34:2–12	382
34:3	400
34:3–5	400
34:5	400
34:6	400
34:7–9	400
34:8	400
34:10–12a	400
34:13–15	400
34:13–29	400
34:16–29	19, 35, 398, 401
34:17	401
34:18–29	401
34:19	401
35	408, 415
35:1–3	409
35:1–8	18, 19, 35, 330, 398, 402, 414
35:1–34	406–8
35:2–3	78
35:4	409
35:4–5	409
35:5	409
35:6	409
35:6–8	409
35:8	409
35:9–15	411
35:9–34	19, 35, 398, 409, 410, 411, 413
35:9–36:13	27
35:12	411
35:16–18	411
35:16–21	411
35:16–34	411
35:19	408, 410, 411
35:20–21	411
35:21	411
35:22–23a	411
35:22–25	411, 414
35:23	412
35:23b	412
35:24–25	411
35:25b	412, 415
35:26–28	412
35:30	411, 413, 415
35:31	413
35:32	413
35:32–34	18
35:33	413, 415, 416
35:33–34	21, 22, 413
35:34	26, 413
36	421
36:1	418
36:1–4	418, 419
36:1–9	215
36:1–12	19, 35, 398
36:1–13	417–18
36:2	419
36:3	419
36:4	419
36:5	419, 421
36:5–9	419
36:6	419
36:6–9	419
36:8	18
36:10	20, 25, 327, 421
36:10–12	419
36:11	220
36:13	18, 22, 25, 35, 327, 398, 420

Deuteronomy

1–3	3, 392
1:22	195
1:30–33	199
1:36	202
1:36–38	202
1:37	13, 271
1:38	202
2:4–5	280
2:9	312
2:11	305
2:13–3:29	279
2:14	6, 51, 187, 327
2:19	280
2:24	280
2:32–35	282
2:34	281
2:35	369
3:3–6	281
3:6–7	282
3:12	383
3:26	13, 271
3:29	280
4:15	185
4:21	13, 271
4:24	88, 318
4:30	308
4:36	14
4:37–38	383

Reference	Page
4:41–43	410
5:9	318
5:24	199
6:8–9	216
6:14–15	316
6:16	202
7:1–2	278, 399
7:1–3	185, 281
7:1–5	399
7:2–6	282
7:7	30
7:8	320
7:22	30
8:5	14
8:7–9	197
8:7–10	255
8:11–20	354
8:15	278
8:19	316
9:2	196
9:3–5	282
10:8	169
10:20	108
12:6–7	356
12:7	117
12:7–18	117, 118
12:9	170
12:10	170
12:11–12	356
13:12–16	282
14	253
14:22–23	252
14:22–26	356
14:22–27	253
14:28–29	253
16:3	349
16:10	350
16:11	351
16:14	352
16:16	350, 352
16:19	294
17:8	114
18:2	3
18:10	289
19:1–13	410
19:4	411
19:4–5	411
19:5	412
19:6	411, 415
19:16–18	412
19:20–21	412
19:24	412
19:25a	412
20:10–15	282
20:14	369, 372
20:16–18	282, 399
21:1–9	260
21:5	122, 125
21:10–13	370
21:10–14	372
21:18	14
21:22–23	317, 321
22:13–21	372
23:4–5	3
23:9–14	92
23:21	360
24:5	107
24:8	73, 189
24:9	3, 189
24:16	201
25:5–6	372, 418
25:9	187
25:17–18	309
25:19	309
26:1–10	254
26:10	351
26:12–15	253
27:15–26	106
27:30–33	253
28:1–2	123
28:1–4	121
28:3–9a	123
28:9–10	123
28:9b	123
28:10–13a	123
28:13b–14	123
30:20	108
31:7b–8	338
31:9	3, 4
31:14	339
31:16	319
31:20	199
31:22–26	4
31:23	339
31:24	3
31:29	308
32:16	318
32:48–52	337

33:10	243
34:1	279, 337
34:1–6	279
34:1–9	337, 401
34:8	271
34:9–12	338

Joshua

1:14	196
2	421
2:9	200
2:9–11	293
2:11	338
3	5
3:3	169
3:5	114
4:7	169
4:12	383, 386
4:13	383
5:1	279
5:11	338
6	327
6:2	196
6:2–7	371
6:4	160
7:3–9	54
9:20	105
10:1–5	371
10:2	196
10:5–6	279
10:13	279
12:1–6	384
12:14	277
13–19	155
13:8–12	384
13:15–28	382, 384
13:21	289
13:25	383
13:29–30	280
13:29–31	384
13:30–31	383
14:6–15	332, 401
15:18–19	335
15:21	204
15:30	204
18:1–10	401
18:6–11	330
18:10	330
18:10a	401
19:1	328
19:10	328
19:17	328, 401
19:19	401
19:49–50	401
20:1–9	410
20:7–8	411
21:1–48	409
21:13	409
21:39	384
21:44	170
22:1–4	386
22:8	373
22:16, 18–19	104
22:26	212

Judges

1:16	168, 310
1:16–17	277
2:6–19	402
2:6–23	399
2:10–13	316
2:10–12a	354
2:11	317
3:10	177
3:27–28	162
4:11	168
5:23	196
6–8	319
11:18	270
13:5	114
14:8	197
18:25	411
18:27	369
18:29	196
20:1	382
21:8–12	372

1 Samuel

1	360
1–2	421
1:3–5	117
1:5	346
1:6–16	106
1:10–11	114
1:11	75, 114, 360, 365
1:19–2:10	114

1:21	117
1:22	114
1:22–28	75
2:22	74
4:3	371
4:4	60, 81
4:5	306
4:8	178
6:7–8	260
6:19	8, 79, 87
7:6	352
7:9	117, 348
10:5–6, 10–11	177
12:3	227
13:8–12	117, 348
14.	365
14:41–42	338
14:44	366
14:45a	366
14:45b	366
15:3–8	309
15:6	310
15:8, 9, 20, 32–33	308
16:20	212
17:12	64
17:47	50
18:12–15	279
18:16	337
19:20–24	177
19:24	307
20:5–6	349
22:17	411
23:9–12	371
24:8	292
24:13	370
25:28	279
29:6	337
30:3	369
30:24	373

2 Samuel

1:18	279
1:24	80
2.	409
2:9	310
2:28	162
3:27	410
5:2	337, 340

6:2	7, 53
6:6–7	8, 73, 79
6:7	87
7:14a	220
8:2	309
8:12	309, 310
8:12–14	309
17:11	308
24.	50, 374
24:2	50

1 Kings

1:15–23	7, 73
1:28	60
1:31	292
2:23	360
3:16	60
4:21–24	400
8:9	241
8:10–11	22
8:22–53	135
8:31–32	102, 105
8:41	213
8:62–63	135
8:62–64	135
8:65	400
10:5	60
11:7	280, 399
11:18	187
11:26–27a	215
11:33	280
12:6	309
16:31–32	317
18:37–39	199
19:9–14	290
20:23, 28	280
22:17–18	177

2 Kings

7:3	92
17:7–16	316
17:9	399
18:4	283

1 Chronicles

2:3	277
2:34–36	336, 418
5:23–24	384

5:25	104
6:3–15	318
6:4	318
6:50–53	318
13:5	400
16:24	199
17:13	220
22:10	220
28:2	7
28:6	220
29:29	279

2 Chronicles

5:10	241
7:1–5	135
7:4–9	135
12:1–2	104
13:1–19	161
13:5	251
13:12–16	161
28:5	369
29:25–28	161

Ezra

3.	346
8:21	360

Nehemiah

5:13	106
7:5	279
7:63	336, 418
8:6	106
8:13–18	353
13:10–11	99, 254

Esther

1:6	80, 216
4:11	7, 73
5:1–2	217
8:4	60
8:15	216

Job

39:9–11	306
42:7–9	147

Psalms

2.	314

2:9	17, 309, 314
3–7	181
4:6	123
4:8	123
6:2	124
9:12, 18	185
10:12	185
13.	181
15.	363
15:4	363, 364, 366
16:5	256
17:8	123
20:1–5	117, 348
22.	181
22:1	182
23:1	340
23:2	170
28:2	122
30:2	124
30:5	23
30:10	123
31.	181
31:5	182
31:16	123
35:13	352, 360
38:2	14
39:11	14
44.	181
44:1–8	50
47:2	309
47:2–4	306
47:5–6	306
50:12–13	346
51.	264
51:2	104
51:17	352
52:9	302
56:12–13	360
57:1	123
58:10–11	370
66:13–16	117, 348
66:13–20	360
67.	26, 213
67:1–2	123
68.	169
68:1	169
68:2–3	169
68:5	169

68:7–10, 12, 14	169
68:19–20	169
68:35	169
73:26	256
74:2	163
78:17–19	202
78:23–25	278
78:29	178
78:30–31	178
78:41	202
78:52	340
78:56	202
78:70–71	340
83:8	310
90:8	103
91	198
94:12	14
95:7–11	24
95:9	202
95:11	206
97:9	309
99:1	60, 81
99:8	370
101:5	103
103:1–18	17
104:16–17	307
105:8	163
105:39	169, 198
105:42	163
106:4	163
106:13–18	14
106:14	202
106:15	178
106:16	232
106:24–33	14
106:32–33	13, 271
106:45	163
106:48	106
110:1	314
110:2	240
118:18	14
119	28, 137
119:49	163
121:5	198
132:2–4	360
135:10–12	281
136:17–22	281
141:2	122
142:5	256
145:15–16	351

Proverbs

3:9	422
3:11–12	15
3:34	185
5:8	109
5:18–19	107, 109
5:20–21	111
5:21	107
7:6–27	109
13:20	402
13:20a	386
15:8	353
16:33	330, 401
18:18	330, 401
18:22	xiii
19:11	235
19:18	14
22:24–25	402
29:17	14
30:8	124

Ecclesiastes

5:4	360
5:5	360, 365

Song of Songs

3:7	81

Isaiah

1:10–15	353
1:11–17	352
1:13–14	349
1:16	377
2:2	308
6:1–3	8, 79
6:3	122, 175
11:6	375
13:1	307
14:2	369
19:11, 13	196
30:3–4	196
40:11	340
46:1	384
49:15–16	161
52–53	89

53. . . . . 89, 90
53:4 90
53:5–12 357
53:5a 90
53:7–8 90
53:8b, 11–12 90
53:12 . . . . .90, 237
56:7 213
59:1 177
61:1–2 60

Jeremiah
3:1–2, 6–9 319
3:15 340
4:6 283
5:9, 29 370
13:23 184
14:10 104
29:22b 106
30:16 197
31:9b 220
36. 4

Lamentations
3:24 256

Ezekiel
3:18–21 246
8:10 399
8:12 399
16:15–34 319
18:23 394
20:41 212
21:21 . . . . .289, 302, 304
21:27 304
23:1–8 319
23:6 80
25:12, 15 370
34:2–10 340
34:4–6 338
34:5 340
44:11 224
44:30 213
48:30–36 65

Daniel
6:16–17 307
8:18–19 307
9:3–5 352

10:3 . . . . .352, 360
10:12 352

Hosea
2:8–9 351
5:14–15 14

Joel
2:17 317
2:22 49

Amos
4:6–11 15
5:21–24 353
7:1–9 200

Micah
5:15 370
6:4 188
7:18 23

Nahum
1:1 307
1:2 370

Habakkuk
1:1 307

Malachi
1:1 307
1:8 116
2:5–6 318
2:8–9 318
3:6 27

Matthew
1:21 195
2:2 314
4:19 206
5:16 25
5:23–24 97
5:33–37 364
5:27–29 110
5:28–29 404
6:9 207
6:10 26
6:11 . . . . .124, 126, 404
6:19 404
6:19–20 295

Scripture Index

6:19–24 26
6:19–34 351
6:21 404
6:24 . . . . 295, 403
6:25–33 123
6:33 65
7:11 123
7:22–23 288
8:17 90
10:10 378
11:28–30 . . . . 170, 422
16:24 386
18:6–7 385
19:21 386
19:29 256
22:39 124
23 235
23:25–26 33
24 376
24:30–31 163
24:31 163
24:37–41 283
24:37–51 376
25:21 . . . . 26, 65
26:13 339
26:17 . . . . 156, 350, 357
26:26–28 156
26:41 20
27:15–26 . . . . 156, 350, 357
27:46 182
27:51 88
27:62–66 350
28:1–10 350
28:18 162
28:18–20 . . . . 22, 27, 205
28:19 162
28:20 . . . . 162, 205

Mark

1:40–45 94
5:21–34 94
5:25–34 94
5:35–43 94
7:6–13 235
7:19 . . . . 264, 377
8:36 . . . . 294, 311
10:45 90
12:31 422
14:3–9 357

Luke

1 421
1:1–4 . . . . 4, 279
1:31–34 177
1:18–20 177
6:35 124
8 . . . . 94, 95
8:43–48 94
9:23 296
9:46 139
14:23 244
14:26 . . . . 120, 236
18:1 163
18:2–5 164
18:6–8a 164
19:1–10 98
19:7 98
19:8 98
19:8–9 97
19:9–10 98
22:1–23 357
22:20 27
22:24 139
22:25–27 139
22:37 90
23:46 182
24 . . . . xvi, xvii
24:25–27 xvi
24:44–45 xvi

John

1:1 . . . . 56, 189
1:4 143
1:12 357
1:14 . . . . 22, 56, 162
1:14a 189
1:20 14
1:29 357
1:51 138
3:14–15 . . . . 276, 283–84
3:16 23
3:17 . . . . 244, 314
3:18 23
3:36 . . . . 23, 314
5:24 23
8:12 144
8:24 23
8:34 56
10:10 314

10:11	340
10:14	340
10:27–30	313
10:30	189
13:5, 12–17	85
14:1–3	23
14:6	7, 138, 244
14:6b	189
14:7–11	138
14:15	25, 111
14:23–24	25
15:1–2	320
15:1–6	202
15:5	66
15:8	320
17	386
17:3	313
17:6–24	337
17:15	126
17:17	126
17:20	387
17:20–23	24
17:20–26	386
17:21–23	126
17:21a	387
17:22–23a	387
17:23b	387
17:24	126
19:34	321
19:36	156
21:15–19	340

Acts

1:8	26
2:1	350
2:44–45	378
4:12	23
5:1–11	23, 103
6:1–4	150
8:32–33	90
12:21–23	23
18:18	364
21:23–24	364

Romans

2:4	23
2:9	376
3:24–26	352
3:25–26	208
5:8	23, 138, 284, 321
6:5–7	55
6:6	56
6:13	56
6:16	56
6:23	23, 56, 284
8:1, 12–17	26
8:18–38	333
8:29	159
8:34	25
8:34–38	25
8:38–39	395
8:39	25
9–11	28
12	28
12:1	28, 111, 152
15:25–28	255

1 Corinthians

1:4–9	23
3:5	188
3:16	26, 93
3:17a	57
5	94
5:5	94
5:7	156, 357
6:9	107
6:9–10	109
6:18–19	57
6:19	22, 57
6:20	57
7:39	421
9:6–18	255
9:12	254
9:13–14	96, 99, 138, 254
9:14	24, 378
10:1–12	14
10:1–13	24
10:5–6	394
10:8	318
10:12	20
14:14–22	403
10:31	120
11:1	386
11:18–22	156
11:27	156
11:30	23
12	24, 65
12:4–31	24

12:12–18	66
12:15–16	139
13.	24
12:12–14	140
12:15–25	65
12:20–27	140
12:27	65, 66
13:1–8a	140
15:33	402

2 Corinthians

1:20–22	23
1:20a	55
4:1–6	272
4:5	188
5:21	152
6:16	26
6:16b–7:1	94
7:1	22, 88, 377
8:1–15	255
8:14	378
9:6	254
9:7	217, 254

Galatians

2:11–14	235
3:8	313
3:14	294
3:16	313
4:4–7	26
4:7	423
6:6	24, 96, 99, 254, 378
6:10	124

Ephesians

1:2	125
1:3	294
1:3–14	125
1:5	357
1:13–14	26
1:15–19	125
2:19–22	140
2:20	66
2:20–21	24
2:20–22	26, 55, 57, 66
2:22	24, 93
3:14–19	125
3:20	400
3:20–21	24

4:1–6	24
4:28	255
5:2	23
5:18–20	111
5:22–33	107
5:25–27	111
6:2	120

Philippians

1:3–11	122, 125
1:6	23, 126
1:15–17	188
1:18	189
2:14–15a	179
4:9	386
4:12–13	126

Colossians

1:9–13	122, 125
1:12–14	26, 404–5
2:16–17	357
3:5	403
3:23	414

1 Thessalonians

1:10	357
2:9	254
4:11	404
5:12–13	24
5:12–13a	86
5:13a	246
5:23–24	23

2 Thessalonians

3:6	385, 402
3:8	254
3:12	404
3:14	94
3:15	403
3:14–15	402

1 Timothy

2:5	25
2:6	25
3:1–7	140, 150
3:1–13	149
3:2	150
3:2–7	150
4:3	404

4:3–4	365
4:12	149, 151
4:16	206
5:4, 8	120
5:17	24, 86, 150
5:20	86, 187, 235
6:10	294
6:10a	294

2 Timothy

2:14, 16–18	377
2:17–19	235
2:19	235
2:21	377
2:22	149

Titus

2:7	149
3:1–2	157
3:3–7	157
3:10–11	94

Hebrews

1:3	138, 206
1:5	314
1:6	151
1:13	314
3	422
3–4	29, 332, 394, 422
3:1	423
3:1–2	138
3:1–6	24
3:1–11	189
3:2, 5	186
3:6–4:13	24
3:7–11	24
3:7–19	422
3:7–4:2	14
3:7–4:13	272
3:12	206, 332
3:13	332
4:1	332
4:1–11	206
4:2–3	206
4:14–16	244
4:5	206
4:11	332
4:14–16	29

4:16	333
6:13–20	23
7:23–25	25
7:25	219, 237, 244
7:26	416
7:27	237, 416
7:28a	273
8:1	416
8:6–13	27
9:4	241
9:7	352, 358
9:12	25, 358, 416
9:13–14	264
9:13–15	26
9:24	25
9:25–10:10	358
9:28	90, 416
10	219
10:1–4	24
10:3	352
10:5–14	24
10:10	416
10:14–22	219
10:19–22	88, 90, 352, 358
10:19–23	244
10:19–31	25
10:24–25	355
10:26–29a	219
10:26–31	110
10:31	17, 23, 219
12:5–6	294
12:5–11	15
12:11	15
12:18–29	22
12:28–29	88
13:4	107
13:8	27
13:17	24, 86, 181, 245, 246, 272

James

1:17	27
2:14–26	25
3:1	73, 245, 272
5:12	364
5:16	23

1 Peter

1:3–5	405

1:3–6 26
1:18–19 89
2:4–10 24
2:5 26
2:9 .... 119, 171
2:9–12 25
2:22–25 89
2:24 90
5:2–4 341
5:3 85

2 Peter

2:15 .... 290, 291, 294, 311
3:9 23

1 John

1:9 .... 95, 120, 152, 264, 416
2:1 25
4:9–10 23
5:3 111

Jude

11 .... 232, 290, 291
11b 294

Revelation

1:12–2:1 22
2:21 23
5:5 64
6:12–17 312
7:15–17 405
7:17 55
8–9 163
11:1–14 312
16:4–7 312
18:19–19:2 312
19:15 314
19:16 64
21:3–4 .... 22, 65
21:12–14 65
22:15 109

Subject Index

* *i* after a page number indicates an illustration
m after a page number indicates a map
t after a page number indicates a table

Aaron
   the budding of the staff of, 240–41
   death of, 270–71
   family of (the priests), 73
   intercession of, 227–28, 231
   the Lord's vindication of, 234–35
   the Lord's vindication of Moses and his anger toward Miriam and, 185–86
   and Miriam's complaint against Moses, 184–85
   and Moses
     the account of the family of, 72–73
     reasons for the severity of God's final punishment of, 271–73
     their obedience and rebellion at Kadesh, 269
adultery, 101–5, 107, 109–10, 206n, 317. *See also* spiritual adultery
affairs, three categories of extramarital, 109
   how to guard against them, 109–10
altar
   animals offered at the dedication of the, 137*t*
   tribal leaders' offerings for the dedication of the, 135–37
   why so much focus on the, 137–38
Amarna letters, 5
Amalek, Balaam's prophecy concerning the fate of, 301, 309
Amenhotep II, 5
ancient warfare, 369, 371
animals
   offered at the altar's dedication, 137*t*
   three types of offerings of, 136
apostasy, 20, 194, 206, 214, 215, 216, 218, 272, 394
apostates, 234

ark of the covenant, 53, 69, 133, 137, 166, 169, 170, 238, 240, 241, 371
   location in the tabernacle and method of transport, 80*t*
   what the ark represents, 169
Ashur and Ebur, Balaam's prophecy concerning the fate of, 300, 310
ass (of Balaam), 290–92
Assyria, 289n8, 310, 316, 390
atonement, and mercy, on the need for a mediator, 15–16
Atrahasis epic, 282
Augustine, Saint, xvii, 124
authority. *See* spiritual authority
avenger of blood, 407, 410, 411, 412, 413, 414–15

Balak (king of Moab), 279, 285–93, 295, 297–310, 312–13, 371
   greeting of Balaam, 292–93
   sequence of events involving the seer Balaam, 303*t*
   summoning of Balaam, 288–90
Balaam (son of Beor), 17, 279, 285–95, 297–313, 367, 371, 372, 395
   the ass of, 290–92
   Balak's summons of, 288–90
   the driving force of his life, 311
   greeted by Balak, 292–93
   how his story is an encouragement, 312–13
   how his story is a warning, 311–12
   the killing of, 367, 371
   oracles of (concerning Israel)
     first message, 297–98, 303–5
     second message, 298–99, 305–6
     third message, 299–300, 306–8

ultimate four oracles, 300–301, 309–10
references to Genesis in describing Israel's blessing, 302t
sequence of events involving the king of Moab and the Israelites, 303t
what lay at the root of his wrong, 294
Balaam Inscriptions, 287–88
baptism, 157
battle
  against the Midianites. *See* Midianites
  on the source of victory in, 281
blessing
  God's desire to bestow, 123
  how we find true, 125–26
  on a priest's responsibility to pronounce (over Israel), 122
  on maintaining hope when it has not yet come, 126–27
  three lines in a priestly, 122–23
  on what it is, 124
blood of Christ, 89, 264
body of Christ, on being committed to the, 66
Book of the Wars of the Lord, 4, 274–75, 279
boundaries of Canaan, 400
bread
  as an offering in the promised land, 213
  of the presence, 141, 142, 143
bronze serpent, 276–77, 278, 283

callings, on respecting others', 24
camp (Israelites')
  arrangement of the outer, 62–64
  laws: how they relate to the church and modern life, 93–94
  on maintaining its ritual purity, 92–93
  on the organization and preparation of the, 7–9
  of Ramesses II at Qadesh, 57i
Canaan
  the boundaries of, 400
  the consequence if Israel failed to dispossess the nations from, 399
  as explored by the twelve spies, 40m
  first use of the word in Numbers, 194
  map of the exodus and conquest of, 39m
  the people's unauthorized and unsuccessful attempt to enter, 203–4, 208
  the twelve scouts explore, 194–96
  two commands of the Lord for Israel once they cross into, 399
  See also land (Canaan); promised land
Canaanites
  Israel's initial victory over the, 277–28
  reasons for the severity of the level of Israel's destruction of the, 281–83
capital punishment, 408, 411n10, 415
captives, taking of, 369, 371
case law(s), 96–97, 101–7
  defined, 96
census(es)
  and authorship, 2
  first- and second-generation numbers, compared, 30–32, 329t
  Israel's second military, 328
  of the Levites (Num 26), 330
  Levite numbers (Num 3–4), 76i
  the Lord's command for a second military, 327–28
  and military divisions of Israel, 50, 51
  on the two different Levite, 78
Christian, what it means to be a, 363–64
Christianity, 124, 313
  special days and celebrations in, 355
church
  how laws concerning the Israelite camp relate to our lives and the, 93–94
  on providing for the, 138, 254–55
  special days and celebrations of the Christian, 355
church bells, 162, 163
cities
  for the Levites, 409
  what it might look like to provide these today, 413–14
  map of the cities or refuge and Levitical, 44m
  of refuge, 410–11
  what we learn about the Lord's view of human life from the law concerning, 414–15
cleansing: how it was and is accomplished, 263–64
cloud of glory, 159, 160, 224, 229, 230
  the lifting of the (from the tabernacle), 167
  the Lord's guidance of the Israelites by the ark and the, 168–69

Subject Index

comparisons, on making 139–40
complaining/complaint, 2, 13, 174–76, 194, 271, 283, 393
  of Israel about the water, and the Lord's response, 268
  of Miriam and Aaron against Moses, 184–85
  how God views, 180
  how it impacts our leaders, and how they should respond, 180–81
  and lamenting, the difference between, 181–82
  what it means to complain, and what complaining leads to, 179
corpses
  on cleansing ceremonial uncleanness that comes from, 259–62, 263–64
  the law for Nazarites, concerning, 115
  why they are ritually defiling, 263
cousins, on the marrying of, 419
cross, 1, 90, 182, 296, 321
crossing of fingers, 263

daily offerings, 348
Dathan and Abiram (Reubenite rebels), 12, 221, 226–27, 228, 232–33, 234, 235, 322, 328, 331, 336
  Moses's detailed interaction with, 226–27
David (king of Israel), 64, 309, 310, 313–14, 400
Day of Atonement, 89, 90, 351–52, 354, 357
  date and offerings required, 347t
  how it foreshadows the work of Jesus, 357
Day of Trumpet Blasts, 351, 354
dead bodies: why they are ritually defiling, 263. *See also* corpses
decisions, on making, 385–86
dedication
  the type that the Lord requires, 119–20
  where the Nazarites lived out wholehearted, 120
defilement of a Nazarite, on unintentional, 115–16
desert of Paran, 165, 167, 184, 190, 191
destruction of the Canaanites, reasons for the severity of the, 281–83
discharge (genital), 91, 92, 259
dishes presented at the altar's dedication, 136t

disobedience
  the hope we can have in our, 207–8
  the theme of the Israelites', 24–25
diviner
  Balaam the. *See* Balaam
  meaning, 302
drink offering(s), 69, 113, 136, 209, 210, 211, 212, 213, 342–45, 348
dying to oneself, 296

Edom
  Balaam's prophecy concerning the fate of, 300, 309
  denial of Israelites' passage through their territory, 270
Egypt
  God's delivery of Israel's slavery in. *See* slavery
  Israel's illogical longing for the food of and/or to return to, 172, 173, 175, 176, 179, 182, 191, 202, 265
  stages in the Israelites' journey out of, 388–90
  wadi. *See* Wadi of Egypt
  See also next
Egyptians, 5, 6, 192, 200, 251, 266, 388
elders
  of Israel, 177–78, 222, 227
  of Midian, 285, 288n3, 289
  of Moab, 285, 289
  New Testament, 86, 140, 149, 150, 151, 341
Eleazar, investiture of, 270n71
'*eleph*, 31
encouragement
  how Balaam's story is an, 312–13
  how God's faithfulness to his promises is an, 332–33
end-time judgment, 283, 379
Er and Onan, 323, 328, 331
Euphrates region, upper, 41m
exodus
  and conquest of Canaan, 39m
  possible route of the 43m
extrabiblical texts, 287
extramarital affairs
  how to guard against them, 109–10
  three categories of, 109

"face to face": meaning of the term, 200n17
faith
    the difference between human religion and biblical, 208
    the scouts' report and undermining of Israel's, 197
    what we learn from Zelophedad's daughters about, 339–40
fear, what keeps us from, 169–70
Festival of Booths, 212, 354. See Festival of Tabernacles
Festival of the Harvest. See Festival of Weeks
Festival of Ingathering. See next
Festival of Tabernacles, 346, 352–53, 356
Festival of Trumpets, date and offerings required, 347t
Festival of Unleavened Bread, 349–50, 351, 354
    date and offerings required, 347t
Festival of Weeks, 343, 346, 350–51, 352, 354
    date and offerings required, 347t
    three different names for the, 350
fidelity, on what motivates us toward marital, 110–11
firstborn
    Israelites, redemption of, 77–78
    the Levites taken by the Lord in place of the, 74–75
firstfruits, 98, 213, 217, 247, 250, 253–54, 255, 343, 350, 422
Focus on the Family, 110n
forgiveness
    does not mean the absence of, 201
    Jesus's provision of rescue and, 90
    one definition of, 208n

Gad, Reuben, and the half tribe of Manasseh, the property inherited by, 384–85
Gadites
    on their presence in the area east of the Jordan, 381
    and Reubenites
        their request of Israel's leaders, and Moses's response, 382–83
        their subsequent proposal to Moses and its acceptance, 383–84
garments, tassels on (as a reminder to obey God), 216, 219–20
gematria, 31
genital discharge. See discharge (genital)
Gershonites, duties of the, 82–83
giving
    how the division of ancient spoils teaches us about, 378
    to the Lord: what we learn from Israel about, 253–54
    to the Lord's servants: what we learn from Israel about, 254–55
    what the Israelites' holy gifts teach us about, 98–99
God
    dwelling in the Israelites' midst, the implications of, 7–8
    on his steadfast faithfulness to his promises, 16–17
    his guiding presence among his people. See cloud of glory
    on his posture toward his people, 294
    his ultimate vision for this world, 375
    how we should respond when he is in our midst, 57
    qualities of a person whose life is pleasing to, 363
    what he calls his people to do, 55–57
    what he requires from his servants, 150–51
    See also King (God); Lord
golden calf incident, 194, 197, 393
grace
    does not make sin safe, 218–19
    how the Lord demonstrates his, 216–17
    the proper response to, 217
grain offerings, 98, 104, 113, 136, 211, 212, 343–45
grumbling, 2, 13, 174, 175, 174–76, 182, 194, 198, 214, 238, 240, 277, 393
    the result of, 179
    See also complaining

Hebron, on the antiquity of, 196n9
high places, 396, 399
high priest
    death of the (Levitical): how it anticipated Jesus, 415–16
    Israelite and Jesus compared and contrasted, 357, 358t
Hobab (Moses's brother-in-law), 165–66, 168, 170–71
High Priestly prayer of Jesus, 126, 386–87

holidays of ancient Israel. *See* special days and celebrations
holy place (tabernacle), 9, 61, 79, 80, 81, 133, 137, 141, 142, 143, 240, 241n4, 249, 253. *See also* most holy place
Holy Spirit, 22, 57, 125, 355
  poured out on the seventy elders, 177
human life, what the laws about cities of refuge teach us about the Lord's view of, 414–15
human religion and biblical faith, the difference between 208
humility, 187, 189, 198, 208, 225, 292
husband
  a jealous, 100–104
  and a wife's vow, 359–60, 361–63, 365
hyperbole, 31, 52, 178, 181, 186, 228n9, 236, 309, 374

idolatry, 218n28, 283n27, 316–17, 319, 394
  on its eradication in and application to modern times, 403–4
  reasons for Israel's strong attraction to, 316
idols, 289, 316, 320, 396, 398, 399, 403–4, 405
impurity
  cleansing and duration of major and minor, 259t
  how Jesus deals with our, 94–95
  ritual purity and, 32–33
  three major types of ritual, 92
incarnation, 162
incest laws, 419
infidelity, how to guard ourselves from marital, 109–10
inheritance
  the hope of our, 422–23
  the Lord's identification of those who would apportion Canaan as an, 401
  our (Christians') eternal, 26, 404–5
  on the patrilineal system of, 335–36
intercession, 200–201, 226, 227–28, 230–31, 237
Israel
  betrayal of the Lord at Moab, 317
  the calling and function of, 171
  on their calling to be a kingdom of priests, 118–19
  on the census and military divisions of, 50, 51–52

Moses's intercession on behalf of, 200–201, 227–28
oracles of Balaam the seer concerning
  first message, 297–98, 303–5
  second message, 298–99, 305–6
  third message, 299–300, 306–8
  ultimate four oracles, 300–301, 309–10
reasons that idols were one of her greatest temptations, 316
three ritual states in ancient, 32
travels of. *See* travel itineraries
See also next
Israelite(s)
  complaining and grumbling of the, 174–76
  departure for the promised land, 167
  Edom's denial of passage of the, 270
  five major themes focused on the, 23–25
  geographical locations of the (and for how long), 51t
  how the Lord guided the, 168–69
  journey to Moab, 278–79
  rebellious response to the twelve spies' evil report, 197–98
  redemption of firstborn, 77–78
  second generation of, 18–20
  four major themes in their story, 18–20
victories
  an initial victory over the Canaanites, 277–78
  on the Jordan's east side, 279–80
See also Israel

Jesus Christ
  God's kingly presence among his people fulfilled in, 162
  as God's Word and a perfect reflection of God, 189
  the good shepherd, 340
  the great high priest, 24, 29
  contrasted with the Israelite high priest, 357, 358t
  High Priestly prayer, 126, 386–87
  how Israel's special days and celebrations prepare us for, 357–58
  as the king who would arise, 313–14
  the laments of, 182
  as the only leader who demonstrates blameless dedication to God, 151–52

the only God-appointed way to know and
draw close to God, 244
as our Passover lamb, 156, 357
the priestly role of followers of, 171
provides rest for our souls, 170
return of, 163
took our judgment on himself, 284
the ultimate demonstration of
substitution, 90
the ultimate redeemer, 395
Jonathan (son of Saul), 366
Joshua (Moses' assistant), 4n8, 5, 20, 173,
177, 190, 191–92, 193, 195, 197,
198–99, 202, 203, 205, 271, 326, 331,
335, 341, 370, 379, 380, 383, 397, 401
commissioning as the leader of Israel,
338–39
on the Lord's command to appoint him as
leader, 338
why he and Caleb were faithful, 332–33
Judaism: understanding of Balaam's rising
king prophecy, 313
judge (Luke 18), the unjust, 163–64
judgment
appearance of God in
for Korah's rebellion, 227–29
for the people's rebellion after deaths of
Korah and the rebels, 230
for the people's rebellion after the spies'
bad report, 199
end-time, 283, 376
on the faithless scouts, 203
of God for the people's grumbling,
175–77, 178
of God for the people's revolt (ch. 14), 199,
201–3
how we can avoid God's, 283–84
the Lord declares a mitigated (after the
revolt of ch. 14), 201–2
on the Lord's patience, mercy, and, 23–24
three observations regarding, 14

Kenites, Balaam's prophecy concerning the
fate of the, 301, 309–10
Kibroth Hattaavah, 174, 178, 388–89, 393,
394, 395
King (God)
of glory, the proper response to a, 161–62
on keeping our lives being centered around
the, 64–65
on the proper posture to have before a holy,
87–88
king of Arad, 274, 277, 389
Kohathites, duties of the, 79–82
Korah
the death of, 229
the people's response to, 235–36
Moses's detailed interaction with, 221, 226
the rebellion of, 225–26, 227, 232

lament, the difference between complaining
and, 181–82
lampstand, lighting of the, 141–42
land
Canaan
two themes that concern the, 25–27
on apportioning the, 329–30, 401
inheritance, 25–26
mission, 26–27
See also Canaan; promised land
of our eternal inheritance, 404–5
and Zelophedad's daughters. See
Zelophedad's daughters
Late Bronze Age, 5, 6, 72
law (in Numbers), teaching and preaching on,
26–27
leaders
how complaining impacts them, and how
they should respond, 180–81
what bad leaders look like, 188
what good leaders look like, 188–89
leadership, what we learn from Moses about
340
leprosy, 92, 186, 187, 263
Levites
carts and oxen for the, 134–35
clans, numbers, placement in the inner
camp, and tabernacle duties, 75–76,
76t, 77, 78–84
duties of the Gershonites, 82–83
duties of the Kohathites, 79–82
duties of the Merarites, 83–84
numbers of males, 76
numbers of those old enough for
tabernacle service, 84
on setting them apart for tabernacle service

Subject Index

stage one, 147
stage two, 147
stage three, 147–48
stage four, 148
stage five, 148
service to the priests in tabernacle duties, 74
the special role of the, 53–54
taken by the Lord in place of the firstborn, 74–75
their primary task, 149
what they are reminders of, 151
why there were age requirements for the, 148–49
livers, examination of (for divination), 289n8
Lord, the
three themes focused on, 21–23
his faithfulness to his covenant promises, 22–23
his holy presence, 21–22
his two main types of responses to mistakes, 394–95
See also God; King (God)
Lord's Supper, 156–57, 350n21
love
how far the Lord's love goes, 321
of money, 294–95
what should be the natural response to God's extravagant, 321

magi, 314
man
on the vows and oaths of a, 361
or woman, what characterizes a godly, 363
Manasseh, the property inherited by Gad, Reuben, and the half tribe of, 384–85
manna, 4, 172, 175–76, 179, 182, 241n4, 395
marching order, 61–62, 167
marital fidelity, on what motivates us toward, 110–11
marital infidelity, how to guard ourselves from, 109–10
marriage
to cousins, 419, 419n8
God's perfect model for, 111
and inheritance of land, 335, 419. *See* Zelophedad's daughters
sex designed for, 107–8

two motivations for honoring the Lord with our bodies in, 110
materialism, 316, 339
measurement, biblical and rough modern equivalent, 213*t*
mediator
atonement and mercy, on the need for a, 15–16
on people's need for a, 25
Meaning of Marriage, The (Keller), 107–8
menstruation, 92, 258
Merarites, duties of the, 83–84
mercy, on the need for a mediator, atonement, and, 15–16
Mesha Stele, 381
messianic prophecy, 300, 309, 313–14
Meribah, 265, 266, 267, 269–70, 334
Merneptah Stele, 6
Middle Assyrian Laws, 408
Midian
the killing of the kings of, 367, 371
the Lord's judgment on, 319. *See also* Midianites
Midianites, 168n8, 184, 288–89, 310, 311, 312, 316, 318n9, 319, 367, 372, 376, 399
dividing the spoils of the, 373–74
how their battle and judgment story is a warning to us, 375–76
the required death of all males and wives, 372
Israel's battle against and spoiling of the, 371
the Lord's command to take vengeance on the, 370
Moses's reaction to Israel's plunder of the, 372
Miriam
and Aaron's complaint against Moses, 184–85
judgment by God for complaining against Moses, 186–87
the Lord's vindication of Moses and his anger toward Aaron and, 185–86
mission, on the relation between the promised land and God's, 26
mistakes
the Lord's two main types of responses to, 394

the role of memories in avoiding future, 393–94
Moab
    Balaam's prophecy concerning the fate of, 300, 309
    the heart of Israel's sins at, 319
    Israel's betrayal of the Lord at, 317
    the Israelites' journey to, 278–79
    king of. *See* Balak
money, on the love of 294–95
monthly offerings, 349
moral purity, 150
Moses
    the account of the family of Aaron and, 72–73
    destined to see but not enter the land of Canaan, 337
    disobedience at Kadesh, and the Lord's subsequent pronouncement of judgment on, 269
    faithful counterresponse to the spies' bad report and Israel's rebellion, 198
    a glimpse into his character as a leader, 177–78
    help for (in carrying the burden of Israel), 176
    prayer for a new leader for God's people, 337
    reasons for the severity of God's final punishment of Aaron and, 271–73
    his response to Korah's rebellion and the people's sin, 221, 225–26, 235
    his response to the people's sin after Korah's rebellion, 235
    intercession of (for Israel), 200–201, 227–28
    the Lord's vindication of
        in the face of Miriam and Aaron's complaints, 185–86
        after Korah's rebellion, 233
    what we learn from him about leadership, 340
most holy place, 7, 9, 53, 60, 61, 73, 79, 80, 81, 88, 137, 240, 243, 358
Mt. Sinai, duration of Israel's encampment at, 167
murder, 27, 406–7, 408, 411, 412n12, 413, 415
musical prayers, 161, 349, 351

Nadab and Abihu, 20, 67, 73, 87, 229, 242n13, 326, 330, 331
narrative (in Numbers), teaching and preaching on, 28–30
nations
    from Canaan, the consequence if Israel failed to dispossess the, 399
    what dispossessing the nations has to do with us today, 402
    why Israel had to dispossess the, 399, 402
Nazarite
    on unintentional defilement of a, 115–16
    vows
        completion of a, 116–18
        three rules for, 114–15
    what Nazarites were reminders of, 118–19
Negev, 190–91, 195, 274, 277, 389
Nephilim, 191, 196
new covenant, 23, 27, 264
New Kingdom period, 390
non-Israelites, why there was a Passover law for, 157
numbers
    in the book of Numbers, four main approaches to understanding, 30–31
Numbers (book)
    advantage of a thematic approach to dividing, 33–34
    author and date of, 2–5
    events in Canaan at the time of, 5
    interpretive challenges
        large numbers in Numbers, 30–32
        ritual purity in Numbers, 32–33
        structure of Numbers, 33–34
    outline (thematic) of, 34–35
    overarching structure and themes of, 6–7
        the three major sections of, 6
            literary and theological themes of the first section (1:1–10:10), 7–10
            literary and theological themes of the second section (10:11–25:18), 10–17
            literary and theological themes of the third section (26:1–36:13), 18–21
    setting of, 5–6
    teaching and preaching from, 27–29
        teaching and preaching on the law, 27–28
        teaching and preaching on Numbers' narrative, 28–30

Subject Index

theological themes summarized and related to the larger biblical story, 21–27
title of, 2

oaths and vows
  cases in which they may be nullified, 365–66
  on making them today, 364–65
  See also specifically vows
old covenant, 264. *See also* Sinai covenant
obedience
  the demonstration of true love and honor, 363
  tassels as a visual reminder of, 216, 219–20
  as a theme in Numbers, 20, 25
  what motivates our, 204–5
  why it matters, 205–6
offerings
  for the altar's dedication, 135–37
  daily, 348
  drink, 69, 113, 136, 209, 210, 211, 212, 213, 342–45, 348
  grain, 98, 104, 113, 136, 211, 212, 343–45
  the Levites' share in the Lord's, 252
  monthly, 349
  the priests' share in the Lord's, 249–51
  required based on Israel's religious calendar, 347*t*
  required of the Levites themselves, 252–53
  Sabbath, 346, 348
  on the soldiers' behalf after the battle with Midian, 374
  three types of animal, 136
  the tribal leaders' first, 134–35

parable of the persistent widow, 163–64
Paran, relationship between the wilderness of Zin and the wilderness of, 187
Passover
  commands for celebrating the second, 154
  date and offerings required, 347*t*
  Festival, 349–40
  how it relates to for Jesus, 357
  lamb. *See* Passover lamb
  laws about celebrating the, 155
  origin of the, 154, 349
  a reminder and celebration of Israel's deliverance from Egyptian slavery, 354
  two positive behaviors modeled by those ritually impure at the time of, 156
  why it was to be regularly celebrated, 156
  why there was a law for non-Israelites, 157
Passover lamb, 74, 156, 357
patience, mercy, and judgment, on the Lord's, 23
patrilineal system of inheritance, 335–36
Paul (apostle), 20, 24, 28, 55, 56, 65, 66, 88, 125, 126–27, 140, 149, 151, 179, 188–89, 235, 246, 254, 294–95, 357, 364, 377, 378, 386, 394, 402–3, 414, 421
Pentateuch, two main approaches to the authorship of, 2–3
Pentecost, 347, 350, 355. *See* Festival of Weeks
Phinehas (priest), 12, 367, 371
  contrasted with Jesus, 321
  the Lord's reward of, 318
  the zeal and righteousness of, 315, 318, 319, 321
plague
  amount of per-person payment to the tabernacle to avoid a, 375
  on the firstborn of Egypt, 74, 154
  on Israel for accusing Moses and Aaron of killing "the Lord's people," 223, 231, 237
  number of deaths from the, 223
  on Israel for wailing about food, 174, 178
  on Israel for worshipping sexual immorality and sacrificing to foreign gods, 315, 317–18
  number of deaths from the, 315, 319
  on the ten fearful spies of Israel, 193
plunder, 161, 193, 198, 203, 277, 367, 368, 369, 371
prayer
  musical, 161, 349, 351
  on persistent, 163–64
preaching
  and teaching from Numbers, 27–29
  and teaching, resources for, 37
priesthood, vindicating tests for the, 233, 240
priestly portions, 97–98, 249
priests
  Aaron's family, 73
  Christians' role as, 171

and Levites, the unique roles of (as a
  theme), 16
and the responsibility to bless God's
  people, 122
See also priestly portions
promised land
  laws for the, 211–13
  in Numbers 26–36, preparing for the, 19*t*
  See also land (Canaan)
promise(s)
  on God's faithfulness to his, 16–17, 22–23
  the most important, 162
  why it matters that God keeps his, 54–55
prophesied: meanings of the word, 177
punishment
  of Israel for sexual immorality, reasons for
    the severity of, 320
  of Moses and Aaron: reasons for the
    severity of God's final, 271–73
purity, moral, 150

Qadesh, 5, 60*i*
quail, 173–74, 176, 178, 179, 395

Rameses (place), 39*m*, 43*m*
Ramses/Ramesses II (person), 5, 60*i*, 81
Rashi (rabbinic scholar), 89
rebellion(s)
  the Lord's response to Korah's, 233–35
  in Numbers 10–25: judgment and
    mediators of, 11–12*t*
  in Numbers 16, 224–33
  six groups of Israelite, 10, 13–14
red heifer, 257, 260, 263
religion and biblical faith, the difference
  between 208
religion, the difference between man-made
  and biblical, 313
religious calendar of Israel, 347*t*
repentance, what it looks like, 98, 203, 377
resources for teaching and preaching, 37
restitution for wrongs, 96–97
Reuben, Gad, and the half tribe of Manasseh,
  the property inherited by, 384–85
Reubenites and Gadites
  their request of Israel's leaders, and Moses's
    response, 382–83
  their subsequent proposal to Moses and its
    acceptance, 383–84

"rites of passage" ceremonies, 116. *See*
  Nazarite: vows
ritual(s)
  for a wife suspected of adultery, 104–7
  impurity. *See* ritual impurity
  purity. *See* ritual purity
  the reason for so much detail in Numbers
    concerning religious, 353–55
  states. *See* ritual states
ritual impurity
  and purity, 32–33
  what it has to do with us, 376–77
ritual purity
  and impurity, 32–33
  on maintaining the Israelite camp's, 92–93
ritual states
  in ancient Israel, three, 32
  what the laws about them mean to us, 264
Rosh Hashanah, 351

Sabbath
  a man who breaks the, 210, 215
  offerings, 346, 348
  a sign of Israel's covenant with the Lord,
    215, 348, 354
"sacred assemblies," 355
sacred contributions, 96, 97, 98–99
Saul (king of Israel), 307n24, 309, 365–66
scapegoat, 89, 358
scouts, the twelve. *See* spies
seer
  Balaam the. *See* Balaam
  meaning, 302
self-denial, 296, 352
self-sufficiency (making it on our own), 143
servant-leadership, 188–89
servants
  what God requires from his, 150–51
  what good servants look like, 189
  what we learn from the Lord's provision for
    his, 255–56
Seti I (Nineteenth Dynasty pharaoh), 5
sex: designed for marriage, 107–9
sexual immorality, 12, 57, 315, 317, 319
sexual practices, how OT laws on marital
  adultery/fidelity relate to modern,
  107–9
shepherd
  Jesus the good, 340

the key to being a good, 341
shofar, 351
sin
  deserves death, 284
  illustration of the penalty for defiant, 215–16
  no safety in, 218–19
  offerings. *See* sin offerings
  unintentional versus defiant, 213–15
Sinai covenant, 27, 215, 255n16, 348
sin offering(s), 112, 113, 115, 129–33, 145, 210, 343–45, 347, 352n25
skin disease, 11, 91, 92, 183, 186, 259, 260
slavery, 48, 49, 55, 56, 75, 151, 154, 155, 156, 179, 182, 198, 253, 320, 349, 351, 354, 357
society, on withdrawing from 120
Solomon (king of Israel), 135, 400
special days and celebrations (of ancient Israel): how they were to be observed, 355–56. *See also individual special days and celebrations by name*
spies (of Israel)
  the bad report of the twelve, 197
  the people's rebellious response and Moses's counterresponse, 197–99
  Canaan as explored by the twelve, 40*m*
  explore Canaan, 194–96
  the names of the twelve, 190
Spirit. *See* Holy Spirit
spiritual adultery, 317, 318
spiritual authority
  the goal of, 85
  the proper response to, 85–87
spiritual leadership
  the difficulty and weight of, 245–46
  New Testament teaching on the importance of respecting those in, 86
  the purpose of, 85, 86
spiritual maturity, 149
spiritual realities, on who has the final say about, 295–96
spoils. *See also* plunder
  ancient taking of, 369
  battle against the Midianites and the taking of, 371
  division of: how it teaches us about modern giving, 378
  of the Midianites

on dividing the, 373–74
  Moses's instruction regarding the, 372
substitute, the role of a, 88–90
substitution, 88–90
  the ultimate demonstration of, 90
Sukkoth (festival), 352. *See* Festival of Tabernacles
suspicion (of a wife's adultery), a husband's, 102–4
  the ritual for, 104–7
"suzerain-vassal" covenant, 49
"symphathetic magic," 277

Taberah, the Israelites' complaints at, 174–75
tabernacle
  confirmation of the Lord's presence in the, 137
  duties
    of the Gershonites, 82–83
    of the Kohathites, 79–82
    of the Merarites, 83–84
  the Israelites' organizational structure in relation to the Lord's, 9*t*
  lampstand, lighting of the, 141–42
  locations of the sacred articles in the, 80*t*
  the people's fear of the, 241
  pictured, 50*i*
  roles, the priests' and Levites', 241–43
  service. *See* tabernacle service
  on setting up and consecrating of the, 134
tabernacle service
  numbers of Levites old enough for, 84
  setting apart the Levites for, 146–48
tassels (as a reminder to obey God), 216, 219–20
teaching and preaching, resources for, 37
Tell Deir 'Alla, 287
Ten Commandments, 241n4, 403
tent of meeting
  the tribes' camping around but keeping a distance from the, 61
  signs that it was the Lord's palace in Israel's midst, 60–61
Thutmose III and Thutmos IV, 5
tithe(s), 248, 249, 252–53, 254, 413, 414. *See also next*
tithing (in modern times), 255n16
travel itineraries
  Assyrian and Egyptian itineraries, 390

the Israelites' travel itinerary, 388–90,
    391–92
  the purpose of the (triggering memories
    of mistakes), 393–94
treason, treasonous acts, 30, 54, 73, 74, 77, 79,
    87, 178, 180, 215–16, 219, 245, 320
  the treasonous, 215, 216, 253, 317
trial by ordeal, 101–2
tribes (of Israel)
  marching order, 59, 61–62, 167
  and proximity to the tent of meeting, 61
  the Transjordan, 42*m*
  on the unity and parity/equality of the,
    9–10, 139–40
  from whom each descended, 52*t*
trumpets, 158–63, 343, 349, 367, 371
  blasts, the day of, 351
  one use of, 160–61
  a second use of, 161
  two basic types, 160
  what a trumpet sound does, 162–63
Tutankhamen, 81n27, 159

unfaithfulness, warnings against, 19–20
unintentional defilement of a Nazarite,
    115–16
unintentional sin versus defiant sin, 213–15
unity
  of God's people, on the necessity of, 23–24
  and parity/equality of the tribes of Israel,
    9–10, 139–40
  on the importance of, 386–87
Urim and Thummim, 371

Valley of Eshkol, 191, 196, 379
victory, -ies
  in battle, on the source of, 281
  an initial victory against the Canaanites,
    277–78
  Israel's victories on the Jordan's east side,
    279–80
vows
  cases in which they could be nullified, 365
  completing a Nazarite, 116–18
  concerning a wife's, 359–60, 361–63, 365
  must be kept at all costs, 363, 365
  and oaths of a man, 361
  and oaths of a woman, 361–63
  three rules for Nazarite, 114–15

See also oaths

Wadi of Egypt, 396, 400n4
warning(s)
  how Balaam's story is a, 311–12
  how God's faithfulness to his promises is a,
    331–32
  against unfaithfulness, 19–20
water(s)
  of cleansing, 145, 147, 257, 258,
    259–261, 368
  at Kadesh
    the people's complaint about the, 268
    the naming of the, 269–70
widow
  has the right to remarry, 421
  parable of the persistent, 163–64
  and vows, 359, 362
wilderness of Zin: relationship to the
    wilderness of Paran, 187
wilderness sojourn, date of the, 5
wilderness wanderings
  geographical locations (and durations) of
    the Israelites during the, 51*t*
  the exodus and, 43*m*
withdrawing from society, 120
woman
  or man, what characterizes a godly, 363
  on the vows and oaths of a, 361–63
worships, the Lord's value of regular, 354

Yom Kippur, 351. *See* Day of Atonement.

Zacchaeus, 98
Zelophedad's daughters
  the case of, 334, 336–37
  inquiry of their clan regarding marriage and
    land inheritance, 418–19
  obedience of, 419–20
  required to marry within their tribal clan to
    ensure the land remains in it, 419
  and the fairness of this restriction,
    420–21
  what these five women model, 421–22
  what we learn from them about faith,
    339–40
Zipporah (Moses's wife), 184
Zoan (in Egypt), 191, 196n9

Author Index

Adeyemo, Tokunboh, 78
Alexander, T. Desmond, 3
Allen, Ronald B., 2, 8, 33, 78, 79, 102, 114, 125, 163, 179, 202, 226, 278, 313, 352, 392, 400
Arnold, Bill T., 3
Ashley, Timothy R., 4, 33, 135, 159, 168, 178, 187, 202, 211, 214, 216, 232, 288, 289, 290, 305, 307, 310, 328, 349, 360, 382, 391, 409, 418
Augustine, xvii, 124
Averbeck, R. E., 4, 141, 249

Bailey, Lloyd R., 122, 194, 277, 289, 392
Beale, Greg K., 89
Bertman, Stephen, 211
Bittles, A. H., 419
Black, M. L., 419
Boda, Mark J., 201
Boniface-Malle, Anastasia, 78, 149, 182, 373
Borowski, Oded, 116
Budd, Philip J., 79, 269

Calvin, John, 61
Carder, David, 109
Carson, D. A., 89
Chadwick, Henry, 124
Coats, George W., 34
Cockerill, Gareth Lee, 241
Cole, R. Dennis, 5–6, 33, 113, 269, 302, 391
Cook, E. M., 78, 83, 136, 178, 212
Currid, John D., 15

Davies, G. J., 390
Delitzsch, Franz, 4
Dozeman, Thomas B., 85, 163
Duguid, Iain M., 1, 94–95, 98, 118, 143, 179, 205, 217, 218, 234, 249, 339, 346, 375, 421–22
Dumbrell, William J., 168

Eichler, Raanan, 81

Enns, Peter, 167

Fee, Gordon D., 156

Gallagher, Maggie, 107
Gane, Roy, 33, 117, 140, 160, 205, 214, 219, 236, 303, 355
Gerstenberger, Erhard, 116
Goetze, Albrecht, 72
Goldstein, Aaron J., 30, 31–32
Gray, George Buchanan, 305
Grisanti, M. A., 4
Gundry, Stanley N., 283

Harrison, R. K., 4, 78
Hobby, Nathan, 255
Hoffmeier, J. K. (James), 4, 30, 390, 391

Imes, Carmen Joy, 123

Jaenicke, Duncan, 109
Jenson, Philip Peter, 80
Joosten, Jan, 220

Keck, Leander, 85
Keil, C. F., 4, 73, 177, 256, 291, 318, 328, 371, 373, 409, 414
Keller, Kathy, 108–9
Keller, Tim (Timothy J.), 56, 108–9, 244
Kidner, Derek, 147, 229, 273, 291
King, Philip J., 419
Kitchen, K. A., 5, 391
Kline, Meredith, 283
Knierim, Rolf P., 34

Laaser, Mark and Debbie, 110
Levine, Baruch, 54, 77, 89, 133, 212, 277, 307
Longman, Tremper, III, 283
Lunn, Nicholas P., 64

Magary, D. R., 4
Masius, André, 256, 414

Matthews, Victor H., 421
McConville, J. Gordon, 204
McMahon, Gregory, 72
Milgrom, Jacob, 32, 54, 72, 91, 107, 117, 133, 168, 178, 197, 200, 216, 218, 220, 252, 261, 263, 277, 290, 310, 351, 360, 372, 375, 382, 383, 390, 392, 409, 416
Moore, Michael S., 289, 302

Noonan, Benjamin J., 81
Noordtzij, A., 4, 103, 328

Olson, Dennis T., 16, 33, 87, 142, 161, 201, 204, 208, 213, 237, 308, 391

Park, Song-Mi Suzie, 374
Pittman, Frank S., 109
Pratt, Richard, 29

Rasmussen, Carl G., 194, 337, 400
Richter, Sandra L., 49
Roth, Martha, 408

Sarna, Nahum M., 53
Sklar, Jay, 1, 3, 15, 16, 27, 28, 29, 33, 51, 53, 55, 56, 60, 73, 75, 77, 80, 82, 86, 90, 92, 97, 104, 105, 106, 107, 114, 116, 117, 141, 142, 154, 155, 168, 201, 212, 214, 215–16, 218, 219, 220, 231, 240, 244, 246, 253, 255, 262, 263, 289, 304, 305, 316, 318, 328, 337, 338, 350, 353, 354, 357, 365, 373, 382, 421

Snell, Daniel C., 316
Speiser, E. A., 374
Sprinkle, Joe, 81, 135, 159, 197, 228, 290, 302, 381
Stager, Lawrence E., 419
Stuart, Douglas K., 74, 138, 151, 201, 316, 412
Stubbs, David L., 33, 34, 94, 118, 208, 267, 295, 309, 327, 335, 337, 340, 421

Tidball, Derek, 28, 415

Van Dam, Cornelis, 348
van der Maas, Ed, 4
Voskamp, Ann, 182

Waite, Linda J., 107
Walton, John, 5
Warren, Rick, 64
Wenham, Gordon J., 3–4, 15, 33, 53, 73, 103, 122, 163, 196, 198, 202, 232, 241, 251, 262, 281, 290, 292, 306, 310, 328, 339, 346, 347, 349, 360, 384, 392, 400, 409, 415, 420
Whybray, Roger N., 3
Wiggershaus, Benjamin, 304
Williams, Michael D., 171
Wright, Christopher J. H., 28, 233, 370

Yadin, Yigael, 61